STATISTICAL CONCEPTS FOR THE BEHAVIORAL SCIENCES

THIRD EDITION

Harold O. Kiess

Framingham State College

Weiling Deng

Jan, 2004

Allyn and Bacon
Boston • London • Toronto • Sydney • Tokyo • Singapore

Executive Editor: Rebecca Pascal
Series Editorial Assistant: Kate Edwards
Senior Marketing Manager: Caroline Croley
Editorial-Production Service: Omegatype Typography, Inc.
Composition and Prepress Buyer: Linda Cox
Manufacturing Buyer: Joanne Sweeney
Cover Administrator: Linda Knowles
Electronic Composition: Omegatype Typography, Inc.

Library of Congress Cataloging-in-Publication Data

Kiess, Harold O.
    Statistical concepts for the behavioral sciences / Harold O. Kiess. —3rd ed.
        p.   cm.
    Includes bibliographical references and index.
    ISBN 0-205-33291-9
        1. Social sciences—Statistical methods.   2. Statistics.   I. Title.
    HA29.K4857   2002
    519.5—dc21

                                                        2001022876

Printed in the United States of America

10   9   8   7   6   5   4   3   2   1   06   05   04   03   02   01

Brief Contents

Contents

Chapter 3   Describing Data: Frequency Distributions and Graphs   30

Chapter 4   Describing Data: Measures of Central Tendency   62

Chapter 9   The Basics of Experimentation and Testing for a Difference between Means   179

Preface

My objective for the first and second editions of this text was to provide a conceptual development of basic statistical methods in the context of their use in behavioral science. To achieve this goal, I placed a strong emphasis on utilizing contemporary research problems in the behavioral sciences. I believe that real problems more adequately illustrate the immediate relevance of statistical analysis in scientific research. For this third edition I have tried to attain the same objective, building on the strengths of the previous two editions.

ORGANIZATION OF THE TEXT

The organization of this edition is designed for continuity in the concepts presented. The uses of statistics are developed and presented in a conceptually logical progression. The first five chapters introduce the need for statistics, the measurement of behavior, displaying scores in frequency distributions graphically, and measures of central tendency and variability. Chapters 6 and 7 introduce the normal distribution, probability, sampling distributions, and using statistics for estimation of parameters. The basics of statistical hypothesis testing are introduced with the z test and the one-sample t test in Chapter 8. Chapters 9 to 12 deal with hypothesis testing for the difference between means using parametric tests. The analysis of variance is emphasized, for it is among the most widely used statistical tests in the behavioral sciences, and students clearly need to be familiar with its use. A thorough introduction is provided for the one-factor between-subjects, one-factor within-subjects, and the factorial between-subjects analyses of variance, including the use of multiple comparison tests and strength of effect measures. In addition, considerable attention is given to the interpretation of an interaction in a factorial design. The order of the remaining chapters has been changed for this edition. Chapters 13 and 14 now present correlation and regression. The first of these chapters introduces both the Pearson and Spearman correlation coefficients. Statistical hypothesis testing with each correlation coefficient is also developed. Chapter 14 then provides an overview of the basics of simple linear regression, building from the discussion of correlation in Chapter 13. The placement of these chapters near the end of the text is somewhat unusual, for many texts include these chapters following a discussion of descriptive statistics. But I believe this common placement poses conceptual difficulties for students. Descriptive statistics, such as the mean and standard deviation, lead naturally to a discussion of statistical tests for the difference between sample means. Interposition of correlation and regression between descriptive statistics and statistical hypothesis testing interrupts this continuity of thought. I elected to maintain the continuity of conceptual development and place the correlation and regression material after the presentation of parametric statistical tests. Chapter 15 concludes the text with a discussion of three nonparametric statistical tests, the chi-square, Mann–Whitney U, and the Wilcoxon signed-ranks tests.

FEATURES

Students attempting to grasp the sometimes difficult conceptual basis of statistics often encounter many problems. To help overcome these problems, the text uses a variety of features to keep the material tied to actual research problems and to permit students to assess their understanding of the material as they proceed through a chapter.

Realistic Problems

All statistical methods are introduced in the context of a problem from behavioral research. Many problems are based on studies drawn from contemporary published research. These studies are referenced fully so that the interested student may read the original research.

Conceptual Development of Statistics

The various statistics are introduced conceptually, often by use of a definitional formula. A problem is then worked using this conceptual approach so that students may see what the statistic does with the data. Using this format, I have tried not to overwhelm students mathematically when introducing a statistic. The mathematics required for elementary statistics is simple, yet many students are intimidated by a first chapter that reviews basic mathematics with no immediate connection to the statistics that use the mathematics. Thus, I have introduced and explained the necessary mathematical concepts when they are needed. For those who need a more complete review of basic mathematical operations, however, such a review is provided in Appendix B.

Testing Your Knowledge and Review Questions

Each chapter contains interspersed Testing Your Knowledge sections and end-of-chapter Review Questions. The questions in these sections provide an opportunity for students to review and test their understanding of the text material. Many of the questions are based on actual research problems. Thus, not only do these questions provide a review, but they also give examples of the uses of the various statistical methods. A number of new questions and problems have been added for the third edition. I strongly encourage students to complete these exercises whenever they are encountered before continuing on in the chapter or to the next chapter.

Sample Journal Formats

For many statistical tests a sample journal report of a statistical analysis is presented with an explanation of the information contained in the report. The sample is followed by exercises on extracting information from journal presentations of the results of a study. For this edition I have included a discussion of the recommendations of the American Psychological Association Task Force on Statistical Inference (Wilkinson & Task Force on Statistical Inference, 1999) as well as the requirements of the *Publication Manual of the American Psychological Association* (1994).

Marginal Definitions and Terms Glossary

Marginal definitions of important terms and a glossary of these terms are included in this edition. Important terms are boldfaced and defined in the text material. These definitions are supplemented by marginal definitions to reinforce learning of the material. A glossary of all these terms is provided in Appendix C.

Symbols Glossary

It is easy to become overwhelmed by the variety of symbols used in statistics. To aid in learning the language of statistics, Appendix D provides a glossary of all the symbols used in this text. Thus, students may easily refresh themselves on the meaning of symbols that they encounter.

Readability

The text is written so that it may be read and studied without interruption by boxed features or optional reading. Each section of the text follows from the previous material. To enhance this continuity, many raw score computational formulas have been placed in chapter supplements at the end of a chapter. Instructors who omit computational formulas in favor of one of the many programs available for computerized statistical analysis may readily do so without loss of continuity in the text material.

New for the Third Edition

In response to suggestions from students, reviewers, and users, a number of changes have been made to make the text more readable and useful to students. The second edition of this text was a major revision from the first. For this third edition I have tried to minimize major organizational changes and placed my focus on improving readability and clarity. But several important changes to content and organization should be noted.

The question of how much discussion of probability should be included in a statistics book is a difficult one to answer. My goal has been to provide sufficient discussion of probability so that students may understand the statistical analysis of data, yet not feel overwhelmed by topics and problems not related to statistical analysis. Chapter 6 now includes a more extensive discussion of probability including empirical and theoretical probability distributions, the probability of mutually exclusive events, and the additivity rule along with additional problems. I have tried to ensure, however, that the discussion and problems maintain a clear relationship to the concepts of statistical analysis.

In Chapter 9 I have added a discussion of the current controversy on the value of statistical hypothesis testing. I believe this discussion will give students a better grasp of both the value and limitations of various statistical analyses.

The chapters on correlation, regression, and nonparametric statistics have been reordered from the previous editions. Chapters 13 and 14 are now Correlation, and Regression and Prediction, respectively. The discussion of nonparametric statistical tests occurs in Chapter 15. I believe this ordering of content will be more congenial to many users but does not change the basic conceptual approach of the text.

Other less extensive changes have also been made. Throughout the text I have tried to smooth out the areas in which users have reported difficulties by rewriting and reorganizing materials. In addition, a number of new problems have been added to the Testing Your Knowledge and chapter Review Questions sections. Finally, the first and second editions of the text contained sections called Statistics in Use, which presented brief summaries of actual research using the statistic being discussed. A number of users indicated these sections disrupted the flow of reading and understanding the material. Accordingly, I have removed these sections from this edition. But I have retained the applied aspects of statistics by incorporating many of these examples of actual research in the text material itself.

I hope that you will find that this text leads to an interesting and rewarding study of statistics. If you have any comments or suggestions on the text, please write to me at the Department of Psychology, Framingham State College, 100 State Street, Framingham, MA 01701-9101 or e-mail hkiess@frc.mass.edu.

ACKNOWLEDGMENTS

Many people have contributed to the three editions of this text. The original idea for the text came from Allen Workman of Allyn and Bacon. He suggested that I use the approach taken in a psychological research methods text, *Psychological Research Methods, A Conceptual Approach*, that I co-authored with my colleague, Dr. Douglas W. Bloomquist, and extend it to a statistics text. Consequently, many of the conceptual ideas used in this text are similar to those developed in that research methods text. I thank Doug Bloomquist for his contributions to the development of those ideas and material and for his willingness to let me use that material in this text. Rebecca Pascal, Allyn and Bacon executive editor for psychology, suggested the preparation of a third edition and provided the impetus and enthusiasm for carrying the project to completion. Her ideas and suggestions have been most useful in revising the text. Also, many thanks to the team at Omegatype Typography for their work on editorial production.

Various professional colleagues have also contributed to the development of the three editions of this text. Their careful scrutiny helped me immensely in clarifying the presentation and avoiding conceptual and mathematical errors. Of course, any inaccuracies remaining are my responsibility alone. I am grateful to the following for their assistance: Paul Amrhein, University of New Mexico; Dennis Cogan, Texas Tech University; Mark Fineman, Southern Connecticut State University; Mike Grelle, Central Missouri State University; Rick Hoyle, University of Kentucky; Arthur D. Kemp, Central Missouri State University; Melanie M. Kercher, Sam Houston State University; Lee Kirkpatrick, College of William and Mary; Robert Lange, University of Central Florida; J. W. Moore, Jr., Marshall University; Jon Rich, California State University at Fullerton; Richard Serkes, Tulsa Junior College; N. C. Silver, University of Central Florida; David D. Simpson, Carroll College; Michael Tirrell, Stonehill College; and Paul Yarnold, Northwestern University Medical School.

I am also grateful to the Biometrika Trustees for permission to reprint several tables from *Biometrika Tables for Statisticians* and to CRC Press for permission to reprint tables from the *CRC Handbook of Tables for Probability and Statistics.*

A final acknowledgment is to the person affected most by the work required to write a book, my wife, Sandra. Without her understanding, tolerance, encouragement, and love over many years, the three editions of this book would never have been completed.

STATISTICAL CONCEPTS
FOR THE
BEHAVIORAL SCIENCES

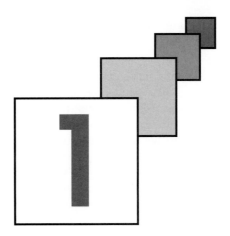

Introduction to Statistics

"Oh that blasted alarm" you mutter as you push the snooze button for a second time. What a short night! As you stumble out of bed, you realize that only a quick shower and a fast breakfast will let you be on time for your 8:00 A.M. class. As you walk to your car, you notice what a pleasant, warm day seems to be in store for this early spring day. Much nicer than yesterday's cold rain and drizzle. As you pull onto the expressway, the traffic is heavier than usual and it's not moving as fast as you had expected. Will you be late for your class? Fortunately, you make your class on time; the lecture today is one of the best of the semester. But you dread your 9:00 A.M. science lab; often it runs so long you don't have time for lunch. But today is different, everything goes smoothly, and you get out in time to have a leisurely, fun lunch with two of your best friends. After lunch, it's off to work at the Big Bargain Department Store. The customers today seem very pleasant in contrast to yesterday, you think maybe it's because of the nice weather. The pleasant customers make the afternoon pass quickly, and soon you are again on the expressway heading for home. Traffic now is lighter than most days; maybe everyone left work earlier today. You have a great deal of school work to do, so after dinner you settle at your desk, hoping for a productive night of studying. And so it is, at least in comparison to many of your attempts to study after dinner. You really feel prepared for that statistics exam coming up at the end of the week. To reward yourself, you watch an hour of television and then you go to bed. Maybe if you go to bed a bit earlier, the night will seem longer.

Perhaps this short vignette represents a typical day in your life, perhaps it does not. In any event, you are probably wondering what this vignette has to do with statistics. Well, for one, it illustrates that you have recognized certain regularities or consistencies in the events of your life: the typical amount of time you have for a shower or breakfast, the normal weather for an early spring day, the characteristic amount of traffic on your drive to college and how long it takes you to get there, the general interest level of a class, the average length of a science lab, the normal amount of fun you have at lunch, the typical behavior of a department store customer, and the normal productivity of a night of studying. The fact that you recognize there are consistencies or regularities in the occurrences of your life indicates you also recognize that there is variability or variation about these regularities. Some nights seem longer than others, showers and breakfasts vary in length from day to day, the weather rarely is normal for the time of the year (in fact as I write this material it is 61 degrees in early January in New England; the normal temperature should be in the mid-30s), traffic may be lighter or heavier, classes vary in interest level from day to day (and from course to course), science labs are sometimes longer and other times shorter than average, the behavior of shoppers is quite variable from person to person, and some study sessions are more productive than others.

This variation among events implies the existence of variables in the environment. A **variable** is any environmental condition or event, stimulus, personal characteristic or attribute, or behavior that can take on different values at different times or with different people. The amount of sleep you obtain, the length of your shower, the amount of traffic on the expressway, the interest level of a class, the length of a science lab, the mood of shoppers, and the productivity of study sessions are all variables. Statistics is the discipline that quantifies the consistency found in a variable and the variability about this

Variable: Any environmental condition or event, stimulus, personal characteristic or attribute, or behavior that can take on different values at different times or with different people.

TABLE 1.1
Conviction rates in French courts as a function of year and the ability
of the defendant to read and write.

Ability of Accused to Read or Write	Year			Average
	1828	1829	1830	
Unable to read or write	0.63	0.63	0.62	0.627
Able to read and write imperfectly	0.62	0.60	0.58	0.600
Able to read and write well	0.56	0.55	0.52	0.543
Has a superior education	0.35	0.48	0.37	0.400

After data of Quetelet. Adapted from Table 5.2, p. 176, *The History of Statistics: The Measurement of Uncertainty before 1900* by S. M. Stigler. Copyright 1986 by the President and Fellows of Harvard College.

consistency. Although this definition of statistics is informal and incomplete, it will serve for the moment.

   You, of course, are not the only person to note the regularity of events in the world. Lambert Adolphe Jacques Quetelet (1796–1874), a Belgian professor with wide-ranging interests, believed that such regularities in variables have causes and that if he could identify the regularities he could then identify their causes. He, thus, set out to identify these regularities. His initial work was to characterize what he called an "average man." To do so, he obtained anthropometric data (that is, bodily measurements) on variables such as height and weight from a large number of French soldiers (Stigler, 1986). His hope was that by characterizing an average person he could find regularities in human attributes and then compare these averages between males and females, or across nationalities, localities, ages, or races. Quetelet's interest in the average person extended also to what he called "moral statistics," regularities in variables such as suicide rates or crime and conviction rates. For example, Quetelet studied conviction rates in French courts over a period of years and categorized the rate of conviction by the accused's ability to read and write. His results are presented in Table 1.1. The numerical values in Table 1.1 represent probabilities. For example, if you were being tried in a French court in 1829 and you were able to read and write only imperfectly, the probability of your being convicted would be .60 (or 6 chances out of 10). Notice there appears to be a clear relationship between the accused's reading and writing abilities and the likelihood that he or she would be convicted of a crime. Quetelet often is called the father of social science for initiating these statistical studies (Dudycha & Dudycha, 1972).

STUDYING STATISTICS: HOW TO USE THIS TEXT

As the introduction illustrates, the study of statistics deals with both the regularities and variability of events that all of us have noticed in our lives. Thus, in one sense we are all novice statisticians. Nevertheless, many people are intimidated by the ideas of statistics and dread the thought of an entire course in statistics. This fear need not be the case, however. Learning statistics is similar to learning a new language. The language of statistics is composed of words, symbols, and formulas. As with any new language it requires serious study to master its components. But with practice and experience it should become as natural to you as your native language. Several features of this text will help you with your study of statistics.

Important Terms and Symbols

Terms and symbols that are especially important for understanding the concepts of a chapter are **boldfaced** in the text. The most important terms are also highlighted in a marginal definition. When you encounter a boldfaced term, you should recognize that it is important to understanding statistics. Don't proceed with your study until you have learned the term. Also, a glossary of terms is provided in Appendix C. If you encounter a term whose meaning you have forgotten, consult this glossary to refresh your memory. A glossary of statistical symbols is provided in Appendix D.

Testing Your Knowledge Sections

Each chapter contains several *Testing Your Knowledge* sections. These sections provide an opportunity to review and test your understanding of the material before you move on to the next section of the chapter. Many of the questions focus on actual research problems; thus, they provide examples of uses of the statistical methods you are studying. Answers for many of the *Testing Your Knowledge* questions are given in Appendix E, *Answers for Computational Problems*.

Review Questions

Review questions are provided at the end of each chapter. As with the *Testing Your Knowledge* questions, I encourage you to complete the chapter review questions and then compare your answers to those given in Appendix E, *Answers for Computational Problems*.

Mathematics Review

The mathematics used in this text is elementary, requiring only the operations of addition, subtraction, multiplication, and division. Mathematical symbols and operations are explained as they are needed. If you encounter difficulties with any of the mathematical operations, a *Mathematics Review* is provided in Appendix B. This review provides a summary of basic mathematical symbols and operations.

WHAT IS STATISTICS?

Data: The scores or measurements of behavior or characteristics obtained from observations of a sample of people or animals.

Statistics: The methods or procedures used to summarize, analyze, and draw inferences from data.

Statistic: A single number used to describe a set of data from a sample or to analyze those data more fully.

Following in the footsteps of Quetelet, behavioral scientists attempt to understand and explain human and animal behavior. They do so by collecting data. **Data** (*data* is plural, *datum* is singular) are the scores or measurements of behavior or characteristics obtained from observations of people or animals. To identify both the consistencies and variability in these data, procedures called *statistics* are applied to the data. **Statistics**, thus, refers to the methods or procedures used to summarize, analyze, and reach conclusions from data. A **statistic** is a single number that may be used to describe a set of data from a sample or to analyze those data more fully.

USING STATISTICS: THREE EXAMPLES

Statistical procedures are used in many different ways in behavioral science. The remainder of this chapter provides examples of three uses of statistical methods in behavioral science. A number of terms are introduced, and you should study and learn these terms, for you will encounter them throughout the text. Don't worry, however, if you don't understand all the details of the examples provided; the use of each approach is discussed more fully in later chapters.

Description and Inference

From our everyday reading, we are familiar with statistical descriptions of large sets of data. For example, Neilsen Media Research reported that in November 1998 women in the United States between the ages of 25 to 54 watched television 4.4 hours per day (Brunner, 1999). This numerical value illustrates two important uses of statistical methods: description and inference. Although the value of 4.4 hours is intended to characterize the population of all 25- to 54-year-old women in the United States, it was not obtained by observing and measuring all the 25- to 54-year-old women in the country. Rather, only a portion, or sample, of all such individuals was observed and measured. The number of hours that each person included in the sample watched television in a day was recorded, providing a set of data. The data from the different women in the sample were then summarized by calculating a single number, a descriptive statistic of 4.4 hours. This statistic is intended to describe the daily amount of time that a typical 25- to 54-year-old woman in the sample watched television. The number of hours of television watching per day for a typical 25- to 54-year-old woman in the population of all women in the United States was then inferred, or estimated, from this statistic.

Population: A complete set of people, animals, objects, or events that share a common characteristic.

The discussion has used the terms *populations* and *samples*. A **population** is a complete set of people, animals, objects, or events that share a common characteristic. For example, all the 25- to 54-year-old women in the United States constitute a population. The common characteristic of this population is that all the individuals included in it are women between the ages of 25 and 54 in the United States. Other examples of populations are all the college students in the United States, all the households in the United States, all the adult females in North Carolina, all the farmers in Nebraska, all individuals who commute on a daily basis to New York City, and all the people who have one or more bank credit cards; each set comprises a population. Any group of individuals may be thought of as a population as long as all those possessing the characteristic common to the population are included in the group.

Behavioral scientists often want to characterize populations with statements such as "the typical American woman watches television 4.4 hours per day" or "the average U.S. male working full time earns $33,748 per year, whereas a female earns only $25,376 per year" (U.S. Bureau of Labor Statistics, April 19, 2000). But it should be obvious that in most instances these characterizations cannot be obtained from measuring all members of the population. Rather, scientists typically use only a sample of the population.

Sample: A subset, or subgroup, selected from a population.

Random sample: A sample in which individuals are selected so that each member of the population has an equal chance of being selected for the sample, and the selection of one member is independent of the selection of any other member of the population.

Descriptive statistics: Statistical procedures used to summarize and describe the data from a sample.

Statistical inference: Estimating population values from statistics obtained from a sample.

Parameter: A number that describes a characteristic of a population.

A **sample** is a subset, or subgroup, selected from a population, often following a set of rules to ensure that the sample is representative of the population. One common form of selecting a sample is random sampling. In a simple **random sample** individuals are selected so that each member of the population has an equal chance of being selected for the sample, and the selection of one member is independent of the selection of any other member of the population. Data are then obtained from members of the sample and a **descriptive statistic** is calculated to describe the data. This descriptive statistic is then used to infer a characteristic of the population. The word *infer* implies reasoning from something known to something unknown. Thus, **statistical inference** is the process of reaching conclusions about unknown population values (e.g., the number of hours per day that a typical 25- to 54-year-old woman watches television), called **parameters**, from statistics obtained from a sample.

There are numerous common examples of statistics used for description and inference. As an illustration, the U.S. Census Bureau collects a variety of information about life in the United States and each year publishes summaries of some of this information in the *Statistical Abstract of the United States.* The 1999 *Statistical Abstract* revealed that

- TVs were found in 98 percent of U.S. households; VCRs were found in 84.6 percent of those households.
- The average person spent $353.30 on clothing and $957.30 on medical care in 1997.
- Fifty-eight percent of males and 54.9 percent of females were married.

Each of these numerical values is a *descriptive statistic,* a number that describes a sample. Realize that it is virtually impossible to count every TV or VCR in the United States, or to ask each person how much he or she spends on clothing in a year. Thus, each of these values is a statistic that estimates a population value. How well these individual descriptive statistics estimate population values depends on how the sample was chosen and how representative it is of the population. The procedures involved in the selection and description of samples and inference to a population are discussed more fully in Chapters 3 through 7.

1. Define: data, descriptive statistics, parameter, population, random sample, sample, statistic, statistical inference, statistics, variable.

2. In a recent election, 600 potential voters of a congressional district were polled to discover whom they planned to vote for in an upcoming election. The results indicated that 312 voters, or 52 percent of the sample, planned to vote for candidate A, 240 voters, or 40 percent, planned to vote for candidate B, and 48 voters, or 8 percent, said they did not plan to vote or had no preference among the candidates. Based on the results of the poll, the researchers estimated that candidate A would win the election with about 52 percent of the total vote.

   a. Explain why descriptive statistics are necessary to summarize the results of this research.

   b. What inferences to a population were made from the statistics obtained?

Experimentation and Statistical Hypothesis Testing

Independent variable: A variable manipulated in an experiment to determine its effect on the dependent variable.

Dependent variable: The variable in an experiment that depends on the independent variable. In most instances the dependent variable is some measure of a behavior.

Research hypothesis: A statement of an expected, or predicted, relationship between two or more variables. In an experiment, a research hypothesis is a predicted relationship between an independent variable and a dependent variable.

Participant or subject: The person who participates in an experiment.

Equivalent groups: Groups of subjects that are not expected to differ in any consistent or systematic way prior to receiving the independent variable of the experiment.

Between-subjects design: A research design in which two or more groups are created.

Behavioral scientists are interested not only in describing and characterizing samples and populations, but they also want to find the causes for individual or group behaviors. One approach to this task is to perform an experiment. To conduct an experiment, a researcher identifies a variable, called an **independent variable**, that he or she thinks affects a person's behavior. The behavior that is expected to be affected by this independent variable is called the **dependent variable**.

For example, I might expect alcohol consumption to affect a person's response to violence: People under the influence of alcohol are expected to be more accepting of violence than people who are not under the influence of alcohol (Gustafson, 1987a). In this instance, alcohol consumption is the independent variable. An experimenter has control over whether a person does or does not consume alcohol, and he or she expects it to affect the acceptance of violence. A measure of the person's acceptance of violence is the dependent variable. Acceptance of violence is presumed to depend on whether or not a person has consumed alcohol. The statement of the researcher's expectation that alcohol consumption will affect the acceptance of violence is called a research hypothesis. A **research hypothesis** is a statement of an expected, or predicted, relationship between two or more variables. In an experiment, a research hypothesis is a predicted relationship between an independent variable and a dependent variable.

The simplest experiment that could be performed to test a research hypothesis relating alcohol consumption to acceptance of violence begins by creating two equivalent groups of people. Scientists refer to the people who participate in research studies as **participants** or **subjects**. I will use these terms interchangeably in the chapters that follow. **Equivalent groups** are groups of subjects that are not expected to differ in any consistent or systematic way prior to receiving the independent variable of the experiment. An experiment in which two or more groups are created is called a **between-subjects design**. After equivalent groups are created, the researcher manipulates, or varies, the independent variable and measures the dependent variable, while controlling all other variables that may affect the dependent variable. In this example, the experimenter might give people in the first group 0.8 milliliter of alcohol per kilogram of body weight mixed with an equal amount of orange juice. Subjects in the second group might be given 1.6 milliliters of plain orange juice per kilogram of body weight. The difference in the drink is the only way in which the two groups are allowed to vary. The dependent variable may be measured by having the participants watch a violent movie and then rate the movie on the acceptability of the violence shown. A score on the rating task is obtained for each person. A **score** is the measurement obtained on the subject's performance of a task. This score is the dependent variable, for we expect it to depend on whether or not the person had consumed alcohol prior to watching the movie. The scores obtained from all the participants provide the **raw data** for the experiment. From these raw data the researcher must decide if the independent variable of consumption of alcohol affected the rating of the acceptability of violence in the movie.

The process by which the experimenter decides if the independent variable had an effect or not involves several steps. The first step is to describe the ratings of each of the two groups by calculating descriptive statistics presenting the typical ratings of participants in each group. This step is identical to the process of description of data discussed earlier in this chapter. Most likely you are already familiar with some common descriptive statistics such as the mode, the median, or the mean.

The second step involves deciding if any observed difference in the descriptive statistics for the two groups of scores is large enough to be attributed to the effect of the independent variable. This step requires using **statistical hypothesis testing**. The purpose of statistical hypothesis testing is to determine the anticipated size of chance differences between the groups.

In an experiment, equivalent groups will always differ in some unpredictable way that I will call a **chance difference**. Chance differences occur between groups in an experiment even if the independent variable has no effect on the dependent variable. In statistical hypothesis testing the difference actually observed between the two groups in the experiment is compared to expected chance differences between the groups. If the possibility of obtaining a chance difference as large as the actual difference found is sufficiently small, then the researcher decides that the observed difference is not a chance difference. Rather, the observed difference is attributed to the effect of the independent variable.

As an example of experimentation and statistical hypothesis testing, consider the following question. Do you sometimes find yourself forgetting some of the tasks that you have to do in a day? I do. No doubt we all do, but might the use of a mnemonic or memory technique help us to better remember our daily schedules? Harris and Blaiser (1997) investigated this question with an experiment requiring people to remember a list of daily tasks. Participants were randomly assigned to create two equivalent groups. Participants in both groups were told a list of 10 tasks, such as return a movie to the video store, return a phone call, get a haircut, and go grocery shopping, and tested for recall of the tasks 24 hours later. The number of tasks each person could recall was the dependent variable. The independent variable was the type of instruction given the individuals. Participants in the control group were not given any instruction on how to go about remembering the tasks. Those in the experimental group, however, were told of the word-pegging memory technique. The word-pegging technique rhymes a number with a word, "one is a bun, two is a shoe, three is a tree, four is a door, five—hive, six—sticks, seven—heaven, eight—gate, nine—wine, ten—

Score: The measurement obtained on the participant's performance of a task.

Raw data: The scores obtained from all the participants before the scores have been analyzed statistically.

Statistical hypothesis testing: Procedures used to determine the anticipated size of chance differences between groups.

Chance difference: A difference between equivalent groups due to random variation.

hen." After the rhyme is learned, the subject attempts to link it to a task with a mental image. For example, if task 1 is to return a movie to the video store, I might imagine the videocassette in a bun. For task 2, returning a phone call, I might imagine a telephone in the shape of a shoe.

Harris and Blaiser hypothesized that the people in the experimental group using the word-pegging technique should recall more tasks than those in the control group. The mean or average number of tasks recalled by the experimental group was 7.1, whereas the mean for the control group was 4.1. To determine if the number of tasks recalled differed by more than chance alone, Harris and Blaiser used a statistical test called analysis of variance. This test indicated that the number of tasks recalled by the two groups differed by more than expected from chance differences alone. People in the experimental group reliably recalled more tasks than participants in the control group, a result in agreement with the research hypothesis. We can better remember the things we have to do by using the word-pegging mnemonic. Now let me think . . . "six is sticks." I need to get a haircut to get rid of those sticks on my head.

Statistical testing is used widely in the behavioral sciences. To understand the concepts involved, however, requires building on knowledge of descriptive statistics, and statistical inference and estimation, topics discussed in Chapters 3 to 7. I discuss statistical testing in Chapters 8 to 13.

TESTING YOUR KNOWLEDGE 1.2

1. Define: between-subjects design, chance difference, dependent variable, equivalent groups, independent variable, participant, raw data, research hypothesis, score, subject.
2. Students learning the basic positions of ballet often have difficulty assuming the correct foot positions. One problem is that of foot pronation, letting the feet roll in when the heels are placed together and the toes pointed laterally outward. To help students overcome this problem, Clarkson, James, Watkins, and Foley (1986) formed two equivalent groups of females who had not previously had ballet training. Both groups were then taught basic ballet positions, and the amount of time the feet pronated was measured. For one group, a buzzer was sounded when the students allowed their feet to pronate. The other group of subjects, however, was not given any feedback about foot pronation. For one test period, the researchers found that subjects given the buzzer feedback had 3.1 seconds of foot pronation, whereas the participants in the no feedback group had 21.8 seconds of foot pronation. A statistical test confirmed that the difference in foot pronation time between the groups was a real and not a chance difference.
   a. Identify the independent variable manipulated by Clarkson et al.
   b. Identify the dependent variable measured.
   c. Explain why this study is an experiment.
   d. Explain why statistical hypothesis testing is necessary in this experiment.

Correlation and Regression

In many instances of behavioral science research an experimenter does not want to or cannot manipulate an independent variable but is interested only in finding whether two or

Covary: Two variables covary when a change in one variable is related to a consistent change in the other variable.

more characteristics of individuals are related to each other or covary. Two variables are said to **covary** if a change in one variable is related to a consistent change in the other variable. For example, if a person's typical level of anxiety is related to his or her use of alcohol, such that high levels of anxiety are related to high use of alcohol and low levels of anxiety are related to low use of alcohol, then anxiety and alcohol usage covary.

To find if two variables covary, we measure a sample of people and obtain two scores from each person, for example, an anxiety score and an alcohol use score. Then a *correlation coefficient* is calculated. A **correlation coefficient** is a statistic that provides a numerical description of the extent of the relatedness of two sets of scores and the direction of the relationship. Values of this coefficient may range from −1.00 to +1.00.

Correlation coefficient: A statistic that provides a numerical description of the extent of the relatedness of two sets of scores and the direction of the relationship.

Statistical hypothesis testing also enters into use with the correlation coefficient. There will always be some chance relationship between scores on two different variables. Thus, the question arises of whether an observed relation, given by the numerical value of the correlation coefficient, is greater than would be expected from chance alone. A statistical test on the correlation coefficient provides an answer for this question.

If the two sets of scores are related beyond chance occurrence, then we may be interested in attempting to predict one score from the other. If you knew a person's anxiety score, could you predict his or her use of alcohol score? And, if you could predict the use of alcohol score, how accurate would your prediction be? Predicting a score on one variable from a score on a second variable involves using **regression analysis**.

Regression analysis: The use of statistical methods to predict one set of scores from a second set of scores.

Correlation and regression analysis techniques are widely used in many areas of behavioral science. As an illustration, to identify what factors might be related to performance on the first test in an introductory psychology course, Woehr and Cavell (1993) and Cavell and Woehr (1994) obtained a variety of measures on 325 students including high school grade point average, the reported number of times a student read a chapter, and the number of hours per week a student watched television. Each of these measures was then correlated with the student's score on the first exam. They found a correlation of +.31 between high school grade point average and the exam score (i.e., a higher grade point average was associated with a higher exam score); a correlation of +.22 between the number of times a student reported reading a chapter and the exam score (i.e., the more times the student read the chapter, the higher the exam score); and a correlation of −.13 between the reported number of hours per week of watching television and the exam score (i.e., the more television watched, the lower the exam score). A statistical test indicated these correlations were not simply chance relationships. The authors suggest these results along with others found in their study may be useful in helping students understand how to improve their test performance. Correlation and regression are discussed more fully in Chapters 13 and 14.

TESTING YOUR KNOWLEDGE 1.3

1. Define: correlation coefficient, covary, regression analysis.
2. Many people believe in paranormal phenomena, such as precognition, extrasensory perception, and psychokinesis. Is the extent of belief in such phenomena related to the type of high school courses taken by such individuals? Tobacyk, Miller, and Jones (1984) measured the belief in paranormal phenomena of 193 eleventh-grade high school students. They also recorded the total number of science courses each student had taken. When

relating the number of science courses to belief in paranormal phenomena, they discovered an inverse relationship. The more science courses a student had taken, the weaker the belief in paranormal phenomena.

a. Explain why correlational statistics are needed in this study.

b. What two sets of measures are used in this study?

WHY ARE STATISTICS NECESSARY?

I have presented three common uses of statistical analysis in behavioral science research. Nagging at you, however, may be the discomforting question of why statistical methods are necessary in the behavioral sciences in the first place. The answer is quite straightforward and the same for each statistical procedure I have presented: It is a delightful fact of life that people differ on many characteristics in varying degrees. It would be a tiresome world if every person were identical to every other person, but such an environment would possess the advantage of requiring no need for statistical techniques. Why? Consider the various uses of statistics that I have introduced.

The first deals with describing numerical measurements obtained from individuals. If all people were alike, then a measurement taken on any one person would describe all other people. Everyone in the United States, for example, would earn exactly $33,748 per year and watch TV 4.4 hours per day. To make an inference to a population, only one person would need to be measured. Accordingly, there would be no need for descriptive statistics to represent a typical score for members of the sample.

The second use discussed deals with statistical hypothesis testing to answer the question of whether an independent variable has an effect on behavior. Think how easy it would be to decide if an independent variable has an effect on behavior if every person's behavior were identical to every other person's. Suppose, for example, that you wanted to know if a particular drug lowers heart rate. Without the drug, everyone's heart rate is 60 beats per minute, and with the drug, everyone's heart rate is 55 beats per minute. Is there any question of whether the drug lowers heart rate? Because there is no chance variation from person to person, there would be no doubt that the drug lowered heart rate. Statistical hypothesis testing would be unnecessary.

Finally, the third use deals with the problem of correlation and regression analysis. Are two behaviors related and, if so, can I predict the occurrence of one behavior from the occurrence of the other? This question only arises because people are different from one another and behave differently in the same situation. If every person were identical to every other person on all behaviors, then all behaviors would be perfectly predictable. Because there would be no variability in behaviors among people, I could predict all behaviors perfectly without using correlation and regression statistics.

An environment with no variability among people and animals would eliminate the need for statistical analysis, but what a boring place it would be. People-watching would be monotonous. Fortunately, we do not have such a world. But a life with both regularities and variability among its peoples requires statistical techniques in order to describe and explain behavior.

SUMMARY

- Statistics refers to the methods or procedures used to summarize, analyze, and draw inferences from data.
- A statistic is a number that may be used to describe the scores from a sample.
- A statistic may also be used to infer the value of a population parameter.
- Statistical hypothesis testing is used to determine if an observed difference between two groups in an experiment is large enough to be attributed to the effect of an independent variable rather than to chance.
- Correlational statistics are used to determine if two sets of scores are related.
- Regression statistics are used to predict one set of scores from another set of scores.

KEY TERMS AND SYMBOLS

between-subjects design (7)
chance difference (8)
correlation coefficient (10)
covary (10)
data (5)
dependent variable (7)
descriptive statistics (6)
equivalent groups (7)

independent variable (7)
parameter (6)
participant (7)
population (5)
random sample (6)
raw data (8)
regression analysis (10)
research hypothesis (7)

sample (6)
score (8)
statistic (5)
statistical hypothesis testing (8)
statistical inference (6)
statistics (5)
subject (7)
variable (2)

REVIEW QUESTIONS

1. Identify four events or occurrences in your life that possess regularity (e.g., the amount of sleep you obtain or the number of hours you work each day). Is there variability as well as regularity in these events?
2. Think of three different populations. What is the common characteristic possessed by the members of each population?
3. A recent research study reported that for males, anger levels and blood pressure are related. Higher levels of anger were related to higher blood pressures.
   a. Which statistical methods discussed in this chapter are used in this study?
   b. Explain why correlational statistics are needed in this study.
   c. What two sets of measures are used in this study?
4. Kawasaki syndrome is a disease of childhood characterized by fever, fissured lips, a bright red tongue, redness of the palms and soles, and a rash. Typical therapy has involved taking aspirin. Recent research, however, has suggested that gamma globulin plus aspirin may be more effective than aspirin alone. To test this research hypothesis, Newburger et al. (1986) randomly assigned 168 children with Kawasaki syndrome to one of two treatment conditions: aspirin or

aspirin plus gamma globulin. They found that after one day of treatment the temperature of children in the aspirin plus gamma globulin treatment group fell an average of 2.3°F, whereas the temperature of the children in the aspirin-only treatment group fell 0.8°F. A statistical test indicated that the difference in the temperature decreases was not a chance difference between the two groups; the aspirin plus gamma globulin group had a greater temperature decrease than the aspirin-only group.

    a. Which statistical methods discussed in this chapter are used in this study?

    b. Identify the independent variable manipulated by Newburger et al.

    c. Identify the dependent variable measured.

    d. Explain why this study is an experiment.

    e. Explain why statistical hypothesis testing is necessary in this experiment.

5. Jacoby (2000) reports that in a nationwide telephone survey of Americans, 72 percent of the males indicated a desire to be wealthy, whereas only 58 percent of females did so. Nineteen percent of the respondents indicated money can buy happiness and 56 percent believed that more money would lead to a less stressful life.

    a. Which statistical methods discussed in this chapter are used in this study?

    b. Explain why descriptive statistics are necessary to summarize the results of this research.

    c. What descriptive statistic was used in this study?

6. For each of the following statements, indicate whether it describes raw data, a statistic, or an inference to a population parameter.

    a. Linda commutes 36 minutes to her work each day.

    b. The average male commuter in the United States spends 42 minutes commuting each day.

    c. A sample of 75 commuters gave an average daily commuting time of 46 minutes.

    d. Benjamin and Anita Houston have $5126 in their bank savings account.

    e. The typical American adult has $6024 in a bank savings account.

    f. A random sample of 50 residents of a small southwestern town provided an average bank savings account of $5692.

7. Think of an instance in which your score on one variable is used to predict your score on a second variable (e.g., your cholesterol level, which is used to predict the chance of heart disease).

Scientific Research

Statistical methods have developed over several thousand years to solve practical problems. In fact, the word *statistics* derives from the Latin *status* or state, for the earliest uses of statistics were for obtaining knowledge of the state or empire. Roman emperors always had a census taken whenever a new territory was conquered. Information from the census, which provided statistics about the population and the valuation of property, was used to levy taxes on the population. Although statistics are still used in this way, their use today has expanded to be an important component in analyzing the data obtained in the scientific study of human and animal behavior. Thus, to understand modern statistical methods, we need to know the basics of the scientific study of behavior.

WHAT IS SCIENCE?

Science is a method for the acquisition of knowledge. The scientific method involves identifying a question, proposing a tentative answer to the question in the form of a research hypothesis, formulating a research design to empirically test the hypothesis, collecting data, analyzing the data, and then reaching a conclusion about the hypothesis from the analyzed data.

Scientific Questions

Empirical data: Scores or measurements based on observation and sensory experience.

A scientific question is one that allows an answer to be obtained by the collection of empirical data. The word *empirical* refers to sensory experience or observation; thus, **empirical data** are scores or measurements based on systematic observation and sensory experience. Each example in Chapter 1 presented research based on a scientific question, for each example allowed an answer to be obtained by collecting empirical data.

Often an experimenter will offer a tentative answer to the question in the form of a research hypothesis. In Chapter 1 a **research hypothesis** was defined as a statement of an expected, or predicted, relationship between two or more variables. For example, Harris and Blaiser (1997) hypothesized that using a mnemonic technique of word pegging would help people to better remember a list of tasks (see page 8). Because a research hypothesis identifies the variables and indicates how they are expected to be related, it directs the researcher in the selection of a research method and the collection of data.

Research Methods

Research method: An approach used to collect data.

Collecting empirical data to test a research hypothesis requires using a research method. A **research method** is an approach the scientist uses to collect data. A variety of methods is used in the behavioral sciences; here I provide only a brief overview of four basic methods. For each of these methods, statistics are used to summarize and analyze the data collected.

Naturalistic Observation

Naturalistic observation: Research involving the observation of behaviors occurring in natural settings.

Naturalistic observation refers to observing behaviors occurring in natural settings without intruding into the situation. As an example of naturalistic observation, Trinkaus (1982, 1983, 1988, 1993, 1997) has systematically observed the behavior of drivers at one intersection over a 15-year period. One of his findings is that compliance with a stop sign has decreased over the observation period. In these observations, the experimenter remained unobtrusive; drivers were not aware that their compliance with a stop sign was being observed. Had the drivers been aware of this observation, they likely would have altered their behavior.

Archival Records

Archival records: Research using existing records.

Archival records research involves answering questions by using existing records. Societies typically collect a variety of information about their members: birth, marriage, and death records; crime reports; census records; and so on. These existing records may provide the data necessary to answer a scientific question. For example, John Graunt (1620–1674), a London shopkeeper, used existing records on births and deaths to identify differences in the causes of death for men and women. More recently, Zusne (1986–1987), interested in the question of whether dying individuals may attempt to delay their death until after an approaching birthday, examined the birthday and deathday records for over 3000 people. These records indicated that such a relationship may exist, but it differs for males and females.

As another example, Thorson (1993) analyzed data from the National Center for Health Statistics on homicide rates in the United States. This research indicated that the homicide rate is greatest in the District of Columbia; about 39 of every 1000 deaths in the District of Columbia are homicides. The rate is lowest in Iowa, where only two deaths of every 1000 are homicides.

Survey Research

Survey research: Research involving obtaining data from either oral or written interviews with people.

Survey research involves obtaining data from either oral or written interviews with people. Survey research is widespread in society. If you have ever filled out a card at a restaurant that asked questions on the quality of the meal or service, or if you have ever completed a product warranty card that asked questions about your income, marital status, and hobbies, then you have participated in survey research. Another familiar example is the surveys at election times that result in political polls.

Experiment

Experiment: A controlled situation in which one or more independent variables are manipulated to observe the effects on the dependent variable.

An **experiment** is a carefully controlled situation in which a scientist manipulates one or more independent variables to observe their effect on the dependent variable. The research of Harris and Blaiser (1997) described in Chapter 1 provides an example of an experiment. The independent variable was the type of instructions given to subjects, either no specific instructions on how to memorize a list or to use a word-pegging memory technique. The dependent variable was the number of tasks each person recalled. The conditions under which the experiment was conducted were carefully controlled so that no variables other than the type of instructions affected the subject's recall of the list of tasks. Properly controlled experiments allow scientists to reach cause-and-effect conclusions about the effect of the independent variable on the dependent variable. If the two groups recall differing numbers of tasks, the cause for this difference must be the independent variable, which is the type of instructions given to the groups. I discuss experiments more fully in Chapter 9, in which the statistical methods needed to analyze an experiment are introduced.

Operational Definitions

Operational definition: A specification of the operations used to make observations, to manipulate an independent variable, or to measure the dependent variable.

Scientific knowledge gained from application of the various research methods must be repeatable and subject to agreement among different observers. Scientific knowledge of a behavior gains strength and generality when other scientists can replicate the behavior in different settings and locations with different participants. For knowledge to be scientific, there must be full communication of ideas and results so that findings can be replicated, criticized, and extended by others. A crucial step in this communication process is to provide an **operational definition** of the procedures used to make observations, to manipulate independent variables, or to measure the dependent variable. As an example, Harris and Blaiser (1997; see page 8) operationally defined a mnemonic technique as having subjects learning to rhyme a number with a word, "one is a bun, two is a shoe, three is a tree, four is a door, five–hive, six–sticks, seven–heaven, eight–gate, nine–wine, ten–hen." Thus, if another scientist wants to extend this research, he or she will know how Harris and Blaiser defined a mnemonic technique.

TESTING YOUR KNOWLEDGE 2.1

1. Define: archival records, empirical data, experiment, naturalistic observation, operational definition, research method, research hypothesis, survey research.
2. For each of the following questions, name the type of research method that you expect would be used to find an answer to the question asked.
   a. What is the opinion of a community concerning the siting of a hazardous waste processing plant within its boundaries?
   b. What is the effect of type of message, either fear inducing or factual, on attitude change?
   c. What is the average age of fathers of firstborn children in Arizona?
   d. How often do 4-year-old children play in groups of three in a nursery school?

MEASUREMENT

Measurement: Assigning numbers to variables following a set of rules.

Answering scientific questions requires measurement of variables. **Measurement** is a process of assigning numbers to variables following a set of rules. Typically, measurements are classified into one of four scales or levels of measurement: nominal, ordinal, interval, or ratio measurements.

Scales of Measurement

Nominal Measurement

Nominal measurement: A classification of the measured variable into different categories.

Nominal measurement is a classification of the measured variable into different categories. As an example, with a nominal measure of the variable of ethnic origin of a person, people may be categorized as Native American, Asian American, African American, Caucasian, or Hispanic and then a number is assigned to name the category (hence, the term *nominal*, which means "to name"), such as 1 = Native American, 2 = Asian American, 3 = African American, 4 = Caucasian, and 5 = Hispanic. Each individual assigned to the same category will be assigned the same number. The number, however, conveys no numerical information; a letter could have been used to identify the category as easily as a number. Many behavioral scientists do not regard nominal measures as actual measurements because the numbers assigned serve the purpose of identification only; they do not provide quantitative information about the variable measured.

Ordinal Measurement

Ordinal measurement: The amount of a variable is placed in order of magnitude along a dimension.

When the amount of a variable is placed in order of magnitude along a dimension, then an **ordinal measurement** scale is used. For example, people may be asked to arrange a series of cartoons on a funniness scale from most to least funny. Often a numerical value of 1 is assigned to the stimulus or individual possessing the greatest amount of the characteristic being measured, a value of 2 to that person or stimulus that exhibits the next greatest amount, and so forth. If, for example, anxiety is measured with an ordinal scale, then the person exhibiting the most anxiety is assigned a 1, the person showing the next largest amount of anxiety a 2, the next a 3, and so on, producing an ordering of people from most to least anxious.

Ordinal scales essentially produce a ranking in which someone or something assigned a rank of 1 possesses more of a variable than one given a rank of 2. Ordinal measures do not, however, permit determining how much of a difference exists in the measured variable between ranks. A small difference in the variable being measured may exist between ranks 1 and 2, but a large difference may exist between ranks 2 and 3. For example, the times for the first three runners of a marathon may be 2 hours 27 minutes, 2 hours 28 minutes, and 2 hours 32 minutes, respectively. The rank order of the finish of these runners is 1, 2, and 3. But the time difference between the first and second finisher is 1 minute, whereas it is 4 minutes between the second- and third-place contestants.

Ordinal scales do not indicate how much of the measured variable exists; they provide information only about the order of individuals or objects on the variable measured. A rank of 1 does not necessarily correspond to a large amount of the variable being measured and the lowest-ranked object or person does not necessarily possess little of the property being measured. A person who is asked to rank order cartoons from most to least funny may find no humor in any of them. Yet, a rank of 1 assigned to a cartoon by this individual conveys the same information as a rank of 1 assigned to a cartoon to by another person who may regard all the cartoons as very funny.

Despite their deficiencies, however, ordinal measures are often a first step in the development of more precise measurements. As an illustration, autism is a disorder that affects a child's language development, thought processes, and responsiveness to social and physical stimulation. However, there has been little research on how children diagnosed as autistic may vary from each other. As a first step in this direction, Dihoff, Hetznecker, Brosvic, Carpenter, and Hoffman (1993) developed an ordinal measurement of the extent of autistic behavior that a child may demonstrate. In this scale, six components of behavior are measured: language ability, responsiveness to the environment, responsiveness to social stimulation, responsiveness to physical stimulation, adaptiveness to the use of materials, and cognitive functioning. Within each component, five levels of functioning were identified, the levels differing on an ordinal scale from the lowest level to the highest level of functioning. For example, the levels within the component of language development are

None
Gestures
Communicative intent
Communicative intent plus words
Other-directed communication

Gestures show greater language development than no language development at all, and communicative intent plus words shows greater language development than only gestures. But I do not know how large the differences are between the categories; hence, the measurement is ordinal.

TESTING YOUR KNOWLEDGE 2.2

1. Define: measurement, nominal measurement, ordinal measurement.
2. Name the four scales of measurement.
3. Identify one deficiency of nominal measurements.
4. What information is provided by a rank of 2 assigned to an individual on a ranking of motivation to achieve?
5. On a rank ordering of 13 people for depression proneness from most to least, Jennifer was ranked 1, Debbi 2, Ena 12, and Marty 13.
   a. Explain why you cannot conclude that Jennifer is very prone to depression and Marty is not at all depression prone.
   b. Is it appropriate to conclude that the difference in depression proneness between Jennifer and Debbi is the same as the difference in depression proneness between Ena and Marty? Explain your answer.

Interval Measurement

Interval measurement: The amount of a variable is ordered along a dimension, and the differences between the assigned numbers represent equal amounts in the magnitude of the variable measured. The zero point of an interval scale is an arbitrary starting point.

If the requirements for ordinal measurement are met, and in addition the differences between the assigned numbers represent equal amounts in the magnitude of the variable measured, then an **interval measurement** is created. An interval measurement, however, has no true zero point for which a value of zero represents the complete absence of the variable measured. A zero value on an interval measurement is an arbitrary starting point that could be replaced by any other value as a starting point.

The Fahrenheit and Celsius temperature scales are examples of interval measurements. Zero degrees does not represent an absence of temperature for either scale. Neither scale contains a true zero point because measured temperatures may fall below zero degrees. It is accurate to state that the difference in temperature between 20°C and 40°C is equivalent to the difference in temperature between 40°C and 60°C, but it is not appropriate to say that 40°C is twice as high a temperature as 20°C. We can see why this difficulty arises by comparing several equivalent Celsius and Fahrenheit temperatures, as follows:

Equivalent Temperatures

°C	°F
20	68
40	104
60	140

Notice that a difference of 20°C is always equal to a difference of 36°F. But because each scale starts with an arbitrary zero point, adjacent scores on one scale do not form ratios equal to adjacent scores on the other scale. For example, a ratio of 40°C/20°C = 2.0, whereas a corresponding temperature ratio of 104°F/68°F = 1.5.

Examples of measurements in the behavioral sciences that definitely achieve an interval level are infrequent. But rating scales, which frequently are used to measure attributes of people, such as personality characteristics, attitudes, marital happiness, fear of objects, motivation to achieve, or leadership ability, are often treated as yielding interval measurement. Rating scales generally present a statement and then a response scale with two extremes and several points between the extremes. For example, in attitude measurement a person may be asked to respond to a statement such as "Strong gun control laws reduce crime" by making a check mark on the scale:

Strongly agree	Agree	Uncertain	Disagree	Strongly disagree

Other forms of rating scales may ask you to rate a person on a set of bipolar adjectives, such as

Dishonest _____ : _____ : _____ : _____ : _____ : _____ : _____ Honest

Attractive _____ : _____ : _____ : _____ : _____ : _____ : _____ Unattractive

Cold _____ : _____ : _____ : _____ : _____ : _____ : _____ Warm

Rating scales may have any number of categories between the extremes; and the scales may be referred to as 5-point, 7-point, or 9-point scales, depending on the number of categories provided. Often the favorability of the adjectives at the end points of the scale is reversed for half the items. Thus, half the favorable adjectives are at the left of the scale and half at the right. This reversal helps to avoid problems of response set, such as checking only the items on the right side of the scale.

After a person has responded on the scale, a numerical value is assigned to each category on the scale, such as

Dishonest _____ : _____ : _____ : _____ : _____ : _____ : _____ Honest
           1   2   3   4   5   6   7

Attractive _____ : _____ : _____ : _____ : _____ : _____ : _____ Unattractive
         7   6   5   4   3   2   1

Cold _____ : _____ : _____ : _____ : _____ : _____ : _____ Warm
         1   2   3   4   5   6   7

In many instances, a series of scales is presented, and the scores on the separate scales are added to yield one score for a person. These scales are called *summated rating scales*. As an illustration, Rotton and Kelly (1985) developed a scale for assessing belief in the effect of a full moon on behavior, the Belief in Lunar Effects Scale. The scale consists of nine statements. For each statement the respondent indicates agreement with the statement by choosing a number between 1 (*strong disagreement*) to 9 (*strong agreement*). For example, one statement on the scale is:

It is a good idea to stay at home when the moon is full.[1]

1	2	3	4	5	6	7	8	9
Strongly disagree			Neither agree nor disagree				Strongly agree	

A score is obtained by summing over the nine statements to yield a total score for the rating scale. The possible range of scores is from 9 (obtained by responding with a 1 to all nine statements) to 81 (obtained by responding with a 9 to all nine statements). Notice that the range of scores that this scale can assume is arbitrary; if the anchor points for each statement ranged from 10 to 90, then the range of the summated rating scale would be 90 to 810.

What level of measurement is represented by scores on the Belief in Lunar Effects Scale and other similar rating scales? It should be clear that the rating for each statement represents at least ordinal measurement. A score of 4 indicates more of a particular characteristic described by the statement than does a 3, and a 3 reflects more than a 2; however, I cannot be certain that the difference between a 4 and 3 represents the same difference in a characteristic as that between 3 and 2. Such ratings do seem to provide more than merely ordinal information, however. I might expect that a respondent subjectively divides the categories into roughly equal intervals between the ends of the scale. Moreover, if the ratings obtained from a person on a number of separate scales are summed, then it seems reasonable to assume that the resulting score provides more than just ordinal information. Gardner (1975) argues that scores from summated scales are in a gray region between ordinal and interval. Thus, a measurement may not necessarily fit neatly into one of the four measurement scales. For statistical analysis, however, researchers often treat rating scales as representing interval measurement.

Ratio measurement: The amount of a variable is ordered along a dimension, the differences between the assigned numbers represent equal amounts in the magnitude of the variable measured, and a true zero point exists, which represents the absence of the characteristic measured.

Ratio Measurement

A **ratio measurement** scale replaces the arbitrary zero point of the interval scale with a true zero point that corresponds to the absence of the variable being measured. With a ratio scale it is possible to state that one thing (e.g., a stimulus, an event, or an individual) has twice, or half, or three times as much of the variable measured than another. Ratio measurement is used in the behavioral sciences when measures such as reaction time or the

[1]Adapted and reproduced with permission of authors and publisher from: Rotton, J., & Kelly, I. W., "A scale for assessing belief in lunar effects: reliability and concurrent validity," *Psychological Reports*, 1985, *57*, 239–245, © Psychological Reports.

amount of time spent on a task are measured. These measures have a true zero point, and the intervals between the units of measurement are equal. For example, if the amount of time a person spends solving a puzzle is measured, the difference between 15 seconds and 25 seconds (i.e., 10 seconds) is equal to the difference between 50 seconds and 60 seconds (again 10 seconds). Furthermore, someone who spends 60 seconds solving a puzzle spends twice as long as someone who spends only 30 seconds.

The magnitude of perceptual illusions may often be measured with a ratio scale. An illusion occurs when our perception of a stimulus does not correspond to its physical characteristics; we misperceive what actually exists. A familiar example is the Müller-Lyer illusion, illustrated in Figure 2.1. Here you may perceive line A to be longer than line B. Both lines are physically equal in length, however. Your perception is in error. The magnitude of this illusion can be measured by finding how much the perceived length of the stimulus differs from its actual length. Perceptual error measured in millimeters (mm) represents a ratio measurement. It is possible for a person to have an error of 0 mm (i.e., no error) when the perceived length of the stimulus does not differ from the actual length. The difference between an error of 5 mm and an error of 8 mm is the same as the difference between errors of 10 mm and 13 mm; in each case the difference is 3 mm. Moreover, an error of 10 mm represents an illusion magnitude that is twice as great as an error of 5 mm.

Qualitative and Quantitative Data

Qualitative data: Data obtained from nominal measurement indicating that variables differ in quality.

Nominal measurement uses numbers to name or assign people or objects to different categories; it does not provide numerical information about the variables categorized. Thus, nominal measurements provide **qualitative data**; the people or objects categorized differ in some quality. Ordinal, interval, and ratio measurements provide **quantitative data**; the

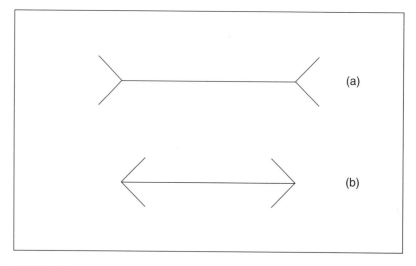

FIGURE 2.1
The Müller–Lyer illusion.

Quantitative data: Data obtained from ordinal, interval, or ratio measurements indicating how much of a variable exists.

numbers assigned to a variable express the amount or quantity of the variable measured. Of the three quantitative measures, behavioral scientists prefer to use interval and ratio measurements, for these measures allow more precise quantification of the underlying attribute or characteristic being measured than do ordinal measurements. Furthermore, because interval and ratio measures permit the use of mathematical procedures such as addition, subtraction, multiplication, and division, they allow the application of more versatile statistical techniques. Consequently, many of the statistical techniques presented in this text are for scores measured on an interval or ratio scale.

TESTING YOUR KNOWLEDGE 2.3

1. Define: interval measurement, qualitative data, quantitative data, ratio measurement.
2. The following scores were obtained on an interval measure of leadership ability: Rosana, 84; Eva, 78; Pierce, 71; Victoria, 65; Nancy, 42; and William, 0.
   a. Is it accurate to conclude that the difference in leadership ability between Rosana and Eva is the same as the difference between Pierce and Victoria? Explain your answer.
   b. Is it accurate to conclude that Rosana possesses twice as much leadership ability as Nancy? Explain your answer.
   c. Is it accurate to conclude that, because of his score of zero, William totally lacks leadership ability? Explain your answer.
3. Several college students participated in a study on sleep in which the amount of time (in minutes) spent in rapid-eye-movement sleep (REM sleep, the dream sleep stage) was measured using an electroencephalogram. On one night, the durations of REM sleep were Dominic, 204 minutes; Greta, 194 minutes; Andre, 175 minutes; Jody, 165 minutes; and Carmen, 102 minutes.
   a. Is it appropriate to conclude that the difference in the amount of REM sleep between Dominic and Greta is the same as the difference between Andre and Jody? Explain your answer.
   b. Is it appropriate to conclude that Dominic spent twice as much time in REM sleep as Carmen? Explain your answer.
   c. Suppose another student, Mandie, spent zero minutes in REM sleep. Is it appropriate to conclude that she had no REM sleep that night? Explain your answer.

Discrete and Continuous Variables

Variables may also be characterized as discrete or continuous.

Discrete Variables

Discrete variable: A variable that can take on only a finite or potentially countable set of values.

A **discrete variable** is one that can take on only a finite or potentially countable set of values. The word *finite* means a definable set of possible values. The number of students at your college is a discrete variable: There may be 5652 students or 5653 students, but not $5652\frac{1}{2}$ students. The number of students may increase or decrease by one whole student, not one-half or one-third student. Thus, the number of students takes on a countable set of values. Typically, variables whose possible values can be counted are discrete variables: the number of people living in a city, the number of children in a family, the number of burglaries in a year, the number of automobiles registered in a state, and so forth.

Continuous Variables

Continuous variable: A variable that can take on an infinite set of values between any two levels of the variable.

A **continuous variable** is one that can take on an infinite set of values between any two levels of the variable. A continuous variable, thus, has an unlimited set of values in the range within which it varies. A measurement of your weight is an example, for you may weigh 135.6 pounds or 135.64 pounds. Your weight is not limited to discrete values such as 135 pounds or 136 pounds although it is possible that you may have a scale that indicates your weight only in whole pounds, such as 135 or 136 pounds. Yet your weight is not limited to these specific values. It may take on any value between 135 and 136 pounds. Similarly, many psychological variables, such as anxiety or intelligence, exist as continuous variables, although they may be measured by scales that assign whole number scores to a person.

Real Limits of a Measurement.

When measurements are made of a continuous variable, specific numerical values are assigned to the amount of the variable present. But the assigned measures only approximate the actual amount of the variable. Consequently, we must be aware of the accuracy of our measurements, regardless of the scale of measurement that we are using. And the accuracy of measurement of a continuous variable is contained in the real limits of the number assigned.

Real limits of a number: The points midway between the number and the next lower and the next higher numbers on the scale used to make the measurements.

Real limits of a measurement are easily understood using measurements of the variable of time. Suppose that you are measuring the amount of time that a person can hold his or her hand in a tub of 40°F water. This task may be used to induce pain safely in experiments dealing with relaxation strategies to increase pain tolerance. Suppose for one subject that you measured a time of 37 seconds by observing the second hand on a stopwatch. How accurate is this measurement? Because you measured to the nearest whole second, the time could not have been 36 or 38 seconds. But might the actual duration have been 37.2 seconds or 36.7 seconds? The answer is yes, for you may have rounded either 36.7 seconds or 37.2 seconds to 37 seconds. The accuracy of this measurement of 37 seconds is given by the real limits of this number. The **real limits of a number** are the points that are midway between the number and the next lower and the next higher numbers on the scale used to make the measurements. For a measured value of 37 seconds, then, the **lower real limit** is 36.5 seconds and the **upper real limit** is 37.5 seconds. The lower real limit of 36.5 seconds is midway between 36 seconds, the next lower measured value on the scale used, and 37 seconds. The upper real limit of 37.5 seconds is midway between 37 seconds and 38 seconds, the next higher measured value on the scale used.

Lower real limit of a number: The point midway between a number and the next lower number.

Upper real limit of a number: The point midway between a number and the next higher number.

Suppose now that you had measured the duration with an electronic stopwatch that provided measurements to the nearest $\frac{1}{100}$ second, such as 37.21 seconds. What are the upper and lower real limits of this measurement? Again, the rule is to find the midpoint between the next lower and the next higher value on the measuring scale used. Thus, the lower real limit is the midpoint between 37.20 (the next lower number) and 37.21 seconds, or 37.205 seconds. The upper real limit is the midpoint between 37.21 seconds and 37.22 seconds (the next upper value), or 37.215 seconds.

Every numerical measurement of a continuous variable has upper and lower real limits associated with it. For example, suppose that I am using the 7-point rating scale illustrated in Figure 2.2. Assume that a person checked a response of 3 on this scale. Following the rules presented earlier, the upper and lower real limits for this score are 2.5 and 3.5, respectively.

How often do you daydream during your statistics class?

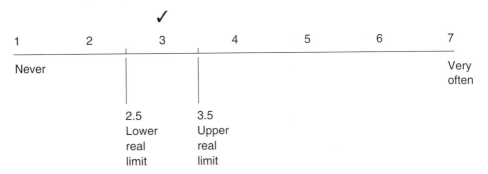

FIGURE 2.2
Upper and lower real limits for a response (indicated by the ✓) on a 7-point rating scale.

The real limits of a measurement are important when plotting frequency distributions of scores and when rounding values in statistical computations. I discuss frequency distributions in Chapter 3.

Rounding: Answers to Computations.   Suppose that you asked three friends to complete the scale shown in Figure 2.2 and obtained the following responses: 4, 4, and 3. To describe the typical response, you found the sum of these numbers, 11, and divided it by 3, or $\frac{11}{3} = 3.666\overline{6}$. The bar ($^-$) over the last 6 indicates that the 6s continue endlessly. How many decimal places should you present in your answer?

One convention is that the final value of a computation should be rounded to two decimal places beyond the value to which the original scores were measured. In the example, the scores were given to the ones (or units) place; a person could check 3 or 4, but not 3.2 or 4.6. Following this rule, the final value of the computation is rounded to two decimal places beyond the ones place, or to 3.67.

Others follow a convention of rounding the final value of a computation to one decimal place beyond the value to which the original scores were measured. Following this approach, the final value of the computation for the example is rounded to one decimal place beyond the ones place, or to 3.7. I illustrate both approaches in text examples.

Rounding: Intermediate Steps in Computations.   If computations require a number of steps prior to obtaining the final answer, then intermediate numerical values should be carried to at least two decimal places beyond the number of decimal places needed for the final answer. For example, if the value of $\frac{11}{3}$ were to enter into further computations, I would not round its value to 3.67. Rather, I carry it to two additional places, 3.6667, for the computations. This approach minimizes rounding error in computations.

Rounding Rules.   Suppose that I have an answer to a computation such as 3.6AB, where the A and B are possible numerical values. For example, if A = 2 and B = 9, then 3.6AB = 3.629. I wish to round this number to two decimal places. Several rules typically are followed when rounding numbers:

- If the number represented by the letter B is greater than 5, increase A by 1 and drop the B value. Following this rule, 3.629 (here $A = 2$ and $B = 9$) is rounded to 3.63.
- If the number represented by the letter B is less than 5, leave the A value as is and drop the B value. Following this rule, 3.623 (here $A = 2$ and $B = 3$) is rounded to 3.62.
- If the number represented by the letter B is exactly 5, increase A by 1 if A is an odd number, but leave its value as is if it is an even number; then drop B. Following this rule, 3.635 (here $A = 3$ and $B = 5$) is rounded to 3.64, but 3.625 (here $A = 2$ and $B = 5$) is rounded to 3.62. Notice, however, that if the number is 3.6251 it is rounded to 3.63, not 3.62.

TESTING YOUR KNOWLEDGE 2.4

1. Define: continuous variable, discrete variable, real limits of a number, lower real limit, upper real limit.
2. Identify each of the following variables being measured as discrete or continuous.
   a. A person's handgrip strength measured in pounds.
   b. The eye contact of an accuser with a defendant in a courtroom measured in seconds.
   c. The number of stotts (leaping vertically with four legs off the ground simultaneously) made by a Thompson's gazelle in a one-hour period.
   d. The length of song (in seconds) by a male songbird during courtship.
   e. The funniness of a set of cartoons measured by the amount of time (in seconds) subjects laugh at them.
   f. The number of altruistic behaviors observed in nursery school children in a one-day period.
   g. The number of friends a child has.
   h. The number of items correct on a statistics examination.
3. Provide the lower real and upper real limits for each of the scores presented.
   a. A height of 152.4 centimeters.
   b. A duration of eye contact of 17.3 seconds.
   c. An assigned rating of 4 on a 7-point scale.
   d. A reaction time of 0.437 second.
   e. An error of 6.9 millimeters on the Müller–Lyer illusion.
   f. A handgrip strength of 67.81 pounds.
4. Round the following values to the number of decimal places indicated.
   a. 27.436 (two decimal places)
   b. 119.0278 (three decimal places)
   c. 1.445 (two decimal places)
   d. 1263.75915 (four decimal places)
   e. 0.352 (two decimal places)
   f. 13.2659 (two decimal places)

SUMMARY

- Statistics are tools used to summarize and analyze data in the scientific study of behavior.
- Scientific research begins by asking a question that can be answered by obtaining empirical data.

- A research method is an approach used to collect data. Four types of research methods are naturalistic observation, archival records, survey research, and experiments.
- Naturalistic observation is research involving the observation of behaviors occurring in natural settings.
- Archival records research uses existing records.
- Survey research involves obtaining data from either oral or written interviews with people.
- An experiment is a carefully controlled situation in which a scientist manipulates one or more independent variables to observe their effect on the dependent variable.
- An operational definition identifies the operations or steps followed to make an observation or to manipulate a variable.
- Measurement is a process of assigning numbers to variables according to a set of rules.
- Nominal measurement is a classification of the measured variable into different categories. Nominal measurement provides qualitative data.
- Ordinal measurement scales place a variable in an ordered set along a dimension.
- Interval scales create equal increments in the magnitude of the variable measured, but they do not have a true zero.
- Ratio scales possess the properties of the interval scale plus a true zero point.
- Ordinal, interval, and ratio measurements provide quantitative data.
- A discrete variable can take on only a finite or potentially countable set of values.
- A continuous variable can take on an infinite set of values between any two levels of the variable.
- The real limits of a number are the points that are midway between the number and the next lower and the next higher numbers on the scale used to make the measurements.

KEY TERMS AND SYMBOLS

archival records (16)
continuous variable (24)
discrete variable (23)
empirical data (15)
experiment (16)
interval measurement (19)
lower real limit of a number (24)

measurement (17)
naturalistic observation (15)
nominal measurement (17)
operational definition (17)
ordinal measurement (18)
qualitative data (22)
quantitative data (22)

ratio measurement (21)
real limits of a number (24)
research method (15)
survey research (16)
upper real limit of a number (24)

REVIEW QUESTIONS

1. Suppose that you were asked to collect data to answer each of the following questions. For each question, indicate what type of research design you would choose and why.

    a. What is the typical amount of time spent on homework by the members of your statistics class?

    b. How often does a basketball player make a free shot when a time-out is called immediately before the shot is made?

    c. Does a sales training program increase the amount of sales by people who have completed the program?

    d. What are the common behaviors of a young child in the check-out line of a supermarket?

2. Suppose that you were asked to measure job stress in a group of employees. How would you operationally define your measure of job stress?

3. The career orientation of police officers was measured by having police officers order four paragraphs describing various career orientations from 1, the paragraph closest to the individual's career orientation, to 4, the paragraph furthest from the individual's career orientation.

    a. What is the variable being measured in this study?

    b. What level of measurement is achieved by the measure used?

4. Professional female golfers were weighed to determine if body weight was related to their game.

    a. What is the variable being measured in this study?

    b. What level of measurement is achieved by the measure used?

    c. The weight of one golfer was reported as 134.6 pounds. What are the upper and lower real limits of this measurement?

    d. Six golfers were weighed to the nearest pound. Their average weight was 127.648 pounds. Round this value.

5. Parents of first-grade children were measured on a personality trait of emotional stability using a rating scale.

    a. What is the variable being measured in this study?

    b. What level of measurement is achieved by the measure used?

    c. Suppose that a person assigned a rating of 8 on a 9-point rating scale for agreement or disagreement with a statement. What are the upper and lower real limits of this measurement?

    d. Suppose that you measured six people on this statement and found their typical rating to be 5.833. Is this result correctly reported with respect to the number of decimal places given? Explain your answer.

6. You are investigating how much time students spend doing homework each day. One student reported she spent 97 minutes working on chemistry.

    a. What level of measurement is achieved by the measure used?

    b. What are the upper and lower real limits of the 97 minutes the student reported spending on homework?

    c. Three students reported spending 97, 68, and 83 minutes on homework, respectively. The average of these three scores is $82.66\overline{66}$. Round this value.

7. Interpersonal values of an individual were measured by having the person order 12 value statements from most to least important. What level of measurement is achieved by the measure used?

8. The behavioral interactions of children at a nursery school with other children at the school were categorized as agonistic (i.e., argumentative or fighting), neutral (i.e., not interacting), or altruistic (i.e., helpful). What level of measurement is achieved by the measure used?

9. Identify each of the following measured variables as discrete or continuous.
   a. The number of students in your statistics class.
   b. The weight loss in pounds by people who have completed a diet and exercise workshop.
   c. The number of left-handed people in a group of 100.
   d. A person's blood pressure measured in millimeters of mercury.

10. Provide the lower and upper real limits for each of the scores presented.
   a. A weight of 141.3 pounds.
   b. A duration of 34 minutes playing a video game.
   c. A golf drive of 175.6 yards.
   d. A body temperature of 98.2°F.
   e. A systolic blood pressure of 109 millimeters of mercury.

11. Round the following values to two decimal places.
   a. 42.255   e. 13.895
   b. 1.165   f. 24.6250
   c. 163.651   g. 19.2751
   d. 27.426

12. A restaurant leaves cards for its patrons to complete after finishing a meal. Each card asks patrons to rate the restaurant on the quality of food, friendliness of service, speed of service, and cleanliness on 5-point scales ranging from poor to excellent. An overall score from 4 to 20 is obtained from each card. What level of measurement is used here? Explain your answer.

13. A psychologist studied how well people could tolerate pain by placing their hand in 40°F water and measuring how long they could keep their hand in the water. She performed two studies.
   a. In study 1, participants were ranked on the duration that they could hold their hand in the water as follows: Lisa, 1; Stacia, 2; Maritza, 3; Robin, 4; and Jody, 5. What level of measurement is used here?
   b. In study 2, the duration of tolerance was measured in seconds with the following results: Lisa, 111.3 seconds; Stacia, 97.8 seconds; Maritza, 71.3 seconds; Robin, 18.7 seconds; and Jody, 13.6 seconds. What level of measurement is used here?

14. In a ranking of health care systems by the World Health Care Organization (Mishra, 2000), the U.S. health care system ranked 37th. The top-ranking health care system was that of France followed by Italy. Japan was ranked 10th and Switzerland 20th.
   a. How much better is France's health care system in comparison to Italy's?
   b. Is Japan's health care system twice as good as Switzerland's? Explain your answer.
   c. What does knowing that the United States ranked 37th tell you about the quality of the U.S. health care system?

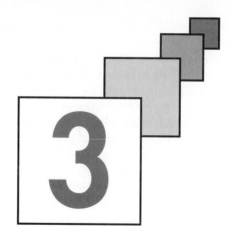

Describing Data: Frequency Distributions and Graphs

Have you ever thought, "If only I could get my anxiety under control I could do much better on examinations"? If so, you are not alone. In recent years, counselors and psychologists have identified test anxiety as a contributor to poor performance for many students. To measure test anxiety, Spielberger (1980) developed the *Test Anxiety Inventory* (TAI). The TAI is composed of 20 statements similar to "I become very uneasy and upset before a big examination." For each statement, the student completing the inventory chooses one of the alternatives, *almost never, sometimes, often, almost always*, that best applies to him or her. After the inventory is completed, a numerical value is assigned to each alternative: *almost never* = 1; *sometimes* = 2; *often* = 3; *almost always* = 4. A score is obtained by adding the numerical values of the alternatives selected. This inventory is, thus, a summated rating scale with a score ranging from 20 to 80. A score of 20 indicates the minimum level of anxiety possible on the TAI and a score of 80 the maximum level. As observed in Chapter 2, summated rating scales probably are in a gray area of measurement. Yet, for statistical purposes, scores from rating scales are often treated as representing interval measurements. I follow this custom with this example.

Suppose a college counselor administers the Test Anxiety Inventory to a sample of 20 students seeking assistance in controlling test anxiety. The scores obtained are portrayed in Table 3.1. Such scores are called **raw data** or **raw scores**, for they are exactly as collected and have not been subjected to statistical analysis. The letter N is used to indicate the total number of scores obtained; thus, N for this example is 20.

Consider a student who obtains a score of 60 on this inventory. What does this score tell us about that student's level of test anxiety? Is it higher or lower than that of the other students completing the inventory? Are you able to answer these questions knowing only this score? The answer to this question is no, for with many measures in behavioral science, an individual score is meaningful only in comparison to other scores. Thus, the first step in analyzing these scores is to arrange them as a frequency distribution. I will first discuss the presentation of quantitative data from interval or ratio measurements.

Raw data or raw scores: The scores obtained from participants before the scores have been analyzed statistically.

N: The total number of scores in a set of scores.

TABLE 3.1
Hypothetical Test Anxiety Inventory scores from 20 students.

61	57
67	55
63	59
60	59
62	59
67	64
59	65
60	62
68	59
64	60

FREQUENCY DISTRIBUTIONS WITH UNGROUPED SCORES

Simple Frequency Distributions

Frequency distribution: A table showing each score in a set of scores and how frequently each score occurred.

Ungrouped frequency distribution: A frequency distribution constructed by listing all possible score values between the lowest and highest scores obtained and then placing a tally mark (/) beside a score each time it occurs.

f: The simple frequency of occurrence of each score in a frequency distribution.

A **frequency distribution** is a table that orders a set of scores from highest to lowest and indicates how often each score occurred. Table 3.2 illustrates an ungrouped frequency distribution for the Test Anxiety Inventory scores presented in Table 3.1. This **ungrouped frequency distribution** was constructed by listing all possible score values between the lowest and highest scores obtained (55 and 68, respectively, column a of Table 3.2) and then placing a tally mark (/) beside a score each time it occurred (shown in column b of Table 3.2). All possible score values in the range from the lowest to the highest score obtained are included in column a, even if the score did not occur. The number of tally marks for each score was counted and entered into column c as the **simple frequency of occurrence of each score** (symbolized by f). Notice that this distribution lets us see that a Test Anxiety Inventory score of 60 is about in the middle of the distribution of scores; about one-half of the scores are less, and about one-half are more.

Relative Frequency Distributions

The frequency of occurrence of scores in an ungrouped frequency distribution may also be presented as relative frequencies. A **relative frequency distribution** is obtained by dividing

TABLE 3.2

Ungrouped frequency distribution for Test Anxiety Inventory scores of Table 3.1.

(a) Score	(b) Tally	(c) Frequency (f)	(d) Relative Frequency (rf)	(e) Percentage Frequency ($\%f$)
68	/	1	.05	5
67	//	2	.10	10
66		0	.00	0
65	/	1	.05	5
64	//	2	.10	10
63	/	1	.05	5
62	//	2	.10	10
61	/	1	.05	5
60	///	3	.15	15
59	/////	5	.25	25
58		0	.00	0
57	/	1	.05	5
56		0	.00	0
55	/	1	.05	5

Relative frequency (*rf*): The frequency of a score divided by the total number of scores obtained.

the frequency of each score by the total number of scores in the distribution. Thus, a **relative frequency** (symbolized by *rf*) is expressed as

$$rf \text{ of a score} = f \text{ of a score}/N.$$

As an example, the relative frequency of occurrence of the score of 60 in Table 3.2 is found by dividing its frequency ($f = 3$) by the total number of scores ($N = 20$), which equals .15.[1] The relative frequency of the TAI scores is presented in column d of Table 3.2.

Percentage Frequency Distributions

Percentage frequency (*%f*): The relative frequency of a score multiplied by 100.

Often relative frequencies are multiplied by 100 to create a **percentage frequency distribution**. The **percentage frequency** of a score (symbolized by *%f*) is found by multiplying the relative frequency of a score by 100, or

$$\%f \text{ of a score} = (rf \text{ of score}) \times 100.$$

The percentage frequency of scores is presented in column e of Table 3.2. Notice that columns c, d, and e of this table present equivalent information about the distribution of scores in Table 3.1. The advantage of having frequencies presented as relative or percentage frequencies is that these values are independent of the total number of scores obtained. Thus, if you had a second sample of 35 scores ($N = 35$) from another group of students, it would be easier to compare the frequency distributions from the two different size samples if the frequency distributions were expressed as either relative or percentage frequencies rather than as simple frequencies alone.

Obtaining Information from a Frequency Distribution

The simple frequencies, relative frequencies, or percentage frequencies presented in Table 3.2 allow us to easily notice that

- The lowest score is 55.
- The highest score is 68.
- The most frequently occurring score is 59.
- Fifteen of the scores are between 59 and 65.

These characteristics of the distribution of scores are not easily seen in the raw scores of Table 3.1.

Example Problem 3.1

Constructing Ungrouped Frequency Distributions

Problem: Psychologists are interested in the perception of ambiguous figures, for they believe that understanding how we perceive these figures will provide knowledge about perception of the everyday world. The Mach pyramid shown in Figure 3.1 is an example of

---

[1]When presenting decimal fractions in this text, I will follow the guidelines of the *Publication Manual of the American Psychological Association* (1994), which indicate that if a decimal fraction cannot be greater than 1, a zero is not used before the decimal point. Thus, relative frequencies are reported without a zero before the decimal point.

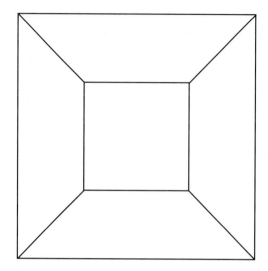

FIGURE 3.1
The Mach pyramid.

an ambiguous figure, for it is reversible in perspective. You may see this figure either as a pyramid with the small square appearing to project out of the page toward you or as a room in perspective with the small square being the far wall. Suppose you timed 25 people over a 1-minute period to see how long each person could see the figure as a pyramid and found the following times (to the nearest whole second):

2, 7, 10, 5, 5, 3, 9, 11, 5, 8, 2, 4, 7, 6, 10, 7, 3, 9, 7, 11, 4, 6, 3, 1, and 8.

Construct an ungrouped simple frequency distribution, relative frequency distribution, and percentage frequency distribution for these scores. What conclusions about the scores may you reach from these distributions?

Solution: The requested frequency distributions are shown in the following table.

Score	Tally	f	rf	$\%f$
11	//	2	.08	8
10	//	2	.08	8
9	//	2	.08	8
8	//	2	.08	8
7	////	4	.16	16
6	//	2	.08	8
5	///	3	.12	12
4	//	2	.08	8
3	///	3	.12	12
2	//	2	.08	8
1	/	1	.04	4

Conclusions: The scores range from 1 to 11 seconds and the most frequently occurring score is 7 seconds. With the exception of the most frequently occurring score of 7, the scores occur about equally throughout their range.

TESTING YOUR KNOWLEDGE 3.1

1. Define: f, frequency distribution, N, percentage frequency distribution, $\%f$, raw data, raw scores, relative frequency distribution, rf, ungrouped frequency distribution.
2. The capability to adapt to differing social situations is a characteristic often found in effective leaders. Suppose you measured 20 people on a scale of adaptability in which scores can range from 0 to 25 and obtained the following scores: 6, 13, 4, 19, 3, 12, 9, 8, 5, 11, 6, 8, 15, 5, 8, 10, 9, 14, 4, and 8.
    a. Construct an ungrouped simple frequency distribution, relative frequency distribution, and percentage frequency distribution for these scores.
    b. What are the lowest and highest scores obtained?
    c. What is the most frequently occurring score?

GROUPED FREQUENCY DISTRIBUTIONS

Grouped frequency distribution: A frequency distribution in which scores are grouped together in class intervals and the frequency of scores occurring within each class is tabulated.

If a large number of scores is collected or if there is a wide range of score values in the data, an ungrouped frequency distribution as illustrated in Table 3.2 can become spread out, making it difficult to see clear patterns in the data. It is useful, then, to construct a **grouped frequency distribution** in which scores are grouped together in class intervals. The class intervals are arranged from highest to lowest, and the frequency of scores occurring within each class is tallied and tabulated. To illustrate grouped frequency distributions, suppose the counselor decided to measure test anxiety in a randomly selected sample of 100 students and obtained the scores in Table 3.3.

Constructing Grouped Frequency Distributions

Class interval: The width of the interval used to group raw scores in a grouped frequency distribution. The size or width of the interval is represented by i.

A grouped frequency distribution places raw scores into class intervals. A **class interval** is a range of score values into which the raw scores are grouped. Table 3.4 presents several grouped frequency distributions of the scores in Table 3.3 using a class interval of size 5. Constructing grouped frequency distributions, such as Table 3.4, requires two decisions: (1) the number of class intervals to be used and (2) the size (or width) of the class interval.

Number of Class Intervals
The number of class intervals to be used is determined by the range of the scores, with 10 to 20 class intervals ordinarily used. The number of intervals usually is chosen so that the size of the class interval is 1, 2, 3, 5, or a multiple of 5. The range of scores in Table 3.3 is from 22 (the lowest score) to 73 (the highest score), or 51. With this range of scores, 10 intervals appear sufficient to group the data.

Size of Class Intervals
After the number of intervals is determined, the size or width of the interval is found by dividing the difference between the largest and smallest score by the number of class intervals to be used.

TABLE 3.3
Hypothetical Test Anxiety Inventory scores
from 100 students.

42	44	41	36	39	50
28	38	44	34	40	46
37	41	22	48	39	37
45	41	32	43	36	60
58	38	35	46	25	60
41	37	41	43	31	47
39	50	38	42	40	36
52	40	47	28	39	73
40	31	52	41	38	43
34	50	48	38	45	46
25	41	55	41	70	37
43	46	41	65	36	46
49	37	28	42	44	34
45	40	36	46	39	29
48	38	41	34	42	40
42	26	44	38	44	37
44	41	55	40		

TABLE 3.4
Grouped frequency distributions for the Test Anxiety Inventory scores of Table 3.3.

(a)	(b) Real Limits		(c)	(d)	(e)	(f)	(g)	(h)	(i)	(j)
Class Interval	Lower	Upper	Midpoint of Interval	Tally	f	rf	$\%f$	cf	crf	$c\%f$
70–74	69.5–74.5		72	//	2	.02	2	100	1.00	100
65–69	64.5–69.5		67	/	1	.01	1	98	.98	98
60–64	59.5–64.5		62	//	2	.02	2	97	.97	97
55–59	54.5–59.5		57	///	3	.03	3	95	.95	95
50–54	49.5–54.5		52	/////	5	.05	5	92	.92	92
45–49	44.5–49.5		47	///////////////	15	.15	15	87	.87	87
40–44	39.5–44.5		42	/////////////////////////////////	33	.33	33	72	.72	72
35–39	34.5–39.5		37	////////////////////////	24	.24	24	39	.39	39
30–34	29.5–34.5		32	building	7	.07	7	15	.15	15
25–29	24.5–29.5		27	ospital	7	.07	7	8	.08	8
20–24	19.5–24.5		22	/	1	.01	1	1	.01	1

X: A symbol used to represent an individual score.

i: The size or width of the class interval in a grouped frequency distribution.

In statistics the letter X is often used to symbolically represent a score. Hence, the **size of the class interval**, represented by i, is found by

$$i = \frac{X_{\text{highest}} - X_{\text{lowest}}}{\text{number of intervals}}$$

where X_{highest} indicates the highest score and X_{lowest} the lowest score in the distribution. Using the raw data of Table 3.3, with $X_{\text{highest}} = 73$ and $X_{\text{lowest}} = 22$, and 10 class intervals, the size of the class interval equals

$$i = \frac{73 - 22}{10} = \frac{51}{10} = 5.10.$$

If this formula leads to a decimal value, such as 5.10, we round to the nearest recommended class size (i.e., 1, 2, 3, 5, or a multiple of 5). For the example, I round i to 5. Should scores be decimals less than 1.0, then I do not round the interval to a whole number. Rather, a decimal interval such as 0.3, 0.5, 0.03, or 0.05 is used.

Constructing the Class Intervals

Two guidelines are used to construct class intervals for the frequency distribution:

- The lowest interval must contain the lowest score.
- The lower limit of the first interval, that is, the lowest possible score value in the first interval, should be evenly divisible by the size of the class interval.

For the scores of Table 3.3, the lowest score is 22. Accordingly, the lowest class interval in column a of Table 3.4 begins with a lower limit of 20, because 20 is the first score less than 22 that is evenly divisible by the class interval of 5. The first class interval is then from 20 to 24. Notice that it is possible for five score values to fall into this interval: 20, 21, 22, 23, and 24; thus, its size or width is 5. The next class interval is 25 to 29. Additional class intervals are calculated up to the point needed to include the highest score, in the example, a class interval of 70 to 74.

Stated limits of a class interval: The highest and lowest scores that could fall into that class interval.

Stated Limits and Real Limits of a Class Interval.   Each interval in column a of Table 3.4 has upper and lower stated and real limits. The **upper and lower stated limits of a class interval** (also called *apparent limits*) are the highest and lowest scores that could fall into that class interval. For example, for the class interval of 40 to 44, the lower stated limit is 40 and the upper stated limit is 44. A numerical score of 40 is the lowest score that may be placed in the interval, and a score of 44 is the highest that may be placed in the interval. Figure 3.2 illustrates the lower and upper stated limits for the class interval of 40 to 44.

Real limit of a class interval: The point midway between the stated limit of a class interval and the stated limit of the next lower or upper class interval.

The real limits of a number were defined in Chapter 2 as the points that are midway between the number and the next lower and higher numbers on the scale used to make the measurements. Real limits exist for the intervals of a grouped frequency distribution also, and these real limits are found similarly to the real limits of a number. The **lower real limit of a class interval** is the point midway between the lower stated limit of the class interval and the upper stated limit of the next lower class interval. For example, for the class interval of 40 to 44 in Table 3.4, the lower stated limit is 40. The upper stated limit of the next

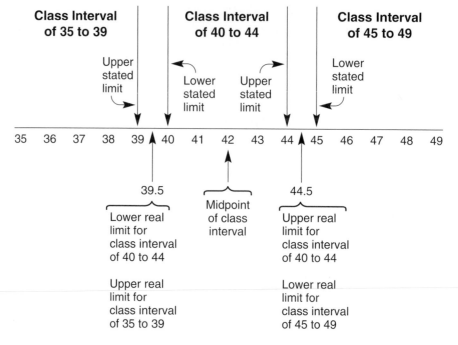

FIGURE 3.2
Illustration of lower and upper stated limits, lower and upper real limits, and the midpoint of a class interval of a grouped frequency distribution.

lower class interval (i.e., the interval of 35 to 39) is 39. Accordingly, the real lower limit of the class interval of 40 to 44 is the midpoint between 39 and 40, or 39.5. This lower real limit is also illustrated in Figure 3.2.

Similarly, the **upper real limit of a class interval** is the point midway between the upper stated limit of that class interval and the lower stated limit of the next higher class interval. The upper real limit of the class interval of 40 to 44 is found by obtaining the midpoint of the upper stated limit of the interval of 40 to 44 (i.e., 44) and the lower stated limit of the next higher class interval, 45 to 49. The lower stated limit of this interval is 45; thus, the upper real limit of the class interval of 40 to 44 is the midpoint of 44 and 45, or 44.5. This upper real limit is also shown in Figure 3.2. Notice that the upper real limit for the class interval of 40 to 44 is also the lower real limit for the next class interval of 45 to 49. The upper and lower real limits of the class intervals are presented in column b of Table 3.4.

Midpoint of a class interval: The point midway between the real limits of the class interval.

Midpoints of Class Intervals.   Each class interval also has a midpoint. The **midpoint of a class interval** is the point midway between the real limits of the class interval. Midpoints of a class interval can be found by adding the values of the real limits of a class interval and dividing the sum by 2. For the class interval of 40 to 44, the midpoint is found by

$$\frac{39.5 + 44.5}{2} = \frac{84}{2} = 42.$$

The midpoints of each class interval are shown in column c of Table 3.4. Although I included both the real upper and lower limits and the midpoint of the class interval in Table 3.4, grouped frequency distributions often are presented with only the class intervals of column a.

Grouped Simple Frequency Distribution

A grouped simple frequency distribution is obtained by tallying scores into the class interval in which they fall (see column d of Table 3.4). For example, a score of 35 is tallied into the class interval of 35 to 39, and a score of 52 is tallied into the class interval of 50 to 54. The tallies in an interval are then summed to obtain the simple frequency (f) for that interval (given in column e of Table 3.4).

Grouped Relative Frequency and Percentage Frequency Distributions

Relative frequency distributions and percentage frequency distributions may also be obtained for grouped frequency distributions. The procedures are similar to those used for an ungrouped frequency distribution.

Grouped relative frequency distribution: A grouped frequency distribution in which the frequency of scores in an interval is divided by the total number of scores in the distribution.

Grouped Relative Frequency Distribution.   A **grouped relative frequency distribution** is found by dividing the frequency of scores in an interval by the total number of scores in the distribution. Thus

$$rf \text{ of scores in an interval} = \frac{f \text{ of scores in interval}}{N}.$$

A grouped relative frequency distribution for the test anxiety scores is presented in column f of Table 3.4.

Grouped percentage frequency distribution: A grouped frequency distribution obtained by multiplying the relative frequency values by 100 to obtain percentages.

Grouped Percentage Frequency Distribution.   A **grouped percentage frequency distribution** is obtained by

$$\%f \text{ of scores in an interval} = rf \text{ of scores in interval} \times 100.$$

The grouped percentage frequency distribution of the Test Anxiety Inventory scores is presented in column g of Table 3.4.

Cumulative Grouped Frequency Distributions

Cumulative Grouped Simple Frequency Distribution.   Each form of frequency distribution discussed may also be presented as a cumulative frequency distribution. The **cumulative frequency of a score** (symbolized as *cf* or ***cum f***) is the frequency of occurrence of that score plus the sum of the frequencies of all the scores of lower value. In a grouped distribution, the **cumulative frequency of a class interval** is the frequency of occurrence of scores in that interval plus the sum of the frequencies of scores of lower class intervals. For example, the cumulative frequency of the class interval of 30 to 34 in Table 3.4 is 15, because a total of 15 scores occur in the intervals 20 to 24 (1 score), 25 to 29 (7 scores), and 30 to 34 (7 scores). The simple cumulative frequency of each class interval is shown in column h of Table 3.4.

Cumulative frequency of a score: The frequency of occurrence of that score plus the sum of the frequencies of all the scores of lower value.

Cumulative frequency of a class interval: The frequency of occurrence of scores in that interval plus the sum of the frequencies of scores of lower class intervals.

Cumulative Grouped Relative and Percentage Frequency Distributions.   Relative frequencies and percentage frequencies may be presented as cumulative frequencies also. The **cumulative grouped relative frequency of a class interval** (symbolized as *crf* or *cum rf*) is the relative frequency of the scores in that interval plus the sum of the relative frequencies of scores of lower class intervals.

Similarly, the **cumulative grouped percentage frequency of a class interval** (symbolized as *c%f* or *cum %f*) is the percentage frequency of the scores in that interval plus the sum of the percentage frequencies of scores of all lower class intervals. The cumulative grouped relative frequencies and percentage frequencies for each class interval of Table 3.4 are presented in columns i and j, respectively.

Cumulative grouped relative frequency of a class interval: The relative frequency of the scores in that interval plus the sum of the relative frequencies of class intervals of lower value.

Cumulative grouped percentage frequency of a class interval: The percentage frequency of the scores in that interval plus the sum of the percentage frequencies of all the class intervals of lower value.

Obtaining Information from a Grouped Frequency Distribution

The several grouped frequency distributions in Table 3.4 indicate that the majority of scores are between 30 to 54. Furthermore, the distributions indicate that about one-third (33 out of 100) of the anxiety scores are in the interval from 40 to 44. However, the exact numerical value of scores is lost in Table 3.4. I cannot determine the exact lowest or highest scores or the most frequently occurring score. But this loss of information is often offset by the greater ease with which we can perceive the general shape of the distribution.

PERCENTILES AND PERCENTILE RANKS

Percentile: The score at or below which a specified percentage of scores in a distribution falls.

Percentile rank of a score: The percentage of scores in a distribution that are equal to or less than that score.

Cumulative frequency distributions are frequently used to find percentiles and percentile ranks. A **percentile** is the score at or below which a specified percentage of scores in a distribution fall. For example, if the 35th percentile on an examination is 70, 35 percent of the scores on the examination are equal to or less than 70. The **percentile rank of a score** indicates the percentage of scores in the distribution that are equal to or less than that score. Thus, in the example, the percentile rank of a test score of 70 is 35. Thirty-five percent of the scores are equal to or less than 70.

The benefit of providing a percentile or the percentile rank for a score is that it provides information about the location of the score with respect to the other scores in the distribution without having to present the distribution itself. Suppose you were one of the 100 students who took the Test Anxiety Inventory and your score was 41. Simply knowing your score does not give you any information about your test anxiety level. Is 41 high or low compared to other students? But if you were told that 41 was the 49th percentile, or the percentile rank for a score of 41 was 49, then you would know that 49 percent of the scores were equal to or less than 41 and your score is at about the middle of the distribution.

Finding the Percentile Rank of a Score

Suppose I want to find the percentile rank of a score of 41 in the distribution portrayed in Table 3.4. This score falls into the class interval of 40 to 44. The cumulative percentage frequency of scores up to the lower real limit of this interval is 39 (from column j, the *c%f*), and the cumulative percentage frequency of scores to the upper real limit of this interval is 72 (from column j). Thus, the percentile rank of 41 will be between 39 and 72. To find the exact percentile rank, I must interpolate the value of 41 in the interval of 40 to 44. The following formula provides this interpolation and calculates the percentile rank of a score:

$$\textbf{Percentile rank} = P_X = \frac{cf_L + [(X - X_L)/i]f_i}{N} \times 100,$$

where

P_X = percentile rank of a score of X.

cf_L = cumulative frequency of scores up to the lower real limit of the interval containing X.

X = the score for which the percentile rank is being found.

X_L = lower real limit of the interval containing X.

i = size of the class interval.

f_i = frequency of scores in the interval containing X.

N = total number of scores in the distribution.

For a score of 41 in Table 3.4, the values for this formula are

$$P_X = P_{41},$$
$$cf_L = 39 \qquad \text{(from column h of Table 3.4),}$$
$$X = 41,$$
$$X_L = 39.5 \qquad \text{(from column b of Table 3.4),}$$
$$i = 5,$$
$$f_i = 33 \qquad \text{(from column e of Table 3.4),}$$
$$N = 100.$$

Substituting these values into the formula, I obtain

$$P_{41} = \frac{39 + [(41 - 39.5)/5]33}{100} \times 100$$

$$= \frac{39 + [(1.5/5)(33)]}{100} \times 100$$

$$= \frac{39 + [(.3)(33)]}{100} \times 100$$

$$= \frac{39 + 9.9}{100} \times 100$$

$$= \frac{48.9}{100} \times 100$$

$$= 48.9.$$

Typically, a percentile rank is rounded to a whole number; thus

$$P_{41} = 49.$$

The percentile rank of a score of 41 is 49; 49 percent of the scores in Table 3.4 are equal to or less than 41. This formula may also be applied to an ungrouped frequency distribution by using $i = 1$.

Finding a Percentile of a Distribution

A second problem is finding a score that corresponds to a specified percentile in a distribution. For example, suppose that I want to find the 49th percentile of the distribution in Table 3.4. I notice that this percentile is a score in the class interval of 40 to 44, for 39 percent of the scores fall below the lower real limit of this interval and 72 percent of the scores fall below the upper real limit. Again I must interpolate to find the exact score that is the 49th percentile. The following formula provides this interpolation and calculates the percentile:

$$\textbf{Percentile} = X_P = X_L + \left(\frac{P(N) - cf_L}{f_i} \right) i,$$

where
X_P = score at a specified percentile (i.e., the score we want to find).
X_L = lower real limit of the interval containing the specified percentile.
P = required percentile given as a proportion between 0 to 1.00.
N = total number of scores in the distribution.
cf_L = cumulative frequency of scores up to the lower real limit of the interval containing X_P.
f_i = frequency of scores in the interval containing X_P.
i = size of the class interval.

For the 49th percentile, these values are

$X_P = X_{49}$,
$X_L = 39.5$ (from column b of Table 3.4),
$P = .49$,
$N = 100$,
$cf_L = 39$ (from column h of Table 3.4),
$f_i = 33$ (from column e of Table 3.4),
$i = 5$.

Substituting these values into the formula, I obtain

$$X_{49} = 39.5 + \left(\frac{.49(100) - 39}{33}\right)5$$

$$= 39.5 + \left(\frac{49 - 39}{33}\right)5$$

$$= 39.5 + \left(\frac{10}{33}\right)5$$

$$= 39.5 + 1.52$$

$$= 41.02.$$

Rounding this value to a whole number, $X_{49} = 41$. The 49th percentile is a score of 41. Forty-nine percent of the scores in the distribution are equal to or less than 41. Again this formula may be used with an ungrouped distribution by using $i = 1$.

Example Problem 3.2

Grouped Frequency Distributions

Problem: Suppose that I investigated the problem of perception of ambiguous figures discussed in Example Problem 3.1 and measured the duration that subjects could see the pyramid in the Mach pyramid figure. I used 50 participants and obtained the following scores (to the nearest whole second): 18, 2, 7, 23, 16, 10, 5, 30, 5, 15, 17, 3, 31, 9, 11, 13, 5, 13, 8, 19, 16, 2, 14, 4, 7, 7, 6, 2, 10, 6, 7, 24, 3, 8, 9, 7, 19, 7, 11, 9, 4, 7, 6, 1, 3, 10, 1, 26, 8, and 5.

    a.   Construct the following grouped distributions for these scores: simple frequency, relative frequency, percentage frequency, simple cumulative frequency, cumulative relative frequency, and cumulative percentage frequency distribution. Include the lower and upper real limits of the class intervals, and the midpoint of each class interval.

    b.   What conclusions about the scores may you reach from these distributions?

    c.   Find the percentile rank of a score of 16 seconds.

    d.   What is the 25th percentile for this distribution?

Solution: a.   The solution requires choosing the number of class intervals to be used, finding the size of the class interval, and then constructing a grouped frequency distribution using these class intervals.

Number of Class Intervals: The range of scores is from 1 to 31 seconds, or 30 seconds. Ten class intervals seem sufficient to group the data.

Size of Class Intervals: $i = (31 - 1)/10 = 3.0$.

Constructing the Distribution: The lowest score obtained is 1 second, and the class interval to be used is 3 seconds. The first class interval then is 0 to 2. This interval contains the lowest score, and the lower stated limit of this interval (i.e., 0) is divisible evenly by the size of the class interval (i.e., 3). The class intervals of the grouped frequency distribution are presented in column a of the following table. The upper and lower real limits for each interval are obtained by finding the points midway between adjacent class intervals. For example, upper and lower real limits for the class interval of 24 to 26 are the points midway between 23 and 24 (lower real limit) and midway between 26 and 27 (upper real limit), respectively. The real limits of each class interval are shown in column b of the table. Midpoints for each class interval are presented in column c. The scores are tallied in column d, and the grouped frequency distributions are presented in columns e through j of the table.

(a)	(b)		(c)	(d)	(e)	(f)	(g)	(h)	(i)	(j)
	Real Limits									
Class Interval	**Lower**	**Upper**	**Midpoint of Interval**	**Tally**	f	rf	$\%f$	cf	crf	$c\%f$
30–32	29.5–32.5		31	//	2	.04	4	50	1.00	100
27–29	26.5–29.5		28		0	.00	0	48	.96	96
24–26	23.5–26.5		25	//	2	.04	4	48	.96	96
21–23	20.5–23.5		22	/	1	.02	2	46	.92	92
18–20	17.5–20.5		19	///	3	.06	6	45	.90	90
15–17	14.5–17.5		16	////	4	.08	8	42	.84	84
12–14	11.5–14.5		13	///	3	.06	6	38	.76	76
9–11	8.5–11.5		10	////////	8	.16	16	35	.70	70
6–8	5.5–8.5		7	/////////////	13	.26	26	27	.54	54
3–5	2.5–5.5		4	/////////	9	.18	18	14	.28	28
0–2	−0.5–2.5		1	/////	5	.10	10	5	.10	10

b. Conclusions: From the simple frequencies (column e), relative frequencies (column f), or percentage frequencies (column g), we see that scores in the interval of 6 to 8 seconds occurred most frequently. The cumulative frequency distributions indicate that .70 or 70 percent of the scores were durations of 11 seconds or less.

c. The percentile rank of a score is found using the formula

$$P_X = \frac{cf_L + [(X - X_L)/i]f_i}{N} \times 100.$$

The values needed to find the percentile rank of a score of 16 are

$$P_X = P_{16},$$
$$cf_L = 38,$$
$$X = 16,$$
$$X_L = 14.5,$$
$$i = 3,$$
$$f_i = 4,$$
$$N = 50.$$

Substituting these values, I obtain

$$P_{16} = \frac{38 + [(16 - 14.5)/3]4}{50} \times 100$$

$$= \frac{38 + (1.5/3)4}{50} \times 100$$

$$= \frac{38 + (.5)4}{50} \times 100$$

$$= \frac{38 + 2}{50} \times 100$$

$$= \frac{40}{50} \times 100$$

$$= .80 \times 100 = 80.$$

The percentile rank of a score of 16 seconds is 80. Eighty percent of the durations are equal to or less than 16 seconds.

d. The 25th percentile is found using the formula

$$X_P = X_L + \left(\frac{P(N) - cf_L}{f_i}\right)i.$$

The values needed to find the 25th percentile are

$$X_P = X_{25},$$

$$X_L = 2.5,$$

$$P = .25,$$

$$N = 50,$$

$$cf_L = 5,$$

$$f_i = 9,$$

$$i = 3.$$

Substituting these values, I obtain

$$P_{16} = 2.5 + \left(\frac{.25(50) - 5}{9}\right)3$$

$$= 2.5 + \left(\frac{12.5 - 5}{9}\right)3$$

$$= 2.5 + \left(\frac{7.5}{9}\right)3$$

$$= 2.5 + 2.5$$

$$= 5.0.$$

A score of 5 seconds is the 25th percentile.

TESTING YOUR KNOWLEDGE 3.2

1. Define: class interval, cumulative frequency of a class interval, cumulative frequency of a score, cumulative grouped percentage frequency of a class interval, cumulative grouped relative frequency of a class interval, cf, $c\%f$, crf, $cum\ f$, $cum\ \%f$, $cum\ rf$, grouped frequency distribution, lower real limit of a class interval, lower stated limit of a class interval, midpoint of a class interval, percentile, percentile rank of a score, upper real limit of a class interval, upper stated limit of a class interval.

2. What is the recommended number of class intervals to use when constructing a grouped frequency distribution?

3. The largest score in a distribution is 88 and the smallest is 14. You plan to construct a grouped distribution with 15 intervals. What will be the size of your class interval?

4. The largest score in a distribution is 95 and the smallest is 62. You want the class interval to be 3. How many intervals will you use?

5. What are the two guidelines for constructing grouped distributions?

6. A grouped frequency distribution has class intervals of 120 to 122, 123 to 125, 126 to 128, 129 to 131, and 132 to 134.
   a. Identify the lower and upper stated limits for the class interval of 123 to 125.
   b. Identify the lower and upper stated limits for the class interval of 129 to 131.
   c. Identify the lower and upper real limits for the class interval of 123 to 125.
   d. Identify the lower and upper real limits for the class interval of 129 to 131.
   e. Find the midpoint of the class interval of 120 to 122.
   f. What is the value of i for this distribution?

7. When approached by a predator, Thompson's gazelles leap straight up with all four feet simultaneously off the ground. This behavior, known as stotting, appears costly to the gazelle, for it delays the onset of flight from the predator. To learn more about stotting, Caro (1986) used naturalistic observation to study gazelles in Serengeti National Park, Tanzania. One measure obtained was the estimated distance of a predator, such as a cheetah, from a gazelle before the first stott occurred. Suppose that he observed 50 instances of a cheetah approaching a gazelle and recorded the following estimated distances (in meters) between the cheetah and the gazelle before the first stott occurred: 47, 61, 72, 63, 56, 54, 67, 75, 91, 72, 83, 140, 31, 37, 25, 38, 57, 62, 49, 205, 66, 39, 43, 81, 66, 72, 42, 29, 190, 64, 76, 54, 38, 67, 61, 33, 48, 55, 59, 68, 18, 49, 37, 83, 70, 154, 91, 50, 58, and 66.
   a. Construct the following grouped distributions for these scores: simple frequency, relative frequency, percentage frequency, cumulative simple frequency, cumulative relative frequency, and cumulative percentage frequency distribution. Include the lower and upper real limits of the class intervals and the midpoint of each class interval. Use 20 class intervals.
   b. What conclusions about stotting distances are you able to reach from the information in the grouped frequency distributions?
   c. Find the percentile rank of a distance of 68 meters.
   d. What is the 50th percentile for this distribution?

PRESENTING FREQUENCY DISTRIBUTIONS GRAPHICALLY

Frequency distributions provide a systematic way of looking at data to understand their characteristics. To further this understanding, the information contained in a frequency distribution is often displayed in the form of a graph, such as a histogram, a frequency polygon, or a stem-and-leaf display. There are several common rules for constructing graphs.

- The two axes of the graph are drawn at right (90°) angles to each other. The horizontal axis is identified as the *x axis* or the *abscissa*. The vertical axis is called the *y axis* or *ordinate*.
- The possible scores, or the class intervals of the possible scores in a grouped frequency distribution, are located along the *x* axis. The measure of frequency (e.g., simple frequency, relative frequency, percentage frequency, cumulative frequency, etc.) is placed on the *y* axis.
- Each axis is labeled so that the reader knows what information is being graphed.
- The origin of each axis is normally at zero. If a part of the scale between the zero origin and the first recorded score or frequency of a score is left off the axis, then a break, indicated by -//-, is inserted into the axis.
- A scale should be chosen for the *y* axis such that the maximum height of the frequency measure is about two-thirds to three-fourths of the width of the *x* axis.

Histograms

Histogram: A form of bar graph in which the frequency of occurrence of scores in a class interval is given by the height of the bar, and the size of each class interval is represented by the width of the bar on the abscissa.

A **histogram** uses the height of a vertical bar to show the frequency of occurrence of scores in a class interval. The size of each class interval is represented by the width of the bar on the abscissa. Histograms are usually drawn only for grouped frequency distributions, and the measure of frequency typically used is either the simple frequency tabulation or the relative frequency for a class interval (columns e and f of Table 3.4, respectively). A histogram of the grouped simple frequency of the Test Anxiety Inventory scores is presented in Figure 3.3. To construct a histogram, the midpoints of the class intervals or the class intervals

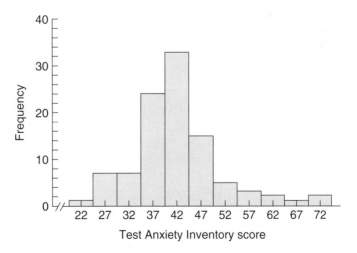

FIGURE 3.3
Simple frequency histogram of Test Anxiety Inventory scores of Table 3.3.

themselves are plotted on the abscissa. The bar that represents the frequency of each interval is centered on the midpoint of the class interval, and the vertical sides of each bar are drawn at the real limits of each class interval. Scores on the abscissa are usually indicated by the numerical value of the midpoint of each class interval, as illustrated in Figure 3.3 and Figure 3.5. The frequency of occurrence of scores is plotted on the ordinate and the height of each bar is drawn to the frequency of the class interval it represents.

Frequency Polygons

Frequency polygon: A graph constructed by placing the midpoints of each class interval of a frequency distribution on the abscissa and indicating the frequency of a class interval by placing a dot at the appropriate frequency above the midpoint. The dots are connected with straight lines.

A **frequency polygon** is constructed by placing the midpoints of each class interval on the abscissa and indicating the frequency of a class interval by placing a dot at the appropriate frequency above the midpoint. The dots are then connected by straight lines. Figure 3.4 portrays a frequency polygon of the grouped Test Anxiety Inventory scores of Table 3.4. The frequency measure used is the simple frequency tabulation in column e of the table. Notice in Figure 3.4 that one extra class interval containing no scores has been included at each end of the distribution, and the frequency polygon has been brought to zero at each end of the graph (at the midpoints of 17 and 77). This practice is commonly followed in the construction of frequency polygons.

Relative Frequency Histograms and Polygons

Histograms and frequency polygons may be constructed using relative frequencies in place of the simple frequencies used in Figures 3.3 and 3.4. A histogram and a frequency polygon of the Test Anxiety Inventory scores using relative frequencies (from column f of Table 3.4) are presented in Figures 3.5 and 3.6, respectively.

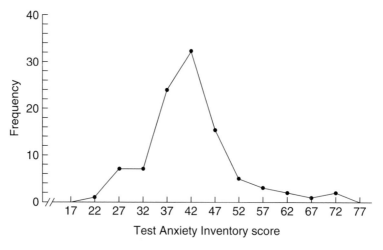

FIGURE 3.4
Simple frequency polygon of Test Anxiety Inventory scores of Table 3.3.

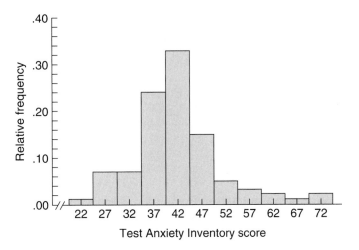

FIGURE 3.5
Relative frequency histogram of Test Anxiety Inventory scores of Table 3.3.

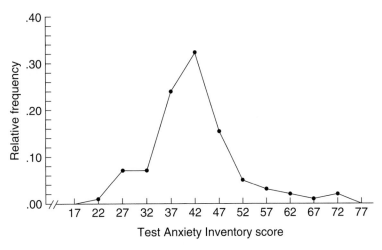

FIGURE 3.6
Relative frequency polygon of Test Anxiety Inventory scores of Table 3.3.

The benefit of using relative frequencies for a histogram or frequency polygon is that the relative frequency values indicate the proportion of scores falling in the various class intervals. Thus, if two different frequency distributions, each based on a different total number of scores, are being compared, relative frequencies make direct comparison easier than simple frequencies.

Obtaining Information from a Histogram or a Frequency Polygon

The histogram and frequency polygon present the same information as does a frequency distribution. The advantage of histograms and frequency polygons is that the information presented is often more easily grasped visually. From any of Figures 3.3, 3.4, 3.5, or 3.6, you can see that the peak of the distribution of the anxiety scores is in the low 40s, and more scores are closer to the bottom of the anxiety scale score (i.e., 20) than to the top (i.e., 80). A few scores, however, tail off in the direction of high test anxiety.

Stem-and-Leaf Displays

Stem-and-leaf display: A display of data in which the first (or second) digit of a score is the stem and the second (or last) digit is the leaf.

The **stem-and-leaf display**, developed by John Tukey (1977), combines the qualities of a frequency distribution and a graphic display of the data. Table 3.5 presents a simple stem-and-leaf display of the Test Anxiety Inventory scores of Table 3.3. In this display, the numbers in the column to the left are the **stems** and represent the first digit of a score. For example, 3 is the stem for a score of 35. The numbers in the right column are the **leaves** and represent the second digit of the score, in the example of 35, a 5. For example, the topmost row with a stem of 7 and leaves of 0 and 3 represents the scores of 70 and 73, respectively. If scores involve three digits, such as a score of 321 seconds, then the first two digits (i.e., 32) are used to form the stem, and the last digit (i.e., 1) is the leaf.

Table 3.5, however, is difficult to read with the long lines of leaves after each stem, especially the stems of 3 and 4. To avoid this difficulty, simple stem-and-leaf displays may be modified to display fewer leaves on each line. Table 3.6 illustrates a modified stem-and-leaf display in which each stem has been given five lines. Notice the column with ., *t*, *f*, *s*, and * that follows the numerical value of the stem. In this display, the leaves on the line preceded by the period (.) are 0 and 1, those on the line preceded by *t* are 2 and 3 (the *t* stands for *t*wo and *t*hree), those on the line preceded by *f* are 4 and 5 (*f* for *f*our and *f*ive), those on the line preceded by *s* are 6 and 7 (*s* for *s*ix and *s*even) and those on the line preceded by the asterisk are 8 and 9. This modification makes the table easier to read and allows us to more easily see the shape of the distribution.

TABLE 3.5
Stem-and-leaf display of Test Anxiety Inventory scores presented in Table 3.3.

Stem	Leaf
7	03
6	005
5	00022558
4	000000011111111111222223333444444555666666778889
3	1124444566666777777888888899999
2	25568889

TABLE 3.6
Modified stem-and-leaf display of
Test Anxiety Inventory scores
presented in Table 3.3.

Stem	Leaf
t	3
7 •	0
6 *	
s	
f	5
t	
6 •	0 0
5 *	8
s	
f	55
t	22
5 •	000
4 *	8889
s	66666677
f	444444555
t	222223333
4 •	00000001111111111
3 *	888888899999
s	66666777777
f	44445
t	2
3 •	11
2 *	8889
s	6
f	55
t	2
2 •	

Stem-and-leaf displays are constructed easily from the raw data, and no information is lost in the process, as occurs in a grouped frequency distribution; all the raw scores can be reconstructed from the display. From an examination of Table 3.6 you can quickly determine that the scores vary from 22 to 73 and that a score of 41 occurs most frequently.

As another illustration of a stem-and-leaf display, I offered the example of a summated rating scale called the Belief in Lunar Effects Scale in the discussion of interval measures in Chapter 2. This scale was developed by Rotton and Kelly (1985) to measure belief in the effect of a full moon on behavior. The minimum score on this scale is 9, indicating minimal or no belief in lunar effects, and the maximum score is 81, indicating maximum belief in lunar effects. Rotton and Kelly administered this scale to 157 undergraduate college students, and the scores they obtained are portrayed in the following stem-and-leaf display.

Stem		Leaf
7	•	12
	*	59
6	•	0011114
	*	5666668999
5	•	000111111222334
	*	5555555556666788888899
4	•	001111223333344444
	*	56666677788899999
3	•	0000112223344444
	*	55667777899999
2	•	00001122234444
	*	556666778888899
1	•	122334

Source: Adapted and reproduced with permission of authors and publisher from: Rotton, J., & Kelly, I. W. Scale for assessing belief in lunar effects: reliability and concurrent validity. *Psychological Reports*, 1985, 57, 239–245. © Psychological Reports.

The stem represents the 10s value of the score and the leaf the 1s value of the score. Thus, a stem of 3 and a leaf of 7 is a score of 37. In this stem-and-leaf display the period is used to denote leaf values from 0 through 4 and the asterisk is used to indicate leaf values from 5 through 9. For example, scores with a stem of 1 are given in the table as

	*	556666778888899
1	•	122334

The leaf values in the row preceded by the period range from 1 to 4. When preceded by their stem of 1, these values become scores of 11, 12, 12, 13, 13, and 14, respectively. The leaf values in the row preceded by the asterisk (*) also have a stem of 1, but they are leaf values from 5 through 9. When preceded by their stem of 1, these values become 15, 15, 16, 16, 16, 16, 17, 17, 18, 18, 18, 18, 18, 19, and 19, respectively.

From this stem-and-leaf display we can see that the range of scores obtained was from 11 to 72, and the most frequently occurring score was 45, with nine occurrences. No information is lost in this display, for each of the 157 scores may be reconstructed from the display.

GRAPHIC PRESENTATION OF QUALITATIVE DATA

The discussion to this point has dealt with the graphic presentation of quantitative data. Qualitative data, however, indicate only that the variable measured differs in quality. As an example, Trinkaus, in a series of studies using naturalistic observation (1982, 1983, 1988, 1993, 1997), categorized driver's behavior at a highway stop sign into one of three categories: 1, coming to a full stop; 2, coming to a rolling stop; and 3, not stopping at all. These categories differ qualitatively; they label the behavior, but they do not tell us how it differs in amount. Trinkaus counted the number of occurrences of each behavior and found the percentage frequencies of occurrence of each category. These percentage frequencies can be presented graphically in the form of a **bar graph**, as shown in Figure 3.7, which presents data representative of those reported by Trinkaus.

Bar graph: A graph used to present a frequency distribution when the variable measured is qualitative in nature. The frequency of occurrence of scores in a category is given by the height of the bar.

A bar graph is similar to a histogram, except the bars are separated on the X axis to indicate that the categories do not represent a continuous measurement. The distance between the bars is arbitrary but is the same for each bar. Either simple frequencies, relative frequencies, or percentage frequencies (as illustrated in Figure 3.7) may be used to indicate

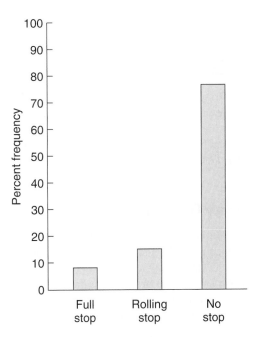

FIGURE 3.7
Percentage frequency of occurrence of three categories of stop sign behavior representative of that reported by Trinkaus (1982, 1983, 1988, 1993, 1997).

the frequency of occurrence of each category. From this graph we easily note that the most frequently occurring behavior at the intersections observed was category 3, not stopping at all.

1. Define: bar graph, frequency polygon, histogram, stem-and-leaf display.
2. Question 7a of Testing Your Knowledge 3.2 required you to construct a frequency distribution of the estimated distance of a predator from a gazelle when the gazelle first stotted. Use that frequency distribution to answer question 2a and b.
    a. Construct a histogram and a frequency polygon for the estimated distances using the simple frequencies of a grouped distribution with a class interval of 10 meters.
    b. Construct a relative frequency histogram and a relative frequency polygon from the grouped distribution of question 2a.
    c. What conclusions do you reach about stotting distances from the graphs that you have constructed?
3. Construct a stem-and-leaf plot of the 50 distance estimates given in question 7 of Testing Your Knowledge 3.2.
    a. What is the shortest distance recorded?
    b. What is the longest distance recorded?
    c. What is the most frequently occurring distance?

SHAPES OF FREQUENCY DISTRIBUTIONS

A distribution of scores may take on any of a variety of shapes. Thus, there usually is no simple way to describe precisely the shape of a frequency distribution in a word or two. There are, however, some general descriptive terms that apply to the shape of a distribution and that help to describe a distribution in words. To illustrate, Figure 3.8 presents examples of several different shaped frequency polygons.

Symmetrical Frequency Distributions

Symmetrical frequency distribution: A frequency distribution that, when folded in half about a midpoint, produces two halves identical in shape.

A **symmetrical frequency distribution**, if it were folded in half about a midpoint, would produce two halves identical in shape. One side of the distribution is a mirror image of the other. Distributions (a), (b), and (c) in Figure 3.8 are symmetrical distributions, but distributions (d) and (e) are not symmetrical; they are **asymmetrical**. The symmetrical bell-shaped or normal distribution shown in Figure 3.8a is of special importance in the behavioral sciences. I discuss it more fully in Chapter 6.

Skewness

It is rare to obtain a perfectly symmetrical distribution of raw data for a given measure. Instead, a frequency distribution is likely to be asymmetrical or skewed. In a **skewed distri-**

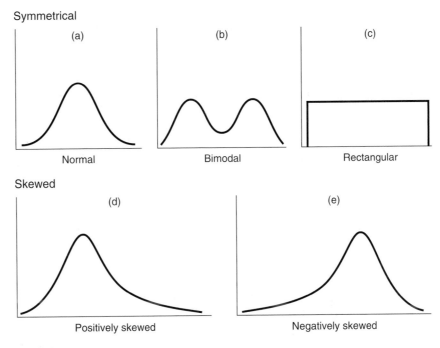

Symmetrical

(a)

Normal

(b)

Bimodal

(c)

Rectangular

Skewed

(d)

Positively skewed

(e)

Negatively skewed

FIGURE 3.8
Shapes of hypothetical frequency distributions.

Skewed distribution: A frequency distribution in which scores are clustered at one end of the distribution, with scores occurring infrequently at the other end of the distribution.

bution, scores are clustered at one end of the distribution, with scores occurring infrequently at the other end (or tail) of the distribution. A distribution is described as **positively skewed** if the tail occurs for the high scores at the right of the distribution (Figure 3.8d) or **negatively skewed** if the tail occurs for the low scores at the left of the distribution (Figure 3.8e).

Modality

Mode: The most frequently occurring score in a distribution of scores.

Distributions are also described in terms of the number of modes possessed. The **mode** is the most frequently occurring score in a distribution of scores. A **unimodal distribution** has just one most frequently occurring score (see Figures 3.8a, d, and e). A frequency distribution that has two modes is described as **bimodal** (illustrated in Figure 3.8b). Many behavioral scientists consider a distribution bimodal if it has two distinct peaks, even if the peaks do not represent scores with equal frequencies of occurrence. A **multimodal distribution** has three or more score values that are the most frequently occurring scores. Again, a distribution may be considered multimodal if it has three or more peaks, even if the frequencies of occurrence of each peak are not equal. There is no mode in the flat rectangular distribution illustrated in Figure 3.8c; in such distributions, each score occurs an equal number of times or nearly so. I discuss the mode more fully in Chapter 4.

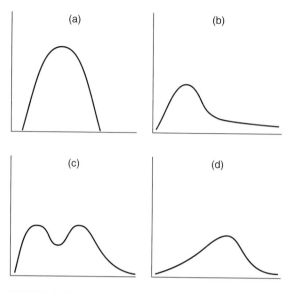

FIGURE 3.9
Frequency distributions for question 2.

TESTING YOUR KNOWLEDGE 3.4

1. Define: asymmetrical distribution, bimodal distribution, mode, multimodal distribution, negatively skewed distribution, positively skewed distribution, skewed distribution, symmetrical frequency distribution, unimodal distribution.
2. Describe the frequency distributions in Figure 3.9 with respect to symmetry, skewness, and modality.

SUMMARY

- A frequency distribution is a table showing each score obtained by a group of individuals and how frequently each score occurred.
- Frequency distributions are used to organize raw data.
- An ungrouped frequency distribution may be used when there is not a large number of scores in the data set.
- Grouped frequency distributions are used when the number of scores becomes large or the scores extend over a wide range of values.
- Ungrouped or grouped frequency distributions may be portrayed as simple, relative, or percentage frequencies.
- A percentile is the score at or below which a specified percentage of scores in a distribution fall.

- The percentile rank of a score indicates the percentage of scores in the distribution that are equal to or less than that score.
- Frequency distributions may be presented graphically as histograms, frequency polygons, or stem-and-leaf displays.
- Qualitative data may be presented graphically in a bar graph.
- Shapes of frequency distributions are described in terms of their symmetry, skewness, and modality.

KEY TERMS AND SYMBOLS

asymmetrical frequency
   distribution (54)
bar graph (53)
bimodal distribution (55)
class interval (35)
cumulative frequency of a class
   interval (39)
cumulative frequency of a score
   (cf or $cum f$) (39)
cumulative grouped percentage
   frequency of a class interval
   ($c\%f$ or $cum\%f$) (40)
cumulative grouped relative
   frequency of a class interval
   (crf or $cum\ rf$) (40)
f (32)
frequency distribution (32)
frequency polygon (48)
grouped frequency distribution
   (35)

grouped percentage frequency
   distribution (39)
grouped relative frequency
   distribution (39)
histogram (47)
i (37)
lower real limit of a class
   interval (37)
lower stated limit of a class
   interval (37)
midpoint of a class interval (38)
mode (55)
multimodal distribution (55)
N (31)
negatively skewed distribution (55)
percentage frequency
   distribution ($\%f$) (33)
percentile (40)
percentile rank of a score (40)
positively skewed distribution (55)

raw data (31)
raw scores (31)
real limits of a class interval (37)
relative frequency distribution
   (32)
relative frequency (rf) (33)
skewed distribution (54)
stated limits of a class interval
   (37)
stem-and-leaf display (50)
symmetrical frequency
   distribution (54)
ungrouped frequency
   distribution (32)
unimodal distribution (55)
upper real limit of a class
   interval (38)
upper stated limit of a class
   interval (37)
X (37)

REVIEW QUESTIONS

1. Hicks, Mistry, Lucero, Marical, and Pellegrini (1990) reported that a survey of college students indicated they were obtaining an average of 6.87 hours (or 412 minutes) of sleep per night. You are curious if this value still holds today. Hence, you ask 50 college undergraduates to record how long they slept for one night. The sleeping times you obtained, in minutes, were 440, 223, 309, 427, 463, 275, 315, 290, 356, 407, 399, 263, 417, 328, 377, 406, 275, 316, 391, 350, 422, 431, 382, 350, 371, 410, 295, 305, 327, 400, 227, 275, 340, 364, 279, 300, 412, 388, 296, 320, 342, 371, 258, 470, 496, 384, 439, 284, 351, 417.

a. Construct a grouped percentage frequency distribution and grouped cumulative percentage frequency distribution for these scores. Use 14 class intervals.

b. Which class interval contains the most scores? Is the midpoint of this interval in agreement with the 412 minutes reported in the survey?

c. Estimate from the grouped cumulative frequency distribution the amount of time that divides the distribution in half, that is, the amount of time that places 25 people above it and 25 people below it.

d. Find the 50th percentile of this distribution. Does it agree with your estimate from question 1c?

e. What is the percentile rank of a score of 431 minutes?

f. Construct a histogram and a frequency polygon using simple frequencies from the distribution you found in question 1a.

g. Describe the shape of the distribution in terms of its skewness and modality.

2. Male bowerbirds build elaborate nests decorated with shells, colorful leaves, and blue feathers from parrots, for success in mating is related to the number of decorations on the bower. It has often been observed that male bowerbirds steal decorations from the bowers of other birds and use them to decorate their own nest. Borgia and Gore (1986) observed this stealing behavior among 59 bowerbirds in New South Wales, Australia. They marked feathers in a bower and recorded which feathers had been stolen from other bowers. Suppose that over the duration of their observation period they recorded the following number of feathers stolen by each bird: 0, 8, 17, 0, 21, 2, 6, 14, 1, 10, 3, 0, 26, 37, 47, 4, 0, 6, 21, 3, 6, 6, 51, 8, 11, 0, 0, 4, 2, 5, 9, 4, 6, 24, 4, 1, 18, 63, 1, 5, 6, 4, 7, 12, 5, 3, 4, 3, 15, 46, 0, 5, 0, 26, 5, 17, 1, 58, 9.

a. Construct a grouped relative frequency distribution and a cumulative grouped relative frequency distribution for these scores. Use 13 class intervals.

b. Which class interval contains the most scores?

c. Find the 50th percentile of this distribution.

d. What is the percentile rank of a score of 24?

e. Construct a stem-and-leaf plot for this distribution. What are the lowest and highest scores in this distribution? What is the most frequently occurring score?

f. Construct a histogram and a frequency polygon using simple frequencies from the distribution that you found in question 1a.

g. Describe the shape of the distribution in terms of its skewness.

3. Suppose that you observed male and female drivers in a mall parking lot and counted the frequency with which they illegally parked in handicapped parking areas. Over a 3-day period you observed that 12 of every 100 male drivers and 7 of every 100 female drivers parked illegally. Construct a bar graph of the relative frequency of illegal parking in handicapped spaces by male and female drivers.

4. Sturgeon and Beer (1990) report that an attendance policy of rewarding students who attend school regularly by exempting them from semester tests increases attendance in comparison to no such policy. Suppose that you compare attendance at two high schools, one that has a reward policy in effect and one that does not, and you obtain the following simple frequency distribution of absences:

Number of Days Absent	Reward Policy School	No Reward Policy School
More than 25	2	6
24–25	0	6
22–23	2	1
20–21	0	8
18–19	1	0
16–17	0	4
14–15	2	22
12–13	0	10
10–11	3	18
8–9	8	20
6–7	4	3
4–5	13	14
2–3	23	34
0–1	42	54
Total	100	200

    a.   Construct a relative frequency distribution for each school.
    b.   What is the 50th percentile for each school?
    c.   What is the percentile rank for four absences at each school?
    d.   Do the schools appear to differ in absence rates? Describe the distributions.

5.   As the pace of life becomes more hectic, it seems there is more and more for each of us to remember each day. As part of a study of memory under natural conditions, a psychologist asked 90 college students to keep a record of the things they had to remember to do on a typical weekday. Suppose the psychologist presented the results in the following stem-and-leaf plot.

Stem		Leaf
2	*	888899
	s	66667
	f	44555
	t	2222333
2	•	0000000111111
1	*	888999999
	s	6666677777
	f	44455555
	t	2233333
1	•	0001111
0	*	888999
	s	6677
	f	555
	t	
0	•	

    a. Create a table of raw scores for the students who gave responses of between 14 to 19 things to remember.

    b. What is the lowest and the highest score reported?

    c. What is the most frequently occurring score?

    d. Place the scores in a histogram. Use a class width of $i = 2$.

    e. In comparison to the stem-and-leaf plot, what information is lost when the scores are placed into a histogram?

6. It was reported in Chapter 1 that women in the United States between the ages of 25 to 54 typically watch TV for 4.4 hours per day (264 minutes). As a class project, members of a social psychology class interviewed 100 women ages 25 to 54 and asked them to estimate the amount of time they watched TV per day. Their estimates in minutes are shown in the following grouped frequency distribution.

Class Interval	Tally
510–539	/
480–509	
450–479	//
420–449	/////
390–419	//////
360–389	/////
330–359	/////////
300–329	////////
270–299	/////////
240–269	//////////
210–239	/////////
180–209	///
150–179	///////
120–149	//
90–119	/////////
60–89	/////
30–59	///////
0–29	////

    a. What is the width (i) of the class interval used in the preceding table?

    b. What are the lower and upper real limits for the class interval of 210 to 239?

    c. What is the midpoint of the class interval of 210 to 239?

    d. Construct a grouped simple frequency and cumulative frequency distribution for these scores.

    e. What is the 75th percentile of this distribution?

    f. What is the percentile rank for a score of 264 minutes spent watching TV?

7. Twenty-five patrons of a health club were asked to estimate how long they exercised each day. The estimates given in minutes were 67, 73, 79, 78, 50, 80, 98, 88, 79, 71, 57, 81, 41, 65, 50, 71, 91, 75, 60, 79, 79, 71, 65, 85, and 64.

a. Using a class width of $i = 5$, construct a grouped relative frequency and a cumulative relative frequency distribution for the scores. What should be the lower stated limit of the first class interval? Why?

b. Describe the shape of the distribution.

c. What is the percentile rank of a score of 78 minutes?

d. Suppose a person would like to exercise sufficiently long each day so that she is among the top 25 percent of the people in the distribution. What would be the minimum amount of time she would need to exercise to achieve this goal?

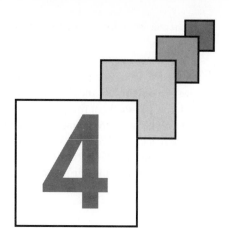

Describing Data: Measures of Central Tendency

Frequency distributions and graphs present a great deal of information about the shape of a distribution of scores and the range of scores obtained. Often, however, a scientist needs to describe a distribution of scores with only one number. These numbers are called **descriptive statistics** for they describe the raw data with a single number. Two types of descriptive statistics are commonly used. One type, called **measures of central tendency**, indicates the typical score obtained, and the other, called **measures of variability** or *measures of dispersion*, indicates the amount of variation or dispersion around the typical score.

Measures of central tendency: Numbers that represent the average or typical score obtained from measurements of a sample.

Measures of central tendency and variability have two uses. Their first is to describe the scores of a sample. Their second use is to estimate or infer characteristics of the population from which the sample was selected. For example, the researcher of Chapter 3 may be interested in estimating the typical level of test anxiety in the population of students at her college. One way to do so would be to base this estimate on a descriptive statistic obtained from the scores of her sample of 100 students.

Measures of variability: Numbers that indicate how much scores differ from each other and the measure of central tendency in a set of scores.

The remainder of this chapter is concerned with the descriptive use of measures of central tendency. Measures of variability and the use of descriptive statistics for inferring population characteristics are introduced in Chapters 5 and 7, respectively. There are three measures of central tendency in common use: the mode, median, and mean.

MODE

Mode: The most frequently occurring score in a distribution of scores.

Unimodal: A distribution with one mode.

Bimodal: A distribution with two modes.

Multimodal: A distribution with more than two modes.

The **mode** is the most frequently occurring score in a distribution of scores. The mode is found by inspecting a simple, ungrouped frequency distribution and observing which score occurs most often. For example, in Table 3.2 (page 32) the most frequently occurring test anxiety score is 59, with five occurrences. Accordingly, the mode for this distribution is 59. Because there is only one mode for this set of scores, this distribution is said to be **unimodal**. A distribution of scores may be **bimodal** (i.e., have two modes) or even **multimodal** (i.e., have more than two modes). Recall that one way of describing the shape of a frequency distribution is on the basis of modality. Unimodal and bimodal distributions are shown in Figure 3.8.

Although the mode is computed easily from a simple ungrouped frequency distribution, it is rarely used or reported as a measure of central tendency in behavioral science research. One reason for this rarity of use is that a distribution may have more than one mode. And, if more than one mode exists, which is a more typical score? Thus, the mode may not provide one typical score to characterize a distribution.

A second reason for the infrequent use of the mode is that a change in only one score may change the mode of a distribution dramatically. Suppose, for example, that you gave individuals a test of short-term memory by asking a person to repeat back as many as possible of 10 digits from a list. Assume that you obtained the following numbers of digits given back from six people:

Participant	Number of Digits
1	5
2	6
3	7
4	7
5	8
6	9

The mode of this distribution is 7, for two people repeated back seven digits. Suppose, however, that participant 4 repeated back only five digits instead of seven. Now the mode of the distribution is 5 rather than 7. The change of only one score shifted the mode considerably. As another instance, suppose participant 3 had recalled ten digits instead of seven. Now the distribution possesses no mode, for each score occurs an equal number of times. Because the mode is so dependent on only a few scores, it is not a stable measure of central tendency.

MEDIAN

Median (Mdn): A score value in the distribution with an equal number of scores above and below it. The median is the 50th percentile in a distribution.

The **median** (abbreviated **Mdn**) corresponds to a score value in the distribution that has an equal number of scores above and below it. The median, thus, represents the 50th percentile in a distribution. For most distributions of scores, there are simple ways of finding the median.

Calculating the Median with an Odd Number of Scores: No Tied Scores near the Median

For an odd number of scores in a distribution with no tied scores near the median, the median is usually determined by finding the middle score in the frequency distribution. As an example, for seven Test Anxiety Inventory scores of 22, 34, 36, 37, 38, 44, 72, the median is 37. This value is the fourth score and falls in the middle of the distribution of the seven scores. Three scores are less than 37 and three scores are greater than 37. Notice, essentially, that a counting procedure is used to determine a median. The numerical values of the scores that go into the count are not utilized in determining the value of the median.

Calculating the Median with an Even Number of Scores: No Tied Scores near the Median

With an even number of scores in a distribution and no tied scores near the median, the median is conventionally taken as the value that lies midway between the two middle scores in the frequency distribution. Consider, for example, six Test Anxiety Inventory scores: 34, 35, 37, 38, 44, 72. The median for these scores is 37.5, a value that falls halfway between 37 (the third score) and 38 (the fourth score). One-half of the six scores lie below a value of 37.5 and one-half lie above it.

Example Problem 4.1

Finding the Median

Problem: Studies investigating visual perception of real-world scenes sometimes present an individual with a picture of a scene for study and then ask the person to recall details of the scene. Suppose that you followed this procedure with 18 subjects and found the following number of details recalled by each person: 7, 3, 7, 9, 6, 10, 14, 3, 6, 9, 14, 9, 8, 5, 4, 6, 9, 13. Find the median.

Solution: Eighteen scores are given in the distribution; thus, the median is the score with nine scores on either side of it. Accordingly, the median is midway between the ninth and tenth scores when the scores are placed in a frequency distribution, as shown next.

Score	f	
14	2	
13	1	
12	0	
11	0	9 scores
10	1	
9	4	
8	1	
7	2	7.5 = median
6	3	
5	1	
4	1	
3	2	9 scores
2	0	
1	0	
0	0	

The ninth score is 7 and the tenth score is 8; thus, the median is 7.5, midway between the scores of 7 and 8.

Calculating the Median with the Percentile Formula

When there are identical (i.e., tied) scores in the region of the median, the simple methods for obtaining the median will not work. In this instance the percentile formula may be applied to obtain the median for the median is the 50th percentile in a distribution. Recall from Chapter 3 that a percentile represents the value below which a certain percentage of scores in a distribution lies. For a median, 50 percent of the scores fall below its value. Accordingly, the median may be obtained from a grouped frequency distribution using the percentile formula given in Chapter 3:

$$\text{Median} = Mdn = X_{50} = X_L + \left(\frac{.50(N) - cf_L}{f_i} \right) i,$$

where
X_{50} = median score we want to find.
X_L = lower real limit of the interval containing the 50th percentile.
N = total number of scores in the distribution.
cf_L = cumulative frequency of scores up to the lower real limit of the interval containing the median.
f_i = frequency of scores in the interval containing the median.
i = size of the class interval.

Characteristics of the Median

The median essentially is obtained by counting scores, ignoring numerical values except for the score that is the median. Therefore, the median is not influenced by the numerical value of extreme scores in a distribution. As an example, the median for each distribution that follows is 37 (in boldface):

Distribution

A	B	C
22	34	22
34	34	34
35	35	35
37	**37**	**37**
39	39	39
44	44	44
44	109	117

The median ignores the extreme scores in the tails of distributions *B* and *C*. This characteristic makes the median a desirable measure of central tendency for a skewed distribution. For example, the median is often reported for the typical income for a population because incomes are heavily positively skewed. There are only a few people who have incomes in the many millions of dollars. If the numerical values of these incomes were included in the measure of typical income, it would be too high to be representative of an average person. The median, however, is not affected by these few large incomes and, thus, provides a measure of central tendency representative of a typical income.

TESTING YOUR KNOWLEDGE 4.1

1. Define: bimodal distribution, descriptive statistics, measures of central tendency, *Mdn*, median, mode, multimodal distribution, unimodal distribution.
2. Identify two uses of descriptive statistics.
3. Assume that a researcher measured self-esteem in 25 seventh-grade girls. The girls rated their self-esteem on a scale ranging from 10 (lowest self-esteem) to 70 (highest self-esteem). The scores obtained were 49, 53, 67, 20, 27, 36, 49, 27, 61, 17, 49, 50, 29, 56, 65, 27, 48, 24, 49, 15, 32, 66, 46, 24, and 38.
   a. Find the mode for this distribution.
   b. Is this distribution unimodal, bimodal, or multimodal?
4. Assume that one of the girls with a score of 49 in question 3 had instead obtained a score of 27.
   a. Find the mode for this distribution.
   b. Is this distribution unimodal, bimodal, or multimodal?
5. Assume that one of the girls with a score of 49 in question 3 had instead obtained a score of 24.
   a. Find the mode for this distribution.
   b. Is this distribution unimodal, bimodal, or multimodal?

6. What limitation of the mode as a descriptive statistic is illustrated by your answers to questions 4 and 5?
7. Find the median for the set of scores in question 3.
8. Assume that the experimenter measured one additional seventh-grader in question 3 and obtained a score of 28. Include this score in the distribution and find the median of the distribution.
9. Assume the original distribution of 25 scores in question 3. Suppose, however, that the scores of 61, 65, 66, and 67 were changed to 51, 55, 56, and 57, respectively. What is the median of this new distribution of scores?
10. Compare your answers to questions 7 and 8 and to questions 7 and 9. What limitations of the median as a measure of central tendency are illustrated by your answers?

SAMPLE MEAN

Sample mean ($\overline{X}$): The sum of a set of scores divided by the number of scores summed.

The most familiar measure of central tendency is the sample mean. The **sample mean**, often called the **arithmetic mean**, or simply the **mean**, is the sum of a set of scores divided by the number of scores summed. Stated in statistical notation,

$$\text{Sample mean} = \overline{X} = \frac{\sum X}{N}$$

where

$\overline{X}$ = mean (pronounced "X-bar").

$\sum$ = summation sign (the Greek capital letter sigma); it indicates summing or adding up of a set of numbers.

X = score for any individual.

N = number of scores in the sample.

In journal articles following the style of the *Publication Manual of the American Psychological Association* (4th ed., 1994), the sample mean is often represented by the symbol M rather than $\overline{X}$. I will use M when presenting sample journal reports but will use the traditional $\overline{X}$ for text material.

Calculating the Sample Mean

Assume that I obtained the following six Test Anxiety Inventory scores: 34, 35, 37, 38, 44, and 40. The sample mean for this set of scores is obtained as follows.

First, I find the sum of the scores, or

$$\sum X = 34 + 35 + 37 + 38 + 44 + 40 = 228.$$

The number of scores, N, equals 6. To find the mean of the scores, I divide the sum, 228, by 6, or

$$\overline{X} = \frac{\sum X}{N} = \frac{228}{6} = 38.0.$$

The mean of the 100 TAI scores in Table 3.3 is found by summing the 100 scores and then dividing the sum by 100. In notation,

$$\overline{X} = \frac{42 + 28 + 37 + \cdots + 29 + 40 + 37}{100}$$

$$= \frac{4164}{100} = 41.64 = 41.6.$$

Example Problem 4.2

Calculating the Mean

Problem: Suppose that you obtained the following 18 scores in a picture recall task, as discussed in Example Problem 4.1: 7, 3, 7, 9, 6, 10, 14, 3, 6, 9, 14, 9, 8, 5, 4, 6, 9, 13. Find the mean of these scores.

Statistic to Be Used: $\overline{X} = \dfrac{\sum X}{N}$.

Solution: The first step is to obtain $\sum X$, which equals

$$7 + 3 + 7 + 9 + 6 + 10 + 14 + 3 + 6 + 9 + 14 + 9 + 8 + 5 + 4 + 6 + 9 + 13 = 142.$$

N is the number of scores added, or 18 in this example. Accordingly,

$$\overline{X} = \frac{\sum X}{N} = \frac{142}{18} = 7.89 = 7.9.$$

Characteristics of the Sample Mean

Calculating the mean requires the numerical value of every score in the distribution. Thus, any change of a score in a distribution will necessarily change the value of the mean for that distribution. For example, consider seven TAI scores: 26, 26, 26, 30, 34, 40, 42. The mode of this distribution is 26, the median 30, and the mean 32. If only one score, for example, 40, changes to a 43, the mode remains 26 and the median 30, but the mean is now 32.4. Because the mean depends on the magnitude of each score, extreme scores in a distribution affect the value of the mean and distort its value as a measure of central tendency. Suppose, for instance, that the 40 in the distribution of seven TAI scores changes not to a 44 but to a 78. The mode and the median of the distribution remain 26 and 30, respectively. But the mean has increased to 37.4. Accordingly, if a distribution includes a few extreme scores, the mean may not be a representative typical score.

A second characteristic of the mean is that the differences of a set of scores from the mean of those scores sum to zero. Notationally,

$$\sum (X - \overline{X}) = 0.$$

This notation indicates that if I subtract the mean from each score in a set of scores and then sum the differences, the sum of the differences will be zero. Table 4.1 illustrates this relation. Column a of Table 4.1 portrays seven Test Anxiety Inventory scores with a mean of 35.0. The numerical value of the mean is subtracted from each of the seven scores in column b of the table. The sum of column b, $\sum (X - \overline{X})$, is zero.

For any set of scores, the value of $\sum (X - \overline{X})$ will always be zero. But the value of $\sum (X - \overline{X})^2$ will not be zero unless each score in the distribution is equal to the mean. This value is calculated in column c of the table, where each difference (often referred to as a *deviation*) of a score from the mean is squared (i.e., multiplied by itself). For example, the score of 22 differs from $\overline{X}$ by -13, and $(-13)^2 = 169$. The total of the scores in column c, $\sum (X - \overline{X})^2$, is 264. The value of $\sum (X - \overline{X})^2$ is used frequently in statistical calculations and is called a **sum of squares** (abbreviated *SS*). Thus,

Sum of squares (SS): A numerical value obtained by subtracting the mean of a distribution from each score in the distribution, squaring each difference, and then summing the differences.

$$\text{Sum of squares} = SS = \sum (X - \overline{X})^2.$$

It can be demonstrated mathematically that the sum of the squared deviations of the scores from the mean [i.e., $\sum (X - \overline{X})^2$] is smaller than the squared deviation of the scores from any other statistic, such as the median or the mode. This property allows the mean to be used in several very important statistical techniques discussed in later chapters.

Journal Presentation of the Sample Mean

Statisticians typically use $\overline{X}$ to indicate the sample mean. Many behavioral science journals, however, follow the editorial style of the *Publication Manual of the American Psychological Association* (American Psychological Association, 1994) in which the sample mean is

TABLE 4.1
Set of seven scores (column a) with a mean of 35.0. Column b shows the value of $X - \overline{X}$ for each score. In column c the $X - \overline{X}$ deviation is squared for each score.

(a) X	(b) $X - \overline{X}$	(c) $(X - \overline{X})^2$
22	$22 - 35 = -13$	169
34	$34 - 35 = -1$	1
35	$35 - 35 = 0$	0
35	$35 - 35 = 0$	0
37	$37 - 35 = +2$	4
38	$38 - 35 = +3$	9
44	$44 - 35 = +9$	81
$\overline{X}$ 35.0	Sum 0	264

M: The symbol used for the sample mean in publications following the editorial style of the *Publication Manual of the American Psychological Association* (1994).

represented by an italicized *M*. Thus, in a journal publication you may expect to find a presentation such as

The mean number of pictures recalled by the experimental group (*M* = 7.9) was greater than the mean number recalled by the control group (*M* = 4.6).

In a typewritten or word-processed manuscript, underlining is used to indicate a statistical symbol; thus, in a manuscript such as a laboratory report the presentation would appear

```
The mean number of pictures recalled by the experi-
mental group (M = 7.9) was greater than the mean num-
ber recalled by the control group (M = 4.6).
```

POPULATION MEAN

Population mean (μ): The sum of all the scores in a population divided by the number of scores summed.

A mean for a population of scores is calculated similarly to the sample mean except that *N* represents the number of scores in the population and the value of the mean is represented by the Greek letter **μ** (mu, the 12th letter of the Greek alphabet, pronounced "mew") rather than $\overline{X}$. Thus, a **population mean** is given by

$$\text{Population mean} = \mu = \frac{\sum X}{N_{\text{population}}}.$$

In most instances μ will be estimated from $\overline{X}$ because we cannot measure all the scores in a population. I discuss the characteristics of the sample mean as an estimator of the population mean more fully in Chapter 7.

TESTING YOUR KNOWLEDGE 4.2

1. Define: *M*, μ, *N*, population mean, $\sum$, sample mean, sum of squares, *SS*, $\sum X$, $\overline{X}$.
2. Assume you obtained the following scores: 97, 90, 86, 93, 76, and 86.
   a. Find the mean for the scores.
   b. Demonstrate that $\sum (X - \overline{X}) = 0$ for these scores.
   c. Find the value of $\sum (X - \overline{X})^2$ for these scores.
3. Assume that a researcher measured self-esteem in seventh-grade girls and obtained the scores 49, 53, 67, 20, 27, 36, 49, 27, 61, and 28.
   a. Find the mean of these scores.
   b. Suppose that the experimenter measured one additional seventh-grader and obtained a score of 17. Include this score in the previous distribution and find the mean of the distribution.
   c. Suppose that the score of 67 was changed to 27 so that the scores obtained were 49, 53, 27, 20, 27, 36, 49, 27, 61, and 28. What is the mean of this new set of scores?
   d. Compare your answers for questions 3a, b, and c. What characteristic of the mean is illustrated by your answers?

COMPARING MEASURES OF CENTRAL TENDENCY

Which is the "best" average score? There is no simple answer to this question. Which measure of central tendency is best depends on the intended use for the statistic. Measures of central tendency have both descriptive and inferential uses.

Descriptive Uses of Measures of Central Tendency

The choice of which measure of central tendency to use as a descriptive statistic depends on the scale of measurement realized in the scores and the shape of the frequency distribution of the scores.

Scale of Measurement of the Scores

Nominal Scale.   A nominal measurement merely places responses into categories; a response occurred or it did not occur. The only measure of central tendency that may be used with a nominal measurement is the mode—the category that occurs most frequently.

Ordinal Scale.   Ordinal measures place scores in order of magnitude, but there is no assurance that on the underlying variable being measured the intervals between adjacent scores are equal. Consequently, a median score may be obtained. The median divides the distribution of scores into two equal halves. A modal score, should one occur, may also be obtained.

Interval and Ratio Scales.   In both interval and ratio measures the intervals between adjacent scores are assumed to represent equal intervals on the variable being measured. Thus, it is appropriate to compute a mean on scores that represent either interval or ratio measurement. It is also appropriate to find the median and the mode for scores at this level.

Shape of the Distribution of Scores

How well a measure of central tendency characterizes a distribution also depends on the shape of the distribution. Figure 3.8 presented shapes of several typical distributions of scores. If a distribution is unimodal and symmetric, such as the normal distribution of Figure 3.8a, then the mode, median, and mean are identical values. Each statistic characterizes the distribution of scores equally well. Often, however, obtained distributions are not unimodal and symmetric; they may be either positively or negatively skewed. In a skewed distribution, the mode, median, and mean will differ from each other. Because the mean is responsive to the extreme scores of a skewed distribution, it will move more in the direction of the extreme scores than either the mode or the median. Thus, the direction of the difference between the mean and median will reveal whether the distribution is positively or negatively skewed. In a negatively skewed distribution the mean will have a lower value than the median; similarly, a few extreme high scores in a positively skewed distribution will increase the value of the mean with respect to the median. Figure 4.1 illustrates the relative locations of the median and mean in positively and negatively skewed distributions. As you can see from this figure, if a distribution is seriously skewed, with a large difference

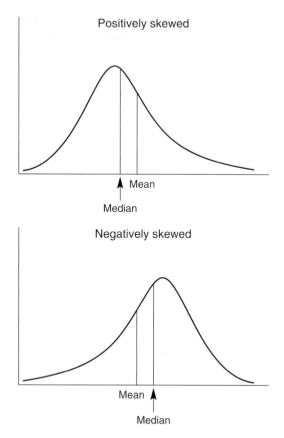

FIGURE 4.1
The relative locations of the median and mean in
positively and negatively skewed distributions.

between the mean and median values, the median usually provides a better measure of central tendency than does the mean. A distribution of the salaries of major league baseball players illustrates this point. For one American League team, the range of annual salaries is from $109,000 to $5,155,250 (Cafardo, 1994). The mean of this distribution is $1,357,163, but the median is $500,000. The distribution is severely positively skewed; only 8 of the 25 players on the team earn more than the mean. Thus, characterizing the typical salary of the players on this team by the mean provides a misleading representation, for half the players earn $500,000 or less (Fudin & Levinson, 1994).

Whenever description is important, I recommend presentation of all three measures of central tendency for a distribution of scores. As you read behavioral sciences literature, however, you will find that the mean is the most widely presented descriptive measure of central tendency, and the mode is provided only rarely. This choice of the mean often is not based on its superior descriptive characteristics; rather the mean is the most useful of the three measures of central tendency as an inferential statistic. And, as you will see, inference is an important aspect of statistical analysis.

Do Some Distributions Not Have a Central Tendency?

Bimodal distributions cannot be adequately described by a single measure of central tendency, especially when the modal scores are widely separated. Suppose, for example, that a researcher obtains a distribution of Test Anxiety Inventory scores such as that shown in Table 4.2. This distribution is clearly bimodal, with a mode at 34 and another at 58. The median of the distribution is 45.5 and the mean is 45.8. But no one obtained scores near either the median or the mean. Neither the median nor the mean represents the test anxiety of a typical person in this sample. In this instance, the modes of 34 and 58 present the best description of typical scores.

TABLE 4.2
Bimodal distribution of 26 Test Anxiety Inventory scores.

Score	Tally	f	
61	/	1	
60			
59	//	2	
58	/////	5	Mode
57	///	3	
56	/	1	
55	/	1	
54			
53			
52			
51			
50			
49			
48			
47			
46			
45			$\overline{X} = 45.8,\quad Mdn = 45.5$
44			
43			
42			
41			
40			
39			
38			
37			
36	/	1	
35	///	3	
34	/////	5	Mode
33	//	2	
32	/	1	
31	/	1	

Consider another example. For a recent year the Department of Agriculture reported that the per capita consumption of chewing tobacco in the United States was 1.33 pounds per person. Does this statistic describe you? If you do not chew tobacco, this number is much too high. But if you do chew tobacco, the value likely is far too low. The distribution of chewing tobacco use is bimodal. A minority of the population uses chewing tobacco, and their consumption is considerably in excess of 1.33 pounds per year. The majority of the population does not chew tobacco, and their modal use is zero pounds per year.

Inferential Uses of Measures of Central Tendency

The choice of a measure of central tendency is determined in part by whether the statistic is to be used for subsequent inferential purposes. In Chapter 1, I indicated that population parameters are often estimated by statistics obtained from a sample. The sample mean, $\overline{X}$, is the best estimator of a population mean, represented by the Greek letter μ. Consequently, the sample mean enters into a number of important statistical tests. Because the mean is so useful for inference, then, behavioral scientists often use the mean to describe their data. I discuss the characteristics of the sample mean as an estimator of the population mean more fully in Chapter 7.

TESTING YOUR KNOWLEDGE 4.3

1. Which measure of central tendency would you choose to achieve each of the following?
   a. Provide a value that is the 50th percentile in a distribution.
   b. Minimize the sum of the squared difference of each score in the distribution from the measure of central tendency.
   c. Describe the most frequently occurring score in a distribution.
   d. Utilize the numerical value of each score in its computation.
2. A distribution is severely negatively skewed. Would you expect the mean to be smaller than, equal to, or larger than the median? Explain your answer.
3. The mean of a distribution is considerably larger than the median. Do you expect the distribution to be symmetrical, negatively skewed, or positively skewed? Why?

SUMMARY

- Measures of central tendency may be used for both descriptive and inferential purposes.
- The mode, median, and sample mean are the three commonly used measures of central tendency.
- The mode is the most frequently occurring score in a distribution of scores.
- The median is a score in the distribution with an equal number of scores above and below it.
- The sample mean is found from $\sum X / N$.
- The population mean is found from $\sum X / N_{population}$.
- The mean is the most used measure of central tendency for inferential purposes.
- The appropriate use of each statistic for descriptive purposes depends on the scale of measurement achieved and the shape of the frequency distribution of the scores.

KEY TERMS AND SYMBOLS

bimodal distribution (63)
descriptive statistics (63)
measures of central
    tendency (63)
measures of variability (63)

median (*Mdn*) (64)
mode (63)
multimodal distribution (63)
population mean (μ) (70)
sample mean (*M* or $\overline{X}$) (67)

$\sum$ (summation) (67)
sum of squares (69)
unimodal distribution (63)
$\sum (X - \overline{X})^2$ (69)

REVIEW QUESTIONS

1. Rotton and Kelly (1985) developed a scale called the Belief in Lunar Effects Scale to measure a person's belief in the effect of a full moon on behavior. Scores on this scale may range from 9 to 81. For one sample of individuals they report a mean of 37.9 and a median of 39. From this information, would you judge the distribution of scores to be approximately symmetrical or skewed? Why?

2. A U.S. Census Bureau report indicates that in 1992 the mean income for male lawyers and judges was $94,757, whereas the median income was $78,052. Is this distribution of incomes skewed? If you think it is skewed, in which direction is it skewed? Why?

3. Egli and Meyers (1984) surveyed 151 teenagers at a video-game arcade. The results revealed that the individuals played a mean of 5.2 hours per week, with a median of 2.5 hours per week. Is the distribution of hours played per week skewed? If you think it is skewed, in which direction is it skewed? Why?

4. Researchers in behavioral medicine are interested in psychological methods of controlling pain. To induce pain safely in their participants, they may use the cold pressor task. One form of this task involves having a person immerse a hand in cold water and then timing how long the person can tolerate the pain induced. Suppose that an experimenter had each of 17 people place a hand in a tub of 40°F water and then timed how long the person could hold his or her hand in the water before the pain became too intense to endure. The experimenter replicated the study four times and obtained the following four sets of scores (the scores represent time in seconds):

   Set 1:   35, 39, 38, 30, 37, 43, 30, 38, 41, 52, 25, 44, 33, 41, 38, 56, and 37.
   Set 2:   20, 28, 26, 29, 60, 21, 37, 30, 28, 57, 29, 25, 63, 26, 32, 30, and 28.
   Set 3:   45, 23, 57, 50, 47, 52, 20, 53, 50, 30, 52, 60, 52, 49, 52, 49, and 53.
   Set 4:   52, 23, 40, 60, 52, 21, 20, 52, 50, 23, 55, 26, 28, 53, 26, 49, and 26.

   For each set of scores:

   a. Construct an ungrouped simple frequency distribution. Use this frequency distribution to make a judgment about the shape of the distribution of the scores.

   b. Calculate the mode, median, and mean.

   c. Compare the measures of central tendency. Is the distribution skewed? Explain how you reached a decision. Does your answer from this comparison agree with your judgment from the frequency distribution constructed for question a?

d. Do you think one of the measures of central tendency describes the scores better than the others? If so, which measure and why?

5. Your statistics professor plans to grade you on the basis of five examinations each worth 100 points. She informs you that your grade will be based on the central tendency of your scores and that you will have to choose whether you want your grade based on the modal, median, or mean score. Suppose the grades of three students in the class are as follows:

	Exam				
	1	**2**	**3**	**4**	**5**
Roberto	35	40	65	90	90
Dimitrios	10	50	65	80	85
Karen	56	56	67	78	98

If you were each of these students, which measure of central tendency would you choose to determine your course grade? Explain the reason for your choice for each student.

6. Gross (1993) surveyed students at a large midwestern university to find the extent of alcohol consumption among college males and females. One question on the survey asked the respondents to indicate the number of drinks consumed each week. Gross found that, among students 21 years or older, men reported having a mean of 23.9 drinks per week and women a mean of 7.5 drinks per week.

a. Critique the use of a mean as a measure of central tendency of drinking behavior. Specifically, do you think the distribution of estimated drinks was skewed? If so, in which direction?

b. Which measure of central tendency do you think may be a better measure to use in this instance?

7. Simple reaction time, the amount of time it takes to respond to a simple stimulus such as a light or tone, is a measure of a person's recovery from general anesthesia. Suppose that you measured eight surgery patients 2 hours after they received general anesthesia for minor surgery and found the following reaction times in milliseconds: 782, 793, 793, 817, 832, 847, 866, 893. A ninth patient was not sufficiently recovered to provide a reaction time; thus, this subject was assigned an infinite reaction time.

a. If you wanted to include the scores of all nine patients, which measure or measures of central tendency could you calculate?

b. What is the numerical value of that measure?

8. The U.S. Census Bureau reports that the median age at first marriage for males in 1998 was 26.7 years. Explain why the median rather than the mean was reported for this statistic.

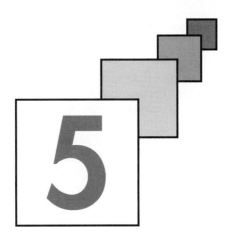

Describing Data: Measures of Variability

Variability refers to how much scores differ from each other and, thus, from the measure of central tendency in a distribution. The more the scores differ from each other, the more they will also differ from the measure of central tendency and the more variability there is in the distribution. Conversely, the less that scores differ from each other in a distribution, the less they will differ from the measure of central tendency and the less the variability of the distribution. Thus, a measure of central tendency tells only part of the story about the scores obtained from a sample of individuals. The mode, median, or mean alone does not indicate how much dispersion or variability there is among the scores in the distribution.

To illustrate the concept of variability, suppose that a researcher measured three different groups of nine subjects each on the amount of time that the subjects laughed while reading a book of cartoons. The scores she obtained, in seconds, are portrayed in Table 5.1. The mode, median, and mean for each group are 41.0. But it should be apparent that the distributions are very different, and the measures of central tendency are not equally representative of the scores in each group. In group 1 each score is equal to 41; thus, there is no variability among the scores. Consequently, each measure of central tendency perfectly represents the scores in the distribution. But the scores in group 1 would be a rare outcome if actual duration-of-laughter scores were obtained from nine subjects. In group 2 there is little variability among the scores. The scores are clustered closely around the measure of central tendency; no score differs more than 3 seconds from 41 seconds. Thus, each measure of central tendency is reasonably representative of all individuals in this group, for there is little variability among the individual scores.

The situation is different in group 3. Here there is more variability in the amount of laughter. The scores differ considerably from each other and some scores differ by as much

TABLE 5.1
Duration-of-laughter scores in seconds for three groups of nine subjects each.

	Group		
	1	2	3
	41	38	21
	41	39	26
	41	40	33
	41	41	41
	41	41	41
	41	41	41
	41	42	50
	41	43	51
	41	44	65
Mode	41	41	41
Mdn	41	41	41
$\overline{X}$	41	41	41

as 20 seconds from the measures of central tendency of 41 seconds. Clearly, any measure of central tendency for this set of scores is not as representative of the scores as are the measures of central tendency for groups 1 and 2.

As with measures of central tendency, the variability of scores must be quantified. Accordingly, there are several statistics to describe the variability of scores in a distribution.

RANGE MEASURES OF VARIABILITY

One form of a measure of variability provides an interval containing a certain percentage of the scores in a distribution. Three such measures are commonly used, the range, the interquartile range, and the semi-interquartile range.

Range

Range: The numerical difference between the lowest and highest scores in a distribution.

The simplest measure of variability for a set of scores, the **range**, is found by

$$\text{Range} = X_{\text{highest}} - X_{\text{lowest}},$$

where X_{highest} represents the highest score and X_{lowest}, the lowest score in a distribution. For group 3 of Table 5.1, $X_{\text{highest}} = 65$ and $X_{\text{lowest}} = 21$; thus, the range for this group is $65 - 21$, or 44. The range for scores in group 2 is $44 - 38$, or 6, and the range of scores for group 1 is $41 - 41$, or 0. For the 100 Test Anxiety Inventory scores given in Table 3.3, the highest score is 73 and the lowest score is 22. Thus, the range for this distribution is $73 - 22$, or 51 rating scale points.

Characteristics of the Range

The range describes the overall spread between the highest and lowest scores in a distribution. Any change in either the highest or lowest score will affect the range, even though all other scores may remain unchanged. Thus, the range is a relatively unstable measure of variability. Moreover, the larger the size of the sample is, the more likely it is that one deviant score may be obtained to inflate the value of the range. The virtue of the range is its easy computation, but because of its lack of stability, it is not a frequently reported measure of variability.

Interquartile Range and Semi-Interquartile Range

Interquartile range (IQR): The range of values for the middle 50 percent of the scores in a distribution.

X_{75}: Score corresponding to the 75th percentile of a distribution.

X_{25}: Score corresponding to the 25th percentile of a distribution.

The **interquartile range (IQR)** describes the range of values for the middle 50 percent of the scores in a distribution and is often used with ordinal measurements. It is obtained by subtracting the score corresponding to the 25th percentile (X_{25}) from the score that falls at the 75th percentile (X_{75}). In notation, the interquartile range is

$$\text{Interquartile range} = IQR = X_{75} - X_{25}.$$

Values of X_{75} and X_{25} may be obtained using the formula in Chapter 3 for finding a specified percentile of a distribution (p. 42).

Semi-interquartile range (SIQR): One-half of the interquartile range.

The **semi-interquartile range (*SIQR*)** is one-half of the interquartile range, or

$$\text{Semi-interquartile range} = SIQR = IQR/2 = (X_{75} - X_{25})/2.$$

Characteristics of the *IQR* and the *SIQR*

The *IQR* provides the range of scores typical for the middle 50 percent of the individuals grouped around the median. Because the *IQR* excludes the top 25 percent and the bottom 25 percent of the scores in a distribution, its value is unaffected by extreme scores of a skewed distribution. Obviously, the interquartile range will be smaller than the range for a set of scores. For example, for the TAI scores of Table 3.3, $X_{75} = 45$ and $X_{25} = 37$ (rounded to the nearest whole number). Thus, the *IQR* is

$$IQR = X_{75} - X_{25} = 45 - 37 = 8,$$

whereas the range for these scores is 51. Although the full range of the TAI scores of Table 3.3 is large, the range for the middle 50 percent of the scores is relatively small.

The *SIQR* describes the average spread of scores for 25 percent of the scores above and below the median. Only when the distribution is symmetrical, however, will the *SIQR* represent exactly the range of scores for the 25 percent of scores above the median and the 25 percent of scores below the median. As an example, for the TAI scores in Table 3.3, the *SIQR* is 8/2, or 4. This *SIQR* indicates that the middle 50 percent of the scores in the distribution does not extend more than about 4 rating points above or 4 rating points below the median. Notice that the preceding statement is qualified with the word *about*. Because the frequency distribution for the TAI scores is slightly skewed, this semi-interquartile range does not include exactly 25 percent of the scores on each side of the median.

TESTING YOUR KNOWLEDGE 5.1

1. Define: interquartile range, range, semi-interquartile range, variability, X_{25}, X_{75}.
2. The highest score on a class test is 98 and the lowest is 54. The 75th percentile score on the test is 92, and the 25th percentile score is 74. Find the range, *IQR*, and *SIQR* for these scores.
3. On a test of complex reaction time, the longest score is 929 milliseconds (ms) and the shortest score is 642 ms. The 75th percentile score is 809 ms and the 25th percentile score is 724 ms.
   a. Find the range, *IQR*, and *SIQR* for these scores.
   b. What information about the scores is given by the *IQR*?
   c. What information about the scores is given by the *SIQR*?
4. Explain why the range is a relatively unstable measure of variability.
5. Explain why the *IQR* is a more stable measure of variability than is the range.

MEASURES OF VARIABILITY ABOUT THE SAMPLE MEAN

The range, *IQR*, and *SIQR* each provide an interval containing a certain percentage of the scores (e.g., 100 percent for the range) around the central location in a distribution. But none of these statistics utilizes all the scores in the distribution for its computation. However, two important measures of variability, the *variance* and the *standard deviation,* utilize all the scores to measure variability about the mean.

In Chapter 4 I obtained the *deviation* or difference of each score in a distribution from the mean of the distribution (see Table 4.1). That is, I calculated $X - \overline{X}$ for each score. This deviation provides a measure of how much a score differs from a mean. If a score is equal to the mean, then $X - \overline{X}$ will be zero. But if the score is not equal to the mean, then $X - \overline{X}$ will take on a numerical value, and the more that X differs from $\overline{X}$, the larger $X - \overline{X}$ will become. We might then propose to obtain a measure of variability by adding up the deviations of all the scores in a distribution and dividing the sum by the number of scores. But as illustrated in column b of Table 4.1, the sum of $X - \overline{X}$ deviations for a distribution of scores will always equal zero; that is, $\sum (X - \overline{X}) = 0$. This problem can be avoided by squaring each deviation value [i.e., $(X - \overline{X})^2$] before summing and dividing. Then the value of $\sum (X - \overline{X})^2$ will be zero only if each $X - \overline{X}$ value is zero. This procedure is used to derive the variance and, subsequently, the standard deviation. I first present the formulas for the variance and standard deviation and how to use them; then I discuss their interpretation.

Variance

Sample Variance

Sample variance (S^2): A descriptive measure of the variance of a sample of scores.

The **sample variance** of scores is represented in notation as S^2 and defined as

$$\text{Sample variance} = S^2 = \frac{\sum (X - \overline{X})^2}{N}.$$

To calculate S^2:

1. Subtract the mean from each score [i.e., $(X - \overline{X})$].
2. Square each resulting difference [i.e., $(X - \overline{X})^2$].
3. Add all the squared difference values [i.e., $\sum (X - \overline{X})^2$.
4. Divide the sum by N, the number of scores in the sample.

Population Variance

If N is equal to the population and the population mean, μ, is known, then substituting μ for X in the formula for the variance provides the variance of the population. The population variance is represented by σ^2 (the Greek letter *sigma,* squared) to indicate that this variance represents a population parameter rather than a statistic obtained from a sample. Thus, the

Population variance (σ^2): The variance obtained by measuring all scores in a population.

population variance is given by

$$\text{Population variance} = \sigma^2 = \frac{\sum (X - \mu)^2}{N_{\text{population}}},$$

where X = the individual score of a member of the population.

μ = the population mean of the scores.

$N_{\text{population}}$ = the total number of scores in the population.

As I have pointed out, however, it usually is impractical to measure all members of a population and, thus, μ will not be known. Consequently, σ^2 typically is estimated from a sample as discussed next.

Estimated Population Variance

The formula for S^2 provides the variance of a sample of scores from a population. However, this value is not used to estimate a population variance, σ^2, because it consistently underestimates the actual value of σ^2 and provides a biased estimate of σ^2. This bias may be corrected by using $N - 1$ instead of N as the denominator in the formula for the sample variance. Thus, the sample variance that is used to determine the **estimated population variance** is represented in notation as s^2 and defined as

Estimated population variance (s^2): The variance obtained from a sample of scores that is used to estimate the population variance for those scores.

$$\text{Estimated population variance} = s^2 = \frac{\sum (X - \overline{X})^2}{N - 1}.$$

As noted in Chapter 4, the sum of squared deviations, $\sum (X - \overline{X})^2$, in the numerator of this formula is called the **sum of squares** and is represented by the symbol **SS.** Thus, the estimated population variance also is defined as

$$\text{Estimated population variance} = s^2 = \frac{SS}{N - 1}.$$

For most purposes the estimated population variance, s^2, is more useful than the sample variance, S^2, and is more widely used than S^2. Thus, from this point on when I discuss the variance I will be referring to s^2 unless I specifically indicate I am using S^2. I discuss the characteristics of s^2 and S^2 as estimates of σ^2 more fully in Chapter 7.

Standard Deviation

Sample Standard Deviation

Sample standard deviation (S): The square root of the sample variance.

The standard deviation of a sample of scores, known as the **sample standard deviation,** is symbolized by S, and is the square root of the sample variance, or

$$\text{Sample standard deviation} = S = \sqrt{S^2} = \sqrt{\frac{\sum (X - \overline{X})^2}{N}}.$$

Population Standard Deviation

Population standard deviation (σ): The square root of the population variance.

If N is equal to the population and the population mean, μ, is known, then the **population standard deviation**, represented by σ, is given by

$$\text{Population standard deviation} = \sigma = \sqrt{\sigma^2} = \sqrt{\frac{\sum (X - \mu)^2}{N_{\text{population}}}}.$$

However, because μ typically is unknown, the value of σ is usually estimated from the sample.

Estimated Population Standard Deviation

Estimated population standard deviation (s): The square root of the estimated population variance.

The **estimated population standard deviation**, s, is the square root of the estimated population variance, or

$$\text{Estimated population standard deviation} = s = \sqrt{s^2} = \sqrt{\frac{\sum (X - \overline{X})^2}{N - 1}}.$$

In sum of squares notation,

$$s = \sqrt{\frac{SS}{N - 1}}.$$

To calculate s:

1. Subtract the mean from each score [i.e., $(X - \overline{X})$].
2. Square each resulting difference [i.e., $(X - \overline{X})^2$].
3. Add all the squared difference values [i.e., $\sum (X - \overline{X})^2$].
4. Divide the sum by $N - 1$, the number of scores in the sample minus one.
5. Take the square root of the resulting quotient.

For most purposes the estimated population standard deviation, s, is more useful than the sample standard deviation, S, and when I use the term *standard deviation*, I will be referring to s.

Example Problem 5.1

Calculating the Estimated Population Variance and Standard Deviation with the Definitional Formula

Problem: Find the estimated population variance and standard deviation of the nine duration-of-laughter scores of group 2 in Table 5.1 using the definitional formula for s^2.

Statistic to Be Used: $s^2 = \sum (X - \overline{X})^2 / (N - 1)$.

Solution: The steps necessary in the calculation of s^2 and s are illustrated in the following table. I first find s^2. The formula requires obtaining the sum of squares, SS or $\sum (X - \overline{X})^2$. The nine scores are given in column a. The mean for these scores is 41, and this value is presented in column b. The first step is to subtract this mean from each score as illustrated in column c. The second step is to square the difference for each score as shown in column d. The squared differences are added together, and this sum, given at the bottom of column d, is 28. This sum is the $\sum (X - \overline{X})^2$, or SS, needed for the numerator of s^2. The last step is to divide the SS by $N - 1$. Because nine scores were used, $N = 9$ and $N - 1 = 8$. Accordingly, $s^2 = 28/8 = 3.50$. Notice that, because the deviation of each score from the mean is squared, s^2 must always be either zero or a positive number. A negative s^2 indicates a mistake in calculations.

(a) X	(b) $\overline{X}$	(c) $(X - \overline{X})$	(d) $(X - \overline{X})^2$
38	41	-3	9
39	41	-2	4
40	41	-1	1
41	41	0	0
41	41	0	0
41	41	0	0
42	41	$+1$	1
43	41	$+2$	4
44	41	$+3$	9
	Sum	0	28

The estimated population standard deviation, s, is the square root of s^2. Thus, $s = \sqrt{3.50} = 1.87$ seconds. Notice that the units attached to s, seconds, are the same as those of the raw scores. It is important to remember to take the square root of s^2 when finding s, for a common error in calculating s is failing to take the square root of s^2.

Summary of Computational Steps

1. Find the mean of the scores in column a and then list this value in column b as shown.
2. Subtract the mean in column b from each score in column a. The difference is shown in column c.
3. Square each difference in column c. The result of this squaring is shown in column d.
4. Sum the squared differences of column d.
5. Divide the sum of column d by $N - 1$. The resulting value is s^2.
6. Take the square root of s^2 to obtain s.

Computational Formula for the Estimated Population Variance and Standard Deviation

The definitional formula for the variance best conveys conceptually what s^2 is. The formula is easy to use when only a few scores are involved and the scores and the mean of the scores are whole numbers. When decimal values are obtained with either the scores or the mean, or if a large number of scores is involved, the computations become more cumbersome. Then it is often easier to calculate s^2 with a formula that is equivalent algebraically to the definitional formula. The computational formula for s^2 is

$$\text{Estimated population variance} = s^2 = \frac{\sum X^2 - [(\sum X)^2/N]}{N - 1}.$$

The estimated population standard deviation is obtained by taking the square root of s^2, or

$$\text{Estimated population standard deviation} = s = \sqrt{s^2} = \sqrt{\frac{\sum X^2 - [(\sum X)^2/N]}{N - 1}}.$$

Example Problem 5.2

Calculating the Variance and Standard Deviation with the Computational Formula

Problem: Find the variance and standard deviation of the nine duration-of-laughter scores of group 2 in Table 5.1 using the computational formula for s^2.

Statistic to Be Used

$$s^2 = \frac{\sum X^2 - [(\sum X)^2/N]}{N - 1}$$

Solution: The steps in calculating s^2 using this formula are illustrated in the following table. The nine scores are presented in column a. The formula requires obtaining two values from the scores, the sum of all the scores (i.e., $\sum X$) and the sum of the values of each score squared (i.e., $\sum X^2$). The sum of the scores, $\sum X$, is 369 and is presented at the bottom of column a. The value of each score squared is given in column b [e.g., $(38)^2 = 1{,}444$]. The sum of the squared scores, $\sum X^2$, is 15,157 and is shown at the bottom of column b. Nine scores were used; thus, $N = 9$ and $N - 1 = 8$.

	(a) X	(b) X^2
	38	1,444
	39	1,521
	40	1,600
	41	1,681
	41	1,681
	41	1,681
	42	1,764
	43	1,849
	44	1,936
Sum	369	15,157

Substituting these values into the formula, I obtain

$$s^2 = \frac{15{,}157 - [(369)^2/9]}{9 - 1}$$

$$= \frac{15{,}157 - (136{,}161/9)}{8}$$

$$= \frac{15{,}157 - 15{,}129}{8}$$

$$= \frac{28}{8} = 3.50.$$

This value of s^2, 3.50, is identical to that obtained in Example Problem 5.1 using the definitional formula of s^2. Again, $s = \sqrt{s^2} = \sqrt{3.50} = 1.87$ seconds.

Finding the Variance and Standard Deviation with a Calculator

After you have become familiar with the variance and standard deviation, it is likely you will calculate the variance and standard deviation for small sets of data by using a hand calculator. Most calculators have built-in programs for computation of these statistics, as well as $\overline{X}$, but their use varies slightly from calculator to calculator. Thus, you will need to read the instruction manual for the calculator you are using. Many calculators will also provide the values of $\sum X$, $\sum X^2$, and N that are used in the computational formulas. The symbols used to identify the different variances may vary from those used in this text. The estimated population standard deviation is often, but not always, symbolized by s as is done in this text. The sample standard deviation, however, is often symbolized by σ or SD. Obviously, it is important to know which of these symbols is used on your calculator.

Review of Symbols and Formulas

I have introduced a number of symbols and formulas up to this point. They are reviewed here.

S^2 The variance of a sample. S^2 is a purely descriptive statistic for a sample.

S The standard deviation of a sample. S is a purely descriptive statistic for a sample.

s^2 The estimated population variance. This statistic is used to estimate a population variance.

s The estimated population standard deviation. This statistic is used to estimate a population standard deviation.

σ^2 The population variance, a parameter calculated on all scores in a population.

σ The population standard deviation, a parameter based on all scores in a population.

The estimated population variance, s^2, and standard deviation, s, are the statistics typically calculated on a sample of scores. Table 5.2 presents the definitional, computational, and sum of squares formulas for both s^2 and s. Each formula provides the same numerical value of the statistic when applied to a set of data.

Interpreting the Variance and the Standard Deviation

The standard deviation is presented as a descriptive statistic in reports of research more often than the variance. One reason for this greater use is that, because the standard deviation is the square root of the variance, it provides a measure of the variability of scores in the original units of the scores. In Example Problems 5.1 and 5.2, s^2 is 3.50 seconds squared, a value not easily interpreted. The value of s, however, is 1.87 seconds, the same units (i.e., seconds) that the raw scores were measured in. Thus, the focus in this section is on the interpretation of s. The variance, however, is used in statistical hypothesis testing methods and is discussed more fully in Chapters 10 through 12.

TABLE 5.2
Definitional, computational, and sum of squares formulas for the estimated population variance and standard deviation.

	Formula		
	Definitional	**Computational**	**Sum of Squares**
Variance, s^2	$\dfrac{\sum(X-\bar{X})^2}{N-1}$	$\dfrac{\sum X^2 - [(\sum X)^2/N]}{N-1}$	$\dfrac{SS}{N-1}$
Standard deviation, $s = \sqrt{s^2}$	$\sqrt{\dfrac{\sum(X-\bar{X})^2}{N-1}}$	$\sqrt{\dfrac{\sum X^2 - [(\sum X)^2/N]}{N-1}}$	$\sqrt{\dfrac{SS}{N-1}}$

The standard deviation provides a measure of the *average* of how much scores in a distribution differ from the mean. If all the scores in a distribution are equal to the mean, such as those of group 1 of Table 5.1, then s will equal zero. Thus, the average amount by which the scores in group 1 differ from the mean is zero. In this case, if you use $\bar{X}$ to predict any of the scores in the distribution, there will be zero error in your prediction. If you see a value of s equal to zero, then you know that all scores in the distribution are equal to the sample mean, and the mean is a perfect predictor of all the scores.

On the other hand, if at least one score in the distribution is not equal to the mean, then s will take on a value greater than zero. And the value of s will increase as the variability of the scores increases. You can see this increase in s with increasing variability of scores by comparing the distributions of groups 2 and 3 of Table 5.1. Notice that the scores of group 3 are more variable about the mean of 41 than are the scores in group 2. For scores in group 2, $s = 1.87$ seconds, whereas in group 3, s is 13.44 seconds. Thus, for group 2 the average amount by which scores differ from $\bar{X}$ is 1.87 seconds, and in group 3 it is 13.44 seconds. If you use $\bar{X} = 41$ seconds to predict any of the scores in group 2, your prediction will be in error by about 1.87 seconds, whereas for group 3 such a prediction will be in error by about 13.44 seconds.

A second interpretation of s involves describing scores in terms of how many standard deviations they are away from the mean of a distribution. For many distributions, a majority of the scores are within one standard deviation of the mean. As an example, the mean for the 100 Test Anxiety Inventory scores of Table 3.3 is 41.64, and s for this distribution is 8.66. The scores within one standard deviation of $\bar{X}$ are scores from 32.98 to 50.30. These values are the distance encompassed by one standard deviation below the mean (i.e., $\bar{X} - 1s = 41.64 - 8.66 = 32.98$) to one standard deviation above the mean (i.e., $\bar{X} + 1s = 41.64 + 8.66 = 50.30$). Counting the scores of Table 3.3, I find that 79 of the 100 scores fall into this interval. If the distribution is normally shaped (as in Figure 3.7a), then knowledge of the standard deviation provides even more information about the scores in the distribution. This interpretation of s is discussed in Chapter 6.

This analysis can be applied to an example from behavioral sciences literature. McKelvey and McKenry (2000) studied the effects of divorce on the psychosocial well-being of a mother using a sample of 235 black and 662 white divorced or separated mothers. To describe the typical age and income of these samples, they presented means and standard deviations for each variable. The mean age of the black mothers was 35.9 years with an s of 7.6 years. The mean age of the white mothers was 35.0 years with an s of 7.4 years. With respect to total income, the black mothers had a mean of \$11,987 with an s of \$11,848; for the white mothers the mean was \$15,296 with an s of \$15,819.

From these descriptive statistics if I state that the typical black mother studied in this research was 35.9 years old, I will be in error by an average of 7.6 years. But I can anticipate that the age of the majority of these women was within one standard deviation of the mean, or between 28.3 (i.e., 35.9 minus 7.6) to 43.5 (i.e., 35.9 plus 7.6) years old. It is unlikely that many of these women were in their sixties for if they had been this old, then such large differences from the mean of 35.9 years would have increased the value of the standard deviation. A similar analysis holds for the ages of the white women. On the other hand, the standard deviations for total income are very large in comparison to the mean of total income for each group. In fact, the s of \$15,819 for the white women is actually larger than the mean for these women. If I take the range of income within one s of this mean, I obtain a range of −\$523 (\$15,296 minus \$15,819) to \$31,115 (\$15,296 plus \$15,819). Obviously, a negative income is impossible (even though you may sometimes spend more than you make, the minimum income you can earn is zero); thus, the implication of this relationship is that the data for the total income must have been heavily positively skewed.

Notice also that a score can be described by indicating how many standard deviations it is above or below the mean. For example, if a distribution of scores has a mean of 80 and a standard deviation of 6, then a score of 86 is one standard deviation above the mean and a score of 74 is one standard deviation below the mean. Chapter 6 explains this use of the standard deviation more fully.

What Is a Large Amount of Variability?

No simple rule is used to determine whether a value for any measure of variability reflects a small or large amount of variability in a distribution of scores. Whether the variability is extensive or not is relative to the possible range of scores that can be obtained on the variable and the mean of the scores. For example, Senders (1958) points out that a standard deviation of 3 inches in the length of 100 electric utility poles would not be unusual, for the mean length of a utility pole is very large. If you were measuring the length of people's noses, however, a standard deviation of 3 inches would be alarming! You might expect you had found a new species. In relation to the average length of a person's nose, a standard deviation of 3 inches would be very large.

Journal Presentation of Measures of Variability

The estimated population standard deviation, s, is the measure of variability commonly presented in journal presentations of research. Journals that follow the editorial style of the *Publication Manual of the American Psychological Association* (1994) use an italicized *SD* to indicate this standard deviation. Thus, in a journal publication you may expect to find a presentation such as

The mean duration of laughter to the cartoons was 41.0 s $(SD = 1.87\ s)$.

In a word-processed manuscript, the presentation would appear as

```
The mean duration of laughter to the cartoons was
41.0 s (SD = 1.87 s).
```

TESTING YOUR KNOWLEDGE 5.2

1. Define: estimated population standard deviation, estimated population variance, sample standard deviation, sample variance, sum of squares, s, s^2, SS, σ, σ^2.
2. Homan, Topping, and Hall (1986) investigated the effect on test scores of a teacher's oral reading of a test to students compared to students reading the test by themselves. Suppose that you, too, were interested in this problem and created two different groups of students. One group of students read the test by themselves, whereas you read the test out loud to the other group of students. You obtained the following two sets of scores on the test (the minimum score is 0 and the maximum is 100):

<table>
<tr><th colspan="2">Group</th></tr>
<tr><th>Read by Themselves</th><th>Read by Teacher</th></tr>
<tr><td>60</td><td>51</td></tr>
<tr><td>50</td><td>74</td></tr>
<tr><td>64</td><td>64</td></tr>
<tr><td>53</td><td>63</td></tr>
<tr><td>61</td><td>52</td></tr>
<tr><td>65</td><td>45</td></tr>
<tr><td>60</td><td>50</td></tr>
</table>

   a. Find $\overline{X}$, s^2, and s for each group using the definitional formula for s^2 as illustrated in Example Problem 5.1.
   b. Find $\overline{X}$, s^2, and s for each group using the computational formula for s^2 as illustrated in Example Problem 5.2.
   c. From the values of s and s^2 obtained, which group has more variable scores?
   d. If you use $\overline{X}$ to predict a typical score in the read-by-teacher group, what would be the average error in your prediction?
3. Many psychologists are interested in the concept of personal space, the idea that each person has an invisible boundary or space around him or her that the individual does not want strangers to encroach upon. One approach to the investigation of this phenomenon has been to invade a person's personal space in a public place, such as a college library or cafeteria, by having an experimenter sit in an empty chair next to the person. An accomplice of the experimenter then covertly times how long the person remains seated next to the experimenter who has invaded his or her personal space. Suppose that a male experimenter invaded the personal space of 10 college-aged males and 10 college-aged females while they were seated in a library. The amount of time (in minutes) that each person stayed seated next to the experimenter was recorded as follows:

	Gender of Person	
	Male	**Female**
	10.6	8.6
	19.8	4.7
	4.3	9.1
	21.6	6.3
	15.7	2.4
	8.1	7.0
	26.4	7.8
	17.9	10.5

a. Find $\overline{X}$, s^2, and s for each group. Use the computational formula for s^2 as illustrated in Example Problem 5.2.

b. From the values of s and s^2 obtained, which group has more variable scores?

c. What is the average error in describing a male as taking 15.55 minutes to move after his personal space was invaded?

d. If you use the mean of a group to predict the typical behavior of a subject, will you make more accurate predictions for males or females? Explain your answer.

A COMPARISON OF MEASURES OF VARIABILITY

To aid in comparing measures of variability, Table 5.3 presents each measure of variability for the TAI scores of Table 3.3. It is evident that the values differ from each other considerably. Because each measure conveys different information about the scores, the numerical values of different measures are not directly comparable to each other. The range, IQR, and the $SIQR$ provide intervals containing a certain percentage of participants' scores; 100 percent for the range, the middle 50 percent for the interquartile range, and 25 percent on each side of the median for the semi-interquartile range. The variance and standard deviation provide an index of the average amount by which scores deviate from the mean. For all measures of variability, however, the smaller the value is the less dispersion there is among the scores. If all individuals had the same scores and there were no variability at all, then the value for each measure would be zero.

TABLE 5.3
Comparison of measures of variability for the 100 Test Anxiety Inventory scores of Table 3.3.

Measure of Variability	**Value**
Range	51
Interquartile range (IQR)	8
Semi-interquartile range ($SIQR$)	4
Estimated population standard deviation (s)	8.66
Estimated population variance (s^2)	74.92

THE CHOICE OF DESCRIPTIVE STATISTICS

I have discussed a variety of statistics used to describe the average score and the variability of scores from a sample. Researchers, however, usually select only one measure of central tendency and one measure of variability to summarize their data from a study. The choice of which descriptive statistic to use to summarize data depends principally on three considerations: (1) the scale of measurement represented by the scores, (2) the shape of the frequency distribution of the scores, and (3) the intended use of the descriptive statistics for further statistical analysis. Table 5.4 summarizes the recommended measures depending on the scale of measurement and the shape of the distribution.

Scale of Measurement

Nominal Measurement

With nominal measurement, responses are classified into categories, and all responses within a category are equated behaviorally. Consequently, nominal data usually are described only in terms of frequencies (i.e., how many individuals in a group were assigned to one category or another) or percentages. Thus, nominal measurement is not included in Table 5.4.

Ordinal Measurement

With ordinal data the median is the most appropriate measure of central tendency, regardless of the shape of the frequency distribution or what further statistical analyses are intended. When the median is used as the measure of central tendency, typically the range, the interquartile range, or the semi-interquartile range is used as a measure of variability.

Interval and Ratio Measurement

When the frequency distribution of scores is approximately symmetric, the mean is the preferred measure of central tendency for interval and ratio measures. The estimated population standard deviation is the measure of variability commonly used with the mean.

TABLE 5.4

Recommended measures of central tendency and variability given scales of measurement of the scores and the shape of the frequency distribution.

	Shape of the Frequency Distribution			
	Approximately Symmetrical Unimodal		*Skewed Unimodal*	
Scale of Measurement	**Measure of Central Tendency**	**Measure of Variability**	**Measure of Central Tendency**	**Measure of Variability**
Ordinal	*Mdn*	*SIQR*	*Mdn*	*SIQR*
Interval or ratio	$\overline{X}$	*s*	*Mdn*	*SIQR*

Shape of the Frequency Distribution

The shape of the frequency distribution is usually a determinant in the choice of the descriptive statistics only when the dependent variable is measured with an interval or ratio scale of measurement. If the distribution of scores is approximately symmetrical, then the sample mean and standard deviation are the preferred statistics. But if the distribution of scores is considerably skewed, then the median and semi-interquartile range may be the descriptive statistics of choice.

Further Data Analysis

The choice of measures of central tendency and variability is also determined by whether the descriptive statistics are to be used for statistical inference. For inferential purposes, the mean, estimated population standard deviation, and estimated population variance are used because they are related to the known characteristics of the normal distribution. These relationships are discussed in Chapter 6. Hence, behavioral scientists may use the sample mean and standard deviation to summarize their data when considerations of level of measurement and shape of the frequency distribution might dictate against it. The issue of making inferences from the data sometimes overrides these other considerations. For this reason, you will find that the mean and standard deviation are the most frequently utilized descriptive statistics in behavioral research.

TESTING YOUR KNOWLEDGE 5.3

1. For each of the following distributions of scores, indicate the measure of central tendency and variability that would provide the most appropriate description of the scores.
    a. The scores represent interval measurement and the distribution is heavily negatively skewed.
    b. The scores represent ordinal measurement and the distribution is approximately symmetric.
    c. The scores represent ratio measurement and the distribution is approximately symmetric.
    d. The scores represent ordinal measurement and the distribution is heavily positively skewed.
    e. The scores represent interval measurement and the distribution is approximately symmetric.
    f. The scores represent interval measurement and the distribution is heavily positively skewed.
    g. The scores represent ratio measurement and the distribution is heavily negatively skewed.

SUMMARY

- Measures of variability quantify how much scores differ from each other and the measure of central tendency of a distribution.
- The range is found by $X_{highest} - X_{lowest}$.
- The interquartile range is the interval between the 25th and 75th percentiles of a distribution.

- The semi-interquartile range is one-half the interquartile range.
- The sample variance, S^2, is defined as $\sum (X - \overline{X})^2/N$.
- The population variance, σ^2, is defined as $\sum (X - \mu)^2/N_{\text{population}}$.
- The estimated population variance, s^2, is defined as $\sum (X - \overline{X})^2/(N - 1)$.
- The square root of the variance provides the standard deviation. The square root of S^2 provides the sample standard deviation, the square root of σ^2 provides the population standard deviation, and the square root of s^2 provides the estimated population standard deviation.
- The estimated population variance and standard deviation are the most frequently used measures of variability.
- The choice of a measure of variability depends on the scale of measurement represented in the scores, the shape of the frequency distribution of the scores, and what further data analysis is intended.

KEY TERMS AND SYMBOLS

estimated population standard
  deviation (s) (83)
estimated population variance
  (s^2) (82)
interquartile range
  (IQR) (79)

population standard deviation
  (σ) (83)
population variance (σ^2) (81)
range (79)
sample standard deviation (S) (82)
sample variance (S^2) (81)

semi-interquartile range
  ($SIQR$) (80)
sum of squares (SS) (82)
variability (78)
X_{25} (79)
X_{75} (79)

REVIEW QUESTIONS

1. Is a student's perception of the expertness of a professor related to the professor's gender? Suppose that you had 20 male college juniors rate the expertness of a male professor giving a lecture. To rate expertness, you used the Teacher Rating Form, a summated rating scale (McCarthy & Schmeck, 1982). Scores on this scale may range from 12 (perceived as very inexpert) to 84 (perceived as very expert). The 20 scores you obtained were 50, 65, 44, 47, 52, 55, 35, 43, 43, 50, 60, 40, 45, 50, 45, 57, 47, 53, 54, and 57.
   a. Find the Mdn, $\overline{X}$, IQR, and s for this distribution.
   b. From a purely descriptive view, does the Mdn or $\overline{X}$ appear to be a better measure of central tendency for these scores? Explain your answer.
2. Suppose now that you had 20 male college juniors rate the expertness of a female professor giving the same lecture as the male professor of question 1, and you obtained the following expertness scores: 50, 80, 44, 47, 52, 55, 17, 43, 43, 50, 60, 40, 45, 50, 45, 57, 47, 53, 54, and 57.
   a. Find the Mdn, $\overline{X}$, IQR, and s for this distribution.
   b. From a purely descriptive view, does the Mdn or $\overline{X}$ appear to be a better measure of central tendency for these scores? Explain your answer.

   c. The value of s increased considerably in this set of scores compared with the value of s for question 1. The IQR did not change, however. Explain this outcome.

3. For each of the following statements, which measure of variability is described?

   a. It provides an interval that contains 100 percent of the scores.

   b. Its value is found by subtracting the 25th percentile score from the 75th percentile score.

   c. It provides an interval that contains about 25 percent of the scores above and below the median.

   d. It provides the average squared deviation of a score from the mean of the distribution and it estimates for the population.

   e. It provides the square root of the average squared deviation of a score from the mean of the distribution and it estimates for the population.

   f. It provides an interval that contains the middle 50 percent of the scores in a distribution.

   g. Its value depends on only two scores in the distribution.

   h. Its value is found by the formula $\sum (X - \overline{X})^2/N$.

   i. Its value is found by the formula $\sum (X - \overline{X})^2/(N - 1)$.

   j. Its value is found by the formula $\sqrt{\sum (X - \overline{X})^2/N}$.

   k. Its value is found by the formula $\sqrt{\sum (X - \overline{X})^2/(N - 1)}$.

   l. Its value is found by the formula $(X_{75} - X_{25})/2$.

   m. Its value is found by the formula $\sqrt{\sum (X - \mu)^2/N_{\text{population}}}$.

   n. Its value is found by the formula $\sum (X - \mu)^2/N_{\text{population}}$.

4. Question 6 of the Review Questions for Chapter 4 presented partial results of a survey by Gross (1993) on drinking behavior by college students and reported that men over 21 years old estimated having a mean of 23.9 drinks per week and women a mean of 7.5 drinks per week. The standard deviations associated with these means were 15.4 drinks per week for the men and 8.7 drinks per week for the women.

   a. If you predicted that the typical college male over 21 years old had 23.9 drinks per week, what would be the average error of your prediction?

   b. Would you judge these standard deviations to indicate a large or small amount of variation in the estimates given?

   c. What information do these standard deviations give you about the appropriateness of the mean as a measure of central tendency for the distributions of scores obtained in this survey?

5. Question 7 of the Review Questions for Chapter 4 presented simple reaction times of eight of nine surgical patients 2 hours after the administration of general anesthesia. The ninth patient was not recovered sufficiently to respond to a stimulus and was assigned an infinite reaction time. If you wanted to include the scores of all nine subjects, what measure of variability could you calculate on these scores? Explain your choice of measure.

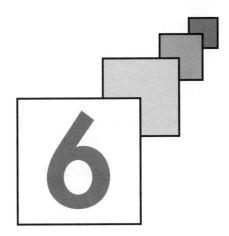

The Normal Distribution, Probability, and Standard Scores

The focus in Chapters 3 to 5 has been on organizing and describing scores from a sample selected from a population. I now turn to a discussion of populations and their characteristics, with emphasis on one population distribution, the normal distribution. In Chapter 1, I defined a **population** as a complete set of people, animals, objects, or events that possess a common characteristic. A **sample** is some subset or subgroup selected from a population. Chapters 3, 4, and 5 discussed organizing and describing the scores from a sample by using frequency distributions and descriptive statistics such as the median, mean, semi-interquartile range, and standard deviation. However, as discussed in these chapters, the scores of a population, too, may be described by the mean and standard deviation. To indicate that I measured an entire population, however, I symbolized the population mean as μ and the standard deviation as σ. Moreover, the values obtained are not called *statistics*; rather they are called *parameters*. A **parameter** is a number, such as a mean or standard deviation, that characterizes a population. The purpose of this change in terminology is to ensure that it is clear whether we are discussing a sample or a population. It is important to understand this distinction, for the normal distribution that I discuss next is a population distribution and is characterized by μ and σ rather than by $\overline{X}$ and s. This difference in notation for samples and populations is summarized in Table 6.1.

NORMAL DISTRIBUTION

Normal distribution: A theoretical mathematical distribution that specifies the relative frequency of a set of scores in a population.

One population distribution of importance to the behavioral sciences is the normal distribution. The **normal distribution** is a theoretical mathematical distribution that specifies the relative frequency of a population of scores. The frequency distribution for a normally distributed set of scores can be described completely by knowing only the mean (μ) and the standard deviation (σ) of the distribution. A normal distribution with $\mu = 70$ and $\sigma = 10$ is illustrated in Figure 6.1. The distribution shown is a mathematical distribution that does not represent any actually measured population of scores. No real population of scores is distributed so precisely that it will be exactly normal. But it will be useful at times to assume that some populations of scores are approximately normally distributed. In this chapter, however, I focus on the normal distribution as a theoretical mathematical distribution.

TABLE 6.1
Notation for samples and populations.

	Sample	Population
Descriptive characteristics	Statistics	Parameters
Mean	$\overline{X}$	μ
Standard deviation	s	σ
Variance	s^2	σ^2

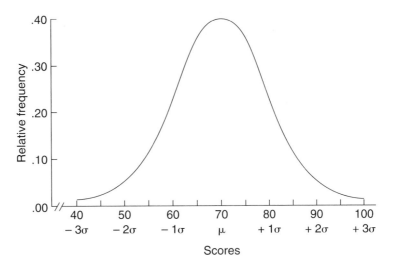

FIGURE 6.1
A normal distribution with $\mu = 70$ and $\sigma = 10$.

The Normal Distribution and the Behavioral Sciences

The normal distribution developed from the work of Jakob Bernoulli (1654–1705), Abraham de Moivre (1667–1754), Pierre Remond de Montmort (1678–1719), Karl Friedrich Gauss (1777–1855), and others. Their interests were in developing mathematical approximations for probabilities encountered in various games of chance or in the distribution of errors to be expected in observations, such as in astronomy or physics. The normal distribution soon became an important distribution to statisticians because many problems in statistics can be solved only if a normal distribution is assumed.

The normal distribution also gained importance for behavioral scientists because it is reasonable to assume that any behavioral measures determined by a large number of independent variables will be approximately normally distributed for a population. Many human capabilities, such as mathematical ability or verbal skills, are determined by a number of independent factors—genetic heritage, parental encouragement, schooling, a particular teacher, social class, cultural forces, and so forth. Consequently, measurements of such abilities are likely to be approximately normally distributed in a population. I stress the word *approximately*, for no actual set of scores is exactly normally distributed.

Properties of the Normal Distribution

The normal distribution possesses the properties of being symmetrical, asymptotic, and continuous.

Symmetrical

A theoretical normal distribution is **symmetrical** about its mode, median, and mean. In a normal distribution, then, the mode, median, and mean are equal to each other.

Asymptotic

Notice from Figure 6.1 that the tails of the normal distribution approach closer to the base line, or abscissa, as they get farther away from μ. The distribution, however, is **asymptotic**; the tails never touch the base line, regardless of the distance from μ.

Continuous

The normal distribution is **continuous** for all scores between plus and minus infinity. This means that, for any two scores, I can always obtain another score that lies between them.

Area under the Normal Distribution

The normal distribution is a theoretical relative frequency distribution. Recall from Chapter 3 that the relative frequency of a score is the frequency of occurrence of the score divided by the total number of scores in a distribution. Thus, relative frequency is expressed as a proportion, and the total cumulative relative frequency in a distribution is 1.0 (see column i of Table 3.4). Because the normal distribution is a relative frequency distribution, the total area under the distribution is equal to 1.0. That is, the relative frequencies of the scores in a normal distribution cumulate to 1.0.

In all normal distributions, specific proportions of scores are within certain intervals about the mean. In any normally distributed population, .3413 of the scores is in an interval between μ and μ plus one standard deviation (i.e., between μ and $\mu + 1\sigma$). The proportion .3413 can be expressed as a percent by multiplying by 100; thus .3413 equals 34.13 percent. Hence, I can say that 34.13 percent of the scores in a normal distribution are in an interval between μ and μ plus one standard deviation. Because the distribution is symmetrical, the same proportion of scores is within an interval between μ and μ minus one standard deviation (i.e., between μ and $\mu - 1\sigma$). This relationship is shown in Figure 6.2. The interval from one to two standard deviations above the mean (i.e., the interval from $\mu + 1\sigma$ to $\mu + 2\sigma$) contains .1359 or 13.59 percent of the scores. Similarly, an interval from one to two standard deviations below the mean (i.e., the interval from $\mu - 1\sigma$ to $\mu - 2\sigma$) also contains .1359 of the scores. Because the normal distribution is symmetrical, corresponding intervals above and below the mean always contain equal areas. Notice from Figure 6.2 that scores more than two standard deviations above μ occur only .0228 of the time (i.e., .0215 + .0013 = .0228), as do scores more than two standard deviations below μ. These relationships hold for any normal distribution regardless of the specific values of μ and σ.

The areas under the normal distribution may also be added so that, for example, the interval from the mean minus one standard deviation to the mean plus one standard deviation (i.e., from $\mu - 1\sigma$ to $\mu + 1\sigma$) contains .3413 + .3413 or .6826 of the scores. Similarly, within plus or minus two standard deviations around the mean (the interval from $\mu - 2\sigma$ to $\mu + 2\sigma$), .1359 + .3413 + .3413 + .1359 or .9544 of the scores occur. Extending the range to three standard deviations around the mean (the interval from $\mu - 3\sigma$ to $\mu + 3\sigma$) encompasses .0215 + .1359 + .3413 + .3413 + .1359 + .0215 or .9974 of the scores.

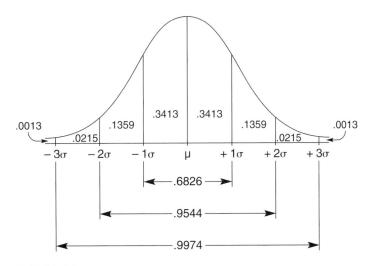

FIGURE 6.2
Relative frequencies of scores in certain intervals of a normal distribution.

These relationships also are illustrated in Figure 6.2. Again, the proportions remain the same regardless of the values of μ and σ.

To illustrate these relationships, suppose that a population of scores is normally distributed with $\mu = 100$ and $\sigma = 15$. A score of 85 is one standard deviation below the mean (i.e., $\mu - 1\sigma = 100 - 15 = 85$), and a score of 115 is one standard deviation above the mean (i.e., $\mu + 1\sigma = 100 + 15 = 115$) in this distribution. Accordingly, .6826 of the scores in this distribution is within the interval of 85 to 115. Similarly, .9544 of the scores will have values between 70 and 130 (the interval from $\mu - 2\sigma$ to $\mu + 2\sigma$), and .9974 of the scores will have values from 55 to 145 (the interval from $\mu - 3\sigma$ to $\mu + 3\sigma$).

As another example, suppose that I have a second normally distributed population of scores with $\mu = 50$ and $\sigma = 5$. In this distribution, .6826 of the scores is in the interval from 45 to 55 (the interval from $\mu - 1\sigma$ to $\mu + 1\sigma$), .9544 in the interval from 40 to 60 (the interval from $\mu - 2\sigma$ to $\mu + 2\sigma$), and .9974 in the interval from 35 to 65 (the interval from $\mu - 3\sigma$ to $\mu + 3\sigma$).

To summarize, in a normal distribution the following relations hold between μ, σ, the proportion of scores, and the percentage of scores contained in certain intervals about the mean:

Interval	Proportion of Scores in Interval	Percentage of Scores in Interval
$\mu - 1\sigma$ to $\mu + 1\sigma$	.6826	68.26
$\mu - 2\sigma$ to $\mu + 2\sigma$	.9544	95.44
$\mu - 3\sigma$ to $\mu + 3\sigma$	.9974	99.74

In the next section you will learn to use a table to look up the proportion of scores that falls in certain intervals about the mean of a normal distribution; thus, the values given here do not have to be memorized. It is useful to remember approximate values, however, so that when solving problems you can estimate answers to check on the correctness of your calculations. Thus, it is helpful to remember the following approximations:

- The interval $\mu - 1\sigma$ to $\mu + 1\sigma$ contains approximately 68 percent of the scores.
- The interval $\mu - 2\sigma$ to $\mu + 2\sigma$ contains slightly more than 95 percent of the scores.
- The interval $\mu - 3\sigma$ to $\mu + 3\sigma$ contains over 99 percent of the scores.

TESTING YOUR KNOWLEDGE 6.1

1. Define: asymptotic, continuous distribution, μ, normal distribution, parameter, population, sample, symmetrical, σ, statistic.
2. Identify three properties of the normal distribution.
3. Why may scores obtained from an actual population of people never be exactly normally distributed? *Hint:* Think of the properties of the normal distribution.
4. Assume that you have a normally distributed population of scores with $\mu = 200$ and $\sigma = 20$. Indicate the proportions of scores that will be contained within each of the following intervals (use Figure 6.2).

Interval

a.	200 to 220		**g.**	180 to 260
b.	200 to 240		**h.**	160 to 240
c.	200 to 260		**i.**	140 to 260
d.	180 to 200		**j.**	220 to 240
e.	160 to 200		**k.**	220 to 260
f.	140 to 200		**l.**	140 to 160

STANDARD NORMAL DISTRIBUTION

Knowing the mean and standard deviation of a normal distribution provides precise information about the proportion of scores contained within certain intervals on that distribution. Because the normal distribution is defined by a mathematical equation, I can determine the exact relative frequency for any interval of scores on the distribution. A problem faced, however, is that I have to utilize a complex mathematical equation employing the value of μ and σ for the distribution of scores of interest. Fortunately, there is a simple way around this problem. The solution is to transform a normal distribution with mean μ and standard deviation σ (e.g., $\mu = 20$, $\sigma = 2$) into a standard form with $\mu = 0$ and $\sigma = 1$. Then, if I use only one standard normal distribution, with $\mu = 0$ and $\sigma = 1$, I can solve the equation for score values and table the relative frequencies found. Subsequently, I could simply look up the relative frequency or cumulative relative frequency of scores in a table, rather than using the equation of the normal distribution.

Standard normal distribution: A normal distribution with $\mu = 0$ and $\sigma = 1$.

The **standard normal distribution** (also called the *unit normal distribution*) has a mean of zero ($\mu = 0$) and a standard deviation of one ($\sigma = 1$). A score from a normally distributed variable with any **μ** and **σ** may be transformed into a score (z) on the standard normal distribution by employing the relation

$$z = (X - \mu)/\sigma$$

where

z = standardized score.

X = raw score from the population.

μ = mean of the normal distribution from which the score X was obtained.

σ = standard deviation of the normal distribution from which the score X was obtained.

When numerical values are substituted into the formula, I will refer to the value of z obtained as z_{obs} where the subscripted *obs* refers to the value of z observed from the value of X. I use this terminology so that it is clear whether I am discussing a value of z obtained from substituting scores into the formula (z_{obs}) or the values of z found in Table A.1, which are explained in the next section. z is often called a **standard normal deviate** because it expresses the value of a score on the standard normal distribution. A standard normal distribution is illustrated in Figure 6.3. The figure includes the proportion of scores between the illustrated z scores. Notice that because $z = +1$ indicates a score one standard deviation above the mean, the proportion of scores between $z = 0$ and $z = +1$ is .3413, the same as the proportion of scores between μ and μ + 1σ on Figure 6.2.

Standard normal deviate:
The value of z_{obs} when a score is transformed into a score on the standard normal distribution.

     To demonstrate the use of the standard normal distribution, suppose that a score of 115 (i.e., $X = 115$) is obtained from a normally distributed set of scores with μ = 100 and σ = 15. This score is converted to a z_{obs} by

$$z_{obs} = \frac{X - \mu}{\sigma}$$

$$= \frac{115 - 100}{15}$$

$$= \frac{15}{15} = +1.0.$$

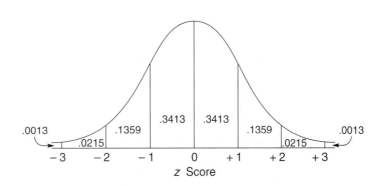

FIGURE 6.3
The standard normal distribution with μ = 0 and σ = 1.0. The proportion of scores between the identified z values is shown.

TABLE 6.2

Transformation of scores from a normal distribution with $\mu = 75$ and $\sigma = 10$ to z scores on a standard normal distribution.

Score (X)	z
105	+3.0
100	+2.5
95	+2.0
90	+1.5
85	+1.0
80	+0.5
75	0.0
70	−0.5
65	−1.0
60	−1.5
55	−2.0
50	−2.5
45	−3.0

For the original score of 115, the transformed standard normal score is +1.0. The z_{obs} score of +1.0 indicates that the original score of 115 is one standard deviation (i.e., 15) above the mean (i.e., 100) of the normal distribution from which it was obtained.

The transformation of a score to a z score on the standard normal distribution locates the original score (i.e., X) in terms of how many standard deviations the score is away from the mean. The score of 115 that I used as an example is $+1.0\sigma$ units away from the mean of its distribution. Consider the scores in Table 6.2 and their corresponding z_{obs} values. These scores were obtained from a normal distribution with $\mu = 75$ and $\sigma = 10$. Attempt to calculate some of the z_{obs} scores given. Notice that the z_{obs} value for any score is simply how many standard deviation units the score is above or below the mean of zero on the standard normal distribution.

A note of caution is in order here. Transforming a score, X, into a z score precisely locates the original score on the standard normal distribution only if the score is from a normally distributed set of scores. If the score is from a nonnormal distribution, such as a rectangular distribution or a bimodal distribution, then converting the score into a z score does not make the original score normally distributed.

Using a Table of the Standard Normal Distribution

The advantage of transforming scores into z scores on a standard normal distribution is that the proportion of scores occurring between values of z is known and tabled. These proportions are presented in Table A.1 of the Appendix. A portion of Table A.1 is illustrated in Table 6.3. Column a lists values of z and column b presents the area between $z = 0$ and the

TABLE 6.3
Proportion of area under the normal distribution between $z = 0.95$
and $z = 1.10$. Column a lists values of z; column b presents the
area between $z = 0$ and the value of z listed in column a; column c
provides the area beyond the value of z in column a to infinity.

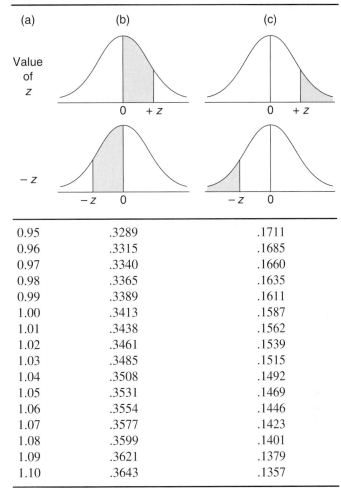

(a) Value of z	(b)	(c)
0.95	.3289	.1711
0.96	.3315	.1685
0.97	.3340	.1660
0.98	.3365	.1635
0.99	.3389	.1611
1.00	.3413	.1587
1.01	.3438	.1562
1.02	.3461	.1539
1.03	.3485	.1515
1.04	.3508	.1492
1.05	.3531	.1469
1.06	.3554	.1446
1.07	.3577	.1423
1.08	.3599	.1401
1.09	.3621	.1379
1.10	.3643	.1357

Source: Reprinted with permission from Table II.1, The normal probability function and related functions. *CRC Handbook of Tables for Probability and Statistics* (2nd ed., 1968). Copyright CRC Press, Boca Raton, Florida.

value of z listed in column a. The shaded area in the small figure at the top of the column
illustrates this area. Column c provides the area beyond the value of z in column a to infinity. Again, the small figure at the top of the column illustrates this area. Because the normal
distribution is symmetrical, negative values of z encompass areas identical to positive values of z. Thus, negative values of z are not tabled.

To demonstrate using this table, consider a normally distributed set of scores with $\mu = 100$ and $\sigma = 15$. Suppose a score of 115 is obtained from this distribution. What proportion of scores is equal to or less than 115? To solve this problem I convert the score of 115 to a z score as follows:

$$z_{obs} = \frac{X - \mu}{\sigma} = \frac{115 - 100}{15} = +1.0.$$

Notice that because this value of z is obtained from a raw score of 115, it is identified as z_{obs} to distinguish it from the values of z given in Table 6.3. To help visualize the solution to the problem, it is useful to draw a figure of the standard normal distribution and indicate on it the raw scores and the z_{obs} values of those scores as shown in Figure 6.4. The answer to the problem requires that I obtain the area of the distribution from $z = -\infty$ to $z = +1.0$. One-half (or .5000) of the scores in the distribution are below $z = 0$. Column b of Table 6.3 indicates that .3413 of the scores are between $z = 0$ and $z = +1.0$ (see the axis labeled c on Figure 6.4). Thus, the answer to the problem is the proportion of scores from $z = -\infty$ to $z = 0$ (i.e., .5000) plus the proportion of scores from $z = 0$ to $z = +1.0$ (.3413 from column b of Table A.1) or .8413. The proportion of scores equal to or less than 115 is .8413 or, expressed as a percentage, 84.13 percent.

Suppose that I now want to know the proportion of scores equal to or greater than 115. I may obtain this proportion in one of two ways. First, because I have already found that

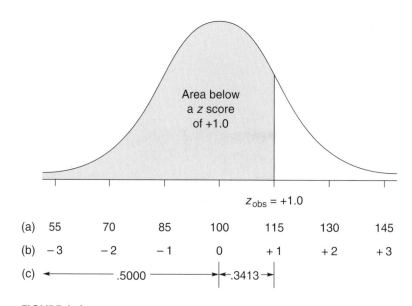

FIGURE 6.4
Location of a score of 115 from a normal distribution with $\mu = 100$ and $\sigma = 15$ on the standard normal distribution. The labels on the X axis show (a) the raw scores, (b) z_{obs} scores corresponding to the raw scores, and (c) the proportion of scores from $z = -\infty$ to $z = 0$ and from $z = 0$ to $z = +1$.

84.13 percent of the scores will be equal to or less than 115, the remaining area under the normal distribution must indicate the number of scores that will be equal to or greater than 115. I find this proportion by subtracting .8413 from 1.000, the total area of the distribution. Accordingly, $1.000 - .8413 = .1587$, the proportion of scores equal to or greater than 115.

If I had not previously found that .8413 of the scores is equal to or less than 115, then I could solve the problem by recognizing that the proportion requested is the area of the distribution beyond $z = +1.0$. Using Table 6.3, I find the value of $z = 1.00$ in column a. I then read across to column c, which presents the proportion of scores beyond z. For $z = +1.0$, this value is .1587. Thus, .1587 of the scores, or 15.87 percent, is equal to or greater than 115.

Consider another problem from this distribution. What proportion of scores in this distribution is equal to or less than 82? To solve the problem I convert 82 to a z score, $z_{obs} = (82 - 100)/15 = -1.2$. This z_{obs} indicates that a score of 82 is 1.2 standard deviations below the mean of the distribution. The raw scores of the distribution and the $z_{obs} = -1.2$ are shown in Figure 6.5. I then obtain the proportion of scores below z equal to -1.2. Notice that from the figure alone I can estimate that this proportion will be very small. Because the standard normal distribution is symmetrical, as many scores lie beyond $z = -1.2$ as lie beyond $z = +1.2$, I look up $z = +1.2$. This value is not included in Table 6.3, however; thus, I use the complete table of proportions of area under the normal distribution given in Table A.1. I find $z = 1.2$ in column a and read across to the value of .1151 in column c. Thus, .1151 of the scores or 11.51 percent is equal to or less than 82. Other uses of the standard normal distribution are given in Example Problem 6.1.

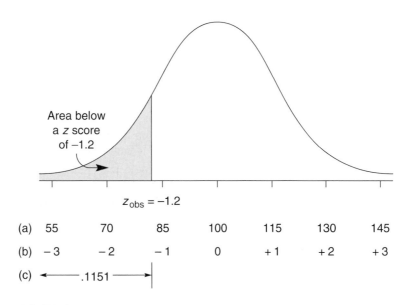

FIGURE 6.5
Location of a score of 82 from a normal distribution with $\mu = 100$ and $\sigma = 15$ on the standard normal distribution. The labels on the X axis show (a) the raw scores, (b) z_{obs} scores corresponding to the raw scores, and (c) the proportion of scores from $z = -\infty$ to $z = -1.2$.

Example Problem 6.1

Using the Standard Normal Distribution

Assume a normally distributed population with $\mu = 80$ and $\sigma = 5$.

Problem: What proportion of scores in this distribution is equal to or greater than 88?

Statistic to Be Used: $z = (X - \mu)/\sigma$.

Solution: The score of 88 must be converted into z_{obs}. Then Table A.1 is used to obtain the proportion of scores equal to or greater than z_{obs}. Substituting numerical values into the formula for z, I obtain

$$z_{obs} = \frac{88 - 80}{5} = \frac{8}{5} = +1.6.$$

Column c of Table A.1 indicates that the area of the standard normal distribution equal to or greater than $z = +1.6$ is .0548. Hence, the proportion of scores equal to or greater than 88 is .0548. Thus, out of every 1000 scores in the population, 54.8 are equal to or greater than 88.

Problem: What proportion of scores in this distribution is between 83 and 87?

Solution: Both 83 and 87 must be converted to z_{obs} scores. Then I obtain the area of the standard normal distribution between the two values of z_{obs}. Substituting numerical values, I obtain

$$z_{obs} \text{ for } 83 = \frac{83 - 80}{5} = \frac{3}{5} = +0.6,$$

$$z_{obs} \text{ for } 87 = \frac{87 - 80}{5} = \frac{7}{5} = +1.4.$$

The raw scores and the corresponding z_{obs} scores are shown in Figure 6.6. From column b of Table A.1, for $z_{obs} = +0.6$, the proportion of scores between $z = 0$ and $z = 0.6$ is .2257. For $z_{obs} = +1.4$, the proportion of scores between $z = 0$ and $z = +1.4$ is .4192. The area of the distribution between these two values of z provides the proportion of scores between 83 and 87. To obtain this area, I subtract .2257 from .4192. The result is .1935 (see the axis labeled c in Figure 6.6). Thus, the proportion of scores that is in the interval from 83 to 87 is .1935. For every 1000 scores, 193.5 are between scores of 83 to 87.

Problem: What proportion of scores is between 65 and 74?

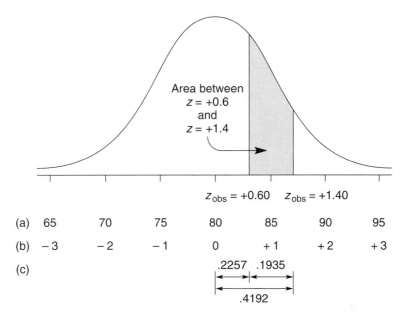

FIGURE 6.6
Location of scores of 83 and 87 from a normal distribution with $\mu = 80$ and σ = 5 on the standard normal distribution. The labels on the X axis show (a) the raw scores, (b) z_{obs} scores corresponding to the raw scores, and (c) the proportion of scores from $z = 0$ to $z = +0.6$ and from $z = 0$ to $z = +1.4$.

Solution: This problem is solved identically to the previous problem. Both 65 and 74 must be converted to z_{obs} scores. Then I find the area of the standard normal distribution between the values of z_{obs} for the two scores. Substituting numerical values, I obtain

$$z_{obs} \text{ for } 65 = \frac{65 - 80}{5} = \frac{-15}{5} = -3.0,$$

$$z_{obs} \text{ for } 74 = \frac{74 - 80}{5} = \frac{-6}{5} = -1.2.$$

The raw scores and the corresponding z_{obs} scores are shown in Figure 6.7. Column b of Table A.1 indicates that .4987 of the scores is between $z = 0$ and $z = -3.0$. For $z_{obs} = -1.2$, .3849 of the scores is between $z = 0$ and $z = -1.2$. I obtain the proportion of scores between $z = -3.0$ and $z = -1.2$ by subtracting .3849 from .4987. This value is .1138 (see the axis labeled c in Figure 6.7). The proportion of scores in the interval from 65 to 74 is .1138. For every 1000 scores in the population, 113.8 are between 65 to 74.

Problem: What range of scores includes the middle 80 percent of the scores on the distribution?

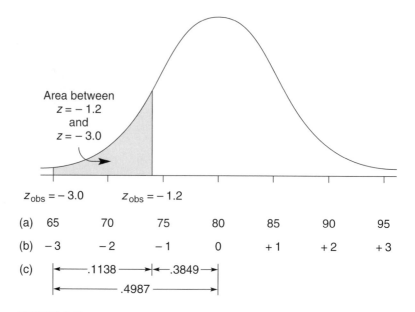

$z_{obs} = -3.0$ $z_{obs} = -1.2$

(a)   65   70   75   80   85   90   95

(b)   − 3   − 2   − 1   0   + 1   + 2   + 3

(c)   ◄——.1138——►◄—.3849—►
                      ◄———— .4987 ————►

FIGURE 6.7
Location of scores of 65 and 74 from a normal distribution with $\mu = 80$ and $\sigma = 5$ on the standard normal distribution. The labels on the X axis show (a) the raw scores, (b) z_{obs} scores corresponding to the raw scores, and (c) the proportion of scores from $z = 0$ to $z = -3.0$ and from $z = 0$ to $z = -1.2$.

Solution: This problem is solved by finding areas in column b of Table A.1 that include a proportion of .40 or 40 percent of the scores on each side of the mean, determining the z value for these scores, and then solving the formula for z to obtain values of X. Figure 6.8 illustrates the proportions and scores that I need. To find the z that includes .40 of the scores between $z = 0$ and its value, I read down column b until I find the proportion closest to .40. This area is .3997, which corresponds to a z of 1.28. Thus, scores that result in z values between 0 to $+1.28$ occur with a relative frequency of .3997, and scores that result in z values between 0 to -1.28 also occur with a relative frequency of .3997. The total area encompassed by scores between $z = -1.28$ to $z = +1.28$ is $.3997 + .3997 = .7994$, or approximately .80. The last step is to obtain the values of X that correspond to $z = -1.28$ and $z = +1.28$. To find these values, I substitute numerical values of z, μ, and σ into the formula $z = (X - \mu)/\sigma$ and solve for X.

For $z_{obs} = +1.28$,

$$+1.28 = \frac{X - 80}{5}.$$

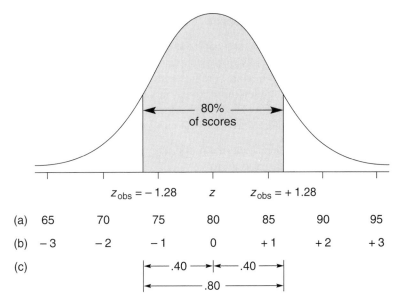

FIGURE 6.8
Illustration of finding scores that include the middle 80 percent of the scores from a normal distribution with $\mu = 80$ and $\sigma = 5$ on the standard normal distribution. The labels on the X axis show (a) the raw scores, (b) z_{obs} scores corresponding to the raw scores, and (c) the proportion of scores from $z = 0$ to $z = -1.28$ and from $z = 0$ to $z = +1.28$.

Solving this equation for X,

$$(+1.28)5 = X - 80$$
$$X = 5(1.28) + 80 = 86.4.$$

For $z_{obs} = -1.28$,

$$-1.28 = \frac{X - 80}{5}.$$

Solving this equation for X,

$$(-1.28)5 = X - 80$$
$$X = 5(-1.28) + 80 = 73.6.$$

Hence, the middle 80 percent of the scores is between 73.6 to 86.4.

An Example of the Use of z Scores

Scores on tests standardized on a large number of people are often considered approximately normally distributed and may be expressed as values of z, thus indicating exactly where a particular score lies with respect to the rest of the scores in the distribution. As an example, the Jenkins Activity Survey (Jenkins, Zyzanski, & Rosenman, 1979) measures so-called Type A–Type B behavior patterns. This survey is a paper-and-pencil questionnaire about typical activities with questions similar to:

When stuck in a traffic jam in your car, do you ever blow the horn to express your frustration?

_____

Never   Occasionally   Frequently   Almost always

People characterized as Type A are thought of as extremely competitive, aggressive, impatient, and quickly irritated and are expected to answer with "frequently" or "almost always." Type B individuals, on the other hand, are characterized as noncompetitive, nonaggressive, patient, and calm in the face of delays and frustrations and are expected to answer with "occasionally" or "never."

Yarnold, Grimm, and Mueser (1986) hypothesized that Type A individuals would conform less to group consensus than Type B individuals when judging line length in a social conformity situation. To test this research hypothesis, they selected two groups of people, extreme Type A individuals and extreme Type B individuals based on Jenkins Activity Survey scores. They report that the mean z score on the Jenkins Activity Survey for the Type A individuals was $+1.22$ (positive z scores indicate Type A behavior) and the mean z score for Type B individuals was -1.38 (negative z scores indicate Type B behavior). This information on the mean z scores for each group permits us to precisely locate each group on the Type A–Type B dimension of the Jenkins Activity Survey. From column c of Table A.1, I find that only about .11 of the values of z on a standard normal distribution is equal to or exceeds $z = +1.22$. Thus, a z of $+1.22$ places the group mean at the 89th percentile of scores in Type A behavior. Likewise, for a z of -1.38 I notice that only about .08 of the scores is below this value on the Type B dimension. The goal of achieving groups extreme in either Type A or Type B behavior was met. The results of the study supported the hypothesis; Type B individuals conformed to a group consensus twice as often as Type A subjects.

TESTING YOUR KNOWLEDGE 6.2

1. Define: standard normal deviate, standard normal distribution, z, z_{obs}.
2. For each of the following values of X, μ, and σ, obtain the value of z_{obs}. Then use Table A.1 to find the area between $z = 0$ and z_{obs} and the area beyond z_{obs}.

	μ	σ	X
a.	73	4.2	81
b.	127	11.6	121
c.	17	1.3	18
d.	50	6.0	39
e.	5	0.4	5.7
f.	256	35.0	212

3. Solve the following problems using the approach illustrated in Example Problem 6.1. You have conducted a large-scale testing project measuring students on a test of reasoning with verbal analogies. Assume that the test scores are normally distributed with $\mu = 72$ and $\sigma = 8$.
   a. What proportion of scores in the distribution is equal to or greater than 86?
   b. What proportion of scores in the distribution is between 80 and 90?
   c. What proportion of scores in the distribution is between 60 and 70?
   d. What range of scores includes the middle 90 percent of scores on the test?

PROBABILITY

I have discussed the normal distribution as a theoretical relative frequency distribution, but it also is a probability distribution of a continuous variable. The concepts associated with probability represent an important component of statistics; however, only some very fundamental aspects of probability are needed to understand the following chapters. In this section I introduce the basics of probability needed to understand probability distributions and their use in statistics.

The daily activities of living provide an intuitive sense of probability. For example, have you ever received a letter similar to the following?

Urgent Notification—Reply Immediately. You are the lucky winner of one of the following prizes:

A Brand-New Luxury Town Car, Value $42,000
A Two-Week, All-Expenses-Paid Vacation in Hawaii, Value $6500
A Wide-Screen TV with Stereo Sound, Value $1995
An Easy-Use Microwave Oven, Value $275
A Top-Quality, 35mm Camera, Value $75
A Whiz-Bang Home Computer, Value $749

All you need to do to claim your prize is visit beautiful LAZY ACRES VACATION RESORT and see the MAGNIFICENT home sites available for your purchase. You will definitely win one of the above prizes when you visit our STUNNING resort.

Visions of a luxurious town car or a delightful two-week vacation may begin to fill your thoughts. Those beautiful visions are shattered, however, when you read the small print on the second page of the letter. Here you find your chances of winning each gift and often they are expressed as follows:

Prize	Number of Awards/1,000,000 Visitors
1 car	1
2 vacation	20
3 TV	34
4 microwave	66
5 camera	999,845
6 computer	34

Assuming that each visitor has an equal chance of winning one prize, which prize do you think it is most likely you will win? Which prize do you think it is least likely that you will win? Even if you haven't studied probability formally, you likely will say "Forget prize 1, the town car, I'll take a picture of it with my camera, prize 5." Only one visitor out of a million wins a car, whereas 999,845 visitors out of a million win a camera. Obviously, the chances are that you will win the camera, not the car.

Suppose that you are asked what is the probability that you will win a TV. It's likely you will answer something similar to "I have 34 chances in a million." In effect, what you have indicated is that the probability of winning a specific prize is found by dividing the numbers of that prize to be awarded by the total number of prizes to be given, or

$$\text{Probability of winning a specific prize} = \frac{\text{Number of the specific prize to be awarded}}{\text{Total number of prizes awarded}}.$$

Applying this formula to prize 3, I obtain the probability of winning a TV as 34/1,000,000, or .000034. If I apply this formula to each of the prizes, I obtain the following probability distribution for the prizes:

Prize	Number of Awards/1,000,000 Visitors	Probability of Winning
1	1	.000001
2	20	.000020
3	34	.000034
4	66	.000066
5	999,845	.999845
6	34	.000034

You may notice that the formula for the probability of a prize looks much like the formula for relative frequency given in Chapter 3. In fact, this probability formula is a specific application of the relative frequency formula. If we call each possible occurrence in this distribution of prizes an **outcome**, then there are 1,000,000 possible outcomes for the distribution. Each outcome is equally probable, for each has a probability of occurrence of 1/1,000,000 or .000001. An **event** is the occurrence of a set of outcomes of interest. For example, if we consider the event of winning prize 5, then there are 999,845 outcomes that comprise this event. If the event of interest is winning either prize 3 or prize 4, then there are 34 outcomes for prize 3 and 66 outcomes for prize 4, for a total of 100 outcomes that comprise the event. Notice that the event of winning prize 5 is much more probable than the event of winning prize 2, for there are 999,845 outcomes out of a possible 1,000,000 that comprise the event of winning prize 5, whereas there are only 20 outcomes out of a possible 1,000,000 that comprise the event of winning prize 2. In a more general sense, if the occurrence of each outcome in a distribution is equally likely, then the **probability (p) of occurrence of an event** is defined as

Outcome: Each possible occurrence in a probability distribution.

Event: The occurrence of a specified set of outcomes in a probability distribution.

Probability of occurrence of an event (p):

$$p(\text{event}) = \frac{\text{number of outcomes comprising the event}}{\text{total number of possible outcomes}}$$

$$p \text{ (event)} = \frac{\text{number of outcomes comprising the event}}{\text{total number of possible outcomes}}.$$

The letter p is used to indicate the probability of occurrence of an event, and the result of applying this formula usually is expressed as a decimal, for example,

$$p(\text{prize 4}) = .000066,$$

Discrete outcomes:
Outcomes in a distribution that have a countable set of values.

although probabilities may also be expressed as percentages or fractions. This formula provides the probability for **discrete outcomes**, outcomes that have a countable set of values, such as the number of computers to be awarded per 1 million visitors. Thus, the probabilities associated with the awarding of each prize constitute a discrete probability distribution.

As another example of a discrete probability distribution, consider the 100 Test Anxiety Inventory scores in Table 3.3. Suppose I am interested in finding that if I were to randomly select one score from this set of scores, what is the probability it would be between 45 to 49? This question asks for the probability of an event of a score occurring between 45 and 49. Thus, the outcomes that are included in this event are scores of 45, 46, 47, 48, and 49. To find the probability of this event, I must find the total number of outcomes associated with these scores. I can find these outcomes by examining the frequency distribution of these scores in column e of Table 3.4. This column indicates that 15 scores are included in the class interval of 45 to 49. Given there are 100 total scores in the distribution, the probability that a score is between 45 to 49 is

$$p(\text{score between 45 to 49}) = 15/100 = .15.$$

I may also state this probability as

$$p(45 \leq X \leq 49) = .15.$$

where $\leq$ = "less than or equal to" symbol. The number preceding the $\leq$ is less than or equal to the number following the $\leq$.

        X = score selected.

This statement is read "the probability that X is equal to or greater than 45 (i.e., $45 \leq X$) and equal to or less than 49 (i.e., $X \leq 49$) is .15." I can go directly to this probability in Table 3.4 by using the relative frequency for these scores given in column f, which indicates that the relative frequency of scores between 45 to 49 is .15. Notice that this probability could also be found from the relative frequency histogram and the relative frequency polygon of the Test Anxiety Inventory scores, Figures 3.5 and 3.6, respectively.

Properties of Discrete Probability Distributions

Probability distributions possess several properties that you likely are aware of already and that have been introduced in the two examples we have discussed. The first is that for any probability distribution, the probability of an event must be between .00 to 1.00. An event with $p(\text{event}) = .00$ is certain not to occur and an event with $p(\text{event}) = 1.00$ is certain to occur. Figure 6.9 presents the probabilities of some events. Few events are absolutely certain in life and possess a probability equal to 1.00, and few are absolutely impossible and

FIGURE 6.9

A probability scale and the probabilities of some events.

Probability

1.00	Probability that you will eventually die.
.90	
	.86 Probability that at birth a female will live to age 60 (86 out of every 100 live female births are alive at age 60, $p = 86/100 = .86$).[1]
.80	.81 Probability that at birth a male will live to age 60 (81 out of every 100 live male births are alive at age 60, $p = 81/100 = .81$).[1]
.70	
	.64 Probability that an adult resident of the United States chosen at random has at least one credit card.[2]
.60	
.50	.50 Probability that a toss of a fair coin will result in a head $(p = 1/2 = .5)$.
.40	
.30	
	.23 Probability that a married couple family selected at random in the United States will be comprised of four people.[4]
.20	
.10	
	.077 Probability of drawing a king from a deck of playing cards $(p = 4/52 = .077)$.
	.000000005 Approximate probability of winning a national magazine sweepstakes.[3]
.00	The probability that you will live forever.

[1] 1980 Commissioners Standard Ordinary (CSO) Mortality Table (The Wizards, 1989).
[2] The Way, 1985.
[3] Artis, 1993.
[4] Calculated from U.S. Census Bureau data.

possess a probability equal to .00. This range of probability from .00 to 1.00 corresponds to the characteristic of a relative frequency distribution that the cumulative relative frequencies (*crf*) range from 0 to 1.00 (see column i of Table 3.4).

The second property is that the individual probabilities associated with the total number of outcomes in a probability distribution add to 1.00. This characteristic of probability distributions can be easily seen in Table 3.4 by noting that the cumulative relative frequency of the Test Anxiety Inventory scores adds to 1.00 (see column i). If you visit the Lazy Acres Vacation Resort, then the probability of winning a prize is 1.00.

The third property is that the probability of an event comprised of mutually exclusive outcomes can be found by adding the probabilities of the outcomes comprising the event. **Mutually exclusive outcomes** are outcomes that cannot occur at the same time. In the example, the outcomes of a person winning both prize 2 and prize 5 are mutually exclusive. A person can win one prize or the other, but not both. Similarly, a person cannot have scores of both 53 and 67 on the Test Anxiety Inventory. These outcomes are mutually exclusive. As an example, suppose I am interested in finding that if I were to randomly select one score from the distribution of Test Anxiety Inventory scores in Table 3.4, what is the probability it would be 45 or greater? This question can be answered by examining the simple frequency distribution in column e of Table 3.4. Notice that there are 28 scores that are 45 or more. I obtain this value simply by adding the frequencies of scores in column e that are 45 or more (i.e., $15 + 5 + 3 + 2 + 1 + 2 = 28$). Thus, the probability of selecting a score of 45 or more is $28 \div 100$ or .28. Using probability notation,

$$p(X \geq 45) = .28.$$

I could also obtain this probability from Table 3.4 by adding the relative frequencies of column f for scores of 45 or greater (i.e., $.15 + .05 + .03 + .02 + .01 + .02 = .28$).

This example illustrates the concept that if two or more outcomes are mutually exclusive, then to find the probability of the event of one of those outcomes occurring, we add the probability associated with each outcome. In probability terminology, if A and B represent two mutually exclusive outcomes from a probability distribution, then the probability of either A or B occurring is the probability of A plus the probability of B, or

$$p(A \text{ or } B) = p(A) + p(B).$$

This relationship is known as the *additivity rule* for the probability of mutually exclusive outcomes.

As another example of the application of this formula, suppose I again randomly sample one Test Anxiety Inventory score and want to know the probability it will either be between 20 to 24 or between 70 to 74. These outcomes are mutually exclusive because one score cannot both be between 20 to 24 and 70 to 74. Using the frequency distribution shown in Table 3.4, the probability of randomly selecting a score either between 20 to 24 or between 70 to 74 is the relative frequency for scores in the class interval 20 to 24 (i.e., .01) plus the relative frequency for scores in the class interval 70 to 74 (i.e., .02), or a total probability of .03. In probability notation,

$$p(\text{selecting a score between 20 to 24 or 70 to 74}) = p(20 \text{ to } 24) + p(70 \text{ to } 74)$$
$$= .01 + .02 = .03.$$

Mutually exclusive outcomes: Outcomes that cannot occur at the same time.

This additivity rule becomes very important later in this chapter and in following chapters on hypothesis testing.

Theoretical and Empirical Probability

Theoretical probability distribution: A probability distribution found from the use of a theoretical probability model.

There are two ways in which we can determine the probability of an outcome, **theoretically** and **empirically**. For certain outcomes we can reason the probability of occurrence of that outcome and determine a **theoretical probability distribution**. As a simple example, the probability of the toss of a fair coin resulting in a head showing can be determined theoretically. There are two possible outcomes of a coin toss, a head or a tail. If the coin is fair, then each is equally likely. Hence, the probability of a single toss resulting in a head showing is one outcome out of the two possible, or p(head showing) = ½ = .5. Theoretical probability models often are more complex than this, however. An example occurs in the next section in which I discuss the standard normal distribution as a theoretical probability distribution.

Empirical probability distribution: A probability distribution found by counting actual occurrences of an event.

For other outcomes, however, such as the probability that if you are a female you will live to be 60 years old, I cannot reason a theoretical probability. To obtain this probability we use actual occurrences of the event to determine an **empirical probability distribution**. As an example, the life insurance industry uses the Commissioners Standard Ordinary Mortality Table to determine longevity rates for residents of the United States (The Wizards, 1989). This table is developed empirically over a long duration by recording mortality rates at various ages for males and females. The table indicates that for every 10,000,000 live female births in the United States, 8,603,801 females are still alive at age 60. Thus, the probability at birth that a female in the United States will live to age 60 is

$$p(\text{female living to age 60}) = \frac{8,603,801}{10,000,000} = .86.$$

Of course, this value of p will change as mortality rates change due to improved health care and nutrition. Likewise, I can only determine the probability of particular Test Anxiety Inventory scores by actually measuring people with this inventory. Behavioral scientists have occasion to use both theoretical and empirical probabilities, but the emphasis in this text is on theoretical distributions such as the standard normal distribution.

In the following chapters we will be concerned with problems of statistical inference—reaching conclusions about populations based on measures obtained from samples drawn from those populations. In doing so, however, we will never be absolutely sure of the correctness of our conclusions; thus, our inferences will utilize probability statements.

The Standard Normal Distribution as a Probability Distribution

The normal distribution is a theoretical relative frequency distribution. Thus, it is also a probability distribution. But it is a slightly different probability distribution than the discrete probability distribution just introduced. A score, X, in a normal distribution is a continuous variable, one that can take on an unlimited set of values in the range within which it varies. As an example, suppose that the scores to which a theoretical normal distribution is being applied are body weights. What is the probability of finding a person who weighs exactly 123 pounds? Weight is a continuous variable, however, and some people may weigh 123.3 pounds, or perhaps 123.36, or even 123.364 pounds. Conceptually, at least, I might find someone weighing 123.3642193 pounds if I could measure so precisely. Is a weight of 123.3 pounds to be considered 123 pounds? What of a weight of 123.00001 pounds? In principle, I can never obtain a weight of exactly 123 pounds, for I could always measure weight to a greater degree of accuracy and find that it was not exactly 123 pounds.

Following this line of reasoning, the probability of occurrence of an exact value of a continuous score is zero. But the probability of the score falling within a certain interval is not zero. Although I cannot obtain a weight of exactly 123 pounds, I can obtain a weight in the interval between 122.5 and 123.5 pounds. For example, regardless of the number of decimal places to which I may carry my measurements, a weight of 123.36 (or even 123.3642193) will always fall into the interval between 122.5 and 123.5 pounds. Thus, the probability function specified by the normal distribution does not provide probabilities for discrete values of X; rather it provides probabilities that the value of X will fall within a certain interval. The probability is provided by the area under the distribution encompassed by the interval.

As an example of the normal distribution used as a probability distribution, consider the following problem. Suppose you know that a set of scores is normally distributed with $\mu = 150$ and $\sigma = 8$. If you were to randomly select a score from this distribution, what is the probability of obtaining a score between 150 and 158? To answer this question, I first transform the distribution into the standard normal distribution with $\mu = 0$ and $\sigma = 1$ using $z = (X - \mu)/\sigma$. Thus, the score of 150 becomes $z = 0$, and the score of 158 becomes $z = +1.0$. The question then resolves to what is the probability of obtaining a score with a value between $z = 0$ and $z = +1.0$? The answer is the area under the standard normal distribution between $z = 0$ and $z = +1.0$, or .3413 (obtained from column b of Table A.1). Accordingly, the probability of obtaining a score between 150 and 158 is .3413 or $p(150 \leq X \leq 158) = .3413$.

Example Problem 6.2

Using the Standard Normal Distribution as a Probability Distribution

Assume that you have the normally distributed population described in Example Problem 6.1 with $\mu = 80$ and $\sigma = 5$. The problems that follow are identical to those in Example Problem 6.1 except that they ask for probabilities rather than proportions of scores. It may be useful to refer to the figures associated with Example Problem 6.1 to follow the solutions presented.

Problem: What is the probability that a score in this distribution is equal to or greater than 88?

Statistic to Be Used: $z = (X - \mu)/\sigma$.

Solution: The score of 88 must be converted into a z_{obs}. Then Table A.1 is used to obtain the proportion of scores equal to or greater than z_{obs}. This proportion represents the probability requested. Substituting numerical values into the formula for z, I obtain

$$z_{obs} = \frac{88 - 80}{5} = \frac{8}{5} = +1.6.$$

Column c of Table A.1 indicates that the area of the standard normal distribution equal to or greater than $z = +1.6$ is .0548. Thus, the probability of a score being equal to or greater than 88 is .0548 or, written as a probability statement, $p(X \geq 88) = .0548$.

Problem: What is the probability that a score in this distribution is between 83 and 87?

Solution: Both 83 and 87 must be converted to z_{obs} scores. Then I find the area of the standard normal distribution between the two values of z_{obs} (see Figure 6.6). Substituting numerical values, I obtain

$$z_{obs} \text{ for } 83 = \frac{83 - 80}{5} = \frac{3}{5} = +0.6,$$

$$z_{obs} \text{ for } 87 = \frac{87 - 80}{5} = \frac{7}{5} = +1.4.$$

From column b of Table A.1, we see that for $z_{obs} = +0.6$ the proportion of scores between $z = 0$ and $z = +0.6$ is .2257. For $z_{obs} = +1.4$, the proportion of scores between $z = 0$ and $z = +1.4$ is .4192. The area of the distribution between these two values of z provides the proportion of scores between 83 and 87. To obtain this area, I subtract .2257 from .4192. The result is .1935. This proportion represents the probability requested. Thus, the probability of a score falling into the interval from 83 to 87 is .1935. In probability terms, $p(83 \leq X \leq 87) = .1935$.

Problem: What is the probability that a score in this distribution is between 65 and 74?

Solution: Both 65 and 74 must be converted to z_{obs} scores. Then I find the area of the standard normal distribution between the two values of z_{obs} (see Figure 6.7). Substituting numerical values, I obtain

$$z_{obs} \text{ for } 65 = \frac{65 - 80}{5} = \frac{-15}{5} = -3.0,$$

$$z_{obs} \text{ for } 74 = \frac{74 - 80}{5} = \frac{-6}{5} = -1.2.$$

Consulting column b of Table A.1 and recalling that, because the standard normal distribution is symmetrical, the same relations hold for negative z scores as for positive z scores, I find that .4987 of the scores lies between $z = 0$ and $z = -3.0$. For $z_{obs} = -1.2$, .3849 of the scores lies between $z = 0$ and $z = -1.2$. Accordingly, I obtain the proportion of scores between $z = -3.0$ and $z = -1.2$ by subtracting .3849 from .4987, which equals .1138. This proportion represents the probability requested; hence, $p(65 \leq X \leq 74) = .1138$.

TESTING YOUR KNOWLEDGE 6.3

1. Define: discrete outcome, empirical probability, event, mutually exclusive outcome, probability of an event, theoretical probability, outcome.
2. What is the formula for the probability of occurrence of an event?
3. You have purchased a ticket for a raffle of a bicycle. The ticket states that one bicycle will be raffled off for every 700 tickets sold. Assuming each ticket has an equal chance of being selected, what is the probability that you will win a bicycle?
4. For each of the following values of X, μ, and σ, obtain the value of z. Then use Table A.1 to find the probability of a score being equal to or larger than the score given.

	μ	σ	X
a.	73	4.2	81
b.	127	11.6	121
c.	17	1.3	18
d.	50	6.0	39
e.	5	0.4	5.7
f.	256	35.0	212

5. You have conducted a large-scale testing project measuring students on a test of reasoning with verbal analogies. Assume that the distribution of test scores is normally distributed, with $\mu = 72$ and $\sigma = 8$.
   a. What is the probability of a score in the distribution being equal to or greater than 84?
   b. What is the probability of a score in the distribution falling between 78 and 86?
   c. What is the probability of a score in the distribution falling between 64 and 70?

STANDARD SCORES

We have seen that we can take a normally distributed raw score and transform it into a score on the standard normal distribution by using the formula

$$z = \frac{X - \mu}{\sigma}.$$

The z is a standard score that can be used for comparing scores from two different normal distributions. For example, suppose that a person obtained a score of 75 on a test with $\mu = 70$ and $\sigma = 5$ and a score of 110 on a second test with $\mu = 100$ and $\sigma = 10$. Assume that scores on both tests are normally distributed. For the scores of 75 and 110, z_{obs} is $+1$ for each. On both tests the individual scored one standard deviation above the mean. Accordingly, the person's standing in relation to other scores on the tests is identical for both tests; he or she has obtained a score one standard deviation above the mean.

It would be useful to make a similar transformation on scores from a sample, even if the scores were not normally distributed. I may make such a transformation using the formula

$$z = \frac{X - \overline{X}}{S},$$

where
X = score of interest.
$\overline{X}$ = mean of the sample of scores.
S = sample standard deviation using the formula

$$S = \sqrt{\frac{\sum (X - \overline{X})^2}{N}}.$$

Standard score: A score obtained by using the transformation $z = (X - \overline{X})/S$.

The z value obtained from this formula is often called a **standard score**. This formula transforms a score into a number indicating how far away from the mean of the sample the score is in standard deviation units. To illustrate, suppose that I gave a statistics test and a history test to five students and obtained the raw and z scores given in Table 6.4. Standard scores were obtained using the formula given previously. For example, Amalia's raw score on the statistics test was 91. The mean on the test was 72.0 and S was 14.2. Thus, Amalia's z score is found as

$$z_{obs} = \frac{X - \overline{X}}{S} = \frac{91 - 72.0}{14.2} = \frac{19.0}{14.2} = +1.34.$$

By knowing the standard score, I know Amalia's score with relation to the class mean; it is 1.34 standard deviations above the mean.

With standard scores I can easily compare scores from one test to the other, something I cannot do from the raw scores alone. For example, Jeff is 1.06 standard deviation

TABLE 6.4
Raw scores and standard scores for five students on a statistics test and a history test.

| | Test | | | |
| | Statistics | | History | |
Person	Raw Score	z Score	Raw Score	z Score
Amalia	91	+1.34	93	+1.18
Denise	62	−0.70	79	0.00
Jeff	87	+1.06	73	−0.50
Hans	56	−1.13	90	+0.92
Matt	64	−0.56	60	−1.60
$\overline{X}$	72.0		79.0	
S	14.2		11.9	

units above the mean on his statistics test, but 0.50 standard deviation units below the mean on his history test. Positive standard scores indicate scores above the sample mean, scores of 0 (such as the history score of Denise) are equal to the sample mean, and negative standard scores are below the sample mean. You should note, however, that, because this z is obtained from a sample of scores, it will not possess the same characteristics with respect to the normal distribution as the z obtained by $z = (X - \mu)/\sigma$. Nevertheless, standard scores are often used when reporting test results, for the score provides the person's relative standing with respect to others taking the same test. The standard score conversion does not change the shape of the distribution of scores, however. If the distribution of raw scores was skewed, then the distribution of standard scores will remain skewed.

SUMMARY

- The normal distribution is a theoretical relative frequency distribution; no measured scores are exactly normally distributed. It is often useful, however, to assume that some behavioral measures are approximately normally distributed.
- A score from a normal distribution can be transformed into a value on the standard normal distribution with $\mu = 0$ and $\sigma = 1$ by the relation

$$z = (X - \mu)/\sigma.$$

- The probability of a discrete event is found by:

$$p(\text{event}) = \frac{\text{number of outcomes comprising the event}}{\text{total number of possible outcomes}}.$$

- For any probability distribution, the probability of an outcome must be between .00 and 1.00.
- The individual probabilities associated with the total number of outcomes in a probability distribution add to 1.00.
- If A and B are mutually exclusive outcomes, then $p(A \text{ or } B) = p(A) + p(B)$.
- The standard normal distribution is a probability distribution specifying the probabilities associated with scores falling into a certain interval of the distribution. It can be used with normally distributed scores to either obtain the proportion of scores that will fall within specified intervals, or to find the probability of scores occurring within specified intervals.
- Raw scores from a sample may be transformed into standard scores using the formula

$$z = (X - \overline{X})/S.$$

This formula transforms a score into a number indicating how far away from the mean the score is in standard deviation units. It does not change the shape of the distribution of the raw scores.

KEY TERMS AND SYMBOLS

asymptotic distribution (98)
continuous distribution (98)
discrete outcome (113)
empirical probability
   distribution (116)
event (112)
mutually exclusive outcomes
   (115)
μ (96)

normal distribution (96)
outcomes (112)
parameter (96)
population (96)
probability of occurrence of an
   event (p) (112)
sample (96)
σ (96)
s (96)

standard normal deviate (101)
standard normal distribution (100)
standard score (120)
symmetrical distribution (98)
theoretical probability
   distribution (116)
$\overline{X}$ (96)
z (101)
z_{obs} (101)

REVIEW QUESTIONS

1. Intelligence tests often involve measures of digit span, ability to follow instructions, vocabulary, analogy completion, picture completion, logical reasoning, and mathematical calculation. Explain why you would expect intelligence test scores to be approximately normally distributed in the population.

2. Measures of reaction time, the amount of time that it takes to initiate a response after the onset of a stimulus, typically are not normally distributed. Rather, the distribution of obtained scores often looks like a reversed letter J with most scores relatively short and only a few long scores. Explain why you would expect these scores to be distributed as they are.

3. Over the years, thousands of scores have been collected for the Wechsler Adult Intelligence Scale. Assume that the distribution of these scores is normal with $\mu = 100$ and $\sigma = 15$.
    a. What proportion of intelligence scores is equal to or greater than 115?
    b. What proportion of intelligence scores is less than 70?
    c. What proportion of intelligence scores is less than 60?
    d. What proportion of scores is between 100 to 120?
    e. What proportion of scores is between 75 to 100?
    f. What interval of scores includes the middle 80 percent of scores on the test?
    g. If you select a person at random, what is the probability that his or her intelligence score will be between 90 to 120?
    h. If you select a person at random, what is the probability that his or her intelligence score will be equal to or less than 80?
    i. If you select a person at random, what is the probability that his or her intelligence score will be equal to or greater than 125?
    j. If you select a person at random, what is the probability that his or her intelligence score will be equal to or greater than 140?

4. You have been summoned, along with 64 other people, to a courthouse as a prospective jury member. To choose members of the jury, names are put in a box and drawn one at a time.

    a. What is the probability that your name will be the first chosen?

    b. If your name is not among the first eight chosen, what is the probability that it will be chosen ninth, assuming that the names of the first eight people chosen are removed from the box?

5. Example Problem 3.2 presented a frequency distribution for the number of seconds a subject in an experiment could see a pyramid in the Mach pyramid figure (see Figure 3.1). Use this frequency distribution to answer the following questions.

    a. What is the probability a subject in this experiment will see the pyramid for 18 to 20 seconds?

    b. What is the probability a subject in this experiment will see the pyramid for 24 seconds or more?

    c. What is the probability a subject in this experiment will see the pyramid for 8 seconds or less?

6. The research of Yarnold et al. (1986) comparing Type A and Type B individuals in conformity to group consensus was presented in this chapter to illustrate one research use of z scores. Recall that to obtain Type A or Type B individuals, Yarnold et al. chose people based on their scores on the Jenkins Activity Survey. Assume the population mean for the Jenkins Activity Survey is 0 and population standard deviation is 10. Suppose you were interested in following up on Yarnold's work. To obtain Type A subjects you want to select people with Jenkins Activity Survey scores greater than +13 and to obtain Type B individuals you want to select people with Jenkins Activity Survey scores less than −13. Assume that scores on the Jenkins Activity Survey are normally distributed.

    a. What is the probability of selecting a person at random with a Jenkins Activity Survey score of +13 or more?

    b. What is the probability of selecting a person at random with a Jenkins Activity Survey score of −13 or less?

    c. What is the probability of selecting a person at random with a score between −13 and +13?

7. Assume that the mean weight of American males between 21 to 30 years old is 156 pounds with a standard deviation of 8 pounds.

    a. What proportion of 21- to 30-year-old males weighs 144 pounds or less?

    b. What proportion of 21- to 30-year-old males weighs 170 pounds or more?

    c. What proportion of 21- to 30-year-old males weighs between 140 to 172 pounds?

    d. If you select a 21- to 30-year-old male at random, what is the probability that his weight will be between 144 to 168 pounds?

    e. If you select a 21- to 30-year-old male at random, what is the probability that his weight will be 150 pounds or less?

    f. If you select a 21- to 30-year-old male at random, what is the probability that his weight will be 160 pounds or more?

8. Suppose that you observed six students on the mean amount of time spent playing video games per week (in hours) and their semester grade point average (GPA) and found the following values:

Student	Video Games	GPA
Alex	6	2.5
Lauren	8	2.0
Yvonne	0	3.9
Laval	15	3.4
Bonnie	3	3.1
Jason	16	1.3

   a. Compute the mean and sample standard deviation for each set of scores and then transform each score into a standard score.

   b. Lauren has a standard score of 0 for time spent playing video games. What does this score tell you about the time she spends playing video games each week?

   c. What information does Yvonne's standard score for GPA tell you about her GPA?

   d. What does a negative standard score for GPA indicate?

   e. What does a positive standard score for video game playing time indicate?

9. You recently had examinations in both English Literature and World History. Your grades on the exams and the class mean and standard deviation (S) are as follows:

	English Literature	World History
Your score	88	70
Class mean	83	65
Class S	6	5

In comparison to other members of the class, on which exam did you do better? What is the reason for your answer?

10. The U.S. Census Bureau (1998, March) reports that for families in the United States, family size is distributed as shown in the following relative frequency distribution.

Family Size—Number of People	Relative Frequency
2	.427
3	.230
4	.206
5	.092
6	.029
7 or more	.016

   a. If you select a family at random, what is the probability there will be exactly four people in the family?

b. If you select a family at random, what is the probability there will be six or more people in the family?

11. The following frequency distribution presents the distribution of the ages of husbands in the United States in 1998 (U.S. Census Bureau, 1998, March).

Age	Relative Frequency
24 or younger	.023
25–34	.178
35–44	.257
45–54	.217
55–59	.079
60–61	.029
62–64	.040
65–69	.062
70–74	.049
75–79	.039
80–84	.019
85 or older	.008

a. If you select a family at random, what is the probability the husband will be 44 or younger?

b. If you select a family at random, what is the probability the husband will be either 34 or younger or 75 or older?

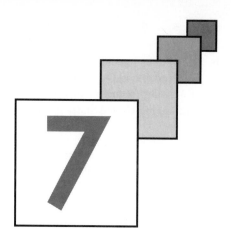

Using Statistics for Inference and Estimation

In this chapter I discuss using descriptive statistics to estimate population parameters. As pointed out in Chapter 1, behavioral scientists often want to generalize their results to a larger population beyond the observations in the sample. For example, polling organizations want to predict the outcome of an election. But pollsters cannot possibly evaluate the opinions of all the members of a large voting population. They measure a sample from a voting population and then generalize to the population. Similarly, it is usually not possible to measure the amount of alcohol consumption, attitudes toward birth control, use of automobile seatbelts, or any other behaviors among all members of a large population. Estimates must be made from the descriptive statistics obtained from a sample of the population. Estimating population parameters from descriptive statistics requires making inferences from sample data. **Inference** is a process of reasoning from something known to something unknown. **Statistical inference** is estimating unknown population parameters from known sample statistics. I first discuss the characteristics of the sample mean $(\overline{X})$ as an estimate of a population mean (μ). Then I discuss the estimated population variance (s^2) and standard deviation (s) as estimates of the population variance (σ^2) and standard deviation (σ), respectively. Finally, I turn to determining the accuracy of $\overline{X}$ as an estimate of μ.

Statistical inference: Estimating population values from statistics obtained from a sample.

$\overline{X}$ AS A POINT ESTIMATOR OF μ

Point estimation: Estimating the value of a parameter as a single point from the value of a statistic.

The sample mean $(\overline{X})$ is often used as a point estimate of a population mean (μ). **Point estimation** is estimating the value of a parameter as a single point from the value of a statistic. Consider the measurement of test anxiety introduced in Chapter 3. The counselor randomly selected 100 students from the population of students at her university and measured their test anxiety. The mean for the sample of scores presented in Table 3.3 is 41.6 and the standard deviation is 8.66. This sample mean of 41.6 may be used as an unbiased and consistent estimator of μ, the mean test anxiety of the population from which the sample was selected.

Unbiased Estimator

Unbiased estimator: A statistic with a mean value over an infinite number of random samples equal to the parameter it estimates.

An **unbiased estimator** is a statistic for which, if an infinite number of random samples of a certain size is obtained, the mean of the values of the statistic equals the parameter being estimated. The mean, $\overline{X}$, obtained from a sample selected from a population is an unbiased estimator of that population mean, μ, because, if we take all possible random samples of size N from a population, then the mean of the sample means equals μ. On the other hand, the sample variance, S^2, is a *biased* estimator of σ^2 for it consistently underestimates σ^2. The estimated population variance, s^2, however, provides an unbiased estimate of σ^2.

Consistent Estimator

Consistent estimator: A statistic for which the probability that the statistic has a value closer to the parameter increases as the sample size increases.

A **consistent estimator** is a statistic for which the probability that the statistic has a value closer to the parameter increases as the sample size increases. Because it is a consistent estimator, a sample mean based on 25 scores has a greater probability of being closer to μ than does a sample mean based on only 5 scores. This characteristic makes intuitive sense for the sample mean. As sample size increases, more scores from the population are included in the calculation of $\overline{X}$, and I, thus, expect $\overline{X}$ to better estimate μ. If I were to sample the whole population of interest so that the sample comprised the entire population, then $\overline{X}$ would be the same as μ and there would be no error in the estimate.

Accuracy of Estimation

Although $\overline{X}$ is an unbiased and consistent estimator of μ, we should not overlook the fact that an estimate is just an approximate calculation. It is unlikely in any estimate that $\overline{X}$ will be exactly equal to μ. Whether $\overline{X}$ is a good estimate of μ depends on the sampling method, the sample size, and the variability of scores in the population.

Sampling Method

Any sample from a population will provide some idea about characteristics of that population. Indeed, in the absence of any other information, $\overline{X}$ provides the "best guess" about the value of the corresponding μ. But to ensure that $\overline{X}$ is a good estimate of μ, the characteristics of the sample should be similar to those of the population of interest. A number of representative sampling methods has been developed in an attempt to ensure that the sample represents the population from which it is selected. I discuss two methods here.

Simple random sampling:
Selecting members from a population such that each member of the population has an equal chance of being selected for the sample, and the selection of one member is independent of the selection of any other member of the population.

Simple Random Sampling.   **Simple random sampling** (often called **random sampling**) is defined as the process of selecting members from a population such that:

1. Each member of the population has an equal chance of being selected for the sample.
2. The selection of one member is independent of the selection of any other member of the population.

A random sample is one selected without bias; therefore, the characteristics of the sample should not differ in any systematic or consistent way from the population from which the sample was drawn. But random sampling does not guarantee that a particular sample will be exactly representative of a population. Because samples are usually much smaller than a population, we cannot expect the characteristics of the sample to be distributed exactly the same as in the population; some random samples will be more representative of the population than others. Random sampling does ensure, however, that in the long run (i.e., over an infinitely large number of samples) such samples will be representative of the population.

Stratified random sampling: A sampling method in which members of a population are categorized into homogeneous subgroupings called strata. Members of the population are randomly sampled from the strata in the proportion to which the strata occur in the population.

Stratified Random Sampling.   With **stratified random sampling**, members of a population are categorized into homogeneous subgroups called *strata*. The word *stratum* (stratum is singular, strata is plural) refers to a layer or level of similar things. Hence, the members within a stratum are homogeneous or similar on some characteristics such as gender, age, or educational level. Members of the population are then randomly selected from the strata in the proportion to which the strata occur in the population. To illustrate, consider a population of students at a university. There are various possible homogeneous subgroups within this population, such as the subgrouping of year in college. The population may be stratified, or put into levels, on the basis of year in college—first, second, third, or fourth. The members of each college-year subgroup are homogeneous, or alike, on the characteristic of year in college. Obviously, there are many possible additional subgroupings, such as gender, academic major, or possessing a part-time job.

Suppose that I stratify the population of students based on their year in college and find the following percentage of students in each stratum (i.e., level or subgroup): first year, 40 percent; second year, 25 percent; third year, 20 percent; and fourth year, 15 percent. Simple random sampling from this population ensures that if I draw many samples the proportion of students in the population for each class year would be represented in similar proportions in the sample. But such proportionality would be unlikely to exist in any single sample. A stratified random sample, however, selects individuals in proportion to the frequency of the stratum in the population. If second-year students represent 25 percent of the population, then 25 percent of the sample will be randomly selected from this stratum. When strata can be identified in a population and when membership in a particular stratum is related to the behavior being measured, then a stratified random sample will likely provide a more representative sample than will simple random sampling.

Sample Size

The discussion of consistent estimators indicated that larger samples are more likely to produce a sample mean closer to the value of the population mean than are smaller samples. Thus, for consistent estimators, sample size is related to the accuracy of the estimate obtained.

Variability in Population Measures

Consider the unlikely possibility that the scores for all members of a population are exactly the same. Thus, every score is equal to the mean of the population, and σ for the population is zero. Under this condition, it is evident that the $\overline{X}$ obtained from a sample of any size will equal μ. There will be no error in the sample estimate. On the other hand, consider a population that has extensive variation among the scores measured and σ is very large. Although it should occur infrequently, by chance alone the scores in one random sample may consist principally of low values. The resulting $\overline{X}$, then, would differ considerably from μ. Similarly, an inaccurate estimate of μ would be obtained if primarily high scores were randomly sampled from the population. Thus, the accuracy of $\overline{X}$ as a point estimate of μ is related to the amount of variability in the population. The larger the population standard deviation is the less likely that a particular sample mean will be an accurate estimate of the population mean.

Nonrandom Sampling

As the discussion has indicated, the sampling method is crucial in determining how well the sample represents the population. Many polls and surveys, however, use nonrandom sampling methods. In this age of instant communication it seems that many of us are interested in what others think about an issue and a whole new industry of immediate polling has arisen to satisfy this urge. Newspapers and TV stations offer call-in polls on topics of the day. Internet news sites offer similar opportunities. Each of these polls collects information from a sample—those people who respond to the poll. But how useful are these polls for making inferences to the larger population containing the sample? Unfortunately, the answer is that they are not very useful for several reasons.

First, as indicated earlier, the population must be clearly defined. Recall from Chapter 1 that a population is a complete set of people, animals, objects, or events that share a common characteristic. In order to make inferences to a population from a sample, we must know what the common characteristic of the population is so that we can assure that all members of the sample possess this characteristic. Second, the sample must represent the population and a systematic procedure must be followed for selecting the sample. Neither of these requirements is met when individuals self-select into the sample by deciding they want to call their response in to a newspaper or TV station, or to complete a poll on the Internet. For example, a poll on a major World Wide Web site asked people in the United States to indicate how far they planned to travel on a particular long summer holiday weekend. The poll was made available on the Friday of the weekend. Of the approximately 20,000 people who responded, about 78 percent indicated they had no plans to travel for the weekend. How confident can we be that this number represents travel plans for Americans in general for this weekend? Unfortunately, the sample for this poll is self-selected, representing only those interested enough to respond. Furthermore, because many people were already traveling before the poll was made available, they were unable to respond to the poll indicating they had travel plans. Thus, we cannot define the population which this sample represents. No inference to a population is reasonable from this sample. Such polls and surveys are scientifically useless.

TESTING YOUR KNOWLEDGE 7.1

1. Define: consistent estimator, point estimation, simple random sampling, statistical inference, stratified random sampling, unbiased estimator.
2. Suppose that a population of individuals with anxiety disorders contains 27 percent generalized anxiety disorder, 23 percent agoraphobia, 19 percent simple phobia, 22 percent panic disorder, and 9 percent obsessive–compulsive disorder. You plan to draw a stratified random sample from this population using the types of disorders as strata.
   a. What proportion of your sample would be in each stratum?
   b. If you drew a sample of 100 individuals, how many people would be in each stratum?
   c. If you drew a single simple random sample, how many people would be in each stratum?

ESTIMATING THE POPULATION VARIANCE AND STANDARD DEVIATION

Variance

The population variance, σ^2, was defined in Chapter 5 as

$$\sigma^2 = \frac{\sum (X - \mu)^2}{N_{\text{population}}}.$$

As you know, however, it is usually impractical to measure all members of a population; thus, σ^2 is typically estimated from a sample. Thus, as I discussed in Chapter 5, an **unbiased and consistent estimator of σ^2** is provided by

$$s^2 = \frac{\sum (X - \overline{X})^2}{N - 1}.$$

Notice in this formula that the denominator is $N - 1$ rather than N. As pointed out in Chapter 5, the sample variance given by

$$S^2 = \frac{\sum (X - \overline{X})^2}{N}$$

is a biased estimator of σ^2; typically, it underestimates the value of σ^2. Consequently, unless I indicate differently, s^2 is used as the variance in subsequent chapters.

Standard Deviation

The estimated population standard deviation, s, is used as an estimator of σ. In contrast to s^2 as an estimator of σ^2, s is not an unbiased estimator of σ. Rather, s slightly underestimates σ. But because the bias in s is small and becomes smaller as sample size increases, most researchers use s when it is necessary to estimate σ.

SAMPLING DISTRIBUTION OF THE MEAN: DETERMINING THE ACCURACY OF AN ESTIMATE

The accuracy of a point estimate of a population mean depends on both sample size and the population standard deviation. Unless the sample includes all the scores in the population or there is no variability of scores in the population, $\overline{X}$ likely will be in error in estimating μ. Although we cannot know for sure just how accurate a point estimate of a population parameter is, we can determine the amount of error to be expected in the estimate by using the concept of a sampling distribution.

Sampling distribution: A theoretical probability distribution of values of a statistic resulting from selecting all possible samples of size N from a population.

Sampling distribution of the mean: The distribution of $\overline{X}$ values when all possible samples of size N are selected from a population.

A **sampling distribution** is a theoretical probability distribution of values of a statistic resulting from selecting all possible samples of size N from a population. For example, the **sampling distribution of the mean** is the distribution of values of $\overline{X}$ obtained when all possible samples of size N are drawn from a population and $\overline{X}$ calculated for each sample. Most sampling distributions are determined theoretically from a mathematical equation, for I can never actually select all possible samples from a population. Each statistical test introduced in the following chapters requires a knowledge of the sampling distribution for the statistic used. These sampling distributions are theoretical sampling distributions obtained from mathematical equations.

Although statistical tests use theoretical sampling distributions, I will generate several empirical sampling distributions of the mean to illustrate the concepts involved. An empirical sampling distribution of the mean may be obtained by selecting a number of samples of size N from a population, calculating $\overline{X}$ for each sample, and then plotting a frequency distribution of the means obtained. For this illustration, I generated a population of 100 scores ranging from 8 to 20 with $\mu = 14.0$ and $\sigma = 2.14$. A frequency polygon of the 100 scores in the population is shown in Figure 7.1. As you can see, the distribution of scores in the population is symmetrical and unimodal.

Empirical sampling distributions of the mean were obtained for three different sample sizes, $N = 2, N = 5$, and $N = 10$, by selecting simple random samples with replacement from this population with the aid of a computer. For each sample size, 100 random samples were selected and $\overline{X}$ for each sample was calculated. Each sample mean for a particular sample size was then placed on an ungrouped frequency distribution as shown in Figure 7.2. Each distribution in this figure, (a), (b), and (c), represents an empirical sampling distribution of the mean based on 100 samples of each sample size ($N = 2, N = 5$, and $N = 10$, respectively).

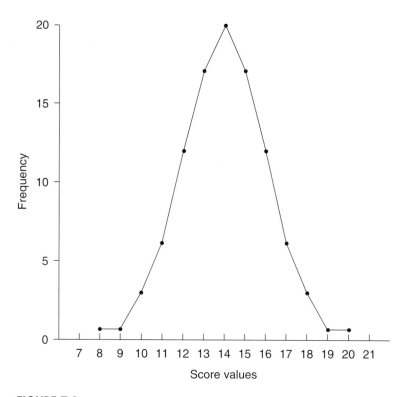

FIGURE 7.1
Frequency distribution for a population of 100 scores with $\mu = 14.0$ and $\sigma = 2.14$.

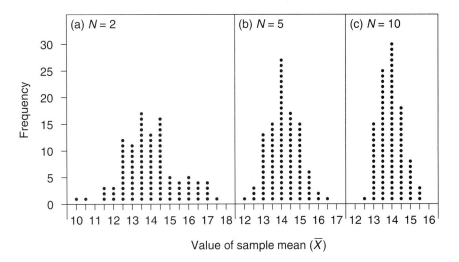

FIGURE 7.2
Three empirical sampling distributions of the mean for 100 samples drawn from the population of scores presented in Figure 7.1. The sample sizes are (a) $N = 2$, (b) $N = 5$, and (c) $N = 10$.

Characteristics of the Sampling Distribution of the Mean

The empirical sampling distributions in Figure 7.2 illustrate several characteristics of the theoretical sampling distribution of the mean. Recall that a frequency distribution can be summarized in terms of its shape and measures of central tendency and variability. Because the sampling distribution of the mean is a frequency distribution, it, too, can be described in terms of its shape, mean, and standard deviation.

Shape of a Sampling Distribution of the Mean
The three sampling distributions in Figure 7.2 are relatively symmetrical and unimodal. Any variations from symmetry are simply chance variation in the values of $\overline{X}$ obtained in sampling. Notice that the distribution becomes more peaked and less spread out as the sample size increases (compare $N = 2$ to $N = 10$). A principle known as the **central limit theorem** applies to the shape of the sampling distribution of the mean: **As sample size increases, the sampling distribution of the mean will approach a normal distribution**. This approximation of the normal distribution by the sampling distribution of the mean occurs whether the shape of the distribution of raw scores in the population is symmetrical or skewed.

How large must N be before the sampling distribution of the mean approaches a normal distribution? The answer depends on the shape of the distribution of raw scores in the population. The population I sampled from is not normally distributed but is unimodal and symmetrical (see Figure 7.1). From such a distribution, the empirical sampling distribution of the mean for sample sizes as small as $N = 5$ or $N = 10$ begins to approach the shape of

Central limit theorem: A mathematical theorem stating that, as sample size increases, the sampling distribution of the mean approaches a normal distribution.

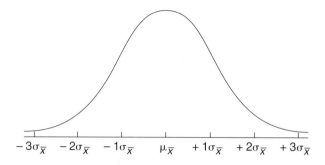

FIGURE 7.3
Theoretical sampling distribution of the mean with mean $\mu_{\overline{X}}$ and standard error $\sigma_{\overline{X}}$.

a normal distribution (see Figures 7.2b and 7.2c). If the distribution of scores in the population is skewed, then the sample size must be larger for the sampling distribution of the mean to approximate a normal distribution. For population distributions that are not heavily skewed, many statisticians consider a sample size of 30 ($N = 30$) to lead to a sampling distribution of the mean that will be approximately normally distributed.

A theoretical sampling distribution of the mean based on the central limit theorem is shown in Figure 7.3. Observe that this distribution is symmetrical, unimodal, and normal. I will use this and other theoretical sampling distributions in developing inferential statistical tests in following chapters. Empirical sampling distributions, such as those presented in Figure 7.2, are typically used only to help understand the concept of a sampling distribution.

Mean of a Sampling Distribution of the Mean

$\mu_{\overline{X}}$: Mean of a theoretical sampling distribution of the mean.

$\overline{X}_{\overline{X}}$: Mean of an empirical sampling distribution of the mean.

The mean of the sample means (represented by $\mu_{\overline{X}}$) in a theoretical sampling distribution will be equal to the population mean. In an empirical sampling distribution of the mean, however, the mean of the sample means (represented by $\overline{X}_{\overline{X}}$) will not be exactly equal to the population mean. This point is illustrated by the empirical sampling distributions of Figure 7.2. The means of the sample means in the three sampling distributions are not exactly equal to 14.0, the mean of the parent population. The mean values are $\overline{X}_{\overline{X}} = 13.96$, $\overline{X}_{\overline{X}} = 14.14$, and $\overline{X}_{\overline{X}} = 13.99$ for distributions in parts (a), (b), and (c), respectively.

Sampling Error and the Standard Error of the Mean

Sampling error: The amount by which a sample mean differs from the population mean.

Sampling Error.   Each sample mean in Figure 7.2 is an estimate of the population mean of 14. As you can see, some of the sample means provide more accurate estimates of this μ than do other sample means. **Sampling error** is the amount by which a particular sample mean differs from the population mean (i.e., $\overline{X} - \mu$). If $\overline{X} = \mu$, then $\overline{X} - \mu = 0$, and there is no sampling error in the estimate. Figure 7.2 illustrates that sampling error is related to sample size; the larger the sample size, the smaller the sampling error. The values of the 100 sample means in Figure 7.2a, with each mean based on two scores, are more variable than the sample means in Figures 7.2b and c, which were obtained from either 5 or 10 scores, respectively. Thus, more sampling error is evident in Figure 7.2a than in either Figure 7.2b or c.

Standard Error of the Mean. The variability among the sample means in a sampling distribution of the mean is described by the standard deviation calculated on the values of the sample means. This standard deviation is called the **standard error of the mean**, or simply the **standard error**, to distinguish it from the standard deviation calculated on a population of raw scores. The standard error of the mean, symbolized as $\sigma_{\overline{X}}$, is equal to the standard deviation of the population divided by the square root of the size of the sample. In notation,

Standard error of the mean ($\sigma_{\overline{X}}$): The standard deviation of the sampling distribution of the mean found by dividing σ by the square root of the size of the sample.

$$\text{Standard error of the mean} = \sigma_{\overline{X}} = \frac{\sigma}{\sqrt{N}}$$

where σ = standard deviation of scores in the population
N = size of the sample.

The standard error of the mean, $\sigma_{\overline{X}}$, is a standard deviation, just as σ is a standard deviation. But $\sigma_{\overline{X}}$ is a standard deviation of a distribution of sample means rather than a standard deviation of the raw scores in a population, as is σ.

Look at Figure 7.3, the theoretical sampling distribution of the mean. Notice that I have indicated its mean as $\mu_{\overline{X}}$ and its standard deviation as $\sigma_{\overline{X}}$. In Chapter 6, I discussed the area under the normal distribution and explained how to find the proportion of scores within certain areas of the distribution (see pages 98–100). Because the sampling distribution of the mean is a normal distribution, the same relationships hold for this distribution. In this instance, however, it is not raw scores that are contained in the intervals but sample means. Thus, the following relationships hold between $\mu_{\overline{X}}$, $\sigma_{\overline{X}}$, and the proportion of means in certain intervals about $\mu_{\overline{X}}$.

Interval	Proportion of Means in Interval
$\mu_{\overline{X}} - 1\sigma_{\overline{X}}$ to $\mu_{\overline{X}} + 1\sigma_{\overline{X}}$	.6826
$\mu_{\overline{X}} - 2\sigma_{\overline{X}}$ to $\mu_{\overline{X}} + 2\sigma_{\overline{X}}$	.9544
$\mu_{\overline{X}} - 3\sigma_{\overline{X}}$ to $\mu_{\overline{X}} + 3\sigma_{\overline{X}}$	.9974

Notice I have used $\mu_{\overline{X}}$ in these intervals because I am using the sampling distribution of the mean. Because $\mu_{\overline{X}}$ is equal to μ, however, I could write the relationships using μ in place of $\mu_{\overline{X}}$, as in the next example.

To illustrate the use of these relationships, suppose that a population of scores has $\mu = 50$ and $\sigma = 6$, and random samples of $N = 9$ are drawn from this population. The standard error of the mean for this sampling distribution is found by

$$\sigma_{\overline{X}} = \frac{\sigma}{\sqrt{N}} = \frac{6}{\sqrt{9}} = \frac{6}{3} = 2.$$

This value, $\sigma_{\overline{X}} = 2$, is the standard deviation of the sampling distribution of the mean for samples of size $N = 9$ from a population with $\sigma = 6$. Thus, in the theoretical sampling distribution of the mean for samples of $N = 9$ from this population, .6826 of the sample means are in the interval of $\mu - 1\sigma_{\overline{X}}$ (i.e., $50 - 2 = 48$) to $\mu + 1\sigma_{\overline{X}}$ (i.e., $50 + 2 = 52$), or the interval from 48 to 52. The interval of $\mu - 2\sigma_{\overline{X}}$ (i.e., $50 - 4 = 46$) to $\mu + 2\sigma_{\overline{X}}$ (i.e., $50 + 4 = 54$), or the interval from 46 to 54, contains .9544 of the sample means, and .9974 of the values of $\overline{X}$ will be in the interval of $\mu - 3\sigma_{\overline{X}}$ (i.e., $50 - 6 = 44$) to $\mu + 3\sigma_{\overline{X}}$ (i.e., $50 + 6 = 56$), or from 44 to 56. This knowledge will be useful in determining the accuracy of a single value of $\overline{X}$ as an estimate of μ.

Using the Standard Normal Deviate with the Sampling Distribution of the Mean

The sampling distribution of the mean is normally distributed with mean, μ, and standard error, $\sigma_{\overline{X}}$. I may convert a value of $\overline{X}$ from a sampling distribution of the mean to a score on the standard normal distribution by

$$z = \frac{\overline{X} - \mu}{\sigma_{\overline{X}}}.$$

This z score may be used with the sample mean just as it was for an individual score in Chapter 6. Example Problem 7.1 illustrates its use.

Example Problem 7.1

Using the Sampling Distribution of the Mean

Problem: Suppose that I have a normally distributed population of scores with $\mu = 80$ and $\sigma = 12$. I plan to draw a large number of random samples of size 16 ($N = 16$) from this population and compute the mean for each sample. What proportion of the sample means will be equal to or greater than 82?

Solution: The solution to this problem requires recognizing that the sampling distribution of the mean is normally distributed with $\mu = 80$ and $\sigma_{\overline{X}} = 12/\sqrt{16} = 12/4 = 3.0$. The proportion of sample means in any interval on the theoretical sampling distribution is found by converting the value of the sample mean (i.e., 82) to a value on the standard normal distribution and looking up the appropriate proportion in the standard normal table, Table A.1. The sample mean is converted to a z_{obs} value by

$$z_{obs} = \frac{\overline{X} - \mu}{\sigma_{\overline{X}}} = \frac{82 - 80}{3.0} = \frac{2}{3.0} = +0.67.$$

Values of the sample means and the z_{obs} for a sample mean of 82 are shown in Figure 7.4. Column c of Table A.1 indicates that the area beyond $z = +0.67$ is .2514 (shown on the axis labeled c in Figure 7.4). Thus, .2514 of the sample means is expected to be equal to or greater than 82. I may write this conclusion in probability terms as

$$p(\overline{X} \geq 82) = .2514.$$

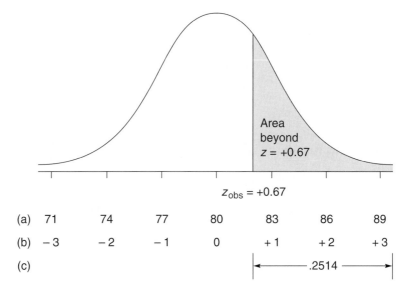

(a)   71   74   77   80   83   86   89

(b) − 3   − 2   − 1   0   + 1   + 2   + 3

(c) |◄———— .2514 ————►|

FIGURE 7.4
Location of a sample mean of 82 on a sampling distribution of the mean with
$\mu = 80$ and $\sigma_{\overline{X}} = 3$. The labels on the X axis show (a) values of the sample
means, (b) z_{obs} scores corresponding to values of the sample means, and
(c) the proportion of sample means equal to or greater than 82.

ESTIMATING THE STANDARD ERROR OF THE MEAN

The sampling distribution of the mean provides a method of finding the variability expected
among sample means. But there is an apparent limit to the use of this knowledge. The population standard deviation, σ, is a population parameter, and any population parameter typically is unknown. How, then, can I determine the standard error of the mean, $\sigma_{\overline{X}}$, if I don't
know σ?

      The answer to this question lies in estimating σ from the scores of a sample, just as I
have estimated μ from $\overline{X}$. In this instance the estimated population standard deviation (s) is

**Estimated standard error
of the mean ($s_{\overline{x}}$):** The
standard error of the mean
estimated by using s to estimate
σ.

used to estimate σ to obtain an estimated standard error of the mean. The **estimated standard error of the mean**, identified as $s_{\overline{x}}$, is based on the estimated population standard
deviation and is expressed in notation as

$$\text{Estimated standard error of mean} = \text{estimated } \sigma_{\overline{X}} = s_{\overline{X}} = \frac{s}{\sqrt{N}},$$

where s is obtained from the scores of a sample and N is the sample size. Thus, $s_{\overline{x}}$ is the estimated standard deviation of the sampling distribution of the mean. In a journal report, this
standard error is often identified as SE, rather than $s_{\overline{X}}$.

It is important to understand the distinction between $\sigma_{\overline{X}}$ and $s_{\overline{X}}$. The $\sigma_{\overline{X}}$ is a fixed value that can be determined when σ is known. Because I seldom know σ, however, I typically estimate $\sigma_{\overline{X}}$ by $s_{\overline{X}}$. The $s_{\overline{X}}$, because it is based on the value of s from a sample, will vary from sample to sample. Different random samples from the same population will produce different values of s because of the chance differences in scores that occur from one sample to another. Nevertheless, the scores of the sample provide the only basis for estimating $\sigma_{\overline{X}}$.

Factors Affecting the Value of $s_{\overline{X}}$

The formula for $s_{\overline{X}}$, $s/\sqrt{N}$, shows how the variability of sample means in a sampling distribution is related to (1) the variability of scores in the population and (2) the size of the sample. The more variable the scores in the population are, the larger the s of the scores in the sample. And, as s increases, $s_{\overline{X}}$ does also. However, increasing the sample size (N) increases the denominator of the formula for $s_{\overline{X}}$, which contributes to making the standard error smaller. Thus, I can expect to obtain a smaller $s_{\overline{X}}$ with large random samples from populations in which the variability of scores is small. Although an investigator can control sample size, often little can be done to reduce the variation of scores in the population. Thus, to decrease the value of $s_{\overline{X}}$, behavioral scientists often resort to using larger sample sizes.

Use of $s_{\overline{X}}$

The standard error is used to measure the amount of sampling error in the sampling distribution of the mean. Therefore, $s_{\overline{X}}$ may be used to determine how well an obtained sample mean estimates a population mean. The smaller $s_{\overline{X}}$ is, the more confident I can be that $\overline{X}$ does not differ substantially from the population mean. In Chapter 8, I will use $s_{\overline{X}}$ to make precise statements about the accuracy with which $\overline{X}$ estimates μ. To simplify the discussion in the remainder of this chapter, however, I assume that $\sigma_{\overline{X}}$ is known to us. You should remember, however, that in practice $\sigma_{\overline{X}}$ will not be known and $s_{\overline{X}}$ must be used in its place.

Review of Types of Distributions

Table 7.1 summarizes the several types of distributions discussed to this point and the symbols used to identify the characteristics of the distributions. Distributions may be composed of either raw scores or of means of samples drawn from a population.

- A distribution of raw scores in a population is obtained by measuring all members of a population. If I were able to measure a population, I would be able to calculate the population mean, μ, standard deviation, σ, and variance, σ^2.
- The distribution of raw scores of a sample selected from a population is described by the sample mean, $\overline{X}$, standard deviation, s, and variance, s^2. These statistics may be used to estimate the corresponding parameter of the population from which the sample was selected.
- A sampling distribution of the mean is a distribution of means of samples selected from a population. The theoretical sampling distribution of the mean for a given

TABLE 7.1
Summary of types of distributions and their characteristics.

Type of Distribution	Obtained by	Mean	Standard Deviation	Variance
Raw scores				
Population	Measuring all members of the population	μ	σ	σ^2
Sample	Selecting and measuring a sample from a population	$\overline{X}$	s	s^2
Sampling distribution of the mean				
Theoretical	Theoretically from a mathematical equation	$\mu_{\overline{X}}$	$\sigma_{\overline{X}}$	$\sigma_{\overline{X}}^2$
Empirical	Empirically by drawing samples from a population	$\overline{X}_{\overline{X}}$	$s_{\overline{X}}$	$s_{\overline{X}}^2$

sample size is obtained from a mathematical equation. The mean of a theoretical sampling distribution of the mean is given by $\mu_{\overline{X}}$, which is equal to μ of the population from which the samples were selected. The standard deviation of a sampling distribution of the mean is given by $\sigma_{\overline{X}}$ and the variance by $\sigma_{\overline{X}}^2$. Typically, μ and $\sigma_{\overline{X}}$ are estimated from $\overline{X}$ and $s_{\overline{X}}$ obtained from a sample.

- Empirical sampling distributions of the mean are obtained by actually selecting samples from a population and then plotting a frequency distribution of the sample means. The major function of empirical sampling distributions is to assist in understanding the concept of a sampling distribution; they typically are not used in actual research.

TESTING YOUR KNOWLEDGE 7.2

1. Define: central limit theorem, estimated standard error of the mean, $\mu_{\overline{X}}$, sampling distribution, sampling distribution of the mean, sampling error, $\sigma_{\overline{X}}$, standard error of the mean.
2. Is the value of S^2 obtained by $S^2 = \sum (X - \overline{X})^2 / N$ an unbiased estimator of σ^2? If it is biased, how is it biased?
3. Is the value of s^2 obtained by $s^2 = \sum (X - \overline{X})^2 / (N - 1)$ an unbiased estimator of σ^2? If it is biased, how is it biased?
4. Is the value of s obtained by $s = \sqrt{\sum (X - \overline{X}) / (N - 1)}$ an unbiased estimator of σ? If it is biased, how is it biased?

5. Distinguish between an empirical and a theoretical sampling distribution of the mean.

6. State the central limit theorem.

7. Suppose you plan to select 100 random samples of size 25 ($N = 25$) from a population of intelligence test scores with $\mu = 100$ and $\sigma = 15$.
   a. What proportion of the sample means do you expect to be between 97 and 103?
   b. What proportion of the sample means do you expect to be greater than 103?
   c. What proportion of the sample means do you expect to be less than 94?
   d. What proportion of the sample means do you expect to be greater than 105?
   e. What proportion of the sample means do you expect to be between 100 and 105?

8. Suppose you have a sample of scores for time on target of a tracking task. In this task, a person must follow a moving target with a mouse on a computer screen. The amount of time the person follows the target during a trial is recorded. The s for the distribution of these scores is 18.0 seconds.
   a. Find the value of $s_{\overline{X}}$ for sample sizes of 4, 9, and 36.
   b. What relationship between the value of $s_{\overline{X}}$ and sample size is illustrated by these samples?

9. Suppose you have three different samples of scores of time on target during a tracking task as described in question 8. The values of s for the three samples are 10, 15, and 20 seconds, respectively. The sample size is 25 ($N = 25$).
   a. Find the value of $s_{\overline{X}}$ for each sample.
   b. What relationship between variability of scores and the value of $s_{\overline{X}}$ is illustrated by these samples?

10. You plan to select equal size samples from two different populations of scores, A_1 and A_2. Population A_1 has a σ of 17.0 and population A_2 has a σ of 30.0. Which population, A_1 or A_2, do you expect will lead to a sample with a larger value of $s_{\overline{X}}$? Explain your answer.

INTERVAL ESTIMATION OF THE POPULATION MEAN

Confidence interval: A range of score values expected to contain the value of μ with a certain level of confidence.

The sample mean is an unbiased and consistent estimator of μ. If we were to estimate the mean of a population from which a sample was drawn, the best point estimate of μ would be $\overline{X}$. But, as I have discussed, a point estimate of μ will likely be in error; the value of μ will not be equal to the value estimated by $\overline{X}$. To gain confidence about the accuracy of an estimate, we may estimate not only a point value for μ, but we may also construct a **confidence interval** for the estimate by providing a range of values expected to contain μ. For example, rather than estimating the population mean of Test Anxiety Inventory scores as exactly 41.6, a researcher may estimate that an interval from 39.9 to 43.3 contains the value of μ. A level of confidence, or probability value, can be attached to this estimate so that, for example, the scientist can be 95 percent confident that the interval encompasses μ. The lower (e.g., 39.9) and upper (e.g., 43.3) scores of the interval are called **confidence limits**. Let us see how such intervals are constructed and what it means to say that an experimenter is 95 percent confident that the interval includes the value of μ.

Confidence limits: The lower and upper scores defining the confidence interval.

Constructing a Confidence Interval

Return to Figure 7.3, the theoretical sampling distribution of the mean. Recall that $\sigma_{\overline{X}}$ is the standard deviation of this sampling distribution and that the distribution is normally distributed. Using this knowledge, I illustrated earlier in this chapter that the interval from $\mu_{\bar{X}} - 1\sigma_{\bar{X}}$ to $\mu_{\bar{X}} + 1\sigma_{\bar{X}}$ contains .6826 of the sample means that could be drawn from this population. Suppose I now asked, if you were to draw one sample and find $\bar{X}$ for that sample, what is the probability that $\bar{X}$ would fall into the interval between $\mu_{\bar{X}} - 1\sigma_{\bar{X}}$ to $\mu_{\bar{X}} + 1\sigma_{\bar{X}}$? The answer is .6826, for .6826 of the sample means has values between $\mu_{\bar{X}} - 1\sigma_{\bar{X}}$ and $\mu_{\bar{X}} + 1\sigma_{\bar{X}}$. Accordingly, if you were to draw a sample, the probability that its mean would be between $\mu_{\bar{X}} - 1\sigma_{\bar{X}}$ and $\mu_{\bar{X}} + 1\sigma_{\bar{X}}$ is .6826. Notice that to answer the question I constructed an interval about $\mu_{\bar{X}}$ (or μ, because $\mu_{\bar{X}}$ is equal to μ) using values of $\sigma_{\bar{X}}$ and then applied known properties of the normal distribution. But in most instances μ is unknown, and I estimate μ with $\bar{X}$. Suppose that I follow the same procedure of constructing an interval around μ, but use $\bar{X}$ to estimate μ. Thus, I obtain an interval of $\bar{X} - 1\sigma_{\bar{X}}$ to $\bar{X} + 1\sigma_{\bar{X}}$. The question I now ask is not whether this interval contains the value of $\bar{X}$, for I already know $\bar{X}$, but does the interval contain μ? I can answer this question with a probability statement also. If the probability that the interval $\mu_{\bar{X}} - 1\sigma_{\bar{X}}$ to $\mu_{\bar{X}} + 1\sigma_{\bar{X}}$ contains $\bar{X}$ is .6826, then it is also true that the probability that the interval $\bar{X} - 1\sigma_{\bar{X}}$ to $\bar{X} + 1\sigma_{\bar{X}}$ contains μ is .6826.

The interval of $\bar{X} - 1\sigma_{\bar{X}}$ to $\bar{X} + 1\sigma_{\bar{X}}$ is a 68 percent (rounding .6826 and then multiplying by 100 to obtain percent) confidence interval. The limits, or extremes, of this interval, $\bar{X} - 1\sigma_{\bar{X}}$ and $\bar{X} + 1\sigma_{\bar{X}}$, are the confidence limits. I can interpret this interval by thinking that, if I were to repeatedly draw samples and calculate a mean for each sample and then construct an interval of plus or minus one $\sigma_{\bar{X}}$ about each $\bar{X}$, 68 percent of the intervals would contain the value of μ. Thus, any one of the intervals has a probability of .68 (or a 68 percent chance) of including μ. Notice that, because μ is a population parameter and, thus, a specific value, it is either contained or not contained in the interval. Consider a numerical example to illustrate this discussion.

Suppose that I have a population with $\mu = 40$ and $\sigma = 10$. I draw a sample of size 25 ($N = 25$) from this population and obtain $\bar{X} = 41.5$. Then $\sigma_{\bar{X}} = \sigma/\sqrt{N} = 10/\sqrt{25}$, which equals 2.0. A 68 percent confidence interval for μ is obtained by finding the interval from $\bar{X} - 1\sigma_{\bar{X}}$ to $\bar{X} + 1\sigma_{\bar{X}}$. Substituting values of $\bar{X} = 41.5$ and $\sigma_{\bar{X}} = 2$, the resulting confidence interval is 39.5 (i.e., $\bar{X} - 1\sigma_{\bar{X}} = 41.5 - 2 = 39.5$) to 43.5 (i.e., $\bar{X} + 1\sigma_{\bar{X}} = 41.5 + 2 = 43.5$). I can be 68 percent confident that this interval contains the value of μ. And, in this instance, it does. Suppose, however, that $\bar{X}$ had been 44.0 rather than 41.5. Then the 68 percent confidence interval is 42.0 (i.e., $\bar{X} - 1\sigma_{\bar{X}} = 44 - 2 = 42.0$) to 46.0 (i.e., $\bar{X} + 1\sigma_{\bar{X}} = 44 + 2 = 46.0$). Again, I can be 68 percent confident that this interval contains μ. But in this instance the interval does not contain $\mu = 40$. In practice, of course, I cannot know for sure if the confidence interval contains μ or not, for I do not know the value of μ. If I did know μ, then I would not need to estimate its value. I can only have a certain level of confidence that the interval actually does contain the value of μ.

Confidence intervals used in actual research are typically 95 percent or 99 percent confidence intervals, rather than 68 percent confidence intervals. I find the limits for these intervals by using the properties of the standard normal distribution with $\mu = 0$ and $\sigma = 1$. From Table A.1, I find that an interval from $z = -1.96$ to 0 contains .4750 of the values of z, and an interval of $z = 0$ to $z = +1.96$ also contains .4750 of the values of z. Thus, an interval of $z = -1.96$ to $z = +1.96$ will contain .95 of the values of z (i.e., $.4750 + .4750 = .95$). Accordingly, a **95 percent confidence interval for the population mean** is obtained by

$$\bar{X} - 1.96\sigma_{\bar{X}} \text{ to } \bar{X} + 1.96\sigma_{\bar{X}}.$$

For a 99 percent confidence interval, I find that an interval from $z = -2.58$ to 0 contains .4951 of the values of z, and an interval of $z = 0$ to $z = +2.58$ also contains .4951 of the values of z. Thus, an interval of $z = -2.58$ to $z = +2.58$ will contain .99 of the values of z (i.e., $.4951 + .4951 = .9902$, or .99). Hence, a **99 percent confidence interval for the population mean** is obtained by

$$\overline{X} - 2.58\sigma_{\overline{X}} \text{ to } \overline{X} + 2.58\sigma_{\overline{X}}.$$

For the example with $\overline{X} = 41.5$ and $\sigma_{\overline{X}} = 2$, a 95 percent confidence interval equals

$$41.5 - 1.96(2) \text{ to } 41.5 + 1.96(2),$$

which equals

$$41.5 - 3.92 \text{ to } 41.5 + 3.92 \quad \text{or} \quad 37.6 \text{ to } 45.4.$$

The 99 percent confidence interval equals

$$41.5 - 2.58(2) \text{ to } 41.5 + 2.58(2),$$

which equals

$$41.5 - 5.16 \text{ to } 41.5 + 5.16 \quad \text{or} \quad 36.3 \text{ to } 46.7.$$

One aspect of this discussion may be puzzling. I have been estimating μ, a population parameter, because I cannot measure the population to obtain the value of this parameter. Yet, in constructing confidence intervals, I have used the value of σ, another parameter, to find $\sigma_{\overline{X}}$. Why should I know the value of σ when I do not know μ? The answer is that I would not; I would estimate $\sigma_{\overline{X}}$ from $s_{\overline{X}}$. I assumed knowledge of $\sigma_{\overline{X}}$ to simplify the introduction of interval estimation. But, in practice, $s_{\overline{X}}$, rather than $\sigma_{\overline{X}}$, is used to determine the confidence limits. When $s_{\overline{X}}$ is used, confidence intervals are slightly larger than those obtained using $\sigma_{\overline{X}}$. The concepts of interval estimation are identical, however, whether $\sigma_{\overline{X}}$ or $s_{\overline{X}}$ is used. I discuss using $s_{\overline{X}}$ in constructing confidence intervals in Chapter 8.

Example Problem 7.2

Constructing Confidence Intervals When $\sigma_{\overline{X}}$ Is Known

Problem: We have a sample of 30 scores from a population with $\sigma = 13.0$. The sample mean is 71.0. Find the 95 percent confidence interval for μ.

Solution: We find $\sigma_{\overline{X}}$ and then use Table A.1 to find the value of z that defines an interval containing 95 percent of the area on the standard normal distribution.

$$\sigma_{\overline{X}} = \frac{\sigma}{\sqrt{N}} = \frac{13.0}{\sqrt{30}} = \frac{13.0}{5.477} = 2.37.$$

From Table A.1, we find that an interval on the standard normal distribution from $z = -1.96$ to $z = +1.96$ contains 95 percent of the area of the distribution. Thus, the 95 percent confidence interval for μ is given by

$$\overline{X} - 1.96\sigma_{\overline{X}} \text{ to } \overline{X} + 1.96\sigma_{\overline{X}}.$$

Substituting numerical values for $\overline{X}$ and $\sigma_{\overline{X}}$ provides an interval

$$71.0 - 1.96(2.37) \text{ to } 71.0 + 1.96(2.37),$$

which equals 66.4 to 75.6. The 95 percent confidence interval for μ is from 66.4 to 75.6.

TESTING YOUR KNOWLEDGE 7.3

1. Define: confidence interval, confidence limits, interval estimation.
2. You have drawn a sample of 25 scores from a population with $\sigma = 10.0$. The value of $\overline{X}$ is 73.0.
   a. Provide a point estimate of μ.
   b. Construct a 95 percent confidence interval for μ.
   c. Construct a 99 percent confidence interval for μ.
   Assume for questions 2d, 2e, and 2f that the sample size was 100 ($N = 100$) rather than 25.
   d. Provide a point estimate of μ.
   e. Construct a 95 percent confidence interval for μ.
   f. Construct a 99 percent confidence interval for μ.
   g. The confidence intervals based on $N = 100$ are smaller than those based on $N = 25$. Explain why this difference occurs.

SUMMARY

- Statistical inference is a process of drawing conclusions about unknown population values from sample statistics.
- $\overline{X}$ is an unbiased and consistent estimator of μ.
- To provide accurate estimation, a sample should be representative of the population from which it is selected. Representativeness is determined by the method of sampling used.
- s^2 is an unbiased and consistent estimator of σ^2.
- s is used to estimate σ, although it slightly underestimates σ.
- The sampling distribution of the mean is the theoretical distribution of sample means for a given size sample.
- The standard error of the mean is the standard deviation of the sampling distribution of the mean.
- $\sigma_{\overline{X}}$ is found by $\sigma/\sqrt{N}$. In most cases it is estimated by $s_{\overline{X}} = s/\sqrt{N}$.
- The sampling distribution of the mean approaches a normal distribution as sample size increases. Thus, $\sigma_{\overline{X}}$ can be used to find confidence intervals for estimates of μ from $\overline{X}$.
- A confidence interval is a range of score values expected to contain the value of μ with a certain level of confidence. The lower and upper scores defining the confidence interval are called the confidence limits.

KEY TERMS AND SYMBOLS

central limit theorem (133)
confidence interval (140)
confidence limits (140)
consistent estimator (127)
estimated standard error of the
mean ($s_{\overline{X}}$) (137)
$\mu_{\overline{X}}$ (134)
95 percent confidence interval
for the population mean (141)

99 percent confidence interval
for the population mean (142)
point estimation (127)
sampling distribution (131)
sampling distribution of the
mean (131)
sampling error (134)
σ^2 (127)
s (127)

s^2 (127)
simple random sampling (128)
standard error of the mean ($\sigma_{\overline{X}}$)
(135)
statistical inference (127)
stratified random sampling (128)
unbiased estimator (127)
$\overline{X}$ (127)
$\overline{X}_{\overline{X}}$ (134)

CHAPTER SUPPLEMENT: REVIEW OF IMPORTANT SYMBOLS AND FORMULAS

Chapters 4 through 7 have introduced a number of important statistical symbols and formulas. To help your study and understanding of these materials, they are summarized in the following table.

Symbol	Formula	Definition
N		The number of scores in a sample, or the sample size.
$N_{\text{population}}$		The number of scores in a population, or the population size.
X		An individual score in either a sample or a population.
$\overline{X}$	$\dfrac{\sum X}{N}$	The sample mean. X refers to the individual scores in the sample.
μ	$\dfrac{\sum X}{N_{\text{population}}}$	The population mean. X refers to the individual scores in the population.
S^2	$\dfrac{\sum (X - \overline{X})^2}{N}$	The sample variance. This variance is a biased estimate of the population variance.
S	$\sqrt{\dfrac{\sum (X - \overline{X})^2}{N}}$	The sample standard deviation. This standard deviation is descriptive of the sample, but it is not used to estimate the population standard deviation.
s^2	$\dfrac{\sum (X - \overline{X})^2}{N - 1}$	The estimated population variance. This variance is an unbiased estimate of the population variance.
s	$\sqrt{\dfrac{\sum (X - \overline{X})^2}{N - 1}}$	The estimated population standard deviation. This standard deviation is the formula most frequently used to calculate the standard deviation. Unless indicated otherwise, it is the standard deviation used in this text.
SS	$\sum (X - \overline{X})^2$	The sum of squares.
σ^2	$\dfrac{\sum (X - \mu)^2}{N_{\text{population}}}$	The population variance. X refers to individual scores in the population.
σ	$\sqrt{\dfrac{\sum (X - \mu)^2}{N_{\text{population}}}}$	The population standard deviation. X refers to individual scores in the population.

Symbol	Formula	Definition
$\mu_{\overline{X}}$		The mean of the theoretical sampling distribution of the mean. This mean is equal to the population mean, μ.
$\overline{X}_{\overline{X}}$		The mean of an empirical sampling distribution of the mean.
$\sigma_{\overline{X}}$	$\dfrac{\sigma}{\sqrt{N}}$	The standard error of the mean for a sample of size N. The standard error of the mean is the standard deviation of the sampling distribution of the mean.
$s_{\overline{X}}$	$\dfrac{s}{\sqrt{N}}$	The estimated standard error of the mean for a sample of size N.
z	$\dfrac{X - \mu}{\sigma}$	The standard normal deviate. This formula converts a normally distributed raw score X to a z score in the standard normal distribution. The value of z_{obs} obtained with this formula can be used with the standard normal distribution of Table A.1.
z	$\dfrac{X - \overline{X}}{S}$	A standard score. This formula converts a raw score into a z score that describes how far above or below the sample mean the raw score is. z scores obtained using this formula *cannot* be used with the standard normal distribution of Table A.1.
z	$\dfrac{\overline{X} - \mu}{\sigma_{\overline{X}}}$	This formula converts a sample mean to a z score in the standard normal distribution. The value of z_{obs} obtained with this formula can be used with the standard normal distribution of Table A.1.

REVIEW QUESTIONS

1. Match the statistic with the parameter it estimates.

	Statistic	Parameter
a.	s	μ
b.	$\overline{X}$	$\sigma_{\overline{X}}$
c.	s^2	σ
d.	$s_{\overline{X}}$	σ^2

2. You select two samples from a population with mean μ. Sample 1 is of size $N = 10$. Sample 2 is of size $N = 24$. Which sample mean do you expect to be closer to the value of μ? Why?

3. A researcher is taking a poll to predict the outcome of a city election. She knows that the voting population of the city is composed of 34 percent registered Democrats, 29 percent registered Republicans, and 37 percent independents. Which type of sampling, simple or stratified random sampling, will more likely lead to a representative sample of voters? Why?

4. A problem of concern to scientists in the twenty-first century is the issue of global warming and the potential contribution of human behaviors to this phenomenon. How concerned, however, is the average person? One well-known World Wide

Web polling site asked visitors to respond to a question about their concern with global warming. Of the approximately 25,000 responses to the question, about 56 percent of the respondents indicated that they, too, were concerned about the potential effects of global warming. The remaining respondents indicated they were not concerned about the issue. Each day at least several hundred thousand people visit this site. What conclusions can you reach from this poll about people's concern with the problem of global warming? Explain your answer.

5. To estimate the number of cigarettes smoked per day by smokers in a high school population, you randomly sample 16 students from among those who identify themselves as smokers. You find that the sample mean for this group is 9.0 cigarettes per day.
    a. Provide a point estimate of the population mean.
    b. Suppose that $\sigma = 3.1$ cigarettes per day. Find the 95 percent confidence interval of the mean.

6. Suppose that the mean number of hours of sleep for a population of college students is 7.1 hours, with $\sigma = 1.2$ hours. You randomly sample 16 college students and determine the mean hours of sleep for this sample.
    a. What is the standard error of the mean for samples of size $N = 16$?
    b. What is the probability that the mean of your sample will be equal to or greater than 8.0 hours?
    c. What is the probability that the mean of your sample will be equal to or less than 6.8 hours?
    d. What is the probability that the mean of your sample will be between 6.5 to 7.7 hours?

7. What is the difference between s and $s_{\overline{X}}$?

8. Zuckerman (1979) developed a scale to measure sensation seeking. People who are high in sensation seeking appear to be easily bored and have a high need to participate in new and sometimes risky activities. Scores on the scale can range from 10 to 40, with higher scores indicating a higher need for sensation seeking. Suppose that the population mean for college student athletes is 23.0, with $\sigma = 4.0$. You have measured five samples (samples A to E) of college-student athletes on this scale. Each of your samples was of a different size, as indicated next.

Sample	N
A	4
B	9
C	16
D	25
E	100

For each sample size:
    a. Calculate $\sigma_{\overline{X}}$.
    b. Find the probability that your sample mean will be equal to or greater than 25.
    c. What relationship between $\sigma_{\overline{X}}$ and N is illustrated in this example?
    d. For each sample size, find the probability that your sample mean will be between 23 and 25.

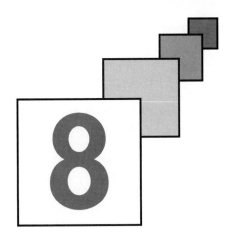

Introduction to Statistical Hypothesis Testing: The *z* Test and the One-Sample *t* Test

In previous chapters I described the use of statistics for organizing and describing data and for estimating population parameters. In this chapter, I turn to the use of statistics for hypothesis testing.

Consider the following problem. Human factors is an area of behavioral science that attempts to match machines and technology to human capabilities. Human factors psychologists often take measurements of physical characteristics of people so that they can design seats, controls, or display devices to fit the person. As an example, assume that you are in charge of interior design for a major truck manufacturer. For years the seats in your trucks have been designed for a population of drivers with a mean popliteal height of 42.0 centimeters (cm) and a σ of 3.0 cm. Popliteal height (pronounced as three syllables: *pop lit eal*, with emphasis on *lit*), is the vertical distance from the underside of the thigh to the floor of a seated driver.

Recently, your company has begun selling its trucks worldwide and has received complaints that the seats are uncomfortable. You hypothesize that perhaps drivers in some countries differ in popliteal height from the population for which the seat is designed. To test this hypothesis, you obtain a sample of 25 drivers of your truck, sampled randomly and independently from the population of drivers in a country from which you have received complaints. The mean popliteal height for this sample of drivers is 44.0 cm. Obviously, this sample mean of 44.0 cm is not the same as the population mean of 42.0 cm. But what does this difference tell you about the population from which the sample was selected? There are two possibilities. The first is that the population from which the sample was drawn actually has a mean popliteal height of 42.0 cm, and your sample mean of 44.0 cm differs from this μ only because of sampling error. By chance you selected a sample with a mean popliteal height greater than 42.0 cm.

The second possibility is that this sample mean represents a population with a μ other than 42.0 cm. The population of drivers in this country has a mean popliteal height different from 42.0 cm. Which of these two possibilities should you select as representing the situation existing in the country from which the sample was selected?

I have posed a problem that requires statistical hypothesis testing to arrive at a choice of which of the two possible situations described is more probable. In statistical terms, this problem requires using a statistical hypothesis test to decide whether the sample mean of 44.0 cm differs significantly from a population mean of 42.0 cm. Figure 8.1 illustrates the problem.

STATISTICAL HYPOTHESIS TESTING

Parametric and Nonparametric Tests

Parametric Tests

Parametric test: A statistical test involving hypotheses that state a relationship about a population parameter.

Parametric tests involve hypotheses that make a statement about a population parameter such as μ or σ^2. Parametric tests often assume certain conditions are true for the scores in the population from which a sample is drawn. As I introduce specific parametric tests, I also identify the assumptions of these tests. In this chapter, I introduce statistical hypothesis test-

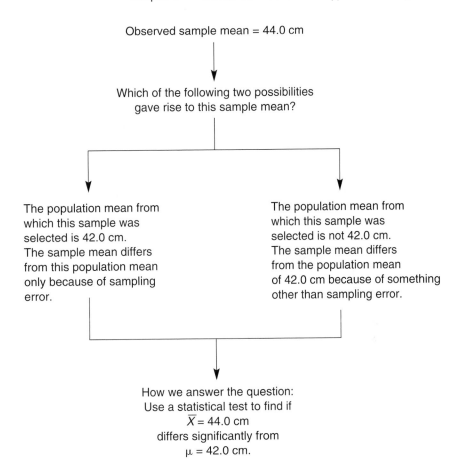

FIGURE 8.1
Two possible situations that may give rise to an observed sample mean.

ing using two different parametric tests, the one-sample z and the one-sample t tests. Other parametric tests are introduced in Chapters 9 through 12.

Nonparametric Tests

Nonparametric test: A statistical test involving hypotheses that do not state a relationship about a population parameter.

Nonparametric tests involve hypotheses that do not make statements about a population parameter. Typically, nonparametric tests make no assumptions about the distribution of scores in the population from which the sample is drawn. For this reason, they are also referred to as *distribution-free tests*. Nonparametric tests are often used when the assumptions necessary for parametric tests are not met by the data. For many, but not all, parametric statistical tests, there are alternative nonparametric tests for analyzing the same data. Several nonparametric tests are presented in Chapter 15. The fundamental concepts of statistical hypothesis testing, though, are much the same for both parametric and nonparametric tests.

Statistical Hypotheses

Statistical hypothesis: A statement about a population parameter (for a parametric test).

Statistical hypothesis testing, parametric and nonparametric, begins with stating a statistical hypothesis. For a parametric test, a **statistical hypothesis** is a statement about a population parameter. This statement may or may not be true; it is made simply to establish a testable condition. For example, I may hypothesize that the mean for the population from which I obtained the sample of 25 popliteal height measures is 42.0 cm. In actuality, the population mean may or may not be 42.0 cm; I simply am proposing that it is 42.0 cm and that I will test this hypothesis. Statistical tests require that two hypotheses be formulated, the null and the alternative hypothesis.

Null Hypothesis

Null hypothesis: A statement of a condition that a scientist tentatively holds to be true about a population; it is the hypothesis that is tested by a statistical test.

The **null hypothesis** is a statement of a condition that tentatively I hold to be true about a population; and it is the hypothesis that is tested by a statistical test. Null hypotheses usually are written in symbolic or notational form using H_0 to indicate that a hypothesis, such as $\mu = 42.0$ cm, is being offered. In statistical notation, the expression of the null hypothesis that $\mu = 42.0$ cm is H_0: $\mu = 42.0$ cm. The subscripted zero is often pronounced "naught"; thus, we say "*H* naught: mu equals 42.0 centimeters." The word *null* implies there is no difference. Its use becomes clearer in Chapter 9 in which I propose a null hypothesis of no difference between two population means.

Alternative Hypothesis

Alternative hypothesis: A statement of what must be true if the null hypothesis is false.

The **alternative hypothesis** is a statement of what must be true if the null hypothesis is false. In the example, if H_0: $\mu = 42.0$ cm is not true, then the alternative must be μ does not equal 42.0 cm. This alternative hypothesis is identified as H_1 and written as H_1: $\mu \neq 42.0$ cm, where $\neq$ is the symbol for "does not equal." Hence, H_1: $\mu \neq 42.0$ cm is read as "*H* one: mu does not equal 42.0 centimeters."

Properties of Statistical Hypotheses

Every statistical test requires null and alternative hypotheses. These hypotheses must be expressed so that:

- They are mutually exclusive. *Mutually exclusive* means both hypotheses cannot be true at the same time. For example, it is impossible for H_0: $\mu = 42.0$ cm and H_1: $\mu \neq 42.0$ cm to be true simultaneously for the same population.
- They include all possible values of the parameter involved in the hypothesis. The hypotheses H_0: $\mu = 42.0$ cm and H_1: $\mu \neq 42.0$ cm meet this requirement; between them they include all possible values of μ for the population of interest.

Because of these characteristics, one of the two hypotheses must represent the true condition in the population. For the example, the population mean either is 42.0 cm and

H_0: $\mu = 42.0$ cm is true, or it is not, and the alternative hypothesis, H_1: $\mu \neq 42.0$ cm, is true.

In summary, for the example problem the statistical hypotheses are

$$H_0: \mu = 42.0 \text{ cm} \qquad \text{(null hypothesis)}$$
$$H_1: \mu \neq 42.0 \text{ cm} \qquad \text{(alternative hypothesis)}.$$

Function of the Statistical Hypotheses

The function of the null hypothesis in a statistical test is to establish a condition under which the sampling distribution of a statistic may be obtained. In Chapter 7 I defined a sampling distribution of the mean as the distribution of $\overline{X}$ values when all possible samples of size N were selected from a population and $\overline{X}$ calculated for each sample. For example, assuming H_0: $\mu = 42.0$ cm is true, and $\sigma = 3.0$ cm for a population, I may obtain the sampling distribution of $\overline{X}$ for samples of size 25 from this population. This sampling distribution, shown in Figure 8.2, is normally distributed with $\mu_{\overline{X}} = 42.0$ cm and a standard error equal to $\sigma_{\overline{X}}$ where

$$\sigma_{\overline{X}} = \frac{\sigma}{\sqrt{N}} = \frac{3.0}{\sqrt{25}} = \frac{3.0}{5} = 0.6.$$

In this distribution a sample mean of 44.0 cm falls beyond three standard errors of the mean away from $\mu_{\overline{X}}$. Accordingly, under the condition established by H_0: $\mu = 42.0$ cm, a sample with a mean of 44.0 cm is a very infrequent occurrence if samples of size 25 are drawn from this population. Hence, I might be inclined to reject the null hypothesis, H_0: $\mu = 42.0$ cm, if I obtained a sample mean of 44.0 cm. This $\overline{X}$ is a statistically rare event if

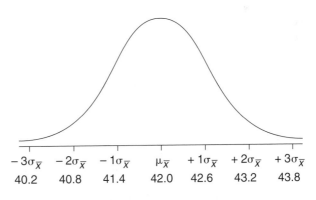

Popliteal height (cm)

FIGURE 8.2
Theoretical sampling distribution of the mean for samples of $N = 25$ from a population with $\mu_{\overline{X}} = 42.0$ cm and $\sigma_{\overline{X}} = 0.6$ cm.

H_0 is true. But, before I can definitely make a decision on whether to treat H_0 as true or not, I must

- Identify the probability of obtaining a value of $\overline{X}$ as large or larger than 44.0 cm if H_0: $\mu = 42.0$ cm is true. This step requires using a test statistic.
- Define what I mean by a statistically rare event. This step requires choosing a significance level.

A Test Statistic: z

Test statistic: A number calculated from the scores of the sample that allows testing a statistical null hypothesis.

A **test statistic** is a number calculated from the scores of the sample that allows us to test a null hypothesis. For the example, we want a test to find the probability of occurrence of a sample mean as large or larger than 44.0 cm if H_0: $\mu = 42.0$ cm is true. Because the sampling distribution of the mean illustrated in Figure 8.2 is normally distributed with $\mu = 42.0$ cm and $\sigma_{\overline{X}} = 0.6$, I can transform any value of $\overline{X}$ into a value on the standard normal distribution by using the test statistic

$$z = \frac{\overline{X} - \mu}{\sigma_{\overline{X}}}$$

where $\overline{X}$ = sample mean.
     μ = hypothesized population mean.
     $\sigma_{\overline{X}}$ = standard error of the mean.

The value of z locates the sample mean on the standard normal distribution. Notice that this formula is identical to that given for z in Chapter 7.

The value of z_{obs} with $\overline{X}$ of 44.0 cm, the value of μ hypothesized to be 42.0 cm, and $\sigma_{\overline{X}} = 0.6$ cm is

$$z_{obs} = \frac{\overline{X} - \mu}{\sigma_{\overline{X}}} = \frac{44.0 - 42.0}{0.6} = \frac{2.0}{0.6} = +3.33.$$

The z statistic is identified as z_{obs} because it is observed from the value of $\overline{X}$ of the sample. From the sampling distribution of the z statistic given in Table A.1, I find that the probability of z being as large as or larger than $+3.33$ is .0004 (see column c of Table A.1 for $z = 3.33$). Consequently, the probability of obtaining $\overline{X} = 44.0$ cm or larger from a sample of size 25 is equal to .0004 if H_0: $\mu = 42.0$ cm is true. In other words, if I were to randomly select 10,000 samples of $N = 25$ from a population with $\mu = 42.0$ cm and $\sigma = 3.0$, I would expect only four of the 10,000 sample means to be as large as or larger than 44.0 cm. Thus, if H_0: $\mu = 42.0$ cm is true, obtaining a sample with $\overline{X}$ equal to 44.0 cm would be a statistically rare event. If I had obtained this $\overline{X}$, I certainly would reject the hypothesis that it was drawn from a population with a mean popliteal height of 42.0 cm, and I would accept the alternative hypothesis that $\mu \neq 42.0$ cm.

The logic of this decision making is that if the population mean is 42.0 cm then obtaining a sample with a mean of 44.0 cm would occur only four times out of every 10,000 samples selected. Although obtaining $\overline{X} = 44.0$ cm is a possible event if $\mu = 42.0$ cm, it is not a very probable event. It would be a more probable event if the population mean were something other than 42.0 cm. Thus, I reject H_0 and accept H_1. This decision may be in error; it is possible to obtain $\overline{X} = 44.0$ cm if $\mu = 42.0$ cm, but it is not very probable.

Suppose, however, that I had obtained a sample mean of 42.5 cm, instead of 44.0 cm. Here the value of z is

$$z_{obs} = \frac{42.5 - 42.0}{0.6} = \frac{0.5}{0.6} = +0.83.$$

From column c of Table A.1, I find that the probability of obtaining a value of $z = +0.83$ or larger is equal to .2033. Thus, if H_0 were true and I drew 10,000 samples of $N = 25$, 2033 of them would have values of $\overline{X}$ equal to or larger than 42.5 cm. Is a sample mean of 42.5 cm a statistically rare event if H_0: $\mu = 42.0$ cm is true? What decision would you make about the null hypothesis in this instance? Would you reject H_0: $\mu = 42.0$ cm and accept H_1: $\mu \neq 42.0$ cm? Or would you not reject H_0 and, therefore, not accept H_1? To answer these questions, I must define what value of z_{obs} will be considered a statistically rare outcome if H_0 is true. The definition of statistical rareness is given by the significance level adopted.

Significance Levels: Statistical Rareness

Significance level: A probability value that provides the criterion for rejecting a null hypothesis in a statistical test.

Alpha or α: The value of the significance level stated as a probability.

The **significance level** is a probability value that provides the criterion for rejecting a null hypothesis in a statistical test. Significance levels are given as values of **alpha or α**, the first letter of the Greek alphabet. Typically, behavioral scientists use alpha levels of either .05 or .01. Thus, if $\alpha = .05$, values of z_{obs} occurring only five or fewer times in 100 occasions if H_0 is true are sufficiently rare that I am willing to reject H_0 and decide that H_1 is true.

Using the Test Statistic and the Significance Level to Decide about the Statistical Hypotheses

After choosing a test statistic and a significance level, we are ready to decide about the statistical hypotheses. Three steps are involved:

1. Locating a rejection region or regions in the sampling distribution of the test statistic
2. Calculating the value of the test statistic on the sample data
3. Deciding about the statistical hypotheses by observing whether the test statistic falls into a rejection region

Locating Rejection Regions

Rejection region: Values on the sampling distribution of the test statistic that have a probability equal to or less than α if H_0 is true. If the test statistic falls into the rejection region, H_0 is rejected.

The **rejection region** represents values on the sampling distribution of the test statistic that have a probability equal to or less than α if H_0 is true. For the example, the rejection region identifies the values of z that meet the criterion for rejecting H_0.

The sampling distribution of the z statistic with rejection regions located in each tail of the distribution is shown in Figure 8.3. Statistically rare values of z occur at either tail, or

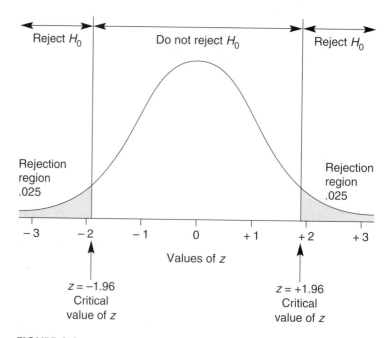

FIGURE 8.3

Sampling distribution of the z statistic illustrating rejection regions for a two-tailed test and $\alpha = .05$. A value of z_{obs} that falls into either rejection region leads to rejecting H_0.

end, of the distribution. For example, z values of either $+3.00$ or -3.00 are equally improbable values of z if H_0 is true. Either large positive or negative values of z for the example problem would cast doubt on the truth of H_0: $\mu = 42.0$ cm. Thus, rejection regions for the z statistic will be in either tail of the sampling distribution. A statistical test with rejection regions in both tails of the sampling distribution of the test statistic is identified as a **two-tailed**, or **nondirectional, test**. A value of z_{obs} falling into either rejection region is improbable or rare if H_0 is true but more likely to occur if H_1 is true. Therefore, if a value of z_{obs} falls into either rejection region, H_0 is rejected and H_1 accepted.

Two-tailed test: A statistical test using rejection regions in both tails of the sampling distribution of the test statistic.

On occasion we may have reason to place the rejection region in only one tail of the sampling distribution of z. In this instance, a **one-tailed**, or **directional, test** is used. The benefit of a one-tailed test is that a smaller value of z_{obs} may fall into the rejection region. I discuss one-tailed tests more fully later in this chapter. For this example, I use a two-tailed test.

One-tailed test: A statistical test using a rejection region in only one tail of the sampling distribution of the test statistic.

Critical value: The specific numerical values that define the boundaries of the rejection region.

Critical Values.   **Critical values** are the specific numerical values that define the boundaries of the rejection region. Critical values for z are found in column c of Table A.1. The first step in finding a critical value is to choose a significance level, such as $\alpha = .05$. For a two-tailed test, rejection regions are located in each tail of the sampling distribution of z. Accordingly, I want the area in each tail of the distribution to equal one-half of α, or

.05/2, which equals .025. What values of z meet the requirement that .025 of the area of the sampling distribution of z lies beyond their values in each tail? Consulting Table A.1, I read down column c until I find the area beyond z equal to .025. When I find this area, I read the corresponding value of z in column a. This value of z is 1.96. Thus, for $\alpha = .05$ the two-tailed critical values are $z = -1.96$ and $z = +1.96$. These critical values of z (symbolized as z_{crit}) locate the rejection regions in the sampling distribution of z, as shown in Figure 8.3.

Decisions about the Statistical Hypotheses

We decide to reject or not reject H_0 by comparing the value of z_{obs} to z_{crit}. A value of z_{obs} equal to or less than $z_{\text{crit}} = -1.96$ or equal to or greater than $z_{\text{crit}} = +1.96$ falls into a rejection region. Values of z_{obs} that fall into a rejection region are statistically rare if H_0 is true, but are more common occurrences if H_1 is true. Thus, a z_{obs} falling into a rejection region leads us to *reject H_0*. If I reject H_0, then I must *accept H_1*. If, however, z_{obs} does not fall into a rejection region, then I *fail to reject H_0*. And if I fail to reject H_0, then I *do not accept H_1*.

Notice that I use the value of z_{obs} to make a decision about H_0; I either reject H_0 or I fail to reject H_0. The decision about H_0 then dictates the decision to be made about H_1. If I reject H_0, then I must accept H_1. On the other hand, if I fail to reject H_0, I cannot accept H_1.

For the example on popliteal height, $z_{\text{obs}} = +3.33$ is larger than $z_{\text{crit}} = +1.96$; thus, it falls into the upper rejection region. Accordingly, I reject H_0: $\mu = 42.0$ cm and accept H_1: $\mu \neq 42.0$ cm. I reject the null hypothesis that the sample was selected from a population with a mean of 42.0 cm. Because the sample mean, $\overline{X} = 44.0$ cm, is greater than the hypothesized population mean of 42.0 cm, I conclude that the mean popliteal height of the current drivers in the country from which I sampled is greater than 42.0 cm. The best point estimate I have of this population mean is the sample mean, $\overline{X} = 44.0$ cm. One reason the truck seats may be uncomfortable is because the population of drivers in some countries has longer popliteal heights than the seats were designed for.

To summarize decision making about the statistical hypotheses:

- If z_{obs} *falls into a rejection region*, then H_0 is rejected and H_1 is accepted.
- If z_{obs} *does not fall into a rejection region*, then H_0 is not rejected and H_1 is not accepted.

Statistically Significant Difference

Statistically significant difference: The observed value of the test statistic falls into a rejection region and H_0 is rejected.

A **statistically significant difference** occurs when the observed value of the test statistic falls into a rejection region and H_0 is rejected. For the z test, a statistically significant difference indicates that we have decided that the sample mean comes from a population with a mean different from the hypothesized population mean.

Statistically significant differences are often reported in the form $z_{\text{obs}} = +3.33$, $p \leq .05$. Often the subscripted *obs* is not used. The symbol $\leq$ implies less than or equal to; thus, $p \leq .05$ is read as "p less than or equal to .05." Often the less-than symbol ($<$) is used in place of the $\leq$ symbol, so the z is reported as $z_{\text{obs}} = +3.33$, $p < .05$. In either case, this report indicates that H_0 was rejected at the .05 significance level because the probability (p) of z_{obs} when H_0 is true is equal to or less than .05. The decisions and conclusions reached from a significant difference with the z test are summarized in the left column of Table 8.1.

TABLE 8.1
Summary of decisions and conclusions in statistical hypothesis testing using the z test for testing a sample mean against an hypothesized population mean. A .05 significance level is used.

If z_{obs} falls into a rejection region for $\alpha = .05$, then:	If z_{obs} does not fall into a rejection region for $\alpha = .05$, then:
Probability of z_{obs} is less than or equal to .05, or $p \leq .05$.	Probability of z_{obs} is greater than .05, or $p > .05$.
H_0 is rejected.	H_0 is not rejected.
H_1 is accepted. The sample mean is treated as being from a population with a mean that is different from the hypothesized population mean.	H_1 is not accepted.
The difference between $\overline{X}$ and the hypothesized μ is statistically significant at the .05 level.	The difference between $\overline{X}$ and the hypothesized μ is nonsignificant at the .05 level.
It is decided that something other than sampling error is responsible for the difference between $\overline{X}$ and the hypothesized μ.	It is decided that sampling error is the most plausible explanation of the difference between $\overline{X}$ and the hypothesized μ.

Nonsignificant Difference

A difference between a sample mean and a population mean is **nonsignificant** if the observed value of the test statistic does not fall into a rejection region. The null hypothesis is not rejected and the observed difference between $\overline{X}$ and the hypothesized μ is treated as due only to sampling error. A nonsignificant difference is indicated by $p > .05$ following the numerical value of z_{obs}. The decisions and conclusions reached from a nonsignificant difference with the z test are summarized in the right column of Table 8.1.

Summary of the Steps of Statistical Hypothesis Testing

All statistical tests require the following:

- Selecting a test statistic, such as z
- Formulating two statistical hypotheses, H_0 and H_1
- Obtaining the sampling distribution of the test statistic assuming that H_0 is true
- Selecting a significance level
- Finding a critical value or values of the test statistic
- Locating a rejection region or regions in the sampling distribution of the test statistic
- Formulating decision rules regarding the statistical hypotheses
- Calculating the value of the test statistic on the sample data

- Deciding to reject or not reject H_0 based on whether the observed value of the test statistic does or does not fall into a rejection region
- Deciding to accept or not accept H_1 based on the decision for H_0

This introduction to statistical hypothesis testing may seem complicated to you, but it soon becomes routine because the same steps are followed for each of the statistical tests presented in this text.

TESTING YOUR KNOWLEDGE 8.1

1. Define: alpha level, α, alternative hypothesis, critical value, H_0, H_1, nonparametric test, nonsignificant difference, null hypothesis, one-tailed test, parametric test, rejection region, significance level, statistical hypothesis, statistically significant difference, test statistic, two-tailed test, z_{crit}, z_{obs}.
2. Identify the two properties of statistical hypotheses.
3. Write H_0 and H_1 in notation for each of the following statements.
   a. The μ for scores on the Wechsler Adult Intelligence Test is 100.
   b. For a population of 25- to 54-year-old women, the mean amount of television watched each day is 4.4 hours.
   c. The mean reaction time of 19-year-old males to a simple stimulus is 423.0 milliseconds.
4. For each of the following, μ represents a population mean, $\sigma_{\overline{X}}$ the standard error of the mean for the population, and $\overline{X}$ a mean of a sample drawn from the population. For each set of values, formulate H_0 and H_1 and find the value of z_{obs}. Then, using Table A.1, determine whether the z_{obs} falls into a two-tailed rejection region at the .05 significance level and indicate your decision for H_0 and H_1.

	μ	$\sigma_{\overline{X}}$	$\overline{X}$
a.	50	4.7	40
b.	100	25.0	70
c.	143	0.4	143.9
d.	87	2.9	92

5. Complete the following problem using a .05 significance level and a two-tailed test. The population mean for an intelligence scale is 100 and $\sigma = 15$. You are the principal of an elementary school in a rural county. For the 121 students in your school, $\overline{X}$ on this scale is 103.4. Does the mean of the students in your school differ significantly from the population mean? In your answer, indicate:
   a. The statistic to be used
   b. The statistical hypotheses
   c. The significance level
   d. z_{crit}
   e. The location of the rejection regions
   f. z_{obs}
   g. Your decision about H_0 and H_1
   h. Your conclusion regarding the mean of your students in relation to a population mean of 100

THE ONE-SAMPLE t TEST

In practice, σ usually is estimated by s, the standard deviation of the scores in the sample. Consequently, $\sigma_{\overline{X}}$ is also estimated from $s_{\overline{X}}$. When I estimate $\sigma_{\overline{X}}$ from $s_{\overline{X}}$, I obtain a new statistic, the t, defined as

$$t = \frac{\overline{X} - \mu}{s_{\overline{X}}}$$

or, substituting $s/\sqrt{N}$ for $s_{\overline{X}}$,

$$t = \frac{\overline{X} - \mu}{s/\sqrt{N}}$$

where
$\overline{X}$ = sample mean.
μ = hypothesized population mean.
$s_{\overline{X}}$ = estimated standard error of the mean obtained from the estimated population standard deviation s.
N = sample size.

This t statistic may be used to test the difference between a sample mean and a hypothesized population mean for statistical significance when $\sigma_{\overline{X}}$ is estimated by $s_{\overline{X}}$. Because only one sample mean is involved, the statistic is called the **one-sample t** to distinguish it from a t test involving two sample means introduced in Chapter 9.

One-sample t test: A t test used to test the difference between a sample mean and a hypothesized population mean for statistical significance when $\sigma_{\overline{X}}$ is estimated by $s_{\overline{X}}$.

The t statistic was developed by the British mathematician William Sealy Gosset shortly after the turn of the twentieth century. Gosset published his work under the pseudonym of "Student." Consequently, the t statistic is often identified as "Student's t."

Sampling Distribution of t

To use the t statistic, I must know its sampling distribution. The sampling distribution of the t differs slightly from the sampling distribution of the z. The z statistic, because it uses the population parameter $\sigma_{\overline{X}}$, has only one sampling distribution, the distribution presented in Table A.1. The t statistic, however, uses s, the **estimated population standard deviation**, defined as

$$s = \sqrt{\frac{\sum (X - \overline{X})^2}{N - 1}}.$$

The calculation of s involves the sample size N; therefore, the sampling distribution of t varies with the sample size or, more specifically, the *degrees of freedom* of the sample.

Degrees of freedom: The number of scores free to vary when calculating a statistic.

Degrees of Freedom

Degrees of freedom (abbreviated **df**) are determined by the number of scores free to vary when calculating a statistic. Several examples will be helpful in understanding what is meant by "scores free to vary" when computing a statistic. Suppose that you are asked to choose three scores between 0 and 100 on a test. You may choose any three scores, say 75, 62, and 97. For this request there are no limitations on the scores that you may choose; each score is free to vary. Accordingly, there are N or 3 *df* for this set of scores. Consider a second request, however, where you are asked to choose three scores, but the sum of the three scores must be 254. Suppose you choose 81 and 78 as your first two scores; they can have any value you want. These two scores are free to vary. Is the third score also free to vary? It is not. Because the three scores must total 254, the third score must be 95; no other score provides a total of 254. Consequently, if you are told that the total of the scores is 254, two scores are free to vary, but the value of the third score is *fixed* by the value of the two scores free to vary and the total of the three scores. Accordingly, if you know the total of the three scores, then there are $N - 1 = 3 - 1 = 2$ degrees of freedom for the three scores.

Applying this reasoning to the calculation of the sample mean, $\overline{X}$ has N *df*. All scores in a set of scores are free to vary when calculating $\overline{X}$. To illustrate, suppose you are asked to calculate the sample mean of a set of five scores, four of which are 7, 10, 3, and 6. Given only this information, you cannot find the mean. The fifth score may assume any value, and you cannot know the value of the fifth score from knowledge of the four scores. Thus, all N scores (where $N = 5$ for this example) are free to vary when calculating the sample mean.

The degrees of freedom for *s*, however, are $N - 1$. To illustrate, suppose that you are asked to calculate *s* on a sample of five scores using the formula

$$s = \sqrt{\frac{\sum (X - \overline{X})^2}{N - 1}}.$$

Suppose that four of the five scores have values of 13, 15, 13, and 12 and that the mean of the five scores is 13.4. I know also that $\sum (X - \overline{X}) = 0$. If I subtract $\overline{X}$ from each of the four known scores, I obtain

$$X - \overline{X}$$

$$13 - 13.4 = -0.4$$
$$15 - 13.4 = +1.6$$
$$13 - 13.4 = -0.4$$
$$12 - 13.4 = \underline{-1.4}$$

Sum $\quad\quad = -0.6$

The sum of these four $X - \overline{X}$ differences is -0.6. When the fifth score is included in the set, this sum must be zero. Thus, the fifth score must result in an $X_5 - \overline{X}$ value of $+0.6$, for $+0.6$ added to -0.6 will equal zero. If $X_5 - 13.4 = +0.6$, then X_5 must equal 14. Accordingly, if $\overline{X}$ is known for the set of five scores, the values of only four of the five scores are free to vary. The value of the fifth score is not free to vary; its value is fixed by the restriction that the value of the mean imposes. Because $\overline{X}$ must be known to calculate *s*, all scores but one are free to vary in calculating *s*. Thus, when calculating either *s* or s^2, a set of N scores possesses $N - 1$ *df*.

We can apply this knowledge of degrees of freedom to the formula for s to write it more briefly. Because $\sum (X - \overline{X})^2$ is also called a *sum of squares (SS)*, and $N - 1$ represents the degrees of freedom when obtaining an SS, the **estimated population standard deviation** can be expressed as the square root of a sum of squares divided by the degrees of freedom, or

$$\text{Estimated population standard deviation} = s = \sqrt{\frac{SS}{df}}.$$

We will find this expression of s useful in later chapters.

Degrees of Freedom for the One-Sample *t* Test

We now apply our knowledge of df to the t test. The estimated standard error of the mean, $s_{\overline{X}}$, is given by $s/\sqrt{N}$. Because s has $N - 1$ df, $s_{\overline{X}}$, too, has $N - 1$ df. Hence, the degrees of freedom for the sampling distribution of the one-sample t statistic are $N - 1$ also.

Sampling Distribution of the *t*

There is a different theoretical sampling distribution of t for each number of df. Because potentially any number of scores can be obtained in a sample, there is an unlimited number of df ranging from 1 to infinity for the t statistic. As an example, Figure 8.4 illustrates the sampling distribution of t for 29 df. Although the shape of the t distribution changes with its degrees of freedom, it is similar to the normal distribution in several respects. Each t distribution is symmetrical, unimodal, and has a mean equal to zero. Consider why these properties arise. When a null hypothesis, such as H_0: μ = some hypothesized value of the population mean, is true, the expected value of t will be zero, because the average $\overline{X} - \mu$ value in a sampling distribution from such a population will be zero. But, even when H_0 is true, values of $\overline{X} - \mu$ will vary around a mean of zero because of sampling error. Furthermore, I expect that $\overline{X}$ will be larger than μ about as often as it will be smaller than μ. In the long run, the $\overline{X} - \mu$ values will be positive and negative equally often when the null hypothesis is true. Consequently, the expected t values will be symmetrical around a mean of zero. For an infinite number of degrees of freedom (a theoretical but not actual possibility) the sampling distribution of t is the same as the normal. All other t distributions are more spread out than a normal distribution.

Why Are Degrees of Freedom Used Rather Than N?   If the df for the one-sample t test are given by $N - 1$, why not present the sampling distribution of t in terms of N rather than df? For the one-sample t statistic, we have gained no advantage by using df rather than N, for the df are always one less than N. The advantage of using df becomes apparent in Chapter 9, however, when I introduce another t statistic used for comparing two sample means. For this t, the df are $N - 2$ rather than $N - 1$. For equal df, however, both t tests possess the same sampling distribution. We will encounter similar instances with other statistics in later chapters.

TESTING YOUR KNOWLEDGE 8.2

1. Write the formula for the one-sample t statistic.
2. Why is the t statistic sometimes called Student's t?

3. You are given seven scores: 73, 42, 51, 68, 49, 62, and 57. How many *df* does this set of scores possess for calculating (a) $\overline{X}$, (b) *s*, and (c) s^2?

4. You plan to compute the one-sample *t* statistic on samples of the following sizes. For each sample, find the *df*. (a) $N = 10$, (b) $N = 16$, (c) $N = 7$, (d) $N = 54$, (e) $N = 120$, (f) $N = 30$.

5. You have two theoretical sampling distributions of *t*, one with 13 *df* and one with 27 *df*. Which distribution will be wider and flatter?

6. Under what conditions will the sampling distribution of the *t* statistic be identical to the sampling distribution of *z*?

Statistical Hypothesis Testing with the One-Sample *t*

The one-sample *t* allows us to determine whether an $\overline{X}$ differs from an hypothesized μ by more than expected from sampling error alone when σ is estimated by *s*. The procedure for statistical hypothesis testing with the *t* is identical to that for the *z* statistic. The necessary steps include the following:

- Formulating H_0 and H_1
- Obtaining the sampling distribution of the *t* statistic, assuming that H_0 is true
- Selecting a significance level
- Finding a critical value or values of *t*
- Locating a rejection region or regions in the sampling distribution of *t*
- Formulating decision rules regarding the statistical hypotheses
- Calculating the value of t_{obs} on the sample data
- Making decisions about H_0 and H_1 from the value of t_{obs}

I illustrate these steps with an example problem. Suppose that a child psychologist studying a group of 30 third-graders in an after-school care program found that for a weekday the children watched an average of 83.0 minutes of television with an *s* of 26.0 minutes. Suppose it is known also that the population mean for time spent watching television by third-graders on a weekday is 95.0 minutes. Does the sample mean of 83.0 minutes differ significantly from the population mean of 95.0 minutes? Because σ is estimated by *s*, the one-sample *t* test will be used to answer this question.

Formulating Statistical Hypotheses

The statistical hypotheses for the one-sample *t* statistic are identical to those of the *z* statistic. The **null hypothesis**, H_0, is stated as an hypothesized value of a population mean. The **alternative hypothesis**, H_1, is a statement that the population mean is not that hypothesized in H_0. For the example, the **statistical hypotheses expressed in notation** are

$$H_0: \mu = 95.0 \text{ minutes,}$$
$$H_1: \mu \neq 95.0 \text{ minutes.}$$

Obtaining the Sampling Distribution of the *t* Statistic

The sampling distribution of *t* depends on the degrees of freedom for the *t* calculated on the sample scores. The *df* for the one-sample *t* are given by $N - 1$. For a mean based on 30 scores, the df for $t = 30 - 1$, or 29. After selecting a significance level and locating rejection regions, I will use these degrees of freedom with a table of the sampling distribution of t to find t_{crit}.

Selecting a Significance Level

The significance level is a probability value that provides the criterion for rejecting H_0. Either the .05 or .01 significance level is typically used in statistical hypothesis testing. For the example, I use $\alpha = .05$.

Locating Rejection Regions for *t*: Two-Tailed Test

A rejection region consists of values in the sampling distribution of t that occur with a probability equal to or less than α when H_0 is true. Thus, the rejection region defines values of t_{obs} that meet the criterion for rejecting H_0.

In a **two-tailed** or **nondirectional test**, rejection regions for the t test are located in either tail of the theoretical sampling distribution, as illustrated in Figure 8.4. When H_0 is true, most values of $\overline{X}$ will differ only slightly from μ and, thus, most values of t will be clustered around zero in the middle of the distribution. Because of sampling error, however, some values of t will be at either end of the distribution even when H_0 is true. These values are obtained when the numerator of the t (i.e., the difference $\overline{X} - \mu$) is large compared to the denominator (i.e., $s_{\overline{X}}$). But these large values of t are rare occurrences if the null hypothesis is true.

On the other hand, if H_1 is true and $\overline{X}$ represents a sample from a population with a mean other than μ, then large values of $\overline{X} - \mu$, and, thus, of t are expected to occur more frequently. Therefore, a rejection region is located in each tail of the theoretical sampling distribution of t, and the total α is divided between the tails. If $\alpha = .05$, then each rejection region includes a probability of $\alpha/2$, or .025. If the value of t calculated on the scores of the sample (identified as t_{obs}) falls into either rejection region, then the null hypothesis is rejected and the alternative hypothesis accepted. By locating a rejection region in each tail of the t distribution, the experimenter covers both possibilities implied by the alternative hypothesis; that is, $\overline{X}$ is greater than μ or $\overline{X}$ is less than μ. The total probability of an outcome in either of the two rejection regions is .05 if H_0 is true.

The two rejection regions for the sampling distribution of t based on 29 df are illustrated in Figure 8.4. For 29 df, if H_0 is true, then the probability that a t will be equal to or less than -2.045 is .025, and the probability that it will be equal to or larger than $+2.045$ is also .025. Any t_{obs} equal to or less than -2.045 or equal to or larger than $+2.045$ falls into a rejection region. This outcome will occur only 5 percent of the time when the null hypothesis is true. The values of -2.045 and $+2.045$ were obtained from a table of critical values of the sampling distribution of t. The use of this table is explained next.

Using the Table of Critical *t* Values

For a particular significance level, the critical t values (identified as t_{crit}) needed for locating the rejection regions depend on the df of t_{obs}. Figures of the sampling distribution of t are useful to visualize how the shape of the t distribution varies with the degrees of freedom, but it is difficult to find exact values of t_{crit} from them. Accordingly, values of t_{crit} for the .05 and .01 significance levels have been calculated and are presented in tables.

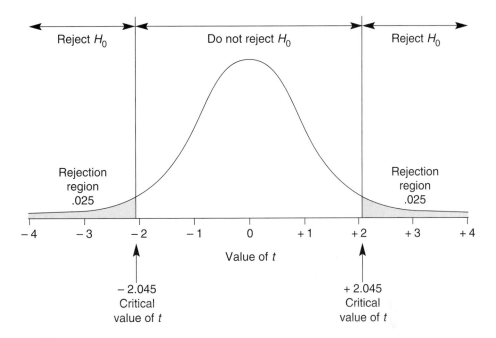

FIGURE 8.4
Two-tailed rejection regions for the t distribution for 29 df and $\alpha = .05$. A value of t_{obs} falling into either rejection region leads to rejection of H_0 and acceptance of H_1.

Table 8.2 presents the two-tailed values of t_{crit} for $\alpha = .05$ and .01. Table 8.2 is part of Table A.2 in the Appendix. The first column lists degrees of freedom for t distributions. The values in any row of the $\alpha = .05$ or .01 columns are the two-tailed values of t_{crit} for the corresponding degrees of freedom for that significance level. For the example with $\alpha = .05$, the two-tailed t_{crit} value for a t_{obs} with 29 degrees of freedom is 2.045. Notice that this value is not preceded by a plus or minus sign. Rather, it is presented as an absolute value of t. For locating rejection regions, however, this value should be treated as both -2.045 and $+2.045$. Similarly, for $\alpha = .01$, the two-tailed t_{crit} value for 29 degrees of freedom is 2.756. Notice that a significance level of .01 imposes a more stringent criterion for rejecting H_0 than does $\alpha = .05$. Any observed $\overline{X} - \mu$ difference will have to be larger to reject H_0 when a .01 significance level is adopted instead of .05.

For more than 30 degrees of freedom, only selected critical values are included in the table. When the df for t_{obs} exceed 30, I recommend that the t_{crit} value used be based on the df in the table closest to but fewer than the degrees of freedom associated with the t_{obs}. For example, if $df = 35$, Table 8.2 shows t_{crit} values for 30 and 40 df but none between. Accordingly, for 35 df I use 30 df to determine the t_{crit} (which is 2.042 for $\alpha = .05$) instead of 40 df. This procedure makes the actual significance level used slightly smaller than .05. If 40 df were used to find the t_{crit} instead, then the significance level would be slightly greater than .05. If t_{obs} falls into the rejection region for 30 df, then it will also fall in the rejection region

TABLE 8.2

Critical values of the *t* distribution for $\alpha = .05$ and $\alpha = .01$. The values provided are for a two-tailed test.

df	$\alpha = .05$	$\alpha = .01$
1	12.706	63.657
2	4.303	9.925
3	3.182	5.841
4	2.776	4.604
5	2.571	4.032
6	2.447	3.707
7	2.365	3.499
8	2.306	3.355
9	2.262	3.250
10	2.228	3.169
11	2.201	3.106
12	2.179	3.055
13	2.160	3.012
14	2.145	2.977
15	2.131	2.947
16	2.120	2.921
17	2.110	2.898
18	2.101	2.878
19	2.093	2.861
20	2.086	2.845
21	2.080	2.831
22	2.074	2.819
23	2.069	2.807
24	2.064	2.797
25	2.060	2.787
26	2.056	2.779
27	2.052	2.771
28	2.048	2.763
29	2.045	2.756
30	2.042	2.750
40	2.021	2.704
60	2.000	2.660
120	1.980	2.617
∞	1.960	2.576

Source: Reprinted from Table 12. Percentage points of the *t*-distribution. *Biometrika Tables for Statisticians*, Volume 1, Copyright 1976, Cambridge University Press. Reprinted by permission of the Biometrika Trustees.

for 40 df. Should t_{obs} (e.g., $t_{obs} = 2.033$) fall between the tabled values for the next lower df (e.g., $t_{crit} = 2.045$ for 30 df) and the next higher df (e.g., $t_{crit} = 2.021$ for 40 df), then a more accurate value of t_{crit} can be interpolated from the tabled values.

Locating a Rejection Region for *t*: One-Tailed Test

In a two-tailed test H_0 is rejected if t_{obs} falls into a rejection region in either tail of the *t* distribution. However, when a research hypothesis predicts a directional relationship among the means (e.g., if the researcher of our example predicted that $\overline{X}$ would be less than μ) and there is no interest in an outcome opposite than predicted (e.g., if $\overline{X}$ greater than μ occurs), then some researchers use a one-tailed test. In a **one-tailed** or **directional test** a rejection region encompassing the entire value of α is located in the tail of the *t* distribution, corresponding to the direction of the outcome predicted by the research hypothesis. Values of t_{crit} for a one-tailed test at the .01 and .05 significance levels are also presented in Table A.2. For 29 df, the one-tailed t_{crit} at the .05 significance level is 1.699. A one-tailed rejection region with $t_{crit} = -1.699$ in the left tail of a *t* distribution is illustrated in Figure 8.5. This rejection region would be appropriate for the example if I had stated the following statistical hypotheses:

$$H_0: \mu \geq 95.0,$$
$$H_1: \mu < 95.0.$$

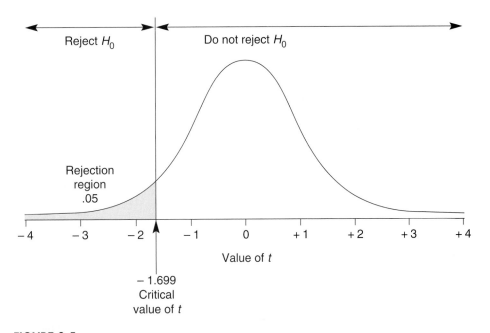

FIGURE 8.5
One-tailed rejection region for the *t* distribution for 29 df and $\alpha = .05$. A value of t_{obs} falling into the rejection region leads to rejection of H_0 and acceptance of H_1.

When Should a One-Tailed Test Be Used?

The advantage of a one-tailed rejection region is that t_{crit} will be smaller because the entire rejection region lies in only one tail of the distribution. Thus, it is easier to reject H_0 because a smaller difference between $\overline{X}$ and μ will result in a t_{obs} falling into the rejection region. This advantage is accompanied by a limitation, however. The decision to adopt a one-tailed or two-tailed rejection region must be made at the time the research is being planned and before the data are collected and analyzed. If a one-tailed rejection region is adopted, then the experimenter cannot reject H_0 from an obtained difference in means opposite in direction to that hypothesized, because no rejection region for such an outcome has been located. I discuss one- and two-tailed tests more fully in Chapter 9. In practice, two-tailed tests are most commonly used; thus, they are used for all examples in this chapter.

Calculating t_{obs}

Calculating t_{obs} requires substituting values of $\overline{X}$, the hypothesized μ, and $s_{\overline{X}}$ into the formula for t. For the example of 30 scores of third-graders watching television, $\overline{X} = 83.0$ minutes, $s = 26.0$ minutes, and $N = 30$. The hypothesized value of μ is 95.0 minutes. The value of $s_{\overline{X}}$ is obtained from $s/\sqrt{N}$; thus,

$$s_{\overline{X}} = \frac{26.0}{\sqrt{30}} = \frac{26.0}{5.477} = 4.75.$$

As a result,

$$t_{obs} = \frac{\overline{X} - \mu}{s_{\overline{X}}}$$

$$= \frac{83.0 - 95.0}{4.75}$$

$$= -2.526$$

with $N - 1 = 29$ df.

Decisions about the Statistical Hypotheses

The decision rules for statistical hypotheses are the same for all statistical tests. Accordingly, for the one-sample t test:

- If t_{obs} falls into a rejection region, then H_0 is rejected and H_1 is accepted.
- If t_{obs} does not fall into a rejection region, then H_0 is not rejected, and H_1 is not accepted.

The two-tailed value of t_{crit} for 29 df and $\alpha = .05$ is 2.045. Consequently, as illustrated in Figure 8.4, a t_{obs} equal to or less than -2.045 or equal to or larger than $+2.045$ falls into a rejection region. The t_{obs} of -2.526 is more extreme than $t_{crit} = -2.045$ and, therefore, falls into the rejection region in the left tail of the distribution. I reject H_0: $\mu = 95.0$ minutes and accept H_1: $\mu \neq 95.0$ minutes. The difference between the sample mean and the population mean is statistically significant at the .05 level. I conclude that the sample mean of 83.0 minutes is from a population with a μ less than 95.0 minutes. The mean amount of TV viewing by the third-graders in the after-school program is significantly less than the population mean of 95.0 minutes per day.

If t_{obs} had fallen between the two critical values of -2.045 and $+2.045$ (e.g., if $\overline{X}$ had been 90.0 minutes and, thus, $t_{obs} = -1.053$), then I would fail to reject H_0 and not accept H_1. The observed difference between the sample mean and hypothesized population mean would be nonsignificant. In this instance there would be no evidence that H_0 is not true.

The decisions about the statistical hypotheses and the conclusions reached from either a statistically significant or a nonsignificant one-sample t test are summarized in Table 8.3.

Assumptions of the One-Sample t Test

The one-sample t test makes the following assumptions of the scores in the sample:

- The scores in the sample are selected randomly from a population of scores and each score is independent of each other score.
- The scores in the population sampled are normally distributed.

In practice, these assumptions may not be met fully by the scores in a sample, yet researchers often proceed to use the t test on the data. I discuss the consequences of this action more fully in Chapter 9.

TABLE 8.3
Summary of decisions and conclusions in statistical hypothesis testing using the one-sample t test. A .05 significance level is used.

If t_{obs} falls into a rejection region for $\alpha = .05$, then:	If t_{obs} does not fall into a rejection region for $\alpha = .05$, then:
Probability of t_{obs} is less than or equal to .05, or $p \le .05$.	Probability of t_{obs} is greater than .05, or $p > .05$.
H_0 is rejected.	H_0 is not rejected.
H_1 is accepted. The sample mean is treated as being from a population with a mean that is different from the hypothesized population mean.	H_1 is not accepted.
The difference between $\overline{X}$ and the hypothesized μ is statistically significant at the .05 level.	The difference between $\overline{X}$ and the hypothesized μ is nonsignificant at the .05 level.
It is decided that something other than sampling error is responsible for the difference between $\overline{X}$ and the hypothesized μ.	It is decided that sampling error is the most plausible explanation of the difference between $\overline{X}$ and the hypothesized μ.

Example Problem 8.1

Using the One-Sample *t* Test

Problem: Several psychologists have hypothesized that in competitive situations some individuals are motivated to avoid being too successful in order to minimize criticism and ostracism by peers. A self-report inventory measuring this motivation to avoid success has been developed by Good and Good (1973). Suppose it is known that the population mean for female college seniors on this inventory is 8.6 for which the range of scores may be from 0, low motivation to avoid success, to 28, high motivation to avoid success. A counselor has developed a workshop dealing with responding to competitive situations. She gives the motivation-to-avoid-success scale to 33 female college seniors who have completed this workshop and obtains a mean of 8.1 with $s = 1.31$. Does this $\overline{X}$ differ significantly from a μ of 8.6 at the .05 level? Use a two-tailed test.

Statistic to Be Used: Because σ is being estimated by s, the one-sample t test is appropriate.

Assumptions for Use

1. The individuals measured are randomly and independently drawn from a population of female college seniors.
2. Motivation-to-avoid-success scores are normally distributed in the population sampled.

Statistical Hypotheses: H_0: $\mu = 8.6$; H_1: $\mu \neq 8.6$.

Significance Level: $\alpha = .05$.

***df* for *t*:** $N - 1 = 33 - 1 = 32$.

Critical Value of *t*: $t_{crit} = 2.042$. A critical value of t for 32 *df* is not presented in Table A.2. I used t_{crit} for the next-lower *df* tabled, 30 *df*.

Rejection Regions: Values of t_{obs} equal to or less than -2.042 or equal to or greater than $+2.042$.

Calculation

$$s_{\overline{X}} = \frac{1.31}{\sqrt{33}} = \frac{1.31}{5.745} = 0.228.$$

Thus,

$$t_{obs} = \frac{\overline{X} - \mu}{s_{\overline{X}}} = \frac{8.1 - 8.6}{0.228} = \frac{-0.5}{0.228} = -2.193.$$

Decision: t_{obs} is more extreme than $t_{crit} = -2.042$ and falls into a rejection region. Thus, I reject H_0 and accept H_1.

Conclusion: The mean motivation to avoid success in the sample of female college seniors who completed the workshop (i.e., $\overline{X} = 8.1$) is significantly less than the population mean of 8.6 of female college seniors.

REPORTING THE RESULTS OF THE ONE-SAMPLE *t* TEST

The *Publication Manual of the American Psychological Association* (1994) requires a report of an inferential statistical test to give the symbol for the statistical test, the *df* for the test, the observed value of the statistic, the alpha level used, and the probability of obtaining the observed value of the statistic or an even more extreme value assuming that the null hypothesis is true (pp. 15–18). Relevant descriptive statistics, such as the sample mean and standard deviation, are also required. I illustrate this style with the results of the example problem of television watching by third-graders.

> The mean daily amount of time spent watching television for the 30 children was 83.0 minutes ($SD = 26.0$ minutes). For alpha equal to .05, a two-tailed one-sample *t* test indicated that the sample mean differed significantly from a hypothesized population mean of 95.0 minutes; $t(29) = -2.53, p < .05$.

In the report:

$\alpha = .05$ Indicates the significance level selected for the test.

$t(29)$ Identifies the test statistic as the *t*. This *t* identifies t_{obs}, although the subscript *obs* is not included. Because the *t* is identified as the one-sample *t*, we know that the test is a comparison of a sample mean against a hypothesized population mean. The degrees of freedom for t_{obs} are shown in parentheses. Thus, we know that 30 scores were used in the calculation of *t* (because $df = N - 1$; thus, $29 = 30 - 1$).

$= -2.53$ The value of t_{obs} (not the t_{crit} value found in Table A.2). The value of *t* should be given to at least two decimal places.

$p < .05.$ Indicates the following:

   a.   The *p* and less than sign ($p <$) indicate that the probability of t_{obs} if H_0 is true is less than (or equal to) .05. This value is the probability of t_{obs} or an even more extreme value of t_{obs} if H_0 is true; it is not necessarily the same as the value of α selected.

   b. H_0: $\mu = 95.0$ minutes was rejected.
   H_1: $\mu \neq 95.0$ minutes was accepted.

   c.   The difference between the sample mean and the hypothesized μ is statistically significant.

d. The sample mean is treated as being from a population with a mean less than the hypothesized $\mu = 95.0$ minutes.

e. If $p > .05$ had been reported, then the greater than sign ($>$) would indicate that H_0 was not rejected and $\overline{X}$ did not differ significantly from the hypothesized μ at the .05 significance level.

TESTING YOUR KNOWLEDGE 8.3

1. Write H_0 and H_1 for the one-sample t test for each of the following statements.
   a. The population mean for time sleeping per night is 493 minutes.
   b. The population mean on an inventory of depression proneness is 36.1.
   c. The population mean on a standardized intelligence test is 100.

2. Using Table A.2, find the values of t_{crit} for the df and value of α indicated. Use a two-tailed test.

	df	α
a.	6	.05
b.	17	.01
c.	23	.05
d.	32	.05
e.	39	.05
f.	75	.01
g.	103	.05
h.	256	.05

3. Indicate whether each of the following t_{obs} does or does not fall into a rejection region. Then indicate your decision for H_0 and H_1. Remember that you *fail to reject* or *reject* H_0, and you *do not accept* or *accept* H_1. Use $\alpha = .05$ and a two-tailed test. The df for each t_{obs} are given in parentheses.
   a. $t_{\text{obs}}(19) = +3.014$
   b. $t_{\text{obs}}(19) = -1.989$
   c. $t_{\text{obs}}(16) = -2.179$
   d. $t_{\text{obs}}(16) = +2.040$
   e. $t_{\text{obs}}(30) = -3.961$
   f. $t_{\text{obs}}(30) = +2.743$
   g. $t_{\text{obs}}(6) = -2.364$
   h. $t_{\text{obs}}(6) = +2.447$
   i. $t_{\text{obs}}(9) = -2.262$
   j. $t_{\text{obs}}(37) = +2.938$
   k. $t_{\text{obs}}(42) = -2.410$

4. Identify the assumptions underlying the use of the one-sample t test.

5. Complete the following problem and answer the questions asked. Use a two-tailed test and .05 significance level. You are interested in how well people can estimate the passage of time without the use of a watch or clock. Accordingly, you ask 11 people to tell you when they think a 7-minute interval has passed without using a watch or clock. The mean of the 11 estimates was 5.8 minutes with $s = 0.8$ minutes. Is your sample mean significantly different from a population mean of 7 minutes? In your answer, indicate the following:
   a. The statistic to be used
   b. The assumptions for its use
   c. The statistical hypotheses

      d. The significance level

      e. The critical value of the test statistic

      f. The rejection regions

      g. The value of t_{obs}

      h. Your decisions about the statistical hypotheses

      i. Your conclusion regarding the sample mean

6. This exercise presents reports of the use of the t test adapted from results of published studies. For each report, answer the following questions:

      a. What is the value of the sample mean?

      b. What is the value of the estimated population standard deviation?

      c. What t test was used in this study?

      d. What are H_0 and H_1 for this t test?

      e. How many scores were obtained in this study?

      f. What is the value of t_{obs} for this study?

      g. What are the df for this t_{obs}?

      h. What is t_{crit} for $\alpha = .05$ and a two-tailed rejection region?

      i. Do you reject or fail to reject H_0?

      j. Do you accept or not accept H_1?

      k. Do you conclude that the sample mean differs significantly from the hypothesized population mean?

Report 1:   The mean weight of the male runners was 70.4 kilograms ($SD = 7.6$ kg). For alpha equal to .05 and a two-tailed test, a one-sample t test indicated that the sample mean did not differ significantly from a hypothesized population mean of 75 kg for 25-year-old males; $t(5) = -1.48, p > .05$.

Report 2:   The mean hospital stay for males age 65 and over with nonterminal diseases was 10.4 days ($SD = 2.3$ days). For alpha equal to .05 and a two-tailed test, a one-sample t test revealed that the sample mean differed significantly from a hypothesized population mean of 8.7 days; $t(24) = +3.70, p < .01$.

IMPORTANT CONSIDERATIONS IN STATISTICAL HYPOTHESIS TESTING

Why We Don't Accept the Null Hypothesis

If a test statistic does not fall into a rejection region, then we do not reject the null hypothesis. This decision is often stated as "we fail to reject the null hypothesis." You may wonder why I use this awkward phrasing; typically, if we do not reject something, then we accept it. Why don't I simply accept the null hypothesis if the test statistic does not fall into a rejection region? To answer this question, I return to the example of the height of a truck seat. The seat was designed for a population of drivers with a popliteal height of 42.0 cm and $\sigma = 3.0$ cm. Suppose again that you obtained a sample of 25 drivers of your truck and found that the mean popliteal height of these drivers was 42.5 cm. The value of z_{obs} for this sample is $+0.83$.

$$z_{obs} = \frac{42.5 - 42.0}{3.0/\sqrt{25}} = +\frac{0.5}{0.6} = +0.83.$$

This z_{obs} does not fall into the rejection region defined by $z_{crit} = $ plus or minus 1.96 for $\alpha = .05$ and is, thus, nonsignificant. I fail to reject H_0: $\mu = 42.0$ cm. But does this decision imply that the mean of the population from which the sample was selected must be exactly 42.0 cm? Obviously, the answer is no; a sample mean of 42.5 cm does not imply that the mean of the population from which the sample was drawn must be 42.0 cm. On the other hand, $\overline{X} = 42.5$ cm also does not provide any evidence that μ may not be 42.0 cm. That is, an $\overline{X}$ of 42.5 cm does not provide evidence that I should reject H_0: $\mu = 42.0$ cm, but neither does it provide evidence that μ is exactly 42.0 cm. It indicates only that I should not reject H_0: $\mu = 42.0$ cm.

Suppose, however, that $\overline{X}$ had been 44.0 cm so that $z_{obs} = +3.33$. This z_{obs} is statistically significant at the .05 level and I reject H_0: $\mu = 42.0$ cm and accept H_1: $\mu \neq 42.0$ cm. It is appropriate to accept H_1 because H_1 states that μ is some value other than 42.0 cm, and $\overline{X} = 44.0$ cm indicates that μ indeed is some value other than 42.0 cm. In this case, the sample mean of 44.0 cm provides the best point estimate of μ for the population of drivers from which the sample was drawn.

The correct decisions about the statistical hypotheses are thus as follows:

- If the test statistic falls into a rejection region, then *reject H_0* and *accept H_1*.
- If the test statistic does not fall into a rejection region, then *fail to reject H_0* and *do not accept H_1*.

Some behavioral scientists feel uncomfortable with the statement of "accepting H_1" because the evidence for believing that H_1 is true is gained only by rejecting H_0. Thus, they prefer to use terminology such as "H_0 is rejected in favor of H_1" or "H_0 is rejected lending support to H_1." However, given the properties of statistical hypotheses, they are mutually exclusive and they include all possible values of the parameter involved, then rejecting H_0 implies that H_1 is accepted. Thus, I will use the terminology of accepting H_1 when H_0 is rejected. But you should realize that some researchers prefer a more tentative statement such as H_1 is supported when H_0 is rejected.

Type I and Type II Errors in Statistical Tests

Type I error: The error in statistical decision making that occurs if the null hypothesis is rejected when actually it is true of the population.

Type II error: The error in statistical decision making that occurs if H_0 is not rejected when it is false and the alternative hypothesis (H_1) is true.

Beta (β): The probability of a Type II error.

Power: The probability of rejecting H_0 when H_0 is false and H_1 is true. The power of a statistical test is given by $1 - \beta$.

A statistical test allows a researcher to either (1) reject H_0 or (2) fail to reject H_0. The decision may be correct or incorrect depending on whether the null hypothesis is in fact true of the population. A **Type I error** occurs if the null hypothesis is rejected when actually it is true. A **Type II error** occurs if I fail to reject H_0 when it is false and H_1 is true. Table 8.4 illustrates these possible errors and correct decisions that may occur with a statistical test.

Type I and Type II errors occur because statistical decision making is probabilistic. If H_0 is true, the probability of a Type I error is given by α. Thus, the probability of making a correct decision and not rejecting H_0 when it is true is provided by $1 - \alpha$. The probability of a Type II error is given by β (the lowercase Greek letter **beta**). Hence, the probability of correctly accepting H_1 when H_1 is true is provided by $1 - \beta$. The value $1 - \beta$ is the power of a statistical test. Therefore, the **power of a statistical test**, or simply, **power**, is the probability of rejecting H_0 when H_0 is false and H_1 is true. The value of β depends on a number of factors, and I discuss these factors in Chapter 9. Each of these probabilities is identified in Table 8.4.

TABLE 8.4
Errors and correct decisions in statistical decision making and the probability associated with each outcome.

	Decision by the Experimenter	
	Fails to Reject H_0	**Rejects H_0, Accepts H_1**
H_0 true	Correct decision: $p = 1 - \alpha$	Type I error: $p = \alpha$
True Situation in the Population		
H_1 true	Type II error: $p = \beta$	Correct decision: $p = 1 - \beta$

A Type I error can occur only when H_0 is true; hence, the probability of making a Type I error depends directly on the significance level selected. Recall that the significance level indicates the probability of obtaining a value of the test statistic (e.g., either z or t) that leads to rejection of H_0 when H_0 is actually true. Accordingly, when alpha is selected for a statistical test, the risk of making a Type I error is established. With $\alpha = .05$, for example, the probability of wrongly rejecting a true H_0 is .05. Similarly, if $\alpha = .01$, then there is only a 1 in 100 chance of making a Type I error by incorrectly rejecting H_0 when it is true. Scientists typically adopt a conservative stance to assure a low probability of making a Type I error in their research. Consequently, the value of α is typically selected to be a small value such as $\alpha = .05$ or $\alpha = .01$.

Statistical and Scientific Significance

Using the word *significant* to characterize the rejection of H_0 in a statistical hypothesis test reflects an unfortunate choice of words by statisticians. The typical connotation to something significant is that it is important. But it is inappropriate to apply this meaning to a statistically significant difference. In statistical testing, significance indicates only that H_0 has been rejected. If H_0 is rejected, the statistical test neither gives a reason for this result nor indicates if the difference is scientifically important. This responsibility rests with the researcher, who must examine carefully the conditions of the study and the nature of the data obtained.

Observed values of the test statistic that do not fall into the rejection region are referred to as **nonsignificant** and not as insignificant. *Insignificant* implies that something is lacking importance or is inconsequential. Yet a nonsignificant difference may be scientifically important. For example, suppose that a program is introduced in an after-school child care center to reduce the amount of television that the children watch. If, in comparing $\overline{X}$ to μ, a nonsignificant difference is found, the implication is that the program was ineffective in changing the children's watching of television, and this may be an important result for the researcher.

USING THE *t* STATISTIC TO CONSTRUCT CONFIDENCE INTERVALS FOR THE POPULATION MEAN

Confidence intervals for the population mean were defined in Chapter 7 as intervals in which we have a certain degree of confidence that the interval contains the population mean. In that chapter I constructed these intervals using $\overline{X}$, z, and $\sigma_{\overline{X}}$. For example, if $\sigma_{\overline{X}}$ is known, a 95 percent confidence interval for the population mean is given by the interval from

$$\overline{X} - 1.96\sigma_{\overline{X}} \text{ to } \overline{X} + 1.96\sigma_{\overline{X}}.$$

Often $\sigma_{\overline{X}}$ is unknown, however, and its value is estimated from $s_{\overline{X}}$. When $s_{\overline{X}}$ is used to estimate $\sigma_{\overline{X}}$, a confidence interval is constructed using the t statistic rather than z. Using t and $s_{\overline{X}}$, the **95 percent confidence interval for the population mean** is given by the interval from

$$\overline{X} - (t_{.05})(s_{\overline{X}}) \text{ to } \overline{X} + (t_{.05})(s_{\overline{X}}),$$

where

$\overline{X}$ = observed sample mean.
$s_{\overline{X}}$ = estimated standard error of the mean obtained from $s/\sqrt{N}$.
$t_{.05}$ = two-tailed value of t_{crit} at the .05 significance level with $N - 1$ degrees of freedom.

Similarly, a **99 percent confidence interval for the population mean** is given by

$$\overline{X} - (t_{.01})(s_{\overline{X}}) \text{ to } \overline{X} + (t_{.01})(s_{\overline{X}}).$$

To illustrate, I find the 95 percent confidence interval for the 30 third-graders' television watching time scores with $\overline{X} = 83.0$ minutes and $s = 26.0$ minutes. Because $N = 30$, there are 29 df for this sample, and the two-tailed value of $t_{\text{crit}}(29)$ at the .05 level is 2.045. The standard error of the mean, $s_{\overline{X}}$, equals $26.0/\sqrt{30}$, or 4.75 minutes. Thus, the 95 percent confidence interval for μ is

$$83.0 - (2.045)(4.75) \text{ to } 83.0 + (2.045)(4.75),$$

or, carrying out the mathematical operations indicated,

$$83.0 - 9.7 \text{ to } 83.0 + 9.7 \text{ minutes,}$$

which equals 73.3 to 92.7 minutes. This interval has a .95 probability of including the value of μ.

Although confidence intervals have not been widely reported in research studies, researchers are now being encouraged to include them in reports of their work (Streiner, 1996; Wilkinson et al., 1999). As an example, Gwartney-Gibbs (1986) studied premarital cohabitation in couples by using archival data from marriage license applications to obtain demographic information on cohabiting and noncohabiting couples. As part of her results, she reported the mean age of marriage for males and females of couples who had either cohabited or had not cohabited prior to marriage. The mean ages were accompanied by 95 percent confidence intervals for the population mean for age. To illustrate, Gwartney-Gibbs presents the following results for cohabiting and noncohabiting females who had not been married previously.

	Cohabiting	Noncohabiting
Mean age at marriage (yr)	22.8	21.7
s (yr)	4.6	4.4
95 percent confidence interval for μ	22.48 to 23.12	21.41 to 21.29

We can be 95 percent confident that μ for age of marriage by cohabiting females falls between 22.48 to 23.12 years for the population from which Gwartney-Gibbs selected her sample. For the noncohabiting females, the 95 percent confidence interval for μ is 21.41 to 21.29 years. The two confidence intervals do not overlap; therefore, Gwartney-Gibbs concluded that cohabiting females typically married at least one-half year later in age than noncohabiting females in the population she studied.

TESTING YOUR KNOWLEDGE 8.4

1. Explain why a researcher does not accept H_0 if t_{obs} does not fall into a rejection region.
2. Answer the following.
   a. What is a Type I error?
   b. What is the probability of making a Type I error if H_0 is true?
   c. What is the probability of making a Type I error if H_0 is false?
   d. What is a Type II error?
   e. Is it possible for an experimenter to make both Type I and Type II errors in the same statistical test? Explain your answer.
3. Distinguish between statistical significance and scientific significance.
4. An experimenter observed the amount of time that adolescents spent playing video games in an arcade. The mean playing time per day for a sample of 23 males was 97 minutes, with a standard deviation of 39 minutes. Construct a 95 percent confidence interval for the population mean for the amount of time male adolescents spent playing video games.

SUMMARY

- Statistical tests may be either parametric or nonparametric.
- Statistical hypothesis testing involves the following steps:
  - Selecting a test statistic (e.g., either z or t).
  - Formulating H_0 and H_1. H_0 is used to find the sampling distribution of the test statistic.
  - Selecting a significance level. The significance level, specified by the value of α, is a probability value that provides the criterion for rejecting H_0 as being true.

- Finding a critical value or values of the test statistic from tabled values. Critical values of the test statistic determine the boundaries of the rejection region or regions.
- Locating a rejection region or regions. The rejection region represents values on the sampling distribution of the test statistic that have a probability equal to or less than α if H_0 is true.
- Formulating decision rules regarding the statistical hypotheses. These rules are:
  —If the test statistic falls into a rejection region, then *reject H_0* and *accept H_1*. The difference between a sample mean and a hypothesized population mean is statistically significant.
  —If the test statistic does not fall into a rejection region, then *fail to reject H_0* and *do not accept H_1*. The difference between a sample mean and a hypothesized population mean is nonsignificant.
- Calculating the observed value of the test statistic from the sample scores.
- Making decisions about H_0 and H_1 based on whether the observed value of the test statistic does or does not fall into the rejection region.
- The z statistic, given by $z = (\overline{X} - \mu)/\sigma_{\overline{X}}$, is used to test a sample mean against a hypothesized population mean when σ is known.
- The t statistic, given by $t = (\overline{X} - \mu)/s_{\overline{X}}$, is used to test a sample mean against a hypothesized population mean when $\sigma_{\overline{X}}$ is estimated from $s_{\overline{X}}$.
- The sampling distribution of the t statistic depends on the df of the t, where the $df = N - 1$.
- Statistical decision making is inherently probabilistic. A Type I error occurs if a true H_0 is rejected. A Type II error occurs if a false H_0 is not rejected.
- The probability of a Type I error is given by α; the probability of a Type II error is given by β.
- The power of a statistical test is the probability of rejecting H_0 when H_0 is false and H_1 is true.
- The t distribution may be used with $s_{\overline{X}}$ to find confidence intervals for the population mean.

KEY TERMS AND SYMBOLS

alpha (α) (153)
alternative hypothesis (H_1) (150)
beta (β) (172)
critical value (154)
degrees of freedom (df) (158)
nonparametric tests (149)
nonsignificant difference (156)
null hypothesis (H_0) (150)
one-sample t test (158)
one-tailed test (154)

parametric tests (148)
power (172)
rejection region (153)
sampling distribution of t (158)
significance level (153)
statistical hypothesis (150)
statistically significant
   difference (155)
t_{crit} (163)

t_{obs} (163)
test statistic (152)
two-tailed test (154)
t statistic (162)
Type I error (172)
Type II error (172)
z (152)
z_{crit} (155)
z_{obs} (152)

REVIEW QUESTIONS

1. What are the requirements that any set of statistical hypotheses must meet?
2. What function does the null hypothesis serve in a statistical test?
3. What is a significance level?
4. What is the critical value of a test statistic?
5. What decision is made regarding H_0 and H_1 if:
   a. The observed value of a test statistic falls into a rejection region?
   b. The observed value of a test statistic does not fall into a rejection region?
6. You have been asked to test whether a sample mean of 73 differs significantly from a hypothesized population mean of 75. What will determine whether you use the z test or the one-sample t test?
7. What decision do you make about the value of a sample mean with respect to a hypothesized population mean if:
   a. z_{obs} falls into a rejection region?
   b. z_{obs} does not fall into a rejection region?
8. For each of the following values of z_{obs}, determine whether the z_{obs} falls into a two-tailed rejection region at the .01 significance level. Then indicate your decision for H_0 and H_1. Remember that you either (1) *fail to reject* or *reject* H_0, and (2) *do not accept* or *accept* H_1. (a) $z_{obs} = +3.71$, (b) $z_{obs} = -2.60$, (c) $z_{obs} = +1.74$, (d) $z_{obs} = -3.05$, (e) $z_{obs} = -1.96$, (f) $z_{obs} = +2.58$.
9. The population mean for a group intelligence scale is 100 and $\sigma = 16$. A school counselor tests seventeen 10-year-olds on this scale and obtains $\overline{X} = 94.1$. Conduct a statistical test on these data to determine if the difference between the population mean and the sample mean is statistically significant. Use a .05 significance level and a two-tailed test.
10. Based on the outcome of a z test, there is a statistically significant difference between a sample mean and a population mean. Explain what is meant by statistical significance in this case.
11. What decision do you make about the value of a sample mean with respect to a hypothesized population mean if:
   a. t_{obs} falls into a rejection region?
   b. t_{obs} does not fall into a rejection region?
12. Indicate whether each of the following t_{obs} does or does not fall into a rejection region. Assume that $\alpha = .01$ and use a two-tailed test. The df for each t_{obs} are given in parentheses.
   a. $t_{obs}(18) = +3.713$
   b. $t_{obs}(7) = -3.015$
   c. $t_{obs}(35) = +2.794$
   d. $t_{obs}(44) = -3.058$
   e. $t_{obs}(74) = -1.960$
   f. $t_{obs}(15) = -2.368$
13. Mothers with young children often complain that they do not get enough sleep. Suppose that you obtained a measure of the typical amount of sleep of nine

mothers of children under 1 year of age and found the following durations (in hours): 6.4, 7.5, 6.9, 7.3, 7.6, 7.1, 6.5, 7.7, and 7.8.

a. Does the mean amount of sleep for these mothers differ significantly from a hypothesized population mean of 7.7 hours sleep per night? Use a two-tailed test and a .05 significance level.

b. Describe your results following the example illustrated in the Reporting the Results of the One-Sample t Test section of this chapter.

c. Could your decision about the statistical hypotheses represent the occurrence of a Type I error?

d. Could your decision about the statistical hypotheses represent the occurrence of a Type II error?

e. Compute the 95 percent confidence interval for the population mean of these scores. Is the hypothesized population mean of 7.7 hours per night included in this interval?

14. A medical researcher attempted to learn if a disease is accompanied by an increase in body temperature. She measured the body temperature of 12 people diagnosed as having the disease and obtained the following temperatures (in °F): 99.3, 99.1, 100.4, 98.4, 98.2, 98.9, 99.7, 100.1, 100.7, 99.0, 98.8, 99.2.

a. Does the mean body temperature of these individuals differ from a hypothesized population mean of 98.6°F? Use a two-tailed test and a .05 significance level.

b. Could your decision regarding the statistical hypothesis represent a Type II error? Explain your answer.

15. For each of the following statements, indicate whether the decision is correct or in error. If an error is made, indicate whether it is a Type I or Type II error.

a. H_0 is true of the population, but on the basis of z_{obs} an experimenter rejects H_0.

b. H_1 is true of the population, but on the basis of z_{obs} an experimenter fails to reject H_0.

c. H_0 is true of the population, and on the basis of z_{obs} the experimenter fails to reject H_0.

d. H_1 is true of the population, and on the basis of z_{obs} the experimenter rejects H_0.

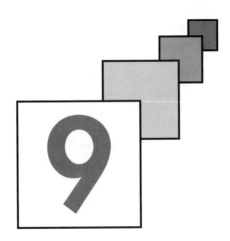

The Basics of Experimentation and Testing for a Difference between Means

THE CONTROVERSY OVER STATISTICAL HYPOTHESIS TESTING
REPORTING THE RESULTS OF A *t* TEST
WITHIN-SUBJECTS DESIGNS AND THE *t* TEST FOR RELATED SCORES
  The *t* Test for Related Scores
  Constructing Confidence Intervals for the Difference between Two
    Related Population Means

Chapter 8 introduced the use of statistical hypothesis testing to determine if a sample mean differs significantly from a hypothesized population mean. In this chapter, I use statistical hypothesis testing to compare two sample means to determine if they differ by more than sampling error alone. One use of this type of statistical hypothesis testing is to analyze the results of experimental research. Chapters 1 and 2 briefly introduced the basic concepts of experimentation; this chapter develops them more fully. The initial discussion will be limited to between-subjects designs. Later in the chapter I discuss within-subjects designs.

A REVIEW OF THE RESEARCH PROCESS

All scientific research begins with asking a question that can be empirically answered. Usually, a scientist will offer a tentative answer to the question in the form of a research hypothesis. A research hypothesis is a statement of an expected or predicted relationship between two or more variables. In an experiment, a research hypothesis is a predicted relationship between an independent variable and a dependent variable. Recall that the independent variable is a variable that the experimenter plans to manipulate to find its effect on the dependent variable. The dependent variable is typically some measured behavior of a person. The form of the research hypothesis indicates to the scientist the type of research design to be used. If the research hypothesis predicts that the manipulation of an independent variable will affect a dependent variable, then an experiment is the appropriate form of research design to empirically test this research hypothesis.

A simple experiment begins by creating equivalent groups of participants. Each group is treated identically except for being given different levels of the independent variable. After the independent variable is manipulated, scores are obtained on the dependent variable. These scores are then analyzed to find if the independent variable had an effect on the dependent variable. Consider an example of this process.

Each year, millions of prescriptions are written for tranquilizers containing the antianxiety drug diazepam. As with many drugs, diazepam has a variety of side effects, both physiological and psychological. One reported psychological effect is that diazepam alters a person's perception of the long-term passage of time (Kleinknecht & Donaldson, 1975). Unrug-Neervoort, Kaiser, and Coenen (1992) hypothesized that diazepam would have similar effects on the judgment of brief time intervals. This research hypothesis predicts that an independent variable, a drug condition, will affect a dependent variable, a person's judgment of the length of a short time interval. To test this hypothesis, Unrug-Neervoort et al. conducted a between-subjects experiment.

The experiment involved creating two equivalent groups of participants. One group, the *placebo control group*, was given a pill containing no active ingredients. The other group, the *experimental group*, was given 15 milligrams (mg) of diazepam. Each group contained 12 people. The dependent variable was a person's judgment of the length of a finger-tapping task. Participants were asked to tap a finger on a counter until told to stop. After ending the tapping, participants were asked to estimate how long they had performed the task. Although both groups tapped for an identical length of time, the placebo control group estimated the duration to be 19.8 sec ($s = 7.6$ sec), whereas the experimental group estimated the length to be 13.6 sec ($s = 4.8$ sec). Unrug-Neervoort et al. statistically analyzed these means using the *t* test for independent groups and found the estimated duration of the experimental group to be significantly shorter than the estimated duration of the placebo control group. Diazepam does affect the perception of short time intervals.

Conducting an experiment requires a number of steps prior to the statistical analysis of the data. These steps are similar in all experiments and include asking a scientific question, formulating a research hypothesis, selecting a research design, selecting participants, creating equivalent groups of subjects, controlling extraneous variables, manipulating the independent variable, and measuring the dependent variable.

Asking a Scientific Question and Formulating the Research Hypothesis

Recall that a scientific question is one that allows an answer to be found by the collection of empirical data. Our example is based on a scientific question: "What is the effect of diazepam on the perception of short intervals of time?" Clearly, this question permits systematic observation to provide an answer. The research hypothesis offers a tentative answer to this question; it states that diazepam will affect a person's judgments of the passage of short time intervals.

Selecting a Research Design

Between-subjects design: An experiment in which two or more groups are created.

The research design is the plan used to guide the collection of data. Testing the research hypothesis of the example requires comparing one group of people who ingest diazepam against another group who do not ingest diazepam. In Chapter 1, I identified this design as a **between-subjects design**. The simplest between-subjects design is one in which only two groups are created, as in the example experiment. This design requires selecting participants and then assigning those participants to create equivalent groups.

Selecting Participants

Random sampling: A sampling method in which individuals are selected so that each member of the population has an equal chance of being selected for the sample, and the selection of one member is independent of any other member of the population.

Random Sampling

An experiment is conducted on a sample from a population. To generalize the results of the experiment beyond the sample used, it is recommended that **random sampling** be used to select participants. But, because of the difficulty of obtaining true random samples, random sampling is rarely achieved in actual experimentation. Often, convenience sampling is used.

Convenience Sampling

Convenience sampling: Obtaining participants from among people who are accessible or convenient to the researcher.

Convenience sampling obtains participants from among people who are accessible or convenient to the researcher. Convenience sampling clearly is not adequate if I am trying to accurately estimate a population mean, such as estimating the outcome of an election from a poll. But the purpose of an experiment is not to estimate a specific value of a population mean; rather, it is to determine if two or more groups differ because of the effect of an independent variable. If the independent variable has an effect, it should occur with any subjects, whether they are randomly selected or not. Thus, provided the groups created are equivalent, convenience sampling typically does not limit the interpretation or importance of an experiment.

Creating Equivalent Groups

Equivalent groups: Groups of participants that are not expected to differ in any consistent or systematic way prior to receiving the independent variable of the experiment.

Equivalent groups are groups in which the participants are not expected to differ in any systematic or consistent way prior to receiving the independent variable. Equivalent groups do not imply that participants in each group will be exactly alike prior to administration of the independent variable; rather, it implies that an unbiased procedure was used to assign individuals to levels of the independent variable. Any differences that may then exist between the groups prior to manipulation of the independent variable will be only chance differences. As I explain later, a *t* test allows us to assess the probability of occurrence of such chance differences.

Random Assignment

Random assignment: A method of assigning participants to treatment groups so that any individual selected for the experiment has an equal probability of assignment to any of the groups, and the assignment of one person to a group does not affect the assignment of any other individual to that same group.

The typical method of creating equivalent groups is to randomly assign participants to treatment conditions. **Random assignment** means that any individual selected for the experiment has an equal chance of being assigned to any one of the treatment groups. Specifically, random assignment satisfies two criteria:

1. The probability of assignment to any of the groups is equal for every individual.
2. The assignment of one person to a group does not affect the assignment of any other individual to that same group.

Random assignment ensures that the effects of variables such as motivation, gender, anxiety, intelligence, and age are distributed without bias among the groups. After random assignment, the groups should not differ in any systematic way before the treatments are given.

In practice, researchers may place some limits on random assignment. They may want to obtain an equal number of people in each group as in the example experiment, or they may want to have each group composed of an equal number of males and females. These limitations still permit the groups to be equivalent, however.

Manipulating the Independent Variable

The **independent variable** is the variable that is manipulated and administered to participants in the different groups in order to determine its effect on behavior. An independent

Independent variable: A variable manipulated in an experiment to determine its effect on the dependent variable.

Level of an independent variable: One value of the independent variable. To be a variable, an independent variable must take on at least two different levels.

Factor: An alternative name for independent variable.

One-factor between-subjects design: A research design in which one independent variable is manipulated and two or more groups are created.

variable must take on at least two different levels. A **level of an independent variable** is one value of the independent variable. An independent variable often is identified as a **factor**, such as factor A, and the levels identified as A_1 and A_2. I then indicate the number of participants in each group by n_{A1} and n_{A2}. Notice that up to now, because we have had only one set of scores to deal with, I have used N to indicate the number of participants in a group. Now, however, I have two groups and use n_A to indicate the number of participants in a group. The total number of participants in the experiment will then be indicated by N.

Each level of the independent variable is administered to one of the groups that has been formed. In the example experiment the independent variable (i.e., factor A) is the drug condition; and there are two levels: level A_1, control, the placebo drug; and level A_2, experimental, the diazepam. Thus, one group (of size $n_{A1} = 12$) was given the placebo drug control, and the other group (of size $n_{A2} = 12$) was given the diazepam. This design is a **one-factor between-subjects design**, for one independent variable is manipulated, and the comparison needed to decide if the independent variable has an effect is between the two different groups of subjects.

Controlling Extraneous Variables

Extraneous variables: Any variables, other than the independent variable, that can affect the dependent variable in an experiment.

Confounded experiment: An experiment in which an extraneous variable is allowed to vary consistently with the independent variable.

Placebo control: A simulated treatment condition.

To ensure that any difference created between the groups is due only to the independent variable, extraneous variables must be controlled. **Extraneous variables** are any variables, other than the independent variable, that can affect the dependent variable. They may arise from characteristics of people such as intelligence, anxiety level, sensitivity to drugs, or motivation; changes in the physical environment in which the experiment is conducted from one person to another; or variations in the experimental procedure from one person to another. To be sure that any difference found between the control and experimental groups is due only to the independent variable manipulated, extraneous variables must not vary in any systematic or consistent way with the independent variable. In a **confounded experiment** an extraneous variable is allowed to vary consistently with the independent variable. When confounding occurs, the effect of the independent variable cannot be separated from the possible effect of the confounded extraneous variable.

In the example experiment, each of the two groups was treated identically except for the administration of the independent variable. To ensure this identical treatment of subjects, Unrug-Neervoort et al. used a placebo control group. In research using drugs, a **placebo control** is a simulated treatment condition in which participants are given a pill or substance that has no active ingredients. Thus, both the placebo control and the experimental group were given a pill. If only the experimental group had been given a pill, then the experiment would have been confounded. People may behave differently simply because they expect a drug to affect them. Thus, when given a drug, behaviors may change for two reasons, (1) the effect of the drug itself and (2) the expectation that the drug will have an effect. By giving the placebo control group a pill with no active ingredients, Unrug-Neervoort et al. controlled for these expectations, for both groups had the same expectations about the effect of the drug. Similarly, both groups were given identical instructions and their time estimates were measured in the same way. Avoiding confounding is vital to conducting a meaningful experiment.

Measuring the Dependent Variable

Dependent variable: The variable in an experiment that depends on the independent variable.

The **dependent variable** is the variable that I expect to be affected by the independent variable. Thus, after the independent variable is manipulated, the dependent variable must be measured for each person. This measurement results in a **score** for each subject. As we have seen in Chapters 2 to 5, the scores are summarized with a measure of central tendency and variability.

The research hypothesis of Unrug-Neervoort et al. predicted that the ingestion of diazepam alters a person's perception of time. The dependent variable was, thus, the perception of time, and it was measured by having subjects estimate how long they had performed a task. These estimates were summarized by presenting the mean and standard deviation of each group. Because I now have two means and two standard deviations, I will use subscripting to identify them. Thus, $\overline{X}_{A1}$ is the mean of the A_1 group, s_{A1} the estimated population standard deviation of the A_1 group, $\overline{X}_{A2}$ the mean of the A_2 group, and s_{A2} the estimated population standard deviation of the A_2 group. For the example, $\overline{X}_{A1} = 19.8$ sec and $s_{A1} = 7.6$ sec for the placebo control group, and $\overline{X}_{A2} = 13.6$ sec and $s_{A2} = 4.8$ sec for the experimental group. The difference between the means was analyzed for statistical significance with a t test for independent groups. I discuss this test later in the chapter.

Figure 9.1 illustrates the various steps of designing and conducting an experiment using the example experiment. Review the steps using this figure.

TESTING YOUR KNOWLEDGE 9.1

1. Define: between-subjects design, confounding, convenience sampling, dependent variable, equivalent groups, extraneous variable, factor, level of an independent variable, one-factor between-subjects design, placebo control, random assignment, random sampling.
2. What is the purpose of creating equivalent groups?
3. What is the difference between random selection of participants and random assignment of participants to treatment groups?
4. When does confounding occur in an experiment?
5. What difficulty does a confounded experiment pose for reaching a conclusion about the effect of an independent variable?
6. An experimenter is investigating the effects of noise on the performance of a tracking task. The task is to use a mouse to keep a cursor on a computer screen on a randomly moving target dot. The dependent variable is the amount of time a person is able to keep the cursor on the dot. The experimenter hypothesized that participants performing the task when no environmental noise is present will keep the cursor on the target for a greater amount of time than participants who perform the task while listening to a loud noise. Each action by the experimenter described next confounds this experiment by letting an extraneous variable vary systematically with the independent variable of noise condition. For each action, identify the extraneous variable confounding the experiment and then explain why the experiment is confounded.
   a. The experimenter assigns ten 20-year-old males to the no-noise condition and ten 60-year-old males to the noise condition.
   b. The experimenter urges the participants in the no-noise condition to try very hard, but does not encourage the participants in the noise condition.

Select a sample of 24 subjects to participate in the experiment.

The subjects are randomly assigned to form equivalent groups.

Group

A_1

Placebo control group: 12 subjects ← Equivalent groups → Experimental group: 12 subjects

A_2

Extraneous variables are controlled.

The independent variable is manipulated.

Group A_1:
Given a placebo pill

Group A_2:
Given a diazepam pill

The subjects perform the finger-tapping task.

The dependent variable is measured:
All subjects estimate how long they performed a task.

Measures of central tendency and variability calculated

$\overline{X}_{A1} = 19.8$ seconds
$s_{A1} = 7.6$ seconds

Measures of central tendency and variability calculated

$\overline{X}_{A2} = 13.6$ seconds
$s_{A2} = 4.8$ seconds

Between-subjects comparison

The effect of the independent variable is determined by comparing the measures of central tendency using a statistical test.

FIGURE 9.1
Aspects of designing and conducting an experiment using a between-subjects design. The figure illustrates the example experiment to determine the effect of diazepam on time perception.

185

    c. The experimenter assigns males to the no-noise condition and females to the noise condition.

    d. The experimenter assigns physical education majors to the no-noise condition and social science majors to the noise condition.

    e. Subjects in the no-noise condition do the experiment between 9:00 to 10:00 A.M., and subjects in the noise condition do the experiment between 4:00 to 5:00 P.M.

DID THE TREATMENT HAVE AN EFFECT?
THE NEED FOR STATISTICAL TESTING

The Implications of Sampling Error for an Experiment

The steps of conducting an experiment are straightforward, yet a problem arises. Any decision about the effect of an independent variable must be made by comparing the sample means with each other. In principle, if the sample means are equal to each other, then the treatment had no effect. On the other hand, if the sample means are not equal to each other, then it seems there is evidence that the treatment had an effect. But, because of sampling error, this decision is not made quite so simply. In Chapter 7, I defined **sampling error** as the amount a sample mean differs from the population mean (i.e., $\overline{X} - \mu$). If you were to draw two samples of subjects from the same population, measure a behavior, and calculate $\overline{X}$ for each sample, because of sampling error it would be unlikely that the two sample means would be equal to each other or to the population mean. This fact was illustrated by the empirical sampling distributions of the mean presented in Figure 7.2.

    What are the implications of sampling error for reaching a decision about the effect of an independent variable in an experiment? Simply that chance differences between the means of different groups drawn from the same population are expected in any experiment, whether or not the independent variable has an effect on the dependent variable. Even if the independent variable has no effect whatsoever, the mean scores of the two treatment groups will differ from each other simply because of sampling error. How, then, does a behavioral scientist answer the following question:

> How large a difference between the sample means is enough to decide that something other than sampling error is at work in the experiment?

The answer is provided by a statistical hypothesis test of the difference between two means.

An Overview of Statistical Hypothesis Testing for the Difference between Two Means

The approach used in statistical hypothesis testing is to assume that $\overline{X}_{A1}$ represents a sample drawn from a population with μ_{A1}, and $\overline{X}_{A2}$ represents a sample drawn from a population with μ_{A2}. Then, assuming that the two population means will be equal (i.e., that $\mu_{A1} = \mu_{A2}$) if the independent variable has no effect, I can find the expected extent of sampling error between the means. The difference between the sample means observed in the experiment is then compared to the differences expected from sampling error alone. If the observed difference is large enough so that it is unlikely to occur from sampling error alone, then I decide that the difference is due not to sampling error but to the effect of the independent variable.

I have introduced a very important point in statistical testing. To decide whether the means of two groups given different levels of an independent variable differ by more than chance, I must first find the extent of *chance differences* between the means, differences expected from sampling error alone. If the observed difference between the sample means is among the commonly occurring chance differences, then I treat the observed difference as a chance difference. The independent variable did not affect the dependent variable. On the other hand, if the observed difference between the means is sufficiently large to be expected rarely by chance, then I decide that the sample means do not differ by chance alone; rather, if the experiment is well designed and not confounded, then I treat the difference as due to the independent variable.

There are many different statistical tests for use with different types of data and research designs; however, basic concepts of hypothesis testing are applicable to all statistical tests. I next introduce the *t* test for two independent groups. This *t* test allows us to statistically test the difference between two sample means when each mean is obtained from a different group of participants.

THE *t* TEST FOR TWO INDEPENDENT GROUPS

The **t test for two independent groups** is defined as

$$t_{\text{ind}} = \frac{(\overline{X}_{A1} - \overline{X}_{A2}) - (\mu_{A1} - \mu_{A2})}{s_{\overline{X}A1 - \overline{X}A2}}.$$

The numerator of t_{ind} indicates how much an observed difference between two sample means (i.e., $\overline{X}_{A1} - \overline{X}_{A2}$) differs from the difference between the two population means (i.e., $\mu_{A1} - \mu_{A2}$) that the sample means are assumed to represent. In most instances, the population means are hypothesized to be equal; thus, the difference between them (i.e., $\mu_{A1} - \mu_{A2}$) is zero, and the numerator of the t_{ind} simplifies to $\overline{X}_{A1} - \overline{X}_{A2}$. The denominator (i.e., $s_{\overline{X}A1 - \overline{X}A2}$) is a measure of error variation called the *standard error of the difference between means*. The standard error of the difference between means is the standard deviation of a sampling distribution of differences between means. To understand this measure of error variation, we must develop the concept of a sampling distribution of differences between two means.

Sampling Distribution of Differences between Means

Consider an experiment in which two levels (A_1 and A_2) of an independent variable are manipulated. Suppose that the independent variable has no effect on the dependent variable. Because the independent variable has no effect, I can simulate this instance by sampling scores from two populations (populations A_1 and A_2) with equal means (i.e., $\mu_{A1} = \mu_{A2}$). Imagine that I conduct this experiment by drawing two samples of size 5 each (i.e., $n_{A1} = 5$, $n_{A2} = 5$), one sample from each population, A_1 and A_2, respectively. This sample size is arbitrary; any sample size would serve to illustrate the point. I calculate the mean for each sample and then subtract $\overline{X}_{A2}$ from $\overline{X}_{A1}$. Suppose that I replicated the hypothetical experiment 100 times and found 100 $\overline{X}_{A1} - \overline{X}_{A2}$ differences. Plotting a frequency distribution of $\overline{X}_{A1} - \overline{X}_{A2}$ values results in an **empirical sampling distribution of differences between means**. The sampling distribution of 100 such differences between means is portrayed in Figure 9.2. This distribution is an empirical sampling distribution of differences between means because I obtained and calculated the values of 100 differences between $\overline{X}_{A1}$ and $\overline{X}_{A2}$. In practice, however, a researcher would not calculate and construct such an empirical sampling distribution. Rather, he or she uses the theoretical sampling distribution of the difference between means as presented in Figure 9.3. A **theoretical sampling distribution of the difference between means** is the distribution of $\overline{X}_{A1} - \overline{X}_{A2}$ differences when all possible pairs of samples of size n are selected from a population and $\overline{X}_{A1} - \overline{X}_{A2}$ found for each pair of samples. Recall from Chapter 7 that the theoretical sampling distribution of the mean possesses important characteristics concerning its shape, mean, and standard error. A theoretical sampling distribution of the difference between means shares these characteristics.

Sampling distribution of the difference between means: The distribution of $\overline{X}_{A1} - \overline{X}_{A2}$ differences when all possible pairs of samples of size n are selected from a population and $\overline{X}_{A1} - \overline{X}_{A2}$ found for each pair of samples.

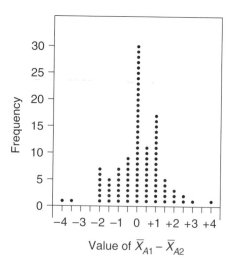

FIGURE 9.2

Empirical sampling distribution of the difference between means ($\overline{X}_{A1} - \overline{X}_{A2}$) for 100 samples drawn from two populations with identical means ($\mu_{A1} = \mu_{A2}$).

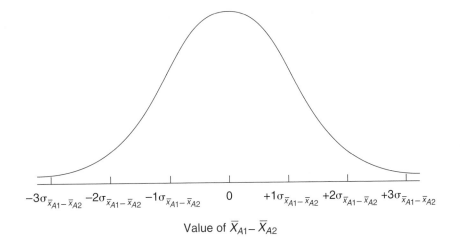

$$-3\sigma_{\bar{x}_{A1}-\bar{x}_{A2}} \quad -2\sigma_{\bar{x}_{A1}-\bar{x}_{A2}} \quad -1\sigma_{\bar{x}_{A1}-\bar{x}_{A2}} \quad 0 \quad +1\sigma_{\bar{x}_{A1}-\bar{x}_{A2}} \quad +2\sigma_{\bar{x}_{A1}-\bar{x}_{A2}} \quad +3\sigma_{\bar{x}_{A1}-\bar{x}_{A2}}$$

Value of $\bar{X}_{A1} - \bar{X}_{A2}$

FIGURE 9.3
Theoretical sampling distribution of the difference between two means when $\mu_{A1} = \mu_{A2}$.

Shape of a Sampling Distribution of Differences between Means

Observe that the empirical sampling distribution in Figure 9.2 is relatively symmetrical and unimodal. Because of the central limit theorem, as sample size increases, a sampling distribution of the difference between means approaches a normal distribution regardless of the shape of the distributions of the underlying populations of scores. This characteristic is present in the theoretical distribution illustrated in Figure 9.3.

Mean of a Sampling Distribution of Differences between Means

The mean of the distribution of an unlimited set of $\bar{X}_{A1} - \bar{X}_{A2}$ differences, $\bar{X}_{\bar{X}_{A1} - \bar{X}_{A2}}$, will be equal to the difference in population means $\mu_{A1} - \mu_{A2}$. Therefore, when $\mu_{A1} = \mu_{A2}$ and, thus, $\mu_{A1} - \mu_{A2} = 0$, the mean of the observed $\bar{X}_{A1} - \bar{X}_{A2}$ values will, in the long run, equal zero, and the observed differences in sample means will be clustered around the difference of zero between the population means. This characteristic is demonstrated in the distribution shown in Figure 9.2. The mean $\bar{X}_{A1} - \bar{X}_{A2}$ difference is $+0.07$. Even with only 100 sets of samples, the mean of the $\bar{X}_{A1} - \bar{X}_{A2}$ difference is very close to the population difference of zero. For the theoretical distribution shown in Figure 9.3, the mean $\bar{X}_{A1} - \bar{X}_{A2}$ difference is zero.

Standard Error of a Sampling Distribution of Differences between Means

Standard error of the difference between means: The standard deviation of a theoretical sampling distribution of $\bar{X}_{A1} - \bar{X}_{A2}$ values.

The standard deviation of a theoretical sampling distribution of $\bar{X}_{A1} - \bar{X}_{A2}$ values is called the **standard error of the difference between means**, or simply the **standard error of the difference**. It is symbolized as $\sigma_{\bar{X}_{A1} - \bar{X}_{A2}}$ as shown in Figure 9.3 and defined as

$$\sigma_{\bar{X}A1 - \bar{X}A2} = \sqrt{\frac{\sigma_{A1}^2}{n_{A1}} + \frac{\sigma_{A2}^2}{n_{A2}}}.$$

Notice that the standard error is found by combining the standard error of the sampling distribution of the mean for each population. Thus, its value will vary with the standard error of the mean for each distribution. In practice, however, σ^2 is not known, and the value of $\sigma_{\overline{X}_{A1} - \overline{X}_{A2}}$ is estimated from the sample variances, s_{A1}^2 and s_{A2}^2. To obtain the estimated standard error of the difference between means, a pooled or combined variance estimate, indicated by s_{pooled}^2, is first obtained from the two sample variances using the following equation:

$$s_{pooled}^2 = \frac{(n_{A1} - 1)s_{A1}^2 + (n_{A2} - 1)s_{A2}^2}{n_{A1} + n_{A2} - 2}.$$

$\rightarrow$ This equation indicates that to obtain s_{pooled}^2 I multiply each sample variance by its degrees of freedom (i.e., $n_A - 1$), add the resulting values, and then divide the sum by the total of the degrees of freedom of the two groups. The next step in obtaining the estimated standard error of the difference between means is to recall from Chapter 7 that the estimated standard error of the mean, $s_{\overline{X}}$, was given by $s/\sqrt{N}$. Notice that this formula could be written as

Estimated standard error of the difference between means: The standard error of the difference between means obtained by using s^2 to estimate σ^2.

$s_{\overline{X}} = \sqrt{(s^2)(1/N)}$. The **estimated standard error of the difference between means**, identified as $s_{\overline{X}_{A1} - \overline{X}_{A2}}$ is found similarly by

$$s_{\overline{X}_{A1} - \overline{X}_{A2}} = \sqrt{s_{pooled}^2 \left[\frac{1}{n_{A1}} + \frac{1}{n_{A2}} \right]}.$$

Substituting the formula for s_{pooled}^2, I obtain

Estimated standard error of the difference between means

$$= s_{\overline{X}_{A1} - \overline{X}_{A2}} = \sqrt{\left[\frac{(n_{A1} - 1)s_{A1}^2 + (n_{A2} - 1)s_{A2}^2}{n_{A1} + n_{A2} - 2} \right] \left[\frac{1}{n_{A1}} + \frac{1}{n_{A2}} \right]}.$$

The estimated standard error of the difference is the denominator of the t statistic. Thus, the value of t indicates how many estimated standard errors away from the mean of the sampling distribution of the difference between $\overline{X}_{A1}$ and $\overline{X}_{A2}$ an observed $\overline{X}_{A1} - \overline{X}_{A2}$ difference lies. For example, suppose that an observed $\overline{X}_{A1} - \overline{X}_{A2} = 3$ and $s_{\overline{X}_{A1} - \overline{X}_{A2}} = 3$. The value of t then equals $3/3$ or 1, indicating that the observed $\overline{X}_{A1} - \overline{X}_{A2}$ difference is one standard error away from the mean of the sampling distribution of $\overline{X}_{A1} - \overline{X}_{A2}$. If an observed $\overline{X}_{A1} - \overline{X}_{A2} = 6$ and $s_{\overline{X}_{A1} - \overline{X}_{A2}} = 3$, then t equals $6/3$ or 2, indicating that the observed $\overline{X}_{A1} - \overline{X}_{A2}$ difference is two standard errors away from the mean of the sampling distribution of the difference between $\overline{X}_{A1}$ and $\overline{X}_{A2}$. Notice that, if an independent variable has no effect and sampling error alone is operating in an experiment, I expect the value of t to be small, whereas if an independent variable has an effect and causes $\overline{X}_{A1}$ and $\overline{X}_{A2}$ to differ, then the value of t should become larger.

TESTING YOUR KNOWLEDGE 9.2

1. Define: empirical sampling distribution of the difference between means, standard error of the difference between means, theoretical sampling distribution of the difference between means.

2. Explain why you cannot simply look at the difference between the mean scores of two groups given different treatments and decide if the difference between the means is due to the independent variable.

3. Calculate $s_{\bar{X}A1 - \bar{X}A2}$ for each of the following sets of scores.

a.

Group	
A_1	A_2
104	99
111	107
120	105
113	110
108	115

b.

Group	
A_1	A_2
77	82
84	86
68	78
71	74
82	69
	79
	80

c.

Group	
A_1	A_2
71	85
82	80
63	73
74	76
68	70
76	67

d.

Group	
A_1	A_2
32	38
37	42
28	29
41	36
35	30
33	37
	36
	39
	34

Statistical Testing with t_{ind}

In using t_{ind} to test for a significant difference between two means, the steps for statistical hypothesis testing outlined in Chapter 8 are followed:

- A null hypothesis, H_0, and an alternative hypothesis, H_1, are formulated.
- The sampling distribution of t assuming H_0 is true is obtained. This distribution is given in Table A.2.
- A significance level is selected.
- A critical value of t, identified as t_{crit}, is found from the sampling distribution of t given in Table A.2.
- Rejection regions are located in the theoretical sampling distribution of the t statistic.
- The t statistic, identified as t_{obs}, is calculated from the sample data.
- A decision to reject or not reject H_0 is made on the basis of whether t_{obs} falls into a rejection region.

Statistical Hypotheses

For a parametric test, a statistical hypothesis is a statement about population parameters. The parameters corresponding to a statistical test of $\overline{X}_{A1}$ and $\overline{X}_{A2}$ are the population means, μ_{A1} and μ_{A2}, respectively. For t_{ind}, the statistical hypotheses are

$$H_0: \mu_{A1} = \mu_{A2} \quad \text{(null hypothesis)},$$

$$H_1: \mu_{A1} \neq \mu_{A2} \quad \text{(alternative hypothesis)}.$$

For two populations of scores, one or the other of these hypotheses must be true.

Null Hypothesis.   The null hypothesis does not specify numerical values for population parameters, which, of course, are unknown. It states only that the population means are equal. Essentially, $H_0: \mu_{A1} = \mu_{A2}$ corresponds to the situation that exists if the independent variable has no effect on the dependent variable. If the independent variable has no effect, then all the participants in the experiment are representative of the same population, and any observed difference between the two sample means is due only to sampling error. Thus, H_0 establishes a situation under which the theoretical sampling distribution of the t statistic may be obtained. By knowing the sampling distribution of t, I can determine how likely or unlikely any value of t_{obs} is if sampling error alone is responsible for the difference between the sample means.

Alternative Hypothesis.   The alternative hypothesis represents the situation if $\overline{X}_{A1}$ and $\overline{X}_{A2}$ differ because the participants in each group are from populations with different means. This situation occurs if the independent variable has an effect. And, if the independent variable has an effect and H_1 is true, then I expect $\overline{X}_{A1}$ and $\overline{X}_{A2}$ to differ by an amount greater than that expected from sampling error alone. Hence, if H_1 is true, the value of t_{obs} should typically be larger than the value of t_{obs} if H_0 is true.

Support for the research hypothesis of the experiment occurs by rejecting H_0 and accepting H_1. Rejecting H_0 and accepting H_1 are decisions that the observed difference in sample means is treated as not due to sampling error but to the effect of the independent variable.

As an example of this reasoning, Unrug-Neervoort et al.'s research hypothesis predicted that ingestion of diazepam would change a person's time perception in comparison to ingestion of a placebo. This hypothesis is supported only if the mean time estimates for the two treatment groups represent populations with different means, the situation stated in the alternative hypothesis. Thus, rejecting H_0 and accepting H_1 provide support for the research hypothesis.

Selecting a Significance Level

The significance level is a probability value that provides the criterion for rejecting a null hypothesis in a statistical test. As you know, behavioral scientists typically choose an alpha of either .05 or .01. By doing so, they have decided that values of t occurring only 5 or fewer times in 100 occasions or only 1 or fewer times in 100 occasions if H_0 is true are statistically rare. I choose $\alpha = .05$ for the example.

Locating Rejection Regions and Finding Critical Values of *t*: Two-Tailed Tests

A rejection region represents values of *t* in the sampling distribution of *t* that have a probability equal to or less than α if H_0 is true. Hence, a rejection region defines values of t_{obs} that meet the criterion for rejecting H_0.

As discussed in Chapter 8, in a **two-tailed** or **nondirectional test**, rejection regions for *t* are located in either tail of the theoretical sampling distribution as illustrated in Figure 9.4. When H_0 is true, most values of *t* will be clustered around 0, for most values of $\overline{X}_{A1} - \overline{X}_{A2}$ will differ only slightly from zero. But some values of *t* will fall in either end of the distribution even when H_0 is true. These relatively large values of *t* occur when the numerator of the *t* (i.e., $\overline{X}_{A1} - \overline{X}_{A2}$) is large compared to the denominator (i.e., the standard error of the difference). These large values of *t* are rare occurrences, however, if H_0: $\mu_{A1} = \mu_{A2}$ is true.

On the other hand, if H_1 is true and $\mu_{A1} \neq \mu_{A2}$, then large positive or negative values of $\overline{X}_{A1} - \overline{X}_{A2}$, and thus of *t*, are expected to occur more frequently. Hence, the rejection regions for the *t* are located in each tail of the theoretical sampling distribution of *t*. The total probability specified by α is divided between both tails of the *t* distribution. If t_{obs} falls into either rejection region, then H_0 is rejected and H_1 accepted. As with the one-sample *t* test, the two-tailed critical values given in Table A.2 define the exact location of the rejection regions. To use this table, we must know the degrees of freedom for t_{obs}.

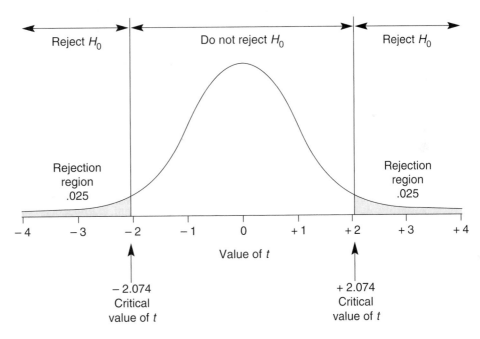

FIGURE 9.4
Illustration of a two-tailed rejection region for the *t* distribution for 22 *df* and α = .05.

Degrees of Freedom for t_{ind}.   Degrees of freedom represent the number of scores that are free to vary when calculating a statistic. In Chapter 8, I demonstrated that s^2 has $N - 1$ df, where N represents the number of scores on which the variance is calculated. For the t_{ind} statistic, $s_{\overline{X}A1 - \overline{X}A2}$ is found by calculating the variances from each group, s_{A1}^2 and s_{A2}^2. Accordingly, the df for t_{ind} are based on the combined df of s_{A1}^2 and s_{A2}^2. When n_{A1} and n_{A2} represent the number of scores in groups A_1 and A_2, respectively, s_{A1}^2 has $n_{A1} - 1$ df and s_{A2}^2 has $n_{A2} - 1$ df. Hence, the combined df for t_{ind} are $(n_{A1} - 1)$ plus $(n_{A2} - 1)$. If N is used to represent the total number of scores in the two groups (i.e., $N = n_{A1} + n_{A2}$), then **the df for t_{ind} are $N - 2$**. Accordingly, for an experiment with 12 scores in each group (i.e., $n_{A1} = 12$, $n_{A2} = 12$, thus $N = 24$), the df for t_{ind} are $24 - 2 = 22$. From Table A.2, t_{crit} for 22 df and $\alpha = .05$ is 2.074. This value of t_{crit} is shown in Figure 9.4, locating the rejection region in each tail of the t distribution.

Locating a Rejection Region: One-Tailed Tests

When a research hypothesis predicts a directional relationship between the means (e.g., that $\overline{X}_{A1}$ should be greater than $\overline{X}_{A2}$) and there is no interest in an outcome opposite the one predicted (e.g., if $\overline{X}_{A1}$ less than $\overline{X}_{A2}$ occurs), then researchers may use a one-tailed or directional test. In a **one-tailed test**, a rejection region including the total value of α is located in the tail of the t distribution corresponding to the direction of the outcome predicted by the research hypothesis. Values of t_{crit} for a one-tailed test at the .01 and .05 significance levels are also presented in Table A.2. For 22 df, the one-tailed t_{crit} at the .05 significance level is 1.717. A one-tailed rejection region with $t_{crit} = +1.717$ in the right tail of a t distribution is illustrated in Figure 9.5. The null and alternative hypotheses for the use of this rejection region are

$$H_0: \mu_{A1} \leq \mu_{A2},$$
$$H_1: \mu_{A1} > \mu_{A2}.$$

There is controversy about the use of one-tailed tests, however. The sampling distribution of t presented in Table A.2 is developed assuming $H_0: \mu_{A1} = \mu_{A2}$ is true. This sampling distribution is symmetric about 0, and positive and negative differences from 0 are expected to occur equally. For a one-tailed test, however, the statistical hypotheses are either

$$H_0: \mu_{A1} \leq \mu_{A2} \text{ and } H_1: \mu_{A1} > \mu_{A2}$$

or

$$H_0: \mu_{A1} \geq \mu_{A2} \text{ and } H_1: \mu_{A1} < \mu_{A2}.$$

But I cannot develop a sampling distribution for t under either of these null hypotheses because there are an infinite number of ways $H_0: \mu_{A1} \leq \mu_{A2}$ or $H_0: \mu_{A1} \geq \mu_{A2}$ could be true. Thus, the sampling distribution for $H_0: \mu_{A1} = \mu_{A2}$ is used to determine critical values of t for one-tailed as well as two-tailed tests. For this and other reasons, some behavioral scien-

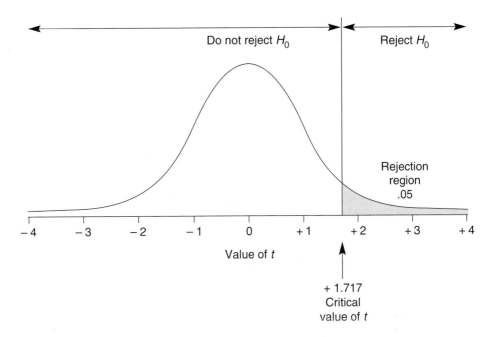

FIGURE 9.5
Illustration of a one-tailed rejection region for the t distribution for 22 df and $\alpha = .05$.

tists recommend against using one-tailed t tests (Gaito, 1977). Consequently, two-tailed tests are used for all examples in this chapter.

Calculating t_{ind}

The definitional formula for t_{ind} is

$$t_{ind} = \frac{(\overline{X}_{A1} - \overline{X}_{A2}) - (\mu_{A1} - \mu_{A2})}{s_{\overline{X}A1 - \overline{X}A2}}.$$

The null hypothesis for t_{ind}, H_0: $\mu_{A1} = \mu_{A2}$, is equivalent to H_0: $\mu_{A1} - \mu_{A2} = 0$. Thus, the difference of $\mu_{A1} - \mu_{A2}$ is hypothesized to be zero, and $\mu_{A1} - \mu_{A2}$ drops from the formula, so

$$t_{ind} = \frac{\overline{X}_{A1} - \overline{X}_{A2}}{s_{\overline{X}A1 - \overline{X}A2}},$$

where $s_{\overline{X}A1 - \overline{X}A2}$ is given by

$$s_{\overline{X}A1 - \overline{X}A2} = \sqrt{\left[\frac{(n_{A1} - 1)s_{A1}^2 + (n_{A2} - 1)s_{A2}^2}{n_{A1} + n_{A2} - 2}\right]\left[\frac{1}{n_{A1}} + \frac{1}{n_{A2}}\right]}.$$

Consequently, for computational purposes,

$$t_{ind} = \frac{\overline{X}_{A1} - \overline{X}_{A2}}{\sqrt{\left[\frac{(n_{A1} - 1)s_{A1}^2 + (n_{A2} - 1)s_{A2}^2}{n_{A1} + n_{A2} - 2}\right]\left[\frac{1}{n_{A1}} + \frac{1}{n_{A2}}\right]}}.$$

To use this formula, I need know only the mean ($\overline{X}_A$), number of subjects (n_A), and estimated population variance (s_A^2) for each group. Use of this formula is illustrated in Example Problem 9.1.

Decisions about the Statistical Hypotheses

Statistically Significant Difference. If t_{obs} falls into a rejection region, then H_0: $\mu_{A1} = \mu_{A2}$ is rejected. Rejection of H_0 implies acceptance of H_1: $\mu_{A1} \neq \mu_{A2}$. The difference between the sample means is *statistically significant*. I conclude that the two sample means involved in t_{obs} are not estimates of the same population mean, and the difference between them is due to something other than sampling error alone. If the experiment has been carefully designed and conducted, then the difference between the sample means is due to the independent variable manipulated. These decisions and conclusions are summarized in the left column of Table 9.1.

TABLE 9.1
Summary of decisions and conclusions in statistical hypothesis testing using the *t* test for two independent groups. A .05 significance level is used.

If t_{obs} falls into a rejection region for $\alpha = .05$, then:	If t_{obs} does not fall into a rejection region for $\alpha = .05$, then:
Probability of t_{obs} is less than or equal to .05, or $p \leq .05$.	Probability of t_{obs} is greater than .05, or $p > .05$.
H_0 is rejected.	H_0 is not rejected.
H_1 is accepted. Each sample mean is treated as being from a different population.	H_1 is not accepted.
The difference between the two sample means is statistically significant at the .05 level.	The difference between the two sample means is nonsignificant at the .05 level.
It is decided that something other than sampling error alone is responsible for the difference between the sample means. In a carefully done experiment the difference is attributed to the independent variable.	It is decided that sampling error alone is the most plausible explanation of the difference between the sample means. There is no evidence that the independent variable had an effect.

Nonsignificant Difference.   If t_{obs} does not fall into a rejection region, then I fail to reject H_0. Failing to reject H_0 implies not accepting H_1. The difference between the sample means is *nonsignificant*. The two sample means are considered to be from populations with identical means, and they differ only because of sampling error. The implication for the experiment is that the independent variable had no effect, and the difference between the sample means is a chance occurrence. These decisions and conclusions are summarized in the right column of Table 9.1.

Assumptions for Use of t_{ind}

The use of t_{ind} rests on the following assumptions:

1. The scores in each sample are drawn randomly from a population of scores and each score is independent of every other score.
2. The scores in the populations sampled are normally distributed.
3. The variances of scores in the populations are equal; that is, $\sigma_{A1}^2 = \sigma_{A2}^2$.

In Chapter 8, I indicated that the assumptions of the t test are often not fully met in actual research; they are violated. Yet researchers may proceed to use the t test on the data. What are the consequences of such violations?

The requirement of the first assumption is that each score in a group be independent of every other score in the group. That is, knowing one person's score in a group will give you no information about any other person's score in the group. This assumption requires that each individual be given only one level of the independent variable and contribute only one score in the experiment. This requirement of independence of scores cannot be violated for t_{ind}. If a person is given both levels of the independent variable and contributes two scores for analysis, then the t test for related scores, discussed later in this chapter, must be used.

The first assumption also indicates that participants are to be selected randomly, but, in actuality, participants in experiments typically are obtained by convenience sampling rather than random sampling. The major impact of convenience sampling is to limit the extent to which the results can be generalized to a population.

Violations of the second (the normal distribution of scores) and the third (the equality of variances, often called the *homogeneity of variances*) assumptions can change the actual probability of making a Type I error from that set by the value of α. But the t test is thought to be *robust* against violations of these assumptions. **Robustness** means that violation of the assumptions has little effect on the probability of making a Type I error. Research by Bradley (1980, 1984) has challenged this robustness notion, however. Bradley argues that there is no one set of conditions under which these assumptions may be violated and robustness of the t test assured. But violations of the normality and equality of variances assumptions are more likely to have minimal effects on the probability of making a Type I error when the following conditions are met:

Robustness: A term used to indicate that violating the assumptions of a statistical test has little effect on the probability of a Type I error.

- The number of subjects in each group is the same.
- The two distributions of scores have about the same shape, and the distributions are neither very peaked nor very flat.
- The significance level is set at .05 rather than .01.

Example Problem 9.1

Using t_{ind} to Find the Effect of Diazepam on Time Estimates

Problem: I use the problem faced by Unrug-Neervoort et al. of the effect of diazepam on time estimates to illustrate calculating t_{ind} when $\overline{X}$ and s are known. Unrug-Neervoort et al. had two treatment groups of 12 people each. The mean time estimate for the placebo control group (A_1) was 19.8 sec, with $s_{A1} = 7.6$ sec. For the experimental group (A_2), the mean time estimate was 13.6 sec, with $s_{A2} = 4.8$ sec. Do these mean time estimates differ significantly at the .05 level? Use a two-tailed test.

Statistic to Be Used

$$t_{ind} = \frac{\overline{X}_{A1} - \overline{X}_{A2}}{\sqrt{\left[\frac{(n_{A1} - 1)s_{A1}^2 + (n_{A2} - 1)s_{A2}^2}{n_{A1} + n_{A2} - 2}\right]\left[\frac{1}{n_{A1}} + \frac{1}{n_{A2}}\right]}}$$

Assumptions
1. The participants were sampled randomly and each participant is independent of every other participant.
2. Time estimate scores are normally distributed in the population.
3. The variances for the time estimate scores are equal in the populations for the two treatment groups.

Statistical Hypotheses: $H_0: \mu_{A1} = \mu_{A2}$,
                                          $H_1: \mu_{A1} \neq \mu_{A2}$.

Significance Level: $\alpha = .05$.

***df* for *t*:** $(n_{A1} - 1) + (n_{A2} - 1) = (12 - 1) + (12 - 1) = 22$, *or* $N - 2 = 24 - 2 = 22$.

Critical Value of *t*: $t_{crit} = 2.074$ from Table A.2.

Rejection Regions: Values of t_{obs} equal to or less than -2.074 or equal to or greater than $+2.074$.

Calculation

$$t_{obs} = \frac{19.8 - 13.6}{\sqrt{\left[\frac{(12 - 1)(7.6)^2 + (12 - 1)(4.8)^2}{12 + 12 - 2}\right]\left[\frac{1}{12} + \frac{1}{12}\right]}}.$$

$$= \frac{+6.2}{\sqrt{\left[\frac{888.80}{22}\right]\left[\frac{2}{12}\right]}} = \frac{+6.2}{2.597} = +2.387.$$

Decision: t_{obs} falls into the rejection region of equal to or greater than $t_{crit} = +2.074$. I reject H_0 and accept H_1.

Conclusion: The two sample means of 19.8 sec and 13.6 sec differ significantly at the .05 level. Because the treatment groups were equivalent before the treatment was administered, the difference between the mean time estimates is treated as due to the effect of the independent variable. The mean time estimates of people given diazepam are shorter than those given a placebo control.

Example Problem 9.2

Using t_{ind} with Raw Scores

Problem: Recent years have seen the call for improvement of education to provide the skills needed for the future. One response to this call has been to use computers to simulate laboratory experiments in science education. Geban, Askar, and Özkan (1992) investigated whether using such computer-simulated experiments in chemistry led to higher chemistry achievement in comparison to a conventional approach in which students performed actual laboratory experiments. They found significantly greater achievement for the computer-simulated teaching method. Suppose that you were interested in replicating this research using 28 high school chemistry students. You randomly assigned the students to one of two equal-sized groups, the conventional teaching group (A_1) and the computer-simulated group (A_2). At the end of the course you measured knowledge of chemistry with an achievement test on which scores could range from 0 to 100. The following scores were obtained.

Teaching Condition	
Conventional (A_1)	**Computer Simulated (A_2)**
74	84
76	75
81	94
90	88
67	69
72	90
84	86
87	97
92	81
70	91
78	83
82	92
75	82
85	93

Do these achievement scores differ significantly at the .05 level? Use a two-tailed test.

Statistic to Be Used: t_{ind}.

Assumptions

1. The students were sampled randomly and each student is independent of every other student.
2. Chemistry achievement scores are normally distributed in the population.
3. The variances for the chemistry achievement scores are equal in the populations for the two treatment groups.

Statistical Hypotheses:

$$H_0: \mu_{A1} = \mu_{A2},$$
$$H_1: \mu_{A1} \neq \mu_{A2}.$$

Significance Level: $\alpha = .05$.

df for t: $(n_{A1} - 1) + (n_{A2} - 1) = (14 - 1) + (14 - 1) = 26$, *or* $N - 2 = 28 - 2 = 26$.

Critical Value of t: $t_{crit} = 2.056$ from Table A.2.

Rejection Regions: Values of t_{obs} equal to or less than -2.056 or equal to or greater than $+2.056$.

Calculation: The first step in the calculation is to find the mean and standard deviation for each group. For the conventional teaching group, $\overline{X}_{A1} = 79.50$ and $s_{A1} = 7.59$. For the computer-simulated group, $\overline{X}_{A2} = 86.07$ and $s_{A2} = 7.74$. Substituting these values into the formula for t_{obs}, I obtain

$$t_{obs} = \frac{79.50 - 86.07}{\sqrt{\left[\frac{(14-1)(7.59)^2 + (14-1)(7.74)^2}{14 + 14 - 2}\right]\left[\frac{1}{14} + \frac{1}{14}\right]}}$$

$$= \frac{-6.57}{\sqrt{\left[\frac{1527.708}{26}\right]\left[\frac{2}{14}\right]}} = \frac{-6.57}{2.899} = -2.266.$$

Decision: t_{obs} falls into the rejection region of equal to or less than $t_{crit} = -2.056$. I reject H_0 and accept H_1.

Conclusion: The two sample means of 79.50 and 86.07 differ significantly at the .05 level. The observed difference between the means is believed to be due to the effect of the teaching condition. The computer-simulated teaching method leads to higher chemistry achievement scores than does the conventional teaching method.

TESTING YOUR KNOWLEDGE 9.3

1. Define: directional test, nondirectional test, one-tailed rejection region, rejection region, t_{crit}, t_{ind}, t_{obs}, two-tailed rejection region.

2. Identify the steps in statistical testing with t_{ind}.
3. Write the statistical hypotheses for t_{ind} for a two-tailed test.
4. To what situation in an experiment does H_0 correspond?
5. To what situation in an experiment does H_1 correspond?
6. Assume that you have two groups of size n_{A1} and n_{A2}, respectively. Complete the following exercise for each set of samples given in the table by (a) finding the df for the t test on the two samples, (b) finding t_{crit} for a two-tailed test for $\alpha = .05$ (if the exact df are not tabled, then use the next lower tabled value), (c) indicating whether the t_{obs} falls into a rejection region, and (d) indicating your decisions with respect to the statistical hypotheses.

Sample Set	n_{A1}	n_{A2}	t_{obs}
1	10	10	2.341
2	8	12	1.763
3	15	15	2.120
4	16	14	3.479
5	35	35	2.912
6	19	16	2.007
7	65	64	2.002
8	75	75	2.193

7. Identify the assumptions underlying the use of t_{ind}.
8. **a.** The t test is said to be robust. What is meant by this term?
   b. Under what conditions is the t test likely to be robust?
9. For problems 1 and 2, answer the following questions. Use a two-tailed test and a .05 significance level for each problem.
   a. State the statistical hypotheses for t_{ind} for these scores.
   b. What is the value of t_{obs}?
   c. What are the df for this t?
   d. What is the value of t_{crit}?
   e. What are the rejection regions for t_{obs}?
   f. Does t_{obs} fall into a rejection region?
   g. What decisions do you make about the statistical hypotheses? Do you reject or fail to reject H_0? Accept or not accept H_1?
   h. Do you conclude that the sample means are from the same or different populations?
   i. Is the difference between the means statistically significant?
   j. Did the groups differ significantly in their estimates of the time they spent waiting? If so, what is the direction of the difference?

Problem 1: Does time seem to pass more slowly when you are expecting a delay before an event occurs? Suppose that to answer this question you randomly assigned a total of 36 subjects to either a control group or an experimental group with $n_{A1} = n_{A2}$. In both groups you told the subjects that the experiment would take only a few minutes and that they were going to fill out a questionnaire on anxiety. Subjects in the control group were told that your assistant would arrive with the questionnaires in a few minutes. Subjects in the experimental group were told that the assistant was delayed and that there would be a short delay. For both groups, however, the assistant arrived in exactly 5 minutes. When your assistant arrived, the subjects were asked to estimate how long they had waited. Suppose that you obtained the following mean time estimates and standard deviations (in minutes) for your groups:

	Group	
	Control	**Experimental**
$\overline{X}$	6.90	8.90
s	1.57	1.71

Problem 2: Suppose that you are interested in answering the same question as in problem 1: Does time seem to pass more slowly when you are expecting a delay before an event occurs? Again, you randomly assign participants to one of two groups. Rather than an equal number in each group, however, you assign 13 participants to the control group and 17 to the experimental group. In all other respects the experiment is identical to that described in problem 1. Suppose that you obtained the following mean estimates and standard deviations (in minutes) for your groups:

	Group	
	Control	**Experimental**
$\overline{X}$	6.60	7.80
s	1.80	1.92

POWER AND t_{ind}

The **power of a statistical test** was defined in Chapter 8 as the probability of rejecting H_0 when H_0 is false. Because rejecting H_0 means that the experimenter accepts H_1 and decides that the independent variable had an effect in his or her experiment, the *power of a statistical test* is the probability that an effect of an independent variable will be detected in an experiment when such an effect is present. An experimenter always wants to maximize the power of a statistical test so that he or she can detect an effect of an independent variable if it is present.

The null hypothesis is rejected when t_{obs} falls into a rejection region, and the larger t_{obs} is, the more likely it will fall into a rejection region. There are several actions we can take to increase the value of t_{obs} and, thus, the power of t_{ind}. We can understand these actions by examining the formula for t_{ind},

$$t_{ind} = \frac{\overline{X}_{A1} - \overline{X}_{A2}}{s_{\overline{X}A1 - \overline{X}A2}}.$$

With this formula there are two ways to increase the value of t_{obs}: (1) increase the difference between $\overline{X}_{A1}$ and $\overline{X}_{A2}$ and (2) decrease the value of $s_{\overline{X}A1 - \overline{X}A2}$.

The first approach is to maximize the effect of the independent variable. That is, I want to manipulate the independent variable in such a way that it makes $\overline{X}_{A1}$ and $\overline{X}_{A2}$ differ as much as possible. For this reason, behavioral scientists often use widely differing levels of the independent variable.

To decrease the value of $s_{\overline{X}_{A1} - \overline{X}_{A2}}$, I may do two things: increase the sample size and decrease the amount of variability in the scores of the samples. To illustrate the relationship of $s_{\overline{X}_{A1} - \overline{X}_{A2}}$ to sample size, suppose that both s_{A1}^2 and $s_{A2}^2 = 36$. Consider also that these values of s^2 came from one of three sample sizes: $n_{A1} = n_{A2} = 3$, $n_{A1} = n_{A2} = 6$, or $n_{A1} = n_{A2} = 9$. Then, substituting the differing values of n_A into the formula for $s_{\overline{X}_{A1} - \overline{X}_{A2}}$:

- For $n_{A1} = n_{A2} = 3$, $s_{\overline{X}_{A1} - \overline{X}_{A2}} = 4.9$.
- For $n_{A1} = n_{A2} = 6$, $s_{\overline{X}_{A1} - \overline{X}_{A2}} = 3.5$.
- For $n_{A1} = n_{A2} = 9$, $s_{\overline{X}_{A1} - \overline{X}_{A2}} = 2.8$.

Here we see that, as the sample size increases, the standard error of the difference decreases. Thus, for a given difference between $\overline{X}_{A1}$ and $\overline{X}_{A2}$, the value of t_{obs} increases as sample size becomes larger and $s_{\overline{X}_{A1} - \overline{X}_{A2}}$ decreases in size. And, as t_{obs} increases, it becomes more likely that t_{obs} will fall into a rejection region and H_0 will be rejected and H_1 accepted.

In general, any treatment effect, no matter how small, may be detected if the sample size is large enough. Thus, a researcher can minimize the probability of making a Type II error by maximizing sample size. But reality must intrude here, for increasing the size of a sample is often costly and time consuming. Moreover, if it takes a sample of 1000 people in each group to detect the effect of an independent variable, then I may expect this independent variable to have a very minimal effect on behavior.

A second step in decreasing $s_{\overline{X}_{A1} - \overline{X}_{A2}}$ is to reduce the variability among the scores in each group. If the scores vary less within the groups, then s_A^2 will decrease for each group and consequently $s_{\overline{X}_{A1} - \overline{X}_{A2}}$ will also decrease. This decrease in $s_{\overline{X}_{A1} - \overline{X}_{A2}}$ will lead to an increase in t_{obs} and, thus, an increase in the probability that t_{obs} will fall into a rejection region. Because of this relationship, experimenters typically carefully control the conditions under which research is conducted to minimize the variability of the scores within each group in an experiment.

MEASURING THE STRENGTH OF A TREATMENT EFFECT

Strength of effect: The strength of an independent variable as measured by one of the strength of effect statistics.

A statistically significant difference indicates that an independent variable has an effect on the dependent variable of the experiment, but it does not indicate the size or strength of that effect. A number of statistics have been developed for measuring the strength of the effect of the independent variable after an experiment has been completed. These statistics are often referred to as **strength of effect measures** or **strength of association measures**. One measure is **eta squared**, represented by η^2, where η is the lowercase Greek letter *eta*. Eta squared is calculated from the t_{obs} value and degrees of freedom for t by

$$\eta^2 = \frac{t_{obs}^2}{t_{obs}^2 + df}.$$

To illustrate, in Example Problem 9.2, t_{obs} for the difference between the conventional and computer-simulated teaching conditions was -2.266, with 26 df. Eta squared for this t_{obs} equals

$$\eta^2 = \frac{t_{obs}^2}{t_{obs}^2 + df} = \frac{(-2.266)^2}{(-2.266)^2 + 26} = \frac{5.1348}{31.1348} = .16 \qquad \text{rounded to two decimal places.}$$

Eta squared is a measure of how much knowing the level of an independent variable that a participant received reduces the error in predicting the participant's score in the sample tested. To illustrate, suppose in Example Problem 9.2 that you were asked to predict a person's score on the achievement test, but you did not know which teaching condition the person was given. In this instance your best prediction would be to use the grand mean ($\overline{X}_G$) of all 28 scores, $\overline{X}_G = 82.79$, as the predicted score. Of course, this prediction will be in error, and the average error will be the standard deviation of the 28 scores around the grand mean. Here I use S rather than s because η^2 is a statistic describing only the sample; it is not an estimate of a population value. The value of S for the 28 scores around the grand mean is 8.09. This value squared [i.e., $(8.09)^2$] equals 65.448 and is the total variance of the sample of 28 scores.

Now suppose that you were asked to predict a person's score, but you were told the teaching condition the subject received. In this instance the best prediction would be the mean of the scores of the teaching condition that the person received, either 79.50 or 86.07. Again your prediction would be in error, but now the average error would be the standard deviation of the group that the participant was in. Again I use S; thus, $S_{A1} = 7.32$ and $S_{A2} = 7.46$. Squaring each S provides the sample variance for each group: $S_{A1}^2 = 53.582$ and $S_{A2}^2 = 55.652$. The mean of these two variances is 54.617 [i.e., $(53.582 + 55.652)/2 = 109.234/2 = 54.617)$]. This value is the average variance of the error when using a teaching condition mean to predict a score. The difference between the variance found using the grand mean (i.e., 65.448) and the average variance using the treatment condition means as predicted scores (i.e., 54.617) is $65.448 - 54.617 = 10.831$. The reduction in variance from the total variance when treatment condition means are used to predict a score is 10.831. Dividing this reduction by the total variance yields $10.831/65.448 = .16$. In other words, when I know the level of an independent variable that a person received and I use the treatment group mean rather than the grand mean to predict a score, the variance of the prediction is reduced by .16, or 16 percent. This value is η^2. Thus, η^2 indicates the proportion of the reduction of the total variance in the dependent variable when I know the level of the independent variable that a participant received. For this reason, η^2 often is interpreted as indicating the proportion of the variance of the dependent variable that can be "accounted for" by the independent variable.

The value of η^2 may range between .00 to 1.00. An η^2 of .00 indicates that knowing the level of an independent variable that a person received does not reduce the error variance of the dependent variable. A prediction of the grand mean is as good a prediction of the person's score as a prediction of the treatment group mean. There is no relation between the level of the independent variable and the score on the dependent variable. On the other hand, η^2 of 1.00 indicates that knowing the level of the independent variable that a person received allows perfect prediction of the participant's score. There will be no error in using the treatment group mean to predict a person's score.

In practice, an η^2 of about .10 to .15 often is treated as revealing a strong treatment effect. This interpretation finds support in published behavioral science research. For example, Haase, Waechter, and Solomon (1982) calculated η^2 on 11,044 tests of statistical significance reported in issues of the *Journal of Counseling Psychology* published between 1970 to 1979. They found a median η^2 value of 0.083. The interquartile range for the η^2 values was 0.043 to 0.268. This result gives some idea of the typical strength of association found in behavioral science research and provides a basis for evaluating a value of η^2. The *Publication Manual of the American Psychological Association* (1994) suggests that measures of the strength of the effect of an independent variable, such as eta squared, be included in a journal report of a statistical test. A sample report is illustrated in Chapter 10.

Example Problem 9.3

Calculating η^2 in an Experiment

Problem: In Example Problem 9.1, t_{obs} for the difference in time estimates between the placebo control and the experimental groups was $+2.387$, with 22 *df*. What is the strength of effect for the independent variable of drug condition?

Solution: The strength of effect is given by η^2, where

$$\eta^2 = \frac{t_{obs}^2}{t_{obs}^2 + df}.$$

Substituting numerical values for t_{obs} and *df*,

$$\eta^2 = \frac{(2.387)^2}{(2.387)^2 + 22} = \frac{5.6978}{5.6978 + 22} = .21 \qquad \text{rounded to two decimal places.}$$

Conclusion: The value of η^2 indicates that knowing the drug condition a person received results in a 21 percent reduction in the total variance of the experiment.

USING THE *t* STATISTIC TO CONSTRUCT CONFIDENCE INTERVALS FOR THE DIFFERENCE BETWEEN TWO INDEPENDENT POPULATION MEANS

A confidence interval for a population mean was defined as an interval in which I have a certain degree of confidence that the interval contains the population mean. In this chapter we have been interested in the difference between two population means. Here I want a confidence interval for the difference between two independent population means, $\mu_{A1} - \mu_{A2}$.

The approach is similar to that used in Chapter 8, except that $\overline{X}_{A1} - \overline{X}_{A2}$ is used in place of $\overline{X}$ and $s_{\overline{X}A1 - \overline{X}A2}$ is used in place of $s_{\overline{X}}$. Accordingly, the **95 percent confidence interval for the difference between two independent population means** is given by the interval from

$$(\overline{X}_{A1} - \overline{X}_{A2}) - t_{.05}(s_{\overline{X}A1 - \overline{X}A2}) \text{ to } (\overline{X}_{A1} - \overline{X}_{A2}) + t_{.05}(s_{\overline{X}A1 - \overline{X}A2}),$$

where $\overline{X}_{A1} - \overline{X}_{A2}$ = difference between the two observed sample means.
$s_{\overline{X}A1 - \overline{X}A2}$ = estimated standard error of the difference between means.
$t_{.05}$ = two-tailed value of t_{crit} at the .05 significance level with $N - 2$ degrees of freedom.

The interval given by this formula has a .95 probability of including the value of $\mu_{A1} - \mu_{A2}$.
Similarly, a **99 percent confidence interval for the difference between two independent population means** is given by the interval from

$$(\overline{X}_{A1} - \overline{X}_{A2}) - t_{.01}(s_{\overline{X}A1 - \overline{X}A2}) \text{ to } (\overline{X}_{A1} - \overline{X}_{A2}) + t_{.01}(s_{\overline{X}A1 - \overline{X}A2}),$$

where $t_{.01}$ is the two-tailed value of t_{crit} at the .01 significance level with $N - 2$ degrees of freedom.

To illustrate the use of these formulas, I find the 95 percent confidence interval for Example Problem 9.1 comparing the time estimates of a placebo control group to a diazepam group. Here $\overline{X}_{A1} = 19.8$ seconds, $\overline{X}_{A2} = 13.6$ sec, and $s_{\overline{X}A1 - \overline{X}A2} = 2.597$ sec. There are 22 degrees of freedom for this example (see Example Problem 9.1); thus, the two-tailed value of t_{crit} at the .05 level is 2.074. The 95 percent confidence interval for $\mu_{A1} - \mu_{A2}$ is

$$(19.8 - 13.6) - (2.074)(2.597) \text{ to } (19.8 - 13.6) + (2.074)(2.597) \text{ sec,}$$

or, carrying out the mathematical operations indicated,

$$6.2 - 5.39 \text{ to } 6.2 + 5.39 \text{ sec,}$$

which equals

$$0.8 \text{ sec to } 11.6 \text{ sec} \qquad \text{rounded to one decimal place.}$$

The interval of 0.8 to 11.6 sec has a .95 probability of including the value of $\mu_{A1} - \mu_{A2}$. I can be 95 percent confident that the difference between the population means of time estimates for a placebo control and a diazepam group is between 0.8 to 11.6 sec.

WHAT DOES A t TEST ACTUALLY TEST?

The t test provides information needed for deciding whether a research hypothesis is or is not supported by the data of the experiment. It is important to recognize, however, that a research hypothesis is not tested directly by the t test. The t test is simply a procedure for testing the statistical hypothesis, H_0: $\mu_{A1} = \mu_{A2}$. Regardless of the independent and dependent variables stated in the research hypothesis, the null and alternative hypotheses for a two-tailed t test are always H_0: $\mu_{A1} = \mu_{A2}$ and H_1: $\mu_{A1} \neq \mu_{A2}$, respectively. A research hypothesis for an experiment, however, is a statement predicting a relationship between an independent variable and a dependent variable. As an example, the statement "it is expected that the time estimates made by subjects given diazepam will be shorter than the estimates made by a placebo control group" is a research hypothesis.

A statistically significant t_{obs} with a nondirectional alternative hypothesis (i.e., H_1: $\mu_{A1} \neq \mu_{A2}$) does not necessarily provide support for the research hypothesis. As an illustration, support for the stated research hypothesis occurs if $\overline{X}_{A1}$, the mean time estimate for the placebo control group, is significantly longer than $\overline{X}_{A2}$, the mean time estimate for the experimental group. But an $\overline{X}_{A1}$ significantly less than $\overline{X}_{A2}$ does not agree with this research hypothesis. Consequently, after obtaining a statistically significant t_{obs}, we must always examine the direction of the difference between the means to find if it agrees or disagrees with the research hypothesis.

STATISTICAL AND SCIENTIFIC SIGNIFICANCE REVISITED

In Chapter 8, I pointed out that in statistical hypothesis testing the word *significant* means only that a null hypothesis has been rejected. But a statistically significant difference between the means in an experiment is not necessarily scientifically important. The scientific importance of an experiment is determined before the data are subjected to statistical analysis. In a well-conceived and well-designed experiment, either a statistically significant or nonsignificant difference may be important scientifically. Indeed, if a particular relationship is predicted between the independent variable and the dependent variable, a failure to find that relationship empirically may have scientific importance. In a poorly designed experiment, however, in which the independent variable is confounded with an extraneous variable, even a statistically significant difference between two sample means cannot be interpreted meaningfully.

THE CONTROVERSY OVER STATISTICAL HYPOTHESIS TESTING

In Chapter 1, I indicated that statistical analysis of data would not be needed if there were no variability among members of a population. But such variability is a fact of life and, thus, provides the need for statistical analysis of data. Statistical hypothesis testing was developed to help scientists make decisions in the context of the variability always found in data. Although statistical hypothesis testing may seem conceptually complex to you, its application to data soon becomes routine and is easily accomplished. It would seem to be a process totally devoid of controversy, but such is not the case. On the contrary, there has been a lively discussion with both critics and defenders of its use (e.g., Abelson, 1997;

Cohen, 1994; Cortina and Dunlap, 1997; Frick, 1996; Hagen, 1997; Harris, 1997; Hunter, 1997; Wainer, 1999). There are varied criticisms of statistical hypothesis testing, some of which are more complex than can be given justice to in an introductory-level text. Essentially, however, many of the critiques focus about the following points:

- Statistical hypothesis testing tests a null hypothesis stating that H_0: $\mu_{A1} = \mu_{A2}$. But it is very unlikely that such a null hypothesis will ever be exactly true.
- Statistical hypothesis testing imposes a dichotomous decision of either rejecting or failing to reject H_0 based on an arbitrary set value of α, usually .05.
- The probability of a Type II error cannot be precisely identified for any study. Thus, when an experimenter fails to reject H_0, she or he may be making a Type II error. Although behavioral scientists have generally thought Type II errors to be less important than Type I errors, this may not necessarily be true of all research problems.
- Statistical hypothesis testing encourages researchers to not carefully examine their data and to use computerized statistical tests they may not fully understand.

There are no simple or noncontroversial responses to these criticisms. Abelson (1997) points out that data analysis is an uncertain process that involves human judgment. All decision making regarding the outcomes of research in the behavioral sciences takes place against a background of error variation due to both measurement and sampling error, and when judging whether two means differ sufficiently to indicate the effect of a treatment, humans are not very good at taking error variation into account without using a statistical test. Two example problems in the next chapter, Example Problems 10.2 and 10.3, illustrate this issue. In Example Problem 10.2, the differences among the means in Table 10.13 look relatively large and a quick visual judgment might lead to an erroneous decision that the independent variable had an effect. But the large amount of error variation in this experiment indicates that the most appropriate interpretation of the differences among the means is that they are due to sampling error and not the effect of the independent variable. In contrast, a visual interpretation of the means in Table 10.14 for Example Problem 10.3 reveals that the means do not appear to differ by much and, thus, may lead us to believe the independent variable was ineffective. But this simple inspection overlooks the small amount of error variation in these scores. The statistical test, however, takes this error variation into account and indicates to us that the difference between the means of the two groups is best accounted for by the effect of the independent variable; it is not a chance difference. Study these problems carefully when you encounter them in the next chapter.

In response to concerns raised by critics of hypothesis testing, the American Psychological Association appointed a Task Force on Statistical Inference to make recommendations regarding the use of statistical analysis in research. This task force made several recommendations relevant to introductory statistical analysis (Wilkinson & the Task Force on Statistical Inference, 1999):

- Researchers should thoroughly describe their data including sample sizes and measures of central tendency and variability.

- Confidence intervals should routinely be provided along with measures of size of effect such as η^2.
- Researchers should be aware of what computerized data analysis programs do with the data. Using two different data analysis programs to verify results is suggested.

Along with these recommendations, I refer you back to the discussion of power earlier in this chapter. That discussion provided several recommendations for increasing the power of a research study and, thus, reducing the possibility of a Type II error.

There is no doubt that questions and criticisms of statistical hypothesis testing will continue to arise in the future. It is likely also that statistical hypothesis testing, perhaps in a modified form, will continue to be used in behavioral science research, for even its severest critics indicate there is no ready replacement for it (Cohen, 1994).

REPORTING THE RESULTS OF A *t* TEST

Following the guidelines of the *Publication Manual of the American Psychological Association* (1994) and the Task Force on Statistical Inference (Wilkinson & the Task Force on Statistical Inference, 1999), the results of Example Problem 9.1 might be described in a published scientific report as follows:

> With an alpha level of .05 and a two-tailed test, the mean time estimate for the placebo control group ($M = 19.8$ s, $SD = 7.6$ s) was significantly longer than the mean estimate of the experimental group ($M = 13.6$ s, $SD = 4.8$ s), $t(22) = +2.39$, $p < .05$, $\eta^2 = .21$. The 95 percent confidence interval for the difference between the two population means is 0.8 to 11.6 s.

In this presentation,

$\alpha = .05$ Indicates the significance level selected for the test.

$t(22)$ Identifies the test statistic as the t. This t is t_{obs}; the subscript *obs* is not utilized. Because two groups were identified in the description, you know the t test is the t_{ind}. The degrees of freedom for t_{obs} are shown in parentheses; thus, scores were analyzed from 24 different participants (because $df = N - 2$).

$= +2.39$ the value of t_{obs} (not the t_{crit} value found in Table A.2).

$p < .05$ Indicates the following:

       a. The probability of t_{obs} if H_0 is true is less than (or equal to) .05. This value is the probability of t_{obs} or an even more extreme value of t_{obs} if H_0 is true; it may not be the same as the value of α selected.

       b. H_0: $\mu_{A1} = \mu_{A2}$ was rejected.
           H_1: $\mu_{A1} \neq \mu_{A2}$ was accepted.

c. The difference between the sample means is statistically significant.

d. Something other than sampling error is responsible for the observed difference in the means. Because this was a controlled experiment, we infer that the difference was due to the drug condition given the participants.

e. If $p > .05$ had been reported, then the greater than ($>$) sign would indicate that H_0 was not rejected and the two sample means did not differ significantly at the .05 significance level. In this instance we would conclude that the drug condition had no effect on time estimation.

$\eta^2 = .21$ Proportion of variance due to the independent variable.

95 percent confidence interval = 0.8 to 11.6 s   This confidence interval is for the difference between the two population means. Alternatively, 95 percent confidence intervals for each for each of the means might have been presented. Occasionally, authors will present the standard error of the mean ($s_{\bar{X}}$ identified as SE) in place of a confidence interval.

TESTING YOUR KNOWLEDGE 9.4

1. Define: effect size, power, strength of association, strength of effect.
2. Two sets of two samples each are obtained. For set 1, $s_{A1} = 6.3$ and $s_{A2} = 7.6$. For set 2, $s_{A1} = 11.7$ and $s_{A2} = 10.3$.
   a. Which set of scores has greater error variation?
   b. If H_1 is true, which set of scores will more likely lead to a Type II error in a statistical test?
   c. Which set of scores will lead to a more powerful statistical test?
3. Which of the following two sample sizes would be expected to lead to a smaller value of $s_{\bar{X}A1 - \bar{X}A2}$ in a t test: $n_{A1} = n_{A2} = 12$, or $n_{A1} = n_{A2} = 20$? Why? Which sample size would lead to a more powerful statistical test?
4. Find η^2 for each of the following values of t_{obs}. The df for each t are presented in parentheses. Each t_{obs} is statistically significant at the .05 level with a two-tailed test.
   a. $t(8) = 2.413$
   b. $t(14) = 2.284$
   c. $t(20) = 2.174$
   d. $t(29) = 2.939$
   e. $t(60) = 2.306$
5. Distinguish between a research hypothesis and a statistical hypothesis.
6. Does a statistically significant difference necessarily mean that a scientifically important result has been found? Explain your answer.
7. The following reports of the use of t_{ind} have been adapted from results of published studies. Answer the following questions for each report:
   a. How many levels of the independent variable were used in this experiment?
   b. How many participants were used in this experiment?
   c. What is the value of the sample mean for each treatment condition?
   d. What is the value of the estimated population standard deviation for each treatment condition?

e.   What is the value of t_{obs}?

f.   What is the value of t_{crit} at the .05 significance level for a two-tailed rejection region?

g.   Do you reject or fail to reject H_0?

h.   Do you accept or not accept H_1?

i.   Is the difference between the means statistically significant or nonsignificant?

j.   To what do you attribute the observed difference in the sample means?

Report 1: With alpha equal to .05 and a two-tailed test, a *t* test indicated that participants correctly detected a larger percentage of targets while listening to the familiar poem ($M = 79.7, SD = 8.57$) than while listening to the unfamiliar poem ($M = 73.0, SD = 5.85$), $t(60) = 3.60, p < .01$.

Report 2: With alpha equal to .05 and a two-tailed test, a *t* test revealed no difference in the number of words recalled after a retention interval of 5 minutes ($M = 22.78, SD = 5.23$) and a retention interval of 0.5 minutes ($M = 24.33, SD = 5.14$), $t(28) = -0.82, p > .05$.

WITHIN-SUBJECTS DESIGNS AND THE *t* TEST FOR RELATED SCORES

Our interest to this point has been with the analysis of between-subjects designs in which each level of the independent variable is given to a different group of participants. A second type of research design is the **within-subjects design** in which a single group of partici-

Within-subjects design: A research design in which one group of participants is exposed to and measured under each level of an independent variable. In a within-subjects design, each person receives each treatment condition.

pants is exposed to and measured under each level of an independent variable. Thus, in a within-subjects design, each participant receives each treatment condition.

Consider the following example of a one-factor within-subjects design. People who quit smoking often report weight gains. To test this report scientifically, Becoña and Vázquez (1998) compared the weights of smokers entering a smoking cessation program at the time they entered the program and 36 months later. They found a statistically significant increase of 2 kilograms (about 4.4 pounds) for people who successfully quit smoking. Suppose you wish to replicate these findings with a group of eight female smokers between the ages of 20 to 24 who successfully quit smoking for a one-year period. Each person was weighed at the time of entering a smoking cessation program (A_1) and 12 months after stopping smoking (A_2); thus, a within-subjects design was used. Suppose you found the weights of the individuals at the time of entering the program and one year later as presented in Table 9.2. Do the weights measured in the two periods differ significantly? To answer this question, we use a *t* test for related scores to compare the means.

The *t* Test for Related Scores

In a within-subjects design the same participants are measured under each treatment condition; thus, the scores in each treatment condition are related. The factors that affect a person's score in one condition will affect that person's score in the other condition. The t_{ind} is not appropriate for this design; rather a *t* **test for related scores** defined as

$$t_{rel} = \frac{\overline{X}_{A1} - \overline{X}_{A2}}{s_D}$$

TABLE 9.2
Weights (in pounds) of eight 20- to 24-year-old females at the time of entering a smoking cessation program (A_1) and one year after quitting smoking (A_2).

Participant	Time of Weight Measurement (A)	
	Entering Program (A_1)	One Year after Stopping (A_2)
1	122.4	127.9
2	117.1	119.4
3	127.8	127.1
4	123.2	126.5
5	112.5	114.6
6	118.7	125.3
7	121.4	119.8
8	131.7	134.2
$\overline{X}_A$	121.85	124.35
s_A	6.03	6.13

is used, where s_D is the standard error of the mean for the difference between each $\overline{X}_{A1}$ and $\overline{X}_{A2}$ score. The formula for s_D is

$$s_D = \sqrt{\frac{\sum D^2 - (\sum D)^2/N_{\text{pairs}}}{N_{\text{pairs}}(N_{\text{pairs}} - 1)}},$$

where D = the difference between the two scores of a participant.
N_{pairs} = the number of pairs of scores, or equivalently, the number of participants.

Substituting the formula for s_D, the **computational formula for t_{rel}** becomes

$$t_{\text{rel}} = \frac{\overline{X}_{A1} - \overline{X}_{A2}}{\sqrt{\frac{\sum D^2 - (\sum D)^2/N_{\text{pairs}}}{N_{\text{pairs}}(N_{\text{pairs}} - 1)}}}.$$

The *df* are equal to $N_{\text{pairs}} - 1$ which represents the number of pairs of scores that are free to vary.

The application of this formula to the scores in Table 9.2 is illustrated in Table 9.3. The steps in this calculation are

1. Find $\overline{X}_{A1}$ and $\overline{X}_{A2}$. For the example, these values are 121.85 and 124.35 pounds, respectively.

TABLE 9.3
Computation of t_{rel} on the scores of Table 9.2.

Participant	Time of Weight Measurement (A)		D	D^2
	Entering Program (A_1)	One Year after Stopping (A_2)		
1	122.4	127.9	−5.5	30.25
2	117.1	119.4	−2.3	5.29
3	127.8	127.1	+0.7	0.49
4	123.2	126.5	−3.3	10.89
5	112.5	114.6	−2.1	4.41
6	118.7	125.3	−6.6	43.56
7	121.4	119.8	+1.6	2.56
8	131.7	134.2	−2.5	6.25
$\overline{X}_A$	121.85	124.35	$\sum D = -20.0$	$\sum D^2 = 103.70$
s_A	6.03	6.13		

$$t_{rel} = \frac{\overline{X}_{A1} - \overline{X}_{A2}}{\sqrt{\dfrac{\sum D^2 - (\sum D)^2/N_{pairs}}{N_{pairs}(N_{pairs} - 1)}}}$$

$$= \frac{121.85 - 124.35}{\sqrt{\dfrac{[103.70 - (-20.00)^2/8]}{[(8)(7)]}}}$$

$$= \frac{-2.50}{0.979} = -2.554 \text{ with 7 } df.$$

2. Find the value of D for each participant by subtracting the person's score in condition A_2 from her score in condition A_1. Maintain the algebraic sign of the difference for each participant. This step is shown in the column headed by D in the table.
3. Square each value of D as shown in the column headed by D^2 of the table.
4. Find $\sum D$ (the sum of column D; −20.0 for the example) and $\sum D^2$ (the sum of column D^2; 103.70 for the example).
5. Determine N_{pairs}. For the example, $N_{pairs} = 8$.
6. Substitute the numerical values into the equation for t_{rel}.
7. Find the df, where $df = N_{pairs} - 1$.

The t_{obs} for the scores of Table 9.2 is −2.554. The remaining steps in using this t_{obs} are identical to those for the t_{ind}. A value of α is selected, the value of t_{crit} found from Table

A.2, and rejection regions are located on the sampling distribution of t. If the value of t_{obs} falls into a rejection region, then

$$H_0: \mu_{A1} = \mu_{A2} \text{ is rejected, and}$$

$$H_1: \mu_{A1} \neq \mu_{A2} \text{ is accepted.}$$

For 7 df and a .05 significance level, t_{crit} for a two-tailed rejection region is 2.365. The rejection region is, thus, composed of values of t_{obs} less than or equal to -2.365 or equal to or greater than $+2.365$. The t_{obs} of -2.554 is less than -2.365; hence, it falls into a rejection region; H_0 is rejected and H_1 accepted. The difference between the sample means is statistically significant at the .05 level. Participants weighed more one year after stopping smoking than they did when entering the smoking cessation program.
    Eta squared is found for this t_{rel} by

$$\eta^2 = \frac{t^2_{obs}}{t^2_{obs} + df}.$$

Substituting numerical values for t_{obs} and df,

$$\eta^2 = \frac{(-2.554)^2}{(-2.554)^2 + 7} = .48.$$

This eta squared indicates that 48 percent of the variance in weight gain is accounted for by the time interval in this study.
    An important point to note from this design is that although there was a statistically significant weight gain over the one-year period, we cannot state it was caused by the cessation of smoking. People often gain weight over time, and the participants might have gained weight even if they had not stopped smoking. To be confident the weight gain was due to the cessation of smoking, another group of similar participants who continued to smoke would have to have their weight measured over a one-year period. Including such a group in this example would have made the discussion more complex, but Becoña and Vázquez (1998) did have such a group and found their weight did not increase significantly in a three-year period.

Constructing Confidence Intervals for the Difference between Two Related Population Means

The **95 percent confidence interval for the difference between two related population means** is given by the interval from

$$(\overline{X}_{A1} - \overline{X}_{A2}) - t_{.05}(s_D) \text{ to } (\overline{X}_{A1} - \overline{X}_{A2}) + t_{.05}(s_D),$$

where $\overline{X}_{A1} - \overline{X}_{A2}$ = the difference between the two sample means.
        s_D = the standard error of the mean for the difference between each X_{A1} and X_{A2} score.
        $t_{.05}$ = the two-tailed value of t_{crit} at the .05 significance level with $N - 1$ degrees of freedom.

The interval given by this formula has a .95 probability of including the value of $\mu_{A1} - \mu_{A2}$. For the example problem, $\overline{X}_{A1} = 121.85$, $\overline{X}_{A2} = 124.35$, $N_{pairs} = 8$, $s_D = 0.979$ (from Table 9.3), and $t_{.05}$ for 7 degrees of freedom equals 2.365. To avoid obtaining a negative difference between sample means, I will subtract $\overline{X}_{A1}$ from $\overline{X}_{A2}$. Substituting numerical values, the 95 percent confidence interval for the difference between μ_{A1} and μ_{A2} is

$$(124.35 - 121.85) - (2.365)(0.979) \text{ to } (124.35 - 121.85) + (2.365)(0.979),$$

which equals an interval of 0.18 to 4.82 pounds. The 95 percent confidence interval for the difference between the population means weight at the time of entering the smoking cessation program and one year after stopping smoking is between 0.18 to 4.82 pounds.

TESTING YOUR KNOWLEDGE 9.5

1. Explain the difference between a between-subjects research design and a within-subjects research design.
2. More and more, people seem to be considering their cars as an extension of their office and many traffic safety experts are concerned that the increasing distractions are leading to more accidents. Suppose in a attempt to provide empirical evidence on this problem, you asked 11 people to drive a simulated trip under two conditions, a control condition with no distractions present and an experimental condition with the participant driving the trip while carrying on a conversation on a cellular telephone. The participants' reaction time to a simulated event requiring braking was measured and you obtained the following reaction times (in milliseconds):

Person	Condition	
	Control	Experimental
1	426	448
2	501	552
3	525	506
4	478	507
5	537	574
6	452	491
7	394	438
8	443	477
9	491	523
10	382	413
11	572	541

Find the mean and standard deviation for each condition; then calculate t_{rel} on the scores and answer the following questions.
a. State the statistical hypotheses for t_{rel} for these scores.
b. What is the value of t_{obs}?
c. What are the df for this t?
d. What is the value of t_{crit}?
e. What are the rejection regions for t_{obs}?
f. Does t_{obs} fall into a rejection region?

g. What decisions do you make about the statistical hypotheses? Do you reject or fail to reject H_0? Accept or not accept H_1?

h. Do you conclude that the sample means are from the same or different populations?

i. Is the difference between the means statistically significant?

j. Did the conditions differ significantly in their reaction times? If so, what is the direction of the difference?

k. What is the value of η^2 for this study?

l. What is the 95 percent confidence interval for the difference between the population means?

SUMMARY

- An experiment requires:
  - Asking a scientific question and formulating a research hypothesis.
  - Selecting subjects.
  - Creating equivalent groups by random assignment.
  - Controlling extraneous variables.
  - Manipulating an independent variable.
  - Measuring the dependent variable.
- The t_{ind} may be used to determine if two sample means from an experiment differ significantly.
- The formula for t_{ind} is

$$t_{ind} = \frac{\overline{X}_{A1} - \overline{X}_{A2}}{s_{\overline{X}A1 - \overline{X}A2}}.$$

  where $s_{\overline{X}A1 - \overline{X}A2}$ is the standard error of the difference between means.
- Statistical hypothesis testing with t_{ind} follows the steps common to all statistical testing.
- The power of a statistical test is the probability of rejecting H_0 when H_0 is false.
- Factors affecting power of the t test include the magnitude of the effect induced by the independent variable, the amount of variability in the measure of the dependent variable, and sample size.
- Eta squared (η^2) is a measure of the strength of association in the sample measured and is calculated from t_{obs}.
- Eta squared indicates the proportion of the total variation in the dependent variable accounted for by the independent variable.
- The 95 percent confidence interval for the difference between two independent population means is given by the interval from

$$(\overline{X}_{A1} - \overline{X}_{A2}) - t_{.05}(s_{\overline{X}A1 - \overline{X}A2}) \text{ to } (\overline{X}_{A1} - \overline{X}_{A2}) + t_{.05}(s_{\overline{X}A1 - \overline{X}A2}).$$

- In a within-subjects design a single group of subjects is exposed to all levels of each independent variable.
- The t_{rel} may be used when there are two levels of an independent variable in a one-factor within-subjects design.

- The formula for t_{rel} is

$$t_{rel} = \frac{\overline{X}_{A1} - \overline{X}_{A2}}{s_D}$$

  where s_D is the standard error of the mean for the difference between each $\overline{X}_{A1}$ and $\overline{X}_{A2}$ score.

- The 99 percent confidence interval for the difference between two related population means is given by the interval from

$$(\overline{X}_{A1} - \overline{X}_{A2}) - t_{.01}(s_{\overline{X}A1 - \overline{X}A2}) \text{ to } (\overline{X}_{A1} - \overline{X}_{A2}) + t_{.01}(s_{\overline{X}A1 - \overline{X}A2}).$$

KEY TERMS AND SYMBOLS

between-subjects design (181)
chance difference (187)
confidence interval for the
   difference between two
   population means (205)
confounded experiment (183)
convenience sampling (182)
dependent variable (184)
directional test (194)
equivalent groups (182)
estimated standard error of the
   difference between means
   $(s_{\overline{X}A1 - \overline{X}A2})$ (190)
eta squared (η^2) (203)
experiment (180)
extraneous variable (183)
factor (183)

independent variable (182)
level of an independent variable
   (183)
95 percent confidence interval
   for the difference between two
   independent population means
   (206)
99 percent confidence interval
   for the difference between two
   independent population means
   (206)
nondirectional test (193)
one-factor between-subjects
   design (183)
one-tailed test (194)
placebo control (183)
random assignment (182)

random sampling (181)
robustness (197)
s_D (212)
s^2_{pooled} (190)
sampling distribution of the
   difference between means
   (188)
standard error of the difference
   between means (189)
strength of effect (203)
t_{crit} (191)
t test for related scores (t_{rel}) (211)
t test for two independent groups
   (t_{ind}) (187)
t_{obs} (191)
two-tailed test (193)
within-subjects design (211)

REVIEW QUESTIONS

1. Suppose that you were interested in finding if noise has any effect on blood pressure. You randomly assigned 22 individuals to either a control or an experimental group ($n_{A1} = n_{A2}$). Subjects in the quiet group (A_1) relaxed in comfortable chairs in a quiet room for 30 minutes. At the end of the 30 minutes you measured their systolic blood pressure (i.e., the blood pressure during the contraction of the heart). Subjects in the noise group (A_2) also sat in the chairs for 30 minutes. During the 30-minute wait, however, they listened to a recording of rush hour traffic noise from a large city. After listening to the noise for 30 minutes, the systolic

blood pressure of these subjects was also recorded. Suppose that you obtained the following blood pressures in millimeters of mercury.

Group	
Quiet	Noise
106	141
117	136
124	124
129	139
115	121
131	119
121	147
115	128
128	115
136	134
127	140

a. Find the mean and standard deviation for each group. Then use a t test to answer the following question: Does noise affect systolic blood pressure? Use a two-tailed test and a .05 significance level.

b. What is the value of η^2 for this experiment? What proportion of the variance in the dependent variable can be accounted for by knowing the level of the independent variable?

c. Find the 95 percent confidence interval for the difference between the two population means.

d. Describe your results following the example illustrated in the Reporting the Results of a t Test section of this chapter.

2. Suppose that you obtained the blood pressures given next for question 1. Does noise affect systolic blood pressure? Use a .05 significance level and a two-tailed test.

Group	
Quiet	Noise
110	116
114	111
106	120
117	119
108	123
116	108
120	122
111	115
115	117
109	101
118	116

3. Pedersen (1987) hypothesized that sex differences exist in the need for privacy among college students. The hypothesis was tested by giving the Privacy Questionnaire (Pedersen, 1979) to male and female college students. One aspect of this questionnaire measures the need for solitude. Scores on this scale may range from 6 (never need solitude) to 30 (usually need solitude). Suppose that the following scores were obtained for 13 males and 17 females.

Gender	
Male (A_1)	**Female (A_2)**
23	16
16	29
13	11
25	14
17	17
21	19
10	18
19	21
24	9
16	15
11	17
22	20
14	14
	24
	23
	25
	24

a. Find the mean and standard deviation for each group. Then use a *t* test to answer the following question: Do males and females differ in the rated need for solitude? Use a two-tailed test and a .05 significance level.

b. Describe your results following the example illustrated in the Reporting the Results of a *t* Test section of this chapter.

4. Psychologists study illusions to better understand how we perceive the world. As one example, the Morinaga misalignment illusion is illustrated in the panel labeled (a) of Figure 10.3 (see page 258). The figure is an illusion because the points of each angle do not appear to be aligned on the same vertical line, although they are. The middle point appears to align with a vertical line different from the line on which the bottom and top angles align. Day and Kasperczyk (1984) investigated the extent of this illusion by asking participants to adjust the center angle so that its point appeared aligned with the points of the top and bottom. The error in the adjustment was measured in millimeters (mm). If a subject aligned the points of the three angles perfectly, then he or she would have 0-mm error and there would be no illusion. On the other hand, if a subject adjusted the center angle so that it appeared aligned, but was not, then the measured error was recorded.

Suppose an experimenter is interested in finding if instructing individuals about the nature of the illusion affects their perception of it. The experimenter first had 12 participants align the points of the angles and measured the amount of error in adjustment for each participant. After participants aligned the points, they were then told about the nature of the illusion and asked to align the points again. Suppose the two error measurements (in millimeters) for each participant were as follows.

	Instructional Condition (A)	
Participant	Before Instructions (A_1)	After Instructions (A_2)
1	1.3	1.4
2	2.1	2.0
3	2.5	2.7
4	1.9	2.0
5	3.0	3.4
6	2.5	2.8
7	1.8	1.6
8	2.4	2.5
9	3.1	3.3
10	3.4	3.4
11	2.5	2.3
12	2.9	2.8

a. Find the mean and standard deviation for each group. Then use a t test to answer the question: Did the instructions affect the magnitude of the illusion perceived? Use a two-tailed test and a .05 significance level.

b. Describe your results following the example illustrated in the Reporting the Results of a t Test section of this chapter.

5. Locus of control refers to the perception a person has over the control of events that affect his or her life. A person with an external locus of control perceives that he or she has little control over these events, whereas a person with an internal locus of control perceives that he or she has a great deal of control over such events. Wiehe (1986) hypothesized that children who have been removed from the custody of their parents might have a more external locus of control than children who live with their biological parents. To test this hypothesis, Wiehe formed two groups from among adolescents in a residential maternity home: 45 pregnant adolescents who had been removed from their biological parents and had become pregnant while in foster care and 45 pregnant adolescents who had become pregnant while living with their biological parents. Each adolescent was given a rating scale to measure locus of control, and Wiehe reported a mean locus of control score of 15.76 ($s = 4.65$) for the foster parents group and a mean score of 12.27 ($s = 5.74$) for the biological parents group. For this measure, higher scores indicate greater external locus of control.

    a. Use a t test to answer this question: Is locus of control related to the type of home of the adolescent? Use a two-tailed test and a .05 significance level.

    b. What is the value of η^2 for this study? What proportion of the variance in the dependent variable can be accounted for by knowing the level of the independent variable?

    c. Find the 95 percent confidence interval for the difference between the two population means.

    d. Describe your results following the example illustrated in the Reporting the Results of a t Test section of this chapter.

6. Hughey (1985) compared the grade point average (GPA) of college students cited for residence hall disruptions with students not involved in residence hall disruptions. The mean GPA of 1794 students involved in disruptions was 1.68 with $s = 0.34$. For 3606 students not involved in disruptions, the mean GPA was 2.19 with $s = 0.83$.

    a. Use a t test to answer this question: Do the GPAs differ significantly? Use a two-tailed test and a .05 significance level.

    b. What is the value of η^2 for this study? What proportion of the variance in the dependent variable can be accounted for by knowing the level of the independent variable?

    c. Find the 95 percent confidence interval for the difference between the two population means.

    d. Describe your results following the example illustrated in the Reporting the Results of a t Test section of this chapter.

7. Many students experience test anxiety that severely interferes with their academic performance. Suppose a college counselor hypothesized that listening to relaxing music before an examination would reduce this anxiety. To test this hypothesis, the therapist selected 34 students with severe test anxiety from a large introductory course. The students were randomly assigned to either a control or an experimental group, with an equal number of subjects in each group. Subjects in the control group spent the hour before the next exam in the course sitting in a quiet lounge where they read magazines. Subjects in the experimental group spent the hour listening to relaxing music. The mean exam grade for the control group was 73.2 ($s_{A1} = 8.4$) and the mean grade for the experimental group was 75.6 ($s_{A2} = 8.7$).

    a. Use a t test to answer this question: Did the groups differ significantly on the mean test grades? Use a two-tailed test and a .05 significance level.

    b. Describe your results following the example illustrated in the Reporting the Results of a t Test section of this chapter.

8. Motivational speakers want to be perceived as trustworthy. One hypothesis is that speakers who exhibit immediacy behaviors such as making eye contact, smiling, and leaning forward will be perceived as more trustworthy than those who do not engage in these behaviors. To test this research hypothesis, suppose a psychologist created two equivalent groups of 13 participants each and each group listened to a speaker giving a short motivational speech. For people in a nonimmediacy group (A_1), the speaker did not engage in any immediacy behaviors while giving the speech. For the immediacy group (A_2), however, the speaker made eye contact, smiled, and leaned forward toward the audience while giving the speech. After the speech was given, participants in both groups rated the speaker on a scale of trust-worthiness ranging from 1 (not at all trustworthy) to 9 (highly trustworthy). Suppose the following ratings were obtained.

Immediacy Condition (A)

No Immediacy Behaviors (A_1)	Immediacy Behaviors (A_1)
4	7
5	6
3	9
4	8
6	8
7	7
7	6
4	4
3	5
5	8
6	7
3	6
5	8

a. Use a t test to answer the question: Is rated trustworthiness affected by the immediacy behaviors of the speaker? Use a two-tailed test and a .05 significance level.

b. What is the value of η^2 for this study? What proportion of the variance in the dependent variable can be accounted for by knowing the level of the independent variable?

c. Find the 95 percent confidence interval for the difference between the two population means.

d. Describe your results following the example illustrated in the Reporting the Results of a t Test section of this chapter.

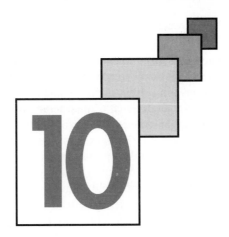

One-Factor Between-Subjects Analysis of Variance

The *t* test introduced many of the important concepts of statistical hypothesis testing in behavioral science research. But the *t* test possesses a major limitation; it can be used to compare the means from only two groups at a time. Many behavioral science experiments, however, are multilevel designs. A **one-factor multilevel design** (also called a **one-way multilevel design**) is an experiment with one independent variable and three or more levels of that independent variable. For these designs, a statistical technique known as **analysis of variance** (abbreviated **ANOVA**) is used as a statistical hypothesis test.

One-factor multilevel design: An experiment with one independent variable and three or more levels of that independent variable.

Analysis of variance is the most widely used statistical test in psychological research. It can be used for both between- and within-subjects designs and for designs in which two or more independent variables are varied. For a one-factor design, analysis of variance may be used in place of the *t* test when only two levels of an independent variable are manipulated. This chapter presents the analysis of variance for the one-factor between-subjects multilevel design, the design in which one independent variable is manipulated, and each level of the independent variable is given to a different group of participants. Its uses in other designs are presented in Chapters 11 and 12.

Analysis of variance (ANOVA): A statistical test used to analyze multilevel designs.

AN EXAMPLE ONE-FACTOR MULTILEVEL DESIGN

What aspects of a stimulus determine how well we remember it? One research hypothesis, the elaboration hypothesis, predicts that the more elaborate the memory representation of a stimulus is the better the stimulus should be remembered (Craik & Tulving, 1975). A second research hypothesis, the effort hypothesis, predicts that stimuli requiring more effort to process and remember will be recalled better than stimuli requiring less effort (Coulter, Coulter, & Glover, 1984). Suppose that we create three different types of drawings of common objects: detailed, outline, and incomplete outline drawings. The elaboration hypothesis predicts that detailed drawings should lead to the most memory elaboration and, thus, be best recalled, with outline and incomplete outline drawings leading to less memory elaboration and, thus, progressively poorer recall. The effort hypothesis, however, leads to an opposite prediction; the incomplete outline drawings require the most effort to process and remember and, thus, they will be best recalled. The detailed drawings require the least effort; hence, they will be the most poorly recalled.

To determine which of these hypotheses best predicts memory for visual stimuli, suppose that we used a one-factor between-subjects design and manipulated the independent variable of type of drawing (factor *A*) over three levels: incomplete outline (A_1), outline (A_2), and detailed (A_3) drawings. The procedures discussed in Chapter 9 for designing and running an experiment were followed. Three equivalent groups were created by randomly assigning five people to each group. The participants in each group were shown a set of drawings of 30 common items. For one group the drawings were detailed, for the second group the drawings were outlines, and for the third group the drawings were incomplete outlines. After viewing each of the 30 drawings for 4 seconds, each person was asked to orally recall as many of the drawings as possible. The number of items recalled by each person, the mean and standard deviation for each group, and the grand mean for the scores are

TABLE 10.1
Hypothetical scores for number of items recalled as a function of type of drawing. The mean ($\overline{X}_A$) and standard deviation (s_A) are provided for each condition. $\overline{X}_G$ is the grand mean of the 15 scores.

	Type of Drawing (Factor A)			
	Incomplete Outline (A_1)	Outline (A_2)	Detailed (A_3)	
	19	14	15	
	13	13	10	
	16	16	11	
	17	12	12	
	20	10	12	
$\overline{X}_A$	17.0	13.0	12.0	$\overline{X}_G = 14.0$
s_A	2.74	2.24	1.87	

Grand mean: The mean of all scores in an experiment.

presented in Table 10.1. The **grand mean**, identified as $\overline{X}_G$, is the mean of all 15 scores in the experiment. Is the number of drawings recalled affected by the type of drawing? To answer this question, I use the one-factor between-subjects analysis of variance.

BETWEEN-GROUPS AND WITHIN-GROUPS VARIATION

The analysis of variance for a one-factor between-subjects design breaks down the total variation in the scores of an experiment into two parts, often called *sources*: (1) a variance that varies with both the systematic effect of an independent variable and sampling error among the group means and (2) a variance that varies only with the within-groups error variation. In the analysis of variance, however, a variance is called a *mean square*. **Mean square** (abbreviated *MS*) is another term for a variance, and it is the name used in analysis of variance.

Mean square: The name used for a variance in the analysis of variance.

Figure 10.1 helps to conceptualize these variances. Panel (a) of this figure presents a frequency distribution of all 15 scores from Table 10.1. The total variation of these scores is the variance of the scores around the grand mean of 14.0. Panels (b), (c), and (d) present frequency distributions of the scores within each group for the incomplete outline, outline, and detailed drawing groups, respectively. Notice that, although the participants within each group received the same treatment condition, the scores within a group vary about the group mean. The within-groups variation is given by the variance of the scores around their respective group means. In analysis of variance, this variation is called **within-groups error variance**, or simply **error variance**, and is measured by MS_{Error}. The term *error* is

Within-groups error variance: The variance of the scores in a group calculated about the group mean.

(a) Total variation in scores: Variation around grand mean

(b) Within-groups error variation: Variation of scores around group mean

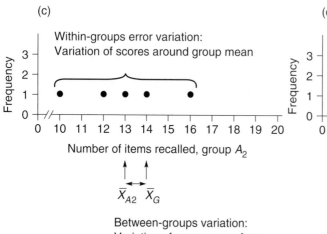

(c) Within-groups error variation: Variation of scores around group mean

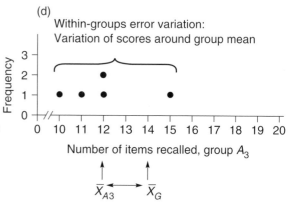

(d) Within-groups error variation: Variation of scores around group mean

FIGURE 10.1

(a) A frequency distribution of all 15 scores from Table 10.1. (b) A frequency distribution of the incomplete outline drawing group (A_1) scores. (c) A frequency distribution of the outline drawing group (A_2) scores. (d) A frequency distribution of the detail drawing group (A_3) scores.

used to indicate that scores within a group are not all identical, even though all subjects within a group received the same treatment.

The variability between groups is reflected in the differences of the group means (i.e., $\overline{X}_{A1}$, $\overline{X}_{A2}$, and $\overline{X}_{A3}$) from the grand mean, $\overline{X}_G$. This variation in group means is called **between-groups variance** and is measured by MS_A.

Between-groups variance:
The variance calculated using the variation of the group means about the grand mean.

The group means in an experiment may differ from each other for two reasons: (1) the effect of an independent variable and (2) sampling error. Thus, MS_A reflects systematic variation among the means of the treatment groups due to the effect of the independent variable and variation due to sampling error. Thus, in the example experiment, the group means $\overline{X}_{A1}$, $\overline{X}_{A2}$, and $\overline{X}_{A3}$ will differ from each other if the type of drawing affects recall, but they will differ also simply from sampling error.

The sorting of the total variation into between-groups variance and within-groups error variance results in a test statistic called F, named after Sir Ronald A. Fisher (1890–1962), a British statistician who developed the concepts of analysis of variance. The F statistic is a ratio of MS_A to MS_{Error} and is expressed as

$$F = \frac{MS_A}{MS_{Error}}.$$

The numerator of the F statistic, MS_A, measures the effect of the independent variable as well as sampling error among the group means. The denominator, MS_{Error}, measures only error variation of scores within treatment conditions. If the independent variable has no effect, then the variation among the treatment group means will be due only to sampling error. Consequently, MS_A and MS_{Error} will be about the same, and F will be about 1.00. But if the independent variable has an effect, it will increase the differences among sample means beyond the differences expected from sampling error alone. In this instance, the between-groups variance of the numerator, MS_A, will be greater than the within-groups variance of the denominator, MS_{Error}, and the F ratio will be larger than 1.00. Thus, F increases in value as a treatment has an effect. Accordingly, the F statistic provides the basis for a statistical hypothesis test.

OBTAINING THE *F* STATISTIC

In the following section I derive the variances that enter into F in order to provide a conceptual understanding of ANOVA. If you were to perform an analysis of variance on an actual set of data, you would use the computationally easier formulas given in the supplement to this chapter or a computer data analysis program. The computational formulas give no insight into the analysis of variance, but they ease considerably the computations involved.

The F statistic requires two measures of the variability of scores, MS_A and MS_{Error}. In Chapter 5, I defined a variance, or a MS, as $SS/(n-1)$, where SS stands for sum of squares. The denominator, $n-1$, corresponds to the degrees of freedom (df) involved in obtaining the variance estimate. Thus, the general formula for a variance providing an unbiased estimate of the population variance is $MS = SS/df$. To obtain MS_A and MS_{Error}, we find SS_A and SS_{Error}, respectively, from the scores and then divide each sum of squares by its df. The first step, obtaining the sums of squares, begins by partitioning a score.

Partitioning a Score

The analysis of variance sorts the total variation of the scores in an experiment into between-groups and within-groups variances by assuming a simple model for a subject's score. Although the example problem uses only three levels of an independent variable, the model introduced here applies to the analysis of variance for any number of levels of a one-factor between-subjects design.

The scores in Table 10.1 are represented symbolically in Table 10.2. The symbols are similar to those used to this point. The independent variable is identified as **factor** A with three levels, A_1, A_2, and A_3. The letter a represents the number of levels of factor A. For Tables 10.1 and 10.2, $a = 3$. A score is represented by X_{ij}, where the subscript i represents a number identifying the participant within a group and the subscript j represents the number of the group, A_1, A_2, or A_3. For example, X_{52} is the fifth person in group A_2. In Table 10.1, this score is 10, or $X_{52} = 10$. When it is not necessary to identify a specific subject, I drop the ij subscripts and simply use X. The sample means for each level of the independent variable are indicated by $\overline{X}_{A1}$, $\overline{X}_{A2}$, and $\overline{X}_{A3}$ or, generally, by $\overline{X}_A$. The grand mean is labeled $\overline{X}_G$. The number of scores in a level of the independent variable is represented by n_A, and the total number of scores in the experiment is represented by N. For Table 10.1, $n_{A1} = 5$, $n_{A2} = 5$, $n_{A3} = 5$, $N = 15$, $\overline{X}_{A1} = 17.0$, $\overline{X}_{A2} = 13.0$, $\overline{X}_{A3} = 12.0$, and $\overline{X}_G = 14.0$. Although analysis of variance does not require an equal number of scores in each treatment condition, having equal numbers simplifies the computations needed. All the examples in the chapter use an equal number of scores in each treatment condition.

The analysis of variance takes the total variation of a score, that is, the total amount by which a score (i.e., X_{ij}) differs from the grand mean of the scores (i.e., $\overline{X}_G$), and partitions, or separates, this total difference into two parts. One part, which becomes the

a: The number of levels of factor A.

n_A: Number of scores in a level of a one-factor design.

TABLE 10.2

Notational representation of scores from the hypothetical experiment in Table 10.1 with three levels of an independent variable, factor A. The means for each level of factor A are represented by $\overline{X}_A$ and the grand mean by $\overline{X}_G$.

Factor A			
A_1	A_2	A_3	
X_{11}	X_{12}	X_{13}	
X_{21}	X_{22}	X_{23}	
X_{31}	X_{32}	X_{33}	
X_{41}	X_{42}	X_{43}	
X_{51}	X_{52}	X_{53}	
$\overline{X}_{A1}$	$\overline{X}_{A2}$	$\overline{X}_{A3}$	$\overline{X}_G$

between-groups variance (i.e., MS_A), varies with an effect of the independent variable and sampling error. The other part, which measures the error of individual scores about their group mean, becomes the within-groups error variance (i.e., MS_{Error}). This model for representing a score can be expressed as

$$\begin{array}{ccc} \textbf{Total variation} & \textbf{Variation due to} & \textbf{Variation due to} \\ \textbf{in a score} = & \textbf{factor } A \textbf{ plus} & + \textbf{ within-groups} \\ & \textbf{sampling error} & \textbf{error} \end{array} \qquad (10.1)$$

In terms of scores, this equation can be written as

$$X - \overline{X}_G \quad = \quad (\overline{X}_A - \overline{X}_G) \quad + \quad (X - \overline{X}_A) \qquad (10.2)$$

Difference of a   **Difference of the**   **Difference of the score**
score from the   **treatment group mean**   **from its treatment**
grand mean   **from the grand mean**   **group mean**

I examine each part of equation 10.2.

Total Variation

The difference of a score from the grand mean (i.e., $X - \overline{X}_G$) is the total variation of that score. As equation 10.2 indicates, a part of this variation is due to the effect of the independent variable and a part of it is due to error variation.

Variation Due to the Effect of the Independent Variable and Sampling Error

The difference between a group mean and the grand mean (i.e., $\overline{X}_A - \overline{X}_G$) varies with the effect of an independent variable and with sampling error. Accordingly, it enters into the computation of MS_A.

Effect of the Independent Variable.   The analysis of variance uses the difference between each group mean and the grand mean to measure the effect of the independent variable. These differences will increase with an effect of the independent variable. A numerical illustration helps to clarify this important point.

Table 10.3 presents three possible outcomes of an experiment involving only three scores in each of two treatment groups. In panel (a) of this table, no treatment effect is present. Each group mean is equal to the grand mean. Furthermore, each of the two $\overline{X}_A - \overline{X}_G$ differences is equal to zero. A treatment effect of $+2$ is added to the scores of A_2 in panel (b); thus, neither group mean is equal to the grand mean. This treatment effect of $+2$ is represented by a value of -1 for the $\overline{X}_{A1} - \overline{X}_G$ difference and a value of $+1$ for the $\overline{X}_{A2} - \overline{X}_G$ difference. Panel (c) presents a treatment effect of $+6$ added to the scores of A_2. In the analysis of variance this effect is broken into a -3 for the $\overline{X}_{A1} - \overline{X}_G$ difference and a

TABLE 10.3

Demonstration that $\overline{X}_A - \overline{X}_G$ responds to the effect of an independent variable in an experiment. Treatment means are represented by $\overline{X}_A$ and the grand mean for each set of scores by $\overline{X}_G$. The difference between each treatment group mean and the grand mean is shown at the bottom of each set of scores.

Panel (a) scores: No treatment effect is present.
Panel (b) scores: A treatment effect of +2 is present.
Panel (c) scores: A treatment effect of +6 is present.

	(a)		(b)		(c)	
	A_1	A_2	A_1	A_2	A_1	A_2
	11	12	11	14	11	18
	12	13	12	15	12	19
	13	11	13	13	13	17
$\overline{X}_A$	12	12	12	14	12	18
$\overline{X}_G$	12		13		15	
	$\overline{X}_{A1} - \overline{X}_G = 0$		$\overline{X}_{A1} - \overline{X}_G = -1$		$\overline{X}_{A1} - \overline{X}_G = -3$	
	$\overline{X}_{A2} - \overline{X}_G = 0$		$\overline{X}_{A2} - \overline{X}_G = +1$		$\overline{X}_{A2} - \overline{X}_G = +3$	

value of +3 for the $\overline{X}_{A2} - \overline{X}_G$ difference. Notice from this illustration that, if a treatment has an effect and causes the group means to differ from each other, the effect will be reflected in the value of the $\overline{X}_A - \overline{X}_G$ differences that can be calculated in an experiment.

Sampling Error.   In addition to any treatment effect, the group means also differ from each other because of sampling error. Even if the independent variable has no effect, I expect a group mean to differ somewhat from the grand mean simply because of sampling error. Thus, any effect of the independent variable in an experiment occurs against a background of sampling error.

Variation Due to Within-Groups Error

The difference of an individual score from its treatment group mean (i.e., $X - \overline{X}_A$) enters into the computation of MS_{Error}. It varies only with within-groups error variation in the experiment. In fact, this difference was used in Chapter 5 as the numerator of the standard deviation and variance, measures of error variation among scores within a group. The numerical value of this difference does not vary with an effect of an independent variable. Because any effect of the independent variable is assumed to equally increase or decrease the scores of all subjects receiving a particular treatment, the treatment group mean will change by an equal amount. Thus, $X - \overline{X}_A$ will remain constant regardless of the effect of an independent variable. For example, for the second person in A_2 of Table 10.3 [i.e., the score represented by $X_{22} = 13$ in panel (a)], the $X - \overline{X}_A$ difference remains a +1 over all panels of the table regardless of the absence or presence of a treatment effect. Thus, the values of $X - \overline{X}_A$ reflect only error variation among the scores within a treatment condition.

Obtaining Mean Squares from Partitioned Scores

Partitioning or breaking a score into parts that measure between-groups and within-groups variation establishes the basis for obtaining the MS_A and MS_{Error} needed for the F statistic. Recall from Chapter 5 that the estimated population variance is given by

$$s^2 = \frac{\sum (X - \overline{X})^2}{N - 1}.$$

Notice that each term in equation 10.2 resembles the numerator of a variance. By using MS in place of s^2, *sum of squares* (SS) to represent $\sum (X - \overline{X})^2$, and df to represent $N - 1$, this variance may be expressed as

$$MS = \frac{SS}{df}.$$

This formula for the variance suggests that if each difference represented in equation 10.2 were squared for each subject and then summed over all scores in an experiment, the result would be a sum of squared differences, or SS, the numerator of a mean square. From equation 10.2, three SS terms can be obtained. The term $X - \overline{X}_G$ leads to SS_{Total}, which represents the total difference of scores from the grand mean. The $\overline{X}_A - \overline{X}_G$ difference leads to SS_A, which is a measure of between-group variation due to an effect of the independent variable and sampling error. Finally, $X - \overline{X}_A$ leads to SS_{Error}, which is a measure of within-group error variation in the experiment.

Obtaining the Three Sums of Squares

I illustrate how equation 10.2 may be used to find these sums of squares by partitioning the score of subject 1 of group A_1 (i.e., X_{11}) of Table 10.1, which is 19. For this score, equation 10.2 becomes

$$X_{11} - \overline{X}_G = (\overline{X}_{A1} - \overline{X}_G) + (X_{11} - \overline{X}_{A1}).$$

Substituting the appropriate numerical values for $X_{11}, \overline{X}_{A1},$ and $\overline{X}_G$ leads to

$$19.0 - 14.0 = (17.0 - 14.0) + (19.0 - 17.0),$$
$$(+5.0) \quad = \quad (+3.0) \quad + \quad (+2.0).$$

The partitioning shows that the score differs from the grand mean (i.e., $X_{11} - \overline{X}_G = +5.0$) as much as it does because of the treatment condition that the subject is in (reflected in $\overline{X}_{A1} - \overline{X}_G = +3.0$) and because of the unsystematic influences of error or chance factors (reflected in $X_{11} - \overline{X}_{A1} = +2.0$).

To obtain the SS, each participant's score is similarly partitioned as shown in Table 10.4 for the 15 scores of Table 10.1. Table 10.4 may appear intimidating, but the computations in the table require only addition, subtraction, and multiplication and proceed in a step-by-step fashion. Follow each step carefully.

TABLE 10.4

Obtaining sums of squares for a one-factor between-subjects analysis of variance. The scores used are those in Table 10.1.

Step 1: **Partition scores for the 15 participants using the following equation.**

		$(X - \overline{X}_G)$	=	$(\overline{X}_A - \overline{X}_G)$	+	$(X - \overline{X}_A)$
Scores	X_{11}	$19 - 14$	=	$(17 - 14)$	+	$(19 - 17)$
in A_1	X_{21}	$13 - 14$	=	$(17 - 14)$	+	$(13 - 17)$
	X_{31}	$16 - 14$	=	$(17 - 14)$	+	$(16 - 17)$
	X_{41}	$17 - 14$	=	$(17 - 14)$	+	$(17 - 17)$
	X_{51}	$20 - 14$	=	$(17 - 14)$	+	$(20 - 17)$
Scores	X_{12}	$14 - 14$	=	$(13 - 14)$	+	$(14 - 13)$
in A_2	X_{22}	$13 - 14$	=	$(13 - 14)$	+	$(13 - 13)$
	X_{32}	$16 - 14$	=	$(13 - 14)$	+	$(16 - 13)$
	X_{42}	$12 - 14$	=	$(13 - 14)$	+	$(12 - 13)$
	X_{52}	$10 - 14$	=	$(13 - 14)$	+	$(10 - 13)$
Scores	X_{13}	$15 - 14$	=	$(12 - 14)$	+	$(15 - 12)$
in A_3	X_{23}	$10 - 14$	=	$(12 - 14)$	+	$(10 - 12)$
	X_{33}	$11 - 14$	=	$(12 - 14)$	+	$(11 - 12)$
	X_{43}	$12 - 14$	=	$(12 - 14)$	+	$(12 - 12)$
	X_{53}	$12 - 14$	=	$(12 - 14)$	+	$(12 - 12)$

Step 2: **Perform the subtractions in step 1 to obtain numerical differences for each participant.**

		$(X - \overline{X}_G)$	=	$(\overline{X}_A - \overline{X}_G)$	+	$(X - \overline{X}_A)$
Scores	X_{11}	$+5$	=	$+3$	+	$+2$
in A_1	X_{21}	-1	=	$+3$	+	-4
	X_{31}	$+2$	=	$+3$	+	-1
	X_{41}	$+3$	=	$+3$	+	0
	X_{51}	$+6$	=	$+3$	+	$+3$
Scores	X_{12}	0	=	-1	+	$+1$
in A_2	X_{22}	-1	=	-1	+	0
	X_{32}	$+2$	=	-1	+	$+3$
	X_{42}	-2	=	-1	+	-1
	X_{52}	-4	=	-1	+	-3
Scores	X_{13}	$+1$	=	-2	+	$+3$
in A_3	X_{23}	-4	=	-2	+	-2
	X_{33}	-3	=	-2	+	-1
	X_{43}	-2	=	-2	+	0
	X_{53}	-2	=	-2	+	0

TABLE 10.4
(Continued)

Step 3: **Square each difference.**

		$(X - \overline{X}_G)^2$	$(\overline{X}_A - \overline{X}_G)^2$	$(X - \overline{X}_A)^2$
Scores	X_{11}	25	9	4
in A_1	X_{21}	1	9	16
	X_{31}	4	9	1
	X_{41}	9	9	0
	X_{51}	36	9	9
Scores	X_{12}	0	1	1
in A_2	X_{22}	1	1	0
	X_{32}	4	1	9
	X_{42}	4	1	1
	X_{52}	16	1	9
Scores	X_{13}	1	4	9
in A_3	X_{23}	16	4	4
	X_{33}	9	4	1
	X_{43}	4	4	0
	X_{53}	4	4	0

Step 4: **Sum the squared differences for each partition over all scores.**

$$\sum_{j=1}^{a=3} \sum_{i=1}^{n_A=5} (X - \overline{X}_G)^2 = \sum_{j=1}^{a=3} \sum_{i=1}^{n_A=5} (\overline{X}_A - \overline{X}_G)^2 + \sum_{j=1}^{a=3} \sum_{i=1}^{n_A=5} (X - \overline{X}_A)^2$$

$$134.00 = 70.00 + 64.00$$

$$SS_{\text{Total}} = SS_A + SS_{\text{Error}}$$

Step 1.   The scores of all 15 subjects in the experiment are partitioned following equation 10.2.

Step 2.   The numerical differences are found for each score.

Step 3.   Each of the positive and negative differences found in step 2 is squared.

Step 4.   The values of the squared differences are summed over the 15 values in each of the columns. The result is three sums of squares:

$$SS_{\text{Total}} = 134.00,$$

$$SS_A = 70.00,$$

$$SS_{\text{Error}} = 64.00.$$

As shown in step 4, the SS_{Total} is represented mathematically by

$$SS_{Total} = \sum_{j=1}^{a=3} \sum_{i=1}^{n_A=5} (X - \overline{X}_G)^2.$$

The double summation sign indicates that the squared differences [i.e., $(X - \overline{X}_G)^2$] are to be summed over all subjects in each treatment group (from the first subject, $i = 1$, to the last subject, n_A, in a particular group) and over all groups (from the first level of the independent variable, $j = 1$, to the last level, a). In the example there are five scores in each group ($n_A = 5$) and three groups ($a = 3$); thus, the summation limits are from $i = 1$ to $n_A = 5$ and from $j = 1$ to $a = 3$, or

$$\sum_{j=1}^{3} \sum_{i=1}^{5}.$$

Because I always sum over all scores in a group and over all groups, the double summation sign without the limits is typically used.

Similarly, to obtain SS_A, the squared differences of the treatment group mean from the grand mean are summed over all scores in the experiment; accordingly,

$$SS_A = \sum \sum (\overline{X}_A - \overline{X}_G)^2.$$

Finally, SS_{Error} is obtained by summing each squared difference of a person's score from the mean of his or her treatment group, or

$$SS_{Error} = \sum \sum (X - \overline{X}_A)^2.$$

An important relationship exists among the sum of squares terms and is shown at the bottom of Table 10.4. The SS_{Total} is equal to the sum of SS_A and SS_{Error}, or

$$SS_{Total} = SS_A + SS_{Error}. \tag{10.3}$$

Thus, the total variation in scores of an experiment, SS_{Total}, is the result of systematic variation that occurs between groups receiving different treatments, SS_A (sometimes identified as $SS_{Between-groups}$ or $SS_{Treatments}$), and error variation that occurs within groups, SS_{Error} (sometimes expressed as $SS_{Within-groups}$).

Finding Degrees of Freedom

The final step in obtaining MS_A and MS_{Error} is to divide each SS by its df. Recall that **degrees of freedom** refers to the number of scores free to vary in the computation of a statistic. The df for each sum of squares of equation 10.3 are easily determined from this definition.

Total Degrees of Freedom.   To find SS_{Total}, the grand mean, $\overline{X}_G$, must be known. Because the total sum of squares is based on the difference of every score in the experiment from the grand mean (i.e., $X - \overline{X}_G$), then one less than the total number of scores are free to vary. To illustrate, the grand mean for the 15 scores in Table 10.1 is 14.0. To obtain SS_{Total}, 14.0 is subtracted from each of the 15 scores. The sum of these 15 differences must equal 0. Thus, any 14 of the 15 scores are free to vary, but the fifteenth score becomes fixed if $\overline{X}_G$ is known. Accordingly, there are 14 df associated with the SS_{Total}. In general, the **total degrees of freedom**, or df_{Total}, are equal to one less than the total number of scores analyzed. In notation,

$$\text{Total degrees of freedom} = df_{Total} = N - 1,$$

where N is the total number of scores in the experiment.

Degrees of Freedom for SS_A.   The SS_A is computed from the differences of the means of the treatment groups (e.g., $\overline{X}_{A1}$, $\overline{X}_{A2}$, and $\overline{X}_{A3}$ for the example) from $\overline{X}_G$. For a research design with three levels of the independent variable and an equal number of scores in each condition, if $\overline{X}_G$ is known, then only two treatment means are free to vary. For example, if I know that $\overline{X}_G = 14.0$, $\overline{X}_{A1} = 17.0$, and $\overline{X}_{A3} = 12.0$, as in Table 10.1, then $\overline{X}_{A2}$ is also known; it must equal 13.0. Any other value of $\overline{X}_{A2}$ would not be consistent with $\overline{X}_G$ equal to 14.0. Accordingly, there are 2 df for SS_A in the example.

In general, the **df for SS_A**, or **df_A**, are equal to one less than the number of levels of the independent variable. In notation,

$$df \text{ for } SS_A = df_A = a - 1,$$

where a is the number of levels of the independent variable A.

Degrees of Freedom for SS_{Error}.   The SS_{Error} is based on subtracting the mean of each treatment group, $\overline{X}_A$, from each score within that treatment group for each group in the experiment. Thus, for each level of the independent variable, after $\overline{X}_A$ is determined, only $n_A - 1$ scores are free to vary within that level. In Table 10.1, if $\overline{X}_A$ is known, only four of the five scores are free to vary within each treatment condition A_1, A_2, and A_3. Because there are three levels of the independent variable and four scores free to vary within each level, there are 12 df for SS_{Error} (4 df for A_1 plus 4 df for A_2 plus 4 df for A_3 equals 12).

In general, where a is the number of levels of the independent variable and there are n_A scores within each level of the independent variable, the **df for SS_{Error}** or **df_{Error}** = $a(n_A - 1)$. Because $(a)(n)$ equals the total number of scores (N), the df_{Error} may also be expressed as N minus a, or

$$df \text{ for } SS_{Error} = df_{Error} = N - a.$$

Additivity of Degrees of Freedom.   The degrees of freedom are additive in the same manner as the corresponding sums of squares values. Thus,

$$df_{Total} = df_A + df_{Error}. \tag{10.4}$$

This relationship holds in the example, for $df_{Total} = 14$, $df_A = 2$, and $df_{Error} = 12$.

Finding Mean Squares from SS and df

The F statistic is a ratio of two mean squares, MS_A and MS_{Error}. The two required MS values are derived from the SS obtained in equation 10.3 and the df value associated with each SS. Specifically, these mean squares are

$$MS_A = \frac{SS_A}{df_A}$$

and

$$MS_{Error} = \frac{SS_{Error}}{df_{Error}}.$$

Although it is possible to obtain the MS_{Total} by dividing the SS_{Total} by the df_{Total}, this value provides no useful information in an analysis of variance and typically it is not calculated. For the scores in Table 10.1, I have found $SS_A = 70.00$ and $SS_{Error} = 64.00$ (see Table 10.4) $df_A = 2$ and $df_{Error} = 12$. Consequently,

$$MS_A = \frac{SS_A}{df_A} = \frac{70.00}{2} = 35.000$$

and

$$MS_{Error} = \frac{SS_{Error}}{df_{Error}} = \frac{64.00}{12} = 5.333.$$

Computing the F Statistic

At the beginning of this chapter the F statistic was defined as

$$F = \frac{MS_A}{MS_{Error}}.$$

For the scores of Table 10.1 $MS_A = 35.000$ and $MS_{Error} = 5.333$. Thus,

$$F_{obs} = \frac{35.000}{5.333} = 6.563 = 6.56 \quad \text{rounded to two decimal places,}$$

where F_{obs} is used to indicate the value of F observed from the scores analyzed. Notice that because MS_A and MS_{Error} are based on sum of squares values, which must always be positive, F, too, must always be positive. A negative value of F indicates a mistake in calculations.

The numerical values of an analysis of variance are frequently summarized in a table identifying the sources of variation; SS, df, and MS values; and the value of F_{obs}. Table 10.5 illustrates how such a summary table is organized using the numerical values obtained from the data of Table 10.1. The value of F is carried to two decimal places in a summary table,

TABLE 10.5

Numerical summary of the analysis of variance on the scores in Table 10.1.

Source	SS	df	MS	F[a]
Type of drawing (A)	70.00	2	35.000	6.56*
Error	64.00	12	5.333	
Total	134.00	14		

*$p < .05$.

[a]Statistically significant values of F are indicated by a probability level footnote on a summary table (i.e., *$p < .05$).

TABLE 10.6

Summary of definitional formulas for a one-factor between-subjects analysis of variance.

Source	SS	df[a]	MS	F
Factor A	$\sum\sum (\overline{X}_A - \overline{X}_G)^2$	$a - 1$	SS_A/df_A	MS_A/MS_{Error}
Error	$\sum\sum (X - \overline{X}_A)^2$	$N - a$	SS_{Error}/df_{Error}	
Total	$\sum\sum (X - \overline{X}_G)^2$	$N - 1$	Not calculated	

[a]a = number of levels of factor A, N = total number of scores.

and values of the SS and MS are carried to two or more decimal places as needed to minimize rounding error. Table 10.6 summarizes the definitional formulas for the SS, df, and MS.

It has taken considerable discussion to derive the F statistic and calculate its value. However, in actual practice, its value is most often found using a computer program or from computational formulas. My goal in this section was not ease of computation but to demonstrate how the F statistic arises from a set of scores. I discuss how to interpret and use this information next.

TESTING YOUR KNOWLEDGE 10.1

1. Define: a, between-groups variance, df_A, df_{Error}, df_{Total}, F, factor A, MS_A, MS_{Error}, N, n_A, one-factor multilevel designs, SS_A, SS_{Error}, SS_{Total}, within-groups variance, $X - \overline{X}_G$, $\overline{X}_A - \overline{X}_G$, $X - \overline{X}_A$.
2. What is the limitation of a t test for analyzing the data of an experiment?
3. What is the test statistic used in analysis of variance?
4. Write the general equation for the F statistic.
5. Into what two sources does a one-factor between-subjects analysis of variance partition or break down the total variation of the scores in an experiment?
6. An experimenter used a one-factor between-subjects experiment with four levels of factor A: A_1, A_2, A_3, and A_4. There were 11 different participants in each level. What are the values of a, n_A, and N?

7. Write the general equation for partitioning scores obtained in a one-factor between-subjects experiment.

8. Explain why the value of $\overline{X}_A - \overline{X}_G$ varies with the effect of an independent variable in an experiment.

9. Explain why the value of $X - \overline{X}_A$ varies with error variation in an experiment.

10. Complete the following equations for a one-factor between-subjects analysis of variance.
    a. $\sum\sum (X - \overline{X}_G)^2 =$
    b. $SS_{Total} =$
    c. $df_A =$
    d. $df_{Error} =$
    e. $MS_A =$
    f. $MS_{Error} =$
    g. $F =$

11. What is the value of SS_{Total} if $SS_A = 50.00$ and $SS_{Error} = 100.00$?

12. What is the value of SS_A if $SS_{Total} = 75.00$ and $SS_{Error} = 50.00$?

13. What is the value of df_{Total} if $df_A = 4$ and $df_{Error} = 75$?

14. What is the value of MS_A if $SS_A = 100.00$ and $df_A = 4$?

15. What is the value of MS_{Error} if $SS_{Error} = 760.00$ and $df_{Error} = 76$?

16. A behavioral scientist used a one-factor between-subjects design with four levels of factor A. There were 11 participants in each level. What are the values of df_A, df_{Error}, and df_{Total}?

17. You conducted an experiment with two levels of an independent variable and three people in each group and obtained the following scores:

Factor A

A_1	A_2
30	34
32	36
28	32

Partition these scores following the approach illustrated in Table 10.4. Find the SS_{Total}, SS_A, and SS_{Error} and the df for each SS. Then complete a numerical summary table for the analysis.

18. You conducted an experiment with three levels of an independent variable and three subjects in each group and obtained the following scores:

Factor A

A_1	A_2	A_3
30	34	37
32	36	35
28	32	33

Partition these scores following the approach illustrated in Table 10.4. Find the SS_{Total}, SS_A, and SS_{Error} and the df for each SS. Then complete a numerical summary table for the analysis.

19. The following two tables are incomplete summary tables for a one-factor between-subjects analysis of variance. Assume an equal number of scores in each level of the inde-

pendent variable. Fill in the missing values in each table by using the relationships among *SS* and *df* given in equations 10.3 and 10.4, respectively, and the formulas in Table 10.6. Then answer these questions for each table.

a. How many levels of the independent variable were used?
b. How many subjects were measured in each treatment group?
c. How many subjects participated in the study?

TABLE 1

Source	SS	df	MS	F
Factor A	50.00	1	—	—
Error	260.00	26	—	
Total	—	—		

TABLE 2

Source	SS	df	MS	F
Factor A	—	3	6.00	—
Error	—	76	—	
Total	170.00	79		

STATISTICAL HYPOTHESIS TESTING WITH *F*

The value of F_{obs} allows us to decide if the treatment means differ significantly. To understand how this decision is made, it is necessary to review briefly the factors influencing MS_A and MS_{Error} and the relationship of MS_A to MS_{Error}.

Factors Affecting the Value of MS_A and MS_{Error}

MS_A

The value of MS_A is given by

$$MS_A = \frac{SS_A}{df_A},$$

where

$$SS_A = \sum\sum (\overline{X}_A - \overline{X}_G)^2.$$

As I indicated in the discussion of partitioning a score, two sources of variation affect the extent of the difference between a group mean and a grand mean and, thus, the value of SS_A in any experiment: (1) the effect of the independent variable and (2) sampling error. Hence, MS_A, too, varies with the effect of the independent variable and sampling error. Because MS_A increases with an effect of an independent variable, it is used as a measure of the systematic variance created by the independent variable.

MS_{Error}

The MS_{Error} is obtained by

$$\frac{\sum\sum (X - \overline{X}_A)^2}{df_{Error}}$$

and measures only the within-groups error variation in an experiment. It is not affected by an independent variable. As I indicated earlier, this result occurs because any systematic changes in scores due to a treatment effect will also be accompanied by a corresponding increase or decrease in the treatment group mean. Thus, the difference between a participant's score and the group mean, $(X - \overline{X}_A)$, will not change with a treatment effect. Hence, MS_{Error} measures only within-groups error variation in the scores of an experiment. The factors affecting each mean square are summarized in Table 10.7.

The Relationship of MS_A and MS_{Error}

Unbiased Estimates.   Both MS_A and MS_{Error} are unbiased estimates of the population variance of scores, σ^2. They are unbiased because to obtain each MS the sum of squares is divided by degrees of freedom rather than by the actual number of scores involved in the computation of the variance. As unbiased estimates, neither MS should be systematically smaller nor larger than σ^2 when error variation alone is responsible for the variability in scores on which the estimate is based.

Independent Estimates. MS_A and MS_{Error} are also independent estimates of the population variance. **Independent estimates** mean that either mean square may change in value without affecting the value of the other, a point demonstrated in the discussion of the factors affecting SS values. These characteristics of MS_A and MS_{Error} lead to the following expectations of the value of F_{obs}.

- **Expected value of F when an independent variable has no effect:** If an independent variable has no effect, then only error variation occurs in an experiment. In this circumstance I expect MS_A and MS_{Error} to estimate only error variation and, thus, to be about equal. Accordingly, the value of F_{obs} should be equal to about 1.00.

TABLE 10.7
Factors affecting MS_A and MS_{Error} in an experiment.

Mean Square	Affected By:
MS_A	The effect of the independent variable Sampling error
MS_{Error}	Within-groups error variation

- **Expected value of F when an independent variable has an effect:** When an independent variable does produce an effect, then MS_A responds to the systematic variation contributed by the independent variable in addition to the existing sampling error. Consequently, MS_A will be larger than MS_{Error}, and F_{obs} will be greater than 1.00. This relationship allows using F in a statistical hypothesis test.

Statistical Decision Making from the F Statistic

Statistical testing with the F statistic follows the familiar steps:

- A null hypothesis, H_0, and an alternative hypothesis, H_1, are formulated.
- The sampling distribution of F, assuming that H_0 is true, is obtained. This distribution is given in Table A.3.
- A significance level is selected.
- A critical value of F, identified as F_{crit}, is found from the sampling distribution of F given in Table A.3.
- A rejection region is located in the sampling distribution of F.
- The F ratio, identified as F_{obs}, is calculated from the sample data.
- A decision to reject or not reject H_0 is made on the basis of whether or not F_{obs} falls into the rejection region.

Statistical Hypotheses

Null Hypothesis.   For an experiment with three levels of an independent variable, the null hypothesis tested in an analysis of variance is that the populations from which the three samples were selected have the same means and is written

$$H_0: \mu_{A1} = \mu_{A2} = \mu_{A3}.$$

This null hypothesis represents the situation that exists if the independent variable has no effect. If H_0 is true for an experiment, then any observed difference among the group means is due only to sampling error.

The number of population means identified in the null hypothesis always corresponds to the number of levels of the independent variable. If an experiment involves five levels of an independent variable, then H_0 is written

$$H_0: \mu_{A1} = \mu_{A2} = \mu_{A3} = \mu_{A4} = \mu_{A5}.$$

Alternative Hypothesis.   The alternative hypothesis, H_1, is

$$H_1: \text{The } \mu_A\text{'s are not all equal,}$$

regardless of the number of population means involved in the null hypothesis. The alternative hypothesis states a situation that exists if the independent variable has an effect.

The Sampling Distribution of F

The decision to reject or not reject H_0 depends on how rare or unlikely a value of F_{obs} would be if H_0 were true. The sampling distribution of a statistic provides the probability of values of the statistic when H_0 is true. Thus, the probability of obtaining a certain value of F_{obs} if H_0 is true is determined from the sampling distribution of the F statistic. There is not just one sampling distribution of F, however, for the sampling distribution of F depends on the number of levels of the independent variable and the number of scores in each treatment group. Specifically, the sampling distribution of F varies with the degrees of freedom for the numerator (i.e., df_A) and the denominator (i.e., df_{Error}) of the F statistic.

As an illustration, the sampling distribution of F for the example experiment with 2 df for the numerator (i.e., 2 df for df_A) and 12 degrees of freedom for the denominator (i.e., 12 df for df_{Error}) is illustrated in Figure 10.2. This distribution is positively skewed and its lowest value is zero; the value of F obtained if the sample means are equal to each other and the resulting MS_A value is zero. The most probable value of F is about 1.00, for if H_0 is true, then MS_A should be about the same as MS_{Error}. There is no upper limit to the values that F may attain; F may take on any value between 0 and positive infinity. Because the probability of obtaining a value of F between 0 and positive infinity is 1.00, the area under the distribution is equal to 1.00.

Selecting a Significance Level

The significance level is a probability value that provides the criterion for rejecting H_0. As I have discussed, the significance level usually adopted in behavioral science research is either $\alpha = .05$ or $\alpha = .01$. I illustrate locating a rejection region for a .05 significance level in Figure 10.2.

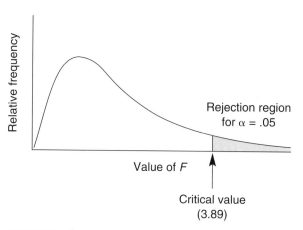

FIGURE 10.2
Theoretical sampling distribution of F for 2 and 12 degrees of freedom. The rejection region for $\alpha = .05$ is illustrated. The F_{crit} from Table A.3 is 3.89.

Locating the Rejection Region for F

The rejection region represents values of F that have a probability equal to or less than α if H_0 is true. Thus, the rejection region identifies values of F_{obs} that meet the criterion for rejecting H_0. The rejection region for F_{obs} is always in the right tail of the sampling distribution for F, as shown in Figure 10.2. We can see why the rejection region is located here by recalling how the value of F_{obs} varies with the effect of an independent variable.

If an independent variable has no effect and, therefore, H_0 is true, then it is expected that MS_A and MS_{Error} will be nearly equal; consequently, F_{obs} should be about 1.00. If the independent variable does have an effect and, therefore, H_0 is not true, then MS_A will be larger than MS_{Error}, and F_{obs} will become greater than 1.00. In order to reject the null hypothesis, then, F_{obs} must be sufficiently larger than 1.00 so that the probability of such a value of F_{obs} occurring if H_0 were true is equal to or less than the alpha level selected. Therefore, the rejection region for F always lies among the larger values of F in the right tail of the distribution.

Critical values of F (identified as F_{crit}) identifying the lower limit of the rejection region for $\alpha = .05$ and $.01$ are presented in Table A.3. A portion of Table A.3a for the .05 significance level is presented in Table 10.8. This table is arranged so that the degrees of freedom for the numerator (i.e., df_A) of the F ratio appear in a row across the top of the table. The degrees of freedom for the denominator (i.e., df_{Error}) appear in the column on the left side of the table.

TABLE 10.8
Values of F_{crit} for $\alpha = .05$.

Degrees of Freedom for Denominator	Degrees of Freedom for Numerator				
	1	**2**	**3**	**4**	**5**
1	161.4	199.5	215.7	224.6	230.2
2	18.51	19.00	19.16	19.25	19.30
3	10.13	9.55	9.28	9.12	9.01
4	7.71	6.94	6.59	6.39	6.26
5	6.61	5.79	5.41	5.19	5.05
6	5.99	5.14	4.76	4.53	4.39
7	5.59	4.74	4.35	4.12	3.97
8	5.32	4.46	4.07	3.84	3.69
9	5.12	4.26	3.86	3.63	3.48
10	4.96	4.10	3.71	3.48	3.33
11	4.84	3.98	3.59	3.36	3.20
12	4.75	**3.89**	3.49	3.26	3.11

Note: This table is only a portion of the complete table presented in Table A.3.

Source: Reprinted from Table 18. Percentage points of the F-distribution (variance ratio). Upper 5 % points. *Biometrika Tables for Statisticians*, Volume 1, Copyright 1976, Cambridge University Press. Reprinted by permission of the Biometrika Trustees.

To locate the value of F_{crit} for the example with 2 degrees of freedom for the numerator and 12 degrees of freedom for the denominator, I find the column for 2 *df* and then locate the row for 12 *df*. This column and row intersect at the value of 3.89 (boldfaced in Table 10.8). This value is F_{crit} and locates the rejection region for F_{obs} with 2 and 12 *df*, as illustrated in Figure 10.2. Any value of F_{obs} with 2 and 12 *df* and equal to or larger than 3.89 lies in the rejection region. Values of *F* equal to or greater than 3.89 occur only five or fewer times in every 100 experiments if H_0 is true.

Decisions about the Statistical Hypotheses

The value of F_{obs} provides the basis for making decisions about the statistical hypotheses. If F_{obs} falls into the rejection region, then H_0 is rejected and H_1 accepted. There is a *statistically significant difference* among the sample means. If F_{obs} does not fall into the rejection region, then I fail to reject H_0 and do not accept H_1. The differences among the sample means are *nonsignificant*.

Statistically Significant Difference.   To illustrate a statistically significant difference, I use the example experiment on the retention of drawings. In this experiment I manipulated three types of drawings to find if the type of drawing affected recall of the items depicted in the drawings. The mean number of items recalled as a function of type of drawing is given next.

	Type of Drawing (*A*)		
	Incomplete Outline (A_1)	**Outline** (A_2)	**Detailed** (A_3)
$\overline{X}_A$	17.0	13.0	12.0

The analysis of variance on the scores of Table 10.1 resulted in $F_{obs}(2, 12) = 6.56$ (see Table 10.5). For 2, 12 *df*, F_{crit} at the .05 level is 3.89. F_{obs} is larger than F_{crit} and, thus, falls into the rejection region. Accordingly, I reject the null hypothesis

$$H_0: \mu_{A1} = \mu_{A2} = \mu_{A3},$$

and accept the alternative

$$H_1: \text{The } \mu_A\text{'s are not all equal.}$$

We conclude that the three sample means are not all from the same population. The independent variable did affect the number of items recalled. Notice, however, that there are many ways for "H_1: The μ_A's are not all equal" to be true. The null hypothesis will be true, for example, if μ_{A1} is greater than either μ_{A2} or μ_{A3}, and μ_{A2} and μ_{A3} are equal, or if μ_{A1} is greater than μ_{A2}, and μ_{A2} is greater than μ_{A3}. Which relationship holds for the pattern of means in the example? The analysis of variance alone does not answer this question with certainty, for rejection of H_0 when there are three or more treatment groups in an experiment simply lets us conclude that there is at least one statistically significant difference among the means. A follow-up with a multiple comparison test is necessary to find the specific significant differences between the means. I discuss this test in a later section of this chapter. The decision-making procedures and corresponding conclusions for a statistically significant difference are summarized in the left column of Table 10.9.

Nonsignificant Difference.   If I fail to reject H_0 and do not accept H_1, then I have no evidence that the null hypothesis is not true. The implication for the experiment is that the independent variable had no effect. Any observed numerical differences among the means are attributed to sampling error. These decisions and conclusions are summarized in the right column of Table 10.9.

Assumptions of One-Factor Between-Subjects Analysis of Variance

Similarly to the t test, the between-subjects analysis of variance is based on three assumptions about the scores obtained in an experiment:

1. The scores in each sample are drawn randomly from a population of scores, and each score is independent of each other score.
2. The scores in the populations sampled are normally distributed.
3. The variances of scores in the populations are equal.

TABLE 10.9

Summary of decisions and conclusions in statistical hypothesis testing using the analysis of variance for a one-factor between-subjects design. A .05 significance level is used.

If F_{obs} falls into the rejection region for α = .05, then:	If F_{obs} does not fall into the rejection region for α = .05, then:
Probability of F_{obs} is less than or equal to .05, or $p \le .05$.	Probability of F_{obs} is greater than .05, or $p > .05$.
H_0 is rejected.	H_0 is not rejected.
H_1 is accepted. The sample means are not all from the same population.	H_1 is not accepted.
At least one difference between the treatment means is statistically significant at the .05 level.	There are no significant differences among the sample means at the .05 level.
It is decided that something in addition to sampling error is responsible for the differences among the sample means. In a carefully done experiment the difference is attributed to the independent variable.	It is decided that sampling error alone is the most plausible explanation of the differences among the sample means. There is no evidence that the independent variable had an effect.
Multiple comparison tests are needed if the independent variable has three or more levels.	No multiple comparison tests are needed.

These assumptions are important because the sampling distribution of F and, therefore, the values of F_{crit} given in Table A.3 are generated from populations that meet these assumptions. In order for the between-subjects analysis of variance to be used, each score in the experiment must be independent of every other score. That is, every participant may be given only one level of the independent variable and contribute only one score in the experiment. If a participant is given more than one level of the independent variable and two or more scores are analyzed for a participant, then the within-subjects analysis of variance must be used. This analysis of variance is discussed in Chapter 12.

The second and third assumptions may not be met by some experiments. Violations of the second (the normal distribution of scores) and the third (the equality of variances) assumption can change the probability of obtaining a particular value of F_{obs} and, thus, affect the probability of making a Type I error. Violations of these assumptions are more likely to have minimal effects on the probability of making a Type I error when the following conditions are met:

- The number of scores in each group is the same.
- The shape of the distributions of the scores for each group is about the same, and the distributions are neither very peaked nor very flat.
- The significance level is set at .05 rather than .01.

TESTING YOUR KNOWLEDGE 10.2

1. Define: F_{crit}, F_{obs}, rejection region.
2. What factors affect the value of MS_A in an experiment?
3. Explain why MS_A increases in value if an independent variable has an effect in an experiment.
4. What factors affect the value of MS_{Error} in an experiment?
5. Explain why the value of MS_{Error} does not change if an independent variable has an effect in an experiment.
6. What value of F_{obs} is expected if an independent variable has no effect in an experiment?
7. What is expected to happen to the value of F_{obs} if an independent variable has an effect in an experiment?
8. Write the statistical hypotheses for the F test for:
   a. Two independent groups.
   b. Four independent groups.
   c. Six independent groups.
9. To what situation in an experiment does H_0 of an analysis of variance correspond?
10. To what situation in an experiment does H_1 of an analysis of variance correspond?
11. What is the lower limit for the value of F if H_0 is true?
12. What is the upper limit for the value of F if H_0 is true?
13. This exercise provides values for df_A, df_{Error}, and F_{obs} for several hypothetical one-factor between-subjects experiments. For each set of values, obtain the value of F_{crit} for a .05 significance level from Table A.3a. Then indicate whether F_{obs} falls into the rejection region and what decision you make with respect to H_0 and H_1. If the exact df are not tabled for df_{Error}, then use the next lower tabled value.

Experiment	df_A	df_{Error}	F_{obs}
1	1	10	5.12
2	2	24	3.29
3	1	24	4.26
4	2	90	3.24
5	2	12	3.94
6	2	15	3.60
7	4	45	1.93
8	3	20	1.46
9	6	63	2.30
10	4	95	2.13

14. Identify the assumptions underlying the use of the one-factor between-subjects analysis of variance.

15. Under what conditions will violation of normality of the distribution of scores in the population have the least effect on Type I errors for a one-factor between-subjects analysis of variance?

INTERPRETING A STATISTICALLY SIGNIFICANT *F* IN A MULTILEVEL DESIGN

Multiple Comparison Tests

Multiple comparison tests: Statistical tests used to make pairwise comparisons to find which means differ significantly from one another in a one-factor multilevel design.

Earlier I indicated that rejecting H_0 when there are three or more levels of an independent variable in an experiment leads us to conclude that there is at least one statistically significant difference among the means. But the analysis of variance alone does not identify specifically which means differ significantly from which other means. To decide which pairs of means differ significantly, we use multiple comparison tests. **Multiple comparison tests** are statistical tests used to make pairwise comparisons to find which means differ significantly from one another in a one-factor multilevel design.

Given the three sample means from the experiment on the effect of type of drawing on recall of details, I can make three two-mean comparisons:

$$\overline{X}_{A1} \quad \text{compared to} \quad \overline{X}_{A2},$$
$$\overline{X}_{A1} \quad \text{compared to} \quad \overline{X}_{A3},$$
$$\overline{X}_{A2} \quad \text{compared to} \quad \overline{X}_{A3}.$$

Pairwise comparisons: Statistical comparisons involving two means.

Because these comparisons each involve two means, they are called **pairwise comparisons**. By performing statistical tests on these three pairwise comparisons, I can find which pairs of means differ significantly.

One way of making pairwise comparisons would be to use t_{ind} to conduct three t tests, one for each comparison. From the outcome of these three tests, I could determine which means differ significantly from each other. The issue is not so easily resolved, however, because of the probability of a Type I error occurring in the comparisons to be made. Recall that a Type I error occurs when H_0 is actually true but is rejected in the statistical hypothesis test. To keep the probability of making a Type I error low, researchers usually set the significance level at .05 or .01. For the overall analysis of variance on the example (reported in Table 10.5), the probability of a Type I error is equal to the value of α, or .05. But when conducting multiple comparisons, an investigator runs many more statistical tests, the exact number depending on the number of comparisons to be made. Consider, for example, conducting a t_{ind} on each of the three pairwise comparisons in the example experiment. For each t test the probability of a Type I error is equal to α. Hence, the probability of making at least one Type I error among the three comparisons is about .14, an unacceptably high value. The **error rate in an experiment** is the probability of making at least one Type I error in the comparisons conducted. The error rate in an experiment increases very rapidly with a growing number of comparisons. As an example, consider using the t test for five pairwise comparisons with $\alpha = .05$ for each comparison. If H_0 is true, then the probability of at least one Type I error in the five comparisons is equal to about .23. This error rate is obviously too high for most researchers. To control this error rate, alternatives to the t test have been developed for making multiple comparisons. I present one specific test for making one type of multiple comparison, post hoc comparisons.

Error rate in an experiment: The probability of making at least one Type I error in the statistical comparisons conducted in an experiment.

Post hoc comparisons: Statistical tests that make all possible pairwise comparisons after a statistically significant F_{obs} has occurred for the overall analysis of variance.

     Post hoc comparisons make all possible pairwise comparisons after a statistically significant F_{obs} has occurred for the overall analysis of variance. The term *post hoc* is Latin for "after this" or "after the fact." Its use here means a comparison made after F_{obs} is statistically significant. If F_{obs} of the overall analysis of variance is nonsignificant and H_0 is not rejected, no further data analysis is needed and post hoc comparisons are not carried out. The next section presents the Tukey HSD test for post hoc comparisons.

The Tukey HSD Test for Post Hoc Comparisons

Critical difference (CD): The minimum numerical difference between two treatment means that is statistically significant.

The Tukey HSD test (HSD represents *honestly significant difference*) provides a **critical difference** (abbreviated **CD**) that specifies the minimum difference between two treatment means that is statistically significant at the α level chosen. The absolute value of an observed difference in a pairwise comparison of means is compared with the Tukey *CD*. If the absolute value of the observed difference between the means is equal to or larger than the *CD*, then the sample means differ significantly and are treated as representing different populations.

    The *CD* for the Tukey HSD test is found from

$$CD = q\sqrt{\frac{MS_{\text{Error}}}{n_A}},$$

where $q =$ the *studentized range statistic*, a numerical value that depends on (1) the level of α selected, (2) the number of levels of the independent variable, and (3) the *df* for MS_{Error} in the analysis of variance. Values of q are given in Table A.4 for $\alpha = .01$ and $\alpha = .05$ for up to 10 levels of an independent variable.

       $MS_{\text{Error}} =$ the error term from the overall analysis of variance.

          $n_A =$ the number of scores in each treatment condition. The values of n_A for each treatment condition must be equal to use this formula.

Obtaining the Tukey CD

I illustrate calculating the Tukey HSD *CD* with the example scores given in Table 10.1 and the analysis of variance of those scores summarized in Table 10.5. The F_{obs}, 6.56, is statistically significant at the .05 level; thus, I reject H_0: $\mu_{A1} = \mu_{A2} = \mu_{A3}$ and accept H_1: The μ_A's are not all equal. The overall analysis of variance indicates that there is at least one significant difference among the three means being compared. To find specifically which means differ from each other, I will calculate the Tukey HSD *CD*.

From the analysis of variance summarized in Table 10.5, $MS_{Error} = 5.333$. The number of scores in each treatment group is 5; thus, $n_A = 5$. The value of q is obtained from Table A.4. This table requires knowing (1) the number of levels of the independent variable a (in the example $a = 3$) and (2) the df_{Error} from the analysis of variance (in this case, 12). At the .05 level, for $a = 3$ and 12 df_{Error}, $q = 3.77$. Substituting these values into the formula for the *CD* leads to

$$CD = q\sqrt{\frac{MS_{Error}}{n_A}} = 3.77\sqrt{\frac{5.333}{5}}$$

$$= 3.9 \quad \text{rounded to one decimal place.}$$

Interpreting the Tukey CD

The *CD* for the Tukey test for the example is 3.9. A difference between two treatment means in Table 10.1 equal to or larger in absolute value (i.e., the value of the difference ignoring the + or − sign) than 3.9 items recalled is statistically significant at the .05 level. The three pairwise comparisons, the absolute values of each comparison, the statistical hypothesis, and the decision for each hypothesis are shown in Table 10.10.

Notice that two pairwise comparisons are larger than 3.9 in absolute value: $\overline{X}_{A1}$ versus $\overline{X}_{A2}$ ($17.0 - 13.0 = 4.0$) and $\overline{X}_{A1}$ versus $\overline{X}_{A3}$ ($17.0 - 12.0 = 5.0$). Each of these comparisons

TABLE 10.10
Application of the Tukey HSD *CD* to the pairwise comparisons of the example experiment. The value of the *CD* = 3.9.

Comparison	Absolute Value of Comparison	Statistical Hypotheses	Decision
$\overline{X}_{A1}$ vs. $\overline{X}_{A2}$ ($17.0 - 13.0$)	4.0	H_0: $\mu_{A1} = \mu_{A2}$ H_1: $\mu_{A1} \neq \mu_{A2}$	Reject Accept
$\overline{X}_{A1}$ vs. $\overline{X}_{A3}$ ($17.0 - 12.0$)	5.0	H_0: $\mu_{A1} = \mu_{A3}$ H_1: $\mu_{A1} \neq \mu_{A3}$	Reject Accept
$\overline{X}_{A2}$ vs. $\overline{X}_{A3}$ ($13.0 - 12.0$)	1.0	H_0: $\mu_{A2} = \mu_{A3}$ H_1: $\mu_{A2} \neq \mu_{A3}$	Fail to reject Do not accept

A_1 = incomplete outline drawing, A_2 = outline drawing, A_3 = detailed drawing.

reveals a statistically significant difference between the means compared. The absolute value of the comparison of $\overline{X}_{A2}$ versus $\overline{X}_{A3}$ ($13.0 - 12.0 = 1.0$) is less than 3.9. Thus, the difference between outline and detailed drawings is nonsignificant. Hence, the Tukey test leads to the conclusion that recall for incomplete outline drawings ($\overline{X}_{A1}$) is significantly greater than recall for outline drawings ($\overline{X}_{A2}$) or detail drawings ($\overline{X}_{A3}$), but recall for outline drawings ($\overline{X}_{A2}$) does not differ from that of detailed drawings ($\overline{X}_{A3}$).

This result provides support for the effort hypothesis of memory processing presented at the opening of this chapter. The incomplete outline drawings, requiring the most effort to process, were best recalled. The result provides no evidence to support the elaboration hypothesis, which predicted that detailed drawings would be best recalled.

Two Instances When a Post Hoc Test Is Not Needed

There are two instances when a post hoc test is not needed. The first is when F_{obs} for the analysis of variance is nonsignificant. A nonsignificant F_{obs} indicates there are no significant differences between any of the means in the analysis; thus, no follow-up test is needed.

The second instance is when there are only two levels of the independent variable. If F_{obs} is significant for this analysis, then $H_0: \mu_{A1} = \mu_{A2}$ is rejected and H_1: The μ_A's are not equal is accepted. Obviously, the only means that can differ significantly in this instance are $\overline{X}_{A1}$ and $\overline{X}_{A2}$. Thus, no further test is needed on these means.

MEASURING THE STRENGTH OF A TREATMENT EFFECT

Similarly to the t test, the analysis of variance indicates whether an independent variable has an effect on the dependent variable of an experiment, but it does not indicate the size of that effect. Again, η^2 may be used as a strength-of-effect measure when a statistically significant value of F_{obs} occurs.

Calculating Eta Squared for the Analysis of Variance

For a one-factor between-subjects analysis of variance, η^2 may be obtained from two alternative formulas. If sums of squares values are known, η^2 is given by

$$\eta^2 = \frac{SS_A}{SS_{Total}}.$$

When only F_{obs} and df are known for an analysis of variance, η^2 can be obtained by

$$\eta^2 = \frac{(df_A)(F_{obs})}{(df_A)(F_{obs}) + df_{Error}}.$$

Example of Calculating η^2 for the One-Factor Between-Subjects Analysis of Variance

An η^2 may be calculated for the example problem either from the SS values or the F_{obs} and df values of the analysis of variance summarized in Table 10.5.

η^2 from *SS* Values

$$\eta^2 = \frac{SS_A}{SS_{\text{Total}}} = \frac{70.00}{134.00} = .52 \qquad \text{rounded to two decimal places.}$$

η^2 from F_{obs} and *df* Values

$$\eta^2 = \frac{(df_A)(F_{obs})}{(df_A)(F_{obs}) + df_{\text{Error}}} = \frac{(2)(6.56)}{(2)(6.56) + 12} = .52 \qquad \text{rounded to two decimal places.}$$

This η^2 indicates that a 52 percent reduction in the total variance of the scores occurs when the means of the levels of the independent variable are used to predict scores in comparison to using the grand mean as the predicted score. This independent variable accounts for a large proportion of the variance in the recall scores.

THE RELATIONSHIP BETWEEN t_{ind} AND *F*

The t_{ind} and the one-factor between-subjects analysis of variance lead to the same statistical decisions when analyzing data from an experiment with two levels of the independent variable. If I reject H_0 with a two-tailed t_{ind} at the .05 level, then I would also reject H_0 with an analysis of variance on the same data. The reason is that $t^2 = F$ or $t = \sqrt{F}$. This relation also holds for the tabled critical values of t and F for the analysis of two sample means when the same significance level is adopted. As an example, for $\alpha = .05$, F_{crit} for 1, 8 *df* is 5.32. The value of t_{crit} for 8 *df* and $\alpha = .05$ in a two-tailed test is 2.306, which is the square root of 5.32. Thus, $(2.306)^2 = 5.32$, and $t^2 = F$. Because of this relationship between t and F, either test may be used for comparing two independent sample means; the tests provide identical outcomes and one is not preferred over the other. The advantage of analysis of variance appears only when three or more treatment conditions are being compared.

Example Problem 10.1

Using the One-Factor Between-Subjects Analysis of Variance with the Tukey HSD Test

Problem: Mood-state-dependent memory refers to the finding that recall of material is improved when one is in the same mood state at the time of recall as at the time of learning (Bower, 1981). Suppose that to study mood-state-dependent memory you create five equivalent groups of 10 people each. For each group you generate a mood state by having participants read a series of statements designed to induce either a happy, sad, or neutral mood state. After the mood state is induced, the participants learn a list of 15 common nouns. Twenty-four hours later the participants return, and you again induce a mood state and have the participants recall the previously learned list of nouns. At this recall session the mood state may be the same or different from the mood state induced at learning. The mood states induced at learning and recall for the five groups are as follows:

Mood State Group

	A_1	A_2	A_3	A_4	A_5
Mood induced at learning	Happy	Sad	Neutral	Happy	Sad
Mood induced at recall	Happy	Sad	Neutral	Sad	Happy

Mood-state-dependent memory predicts that the groups having congruent learning and recall states (i.e., groups A_1, A_2, and A_3) should have greater recall of the list of nouns than groups having different learning and recall mood states (i.e., groups A_4 and A_5). Suppose that you obtained the numbers of items recalled for each group as shown in Table 10.11. Which group means differ significantly from each other at the .05 level?

Solution: The design is a one-factor between-subjects design with five levels of the independent variable, mood state group. The first step in data analysis is to calculate a one-factor between-subjects analysis of variance on the scores. If F_{obs} is statistically significant, I will use the Tukey HSD test to find the statistically significant pairwise differences between the treatment means.

Statistic to Be Used: $F = MS_A/MS_{Error}$.

TABLE 10.11
Number of nouns correctly recalled as a function of mood state group.

	Mood State Group				
	A_1	A_2	A_3	A_4	A_5
	8	14	9	5	6
	12	13	12	9	9
	12	6	7	6	8
	7	9	7	8	8
	10	12	11	4	5
	9	10	6	6	4
	13	8	10	10	5
	8	7	8	3	7
	14	11	13	7	7
	11	9	10	3	3
$\overline{X}_A$	10.40	9.90	9.30	6.10	6.20
s_A	2.37	2.60	2.31	2.42	1.93

Assumptions for Use
1. The subjects were sampled randomly and independently from a population.
2. Item recall is normally distributed in the population.
3. The variances for item recall are equal in the populations sampled.

Statistical Hypotheses: $H_0: \mu_{A1} = \mu_{A2} = \mu_{A3} = \mu_{A4} = \mu_{A5}.$

$H_1:$ The μ_A's are not all equal.

Significance Level: $\alpha = .05.$

df:
$$df_A = a - 1 = 5 - 1 = 4$$
$$df_{Error} = N - a = 50 - 5 = 45$$
$$df_{Total} = N - 1 = 50 - 1 = 49$$

Critical Value of *F*: $F_{crit}(4,45) = 2.61$. A value of 45 *df* for the denominator is not presented in Table A.3a. I used the critical value for the next lower tabled *df* for df_{Error}, 40.

Rejection Region: Values of F_{obs} equal to or greater than 2.61.

Calculation: The analysis of variance may be calculated on the scores using the computational formulas given in the chapter supplement or by using a computer program. The formulas from the chapter supplement were used to obtain the following analysis of variance summary table.

Source	SS	df	MS	F
Mood state group (A)	171.880	4	42.970	7.86*
Error	245.900	45	5.464	
Total	417.780	49		

*p < .05.

Decision: $F_{obs} = 7.86$ falls into the rejection region, I reject $H_0: \mu_{A1} = \mu_{A2} = \mu_{A3} = \mu_{A4} = \mu_{A5}$ and accept $H_1:$ The μ_A's are not all equal. Rejection of H_0 indicates that there is at least one statistically significant difference between the sample means. To find the statistically significant pairwise differences, I use the Tukey HSD test.

Tukey Test: The numerical values needed for this test are found as follows:

- q is obtained from Table A.4. There are five levels of the independent variable and 45 *df* for MS_{Error} from the analysis of variance summary table. Because 45 *df* is not given in Table A.4, I use 40 *df*, the next lower tabled *df* from the 45 *df* for MS_{Error}. Thus, $q = 4.04$ for a .05 significance level.
- MS_{Error}, obtained from the analysis of variance, is 5.464.
- n_A, the number of scores in each of the means to be compared, is 10.

Substituting these numerical values into the formula,

$$CD = q\sqrt{\frac{MS_{\text{Error}}}{n_A}} = 4.04\sqrt{\frac{5.464}{10}}$$

$$= 3.0 \text{ words}, \quad \text{rounded to one decimal place.}$$

A difference between two means equal to or larger in absolute value than 3.0 words is statistically significant at the .05 level. The pairwise comparisons and their absolute values, the statistical hypotheses tested, and the decisions reached on the statistical hypotheses for each comparison are given in Table 10.12.

TABLE 10.12
Application of the Tukey HSD CD to the pairwise comparisons of the five mood state groups. The value of the $CD = 3.0$.

Comparison	Absolute Value of Comparison	Statistical Hypotheses	Decision
$\overline{X}_{A1}$ vs. $\overline{X}_{A2}$ (10.4 − 9.9)	0.5	$H_0: \mu_{A1} = \mu_{A2}$ $H_1: \mu_{A1} \neq \mu_{A2}$	Fail to reject Do not accept
$\overline{X}_{A1}$ vs. $\overline{X}_{A3}$ (10.4 − 9.3)	1.1	$H_0: \mu_{A1} = \mu_{A3}$ $H_1: \mu_{A1} \neq \mu_{A3}$	Fail to reject Do not accept
$\overline{X}_{A1}$ vs. $\overline{X}_{A4}$ (10.4 − 6.1)	4.3	$H_0: \mu_{A1} = \mu_{A4}$ $H_1: \mu_{A1} \neq \mu_{A4}$	Reject Accept
$\overline{X}_{A1}$ vs. $\overline{X}_{A5}$ (10.4 − 6.2)	4.2	$H_0: \mu_{A1} = \mu_{A5}$ $H_1: \mu_{A1} \neq \mu_{A5}$	Reject Accept
$\overline{X}_{A2}$ vs. $\overline{X}_{A3}$ (9.9 − 9.3)	0.6	$H_0: \mu_{A2} = \mu_{A3}$ $H_1: \mu_{A2} \neq \mu_{A3}$	Fail to reject Do not accept
$\overline{X}_{A2}$ vs. $\overline{X}_{A4}$ (9.9 − 6.1)	3.8	$H_0: \mu_{A2} = \mu_{A4}$ $H_1: \mu_{A2} \neq \mu_{A4}$	Reject Accept
$\overline{X}_{A2}$ vs. $\overline{X}_{A5}$ (9.9 − 6.2)	3.7	$H_0: \mu_{A2} = \mu_{A5}$ $H_1: \mu_{A2} \neq \mu_{A5}$	Reject Accept
$\overline{X}_{A3}$ vs. $\overline{X}_{A4}$ (9.3 − 6.1)	3.2	$H_0: \mu_{A3} = \mu_{A4}$ $H_1: \mu_{A3} \neq \mu_{A4}$	Reject Accept
$\overline{X}_{A3}$ vs. $\overline{X}_{A5}$ (9.3 − 6.2)	3.1	$H_0: \mu_{A3} = \mu_{A5}$ $H_1: \mu_{A3} \neq \mu_{A5}$	Reject Accept
$\overline{X}_{A4}$ vs. $\overline{X}_{A5}$ (6.1 − 6.2)	0.1	$H_0: \mu_{A4} = \mu_{A5}$ $H_1: \mu_{A4} \neq \mu_{A5}$	Fail to reject Do not accept

A_1 = happy/happy group, A_2 = sad/sad group, A_3 = neutral/neutral group, A_4 = happy/sad group, and A_5 = sad/happy group.

The absolute values of the comparisons of $\overline{X}_{A1}$ versus $\overline{X}_{A4}$ and $\overline{X}_{A5}$, $\overline{X}_{A2}$ versus $\overline{X}_{A4}$ and $\overline{X}_{A5}$, and $\overline{X}_{A3}$ versus $\overline{X}_{A4}$ and $\overline{X}_{A5}$ exceed the CD of 3.0 words. Each of these differences is statistically significant. The absolute values of the remaining comparisons, $\overline{X}_{A1}$ versus $\overline{X}_{A2}$, $\overline{X}_{A1}$ versus $\overline{X}_{A3}$, $\overline{X}_{A2}$ versus $\overline{X}_{A3}$, and $\overline{X}_{A4}$ versus $\overline{X}_{A5}$ are less than the CD. These comparisons are nonsignificant, and the observed differences between these sample means are best explained by sampling error.

Strength of Effect: $\eta^2 = 171.880/417.780 = .41$.

Conclusion: The Tukey test leads to the conclusion that mood state groups that had congruent learning and recall conditions (i.e., the happy/happy, sad/sad, and neutral/neutral groups) did not differ significantly from each other in recall. Each of these groups, however, recalled significantly more words than did either of the noncongruent mood state groups (i.e., the happy/sad and sad/happy groups). In addition, the happy/sad and sad/happy groups did not differ significantly from each other. Accordingly, the inferred relationship among the population means is

$$(\mu_{A1} = \mu_{A2} = \mu_{A3}) > (\mu_{A4} = \mu_{A5}).$$

The η^2 indicates that knowledge of mood state group reduces the total variance in prediction by 41 percent.

Example Problem 10.2

Using the One-Factor Between-Subjects Analysis of Variance: A Nonsignificant F_{obs}

Problem: Does drinking alcohol make a person more open to the effects of social influence? Gustafson (1987b) hypothesized that it does. To test this hypothesis, he had participants estimate the length of a line that ranged in length from 5 to 100 centimeters. The participants were then given written feedback about the length of the line and asked to give a second estimate of the line's length. Each person estimated the length of 75 lines. For 60 of the 75 estimates, the written feedback indicated to the participant that the first estimate was incorrect. The number of times that each person changed his or her second estimate was recorded as a measure of responsiveness to social influence. Three treatment groups were used. A control group was given a drink of only orange juice 15 minutes before the line-length-estimation task. The second group was a placebo control for expectations associated with a drink of alcohol. People in this group were also given only orange juice 15 minutes before the line-length-estimation task, but they were led to believe that the drink contained alcohol. The subjects in the third group were given 0.8 milliliter of alcohol per kilogram of body weight in an orange juice solution 15 minutes before the task began. Gustafson hypothesized that the individuals in the alcohol and placebo groups would be more responsive to the written feedback and would thus change their second estimates more often than the control group. Suppose that the number of estimates changed for each of 13 participants in a group were as given in Table 10.13. Does alcohol affect the number of estimates changed?

TABLE 10.13
Number of changed estimates as a function of treatment group.

	Treatment Group (A)		
	Control (A_1)	Placebo (A_2)	Alcohol (A_3)
	18	17	31
	2	19	27
	11	26	16
	3	4	24
	26	18	41
	18	23	17
	9	31	12
	24	35	32
	17	11	16
	21	8	19
	14	29	35
	19	25	26
	33	38	17
$\overline{X}_A$	16.50	21.80	24.10
s_A	8.83	10.29	8.81

Solution: The design used is a one-factor between-subjects design with three levels of the independent variable, treatment group. The one-factor between-subjects analysis of variance is the appropriate statistical test for these data. I use a .05 significance level.

Statistic to Be Used: $F = MS_A/MS_{\text{Error}}$.

Assumptions for Use
1. The participants were sampled randomly and independently from a population.
2. The number of changes made in line-length estimates is normally distributed in the population.
3. The variances for the number of changes in line-length estimates are equal in the populations sampled.

Statistical Hypotheses: $H_0: \mu_{A1} = \mu_{A2} = \mu_{A3}$.
H_1: The μ_A's are not all equal.

Significance Level: $\alpha = .05$.

df:

$df_A \quad = a - 1 = 3 - 1 = 2$
$df_{\text{Error}} = N - a = 39 - 3 = 36$
$df_{\text{Total}} = N - 1 = 39 - 1 = 38$

Critical Value of F: $F_{crit}(2,36) = 3.32$. The value of F_{crit} for 2, 36 df is not tabled in Table A.3a; hence, I used F_{crit} for 2, 30 df.

Rejection Region: Values of F_{obs} equal to or greater than 3.32.

Calculation: The analysis of variance was calculated by using the computational formulas given in the chapter supplement. A summary of this analysis is as follows:

Source	SS	df	MS	F
Treatment group (A)	389.898	2	194.949	2.24
Error	3137.846	36	87.162	
Total	3527.744	38		

Decision: $F_{obs} = 2.24$ is less than $F_{crit} = 3.32$ and does not fall into the rejection region; thus, I fail to reject H_0 and do not accept H_1.

Conclusion: The observed differences among the means are nonsignificant; the sample means of 16.5, 21.8, and 24.1 are treated as samples from the same population. There is no evidence for an effect of the independent variable. Individuals given an alcoholic drink do not change their line-length estimates more often than subjects given a placebo drink or only orange juice. The observed differences among the sample means are due only to sampling error. Because the F_{obs} was nonsignificant, there is no need for multiple comparison tests or a strength of association measure.

The results of this example illustrate the need for statistical hypothesis testing to determine whether group means differ by more than chance alone. From a visual examination of the means, it appears that they differ by quite a large amount. But there are also large differences among scores within the groups leading to a considerable amount of error variation as reflected in the relatively large values of the standard deviations for the groups. When there is a large amount of error variation, then we may expect relatively large differences between group means due simply to sampling error, as is the case in this example.

Example Problem 10.3

Using the One-Factor Between-Subjects Analysis of Variance with Two Levels of an Independent Variable

Problem: Review question 4 of Chapter 9 (see page 219) introduced the Morinaga misalignment illusion illustrated in panel (a) of Figure 10.3. As indicated in question 4, the figure is an illusion because the points of each angle do not appear to be aligned on the same vertical line, although they are. Would a similar illusion also be seen if the stimulus figure were rounded as shown in Figure 10.3 (b)? To answer this question, suppose a psychologist created two equivalent groups of 10 people each. The participants in group A_1 were shown the stimulus created from angled points, and those in group A_2 saw a stimulus made from partial circles, as illustrated in Figure 10.3. The error in perception of the stimulus was measured as the dependent variable for both groups. Suppose the error scores given in Table 10.14 were obtained. Does the amount of error perceived depend on the type of figure?

Solution: To find if the means differ significantly, I use the one-factor between-subjects analysis of variance. (Because only two groups are involved, a t_{ind} is also an appropriate statistical test.) I use a .05 significance level.

Statistic to Be Used: $F = MS_A/MS_{Error}$.

Assumptions for Use
1. The participants were sampled randomly and independently from a population.
2. The error in perceiving the illusion is normally distributed in the population.
3. The variances for the perceptual error scores are equal in the populations sampled.

Statistical Hypotheses: $H_0: \mu_{A1} = \mu_{A2}$.

H_1: The μ_A's are not equal.

Significance Level: $\alpha = .05$.

df: df_A $= a - 1 = 2 - 1 = 1$

$df_{Error} = N - a = 20 - 2 = 18$

$df_{Total} = N - 1 = 20 - 1 = 19$

Critical Value of F: $F_{crit}(1,18) = 4.41$.

Rejection Region: Values of F_{obs} equal to or greater than 4.41.

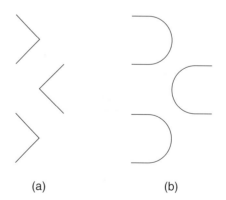

(a)   (b)

FIGURE 10.3
Morinaga misalignment illusion.
(a) Figure shown Group A_1.
(b) Figure shown Group A_2.

TABLE 10.14

Perceived error (in millimeters) as a function of type of figure viewed.

	Type of Figure (A)	
	Angular (A_1)	**Circular (A_2)**
	2.0	1.6
	1.8	1.7
	2.0	1.8
	2.1	1.6
	2.2	1.5
	1.8	1.8
	1.9	1.7
	1.8	1.8
	1.9	1.7
	1.7	1.6
$\overline{X}_A$	1.92	1.68
s_A	0.15	0.10

Calculation: Using the computational formulas given in the chapter supplement, a summary of the analysis of variance is as follows:

Source	SS	df	MS	F
Type of figure (A)	0.288	1	0.28800	16.62*
Error	0.312	18	0.01733	
Total	0.600	19		

*$p < .05$.

Decision: F_{obs} falls into the rejection region; thus, I reject H_0 and accept H_1.

Strength of Effect: $\eta^2 = 0.288/0.600 = .48$.

Conclusion: The means of 1.92 mm and 1.68 mm differ significantly at the .05 level; the mean of 1.92 mm is significantly larger than the mean of 1.68 mm. Because the two groups were equivalent before the independent variable was administered and extraneous variables were controlled, the observed difference between the groups is treated as due to the effect of the independent variable. People see a larger illusion with angular stimuli than with circular stimuli. The Tukey HSD test is not needed because only two means are being compared. The $\eta^2 = .48$ indicates a large effect of the independent variable, accounting for 48 percent of the variance in the dependent variable. If a t_{ind} had been used in place of the analysis of variance, $t_{obs}(18) = 4.077$. This value of t_{obs} is equal to the square root of F_{obs}

$(1,18) = 16.62$. This t is statistically significant at the .05 level and leads to the same conclusion as the analysis of variance. This result, too, illustrates the importance of statistical hypothesis testing in data analysis. At first glance, the group means reveal what appears to be a relatively small difference between them. But notice that there is also relatively little variability among subjects within the groups. With little within-groups error variation, then even small differences between groups may be statistically significant.

REPORTING THE RESULTS OF THE ANALYSIS OF VARIANCE

The *Publication Manual of the American Psychological Association* (1994) requires the report of the results of an analysis of variance to present group means, standard deviations, the value of alpha selected, the observed value of F and its degrees of freedom, the MS_{Error}, and the probability of the observed value of F if H_0 is true. I illustrate this style using the results from the example of the effect of type of drawing on item recall. The analysis of variance for this problem is summarized in Table 10.5. Although I have been using summary tables for analysis of variance, such tables may not be included in journal articles because of their expense to print. If a summary table is not included, the analysis of variance is summarized in text, as illustrated here.

> The mean number of items correctly recalled was 17.0 for the incomplete outline drawings ($SD = 2.74$), 13.0 for the outline drawings ($SD = 2.24$), and 12.0 for the detailed drawings ($SD = 1.87$). With alpha equal to .05, a one-factor between-subjects analysis of variance indicated a significant effect for the type of drawing: $F(2,12) = 6.56$, $MSE = 5.333$, $p < .05$. Post hoc comparisons using the Tukey HSD test ($CD = 3.9$, $\alpha = .05$) indicated significantly more objects recalled for the incomplete outline drawings compared with either the outline drawings or the detailed drawings, but no significant difference in the number of objects recalled for outline drawings compared with the detailed drawings condition. Eta squared for the scores was .52.

In this presentation:

$\alpha = .05$ Indicates the significance level selected for the test.

$F(2, 12)$ Identifies the test statistic as the F; hence, an analysis of variance was used to analyze the data. This F is F_{obs}; the subscript *obs* is not utilized. The df for the numerator (i.e., 2) and the denominator (i.e., 12) of F_{obs} are shown in parentheses. From these df you can determine the number of groups involved and the number of subjects used in the experiment as follows: The df for the numerator equal $a - 1$. In this report, $df_A = 2$; thus $a = 3$. The df for the denominator equal df_{Error}, which equal $N - a$. In the example, $df_{Error} = 12$ and $a = 3$; therefore, $12 = N - 3$ and the total number of subjects in the experiment equals 15.

$= 6.56$ Gives the value of F_{obs} (not the F_{crit} value found in Table A.3). If F_{obs} is less than 1.00, it may be reported simply as $F < 1.00$.

$p < .05$ Indicates that

   a. The probability of F_{obs} if H_0 is true is less than or equal to .05. This value is the probability of F_{obs} or an even more extreme value of F_{obs} if H_0 is true; it may not be the same as the value of α selected.

   b. $H_0: \mu_{A1} = \mu_{A2} = \mu_{A3}$ was rejected.
       H_1: The μ_A's are not all equal was accepted.

   c. At least one difference between group means is statistically significant.

   d. Something other than sampling error is responsible for the observed difference in sample means.

   e. If $p > .05$ had been reported, then the greater than sign would indicate that H_0 was not rejected and the sample means did not differ significantly at the .05 significance level. In this instance I would conclude that the type of drawing did not affect the recall of details.

$MSE = 5.333$ Gives the value of MS_{Error} for the F_{obs}. This value is a measure of the within-group error variation in the scores.

$CD = 3.9$ Gives the critical difference for pairwise comparisons using the Tukey HSD test. The statistically significant pairwise comparisons are then described.

Eta squared $= .52$ Presents the value of η^2, indicating that 52 percent of the variance in the in the recall scores of this experiment is accounted for by the type of drawing. Sometimes a similar strength of association measure, ω^2 (omega squared), is given. The value of ω^2 will be slightly less than η^2.

TESTING YOUR KNOWLEDGE 10.3

1. In Testing Your Knowledge 9.3, problem 1 of question 9 presented an experiment dealing with the effects of an expected delay on the estimation of a time interval. Recall that participants in the control group were not led to expect a delay in the start of an experiment, whereas those in the experimental group were told that the experimenter's assistant was delayed. However, the delay period was 5 minutes for both groups. After the experiment started, participants were asked to estimate how long the delay was. Suppose that you replicated this experiment with a total of 22 people and obtained the following estimates of the 5-minute delay period (in minutes):

Group	
Control	**Experimental**
6	8
7	9
9	11
7	10
6	9
8	8
5	7
9	6
6	10
8	10
7	9

Find the mean and standard deviation for each group, then calculate an analysis of variance on these scores and answer the following questions.

a. State the statistical hypotheses for the F test for these scores.
b. What is the value of F_{obs}?
c. What are the df for F_{obs}?
d. What is F_{crit} at the .05 level?
e. What is the rejection region for F_{obs}?
f. Does F_{obs} fall into the rejection region?
g. What decisions do you make about the statistical hypotheses? Do you reject or fail to reject H_0? Accept or not accept H_1?
h. Do you conclude that the group means are from the same or different populations?
i. Is the difference between the means statistically significant?
j. Did the groups differ in their estimates of the time they spent waiting? If so, what is the direction of the difference?
k. Are multiple comparison tests needed in this experiment? Give the reason for your answer.
l. What is η^2 for this experiment?
m. How much of the variance is accounted for by the independent variable in this experiment?

2. Sadeh, Raviv, and Gruber (2000) investigated sleeping patterns in second, fourth, and sixth grade children. Suppose you also investigated this problem and found the following sleep periods in minutes for groups of second, fourth, and sixth grade girls. There were 14 students in each group. Sleep period is defined as the amount of time from the onset of sleep to awakening in the morning.

	Grade	
2nd	**4th**	**6th**
580	497	525
525	515	506
562	543	475
590	478	493
575	567	537
603	532	532
594	517	480
521	510	501
536	534	472
612	556	463
514	511	521
544	523	517
573	572	477
592	574	515

Find the mean and standard deviation for each group and then calculate an analysis of variance on these scores and answer the following questions.

a. State the statistical hypotheses for the F test for these scores.
b. What is the value of F_{obs}?
c. What are the df for F_{obs}?
d. What is F_{crit} at the .05 level?

e.   What is the rejection region for F_{obs}?

f.   Does F_{obs} fall into the rejection region?

g.   What decisions do you make about the statistical hypotheses? Do you reject or fail to reject H_0? Accept or not accept H_1?

h.   What can you conclude from the overall analysis of variance on these scores?

i.   Are multiple comparison tests needed in this experiment? Give the reason for your answer.

j.   What is the value of the Tukey CD?

k.   Which pairwise differences are statistically significant?

l.   Describe how the groups differ in sleep periods.

m.   What is η^2 for this experiment?

n.   How much of the variance is accounted for by the independent variable in this experiment?

3.   The following exercises present brief reports of one-factor between-subjects analysis of variance. Answer the following questions for each report.

a.   How many levels of the independent variable were used in this experiment?

b.   How many subjects were used in this experiment?

c.   What is the value of F_{obs}?

d.   What is the value of F_{crit} at the .05 significance level?

e.   Do you reject or fail to reject H_0?

f.   Do you accept or not accept H_1?

g.   Is there at least one statistically significant difference between the means?

h.   Which means, if any, differ significantly?

3.1.   The mean number of tones detected while listening to a familiar poetry passage was 79.9 compared to a mean of 73.0 when listening to an unfamiliar poetry passage. With alpha equal to .05, a one-factor between-subjects analysis of variance indicated that the means differed significantly, $F(1, 60) = 14.15$, $MSE = 5.740$, $p < .01$.

3.2.   With alpha equal to .05, no difference was found in the number of words recalled as a function of retention interval, $F(3, 36) = 1.13$, $MSE = 14.342$, $p > .05$.

3.3.   The mean number of typing errors was 18.5 for the group listening to classical music, 29.9 for the group listening to hard-rock music, and 17.5 for the no-music control group. With alpha equal to .05, a one-factor between-subjects analysis of variance indicated a significant effect for the type of music, $F(2, 36) = 33.94$, $MSE = 18.261$, $p < .001$. Post hoc comparisons using the Tukey HSD test ($CD = 4.1$, $\alpha = .05$) indicated significantly more typing errors for the hard-rock music condition than for either the no-music control or the classical-music condition. The no-music and classical-music conditions did not differ significantly.

SUMMARY

- A one-factor multilevel design is an experiment with one independent variable and three or more levels of that independent variable.
- The one-factor between-subjects analysis of variance is used to analyze scores from a one-factor multilevel design.
- The F statistic is given by $F = MS_A/MS_{Error}$.
- A MS is a variance and is found by SS/df.

- MS_A varies with the effect of the independent variable and sampling error.
- MS_{Error} varies with the within-groups error variation.
- If the independent variable has no effect, then MS_A and MS_{Error} estimate only error variation in the scores, and F should be about equal to 1.00.
- When an independent variable has an effect, MS_A increases in value, but MS_{Error} is not affected. The value of F becomes larger than 1.00.
- Using the F statistic in a statistical test follows the usual steps of formulating statistical hypotheses, setting a significance level, locating a rejection region, calculating F_{obs}, and making decisions concerning the statistical hypotheses.
- A statistically significant F_{obs} when three or more levels of an independent variable are manipulated requires a multiple comparison test to follow up the analysis of variance.
- Multiple comparison tests are used to find which means differ significantly from one another in a one-factor multilevel design after a statistically significant F_{obs} has occurred for the overall analysis of variance. A comparison of two means is a pairwise comparison.
- The Tukey test is used for all possible pairwise post hoc comparisons for a set of means. The Tukey test holds the probability of a Type I error equal to or less than α for all possible pairwise comparisons.
- η^2 may be used as a measure of the strength of a treatment effect.

KEY TERMS AND SYMBOLS

a (228)

analysis of variance (ANOVA) (224)

between-groups variance (MS_A) (226)

critical difference (CD) (248)

df for SS_A (df_A) (235)

df for SS_{Error} (df_{Error}) (235)

error rate in an experiment (248)

eta squared (η^2) (250)

F_{crit} (243)

F_{obs} (239)

factor A (228)

grand mean ($\overline{X}_G$) (225)

mean square (MS) (225)

multiple comparison tests (247)

N (235)

n_A (228)

one-factor multilevel design (224)

pairwise comparisons (247)

post hoc comparisons (248)

q (248)

SS_A (231)

SS_{Error} (231)

SS_{Total} (231)

total degrees of freedom (df_{Total}) (234)

Tukey HSD test (248)

within-groups error variance (MS_{Error}) (225)

$X - \overline{X}_A$ (230)

$X - \overline{X}_G$ (231)

$\overline{X}_A - \overline{X}_G$ (225)

CHAPTER SUPPLEMENT: CALCULATING A ONE-FACTOR BETWEEN-SUBJECTS ANALYSIS OF VARIANCE WITH COMPUTATIONAL FORMULAS

Computational formulas for analysis of variance are based on the total of the scores in a treatment group (rather than the treatment mean) and the grand total of the scores in the experiment (rather than the grand mean). Following the notational representation introduced in Table 10.2, an experiment with three levels of an independent variable A and five participants in each level is represented as follows:

Factor A

A_1	A_2	A_3	
X_{11}	X_{12}	X_{13}	
X_{21}	X_{22}	X_{23}	
X_{31}	X_{32}	X_{33}	
X_{41}	X_{42}	X_{43}	
X_{51}	X_{52}	X_{53}	
T_{A1}	T_{A2}	T_{A3}	G (grand total)

where X_{ij} = score of a participant
   T_A = total of scores for a level of the independent variable
   G = grand total of the scores
   n_A = number of scores in a level of the independent variable
   a = number of levels of the independent variable
   N = total number of scores.

Three numerical values are found using these terms:

$[1] = \sum\sum X_{ij}^2$ the sum of all the scores squared,

$[2] = \dfrac{\sum T_A^2}{n_A}$ the sum of each treatment group total squared, divided by the number of scores in a group,

$[3] = \dfrac{G^2}{N}$ the grand total squared, divided by the total number of scores.

Using these numerical values, an analysis of variance is obtained as follows:

Source of Variance	SS	df	MS	F
Factor A	$[2] - [3]$	$a - 1$	$\dfrac{SS_A}{df_A}$	$\dfrac{MS_A}{MS_{\text{Error}}}$
Error	$[1] - [2]$	$N - a$	$\dfrac{SS_{\text{Error}}}{df_{\text{Error}}}$	
Total	$[1] - [3]$	$N - 1$	Not calculated	

To illustrate the computations, I use the example scores given in Table 10.1 for which an analysis of variance is summarized in Table 10.5.

	Factor A		
	A_1	A_2	A_3
	19	14	15
	13	13	10
	16	16	11
	17	12	12
	20	10	12
$T_A =$	85	65	60

$$G = 85 + 65 + 60 = 210$$
$$n_A = 5, a = 3, \text{ and } N = 15$$

The values of the numerical computational terms are

$$[1] = 19^2 + \cdots + 20^2 + 14^2 + \cdots + 10^2 + 15^2 + \cdots + 12^2 = 3074.00$$

$$[2] = \frac{85^2 + 65^2 + 60^2}{5} = \frac{15,050}{5} = 3010.00$$

$$[3] = \frac{210^2}{15} = \frac{44,100}{15} = 2940.00.$$

Then

$$SS_A = [2] - [3] = 3010.00 - 2940.00 = 70.00,$$
$$df_A = a - 1 = 3 - 1 = 2,$$
$$MS_A = \frac{70.00}{2} = 35.000.$$

$$SS_{Error} = [1] - [2] = 3074.00 - 3010.00 = 64.00,$$
$$df_{Error} = N - a = 15 - 3 = 12,$$
$$MS_{Error} = \frac{64.00}{12} = 5.333.$$

$$SS_{Total} = [1] - [3] = 3074.00 - 2940.00 = 134.00,$$
$$df_{Total} = N - 1 = 15 - 1 = 14.$$

$$F_{obs} = \frac{MS_A}{MS_{Error}} = \frac{35.000}{5.333} = 6.56.$$

The summary of the analysis of variance is

Source	SS	df	MS	F
Factor A	70.00	2	35.000	6.56*
Error	64.00	12	5.333	
Total	134.00	14		

*$p < .05.$

The values obtained by this computational approach are identical to those presented in Table 10.5 obtained from the definitional formulas of an analysis of variance.

REVIEW QUESTIONS

1. Music seems to be everywhere in modern society and psychologists have investigated its effects on a variety of performances. As an example, suppose an experimenter created three equivalent groups of eight people each and asked each person to perform a proofreading task on a short research paper. Participants in group A_1 performed the task with no music playing in the background, participants in group A_2 performed the task with a selection of oldies playing in the background, and participants in group A_3 performed the task while listening to hard rock. The dependent variable was the number of errors detected out of a possible 50. Suppose the following scores were obtained:

Treatment Group		
No Music (A_1)	**Oldies** (A_2)	**Hard Rock** (A_3)
40	34	26
41	39	24
39	38	19
36	40	23
35	34	18
32	35	21
31	29	23
34	36	29

a. Find the mean and standard deviation for each group. Then analyze the scores with a one-factor between-subjects analysis to answer the question: Did the music condition affect the number of errors detected by a subject?

Use a .05 significance level. If needed, use the Tukey HSD test for multiple comparisons.

b. What is the value of η^2 for this experiment? What proportion of the variance in the dependent variable can be accounted for by knowing the level of the independent variable?

c. Describe the results of this experiment following the style illustrated in the Reporting the Results of the Analysis of Variance section of this chapter.

2. Elementary school teachers must have many talents, among them the ability to teach children the physical skills needed for certain sports and other skilled activities. To determine how well elementary education majors could learn the necessary skills from instructional videotapes, Morrison and Reeve (1986) created three equivalent groups of participants and varied the instructional videotape shown them. Group A_1 was a control group and saw no videotape. Group A_2 saw a videotape on soccer kicks, and group A_3 saw a videotape on throwing, catching, and striking skills. After viewing the instructional videotape, or no tape for group A_1, all participants were shown a second videotape on throwing, catching, and striking and asked to identify correct performances displayed on the tape. Suppose the following scores were obtained for nine people in each instructional condition.

Instructional Condition

No Videotape (A_1)	Soccer Videotape (A_2)	Throwing, Catching Videotape (A_3)
50	53	61
46	48	58
39	37	49
52	49	56
44	46	45
51	48	66
41	37	58
36	41	64
48	40	57

a. Find the mean and standard deviation for each group. Then analyze the scores with a one-factor between-subjects analysis to answer the following question: Did the instructional condition affect a person's skill to correctly identify throwing, catching, and striking performance? Use a .05 significance level. If needed, use the Tukey HSD test for multiple comparisons.

b. What is the value of η^2 for this experiment? What proportion of the variance in the dependent variable can be accounted for by knowing the level of the independent variable?

    c. Describe the results of this experiment following the style illustrated in the Reporting the Results of the Analysis of Variance section of this chapter.

3. Problem 1 of the Chapter 9 Review Questions dealt with the physiological effects of noise. In the experiment described, subjects either sat in a quiet room for 30 minutes or listened to a recording of traffic noise for 30 minutes. At the end of 30 minutes, their systolic blood pressures were measured and the following scores obtained (in millimeters of mercury).

Group	
Quiet	**Noise**
106	141
117	136
124	124
129	139
115	121
131	119
121	147
115	128
128	115
136	134
127	140

    a. Find the mean and standard deviation for each group. Then analyze the scores with a one-factor between-subjects analysis to answer the following question: Does noise affect systolic blood pressure? Use a .05 significance level.

    b. Compare the value of F_{obs} to the value of t_{obs} for Problem 1 of the Chapter 9 Review Questions. Do you find the expected relationship between t and F?

4. An experimenter used a one-factor between-subjects design with six levels of the independent variable, A_1, A_2, A_3, A_4, A_5, and A_6, and seven participants in each level.

    a. What are the values of a, n_A, and N for this experiment?

    b. What are the values of df_A, df_{Error}, and df_{Total} for the analysis of variance for this experiment?

5. The following tables are incomplete summary tables for an analysis of variance. Assume an equal number of scores in each level of the independent variable. By using the relationships among SS, df, and MS, provide the missing values in each table. Then answer the following questions for each table.

    a. How many levels of the independent variable were manipulated?

    b. How many participants were tested in each treatment condition?

    c. What was the total number of participants in the experiment?

d. Is the value of F_{obs} statistically significant at the .05 level?

e. What decision do you make for H_0 and H_1 for each analysis?

TABLE 1

Source	SS	df	MS	F
Factor A	50.0	2	—	—
Error	270.0	27	—	
Total	—	—		

TABLE 2

Source	SS	df	MS	F
Factor A	60.0	—	12.0	—
Error	—	72	—	
Total	276.0	77		

TABLE 3

Source	SS	df	MS	F
Factor A	—	—	—	3.00
Error	320.0	—	5.0	
Total	365.0	67		

6. Does rejection of H_0 and acceptance of H_1 in an analysis of variance necessarily provide support for a research hypothesis? Explain your answer.

7. You conducted a t_{ind} on two groups and $t_{obs}(18) = 2.000$. If you had analyzed the scores with an analysis of variance, what value of F_{obs} would you have found? Indicate the df for F_{obs}.

8. You conducted an analysis of variance on two independent groups and F_{obs} (1, 22) = 9.00. If you had analyzed the scores with a t_{ind}, what value of t_{obs} would you have found? Indicate the df for t_{obs}.

9. Explain why a statistical test cannot identify the reason for two groups differing significantly.

10. A psychologist was interested in comparing four treatments for a smoking-cessation program. She created four groups of 17 smokers each by random assignment and gave each group a different treatment. The dependent variable measured was the mean time between smoking cigarettes after five weeks of treatment. The treatment groups and the mean time between cigarettes (in minutes) are given in Table 1, and an analysis of variance for these data is presented in Table 2.

TABLE 1

Treatment conditions and mean times between smoking cigarettes (in minutes).

	Treatment Condition	Mean Time
A_1	Control group; no treatment given	24.0
A_2	Behavior modification	38.0
A_3	Cigarettes anonymous club	34.0
A_4	Smoke-Stop gum	28.0

TABLE 2

Analysis of variance summary table for mean time between smoking cigarettes in Table 1.

Source	SS	df	MS	F
Treatment condition	1972.00	3	657.333	21.64*
Error	1944.00	64	30.375	
Total	3916.00	67		

*$p < .01$.

A Tukey HSD gave a $CD = 5.0$ minutes at the .05 significance level.

a.   What is the effect of the treatment conditions on the amount of time between smoking cigarettes?

b.   Describe the results of this experiment following the style illustrated in the Reporting the Results of the Analysis of Variance section of this chapter.

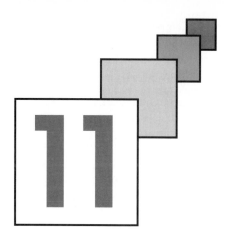

11

Two-Factor Between-Subjects Designs and Analysis of Variance

Many behaviors are determined by two or more independent variables functioning simultaneously. For example, the effect of noise (one independent variable) on reading comprehension (the dependent variable) differs for introverted and extroverted personality types (a second independent variable) (Standing, Lynn, & Moxness, 1990). Or, as another example, memory for a list of noun pairs (the dependent variable) depends on the imagery ability of the person learning the list (one independent variable), the type of image provided to the learner (a second independent variable), and the length of the retention interval (a third independent variable) (O'Brien & Wolford, 1982). One-factor designs do not permit the manipulation of more than one independent variable at a time; thus, to study the influence of two or more independent variables in combination, factorial designs are used.

Factorial design: A research design in which two or more independent variables are varied simultaneously.

Factorial designs are research designs in which two or more independent variables are simultaneously varied. In the simplest factorial design, two independent variables are varied and each independent variable assumes two levels. This design often is called a 2×2 ("two-by-two") design. The first 2 of the 2×2 indicates that there are two levels of the first independent variable (identified as **factor A**), and the second 2 indicates the number of levels of the second independent variable (identified as **factor B**). A $2 \times 2 \times 2$ design is a three-factor design with factors A, B, and C, and each independent variable varies over two levels. There are many possible factorial designs, such as a 2×4 design (two levels of factor A, four levels of factor B), a $3 \times 3 \times 2$ design (three levels of factors A and B, two levels of factor C), and a $2 \times 2 \times 2 \times 2$ design (four factors, A, B, C, and D, with two levels of each). Factorial designs may also be totally between subjects, totally within subjects, or a combination of the two, resulting in a mixed design. In this text I discuss only the two-factor (also called a *two-way*) between-subjects design.

Cell or treatment condition: A combination formed from one level of each independent variable in a factorial design.

The 2×2 between-subjects design is convenient for introducing the statistical data analysis of factorial designs. Table 11.1 illustrates two independent variables or factors identified as A and B, each taking on two levels: factor A with levels A_1 and A_2 and factor B with levels B_1 and B_2. Generally, there are a levels of factor A and b levels of factor B. In the example, $a = 2$ and $b = 2$. The combination of the two independent variables creates four treatment conditions, called *cells*, in the table. Each **cell** or **treatment condition** represents

TABLE 11.1

Plan of a 2×2 between-subjects design. The combination of a level of factor A with a level of factor B forms a treatment condition or cell.

		Factor A	
		A_1	A_2
Factor B	B_1	A_1B_1 treatment condition (A_1B_1 cell)	A_2B_1 treatment condition (A_2B_1 cell)
	B_2	A_1B_2 treatment condition (A_1B_2 cell)	A_2B_2 treatment condition (A_2B_2 cell)

a combination formed from one level of each independent variable, for example, the A_1B_1, $A_1B_2, A_2B_1,$ and A_2B_2 cells. An equal number of participants typically is randomly assigned to each of the treatment conditions. Thus, if 20 participants are used in a 2×2 between-subjects design, five people are assigned to each treatment condition or cell. Each person experiences only one treatment condition.

AN EXAMPLE 2 × 2 BETWEEN-SUBJECTS DESIGN

People generally don't like to give other people bad news. This phenomenon is called the *MUM effect*. Several hypotheses have been proposed to explain this effect. The personal discomfort hypothesis states that the bearer of bad news feels personal discomfort when delivering the bad news and avoids this discomfort by not delivering the news. A second hypothesis, the self-presentational hypothesis, suggests that individuals do not feel discomfort when delivering the bad news; rather, failing to deliver the bad news is a public display to maintain a positive social image. After all, who wants to be known as the bearer of bad news? To test these hypotheses, Bond and Anderson (1987) used a 2×2 between-subjects design. The two independent variables were the visibility of the subject to the person to whom the bad news was to be delivered (subject visibility, factor A) and the type of news to be delivered (type of news, factor B). Each independent variable was manipulated over two levels. For subject visibility, the subject was either not visible (level A_1) or visible (level A_2) to the person to whom the news was to be delivered. The type of news was either good (level B_1) or bad (level B_2). The experimental procedure was as follows. A subject was to administer a multiple-choice intelligence test to another person who, unknown to the subject, was an assistant to the experimenter. The subject and the assistant were in separate rooms joined by a one-way mirror. In the subject-not-visible condition (level A_1), the subject was told that the assistant could not see through the mirror. For the subject-visible condition (level A_2), the subject was told that the assistant could see him or her through the mirror. The type of news was manipulated by the assistant's success on the test. In the good news condition (level B_1), the subject informed the assistant that her performance was in the top 20 percent of the scores on the test. In the bad news condition (level B_2), the subject informed the assistant that her performance was in the bottom 20 percent of the scores on the test. The dependent variable was the latency of feedback of the test score from the subject to the assistant. This latency was the length of time from the completion of the test to the subject's telling the assistant what her score was.

Two different outcomes for the experiment were predicted from the two hypotheses concerning the MUM effect. If the MUM effect occurs because subjects experience personal discomfort, then it should take longer to deliver the bad news than the good news, regardless of whether the subject is or is not visible to the assistant. In other words, the difference between the good (level B_1) and bad (level B_2) news conditions should not depend on whether the subject is visible or not to the assistant. On the other hand, if the MUM effect is simply a public display, then the latency to deliver the bad news should depend on whether the subject is or is not visible to the assistant. That is, an interaction of the independent variables should occur. When good news is delivered, there should be no difference in the latencies of the not visible and visible conditions. When bad news is delivered, however, the latency of the visible condition should be significantly longer than the latency of the not visible condition. Correspondingly, for the not visible condition, there should be no difference between the latencies of the good and bad news conditions. For the visible condition, however, the latency of the bad news condition should be significantly longer than the good news condition.

Suppose five males were randomly assigned to each cell and the latency scores (in seconds) presented in Table 11.2 were obtained. Which prediction, if either, do the results agree with, those of the personal discomfort hypothesis or those of the public display hypothesis?

INFORMATION OBTAINED FROM A FACTORIAL DESIGN

The scores in Table 11.2 are represented notationally in Table 11.3. A score for a subject is represented by X_{ijk}, where the subscripts provide the following information:

$i =$ number identifying the participant within a treatment condition
$j =$ level of the A variable that the participant receives
$k =$ level of the B variable that the participant receives

For example, X_{311} is the score of the third person in the A_1B_1 treatment condition (80 seconds in Table 11.2), X_{421} is the score of the fourth person in the A_2B_1 treatment condition (95 seconds), X_{212} is the score of the second participant in the A_1B_2 treatment condition (87 seconds), X_{522} is the score of the fifth participant in the A_2B_2 treatment condition (115 sec-

TABLE 11.2
Hypothetical response latencies (in seconds) as a function of subject visibility and type of news for 20 subjects in the example 2 × 2 between-subjects experiment.

		Subject Visibility Condition (Factor A)	
		Not Visible (A_1)	Visible (A_2)
Type of News (Factor B)	Good (B_1)	97	70
		90	87
		80	81
		107	95
		80	90
	Bad (B_2)	68	114
		87	96
		92	127
		80	110
		84	115

TABLE 11.3

Notational representation of scores in a 2×2 between-subjects design with two levels of each independent variable and five subjects per cell.

		Factor A	
		A_1	A_2
Factor B	B_1	X_{111} X_{211} X_{311} X_{411} X_{511}	X_{121} X_{221} X_{321} X_{421} X_{521}
	B_2	X_{112} X_{212} X_{312} X_{412} X_{512}	X_{122} X_{222} X_{322} X_{422} X_{522}

onds), and so on. When it is not necessary to identify a specific person, I drop the *ijk* subscripts and simply use X. For each cell there are n_{AB} subjects with a total of N subjects in the experiment. For the example, $n_{AB} = 5$ and $N = 20$. The first step in data analysis begins with computing measures of central tendency, the sample means. Table 11.4 illustrates the cell and main effect means that may be calculated from the example scores.

Cell Means

Cell mean: The mean of the n_{AB} scores for a treatment combination in a factorial design.

The **cell means**, symbolized by $\overline{X}_{A1B1}$, $\overline{X}_{A1B2}$, $\overline{X}_{A2B1}$, and $\overline{X}_{A2B2}$, or, in general, by $\overline{X}_{AB}$, are the means of the n_{AB} scores for a treatment combination (see Table 11.4a). A cell mean indicates the typical performance of participants in a treatment condition. The numerical values of the cell means for the scores of Table 11.2 are presented in Table 11.5 with the standard deviations in parentheses. In a factorial design the standard deviation typically is calculated only for the cell means.

Main Effect Means

Main effect mean: The mean of all subjects given one level of an independent variable, ignoring the classification by the other independent variable in a factorial design.

A **main effect mean** indicates the typical performance of all participants given one level of an independent variable, ignoring the classification by the other independent variable. Thus, there are two sets of main effect means, those for factor A and those for factor B.

Factor A

Main effect of factor A: The difference between $\overline{X}_{A1}$ and $\overline{X}_{A2}$, symbolized by $\overline{X}_{A1} - \overline{X}_{A2}$.

The **main effect means for factor A** are symbolized by $\overline{X}_{A1}$ and $\overline{X}_{A2}$. These means, sometimes called *column means*, are found for all subjects within either level A_1 or A_2, while disregarding the level of factor B that they received. Collapsing the data over levels of factor B

TABLE 11.4

Cell and main effect means in a 2×2 between-subjects design.

(a) Cell means

	Factor A	
	A_1	A_2
Factor B B_1	$\overline{X}_{A1B1}$	$\overline{X}_{A2B1}$
B_2	$\overline{X}_{A1B2}$	$\overline{X}_{A2B2}$

(b) Main effect means for factor A, $\overline{X}_{A1}$ and $\overline{X}_{A2}$

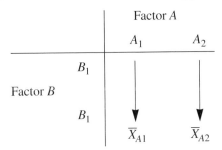

Ignore classification of scores by factor B to obtain main effect means for factor A. The difference between $\overline{X}_{A1}$ and $\overline{X}_{A2}$ is the main effect of factor A.

(c) Main effect means for factor B, $\overline{X}_{B1}$ and $\overline{X}_{B2}$

	Factor A		
	A_1	A_2	
Factor B B_1		$\longrightarrow$	$\overline{X}_{B1}$
B_2		$\longrightarrow$	$\overline{X}_{B2}$

Ignore classification of scores by factor A to obtain main effect means for factor B. The difference between $\overline{X}_{B1}$ and $\overline{X}_{B2}$ is the main effect of factor B.

to obtain main effect means for factor A is shown in Table 11.4b. For the example in Table 11.2, the main effect means for factor A, subject visibility, are based on the 10 scores of participants either not visible or visible to the assistant. Type of news (factor B) is ignored when finding the main effect means of factor A. The numerical values of $\overline{X}_{A1}$ and $\overline{X}_{A2}$ are presented in Table 11.5. The **main effect of factor A** is the difference between $\overline{X}_{A1}$ and $\overline{X}_{A2}$. If factor A has an effect on the dependent variable, then $\overline{X}_{A1}$ and $\overline{X}_{A2}$ will differ from each other, and the value of $\overline{X}_{A1} - \overline{X}_{A2}$ will become larger.

Factor B

Main effect of factor B:
The difference between $\overline{X}_{B1}$ and $\overline{X}_{B2}$, symbolized by $\overline{X}_{B1} - \overline{X}_{B2}$.

A similar logic applies to finding the main effect for independent variable B. The **main effect means for factor B** (sometimes called *row means*), symbolized as $\overline{X}_{B1}$ and $\overline{X}_{B2}$, are

TABLE 11.5

Cell and main effect means for the data of Table 11.2. The numerical values are response latency in seconds. Standard deviations of cell means are given in parentheses.

		Subject Visibility (Factor A)		
		Not Visible (A_1)	Visible (A_2)	Main Effect Means for Type of News ($\overline{X}_B$)
Type of News (Factor B)	Good (B_1)	90.8 (11.56)	84.6 (9.61)	87.7
	Bad (B_2)	82.2 (9.07)	112.4 (11.15)	97.3
	Main Effect Means for Subject Visibility ($\overline{X}_A$)	86.5	98.5	Grand mean 92.5

obtained by collapsing over factor A as shown in Table 11.4c. To find the main effect means for factor B in the example, type of news, the categorization by subject visibility (factor A) is ignored. The numerical values of $\overline{X}_{B1}$ and $\overline{X}_{B2}$ also are presented in Table 11.5. The **main effect of factor B** is the difference $\overline{X}_{B1} - \overline{X}_{B2}$. If factor B has an effect on the dependent variable, then $\overline{X}_{B1}$ and $\overline{X}_{B2}$ will differ from each other, and the value of $\overline{X}_{B1} - \overline{X}_{B2}$ will become larger.

Grand Mean

The **grand mean**, symbolized as $\overline{X}_G$, is the mean of all the scores in the table. For the data in Table 11.2, the grand mean of 92.5 seconds is the mean of all 20 scores. The grand mean typically is not presented as a descriptive statistic, but it is needed in this chapter for developing an analysis of variance for this design.

Interaction of the Independent Variables

Interaction: A situation in a factorial design when the effect of one independent variable depends on the level of the other independent variable with which it is combined.

An **interaction** occurs in a factorial design when the effect of one independent variable (e.g., factor A) depends on the level of the other independent variable (e.g., either B_1 or B_2) with which it is combined. For example, if an interaction occurs in a 2×2 design, then the effect of factor A, the difference in behavior between treatments A_1 and A_2, depends on the level of factor B. Similarly, if an interaction occurs, the effect of factor B, the difference in behavior between treatments B_1 and B_2, depends on the level of factor A. An interaction often is symbolized as $A \times B$, which is read as "A by B" or the "A by B interaction."

The public display hypothesis predicted an interaction for the example experiment. This hypothesis predicted no difference in the response latency between the not visible and visible conditions for good news (i.e., no difference between the A_1B_1 and A_2B_1 cell means). For bad news, however, the hypothesis predicted significantly longer latencies for the visible condition (the A_2B_2 cell mean) compared to the not visible condition (the A_1B_2 cell mean). Notice that the occurrence of an interaction is analyzed by comparing differences among the cell means rather than among the main effect means. I discuss these comparisons more fully later in the chapter.

TESTING YOUR KNOWLEDGE 11.1

1. Define: a, b, cell, cell mean, column mean, factor, factorial design, grand mean, interaction, level of an independent variable, main effect for factor A, main effect for factor B, main effect mean, n_{AB}, N, row mean, treatment condition, $\overline{X}_{AB}$, $\overline{X}_A$, $\overline{X}_B$, $\overline{X}_G$.

2. For each of the following factorial designs, identify how many independent variables are varied and indicate the number of levels for each factor. Then, assuming that the design is a between-subjects design, indicate how many subjects would be needed if 10 subjects were to be tested in each treatment combination.
   Type of design: (a) 3×3, (b) 3×2, (c) 2×3, (d) 6×2, (e) 4×4, (f) $2 \times 2 \times 2$, (g) $2 \times 4 \times 3$, (h) $3 \times 3 \times 2$.

3. Find cell means, main effect means, and the grand mean for the scores in each of the following tables:

TABLE 1

| | Factor A | |
	A_1	A_2
	10	17
	13	23
	8	17
B_1	17	21
	12	19
	20	24
	19	27
	13	21
	10	16
B_1	20	19
	22	30
	17	24

Factor B

TABLE 2

| | Factor A | |
	A_1	A_2
	23	41
	13	22
	28	27
B_1	11	32
	19	26
	20	24
	18	39
	29	28
	33	31
	18	26
B_1	29	34
	36	39
	47	44
	27	35

Factor B

ANALYSIS OF VARIANCE OF A TWO-FACTOR BETWEEN-SUBJECTS DESIGN

The statistical analysis of a factorial design involves hypothesis testing to determine if the main effect means differ significantly from each other for each independent variable and to determine if the interaction of the independent variables is statistically significant. Again, this testing is done with an analysis of variance that partitions the total variation of scores into sources of variation that are independent of each other. The one-factor between-subjects analysis of variance (discussed in Chapter 10) partitions the total variation into two independent sources: that due to the effect of the independent variable (i.e., factor A) and that due to within-groups error variation. In a two-factor between-subjects design, the total variation of scores is partitioned into three between-groups sources and one within-group source. The between-groups sources of variation are the following:

- The variation due to the effect of factor A
- The variation due to the effect of factor B
- The variation due to the interaction of factors A and B, symbolized as $A \times B$

The within-groups source is the within-cells error variation.

The analysis of variance then uses these partitioned scores to generate four mean squares:

MS_A, which varies with the effect of factor A
MS_B, which varies with the effect of factor B
$MS_{A \times B}$, which varies with an interaction of factors A and B
MS_{Error}, which varies with the within-cells variation of the scores

Following this step, three separate F statistics are generated, one for each independent variable and one for interaction, as follows:

Source of Variation	F Statistic
Factor A	$MS_A \div MS_{Error}$
Factor B	$MS_B \div MS_{Error}$
Interaction of $A \times B$	$MS_{A \times B} \div MS_{Error}$

Each of the three F statistics is used in a statistical hypothesis test to find if the source of variation that the F statistic corresponds to is statistically significant.

To provide a conceptual understanding of a factorial analysis of variance, the next section derives the mean squares that enter into these F statistics. If you were to perform a factorial analysis of variance on an actual set of data, however, you would use the computationally easier formulas given in the computational formulas supplement to this chapter or a computer data analysis program.

Partitioning a Score

The factorial analysis of variance finds the mean squares for the three F statistics by partitioning or separating the total variation of the scores in an experiment into parts varying with factor A (between groups), factor B (between groups), the $A \times B$ interaction (between groups), and error variation (within groups). This model for representing a score in a two-factor between-subjects design can be expressed as follows:

Total variation in a subject's score	=	Variation due to factor A plus sampling error	+	Variation due to factor B plus sampling error	+	Variation due to interaction of factors A and B plus sampling error	+	Variation due to within-cells error	(11.1)

In terms of scores, this equation can be written as

$$X - \overline{X}_G = (\overline{X}_A - \overline{X}_G) + (\overline{X}_B - \overline{X}_G) + (\overline{X}_{AB} - \overline{X}_A - \overline{X}_B + \overline{X}_G) + (X - \overline{X}_{AB}) \quad (11.2)$$

Difference of a subject's score from the grand mean	**Difference of factor A main effect mean from the grand mean**	**Difference of factor B main effect mean from the grand mean**	**Interaction: Difference of a cell mean from the grand mean after the main effects of factors A and B have been removed**	**Difference of the subject's score from its cell mean**

I examine each part of equation 11.2.

Total Variation

Similar to the one-factor analysis of variance of Chapter 10, the difference of a score from the grand mean (i.e., $X - \overline{X}_G$) represents the total variation of that score. As equation 11.2 indicates, a part of this variation is due to the effect of each independent variable and the interaction of the independent variables, and a part of it is due to error variation.

Variation Due to the Effect of Factor A and Sampling Error

The difference between a main effect mean of factor A and the grand mean (i.e., $\overline{X}_A - \overline{X}_G$) varies with the effect of factor A and with sampling error among the main effect means of factor A. Its use in a two-factor design is identical to its use in the one-factor between-subjects design to measure the effect of the independent variable. Any effect of factor A is expected to affect all subjects within a level of this factor equally. Thus, an effect of factor A changes the value of the main effect means for factor A. These main effect means will then differ from the grand mean. Hence, the difference $\overline{X}_A - \overline{X}_G$ reflects any effect of factor A (the treatment effect for factor A in equation 11.1). In addition to any treatment effect, the main effect means for factor A will also differ from each other because of sampling error. Therefore, the value of any $\overline{X}_A - \overline{X}_G$ difference reflects both a treatment effect of factor A and sampling error affecting the values of $\overline{X}_A$. Accordingly, it enters into the computation of MS_A.

Variation Due to the Effect of Factor B and Sampling Error

The difference between a main effect mean of factor B and the grand mean (i.e., $\overline{X}_B - \overline{X}_G$) varies with the effect of factor B and sampling error among the main effect means of factor

B. As with factor *A*, any effect of factor *B* is expected to affect all individuals within a level of this factor equally and, thus, change the value of the main effect means for factor *B*, which will then differ from the grand mean. Therefore, the difference $\overline{X}_B - \overline{X}_G$ reflects any effect of factor *B* (the treatment effect for factor *B* in equation 11.1). In addition, the main effect means for factor *B* will differ from each other because of sampling error. Hence, the difference $\overline{X}_B - \overline{X}_G$ reflects both a treatment effect of factor *B* and sampling error affecting the values of $\overline{X}_B$ and, thus, enters into the computation of MS_B.

Variation Due to the Interaction of Factors *A* and *B*

The interaction of factors *A* and *B* is the remaining difference of the cell means from the grand mean after the main effect of each independent variable has been removed. Symbolically, this statement may be represented as follows:

$$A \times B \quad = \quad (\overline{X}_{AB} - \overline{X}_G) \quad - \quad (\overline{X}_A - \overline{X}_G) \quad - \quad (\overline{X}_B - \overline{X}_G),$$

$$\begin{array}{ccccc} \text{Interaction} \\ \text{of } A \text{ and } B \end{array} = \begin{array}{c} \text{Difference of} \\ \text{cell mean from} \\ \text{grand mean} \end{array} - \begin{array}{c} \text{Main effect} \\ \text{of factor } A \end{array} - \begin{array}{c} \text{Main effect} \\ \text{of factor } B \end{array} .$$

The equation indicates that the interaction represents the variation in cell means after the main effect of each independent variable has been removed. This remaining variation in the cell means is due to the interaction of the independent variables and any sampling error among the cell means.

Carrying out the subtractions indicated in the equation results in a simplified expression of the interaction:

$$\overline{X}_{AB} - \overline{X}_A - \overline{X}_B + \overline{X}_G.$$

The interaction is expressed in this form in equation 11.2. This part of the equation enters into the computation of $MS_{A \times B}$.

Variation Due to Within-Cells Error

The difference of a score from its cell mean (i.e., $X - \overline{X}_{AB}$) reflects only within-cells error variation in the experiment. This error is what is left over in the score after the main effects of both factors and their interaction have been taken into account. As in a one-factor analysis of variance, the error reflects the uniqueness of a person's score in a group of individuals all of whom receive the same treatment. It enters into the computation of MS_{Error}.

Obtaining Mean Squares from Partitioned Scores

As discussed in Chapter 10, the partitioning equation provides the basis for obtaining the *SS* and *df* that produce the mean squares for the *F* ratio. The first step is to obtain the *SS* from the scores.

Obtaining Sums of Squares

Following the approach of Chapter 10, sums of squares (*SS*) are obtained by partitioning each score in the form of equation 11.2. To illustrate this partitioning, I use the score for the first person in the not visible/good news treatment condition (i.e., X_{111}) of Table 11.2, which is 97.0. For this score, equation 11.2 becomes

$$X_{111} - \overline{X}_G = (\overline{X}_{A1} - \overline{X}_G) + (\overline{X}_{B1} - \overline{X}_G) + (\overline{X}_{A1B1} - \overline{X}_{A1} - \overline{X}_{B1} + \overline{X}_G) + (X_{111} - \overline{X}_{A1B1}).$$

Substituting numerical values, I obtain

$$97.0 - 92.5 = (86.5 - 92.5) + (87.7 - 92.5)$$
$$+ (90.8 - 86.5 - 87.7 + 92.5) + (97.0 - 90.8)$$

or, carrying out the arithmetic functions indicated,

$$+4.5 = (-6.0) + (-4.8) + (+9.1) + (+6.2).$$

This partitioning shows that this score differs from the grand mean as much as it does because of the systematic effect of the level of factor *A* received (reflected in $\overline{X}_{A1} - \overline{X}_G = -6.0$), the systematic effect of the level of factor *B* received (reflected in $\overline{X}_{B1} - \overline{X}_G = -4.8$), the inter-action of factors *A* and *B* (reflected in $\overline{X}_{A1B1} - \overline{X}_{A1} - \overline{X}_{B1} + \overline{X}_G = +9.1$), and because of the unsystematic influences of within-cells error variation (reflected in $X_{111} - \overline{X}_{A1B1} = +6.2$). A similar partitioning for each of the other scores in Table 11.2 is shown in step 1 of Table 11.6. The remaining steps in the table obtain sums of squares from these partitioned scores. Follow each of these steps carefully.

Step 1:   The scores of all 20 participants in the experiment are partitioned following equation 11.2.

Step 2:   The numerical differences are found for each score.

Step 3:   Each positive and negative difference found in step 2 is squared.

Step 4:   The values of the squared differences are summed over all scores in the experiment. This summing is achieved by adding the 20 values in each of the columns. The result is five sums of squares:

$$SS_{Total} = 4567.000,$$
$$SS_A = 720.000,$$
$$SS_B = 460.800,$$
$$SS_{A \times B} = 1656.200,$$
$$SS_{Error} = 1730.000.$$

The SS_{Total} is the sum of its components; thus,

$$SS_{Total} = SS_A + SS_B + SS_{A \times B} + SS_{Error}. \tag{11.3}$$

TABLE 11.6
Obtaining sums of squares for a two-factor analysis of variance based on the scores of Table 11.2.

Step 1: **Partition the scores for the 20 subjects using the following equation:**

$$X - \bar{X}_G = (\bar{X}_A - \bar{X}_G) + (\bar{X}_B - \bar{X}_G) + (\bar{X}_{AB} - \bar{X}_A - \bar{X}_B + \bar{X}_G) + (X - \bar{X}_{AB})$$

Scores in A_1B_1
$$97.0 - 92.5 = (86.5 - 92.5) + (87.7 - 92.5) + (\ 90.8 - 86.5 - 87.7 + 92.5) + (\ 97.0 - 90.8)$$
$$90.0 - 92.5 = (86.5 - 92.5) + (87.7 - 92.5) + (\ 90.8 - 86.5 - 87.7 + 92.5) + (\ 90.0 - 90.8)$$
$$80.0 - 92.5 = (86.5 - 92.5) + (87.7 - 92.5) + (\ 90.8 - 86.5 - 87.7 + 92.5) + (\ 80.0 - 90.8)$$
$$107.0 - 92.5 = (86.5 - 92.5) + (87.7 - 92.5) + (\ 90.8 - 86.5 - 87.7 + 92.5) + (107.0 - 90.8)$$
$$80.0 - 92.5 = (86.5 - 92.5) + (87.7 - 92.5) + (\ 90.8 - 86.5 - 87.7 + 92.5) + (\ 80.0 - 90.8)$$

Scores in A_2B_1
$$70.0 - 92.5 = (98.5 - 92.5) + (87.7 - 92.5) + (\ 84.6 - 98.5 - 87.7 + 92.5) + (\ 70.0 - 84.6)$$
$$87.0 - 92.5 = (98.5 - 92.5) + (87.7 - 92.5) + (\ 84.6 - 98.5 - 87.7 + 92.5) + (\ 87.0 - 84.6)$$
$$81.0 - 92.5 = (98.5 - 92.5) + (87.7 - 92.5) + (\ 84.6 - 98.5 - 87.7 + 92.5) + (\ 81.0 - 84.6)$$
$$95.0 - 92.5 = (98.5 - 92.5) + (87.7 - 92.5) + (\ 84.6 - 98.5 - 87.7 + 92.5) + (\ 95.0 - 84.6)$$
$$90.0 - 92.5 = (98.5 - 92.5) + (87.7 - 92.5) + (\ 84.6 - 98.5 - 87.7 + 92.5) + (\ 90.0 - 84.6)$$

Scores in A_1B_2
$$68.0 - 92.5 = (86.5 - 92.5) + (97.3 - 92.5) + (\ 82.2 - 86.5 - 97.3 + 92.5) + (\ 68.0 - 82.2)$$
$$87.0 - 92.5 = (86.5 - 92.5) + (97.3 - 92.5) + (\ 82.2 - 86.5 - 97.3 + 92.5) + (\ 87.0 - 82.2)$$
$$92.0 - 92.5 = (86.5 - 92.5) + (97.3 - 92.5) + (\ 82.2 - 86.5 - 97.3 + 92.5) + (\ 92.0 - 82.2)$$
$$80.0 - 92.5 = (86.5 - 92.5) + (97.3 - 92.5) + (\ 82.2 - 86.5 - 97.3 + 92.5) + (\ 80.0 - 82.2)$$
$$84.0 - 92.5 = (86.5 - 92.5) + (97.3 - 92.5) + (\ 82.2 - 86.5 - 97.3 + 92.5) + (\ 84.0 - 82.2)$$

Scores in A_2B_2
$$114.0 - 92.5 = (98.5 - 92.5) + (97.3 - 92.5) + (112.4 - 98.5 - 97.3 + 92.5) + (114.0 - 112.4)$$
$$96.0 - 92.5 = (98.5 - 92.5) + (97.3 - 92.5) + (112.4 - 98.5 - 97.3 + 92.5) + (\ 96.0 - 112.4)$$
$$127.0 - 92.5 = (98.5 - 92.5) + (97.3 - 92.5) + (112.4 - 98.5 - 97.3 + 92.5) + (127.0 - 112.4)$$
$$110.0 - 92.5 = (98.5 - 92.5) + (97.3 - 92.5) + (112.4 - 98.5 - 97.3 + 92.5) + (110.0 - 112.4)$$
$$115.0 - 92.5 = (98.5 - 92.5) + (97.3 - 92.5) + (112.4 - 98.5 - 97.3 + 92.5) + (115.0 - 112.4)$$

Step 2: **Perform the subtractions in step 1 to obtain numerical differences for each subject.**

Scores in A_1B_1

+4.5	=	−6.0	+	−4.8	+	+9.1	+	+6.2
−2.5	=	−6.0	+	−4.8	+	+9.1	+	−0.8
−12.5	=	−6.0	+	−4.8	+	+9.1	+	−10.8
+14.5	=	−6.0	+	−4.8	+	+9.1	+	+16.2
−12.5	=	−6.0	+	−4.8	+	+9.1	+	−10.8

Scores in A_2B_1

−22.5	=	+6.0	+	−4.8	+	−9.1	+	−14.6
−5.5	=	+6.0	+	−4.8	+	−9.1	+	+2.4
−11.5	=	+6.0	+	−4.8	+	−9.1	+	−3.6
+2.5	=	+6.0	+	−4.8	+	−9.1	+	+10.4
−2.5	=	+6.0	+	−4.8	+	−9.1	+	+5.4

Scores in A_1B_2

−24.5	=	−6.0	+	+4.8	+	−9.1	+	−14.2
−5.5	=	−6.0	+	+4.8	+	−9.1	+	+4.8
−0.5	=	−6.0	+	+4.8	+	−9.1	+	+9.8
−12.5	=	−6.0	+	+4.8	+	−9.1	+	−2.2
−8.5	=	−6.0	+	+4.8	+	−9.1	+	+1.8

Scores in A_2B_2

+21.5	=	+6.0	+	+4.8	+	+9.1	+	+1.6
+3.5	=	+6.0	+	+4.8	+	+9.1	+	−16.4
+34.5	=	+6.0	+	+4.8	+	+9.1	+	+14.6
+17.5	=	+6.0	+	+4.8	+	+9.1	+	−2.4
+22.5	=	+6.0	+	+4.8	+	+9.1	+	+2.6

TABLE 11.6
(Continued)

Step 3: **Square each difference.**

	$(X - \overline{X}_G)^2$	$(\overline{X}_A - \overline{X}_G)^2$	$(\overline{X}_B - \overline{X}_G)^2$	$(\overline{X}_{AB} - \overline{X}_A - \overline{X}_B + \overline{X}_G)^2$	$(X - \overline{X}_{AB})^2$
	20.25	36.00	23.04	82.81	38.44
Scores	6.25	36.00	23.04	82.81	0.64
in A_1B_1	156.25	36.00	23.04	82.81	116.64
	210.25	36.00	23.04	82.81	262.44
	156.25	36.00	23.04	82.81	116.64
	506.25	36.00	23.04	82.81	213.16
Scores	30.25	36.00	23.04	82.81	5.76
in A_2B_1	132.25	36.00	23.04	82.81	12.96
	6.25	36.00	23.04	82.81	108.16
	6.25	36.00	23.04	82.81	29.16
	600.25	36.00	23.04	82.81	201.64
Scores	30.25	36.00	23.04	82.81	23.04
in A_1B_2	0.25	36.00	23.04	82.81	96.04
	156.25	36.00	23.04	82.81	4.84
	72.25	36.00	23.04	82.81	3.24
	462.25	36.00	23.04	82.81	2.56
Scores	12.25	36.00	23.04	82.81	268.96
in A_2B_2	1190.25	36.00	23.04	82.81	213.16
	306.25	36.00	23.04	82.81	5.76
	506.25	36.00	23.04	82.81	6.76

Step 4: **Sum the squared differences for each partition over all subjects.**

4567.000	= 720.000	+ 460.800	+ 1656.200	+ 1730.000
SS_{Total}	= SS_A	+ SS_B	+ $SS_{A\times B}$	+ SS_{Error}

This equation indicates that the total variation of the scores in the experiment (SS_{Total}) is the result of variation that occurs from four independent sources: factor A, factor B, the interaction of factors A and B, and the within-cells error.

Finding Degrees of Freedom

Mean squares (*MS*) are obtained by dividing each *SS* by its degrees of freedom. Recall that degrees of freedom are defined as the number of scores that are free to vary in the computation of a statistic. I use this definition to calculate the *df* for each *SS* of equation 11.3.

Total Degrees of Freedom.   To find the SS_{Total}, the grand mean $\overline{X}_G$ must be known. Because the total sum of squares is based on the difference of every score in the experiment from the grand mean (i.e., $X - \overline{X}_G$), then one less than the total number of scores are free to vary when calculating SS_{Total}. In notation,

$$\text{Total degrees of freedom} = df_{Total} = N - 1,$$

where N is the total number of scores in the experiment. With $N = 20$, $df_{Total} = 20 - 1 = 19$.

Degrees of Freedom for SS_A.   The SS_A is computed from the differences of the main effect means of factor A (i.e., $\overline{X}_{A1}$ and $\overline{X}_{A2}$ for the example) from $\overline{X}_G$. For a factorial design with two levels of factor A, if $\overline{X}_G$ is known, then only one main effect mean for factor A is free to vary. In general, the df for SS_A (df_A) are equal to one less than the number of levels of factor A, or

$$\text{Degrees of freedom for } SS_A = df_A = a - 1,$$

where a is the number of levels of independent variable A. For the example, $a = 2$; thus, $df_A = 2 - 1 = 1$.

Degrees of Freedom for SS_B.   The SS_B is computed from the differences of the main effect means of factor B (i.e., $\overline{X}_{B1}$ and $\overline{X}_{B2}$ in the example) from $\overline{X}_G$. For a factorial design with two levels of factor B, if $\overline{X}_G$ is known, then only one main effect mean for factor B is free to vary. Thus, the df for SS_B (df_B) are equal to one less than the number of levels of factor B, or

$$\text{Degrees of freedom for } SS_B = df_B = b - 1,$$

where b is the number of levels of independent variable B. For the example, $b = 2$; thus, $df_B = 2 - 1 = 1$.

Degrees of Freedom for $SS_{A \times B}$.   The $SS_{A \times B}$ is found by subtracting the appropriate main effect means from each cell mean. For a 2×2 design, if each main effect mean is known, then only one cell mean is free to vary. Given one cell mean and knowing the main effect means for factors A and B, you can find the other three cell means. In general,

$$\text{Degrees of freedom for } SS_{A \times B} = df_{A \times B} = (a - 1)(b - 1).$$

In the 2×2 design, $a = 2$ and $b = 2$; thus,

$$df_{A \times B} = (2 - 1)(2 - 1) = 1.$$

Degrees of Freedom for SS_{Error}.   The SS_{Error} is found by subtracting each $\overline{X}_{AB}$ from all the scores within that cell, for all the cells in the experiment. Thus, for each treatment condition, after $\overline{X}_{AB}$ is found, only $n_{AB} - 1$ scores are free to vary within that cell. For example, in Table 11.2 only four of the five scores are free to vary within each cell if each $\overline{X}_{AB}$ is known. Because there are four cells and four scores free to vary within each cell, there are 16 df for the SS_{Error}. In general, where a is the number of levels of factor A, b the levels of factor B, and n_{AB} the number of scores within each cell,

$$\textbf{Degrees of freedom for } SS_{\textbf{Error}} = df_{\textbf{Error}} = ab(n_{AB} - 1).$$

Additivity of Degrees of Freedom.   The degrees of freedom for a factorial analysis are additive in the same manner as they are for the one-factor analysis of variance. Thus,

$$df_{\text{Total}} = df_A + df_B + df_{A \times B} + df_{\text{Error}}. \tag{11.4}$$

This relationship holds in the example, for $df_{\text{Total}} = 19$, $df_A = 1$, $df_B = 1$, $df_{A \times B} = 1$, and $df_{\text{Error}} = 16$.

Obtaining MS from SS and df

Dividing each SS in equation 11.3 by its corresponding df produces the four mean squares needed for the two-factor between-subjects analysis of variance:

$$MS_A = \frac{SS_A}{df_A},$$

$$MS_B = \frac{SS_B}{df_B},$$

$$MS_{A \times B} = \frac{SS_{A \times B}}{df_{A \times B}},$$

$$MS_{\text{Error}} = \frac{SS_{\text{Error}}}{df_{\text{Error}}}.$$

I do not obtain MS_{Total} because it is not used for any F ratios in this analysis.

For the scores in Table 11.2, I have found $SS_A = 720.000$, $SS_B = 460.800$, $SS_{A \times B} = 1656.200$, and $SS_{\text{Error}} = 1730.000$. Furthermore, $df_A = 1$, $df_B = 1$, $df_{A \times B} = 1$, and $df_{\text{Error}} = 16$. Consequently,

$$MS_A = \frac{720.000}{1} = 720.000,$$

$$MS_B = \frac{460.800}{1} = 460.800,$$

$$MS_{A \times B} = \frac{1656.200}{1} = 1656.200,$$

$$MS_{\text{Error}} = \frac{1730.000}{16} = 108.125.$$

Computing the *F* Statistics

An *F* statistic is formed by the ratio of two mean squares, one *MS* varying with the effect of an independent variable, as well with sampling error, and the other *MS* varying only with error variation in the experiment. In the two-factor between-subjects analysis of variance, MS_A varies with factor A, MS_B varies with factor B, $MS_{A \times B}$ varies with the interaction of factors A and B, and MS_{Error} varies only with the within-cells error variation. Thus, three *F* statistics are formed, one for each systematic source of variation in the experiment:

Source of Variation	*F*
Factor A	$\dfrac{MS_A}{MS_{Error}}$
Factor B	$\dfrac{MS_B}{MS_{Error}}$
Interaction of A × B	$\dfrac{MS_{A \times B}}{MS_{Error}}$

Substituting numerical values for the mean squares, I obtain the following *F* statistics:

Source of Variation	*F*
Factor A	$\dfrac{720.000}{108.125} = 6.66$
Factor B	$\dfrac{460.800}{108.125} = 4.26$
Interaction of A × B	$\dfrac{1656.200}{108.125} = 15.32$

I discuss how to use and interpret each *F* shortly.

Table 11.7 provides a summary of the sources of variance in a two-factor between-subjects analysis of variance and the definitional formulas for each *df*, *MS*, and *F* statistic. A numerical summary of the analysis of variance on the data of Table 11.2 is presented in Table 11.8.

TESTING YOUR KNOWLEDGE 11.2

1. Identify the sources of variation in scores from a two-factor between-subjects design.
2. Write the equation to partition a score for the two-factor between-subjects analysis of variance.
3. Explain why the value of $\overline{X}_A - \overline{X}_G$ varies with the effect of factor A in a factorial experiment.
4. Explain why the value of $\overline{X}_B - \overline{X}_G$ varies with the effect of factor B in a factorial experiment.

TABLE 11.7
Summary of formulas for a two-factor between-subjects analysis of variance.

Source	SS	df[a]	MS	F
Factor A	SS_A	$a - 1$	$\dfrac{SS_A}{df_A}$	$\dfrac{MS_A}{MS_{\text{Error}}}$
Factor B	SS_B	$b - 1$	$\dfrac{SS_B}{df_B}$	$\dfrac{MS_B}{MS_{\text{Error}}}$
Interaction of A and B	$SS_{A \times B}$	$(a - 1)(b - 1)$	$\dfrac{SS_{A \times B}}{df_{A \times B}}$	$\dfrac{MS_{A \times B}}{MS_{\text{Error}}}$
Error	SS_{Error}	$ab(n_{AB} - 1)$	$\dfrac{SS_{\text{Error}}}{df_{\text{Error}}}$	
Total	SS_{Total}	$N - 1$	Not calculated	

[a]a = number of levels of factor A; b = number of levels of factor B; n_{AB} = number of scores in each cell; N = total number of scores.

TABLE 11.8
Numerical summary of the analysis of variance on the hypothetical scores of Table 11.2.

Source	SS	df	MS	F
Subject visibility (A)	720.000	1	720.000	6.66*
Type of news (B)	460.800	1	460.800	4.26
$A \times B$	1656.200	1	1656.200	15.32**
Error	1730.000	16	108.125	
Total	4567.000	19		

*$p < .05$.
**$p < .01$.

5. Explain why the value of $\overline{X}_{AB} - \overline{X}_A - \overline{X}_B + \overline{X}_G$ varies with the effect of the interaction of factors A and B in a factorial experiment.
6. Explain why the value of $X - \overline{X}_{AB}$ varies only with within-cells error variation in a factorial experiment.
7. Complete the following equations for a two-factor between-subjects analysis of variance.
   a. $df_A =$
   b. $df_B =$
   c. $df_{A \times B} =$

    d. $df_{Error} =$

    e. $df_{Total} =$

    f. $MS_A =$

    g. $MS_B =$

    h. $MS_{A \times B} =$

    i. $MS_{Error} =$

8. What is the value of SS_{Total} if $SS_A = 40.00$, $SS_B = 70.00$, $SS_{A \times B} = 30.00$, and $SS_{Error} = 100.00$?

9. What is the value of SS_A if $SS_{Total} = 224.00$, $SS_B = 14.00$, $SS_{A \times B} = 64.00$, and $SS_{Error} = 101.00$?

10. What is the value of $SS_{A \times B}$ if $SS_{Total} = 302.00$, $SS_A = 75.00$, $SS_B = 19.00$, and $SS_{Error} = 153.00$?

11. What is the value of SS_{Error} if $SS_{Total} = 98.00$, $SS_A = 14.00$, $SS_B = 7.00$, and $SS_{A \times B} = 17.00$?

12. Find $df_A, df_B, df_{A \times B}, df_{Error}$, and df_{Total} for a 2×3 between-subjects analysis of variance with six subjects in each cell.

13. Find $df_A, df_B, df_{A \times B}, df_{Error}$, and df_{Total} for a 3×2 between-subjects analysis of variance with 13 scores in each treatment condition.

14. What is the value of df_{Total} if $df_A = 3$, $df_B = 1$, $df_{A \times B} = 3$, and $df_{Error} = 72$?

15. Find the numerical values of mean squares for the following SS and df: $SS_A = 14.00$, $SS_B = 26.00$, $SS_{A \times B} = 44.00$, $SS_{Error} = 480.00$, $df_A = 1$, $df_B = 2$, $df_{A \times B} = 2$, and $df_{Error} = 60$.

16. Suppose that you conducted a 2×2 factorial experiment with three participants in each cell and obtained the following scores:

		Factor A	
		A_1	A_2
	B_1	30	34
		32	36
		28	32
Factor B			
	B_2	28	38
		30	34
		26	36

    a. Partition these scores following the approach illustrated in Table 11.6. Obtain the $SS_{Total}, SS_A, SS_B, SS_{A \times B}, SS_{Error}$, and the corresponding degrees of freedom for each partition. Then complete a numerical summary table with values of MS and F.

    b. Why is SS_B equal to zero in this example?

17. Tables 1 and 2 are incomplete summary tables for a factorial between-subjects analysis of variance. Assume an equal number of scores in each cell. Fill in the missing values in each table by using the relationships among SS and df given in equations 11.3 and 11.4, respectively. Then answer these questions for each table.

    a. How many levels of factor A were used?

    b. How many levels of factor B were used?

    c. How many subjects were measured in each cell?

    d. How many subjects participated in the study?

TABLE 1

Source	SS	df	MS	F
Factor A	—	2	16.00	—
Factor B	24.00	1	—	3.00
A × B	—	—	12.00	—
Error	—	—	—	
Total	560.00	65		

TABLE 2

Source	SS	df	MS	F
Factor A	—	2	—	4.50
Factor B	24.00	4	—	1.50
A × B	160.00	—	—	5.00
Error	—	—	4.00	
Total	—	224		

STATISTICAL HYPOTHESIS TESTING WITH THE TWO-FACTOR BETWEEN-SUBJECTS ANALYSIS OF VARIANCE

To understand statistical hypothesis testing using the F statistics obtained from a factorial analysis of variance, we must know what affects MS_A, MS_B, $MS_{A \times B}$, and MS_{Error} in an experiment.

Factors Affecting the Value of Mean Squares in a Factorial Analysis of Variance

Each MS in a factorial analysis is affected by a different source of variation in the experiment. If neither of the independent variables has an effect on the dependent variable and there is no interaction of the independent variables, then each MS estimates only error variation. Under these circumstances, all four mean squares should be approximately equal in value and reflect only the effects of sampling error. But if either or both of the independent variables have a main effect or if they interact, then the effect increases the value of the corresponding MS. For example, if factor A produces a main effect, then MS_A will increase relative to MS_{Error}, but MS_B, $MS_{A \times B}$, and MS_{Error} will not be affected by this main effect. A similar situation holds if factor B has a main effect. If factor B produces a main effect, then MS_B will increase relative to MS_{Error}, but MS_A, $MS_{A \times B}$, and MS_{Error} will not be affected by this main effect. If the independent variables interact, then $MS_{A \times B}$ increases, but MS_A, MS_B, and MS_{Error} will not be affected. The MS_{Error} is not affected by either main effects or interaction of the independent variables. It reflects only within-cells error variance in the experiment. Thus, the value of each MS is independent of the value of the other mean squares.

The four mean squares and the sources of variation affecting them may be summarized as follows:

Mean Square	Affected by:
MS_A	Systematic variance due to factor A Sampling error
MS_B	Systematic variance due to factor B Sampling error
$MS_{A \times B}$	Systematic variance due to the interaction of factors A and B Sampling error
MS_{Error}	Within-cell error variance

To relate this understanding of the factors affecting each MS to the three F statistics of Table 11.8, notice that each F uses MS_{Error} as the denominator and the appropriate MS for the independent variable or the interaction as the numerator. If the independent variable affecting the MS in the numerator of a particular F ratio does not have an effect, then that F ratio should equal about 1.00, for both the numerator and denominator MS will measure only error variation in the experiment. But if the independent variable does have an effect, then the value of the MS for that variable increases, and the value of F for that factor becomes greater than 1.0. This reasoning is identical to that expressed in Chapter 10 for the one-factor analysis of variance.

Statistical Decision Making from the F Statistics

With this understanding of the factors affecting each value of F, we are ready to use each F in a statistical hypothesis test. The steps followed are identical to those discussed in Chapter 10.

- A null hypothesis, H_0, and an alternative hypothesis, H_1, are formulated for each F statistic.
- The sampling distribution of F, assuming that H_0 is true, is obtained for each F value. This distribution is given in Table A.3.
- A significance level is selected.
- A critical value of F, identified as F_{crit}, is found for each of the F statistics from the sampling distribution of F given in Table A.3.
- A rejection region is located in the sampling distribution of F for each F.
- The three F values, identified as F_{obs}, are calculated from the sample data.
- A decision to reject or not reject H_0 for each F_{obs} is made on the basis of whether or not F_{obs} falls into the rejection region.

Statistical Hypotheses

For a two-factor between-subjects analysis of variance, three different null hypotheses are tested, one for each F_{obs}. For a 2×2 factorial analysis of variance, the null (H_0) and alternative hypotheses (H_1) for each F are as follows:

F for:	Statistical Hypotheses
Factor A	H_0: $\mu_{A1} = \mu_{A2}$ H_1: The μ_A's are not equal
Factor B	H_0: $\mu_{B1} = \mu_{B2}$ H_1: The μ_B's are not equal
$A \times B$	H_0: All $(\mu_{AB} - \mu_A - \mu_B + \mu_G) = 0$ H_1: Not all $(\mu_{AB} - \mu_A - \mu_B + \mu_G) = 0$

Main Effects. The null and alternative hypotheses for the main effects of factors A and B are identical in form to the statistical hypotheses for a one-factor analysis. For the main effect of an independent variable, the factorial analysis of variance is treating the data as if they were obtained from a one-factor design as illustrated in Table 11.4. The number of population means identified in H_0 for either factor A or B corresponds to the number of levels of that factor in the experiment. For example, if an experiment involves three levels of factor A, then H_0 for factor A is written as

$$H_0: \mu_{A1} = \mu_{A2} = \mu_{A3}$$

and H_1 as

$$H_1: \text{The } \mu_A\text{'s are not all equal.}$$

The null hypothesis for each factor represents the situation that exists if the independent variable has no effect. If the null hypothesis is true, then any observed difference between the corresponding main effect means is due only to sampling error.

The alternative hypothesis states that the population means are not equal to each other, a situation that exists if the independent variable does have an effect.

Interaction. The null hypothesis for the interaction states that in the population, if no interaction occurs, then the difference of a cell mean, μ_{AB}, from the grand mean, μ_G, will be equal to zero after the main effects of each independent variable [i.e., $(\mu_A - \mu_G)$ and $(\mu_B - \mu_G)$] have been subtracted from it. In other words, this H_0 states that with no interaction of the independent variables the value of each cell mean may be exactly predicted from the main effects of the independent variables. The alternative hypothesis states that this relation is not the case and that the variation in cell means is not predictable from the main effects alone.

Decision Making from the F Value

Making decisions about each of the three sets of hypotheses from the values of F_{obs} is identical to the process followed in a one-factor analysis of variance. A value of α defining the size of the rejection region is chosen prior to conducting the analysis. The sampling distribution of F under H_0 is then determined for each of the three values of F_{obs}, and a rejection region is located in each sampling distribution. This step requires looking up three values of F_{crit} with the appropriate numerator and denominator df in Table A.3a or b, depending on the value of α selected. Then, for each F_{obs}, if F_{obs} is equal to or larger than its corresponding F_{crit} value, the H_0 for that F_{obs} is rejected and H_1 accepted. The difference between the means entering into that value of F_{obs} is statistically significant. If F_{obs} is less than its F_{crit} value, then the decision is to fail to reject H_0 and to not accept H_1 for that source of variance. The difference between the means entering into that value of F_{obs} is nonsignificant. The two sets of decisions for each F_{obs} in a two-factor analysis of variance are summarized in Table 11.9.

I illustrate decision making with the analysis of variance on the example data of Table 11.2, summarized in Table 11.8. In this table, each F_{obs} has 1 df for its numerator and 16 df for its denominator. Hence, each F_{obs} has the same value of F_{crit} and, thus, the same rejection region. This relationship is not necessarily the case in all factorial analyses of variance. Depending on the number of levels of each independent variable, it is possible for each F_{obs} to have a different df for the numerator and, thus, a different rejection region.

TABLE 11.9
Summary of statistical decisions in a two-factor analysis of variance.

F Ratio for:	Value of F_{obs}	Statistical Decision	
Factor A	Less than F_{crit}	Fail to reject H_0 Do not accept H_1	The main effect of factor A is nonsignificant.
	Equal to or greater than F_{crit}	Reject H_0 Accept H_1	The main effect of factor A is statistically significant.
Factor B	Less than F_{crit}	Fail to reject H_0 Do not accept H_1	The main effect of factor B is nonsignificant.
	Equal to or greater than F_{crit}	Reject H_0 Accept H_1	The main effect of factor B is statistically significant.
$A \times B$	Less than F_{crit}	Fail to reject H_0 Do not accept H_1	The interaction of factors A and B is nonsignificant.
	Equal to or greater than F_{crit}	Reject H_0 Accept H_1	The interaction of factors A and B is statistically significant.

For $\alpha = .05$, F_{crit} with 1, 16 df is 4.49 (obtained from Table A.3a). Hence, for each F_{obs} in Table 11.8, the rejection region consists of values of F_{obs} equal to or greater than 4.49. Accordingly, I make the following decisions from this analysis of variance:

Source	F_{obs}	Falls into Rejection Region	Statistical Decision	
Factor A	6.66	Yes	Reject H_0 Accept H_1	The main effect of factor A is statistically significant.
Factor B	4.26	No	Fail to reject H_0 Do not accept H_1	The main effect of factor B is nonsignificant.
$A \times B$	15.32	Yes	Reject H_0 Accept H_1	The interaction of A and B is statistically significant.

Assumptions of Factorial Between-Subjects Analysis of Variance

The factorial between-subjects analysis of variance is based on the same three assumptions about the scores obtained in an experiment as is the one-factor between-subjects analysis.

1. The scores in each sample are drawn randomly from a population of scores, and each score is independent of each other score.
2. The scores in the populations sampled are normally distributed.
3. The variances of scores in the populations are equal.

As I pointed out with a one-factor analysis, the first assumption of independence of scores must be met for a between-subjects analysis of variance to be used. Each participant may contribute only one score in the experiment. The second and third assumptions, however, may not always be met by the data of an experiment. Again, violations of the normality and equality of variance assumptions are more likely to have minimal effects on the probability of making a Type I error when the following conditions are met:

- The number of participants in each cell is the same.
- The shape of the distributions of the scores for each treatment condition is about the same and the distributions are neither very peaked nor very flat.
- The significance level is set at .05.

TESTING YOUR KNOWLEDGE 11.3

1. Identify the factors affecting the value of each MS in a between-subjects factorial analysis of variance.
2. Explain why MS_A increases in value if factor A has an effect in a factorial experiment.

3. Explain why MS_B increases in value if factor B has an effect in a factorial experiment.
4. Explain why $MS_{A \times B}$ increases in value if factors A and B interact in a factorial experiment.
5. Explain why the value of MS_{Error} is not affected by either factors A or B or their interaction in a factorial experiment.
6. What is expected to happen to the value of F_{obs} for factor A if factor A has an effect in an experiment?
7. What is expected to happen to the value of F_{obs} for $A \times B$ if the independent variables interact in an experiment?
8. Identify the steps in statistical testing with a factorial analysis of variance.
9. Write the statistical hypotheses for the following:
   a. A 2×4 between-subjects analysis of variance
   b. A 3×2 between-subjects analysis of variance
   c. A 3×3 between-subjects analysis of variance
10. This exercise provides a brief analysis of variance summary tables for several two-factor between-subjects designs. For each F_{obs}, find F_{crit} for a .05 significance level from Table A.3a and indicate whether F_{obs} falls into the rejection region. Then indicate your decision with respect to H_0 and H_1. If the exact df are not tabled for df_{Error}, use the next lower tabled value.

TABLE 1

Source	df	F_{obs}
Factor A	1	4.63
Factor B	3	2.11
$A \times B$	3	3.97
Error	56	
Total	63	

TABLE 2

Source	df	F_{obs}
Factor A	3	1.42
Factor B	2	3.51
$A \times B$	6	2.37
Error	144	
Total	155	

TABLE 3

Source	df	F_{obs}
Factor A	3	4.12
Factor B	4	2.83
$A \times B$	8	1.87
Error	150	
Total	164	

11. Identify the assumptions underlying the use of the factorial between-subjects analysis of variance.

INTERPRETING A 2 × 2 FACTORIAL ANALYSIS OF VARIANCE

I begin discussion of the interpretation of the results of a factorial design with the steps needed to interpret a statistically significant interaction. I then turn to the interpretation of statistically significant main effects.

The Simple Effect of an Independent Variable

An interaction of two independent variables occurs when the effect of one independent variable depends on the level of the other independent variable with which it is combined. Consequently, a statistically significant interaction in the analysis of variance is interpreted by comparing differences among the cell means in the experiment. The differences between the

Simple effect of an independent variable: The effect of one independent variable at only one level of the other independent variable in a factorial design.

cell means reveal the simple effects of the independent variables. The **simple effect of an independent variable** (sometimes called a **simple main effect**) in a factorial design is the effect of that independent variable at only one level of the other independent variable. Table 11.10 illustrates the four simple effects as well as the two main effects in a 2×2 design. The simple effects for each independent variable are identified in the rectangular boxes between cells. In a 2×2 design there are only two simple effects for each independent variable.

Simple Effects of Factor A

The simple effect of factor A at level B_1 of factor B is given by the difference between the $\overline{X}_{A1B1}$ and $\overline{X}_{A2B1}$ cell means (i.e., $\overline{X}_{A1B1} - \overline{X}_{A2B1}$). This difference reveals the effect of factor A at level B_1 of factor B. Similarly, the simple effect of factor A at level B_2 of factor B is given by the difference between the $\overline{X}_{A1B2}$ and $\overline{X}_{A2B2}$ cell means (i.e., $\overline{X}_{A1B2} - \overline{X}_{A2B2}$). This difference reveals the effect of factor A at level B_2. In finding the numerical values of the simple effects, it is important to maintain a consistency of direction in the comparisons and to retain the sign ($+$ or $-$) of the effect.

TABLE 11.10

Simple and main effects in a 2×2 between-subjects analysis of variance.

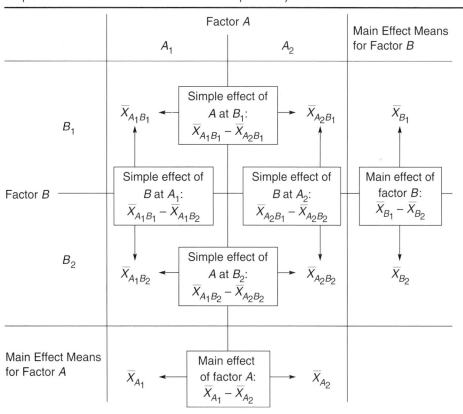

Simple Effects of Factor B

The simple effect of factor B at level A_1 of factor A is given by the difference between the $\overline{X}_{A1B1}$ and $\overline{X}_{A1B2}$ cell means (i.e., $\overline{X}_{A1B1} - \overline{X}_{A1B2}$), and the simple effect of factor B at level A_2 of factor A is given by the difference between the $\overline{X}_{A2B1}$ and $\overline{X}_{A2B2}$ cell means (i.e., $\overline{X}_{A2B1} - \overline{X}_{A2B2}$). Each simple effect indicates the effect of factor B at only one level of factor A.

A Numerical Example of Simple and Main Effects.   The numerical values of the simple and main effect differences from the means of Table 11.5 are presented in Table 11.11. The main effect and simple effect differences between means are shown in the rectangular boxes. For example, the simple effect of subject visibility for good news (the simple effect of factor A at B_1) is $\overline{X}_{A1B1} - \overline{X}_{A2B1}$, which equals $90.8 - 84.6$, or $+6.2$ seconds. Likewise, the simple effect of type of news for the subject-not-visible condition (the simple effect of B at A_1) is $\overline{X}_{A1B1} - \overline{X}_{A1B2}$, which equals $90.8 - 82.2$, or $+8.6$ seconds.

Interpreting Simple Effects When a Statistically Significant Interaction Occurs

If a statistically significant interaction of the independent variables occurs in an analysis of variance, then the two simple effects for a factor are not equal to each other or to the main

TABLE 11.11
Main effect and simple effect differences of latency of response (in seconds) for subject visibility and type of news in the example experiment.

| | Subject Visibility (A) | | |
	Not Visible (A_1)	Visible (A_2)	Main Effect Means for Type of News (B)
Good (B_1)	90.8 ← +6.2 → 84.6		87.7
Type of News (B)	+8.6 ↓	−27.8 ↓	−9.6
Bad (B_2)	82.2 ← −30.2 → 112.4		97.3
Main Effect Means for Subject Visibility (A)	86.5 ← −12.0 → 98.5		

effect for that factor. Thus, if there is a statistically significant interaction, the simple effect of factor A at level B_1, $\overline{X}_{A1B1} - \overline{X}_{A2B1}$, is not equal to the simple effect of factor A at level B_2, $\overline{X}_{A1B2} - \overline{X}_{A2B2}$. In addition, neither simple effect of factor A is equal to the main effect of factor A given by $\overline{X}_{A1} - \overline{X}_{A2}$.

Applying this relationship to the example results in Table 11.11, I find that the simple effect of subject visibility for good news (an effect of $+6.2$ seconds) is not equal to the simple effect of subject visibility for bad news (an effect of -30.2 seconds), and neither simple effect is equal to the main effect for subject visibility (an effect of -12.0 seconds).

A similar relationship applies to the simple effects of factor B. If a statistically significant interaction occurs, then the simple effect of factor B at level A_1, $\overline{X}_{A1B1} - \overline{X}_{A1B2}$, is not equal to the simple effect of B at level A_2, $\overline{X}_{A2B1} - \overline{X}_{A2B2}$. And neither simple effect equals the main effect of factor B given by $\overline{X}_{B1} - \overline{X}_{B2}$.

Applying this relationship to the example results in Table 11.11 indicates that the simple effect of type of news for the subject-not-visible condition (an effect of $+8.6$ seconds) is not equal to the simple effect of type of news for the subject-visible condition (an effect of -27.8 seconds), and neither simple effect is equal to the main effect for type of news (an effect of -9.6 seconds).

Multiple Comparison Tests for a Statistically Significant Interaction.   Each simple effect comparison in Tables 11.10 and 11.11 is a pairwise comparison; two cell means are compared with each other. To determine if the two cell means differ significantly from each other, a multiple comparison test is used to find a **critical difference** (*CD*) for the simple effect. If the observed value of the simple effect is equal to or exceeds the *CD*, then the difference between the cell means is statistically significant.

Again, the **Tukey HSD test** is frequently used for post hoc comparisons of simple effects. The *CD* for this test is given by

$$CD = q\sqrt{\frac{MS_{\text{Error}}}{n_{AB}}}.$$

The value of q is found from Table A.4 and depends on the number of simple effect comparisons to be made and df_{Error}. Because Table A.4 was constructed for a one-factor design, we use the following conversion to enter the table:

Type of Design	Use *q* from Table A.4 Found in the Column for ___ Levels of the Independent Variable:
2×2	3
2×3	5
3×2	5
3×3	7
3×4	8
4×3	8
4×4	10

The MS_{Error} is the value of MS_{Error} calculated in the factorial analysis of variance, and n_{AB} is the number of scores in each cell.

To illustrate this computation for the 2×2 experiment on the effects of subject visibility and type of news, I use the column for $a = 3$ in Table A.4 to find q. With 16 df for MS_{Error} (from Table 11.8) and $\alpha = .05$, the value of q (3,16) is 3.65. $MS_{Error} = 108.125$ from Table 11.8, and n_{AB}, the number of scores entering into each cell mean, is 5. Hence, the numerical value of the Tukey CD is

$$CD = 3.65 \sqrt{\frac{108.125}{5}} = 17.0 \quad \text{seconds rounded to one decimal place.}$$

Any simple effect in Table 11.11 equal to or greater than 17.0 seconds in absolute value is statistically significant at the .05 level. The simple effects of subject visibility for bad news (i.e., -30.2 seconds) and for type of news for the visible condition (i.e., -27.8 seconds) are greater in absolute value than the CD of 17.0 seconds. These simple effects reveal statistically significant differences between the cell means involved. The simple effects for subject visibility for good news (i.e., $+6.2$ seconds) and for type of news in the not visible condition (i.e., $+8.6$ seconds) are less in absolute value than the CD of 17.0 seconds. These simple effects are nonsignificant, and the cell means involved differ only because of sampling error.

Interpreting Main Effects When an Interaction Occurs

When a statistically significant interaction occurs, the main effects for the independent variables may not lend themselves to meaningful interpretation. This condition happens because the main effect of an independent variable is the mean of the simple effects for that variable. For example, with an equal number of scores in each cell, the main effect for subject visibility (-12.0 seconds) in Table 11.11 is the mean of the simple effects for subject visibility for good and bad news (i.e., $[(+6.2) + (-30.2)]/2 = -12.0$ seconds). A similar relationship holds for the main effect for type of news, -9.6 seconds. It is the mean of the simple effects for type of news for the subject-not-visible condition, $+8.6$ seconds, and the subject-visible condition, -27.8 seconds. Accordingly, when an interaction occurs so that the simple effects of an independent variable are not equal to each other, the main effect of that independent variable may not accurately represent the effect of the variable. Such main effects are artifacts of the interaction and do not provide meaningful information about the results of the experiment. An **artifactual main effect**, then, is a main effect that does not give meaningful information about the effect of an independent variable, for it occurs only because of the specific pattern of interaction observed. It is an artificial result of the pattern of simple effects for that variable. Consequently, an important note of caution about interpreting main effects in a factorial design is in order:

Artifactual main effect: A main effect that does not give meaningful information about the effect of an independent variable in a factorial design.

- If a statistically significant interaction occurs in a factorial design, then main effects for either factor A or factor B may be artifactual and may not present meaningful results about the effect of that independent variable.
- If the interaction in a factorial design is nonsignificant, then main effects for either factor A or factor B will present meaningful results about the outcome of that independent variable.

A statistically significant interaction in an analysis of variance does not ensure that the main effects will be artifactual, but it is a warning to examine any significant main effect to find whether it provides meaningful results about the effect of the independent variable. Table 11.12a summarizes these relationships among simple and main effects when a statistically significant interaction occurs.

TABLE 11.12
Interaction and interpretation of simple effects and main effects in a 2 × 2 factorial analysis of variance.

(a) **If F_{obs} for the $A \times B$ interaction falls into the rejection region, then:**
  - The F ratio for interaction is statistically significant.
  - The effect of one independent variable depends on the level of the other independent variable.
  - The simple effect of factor A at B_1 (i.e., $\overline{X}_{A1B1} - \overline{X}_{A2B1}$) is not equal to the simple effect of factor A at B_2 (i.e., $\overline{X}_{A1B2} - \overline{X}_{A2B2}$). The observed difference between the two simple effects for factor A is due to the interaction of the independent variables and not simply to sampling error.
  - The simple effect of factor B at A_1 (i.e., $\overline{X}_{A1B1} - \overline{X}_{A1B2}$) is not equal to the simple effect of factor B at A_2 (i.e., $\overline{X}_{A2B1} - \overline{X}_{A2B2}$). The observed difference between the two simple effects for factor B is due to the interaction of the independent variables and not simply to sampling error.
  - The simple effects of factor A are not equal to the main effect of factor A.
  - The simple effects of factor B are not equal to the main effect of factor B.
  - Each simple effect should be compared to a Tukey CD to find which cell means differ significantly from each other.
  - The main effects for either factor A or factor B may be artifactual and may not present meaningful results about the effect of the independent variable.

(b) **If F_{obs} for the $A \times B$ interaction does not fall into the rejection region, then:**
  - The F ratio for interaction is nonsignificant.
  - The effect of one independent variable does not depend on the level of the other independent variable.
  - The main effects for factor A and factor B will present meaningful results about the outcome of the experiment.
  - The simple effect of factor A at B_1 (i.e., $\overline{X}_{A1B1} - \overline{X}_{A2B1}$) does not differ significantly from the simple effect of factor A at B_2 (i.e., $\overline{X}_{A1B2} - \overline{X}_{A2B2}$). The observed difference between the two simple effects for factor A is due to sampling error.
  - The simple effect of factor B at A_1 (i.e., $\overline{X}_{A1B1} - \overline{X}_{A1B2}$) does not differ significantly from the simple effect of factor B at A_2 (i.e., $\overline{X}_{A2B1} - \overline{X}_{A2B2}$). The observed difference between the two simple effects for factor B is due to sampling error.
  - The simple effects of factor A do not differ from the main effect of factor A. The main effect of factor A provides the best description of the effect of factor A.
  - The simple effects of factor B do not differ from the main effect of factor B. The main effect of factor B provides the best description of the effect of factor B.
  - There is no need to analyze the simple effects with a multiple comparison test.

Interpreting Simple and Main Effects When No Statistically Significant Interaction Occurs

If no statistically significant interaction of the independent variables occurs, then the effect of one independent variable does not depend on the level of the other independent variable. Thus, if no interaction occurs, the simple effect of factor A at level B_1 will be equivalent to the simple effect of factor A at level B_2. Any observed difference between these simple effects is due only to sampling error. Furthermore, if the simple effects of factor A are equivalent to each other, they are also equivalent to the main effect of factor A, and the main effect of factor A provides the best description of the effect of this independent variable.

A similar relationship holds for the simple effects of factor B. If no interaction occurs, then the simple effect of factor B at level A_1 will be equivalent to the simple effect of factor B at level A_2. Any observed difference between these simple effects is due only to sampling error. The simple effects of factor B also are equivalent to the main effect of factor B, and the main effect of factor B provides the best description of the effect of this independent variable. These relationships are summarized in part (b) of Table 11.12.

Putting It All Together: Interpreting the Analysis of Variance on the Example Experiment

Understanding the results of a factorial experiment requires looking at each main effect and the interaction and interpreting them with respect to the decisions made in the analysis of variance. Whenever a statistically significant interaction occurs, as in the example experiment (see Table 11.8), interpretation of the results should start with the interaction.

Interpreting the Interaction of Subject Visibility and Type of News

The value of F_{obs} for interaction = 15.32 in Table 11.8 is greater than the F_{crit} value of 4.49 and, thus, falls into the rejection region. Consequently, H_0 for the interaction of factors A and B,

$$H_0: \text{All } (\mu_{AB} - \mu_A - \mu_B + \mu_G) = 0,$$

is rejected and

$$H_1: \text{Not all } (\mu_{AB} - \mu_A - \mu_B + \mu_G) = 0$$

is accepted. To interpret this interaction, I first apply the Tukey HSD critical difference to the simple effects in Table 11.11. The Tukey CD is 17.0 seconds; thus, any simple effect in Table 11.11 equal to or greater than 17.0 seconds in absolute value is statistically significant at the .05 level.

Turning to Table 11.11, I first examine the simple effects of factor A, subject visibility. The simple effect of factor A at B_1, a difference of $+6.2$ seconds, is less than the CD of 17.0 seconds; this simple effect is nonsignificant. Subject visibility does not have an effect when good news is delivered. The difference between the not visible and visible cell means for good news (90.8 and 84.6 seconds, respectively) is due only to sampling error. The simple effect of factor A at B_2, a difference of -30.2 seconds, however, is greater in absolute value than the *CD* of 17.0 seconds. This simple effect is statistically significant. Bad news is delivered significantly more slowly when the subject is visible (at 112.4 seconds) than when the subject is not visible (at 82.2 seconds).

I now turn to the simple effects of factor *B*, type of news. The simple effect of factor B at A_1, a difference of $+8.6$ seconds, is less in absolute value than the *CD* of 17.0 seconds; this simple effect is nonsignificant. When the subject is not visible, good and bad news are delivered with equal rapidity. The difference between the good and bad news cell means for the not visible subjects (90.8 and 82.2 seconds, respectively) is due only to sampling error. The simple effect of factor B at A_2, a difference of -27.8 seconds, is greater in absolute value than the *CD* of 17.0 seconds; thus, this simple effect is a significant difference. When the subject is visible, bad news is delivered significantly more slowly (at 112.4 seconds) than good news (at 84.6 seconds).

This analysis leads to the following summary of the outcome of this interaction of subject visibility with type of news.

- The effect of subject visibility depends on the type of news delivered.
  - **a.** For good news, there was no significant difference in response latency between visible and not visible subjects (90.8 and 84.6 seconds, respectively).
  - **b.** For bad news, the response latency of visible subjects (112.4 seconds) was significantly longer than the latency of the not visible subjects (82.2 seconds).
- The effect of type of news depends on the subject's visibility.
  - **a.** For not visible subjects, there was no significant difference between good and bad news; not visible subjects delivered good and bad news with equivalent latencies (90.8 and 82.2 seconds, respectively).
  - **b.** Visible subjects took significantly longer to deliver bad news compared to good news, 112.4 seconds versus 84.6 seconds, respectively.

These outcomes are in clear agreement with the predictions offered by the self-presentational hypothesis that the MUM effect is simply a public display to maintain a positive social image.

Graphic Presentation of the Results of the Example Experiment.
In published results of factorial designs, cell means frequently are presented graphically in a figure, rather than in a table such as Table 11.5, for a figure often provides a clearer portrayal of an interaction.

The cell means from Table 11.5 are plotted in Figure 11.1. Each cell mean is identified in this figure, but in published articles the cell means are represented only by a symbol such as filled or open circles, which are labeled in a legend on the figure. When plotting a figure, one of the independent variables is placed on the abscissa (i.e., horizontal axis), and the second independent variable is represented as a function on the figure. The measure of the dependent variable is represented on the ordinate (i.e., vertical axis). Which of the two independent variables is placed on the abscissa? The rule generally followed is that the independent variable that is more quantitative in nature or with a more continuous underlying dimension is plotted on the abscissa. In the example experiment, this variable is factor *B*, the type of news, for type of news may vary over the good–bad dimension in a continuous

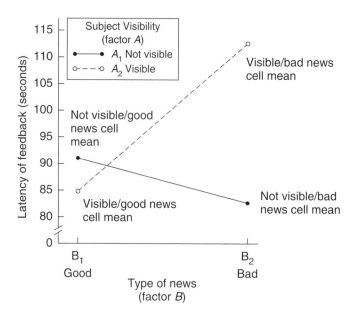

FIGURE 11.1

Latency of response (in seconds) in the example experiment as a function of the type of news (good versus bad) and subject visibility (not visible versus visible). This figure plots the cell means of Table 11.5.

manner; some news may be very good, other news may be very bad, and some news is between these two extremes. Thus, the type of news variable was placed on the abscissa. The second independent variable, subject visibility, varies in a less continuous manner; there is not a continuous gradation from not visible to visible. Accordingly, this independent variable is represented by the two functions within the figure. The filled circles connected by the solid line represent the subject-not-visible condition (A_1) and the open circles connected by the dashed line indicate the subject visible condition (A_2). The dependent variable is represented on the ordinate. Because the shortest latency is 82.2 seconds, the axis is broken (by the ⧸) and the first labeled value begins at 80 seconds.

Figure 11.1 portrays the differing simple effects for each of the two independent variables. When a statistically significant interaction occurs, the effect of one independent variable depends on the level of the other independent variable with which it is combined. This "it depends" nature of an interaction becomes clear from this figure. If you were asked, "What is the effect of subject visibility on response latency?", your answer would be, "It depends on the type of news delivered. For good news there is a nonsignificant difference between the subject-visible and subject-not-visible conditions, but for bad news the subject-visible condition results in a significantly longer response latency than the subject-not-visible condition." Likewise, if you were asked, "What is the effect of type of news on response latency?", your answer would take the form, "It depends on the subject visibility condition. For the subject-not-visible condition there is a nonsignificant difference in the latency of delivery of good and bad news. For the subject-visible condition, however, there is a significantly longer latency for the bad news condition compared to the good news condition."

The lines connecting data points in Figure 11.1 are nonparallel, a distinguishing characteristic of a figure of a statistically significant interaction. Because an interaction indicates that the simple effects of an independent variable are not equal to its main effect, the plot of a statistically significant interaction must show nonparallel lines. But the lines need not cross as they do in Figure 11.1; they will only do so when the simple effects for an independent variable have opposite signs, as in this example.

In practice, it is rare for any two lines in a figure to be exactly parallel. Because of sampling error, the lines will not be precisely parallel, even when there is no statistically significant interaction. Thus, visual inspection alone is not adequate to determine whether an interaction has occurred. An interaction is present in data *only* if a statistically significant F_{obs} is found for the interaction term in an analysis of variance.

Interpreting the Main Effect for Independent Variable A: Subject Visibility

The value of $F_{obs}(1,16) = 6.66$ for the main effect of factor A in Table 11.8 is greater than $F_{crit}(1,16) = 4.49$. This F_{obs} falls into the rejection region and "$H_0: \mu_{A1} = \mu_{A2}$" for subject visibility is rejected, and "H_1: The μ_A's are not equal" is accepted. This decision implies that the main effect for subject visibility (the difference of –12.0 seconds between the main effect means of 86.5 and 98.5 seconds for subject not visible and subject visible, respectively) is statistically significant. This main effect indicates that news is delivered more rapidly in the subject-not-visible condition than it is in the subject-visible condition. But this main effect is artifactual, and the relationship it implies does not hold for both good and bad news. As our examination of the interaction revealed, the subject-visible condition leads to a significantly longer latency only when bad news is delivered. For good news, the latencies under the subject-not-visible and subject-visible conditions do not differ significantly. Thus, although the main effect for subject visibility indicates a longer latency for the subject-visible condition, analysis of the simple effects indicates that this relationship holds only when bad news is delivered; it does not hold for good news. Thus, the main effect for subject visibility does not convey meaningful information about the results of this experiment; it is artifactual.

Interpreting the Main Effect for Independent Variable B: Type of News

The value of F_{obs} for factor B, the type of news, is 4.26. This value of F_{obs} is less than F_{crit} of 4.49 and, hence, "$H_0: \mu_{B1} = \mu_{B2}$" is not rejected and "H_1: The μ_B's are not equal" is not accepted. This decision implies that the main effect for type of news (the difference of –9.6 seconds between 87.7 and 97.3 seconds for good and bad news, respectively) is nonsignificant. From this nonsignificant main effect alone, I would conclude that type of news does not affect the response latency of a participant; the 9.6-second main effect difference between the good and bad news conditions is due to sampling error. But does this conclusion accurately describe the effect of type of news? Again, examination of the simple effects indicates that it does not; type of news does have an effect, but the effect depends on the visibility of the subject. When the participant is not visible to the assistant, there is no significant difference in the response latency between good and bad news (i.e., the difference between 90.8 and 82.2 seconds is due to sampling error); but when the participant is visible to the assistant, the bad news ($\overline{X}_{A2B2} = 112.4$ seconds) is delivered significantly more slowly than the good news ($\overline{X}_{A2B1} = 84.6$ seconds). The statistically significant interaction has made it inappropriate to interpret the nonsignificant main effect for type of news. The personal discomfort hypothesis predicted a statistically significant and meaningful main effect for type of news. It should take longer to deliver bad news than good news, regardless of whether the subject is or is not visible to the assistant. The result of the main effect for type of news in this example is clearly not in agreement with the prediction of the personal discomfort hypothesis.

Patterns of Interaction

The relationship among the cell means in the example experiment is only one of many that may result in a statistically significant interaction. A statistically significant interaction in the analysis of variance indicates only that the simple effect and main effect differences for an independent variable will not be equal. It alone does not provide any further information about the numerous ways in which this result may occur. The exact nature of the interaction can be determined only by carefully analyzing the relationships among the cell means, as I have done for the example experiment.

Measuring the Strength of a Treatment Effect in a Factorial Analysis of Variance

As with the one-factor analysis of variance, the strength of a statistically significant effect in a factorial design may be measured by η^2. Because there are tests for two main effects and the interaction, I obtain three different values of η^2 as follows:

$$\eta^2 = \frac{SS_A}{SS_{\text{Total}}} \qquad \text{for a statistically significant main effect of factor } A.$$

$$\eta^2 = \frac{SS_B}{SS_{\text{Total}}} \qquad \text{for a statistically significant main effect of factor } B.$$

$$\eta^2 = \frac{SS_{A \times B}}{SS_{\text{Total}}} \qquad \text{for a statistically significant interaction of factors } A \text{ and } B.$$

To illustrate the use of η^2 for the example, the interaction provided the only meaningful information in the experiment; thus, η^2 for the interaction based on the SS values from Table 11.8 is

$$\eta^2 = \frac{SS_{A \times B}}{SS_{\text{Total}}} = \frac{1656.200}{4567.000} = .36.$$

This value indicates that 36 percent of the variance in the response latencies is accounted for by the interaction of subject visibility and type of news.

TESTING YOUR KNOWLEDGE 11.4

1. Define: artifactual main effect, main effect, simple effect.
2. Each of the following tables and Figures 11.2 and 11.3 present cell means obtained in an experiment. A summarized analysis of variance is included for each set of means. In the summarized analysis, a statistically significant F_{obs} is indicated by $p < .05$. A nonsignificant F_{obs} is indicated by $p > .05$. When a significant interaction occurs, the Tukey HSD CD for the simple effects is given at the bottom of the analysis of variance summary. Assume that factor A is a teaching method with two levels, computer-assisted (A_1) and noncomputer-assisted teaching (A_2). Factor B is type of material to be learned, mathematical (B_1) or social studies (B_2). The dependent variable is test score. Interpret each set of means by finding the simple and main effects for each independent variable and relating these effects to the summarized analysis of variance. Then answer these questions for each example:
   a. Do the main effect means of factor A differ significantly from each other?
   b. Do the main effect means of factor B differ significantly from each other?
   c. Is there a statistically significant interaction of factors A and B?
   d. What is the effect of teaching method (factor A) on test scores?
   e. What is the effect of type of material (factor B) on test scores?
   f. Do the main effects provide useful information about the results of the experiment?

TABLE 1

		Factor A A_1	Factor A A_2	ANOVA Summary	
Factor B	B_1	91	85	Factor A	$p < .05$
				Factor B	$p > .05$
	B_2	92	87	$A \times B$	$p > .05$

TABLE 2

		Factor A A_1	Factor A A_2	ANOVA Summary	
Factor B	B_1	89	90	Factor A	$p > .05$
				Factor B	$p < .05$
	B_2	81	80	$A \times B$	$p > .05$

TABLE 3

		Factor A A_1	Factor A A_2	ANOVA Summary	
Factor B	B_1	85	94	Factor A	$p < .05$
				Factor B	$p < .05$
	B_2	78	86	$A \times B$	$p > .05$

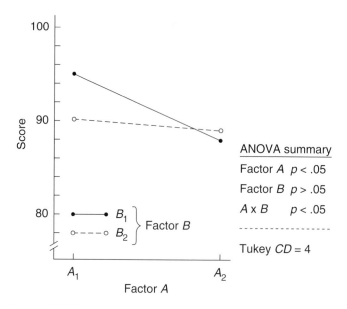

FIGURE 11.2
Outcome of an experiment involving manipulation of factors A and B.

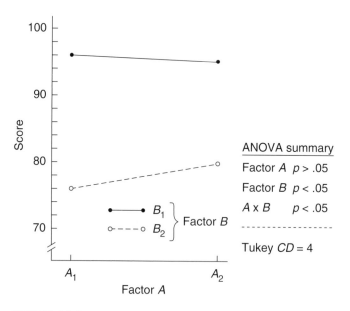

FIGURE 11.3
Outcome of an experiment involving manipulation of factors A and B.

TABLE 4

		Factor A		ANOVA Summary	
		A_1	A_2		
Factor B	B_1	88	75	Factor A	$p > .05$
				Factor B	$p > .05$
	B_2	76	90	$A \times B$	$p < .05$
				Tukey $CD = 4$	

TABLE 5

		Factor A		ANOVA Summary	
		A_1	A_2		
Factor B	B_1	87	88	Factor A	$p < .05$
				Factor B	$p < .05$
	B_2	74	80	$A \times B$	$p < .05$
				Tukey $CD = 4$	

TABLE 6

		Factor A		ANOVA Summary	
		A_1	A_2		
Factor B	B_1	90	80	Factor A	$p < .05$
				Factor B	$p < .05$
	B_2	81	82	$A \times B$	$p < .05$
				Tukey $CD = 4$	

Example Problem 11.1

Analyzing a 2 × 2 Design with a Statistically Significant Interaction and Nonsignificant Main Effects

Problem: Vision and hearing are two independent senses, yet, there may be a common dimension of experience across them. Visual stimuli are sometimes described as loud and sounds as bright. Thus, Lindner and Hynan (1987) hypothesized that the type of music a person listened to would affect the perception of an abstract painting. To test this hypothesis, they varied the type of music a person listened to, either unstructured avant-garde or structured minimalistic music (factor A), and the gender of the participant, male or female (factor B), in a 2 × 2 between-subjects design. While listening to the music, each person viewed eight abstract paintings. After viewing the paintings, the participant rated the paintings on several 7-point rating scales. One rating scale was composed of the adjective pairs *constrained* (1) to *free* (7), *rigid* (1) to *flexible* (2), and *constricted* (1) to *expanded* (7).

Suppose that scores were obtained by summing over the three sets of adjective pairs so that a rating could range from 3 to 21. Assume that the following hypothetical scores were obtained from 24 participants.

	Type of Music (A)	
	Avant-Garde (A_1)	Minimalistic (A_2)
Male (B_1)	4	16
	5	14
	7	17
	6	19
	10	16
	4	20
Gender of Subject (B)		
Female (B_2)	12	5
	15	9
	18	7
	13	6
	16	10
	16	5

Is there an effect of type of music on the ratings of pictures, do males and females differ in the ratings given, and is there an interaction of type of music with gender of the participants? Use a .05 significance level.

Solution: The design used is a 2×2 between-subjects design. The first step is to perform a two-factor between-subjects analysis of variance on the scores to determine if either statistically significant main effects or a statistically significant interaction exists.

Assumptions for Use
1. The participants were sampled randomly and independently from a population.
2. The error in ratings is normally distributed in the population.
3. The variances for the rating scores are equal in the populations sampled.

Statistical Hypotheses

Factor A H_0: $\mu_{A1} = \mu_{A2}$.
                H_1: The μ_A's are not equal.

Factor B H_0: $\mu_{B1} = \mu_{B2}$.
                H_1: The μ_B's are not equal.

$A \times B$ H_0: All $(\mu_{AB} - \mu_A - \mu_B + \mu_G) = 0$.
                H_1: Not all $(\mu_{AB} - \mu_A - \mu_B + \mu_G) = 0$.

Significance Level: $\alpha = .05$.

df:

$$df_A = a - 1 = 2 - 1 = 1$$
$$df_B = b - 1 = 2 - 1 = 1$$
$$df_{A \times B} = (a - 1)(b - 1) = (2 - 1)(2 - 1) = 1$$
$$df_{Error} = ab(n_{AB} - 1) = (2)(2)(6 - 1) = 20$$
$$df_{Total} = N - 1 = 24 - 1 = 23$$

Critical Value of F: Each F_{obs} has 1 df for the numerator and 20 df for the denominator; thus, $F_{crit}(1,20) = 4.35$ from Table A.3a.

Rejection Region: Values of F_{obs} equal to or greater than 4.35.

Calculation: The analysis of variance may be calculated on the scores using the computational formulas given in the chapter supplement or by using a computer program. I used the formulas from the chapter supplement to obtain the following summary table.

Source	df	SS	MS	F
Music (A)	1	13.50	13.50	2.81
Gender (B)	1	1.50	1.50	0.31
A × B	1	541.50	541.50	112.81*
Error	20	96.00	4.80	
Total	23	652.50		

*$p < .01$.

Decisions: Three decisions must be made for the statistical hypotheses of this analysis, one for each F_{obs}.

- Type of music (factor A): $F_{obs} = 2.81$. This F_{obs} does not fall into the rejection region; I fail to reject H_0 and do not accept H_1.
- Gender (factor B): $F_{obs} = 0.31$. This F_{obs} does not fall into the rejection region; I fail to reject H_0 and do not accept H_1.
- Type of music by gender (A × B): $F_{obs} = 112.81$. This F_{obs} falls into the rejection region; I reject H_0 and accept H_1.

Strength of Effect: η^2 for the statistically significant interaction equals $SS_{A \times B}/SS_{Total} = 541.50/652.50 = .83$.

Interpretation and Conclusions: To interpret the statistically significant interaction, I find the Tukey HSD CD for the simple effects and then compare the simple effects to this CD. The numerical values needed for this test are found as follows:

- q is obtained from Table A.4. Using the conversion chart for a 2 × 2 design given with this table, the value of q is obtained for $a = 3$ and 20 df for MS_{Error}. This value is 3.58 for $\alpha = .05$.
- MS_{Error}, obtained from the analysis of variance, is 4.80.
- n_{AB}, the number of scores in each cell, is 6.

Substituting these numerical values into the formula,

$$CD = q\sqrt{\frac{MS_{Error}}{n_{AB}}} = 3.58\sqrt{\frac{4.80}{6}} = 3.2 \quad \text{rating points.}$$

Any simple effect equal to or larger than 3.2 rating points in absolute value is statistically significant at the .05 level.

Table 11.13 presents the cell and main effect means and the simple and main effects for the scores. Each simple effect in this table is larger in absolute value than the $CD = 3.2$ and, thus, is statistically significant. Notice, however, that for each independent variable the simple effects are opposite in sign. The effect of type of music clearly depends on the gender of the participant. Males hearing avant-garde music typically rate the paintings as 6.0 (constrained, rigid, and constricted), but males hearing minimalistic music rate the paintings significantly higher at 17.0 (free, flexible, and expanded). This rating pattern is reversed for females. When listening to avant-garde music, females rate the paintings as 15.0, whereas when listening to minimalistic music they give a significantly lower rating of 7.0. The simple effects for type of music (−11.0 for males, +8.0 for females) are not equal to each other, nor are they equal to the nonsignificant main effect of −1.5 for music.

TABLE 11.13

Main effect and simple effect differences in ratings of paintings as function of type of music and gender of subject.

	Type of Music (A)		
	Avant-Garde (A₁)	Minimalistic (A₂)	Main Effect Means for Gender (B)
Male (B₁)	6.0 ← −11.0 → 17.0		11.5
Gender of Subject (B)	−9.0 ↓	+10.0 ↓	+0.5 ↓
Female (B₂)	15.0 ← +8.0 → 7.0		11.0
Main Effect Means for Type of Music (A)	10.5 ← −1.5 → 12.0		

Similarly, the difference between males and females in rating the paintings depends on the type of music. Females listening to avant-garde music ($\overline{X}_{A1B2} = 15.0$) rate the paintings as significantly more free, flexible, and expanded than do males ($\overline{X}_{A1B1} = 6.0$) listening to avant-garde music. But males listening to the minimalistic music ($\overline{X}_{A2B1} = 17.0$) rate the paintings as significantly higher in this dimension than do females ($\overline{X}_{A2B2} = 7.0$). Thus, the simple effects for gender (–9.0 for avant-garde music, +10.0 for minimalistic music) are not equal to each other or to the nonsignificant main effect of +0.5 for gender of the participants.

The main effects do not provide useful information about the results of this experiment. From the main effects alone, I would conclude that there is no effect for type of music and that males and females do not differ on their ratings. The analysis of the interaction, however, indicates that type of music does have an effect on the ratings given, but the direction of the effect depends on gender. Furthermore, males and females differ in their ratings, but the difference depends on the type of music. The η^2 indicates that 83 percent of the variance in the ratings is determined by the interaction. Predicting scores from the cell means rather than the grand mean reduces the total variance by 83 percent in this sample.

Example Problem 11.2

Analyzing a 2 × 2 Design with a Statistically Significant Interaction and Main Effects

Problem: The keyword method is a memory-enhancement technique in which a person uses a visual image to form an association between two items. One use of this method is in helping to learn the vocabulary of a second language. Suppose that you are asked to learn a list of unfamiliar French words and their English equivalents, such as the French word *boue* and its English equivalent *mud*. Here the keyword might be *boot*, an English word that sounds like the French *boue*. To use the technique, when you hear *boue*, you think of *boot* and then form an image of a person wearing boots and walking through *mud*. A number of studies have shown that the keyword technique enhances learning and immediate recall of a second language vocabulary (Wang, Thomas, & Ouellette, 1992). How long this improved recall lasts, however, is open to question. Wang et al. (1992) found that, although the keyword technique enhanced immediate retention in comparison to rote learning by simple repetition of the words, the keyword subjects also forgot at a greater rate over a one-week retention interval.

Suppose that you are interested in finding if this relationship holds for adult learners as well as for the college students tested by Wang et al. Accordingly, you use a 2 × 2 between-subjects design with learning method, either rote or keyword as factor *A*, and retention interval, either immediate or delayed for one week, as factor *B*. You randomly assigned eight adult learners unfamiliar with French to each treatment condition. People in the rote learning method were told to simply repeat the French words and their English equivalents over and over in order to remember them. In the keyword method, participants were taught the keyword method and given a keyword for each French–English pair. For the immediate-retention condition, recall of the English equivalents was tested 5 minutes after the list was learned. For the delayed-retention groups, participants were tested for recall of the English equivalents one week after they had learned the list. The list of words was 25 items long, so a person's recall score could vary from 0 (no recall) to 25 (perfect recall). Assume that the accompanying hypothetical recall scores were given by the 32 participants. Analyze and describe the results of this experiment.

| | Learning Condition (A) | |
	Rote (A_1)	Keyword (A_2)
Immediate (B_1)	12	25
	9	22
	11	19
	19	23
	16	17
	14	24
	13	20
	15	21
Retention Interval (B)		
Delayed (B_2)	6	9
	7	4
	3	7
	11	11
	5	5
	10	8
	5	12
	8	6

Solution: A two-factor between-subjects analysis of variance is needed to statistically analyze this experiment.

Assumptions for Use

1. The participants were sampled randomly and independently from a population.
2. Recall scores are normally distributed in the population.
3. The variances for the recall scores are equal in the populations sampled.

Statistical Hypotheses

Factor A H_0: $\mu_{A1} = \mu_{A2}$.
            H_1: The μ_A's are not equal.

Factor B H_0: $\mu_{B1} = \mu_{B2}$.
            H_1: The μ_B's are not equal.

$A \times B$ H_0: All $(\mu_{AB} - \mu_A - \mu_B + \mu_G) = 0$.
                H_1: Not all $(\mu_{AB} - \mu_A - \mu_B + \mu_G) = 0$.

Significance Level: $\alpha = .05$.

df:

$$df_A = a - 1 = 2 - 1 = 1$$
$$df_B = b - 1 = 2 - 1 = 1$$
$$df_{A \times B} = (a - 1)(b - 1) = (2 - 1)(2 - 1) = 1$$
$$df_{Error} = ab(n_{AB} - 1) = (2)(2)(8 - 1) = 28$$
$$df_{Total} = N - 1 = 32 - 1 = 31$$

Critical Value of *F*: $F_{crit}(1,28) = 4.20$ for each value of F_{obs}.

Rejection Region: Values of F_{obs} equal to or greater than 4.20.

Calculation: The formulas from the chapter supplement were used to obtain the following summary table.

Source	SS	df	MS	F
Learning condition (A)	148.781	1	148.781	18.59*
Retention interval (B)	830.281	1	830.281	103.73*
A × B	94.531	1	94.531	11.81*
Error	224.125	28	8.004	
Total	1297.718	31		

*$p < .01$.

Decisions

- Learning condition (factor A): $F_{obs} = 18.59$. This F_{obs} falls into the rejection region; I reject H_0 and accept H_1.
- Retention interval (factor B): $F_{obs} = 103.73$. This F_{obs} falls into the rejection region; I reject H_0 and accept H_1.
- Learning condition by retention interval (A × B): $F_{obs} = 11.81$. This F_{obs} falls into the rejection region; I reject H_0 and accept H_1.

Strength of Effect

Learning condition: $\eta^2 = SS_A/SS_{Total} = 148.781/1297.718 = .11$.

Retention interval: $\eta^2 = SS_B/SS_{Total} = 830.281/1297.718 = .64$.

Learning condition × retention interval: $\eta^2 = SS_{A \times B}/SS_{Total} = 94.531/1297.718 = .07$.

Interpretation and Conclusions: I first interpret the interaction by finding the Tukey HSD *CD* for the simple effects and then comparing the simple effects to this *CD*. The numerical values needed for this test are found as follows:

- *q* is obtained from Table A.4 for $a = 3$ and 28 *df* for MS_{Error}. Because 28 *df* are not tabled for MS_{Error}, *q* for the next lower tabled *df*, 24 was used. This value is 3.53 for $\alpha = .05$.
- MS_{Error} is 8.004.
- n_{AB} is 8.

Substituting these numerical values into the formula,

$$CD = q \sqrt{\frac{MS_{\text{Error}}}{n_{AB}}} = 3.53 \sqrt{\frac{8.004}{8}}$$

$$= 3.5 \text{ words}, \quad \text{rounded to one decimal place.}$$

Any simple effect equal to or larger than 3.5 words in absolute value is statistically significant at the .05 level. Table 11.14 presents the cell and main effect means and the simple and main effects for the scores. I first interpret the interaction for each independent variable and then the main effect of that variable.

Learning Condition: The simple effect of learning condition for immediate recall, −7.8, is greater in absolute value than the CD of 3.5 and is statistically significant. The keyword condition ($\overline{X}_{A2B1} = 21.4$ words) results in significantly greater recall than does rote learning for immediate retention ($\overline{X}_{A1B1} = 13.6$ words). For delayed retention, however, the simple effect of learning condition, −0.9, is smaller in absolute value than the CD

TABLE 11.14
Main effect and simple effect differences in number of words correctly recalled as a function of learning condition and retention interval.

	Learning Condition (A)		
	Rote (A₁)	Keyword (A₂)	Main Effect Means for Retention Interval (B)
Immediate (B₁)	13.6 ← −7.8 → 21.4		17.5
Retention Interval (B)	+6.7	+13.6	+10.2
Delayed (B₂)	6.9 ← −0.9 → 7.8		7.3
Main Effect Means for Learning Condition (A)	10.2 ← −4.4 → 14.6		

of 3.5. This simple effect is nonsignificant. Thus, for delayed retention, rote ($\overline{X}_{A1B2} = 6.9$ words) and keyword ($\overline{X}_{A2B2} = 7.8$ words) conditions do not differ significantly. Learning condition has no effect on recall for delayed retention. The $F_{obs}(1, 28) = 18.59$ for the main effect of learning condition is statistically significant, indicating that the main effect means for learning condition ($\overline{X}_{A1} = 10.2$ and $\overline{X}_{A2} = 14.6$) differ significantly. But this significant main effect does not provide meaningful information about the outcome of the experiment. This main effect indicates that people recall more words with the keyword condition, but the analysis of the simple effects for learning condition revealed that this relationship holds only for the immediate-recall interval; it does not hold for the delayed-retention interval. Hence, the main effect of learning condition does not provide a correct description of the effect of learning condition. I, thus, ignore it in the description of the results of the experiment.

Retention Interval: The significant interaction indicates also that the effect of retention interval depends on learning condition. For both levels of learning condition, the simple effects of retention interval ($+6.7$ for rote learning, $+13.6$ for keyword learning) are larger in absolute value than the *CD* of 3.5. These statistically significant simple effects indicate that, for both rote and keyword learning, delayed recall results in significantly less recall than does immediate recall. Examination of the simple effects, however, reveals that the decrease in retention from immediate to delayed recall is greater for the keyword condition (13.6 words) than it is for the rote condition (6.7 words). The statistically significant main effect of retention interval [i.e., $F_{obs}(1, 28) = 103.73, p < .01$] indicates that the main effect means for retention interval ($\overline{X}_{B1} = 17.5$ and $\overline{X}_{B2} = 7.3$) differ significantly. From this significant main effect alone, I conclude that immediate recall leads to greater retention than does delayed retention. This conclusion is correct, for the relationship holds for both rote and keyword conditions. Hence, the main effect for retention interval is meaningful and provides useful information about the results of the experiment. The interpretation of this main effect must be qualified, however, by recognizing that the interaction indicates that the extent of the difference between immediate and delayed recall depends on learning condition.

The η^2 for the main effect of retention interval, .64, indicates that the retention interval accounts for a large proportion of the variance in recall scores. The η^2 for the interaction, .07, indicates that the interaction accounts for a smaller portion of the variance in the recall scores. Because the main effect of learning condition is artifactual, I do not utilize the eta squared for this factor.

REPORTING THE RESULTS OF A FACTORIAL ANALYSIS OF VARIANCE

The style of reporting the results of a factorial experiment follows that used for the one-factor design in Chapter 10. I illustrate using the results of the example problem on the effects of subject visibility (subject visible or subject not visible) and type of news (good or bad) on the latency to deliver the news. Cell means for this experiment are presented in Table 11.5 and the analysis of variance summarized in Table 11.8. Because of the expense of printing tables, the results of an experiment, including cell means and the statistical analysis, are often reported in text format as illustrated here.

An alpha level of .05 was used for all statistical tests. There was a significant interaction of subject visibility with the type of news to be delivered, $F(1, 16) = 15.32$, $MSE = 108.125$, $p < .01$. The Tukey HSD test (critical difference = 17.0 s with $\alpha = .05$) was used for testing the statistical significance of the simple effects. When good news was delivered, the effect of subject visibility was nonsignificant ($M = 90.8$ s, $SD = 11.56$ s for subject not visible, and $M = 84.6$ s, $SD = 9.61$ s for subject visible). For the delivery of bad news, however, the latency of the subject-visible condition ($M = 112.4$ s, $SD = 11.15$ s) was significantly longer than for the subject-not-visible condition ($M = 82.2$ s, $SD = 9.07$ s). The difference in latency between the good and bad news for the subject-not-visible condition was nonsignificant. For the subject-visible condition, however, the latency of the delivery of bad news was significantly longer than the latency for the delivery of good news. Eta squared for the interaction was .36. The main effect of subject visibility was statistically significant, $F(1, 16) = 6.66$, $p < .05$, but was not meaningful. The main effect for type of news was nonsignificant, $F(1, 16) = 4.26$, $p > .05$.

In this presentation:

$\alpha = .05$ Indicates the significance level selected for the statistical tests.

$F(1, 16)$ Identifies the test statistic as the F. The *df* for the numerator and denominator of each F_{obs} reported are shown in parentheses. Three values of F_{obs} are reported, one for each independent variable and one for the interaction of the independent variables. The order in which F_{obs} is reported is not necessarily factor A, factor B, and $A \times B$. Often an experimenter has more interest in the interaction and will present this F_{obs} value first in the description of the results, as illustrated in the example.

$= 15.32$ Gives the value of F_{obs} (not the F_{crit} value found in Table A.3). In some instances, only two of the three F_{obs} obtained in the analysis of variance may be reported. In this case you may assume that the unreported value of F_{obs} was nonsignificant.

$p < .01$ Indicates that
      a. The probability of F_{obs} if H_0 is true is less than or equal to .01. This value is the probability of F_{obs} or an even more extreme value of F_{obs} if H_0 is true; it may not be the same as the value of α selected.
      b. H_0 was rejected and H_1 was accepted.
      c. The F_{obs} was for the interaction term of the analysis of variance; thus, it indicates that the interaction of factors A and B is statistically significant.
      d. Something other than sampling error is responsible for the interaction of factors A and B.

$MSE = 108.125$ Gives the MS_{Error} for the F_{obs}. This value is a measure of the within-cells error variation in the scores.

$CD = 17.0$ Gives the critical difference for simple effect comparisons using the Tukey HSD test. The statistically significant simple effects are then described.

$\eta^2 = .36$ Indicates that 36 percent of the variance in the response latencies in this experiment is accounted for by the interaction of factors A and B. In this example, the interaction provides the only meaningful information about the outcome of the experiment; thus, η^2 is given only for this source of variance.

TESTING YOUR KNOWLEDGE 11.5

Complete these problems using a two-factor between-subjects analysis of variance following the format illustrated in the example problems. Use a .05 significance level for each problem.

1. A psychologist hypothesized that the effect of type of instructions on a person's performance on an anagram solution task would depend on that individual's perceived locus of control. To evaluate this hypothesis, she obtained 12 females who scored low on a locus of control scale (indicating an internal locus of control) and 12 females who scored high on the scale (indicating an external locus of control). Half the females in each group were randomly assigned to one of two instructional conditions, skill or chance instructions. In the skill-instructions condition, participants were told that their performance on an anagram solution task depended on their verbal ability and was under their control. The chance instructions indicated that performance on this task does not depend on verbal ability and is beyond a person's control. The participants then solved a series of anagrams, and the amount of time devoted to the task was recorded. Suppose that the following amounts of time (in seconds) that each person worked on solving the anagrams were obtained:

	Locus of Control (A)	
	Internal (A_1)	External (A_2)
Skill (B_1)	175	115
	202	106
	193	87
	186	93
	150	99
	212	157
Instructions (B)		
Chance (B_1)	125	218
	100	202
	77	196
	101	244
	131	237
	152	180

a. Calculate the cell and main effect means. Then analyze the scores to determine (1) if there is a main effect for either independent variable and (2) if there is an interaction of the independent variables.

b. Describe the effect of type of instructions. If needed, use the Tukey HSD test to determine the statistically significant simple effects.

c. Are you able to meaningfully interpret any statistically significant main effects or are they artifactual?

d. What proportion of the variance in the dependent variable can be accounted for by the interaction of the independent variables?

2. In many jurisdictions, potential jurors are shown a film to acquaint them with the legal process and the nature of the jury system. Suppose that a lawyer was interested in finding out whether the film alters a juror's behavior in comparison to standard oral instructions. Furthermore, the lawyer wanted to know if any effect of the film may depend on the type of crime the juror is to evaluate. To answer these questions, the lawyer conducted a 2×2 between-subjects factorial experiment with nine people in each treatment condition serving as mock jurors. Factor A was the type of instruction given to jurors: A_1, normal oral instructions by a court officer, and A_2, filmed instructions. Factor B was the type of crime that the juror was asked to evaluate; this variable was manipulated by having the participants read a description of an auto theft case (level B_1) or of an aggravated assault case (level B_2). Each participant was then asked to assign a prison term to the defendant described in the case. The prison terms assigned (in months) are given in the accompanying table.

| | Type of Instruction (A) | |
	Normal (A_1)	Filmed (A_2)
Auto Theft (B_1)	15	13
	10	16
	10	9
	14	11
	17	14
	9	8
	8	10
	12	10
	10	12
Type of Crime (B)		
Aggravated Assault (B_2)	25	30
	20	33
	23	26
	20	25
	19	30
	17	35
	18	30
	22	28
	20	32

a. Calculate the cell and main effect means. Then analyze the scores to determine (1) if there is a main effect for either independent variable and (2) if there is an interaction of the independent variables.

b. Describe the effect of type of instructions.

c. Describe the effect of type of crime.

d. Are you able to meaningfully interpret any statistically significant main effects or are they artifactual?

    e.   What proportion of the variance in the dependent variable can be accounted for by the type of crime and the interaction of the independent variables?

3. The following exercises present sample reports of two-factor between-subjects analyses of variance. Answer the following questions for each report.

    a.   How many levels of factor A were varied in this experiment?

    b.   How many levels of factor B were varied in this experiment?

    c.   How many subjects were used in the experiment?

    d.   What is the value of F_{crit} at the .05 significance level for each F_{obs} reported?

    e.   Is the value of F_{obs} for factor A statistically significant?

    f.   Is the value of F_{obs} for factor B statistically significant?

    g.   Is the value of F_{obs} for $A \times B$ statistically significant?

3.1. An alpha level of .05 was used for all statistical tests. The main effect of drug level (factor A) was statistically significant, $F(2, 36) = 9.43, p < .01, MSE = 17.814$. There was also a main effect for retention interval (factor B), $F(1, 36) = 5.60, p < .05$. The interaction was nonsignificant, $F(2, 36) = 2.46, p > .05$.

3.2. An alpha level of .05 was used for all statistical tests. There was a significant gender of athlete (factor A) by type of sport (factor B) interaction on self-esteem ratings, $F(3, 88) = 3.28, p < .05, MSE = 42.163$. In addition, males gave higher-rated self-esteem than females, $F(1, 88) = 4.82, p < .05$. There were no main effect differences among sport types, $F(3, 88) = 1.65, p > .05$.

3.3. An alpha level of .05 was used for all statistical tests. There was a significant interaction of noise condition with personality type $F(1, 56) = 5.33, p < .05, MSE = 26.718$. Neither the main effect for noise condition, $F(1, 56) < 1.0$, nor personality type $F(1, 56) = 1.43$, $p > .05$, was significant.

SUMMARY

- Factorial designs are research designs in which two or more independent variables are varied simultaneously.
- Each cell or treatment condition of a factorial design represents a combination formed from one level of each independent variable.
- Main effect means indicate the typical performance of all individuals given one level of an independent variable, while ignoring the classification by the other independent variable.
- An interaction occurs in a factorial design when the effect of one independent variable depends on the level of the other independent variable with which it is combined.
- Three F statistics are obtained in the two-factor between-subjects analysis of variance.

Source of Variation	F
Factor A	MS_A/MS_{Error}
Factor B	MS_B/MS_{Error}
Interaction of $A \times B$	$MS_{A \times B}/MS_{Error}$

- The steps in statistical testing with these F ratios are identical to those discussed in Chapter 10.
- The simple effect of an independent variable in a factorial design is the effect of that independent variable at only one level of the other independent variable.
- If a statistically significant interaction of the independent variables occurs, then the two simple effects for a factor are not equal to each other or to the main effect for that factor.
- An artifactual main effect is a main effect that cannot be meaningfully interpreted; it occurs only because of the specific pattern of interaction obtained.
- Follow-up tests are needed to statistically analyze the simple effects if a significant interaction is obtained. The Tukey HSD test is used for post hoc comparisons.
- η^2 is used as a measure of the strength of a treatment effect for statistically significant main effects and interaction.

KEY TERMS AND SYMBOLS

a (289)
artifactual main effect (300)
b cell (273)
cell mean ($\overline{X}_{AB}$) (276)
critical difference (CD) (299)
df_A (287)
df_B (287)
$df_{A \times B}$ (287)
df_{Error} (287)
df_{Total} (287)
factor A (273)
factor B (273)

factorial design (273)
grand mean ($\overline{X}_G$) (278)
interaction ($A \times B$) (278)
main effect for factor A (276)
main effect for factor B (277)
main effect mean (276)
MS_A (280)
MS_B (280)
$MS_{A \times B}$ (280)
MS_{Error} (280)
n_{AB} (311)

simple effect of an independent
    variable (296)
SS_A (283)
SS_B (283)
$SS_{A \times B}$ (283)
SS_{Error} (283)
SS_{Total} (283)
treatment condition (273)
Tukey HSD test (299)
$\overline{X}_A$ (297)
$\overline{X}_B$ (297)

CHAPTER SUPPLEMENT:
CALCULATING A TWO-FACTOR BETWEEN-SUBJECTS
ANALYSIS OF VARIANCE WITH COMPUTATIONAL FORMULAS

This supplement provides the computational formulas for a two-factor between-subjects analysis of variance with an equal number of participants in each cell. The notational representation with two levels of each factor and five scores per cell is as follows:

Factor A

		A_1		A_2		
	B_1	X_{111} X_{211} X_{311} X_{411} X_{511}	T_{A1B1}	X_{121} X_{221} X_{321} X_{421} X_{521}	T_{A2B1}	T_{B1}
Factor B	B_2	X_{112} X_{212} X_{312} X_{412} X_{512}	T_{A1B2}	X_{122} X_{222} X_{322} X_{422} X_{522}	T_{A2B2}	T_{B2}
		T_{A1}		T_{A2}		G

where X_{ijk} = score of a participant.
T_A = total of scores for a level of factor A.
T_B = total of scores for a level of factor B.
T_{AB} = total of scores in a cell.
G = grand total of scores.
n_{AB} = number of scores in a cell.
a = number of levels of factor A.
b = number of levels of factor B.
N = total number of scores.

Five numerical values are found using these terms:

$[1] = \sum \sum \sum X_{ijk}^2$ the sum of all the scores squared
(the $\sum \sum \sum$ indicates that the squared scores are summed over all scores in a cell, then over all levels of factors A and B),

$[2] = \dfrac{\sum \sum T_{AB}^2}{n_{AB}}$ the sum of each cell total squared divided by the number of scores in a cell,

$[3] = \dfrac{\sum T_A^2}{bn_{AB}}$ the sum of each level total for factor A squared divided by the number of scores entering into each total,

$[4] = \dfrac{\sum T_B^2}{an_{AB}}$ the sum of each level total for factor B squared divided by the number of scores entering into each total,

$[5] = \dfrac{G^2}{N}$ the grand total squared divided by the total number of scores.

Using these numerical values, an analysis of variance is obtained as follows:

Source of Variance	SS	df	MS	F
Factor A	[3] − [5]	$a - 1$	$\dfrac{SS_A}{df_A}$	$\dfrac{MS_A}{MS_{\text{Error}}}$
Factor B	[4] − [5]	$b - 1$	$\dfrac{SS_B}{df_B}$	$\dfrac{MS_B}{MS_{\text{Error}}}$
$A \times B$	[2] − [3] − [4] + [5]	$(a - 1)(b - 1)$	$\dfrac{SS_{A \times B}}{df_{A \times B}}$	$\dfrac{MS_{A \times B}}{MS_{\text{Error}}}$
Error	[1] − [2]	$ab(n_{AB} - 1)$	$\dfrac{SS_{\text{Error}}}{df_{\text{Error}}}$	
Total	[1] − [5]	$N - 1$	Not calculated	

To illustrate the computations, I use the example scores given in Table 11.2 for which an analysis of variance is summarized in Table 11.8.

	Factor A			
	A_1		A_2	
B_1	97 90 80 $T_{A1B1} = 454$ 107 80		70 87 81 $T_{A2B1} = 423$ 95 90	$T_{B1} = 877$
Factor B				
B_2	68 87 92 $T_{A1B2} = 411$ 80 84		114 96 127 $T_{A2B2} = 562$ 110 115	$T_{B2} = 973$
	$T_{A1} = 865$		$T_{A2} = 985$	$G = 1850$

and $n_{AB} = 5$, $a = 2$, $b = 2$, and $N = 20$.

The values of the numerical computational terms are

$$[1] = 97^2 + \cdots + 80^2 + 70^2 + \cdots + 90^2 + 68^2 + \cdots + 84^2 + 114^2 + \cdots + 115^2$$
$$= 175,692.000$$

$$[2] = \frac{(454)^2 + (423)^2 + (411)^2 + (562)^2}{5} = \frac{869,810.00}{5} = 173,962.000$$

$$[3] = \frac{(865)^2 + (985)^2}{(2)(5)} = \frac{1,718,450.00}{10} = 171,845.000$$

$$[4] = \frac{(877)^2 + (973)^2}{(2)(5)} = \frac{1,715,858.00}{10} = 171,585.800$$

$$[5] = \frac{1850^2}{20} = \frac{3,422,500.00}{20} = 171,125.000$$

Then

$$SS_A = [3] - [5] = 171,845.000 - 171,125.000 = 720.000,$$
$$df_A = a - 1 = 2 - 1 = 1,$$
$$MS_A = \frac{720.000}{1} = 720.00.$$

$$SS_B = [4] - [5] = 171,585.800 - 171,125.000 = 460.800,$$
$$df_B = b - 1 = 2 - 1 = 1,$$
$$MS_B = \frac{460.800}{1} = 460.800.$$

$$SS_{A \times B} = [2] - [3] - [4] + [5]$$
$$= 173,962.000 - 171,845.000 - 171,585.800 + 171,125.000 = 1656.200,$$
$$df_{A \times B} = (a - 1)(b - 1) = (2 - 1)(2 - 1) = 1,$$
$$MS_{A \times B} = \frac{1656.200}{1} = 1656.200.$$

$$SS_{Error} = [1] - [2] = 175,692.000 - 173,962.000 = 1730.000,$$
$$df_{Error} = ab(n_{AB} - 1) = (2)(2)(5 - 1) = 16,$$
$$MS_{Error} = \frac{1730.000}{16} = 108.125.$$

$$SS_{Total} = [1] - [5] = 175,692.000 - 171,125.000 = 4567.000,$$
$$df_{Total} = N - 1 = 20 - 1 = 19.$$

Values of F_{obs} are, thus,

Factor A: $F_{\text{obs}} = \dfrac{MS_A}{MS_{\text{Error}}} = \dfrac{720.000}{108.125} = 6.66,$

Factor B: $F_{\text{obs}} = \dfrac{MS_B}{MS_{\text{Error}}} = \dfrac{460.800}{108.125} = 4.26,$

Interaction of factors A and B: $F_{\text{obs}} = MS_{A \times B}/MS_{\text{Error}}$

$$F_{\text{obs}} = \frac{1656.200}{108.125} = 15.32.$$

The summary of the analysis of variance is

Source	SS	df	MS	F
Subject visibility (A)	720.000	1	720.000	6.66*
Type of news (B)	460.800	1	460.800	4.26
A × B	1656.200	1	1656.200	15.32**
Error	1730.000	16	108.125	
Total	4567.000	19		

*$p < .05$.   **$p < .01$.

The values obtained by this computational approach are identical to those presented in Table 11.8 obtained from the definitional formulas of an analysis of variance.

REVIEW QUESTIONS

Answer questions 1 to 3 by performing a two-factor between-subjects analysis of variance on the scores given.

1. How does level of physiological arousal change when we engage in social exchange with others? To partially answer this question, Wellens (1987) used a 2×2 between-subjects design in which participants were interviewed by an experimenter. One independent variable (factor A) was eye contact of the experimenter with the participant during the interview. Two levels were manipulated: no eye contact (A_1) and eye contact (A_2) made. The second independent variable (factor B) was a manipulation of affect with two levels: positive (B_1) and negative (B_2). In the positive-affect condition, participants were given a written "first impression" of them by the interviewer that was very favorable. For the negative-affect condition, they were given a written first impression of them by the interviewer that was very unfavorable. The dependent variable was the participant's heart rate in beats per minute recorded while the interview was being conducted. Suppose that you replicated this experiment with eight participants per cell and obtained the following heart rates.

	Eye-Contact Condition (A)	
	No Eye Contact (A_1)	Eye Contact (A_2)
Positive (B_1)	75	61
	77	68
	68	71
	72	59
	83	74
	78	66
	70	67
	65	57
Negative (B_2)	79	84
	82	79
	75	88
	77	90
	84	75
	72	75
	78	77
	69	85

Affect Condition (B)

a.   Does the effect of eye contact depend on the level of affect? If so, use the Tukey HSD test for the simple effect comparisons. Describe the relationship that you found.

b.   Does the effect of the affect condition depend on the eye-contact condition? If so, use the Tukey HSD test for the simple effect comparisons. Describe the relationship that you found.

c.   Are you able to meaningfully interpret any main effects or are they artifactual?

d.   What proportion of the variance in the dependent variable can be accounted for by the interaction of the independent variables?

e.   Describe the results of this experiment following the style illustrated in the Reporting the Results of a Factorial Analysis of Variance section of this chapter.

2.   One personality dimension that seems well recognized by most people is that of introversion–extroversion. Extroverts are described as outgoing, sociable, and fun-loving, whereas introverts are described as reserved and less sociable. Because introverts seem more directed toward their own thoughts and ideas, we might suspect that introverts and extroverts may respond differently to external stimulation such as noise. To more fully investigate this issue, Standing, Lynn, and Moxness (1990) used a 2×2 between-subjects design to vary personality type (factor A), introverts (A_1) and extroverts (A_2) and background noise (factor B), quiet (B_1) and noisy (B_2), while participants performed a reading comprehension task. Suppose you conducted a similar study with 12 participants per cell and each person completed a 15-item true–false reading comprehension task. A person's score was the number of items correctly answered. You obtained the following scores:

| | Personality Type (A) | |
	Introvert (A_1)	Extrovert (A_2)
Quiet (B_1)	10	15
	8	14
	12	12
	15	15
	10	11
	9	8
	14	12
	13	8
	14	13
	7	10
	12	9
	11	11
Noisy (B_2)	6	13
	8	8
	11	9
	4	14
	5	13
	8	12
	9	15
	10	11
	9	9
	10	11
	7	12
	11	10

Background Noise (B) (row label at left between the two blocks)

a. What is the relationship between personality type and the effect of background noise? If an interaction occurred, use the Tukey HSD test for the simple effects. Describe the relationship that you found.

b. What is η^2 for the interaction?

c. Are you able to meaningfully interpret any main effects or are they artifactual?

d. Describe the results of this experiment following the style illustrated in the Reporting the Results of a Factorial Analysis of Variance section of this chapter.

3. What is the best approach to teaching phonics to beginning readers? Joseph (2000) tested two new approaches to teaching phonics to first graders, word box instruction and word sort instruction, as well as traditional phonics instruction. Word box instruction provides a child with a rectangle that is divided into sections for each phoneme in a word (a phoneme is the smallest speech sound). In the initial phases of this instruction, as a word is spoken, the child places a token in each section of the rectangle corresponding to the phoneme being sounded.

Word sort instruction involves asking children to sort words into categories based on some common aspect such as spelling or sound. Traditional phonics teaching involves having students give choral readings of words sharing spelling patterns. Suppose you were also interested in the effect of phonics teaching methods but further wanted to know the effects of practice on the methods. Thus, you manipulated three methods of phonics instruction (factor A): traditional (A_1), word box (A_2), and word sort (A_3). You also manipulated amount of practice (factor B) over two levels: one week (B_1) and six weeks (B_2). Nine first-grade children were randomly assigned to each cell. At the end of the practice period, each child was tested on a 30-item spelling test and the following scores were obtained (each score is the number of words correctly spelled):

| | Instructional Method (A) | | |
	Traditional (A_1)	Word Box (A_2)	Word Sort (A_3)
One Week (B_1)	10	16	21
	14	17	24
	16	23	23
	12	19	20
	14	20	23
	13	15	25
	15	19	21
	11	18	26
	13	21	22
Six Weeks (B_2)	15	18	21
	18	24	19
	22	19	20
	18	22	23
	21	21	24
	17	20	24
	18	20	22
	16	22	25
	16	23	20

The left margin also contains the label "Amount of Practice (B)".

a. Does the effect of instructional method depend on the amount of practice? If so, use the Tukey HSD test for the simple effects. Describe the relationship between instructional method and amount of practice that you found.

b. What is η^2 for the interaction?

c. Are you able to meaningfully interpret any main effects or are they artifactual?

d. Describe the results of this experiment following the style illustrated in the Reporting the Results of a Factorial Analysis of Variance section of this chapter.

4. A psychologist used a 2×3 between-subjects design with eight participants in each cell.
   a. What are the values of a, b, n_{AB}, and N for this design?
   b. What are the values of df_A, df_B, $df_{A \times B}$, df_{Error}, and df_{Total} for this design?
5. The following tables are incomplete summary tables for between-subjects factorial analyses of variance. Assume an equal number of scores in each cell. Use the relationships among SS, df, and MS to provide the missing values in each table. Then answer the following questions for each table.
   a. How many levels of factor A were varied?
   b. How many levels of factor B were varied?
   c. How many participants were used in each cell?
   d. What was the total number of participants in the experiment?
   e. Which values of F_{obs} are statistically significant at the .05 level?
   f. What decision do you make for each null and alternative hypothesis for this analysis?

TABLE 1

Source	SS	df	MS	F
Type of task (A)	—	3	5.00	—
Noise level (B)	16.00	—	—	—
A × B	36.00	6	—	—
Error	—	60	2.00	
Total	—	—		

TABLE 2

Source	SS	df	MS	F
Training length (A)	40.00	—	10.00	—
Skill level (B)	—	3	40.00	—
A × B	960.00	—	80.00	—
Error	3200.00	160	—	
Total	—	179		

TABLE 3

Source	SS	df	MS	F
Type of feedback (A)	200.00	—	50.00	—
Task difficulty (B)	—	—	—	—
A × B	—	8	30.00	—
Error	—	—	20.00	
Total	3300.00	149		

6. Suppose that you had people learn a series of sentences and then recall the nouns in the sentences. You manipulated two levels of type of imagery (factor A), ordi-

nary imagery and bizarre imagery, and two levels of the amount of elaboration (factor B), low and high elaboration, of the sentences. Each person had 30 sentences to learn; thus a maximum of 30 nouns could be recalled. The cell means for number of nouns correctly recalled are shown in Table 1. An analysis of variance for these data is presented in Table 2. Assume a between-subjects design with five subjects per cell.

TABLE 1
Mean number of nouns correctly recalled as a function of type of imagery and amount of elaboration.

		Type of Imagery (A)	
		Ordinary (A_1)	Bizarre (A_2)
Amount of elaboration	Low (B_1)	21.4	4.8
	High (B_2)	10.4	18.8

TABLE 2
Analysis of variance summary table for mean number of nouns recalled in Table 1.

Source	SS	df	MS	F
Type of imagery (A)	84.050	1	84.050	4.91*
Amount of elaboration (B)	11.250	1	11.250	0.66
$A \times B$	781.250	1	781.250	45.62**
Error	274.000	16	17.125	
Total	1150.550	19		

*$p < .05$.   **$p < .01$.

A Tukey HSD yielded a $CD = 6.8$ words for the simple effects.
a.   What is the effect of type of imagery on the recall of nouns?
b.   What is the effect of amount of elaboration on the recall of nouns?

7.   A human factors psychologist was interested in the ability of pilots to read aircraft instruments after a period of sleep deprivation. She used two different types of gauges for the pilots to read, analog and digital, as illustrated in Figure 11.4.

The psychologist obtained a sample of pilots, and half were assigned to read the analog gauge and the other half, the digital gauge. For each group, half the pilots were tested after a normal night's sleep and the other half after they had been deprived of sleep for 24 hours. Thus, a 2 × 2 between-subjects design was used with type of gauge, analog or digital, as one independent variable, and amount of sleep deprivation, none or 24 hours, as the second independent variable. The dependent variable was the number of correct readings out of 100 trials. The cell means for the number of correct readings are given in Table 1. An analysis of variance for these data is presented in Table 2.

FIGURE 11.4
Illustration of an analog and a digital gauge.

TABLE 1
Mean number of correct gauge readings as a function of type of gauge and amount of sleep deprivation.

		Type of Gauge (A)	
		Analog (A_1)	Digital (A_2)
Amount of Sleep deprivation (B)	None (B_1)	89.0	91.0
	24 hours (B_2)	72.0	81.0

TABLE 2
Analysis of variance summary for mean correct gauge readings in Table 1.

Source	SS	df	MS	F
Type of gauge (A)	211.750	1	211.750	11.71**
Amount of sleep deprivation (B)	1275.750	1	1275.750	70.56**
A × B	85.750	1	85.750	4.74*
Error	433.920	24	18.080	
Total	2007.170	27		

$*p<.05.$ $**p<.01.$

The *CD* for simple effects using a Tukey HSD test is 5.7 correct readings.
   a. What is the effect of type of gauge on the number of correct readings?
   b. What is the effect of amount of sleep deprivation on the number of correct readings?

One-Factor Within-Subjects Designs and Analysis of Variance

Within-subjects design: A research design in which one group of subjects is exposed to and measured under each level of the independent variable.

Chapter 9 introduced **within-subjects designs** and the t test for related scores. This chapter expands the discussion of within-subjects designs and introduces the analysis of variance for these designs.

In a **one-factor within-subjects design** a single group of subjects is exposed to and measured under each level of the independent variable. Because subjects are measured repeatedly in a within-subjects design, it also is called a *repeated measures design* or a *treatments-by-subjects design*, a reminder that each participant is tested under all levels of the independent variable.

Table 12.1 presents the notation for the scores of a one-factor within-subjects design with four levels of an independent variable and five subjects. The independent variable is identified as factor A with levels A_1, A_2, A_3, and A_4. The number of levels of factor A is represented by a; for Table 12.1, $a = 4$. A score for a subject is represented by X_{ij}, where the subscript i represents a number identifying the subject (e.g., $X_{1j}, X_{2j}, \ldots, X_{5j}$) and the subscript j represents a number identifying the level of the independent variable. Thus, X_{34} represents the score of subject 3 in level 4 of factor A. When it is not necessary to identify a specific subject, I drop the ij subscripts and simply use X. The means for each level of the independent variable are indicated by $\overline{X}_{A1}, \overline{X}_{A2}, \overline{X}_{A3}$, and $\overline{X}_{A4}$, or generally by $\overline{X}_A$. The number of scores in a level of the independent variable is represented by n_A. Notice that n_A is also the number of subjects in a within-subjects design. The total number of scores in the experiment is represented by N. For Table 12.1, $n_A = 5$ and $N = 20$. The mean for a subject over all levels of factor A is represented by $\overline{X}_S$. This mean represents the typical performance of a person over all levels of the independent variable.

AN EXAMPLE ONE-FACTOR WITHIN-SUBJECTS EXPERIMENT

Look at Figure 12.1. Although there are only partially filled circles present, it should appear that there are edges forming a triangle between the dots. These edges are called *subjective*

TABLE 12.1

Notational representation of scores from a one-factor within-subjects design with four levels of the independent variable and five participants.

Subject	Factor A				Means for Subject
	A_1	A_2	A_3	A_4	
S_1	X_{11}	X_{12}	X_{13}	X_{14}	$\overline{X}_{S1}$
S_2	X_{21}	X_{22}	X_{23}	X_{24}	$\overline{X}_{S2}$
S_3	X_{31}	X_{32}	X_{33}	X_{34}	$\overline{X}_{S3}$
S_4	X_{41}	X_{42}	X_{43}	X_{44}	$\overline{X}_{S4}$
S_5	X_{51}	X_{52}	X_{53}	X_{54}	$\overline{X}_{S5}$
Means for Factor A	$\overline{X}_{A1}$	$\overline{X}_{A2}$	$\overline{X}_{A3}$	$\overline{X}_{A4}$	$\overline{X}_G$

contours, for they do not exist in the stimulus itself. Is it possible to use subjective contours to induce an illusion in perception? Suppose that we decide to investigate this question by using several forms of the Ponzo illusion, as did Meyer (1986). Figure 12.2a illustrates the standard Ponzo illusion. This figure is an illusion because the two horizontal lines are physically equal in length, although they do not appear to be equal. The top line should appear longer to you than the bottom line. Figure 12.2b presents a subjective contours version of this illusion. The version in Figure 12.2c provides orientation information, but the solid

FIGURE 12.1
Subjective contours
forming a triangle.

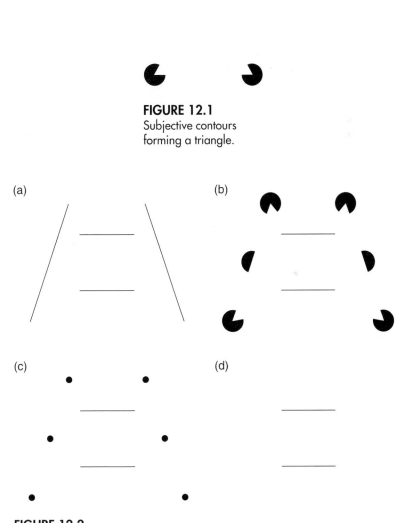

FIGURE 12.2
Four versions of the Ponzo illusion: (a) standard, (b) subjective contours,
(c) solid dots, and (d) control (no illusion).

dots do not introduce a subjective contour. Finally, Figure 12.2d presents a control condition in which no illusion should occur. Suppose that a person is asked to adjust the length of the bottom horizontal line so that it appears equal in length to the top horizontal line, and suppose further that the length of the top line is 14.0 centimeters (cm). If no illusion appears, then the bottom line also should be adjusted to 14.0 cm. If, however, an illusion appears, then the top line should appear to be longer than it really is (i.e., it should appear to be longer than 14.0 cm), and the bottom line should be adjusted to match its perceived length.

Suppose a one-factor within-subjects experiment with four levels of type of illusion (factor A) and five participants is used to test the effect of illusion condition on the perceived magnitude of the illusion. Each person views each of the four stimuli shown in Figure 12.2 and adjusts the bottom horizontal line to look equal in length to the top horizontal line. The adjusted length of the bottom horizontal line, in centimeters, is the dependent variable. Suppose that the scores obtained are those presented in Table 12.2. Is the magnitude of the perceived illusion affected by the illusion condition?

As with between-subjects designs, the analysis of the data in Table 12.2 begins with calculation of descriptive statistics. Thus, treatment means and standard deviations are shown at the bottom of each column in the table. If the independent variable does affect the perception of the illusion, then the treatment means should differ from each other. But, as we know, any differences observed between treatment means must always be viewed against a background of error variation. How much might the means differ by sampling error alone? Again a simple visual inspection of the means does not permit an answer to this question. As I have done for between-subjects designs, I resolve this decision-making problem by using a statistical test, the one-factor within-subjects analysis of variance.

TABLE 12.2
Perceived equal line lengths (in cm) from five subjects viewing four versions of the Ponzo illusion.

Subject	Standard (A_1)	Subjective Contours (A_2)	Solid Dots (A_3)	Control (A_4)	Subject Means
1	16.6	15.8	14.7	14.4	15.38
2	16.9	15.6	15.1	13.8	15.35
3	17.1	16.1	14.8	13.9	15.48
4	17.2	16.3	15.2	14.1	15.70
5	16.8	15.7	15.3	14.3	15.53
$\overline{X}_A$	16.92	15.90	15.02	14.10	
s_A	0.24	0.29	0.26	0.25	

The column span header is **Illusion Condition (A)** over A_1 through A_4.

ONE-FACTOR WITHIN-SUBJECTS ANALYSIS OF VARIANCE

The one-factor within-subjects analysis of variance is used to analyze one-factor multilevel within-subjects designs. If only two levels of an independent variable are manipulated, the one-factor within-subjects analysis of variance may be used in place of t_{rel}. This analysis partitions the total variation of scores in an experiment into three sources:

- The variation due to the effect of **factor A**.
- The variation due to the effect of **factor S**, individual differences among subjects.
- The variation due to the interaction of the treatments with the subjects, symbolized as $A \times S$.

These three partitions are used to obtain three mean squares:

- MS_A, which varies with the effect of factor A and error variation,
- MS_S, which varies with differences among subjects,
- $MS_{A \times S}$, which varies with the interaction of treatments with subjects and provides a measure of the error variation in the experiment.

The F statistic used in the statistical hypothesis test is

$$F = \frac{MS_A}{MS_{A \times S}}.$$

Partitioning a Score and Obtaining Sums of Squares

In this section I discuss the partitioning of scores and obtaining sums of squares for a within-subjects design. Because the approach followed is very similar to that for the between-subjects design, the presentation of the partitioning will be brief.

To understand how sources of variance from a within-subjects design are partitioned, it is useful to think of the within-subjects design as a two-factor design with the independent variable as one factor (factor A) and the subjects being tested as the second factor (factor S, where S represents the subject). Because each participant is tested under each level of the independent variable, a one-factor within-subjects design can be regarded as an $A \times S$ factorial design with a levels of factor A and n_A levels of factor S. Thus, there are $a \times n_A$ conditions, or cells, and each cell represents one level of the independent variable combined with a particular subject. In Table 12.2, there are four levels of factor A and five subjects; therefore, the experiment can be viewed as a 4 (levels of illusion condition) $\times$ 5 (number of subjects) factorial design, producing a total of 20 different treatment-by-subject ($A \times S$) conditions. But only one score is obtained for each $A \times S$ condition.

Thinking of the one-factor within-subjects analysis of variance as a two-factor analysis of variance allows obtaining "main effect" means for factors A and S. Notice in Table 12.2 that means are given for each subject, as well as for each level of the independent variable. Each subject mean is the mean of the scores of a single participant over all the illusion conditions. These means reflect individual differences in the perception of illusions among the participants in the experiment. Although the subject means are relevant to the analysis of variance, these means typically are not reported as descriptive statistics for experiments using a within-subjects design.

Conceptualizing a one-factor within-subjects analysis of variance as a two-factor analysis does not change the nature of the experiment; only one independent variable is manipulated and its effect analyzed. Thinking of the analysis as a two-factor design, however, helps to understand the introduction of the $A \times S$ interaction as the error term for the F statistic.

To obtain the F statistic, the analysis of variance for a within-subjects design takes the total amount by which a score differs from the grand mean and partitions this difference into three components, as follows:

$$
\begin{matrix}
\text{Total} & \text{Variation due to} & \text{Variation due} & \text{Variation} \\
\text{variation} & \text{factor } A \text{ plus} & \text{to individual} & \text{due to} \\
\text{in a} = & \text{error due to the} + & \text{differences} + & \text{interaction} . \quad (12.1)\\
\text{subject's} & \text{interaction of} & \text{among subjects} & \text{of factors} \\
\text{score} & \text{factors } A \text{ and } S & \text{(factor } S) & A \text{ and } S
\end{matrix}
$$

Following the basic approach of analysis of variance, the components of the partitioned scores are squared and summed over subjects and treatment conditions to obtain the sum of squares:

$$ SS_{\text{Total}} = SS_A + SS_S + SS_{A \times S}. \qquad (12.2) $$

These sums of squares indicate that the total variation of the scores in the experiment (given by SS_{Total}) is the result of variation that occurs from factor A (given by SS_A), factor S (given by SS_S), and the interaction of factors A and S (given by $SS_{A \times S}$). For the scores in Table 12.2, this process leads to the numerical values

$$
\begin{aligned}
SS_{\text{Total}} &= 22.926, \\
SS_A &= 21.830, \\
SS_S &= 0.314, \\
SS_{A \times S} &= 0.782.
\end{aligned}
$$

The computational formulas in the Chapter Supplement were used to obtain these values. I examine each sum of squares of equation 12.2.

SS_{Total}

The SS_{Total} represents the total variation of the scores in the experiment. As equation 12.2 indicates, a part of this variation is due to the effect of the independent variable, part is due to individual differences among subjects, and part is due to the treatments-by-subjects interaction.

SS_A

The SS_A varies with the effect of an independent variable and with treatments-by-subjects interaction. As with the one-factor between-subjects design, an effect of an independent variable increases the value of SS_A. In addition, the SS_A responds to any treatments-by-subjects interaction. In a within-subjects design, the treatments-by-subjects interaction is considered to be error variation.

SS_S

The SS_S varies with individual differences among the participants in the experiment. I refer to these differences among subjects as factor S. Notice from Table 12.2 that subject 4 tends to see the largest amount of an illusion over all levels of the independent variable ($\overline{X}_{S4} = 15.70$ cm), whereas subject 2 perceives the least illusion ($\overline{X}_{S2} = 15.35$ cm). The more the subject means differ from each other in an experiment, the larger SS_S becomes.

$SS_{A \times S}$

Treatments-by-subjects interaction (A × S): A situation in a one-factor within-subjects design where the effect of the independent variable depends on the subject.

The interaction of the treatment with the subjects is the remaining variation in a score and affects $SS_{A \times S}$. This **treatments-by-subjects interaction** can be seen in Figure 12.3, which depicts the hypothetical data of Table 12.2. The four types of illusion figures are represented on the abscissa. The functions within the figure depict the four scores obtained from each of the five subjects. The perceived equal line length is longest for all subjects at the standard illusion condition. Thus, there is an apparent effect-of-illusion condition on perceived line length. Because the five functions are not parallel, however, a treatments-by-subjects interaction is present, too. The difference in perceived line length between the illusion conditions is not the same for all subjects. For example, for subject 1, the difference in the standard condition and subjective contour condition scores is $16.6 - 15.8 = 0.8$ cm, but for subject 2 the difference is $16.9 - 15.6 = 1.3$ cm. Thus, the effect-of-illusion condition on perceived line length depends on the subjects. The $SS_{A \times S}$ provides a measure of the extent of the treatments-by-subjects interaction in a within-subjects experiment. But, because only one score is obtained from each person in each treatment condition, the treatments-by-subjects interaction cannot be separated from any error that may be affecting the score. Accordingly, $SS_{A \times S}$ is considered to be a measure of the error variation in a one-factor within-subjects design and is the basis for the error term of the F statistic for this analysis.

Finding Degrees of Freedom

To obtain the mean squares needed for the F statistic, each SS is divided by its corresponding degrees of freedom. The process of finding degrees of freedom is very similar to that for the between-subjects design.

Total Degrees of Freedom

$$df_{\text{Total}} = N - 1,$$

where N is the total number of scores in the experiment. For the example, $N = 20$; thus, $df_{\text{Total}} = 20 - 1 = 19$.

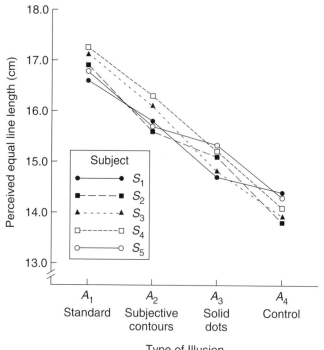

FIGURE 12.3
Perceived equal line lengths (in centimeters) for each subject as
a function of type of illusion.

Degrees of Freedom for SS_A

$$df_A = a - 1,$$

where a is the number of levels of the independent variable A. For the four levels of factor A in the example, $a = 4$; hence, $df_A = 4 - 1 = 3$.

Degrees of Freedom for SS_S

$$df_S = n_A - 1.$$

There are five subjects in the example experiment; accordingly, $n_A = 5$ and $df_S = 5 - 1 = 4$.

Degrees of Freedom for $SS_{A \times S}$

$$df_{A \times S} = (a - 1)(n_A - 1).$$

In the example, $a = 4$ and $n_A = 5$; therefore,

$$df_{A \times S} = (4 - 1)(5 - 1) = 12.$$

Additivity of Degrees of Freedom

The degrees of freedom are additive, so

$$df_{Total} = df_A + df_S + df_{A \times S}.$$

This relationship holds for the example; for

$$df_{Total} = 19, \; df_A = 3, \; df_S = 4, \text{ and } df_{A \times S} = 12.$$

Finding Mean Squares and F

Three mean squares are obtained from the SS in equation 12.2 by dividing each SS by its df:

$$MS_A = \frac{SS_A}{df_A},$$

$$MS_S = \frac{SS_S}{df_S},$$

$$MS_{A \times S} = \frac{SS_{A \times S}}{df_{A \times S}}.$$

MS_{Total} is not calculated because it is not used in the analysis of variance.
For the scores in Table 12.1,

$$SS_A = 21.830,$$
$$SS_S = 0.314,$$
$$SS_{A \times S} = 0.782.$$

The degrees of freedom for these sums of squares are

$$df_A = 3,$$
$$df_S = 4,$$
$$df_{A \times S} = 12.$$

Therefore,

$$MS_A = \frac{21.830}{3} = 7.277,$$

$$MS_S = \frac{0.314}{4} = 0.078,$$

$$MS_{A \times S} = \frac{0.782}{12} = 0.065.$$

The F statistic for the one-factor within-subjects analysis of variance is given by

$$F = \frac{MS_A}{MS_{A \times S}}.$$

Thus, for the scores of Table 12.1,

$$F_{obs} = \frac{7.277}{0.065} = 111.95.$$

This F_{obs} is the only F computed in this analysis; no F is found for factor S. A numerical summary of the analysis of variance on the scores of Table 12.2 is presented in Table 12.3. Computational formulas for this analysis are given in the chapter supplement. Table 12.4 summarizes the sources of variance in a one-factor within-subjects analysis of variance, the SS, df, MS, and F.

TABLE 12.3
Analysis of variance summary table for hypothetical perceived equal line length scores of Table 12.2.

Source	SS	df	MS	F
Type of illusion (A)	21.830	3	7.277	111.95*
Subjects (S)	0.314	4	0.078	
$A \times S$	0.782	12	0.065	
Total	22.926	19		

*$p < .01$.

TABLE 12.4
Summary of formulas for a one-factor within-subjects analysis of variance.

Source	SS	df[a]	MS	F
Factor A	SS_A	$a - 1$	$\dfrac{SS_A}{df_A}$	$\dfrac{MS_A}{MS_{A \times S}}$
Factor S	SS_S	$n_A - 1$	$\dfrac{SS_S}{df_S}$	
$A \times S$	$SS_{A \times S}$	$(a - 1)(n_A - 1)$	$\dfrac{SS_{A \times S}}{df_{A \times S}}$	
Total	SS_{Total}	$N - 1$	Not calculated	

[a] a = number of levels of factor A; n_A = number of scores in a treatment condition or, equivalently, the number of subjects; N = total number of scores.

TESTING YOUR KNOWLEDGE 12.1

1. Define: $A \times S$ interaction, df_A, $df_{A \times S}$, df_S, df_{Total}, factor A, factor S, MS_A, $MS_{A \times S}$, MS_S, n_A, one-factor within-subjects design, repeated measures design, SS_A, $SS_{A \times S}$, SS_S, SS_{Total}, treatments-by-subjects design.

2. Identify the sources of variation in scores from a one-factor within-subjects design.

3. Complete the following equations for a one-factor within-subjects analysis of variance:
   a. $SS_{Total} =$
   b. $df_A =$
   c. $df_S =$
   d. $df_{A \times S} =$
   e. $MS_A =$
   f. $MS_S =$
   g. $MS_{A \times S} =$
   h. $F =$

4. What is the value of SS_{Total} if $SS_A = 74.00$, $SS_S = 29.00$, and $SS_{A \times S} = 96.00$?

5. What is the value of SS_A if $SS_{Total} = 426.00$, $SS_S = 92.00$, and $SS_{A \times S} = 301.00$?

6. What is the value of SS_S if $SS_{Total} = 96.00$, $SS_A = 15.00$, and $SS_{A \times S} = 56.00$?

7. What is the value of $SS_{A \times S}$ if $SS_{Total} = 173.00$, $SS_A = 41.00$, and $SS_S = 36.00$?

8. A psychologist used a one-factor within-subjects analysis of variance with five levels of factor A and 13 participants. What are the values of df_A, df_S, $df_{A \times S}$, and df_{Total}?

9. What is the value of df_{Total} in a one-factor within-subjects analysis of variance if $df_A = 2$ and $df_S = 19$?

10. Find the numerical values of mean squares for the following SS and df: $SS_A = 22.00$, $SS_S = 18.00$, $SS_{A \times S} = 36.00$, $df_A = 2$, $df_S = 9$, and $df_{A \times S} = 18$.

11. Tables 1 and 2 are incomplete summary tables for a one-factor within-subjects analysis of variance. Fill in the missing values in each table by using the relationships among SS and df given in Table 12.4. Then answer these questions for each table.
   a. How many levels of the independent variable were manipulated?
   b. How many scores were obtained in each treatment condition?
   c. How many subjects participated in the study?

TABLE 1

Source	SS	df	MS	F
Factor A	48.00	4	—	—
Factor S	27.00	9	—	
$A \times S$	72.00	—	—	
Total	—	—		

TABLE 2

Source	SS	df	MS	F
Factor A	6.00	—	—	—
Factor S	36.00	12	3.00	
$A \times S$	—	24	—	
Total	78.00	—		

STATISTICAL HYPOTHESIS TESTING WITH F_{obs}

$F_{obs} = MS_A/MS_{A \times S}$ is used to decide if the treatment condition means differ significantly. As the discussion of $SS_{A \times S}$ indicated, the denominator of F, $MS_{A \times S}$, represents the error variation in this analysis. The numerator of F, MS_A, varies with the systematic effect of the independent variable and with any treatments-by-subjects interaction. If the independent variable has no effect and variation in the treatment means is due only to treatments-by-subjects interaction, then the value of MS_A should be about the same as $MS_{A \times S}$, and F_{obs} should be approximately 1.00. If factor A has an effect, however, and the treatment means differ because of both this effect and the treatments-by-subjects interaction, then MS_A will have a value larger than $MS_{A \times S}$, and F_{obs} becomes greater than 1.00.

No F ratio is constructed involving MS_S for individual differences. Although MS_S varies with the extent of the differences among the subjects in the experiment, there is no MS calculated in this analysis that provides an estimate of the chance variation expected among individuals. Therefore, the value of MS_S often is not included in a summary table.

The three mean squares and the sources of variation affecting them may be summarized as follows:

Mean Square	Affected by:
MS_A	**Systematic variance due to factor A**
	Treatments-by-subjects interaction (i.e., error variation)
MS_S	**Systematic variance due to factor S**
$MS_{A \times S}$	**Treatments-by-subjects interaction (i.e., error variation)**

Statistical testing with F follows the now familiar procedure:

- A null hypothesis, H_0, and an alternative hypothesis, H_1, are formulated.
- The sampling distribution of F, assuming that H_0 is true, is obtained. This distribution is given in Table A.3.
- A significance level is selected.
- A critical value of F, identified as F_{crit}, is found from the sampling distribution of F given in Table A.3.
- A rejection region is located in the sampling distribution of F.
- The F statistic, identified as F_{obs}, is calculated from the sample data.
- A decision to reject or not reject H_0 is made on the basis of whether or not F_{obs} falls into the rejection region.

Statistical Hypotheses

Null Hypothesis.   The null hypothesis for a within-subjects design with four levels of factor A is expressed as

$$H_0: \mu_{A1} = \mu_{A2} = \mu_{A3} = \mu_{A4}.$$

This null hypothesis represents the situation that exists if the independent variable has no effect. If H_0 is true, then any observed differences among the treatment means are due simply to error variation. As with the between-subjects design, the number of population means identified in the null hypothesis always corresponds to the number of levels of the independent variable.

Alternative Hypothesis.   The alternative hypothesis is

H_1: **The μ_A's are not all equal,**

regardless of the number of population means involved in the null hypothesis. The alternative hypothesis states a situation that exists if the independent variable has an effect.

Decision Making from the F

The statistical decision-making process in a one-factor within-subjects design is identical to that followed in the one-factor between-subjects analysis of variance. A value of α defining the size of the rejection region for F_{obs} is selected prior to conducting the analysis. The value of F_{crit} with the appropriate numerator and denominator df is then found from Table A.3a or b. If F_{obs} is equal to or larger than F_{crit}, then F_{obs} falls into the rejection region. The null hypothesis is rejected and the alternative hypothesis accepted. There is at least one statistically significant difference among the treatment means. If F_{obs} is less than F_{crit}, then F_{obs} does not fall into the rejection region; the null hypothesis is not rejected and the alternative hypothesis is not accepted. The treatment means do not differ significantly; the observed differences among the means are due to error variation. I conclude that the independent variable did not have an effect. The decisions from F_{obs} and the conclusions that follow are summarized in Table 12.5.

To illustrate the decision process, I use the analysis summarized in Table 12.3 on the example scores of Table 12.2. In this analysis, F_{obs} has 3 (numerator) and 12 (denominator) df. Thus, for $\alpha = .05$, $F_{crit} = 3.49$ (obtained from Table A.3a). The $F_{obs} = 111.95$ is larger than F_{crit} and falls into the rejection region. I reject

$$H_0: \mu_{A1} = \mu_{A2} = \mu_{A3} = \mu_{A4}$$

and accept

$$H_1: \text{The } \mu_A\text{'s are not all equal.}$$

This decision indicates that there is at least one statistically significant difference among the four means of Table 12.2, but it does not indicate specifically which means differ from each other. To find which pairwise comparisons differ significantly, multiple comparison tests are conducted.

TABLE 12.5

Summary of decisions and conclusions in statistical hypothesis testing using the analysis of variance for a one-factor within-subjects design. A .05 significance level is illustrated.

If F_{obs} falls into the rejection region for $\alpha = .05$, then:	If F_{obs} does not fall into the rejection region for $\alpha = .05$, then:
Probability of F_{obs} is less than or equal to .05, or $p \le .05$.	Probability of F_{obs} is greater than .05, or $p > .05$.
H_0 is rejected.	H_0 is not rejected.
H_1 is accepted. The sample means are not all from the same population.	H_1 is not accepted.
At least one difference between the treatment means is statistically significant at the .05 level.	There are no significant differences among the sample means at the .05 level.
It is decided that something in addition to sampling error is responsible for the differences among the sample means. In a carefully done experiment the difference is attributed to the independent variable.	It is decided that sampling error alone is the most plausible explanation for the differences among the sample means. There is no evidence that the independent variable had an effect.
Multiple comparison tests are needed if the independent variable has three or more levels.	No multiple comparison tests are needed.

Multiple Comparison Tests for Within-Subjects Analysis of Variance

The problems and issues of multiple comparison tests for the within-subjects analysis of variance are the same as those discussed in Chapter 10 for the between-subjects analysis of variance. For post hoc comparisons, the **Tukey HSD test** with a critical difference of

$$CD = q\sqrt{\frac{MS_{A \times S}}{n_A}}$$

may be used. Applying this test to the example experiment:

- $MS_{A \times S} = 0.065$ (obtained from Table 12.3).
- $n_A = 5$.
- q at the .05 level for four levels of the independent variable and 12 df for $MS_{A \times S}$ is 4.20 (obtained from Table A.4).

Substituting these values, I obtain

$$CD = 4.20\sqrt{\frac{0.065}{5}} = 4.20\sqrt{0.013} = 0.48 \text{ cm.}$$

TABLE 12.6
Application of the Tukey HSD *CD* to the pairwise comparisons of the example experiment. The value of *CD* = 0.48.

Comparison	Absolute Value of Comparison	Statistical Hypotheses	Decision
$\overline{X}_{A1}$ vs. $\overline{X}_{A2}$ $(16.92 - 15.90)$	1.02	$H_0: \mu_{A1} = \mu_{A2}$ $H_1: \mu_{A1} \neq \mu_{A2}$	Reject Accept
$\overline{X}_{A1}$ vs. $\overline{X}_{A3}$ $(16.92 - 15.02)$	1.90	$H_0: \mu_{A1} = \mu_{A3}$ $H_1: \mu_{A1} \neq \mu_{A3}$	Reject Accept
$\overline{X}_{A1}$ vs. $\overline{X}_{A4}$ $(16.92 - 14.10)$	2.82	$H_0: \mu_{A1} = \mu_{A4}$ $H_1: \mu_{A1} \neq \mu_{A4}$	Reject Accept
$\overline{X}_{A2}$ vs. $\overline{X}_{A3}$ $(15.90 - 15.02)$	0.88	$H_0: \mu_{A2} = \mu_{A3}$ $H_1: \mu_{A2} \neq \mu_{A3}$	Reject Accept
$\overline{X}_{A2}$ vs. $\overline{X}_{A4}$ $(15.90 - 14.10)$	1.80	$H_0: \mu_{A2} = \mu_{A4}$ $H_1: \mu_{A2} \neq \mu_{A4}$	Reject Accept
$\overline{X}_{A3}$ vs. $\overline{X}_{A4}$ $(15.02 - 14.10)$	0.92	$H_0: \mu_{A3} = \mu_{A4}$ $H_1: \mu_{A3} \neq \mu_{A4}$	Reject Accept

For each pairwise comparison a difference between the treatment means larger in absolute value than 0.48 cm is a statistically significant difference at the .05 level. The six pairwise comparisons, the absolute values of each comparison, the statistical hypothesis, and the decision for each hypothesis are shown in Table 12.6 (where A_1 = standard illusion, A_2 = subjective contours illusion, A_3 = solid dots illusion, A_4 = control condition).

The absolute value of each difference is larger than the *CD* of 0.48; thus, each comparison is statistically significant at the .05 level. The standard illusion creates the greatest illusion of the four conditions, the subjective contours create a significantly lesser amount of illusion, the solid dots significantly less illusion, and the control condition the least illusion.

Measuring the Strength of a Treatment Effect

Eta squared may be used as a strength of effect measure for a one-factor within-subjects design. The formula used is modified slightly from that for a between-subjects design,

$$\eta^2 = \frac{SS_A}{SS_A + SS_{A \times S}}.$$

Notice that with this formula, the variability due to individual differences, given by SS_S, is not included in the total variation of the experiment.

For the example, $SS_A = 21.830$ and $SS_{A \times S} = 0.782$. Thus,

$$\eta^2 = \frac{21.830}{21.830 + 0.782} = .97.$$

Ninety-seven percent of the variance in the length of line measures is accounted for by the illusion condition after the variability due to individual differences is removed, a very strong effect of the independent variable.

Assumptions of a Within-Subjects Analysis of Variance

The assumptions for the appropriate use of a one-factor within-subjects analysis are as follows:

1. Each participant is tested under each level of the independent variable.
2. The scores in the sample are drawn randomly from a population.
3. The populations of scores for the different treatment conditions are normally distributed.
4. The population variances of scores for the different treatment conditions are equal.
5. The contribution of the individual differences of a participant remains the same for his or her scores over all treatment conditions.

The first assumption is necessary for the within-subjects analysis of variance to be the appropriate statistical test for the data; it cannot be violated. The second, third, and fourth assumptions are identical to assumptions for a between-subjects analysis of variance. They are sometimes violated in experiments, but the analysis of variance maintains some robustness toward such violations. The fifth assumption states that the person's behavior, independent of the treatment effect, remains stable over all levels of the independent variable. It is likely that this assumption is violated in many cases of behavioral research. The effect of such a violation is to increase the probability of making a Type I error above the value set by the significance level.

Several approaches have been offered for dealing with this increased error rate. The Geisser–Greenhouse correction changes the df used to obtain F_{crit} so that a larger F_{crit} will be used to evaluate F_{obs}. With this correction, F_{crit} is found using 1 df for the numerator and $(n_A - 1)$ df for the denominator in place of the $a - 1$, $(a - 1)(n_A - 1)$ df normally used. Applying the Geisser–Greenhouse correction to the example, $F_{crit}(1, 4) = 7.71$. The $F_{obs}(3, 12) = 111.95$ still is larger than F_{crit} and H_0 is rejected, the same decision made using F_{crit} with 3, 12 df. This approach and others for reducing the error rate if assumption 5 is violated are discussed in Keppel (1991).

An alternative approach is to use the nonparametric Wilcoxon signed ranks test or the Friedman analysis of variance in place of the within-subjects analysis of variance. The Wilcoxon test is presented in Chapter 15.

TESTING YOUR KNOWLEDGE 12.2

1. Identify the factors affecting the value of each MS in a one-factor within-subjects analysis of variance.
2. Explain why MS_A increases in value if factor A has an effect in a one-factor within-subjects experiment.

3. Write the statistical hypotheses for a one-factor within-subjects analysis of variance with five levels of the independent variable.

4. Identify the assumptions underlying the use of the one-factor within-subjects analysis of variance.

Example Problem 12.1

Analyzing a One-Factor Within-Subjects Design with Four Levels of an Independent Variable

Problem: Many tasks require people to be vigilant over a long period, such as an air traffic controller monitoring a radar screen to maintain the proper distance between planes. Thus, psychologists have studied various factors affecting vigilance. As an example, Pfendler and Widdel (1986) had participants monitor a simulated display of the dials in the control room of a ship for a 2½-hour period. As time progressed, their participants took longer to detect changes in the readings of the controls. Suppose that a similar study was conducted requiring individuals to monitor a set of dials for a 4-hour period. The task was to indicate whenever a dial changed its displayed value. The dependent variable measured was the amount of time it took a person to detect the change. The mean detection times (in seconds) for each of the four 1-hour periods for 13 subjects are shown in Table 12.7. Did the detection times increase significantly over time periods?

TABLE 12.7
Mean number of seconds to detect a change in a dial over a four-hour time period for 13 subjects.

Subject	Time Period (in hours) (A)			
	1 (A_1)	2 (A_2)	3 (A_3)	4 (A_4)
1	6.2	6.7	7.4	7.8
2	5.9	4.8	6.1	6.9
3	8.4	8.7	9.9	10.3
4	7.6	7.8	8.7	8.9
5	4.1	4.7	5.4	6.6
6	5.4	5.3	5.9	7.1
7	6.6	6.7	7.2	7.5
8	6.1	5.8	6.4	6.7
9	4.9	5.1	5.2	6.8
10	8.2	8.6	9.3	10.4
11	5.7	5.7	6.5	7.2
12	5.9	6.4	6.9	7.6
13	6.9	6.6	7.1	7.5
$\overline{X}_A$	6.30	6.38	7.08	7.79
s_A	1.24	1.34	1.45	1.28

Solution: The design is a one-factor within-subjects design with four levels of the independent variable, time period. The first step in data analysis is to conduct a one-factor within-subjects analysis of variance on the scores. If F_{obs} is statistically significant, I will use the Tukey HSD test to find the statistically significant pairwise differences between the treatment means.

Statistic to Be Used: $F = MS_A/MS_{A \times S}$.

Assumptions for Use
1. Each participant is tested under each time period.
2. The scores in the sample are drawn randomly from a population.
3. The populations of detection times for the different time periods are normally distributed.
4. The population variances of detection times for the different time periods are equal.
5. The contribution of the individual differences of a subject remains the same for his or her scores over all time periods.

Statistical Hypotheses: $H_0: \mu_{A1} = \mu_{A2} = \mu_{A3} = \mu_{A4}$.
H_1: The μ_A's are not all equal.

Significance Level: $\alpha = .05$.

df:
$$df_A = a - 1 = 4 - 1 = 3$$
$$df_S = n_A - 1 = 13 - 1 = 12$$
$$df_{A \times S} = (a - 1)(n_A - 1)$$
$$= (4 - 1)(13 - 1) = 36$$
$$df_{Total} = N - 1 = 52 - 1 = 51$$

Critical value of F: $F_{crit}(3,36) = 2.92$. A value of 36 df for the denominator is not presented in Table A.3a. I used the critical value for the next lower tabled df for df_{Error}, 30.

Rejection Region: Values of F_{obs} equal to or greater than 2.92.

Calculation: I calculated the analysis of variance using the formulas given in the chapter supplement to obtain the following analysis of variance summary table.

Source	SS	df	MS	F
Time period (A)	18.985	3	6.328	60.85*
Subjects (S)	81.188	12	6.766	
A × S	3.727	36	0.104	
Total	103.900	51		

*$p < .05$.

Decision: $F_{obs} = 60.85$ falls into the rejection region. I reject H_0: $\mu_{A1} = \mu_{A2} = \mu_{A3} = \mu_{A4}$ and accept H_1: The μ_A's are not all equal. Rejecting H_0 indicates that there is at least one statistically significant difference between the treatment condition means. To find the statistically significant pairwise differences, I use the Tukey HSD test.

Tukey Test: The numerical values needed for this test are found as follows:

- q is obtained from Table A.4. There are four levels of the independent variable and 36 df for $MS_{A \times S}$. Because 36 df is not given in Table A.4, I use 30 df, the next lower tabled df from the 36 df for $MS_{A \times S}$. Thus, $q = 3.85$ for a .05 significance level.
- $MS_{A \times S}$, obtained from the analysis of variance, is 0.104.
- n_A, the number of scores in each of the means to be compared, is 13.

Substituting these numerical values into the formula,

$$CD = q \sqrt{\frac{MS_{A \times S}}{n_A}} = 3.85 \sqrt{\frac{0.104}{13}} = 0.34 \text{ second.}$$

Any difference equal to or larger in absolute value than 0.34 second is statistically significant at the .05 level. The pairwise comparisons, their absolute values, the statistical hypothesis tested, and the decision reached on the statistical hypothesis for each comparison are shown in Table 12.8 (where $A_1 = 1$ hour, $A_2 = 2$ hours, $A_3 = 3$ hours, and $A_4 = 4$ hours).

TABLE 12.8
Application of the Tukey HSD CD to the pairwise comparisons of the four time periods. The value of the CD is 0.34.

Comparison	Absolute Value of Comparison	Statistical Hypotheses	Decision
$\overline{X}_{A1}$ vs. $\overline{X}_{A2}$ $(6.30 - 6.38)$	0.08	H_0: $\mu_{A1} = \mu_{A2}$ H_1: $\mu_{A1} \neq \mu_{A2}$	Fail to reject Do not accept
$\overline{X}_{A1}$ vs. $\overline{X}_{A3}$ $(6.30 - 7.08)$	0.78	H_0: $\mu_{A1} = \mu_{A3}$ H_1: $\mu_{A1} \neq \mu_{A3}$	Reject Accept
$\overline{X}_{A1}$ vs. $\overline{X}_{A4}$ $(6.30 - 7.79)$	1.49	H_0: $\mu_{A1} = \mu_{A4}$ H_1: $\mu_{A1} \neq \mu_{A4}$	Reject Accept
$\overline{X}_{A2}$ vs. $\overline{X}_{A3}$ $(6.38 - 7.08)$	0.70	H_0: $\mu_{A2} = \mu_{A3}$ H_1: $\mu_{A2} \neq \mu_{A3}$	Reject Accept
$\overline{X}_{A2}$ vs. $\overline{X}_{A4}$ $(6.38 - 7.79)$	1.41	H_0: $\mu_{A2} = \mu_{A4}$ H_1: $\mu_{A2} \neq \mu_{A4}$	Reject Accept
$\overline{X}_{A3}$ vs. $\overline{X}_{A4}$ $(7.08 - 7.79)$	0.71	H_0: $\mu_{A3} = \mu_{A4}$ H_1: $\mu_{A3} \neq \mu_{A4}$	Reject Accept

Strength of Effect: $\eta^2 = \dfrac{SS_A}{SS_A + SS_{A \times S}} = \dfrac{18.985}{18.985 + 3.727} = .84.$

Conclusion: The only comparison smaller than the $CD = 0.34$ second is between the first and second hours. This difference is nonsignificant; all other differences are statistically significant. Thus, the comparisons reveal that there is no increase in the detection times between the first and second hours of the task, but a statistically significant increase occurs between hours 2 and 3, and between hours 3 and 4. The strength of effect, $\eta^2 = .84$ indicates that the time period accounts for a large proportion of the variance in the detection times after individual differences variability has been removed from the experiment.

Example Problem 12.2

Using the One-Factor Within-Subjects Analysis of Variance with Two Levels of an Independent Variable

Problem: The yawn of a student during class often is interpreted by an instructor as a sign of boredom. But is yawning actually such a sign? To explore this hypothesis, Provine and Hamernik (1986) designed an experiment to test if studying uninteresting material actually increases the frequency of yawning. In this experiment, students saw 30 minutes of rock music videos (A_1, the interesting stimulus) and 30 minutes of a color-bar test pattern without sound (A_2, the uninteresting stimulus) in two different sessions. The number of times a person yawned during the two sessions was observed and recorded. Suppose I replicated this experiment using 11 participants and observed the number of yawns for each session given in Table 12.9. Does the type of video affect the amount of yawning that occurs?

Solution: A one-factor within-subjects analysis of variance is an appropriate statistical test for these data. Because only two treatment conditions are involved, a t_{rel} also would be an appropriate statistical test.

Statistic to Be Used: $F = MS_A / MS_{A \times S}.$

Assumptions for Use
1. Each person is tested under each type of video condition.
2. The scores in the sample are drawn randomly from a population.
3. The populations of yawning scores for the different treatment conditions are normally distributed.
4. The population variances of yawning scores for the different treatment conditions are equal.
5. The contribution of the individual differences of a subject remains the same for his or her scores over both video conditions.

Statistical Hypotheses: $H_0: \mu_{A1} = \mu_{A2}.$

$H_1:$ The μ_A's are not equal.

Significance Level: $\alpha = .05.$

TABLE 12.9
Number of yawns observed as a function of type of video viewed for 11 participants.

Subject	Type of Video (A) Interesting (A_1)	Uninteresting (A_2)
1	5	7
2	2	1
3	4	7
4	3	8
5	0	2
6	4	5
7	7	6
8	6	9
9	3	3
10	1	4
11	8	9
$\overline{X}_A$	3.90	5.50
s	2.47	2.77

df:

$$df_A = a - 1 = 2 - 1 = 1$$
$$df_S = n_A - 1 = 11 - 1 = 10$$
$$df_{A \times S} = (a - 1)(n_A - 1)$$
$$= (2 - 1)(11 - 1) = 10$$
$$df_{\text{Total}} = N - 1 = 22 - 1 = 21$$

Critical Value of F: $F_{\text{crit}}(1, 10) = 4.96$.

Rejection Region: Values of F_{obs} equal to or greater than 4.96.

Calculation: Using the formulas given in the chapter supplement, the summary of this analysis is as follows:

Source	SS	df	MS	F
Type of video (A)	14.728	1	14.728	8.53*
Subjects (S)	120.364	10	12.036	
A × S	17.272	10	1.727	
Total	152.364	21		

*$p < .05$.

Decision: F_{obs} falls into the rejection region; thus, I reject H_0 and accept H_1.

Strength of Effect:
$$\eta^2 = \frac{14.728}{14.728 + 17.272} = .46.$$

Conclusion: The difference between the two treatment means of 3.9 and 5.5 yawns is statistically significant. When viewing the interesting video, individuals yawned less often than when watching the uninteresting video. Because only two means are involved, no multiple comparison test is necessary. The η^2 indicates that 46 percent of the variance in the dependent variable is accounted for by the type of video after individual differences variability has been removed from the experiment.

REPORTING THE RESULTS OF THE ANALYSIS OF VARIANCE

A description of the results of the analysis of the example experiment on illusion condition and perceived line length (see Tables 12.2 and 12.3) following the style of *The Publication Manual of the American Psychological Association* (1994) might be written for the results section of an article as follows:

> The mean perceived equal line lengths for the standard, subjective contours, solid dots, and control illusion conditions were 16.92 ($SD = 0.24$), 15.90 ($SD = 0.29$), 15.02 ($SD = 0.26$), and 14.10 ($SD = 0.25$) cm, respectively. With an alpha level of .05, a one-factor within-subjects analysis of variance indicated that the means differed significantly, $F(3, 12) = 111.95$, $MSE = 0.065$, $p < .01$. A Tukey test on the pairwise comparisons revealed that each illusion condition differed significantly from each other illusion condition, $p < .05$ ($CD = 0.48$ cm). Eta squared for the scores was .97.

Much of the information in this report is similar to that of a between-subjects design. I review this presentation briefly.

Sample means	The obtained values of the sample means and standard deviations are presented in the first sentence. Because only four means were obtained, they are presented in a sentence rather than in a table or a figure.
$\alpha = .05$	Indicates the significance level selected for the test.
$F(3, 12)$	Identifies the name of the test statistic as the F. The numbers shown in parentheses indicate the *df* for the numerator (i.e., 3) and the denominator (i.e., 12) of F_{obs}, respectively.
$= 111.95$	Gives the value of F_{obs}.
$p < .01.$	Indicates that:

    a. The probability of F_{obs} if H_0 is true is less than or equal to .01. This value is the probability of F_{obs} or an even more extreme value of F_{obs} if H_0 is true.

    b. H_0: $\mu_{A1} = \mu_{A2} = \mu_{A3} = \mu_{A4}$ was rejected.
    H_1: The μ_A's are not all equal was accepted.

    c.   There is at least one statistically significant difference among the treatment means.

    d.   Something other than sampling error alone is responsible for a difference in the treatment means.

$MSE =$ 0.065   Gives the value of the $MS_{A \times S}$ for F_{obs}. This MS is the error term for the F ratio.

$CD =$ 0.48 cm   Gives the critical difference for pairwise comparisons using the Tukey HSD test. The statistically significant pairwise comparisons are then described.

$\eta^2 = .97$ Indicates that 97 percent of the variance in the perceived equal line lengths in this experiment is accounted for by the illusion condition after variability due to individual differences has been removed.

CHOICE OF RESEARCH DESIGN: BETWEEN SUBJECTS OR WITHIN SUBJECTS

How does a behavioral scientist decide whether to use a between-subjects or within-subjects research design to evaluate a research hypothesis? Each type of design has its advantages and limitations. In general, there are three concerns when making this decision: (1) the number of participants needed, (2) the anticipated effectiveness of the independent variable, and (3) the possibility of multiple treatment effects occurring.

Number of Participants Needed

A participant in a within-subjects design is measured under each treatment condition; thus, fewer participants are needed than would be required for a corresponding between-subjects design. In the example shown in Table 12.2, five scores are obtained under each of the four levels of illusion condition for a total of 20 scores. But only five people are required to obtain these 20 scores. For a corresponding between-subjects design, 20 different subjects would be needed to obtain the 20 scores. Thus, when participants are difficult to obtain or where obtaining and instructing them requires considerably more time than actually performing the experimental task, the within-subjects design may be advantageous in comparison to a between-subjects design with respect to utilization of subjects.

Effectiveness of the Independent Variable

How easily the effect of an independent variable can be detected in an experiment depends partially on the strength of effect of that variable. A within-subjects design is often more sensitive to detecting the effect of an independent variable than is a between-subjects design. Therefore, a within-subjects design may be preferred when the anticipated effect of the independent variable is weak. The increased sensitivity of the within-subjects design occurs because each subject receives each level of the independent variable and is exposed to all treatment conditions. The within-subjects analysis of variance partitions out the variability due to individual differences among subjects (i.e., the variability due to factor S,

MS_S) so that it does not contribute to the error term for the F (i.e., $MS_{A \times S}$). In a between-subjects design, this variation is included in the MS_{Error}. Thus, the error term in a within-subjects design (i.e., $MS_{A \times S}$) will be smaller than the error term in a between-subjects design (i.e., MS_{Error}). A smaller error term leads to a larger value of F_{obs}, which is more likely to result in the rejection of H_0. Thus, in an experiment where there are large individual differences among subjects and the effect of the independent variable is not expected to be strong, a within-subjects design is more likely to detect the effect of the independent variable than is a between-subjects design.

Multiple Treatment Effects

Multiple treatment effects: Changes in participants' performance in a within-subjects design that are due to being tested in each level of the independent variable.

In a within-subjects design a participant is given each level of the independent variable over a period of time. This sequence of treatments opens the within-subjects design to the possibility of **multiple treatment effects** occurring; the effect of a level of the independent variable may depend on the levels preceding it. Multiple treatment effects include both practice effects and treatment carry-over effects.

Practice effect: A multiple treatment effect that occurs because participants may become more practiced or fatigued on the experimental task.

Practice effects are changes in performance due simply to repeated practice in the experimental task. These changes may result either in improved or impaired performance as the experiment progresses. For instance, in the example experiment measuring the extent of an illusion in four different illusion conditions, participants may become bored with the experiment as it progresses, or they may become more accurate with their estimates as they make more of them. In either case, a person's performance may change whether or not the illusion condition affects behavior.

Treatment carry-over effect: A multiple treatment effect that occurs when the effect of one level of the independent variable carries over to affect performance in the next level of the independent variable.

Treatment carry-over effects are specific effects from one level of an independent variable that may carry over to affect performance on a subsequent level of the independent variable. For example, in the problem of the perception of illusions as a function of the illusion condition, if subjects always saw the control condition last, they may perceive an illusion because they had seen conditions creating illusions prior to the control condition. They have an expectation of seeing an illusion that carries over to the control condition. If they had seen the control condition first without the expectation of seeing an illusion, they would not have perceived it as an illusion.

Practice effects and treatment carry-over effects are important, because if they occur and are not controlled for they confound an experiment. Control for these effects is usually obtained by giving each participant the treatments in a different order.

Each of the issues discussed, the number of participants needed, the anticipated effectiveness of the independent variable, and the possibility of multiple treatment effects occurring must be considered when choosing a research design. The effective use of participants and the greater sensitivity to detecting the effect of an independent variable are advantages of the within-subjects design. The potential for multiple treatment effects occurring, however, is a disadvantage of this design. Multiple treatment effects cannot occur in a between-subjects design, for each person experiences only one level of the independent variable. Thus, when multiple treatment effects are likely to occur in an experiment and cannot be easily controlled through the ordering of treatments, a between-subjects design will likely be used. Because multiple treatment effects occur with many independent variables and cannot be easily controlled in a within-subjects design, behavioral scientists often choose to use between-subjects designs.

TESTING YOUR KNOWLEDGE 12.3

1. Define: multiple treatment effects, practice effect, treatment carry-over effect.
2. When people think of geographical locations, their identification of areas is often affected by a superordinate bias. That is, geographical locations, such as cities, are located within larger geographical areas such as a state or country. The larger geographical areas (i.e., the superordinate locations) then may affect how we think about locations within them. For example, Canada is located north of the United States, yet there are some Canadian cities that are located further south than some U.S. cities. But most people would judge the U.S. cities to be more southerly simply because the United States is south of Canada. Indeed, Friedman and Brown (2000) found that people judged Seattle, Washington, United States, to be considerably south of St. Johns, Newfoundland, Canada, although both cities are at the same latitude. Suppose you are interested in this issue and asked participants to estimate the latitudes of three cities located at essentially the same latitude, Dallas, Texas (United States), Tijuana, Mexico, and Tripoli, Libya. Each person is given instruction and brief practice on estimating latitude and asked to estimate the latitude for each city. The following estimates were obtained:

	City (A)		
Participant	**Dallas (A_1)**	**Tijuana (A_2)**	**Tripoli (A_3)**
1	33	18	20
2	29	27	24
3	35	21	26
4	28	17	19
5	30	18	27
6	40	26	23
7	32	25	25
8	31	19	24
9	30	23	17
10	25	20	21
11	27	20	20
12	36	24	23
13	26	22	18
14	29	23	29

Find the mean and standard deviation for each treatment condition. Then perform a one-factor within-subjects analysis of variance on these scores to determine if a superordinate bias exists in estimating latitudes and answer the following questions.

a. State the statistical hypotheses for the F test for these scores.
b. What is the value of F_{obs}?
c. What are the df for F_{obs}?
d. What is F_{crit} at the .05 level?
e. What is the rejection region for F_{obs}?
f. Does F_{obs} fall into the rejection region?
g. What decisions do you make about the statistical hypotheses? Do you reject or fail to reject H_0? Accept or not accept H_1?
h. Do you conclude that the means are from the same or different populations?
i. Is there a statistically significant difference between at least one pair of means?

  j. Are multiple comparison tests needed in this experiment? Give the reason for your answer.

  k. What is the value of the Tukey *CD*?

  l. Which pairwise differences are statistically significant?

  m. What is η^2 for this experiment?

  n. Describe the results of this experiment following the style illustrated in the Reporting the Results of an Analysis of Variance section of this chapter.

Exercises 3 and 4 present sample reports of one-factor within-subjects analysis of variance. Answer the following questions for each exercise.

  a. How many levels of the independent variable were used in this experiment?

  b. How many subjects were used in this experiment?

  c. What is the value of F_{obs}?

  d. What is the value of F_{crit} at the .05 significance level?

  e. Do you reject or fail to reject H_0?

  f. Do you accept or not accept H_1?

  g. Is there at least one statistically significant difference between the means?

  h. Which treatment conditions, if any, differ significantly?

3. The mean reaction time for the simple stimulus condition was 396 milliseconds (ms), whereas the mean for the complex stimulus condition was 412 ms. With alpha equal to .05, a one-factor within-subjects analysis of variance revealed a significant difference between the means, $F(1, 18) = 4.76$, $MSE = 510.924$, $p < .05$.

4. The mean number of faces correctly recognized was 13.9 on trial 1, 14.6 on trial 2, and 14.1 on trial 3. With alpha equal to .05, a one-factor within-subjects analysis of variance indicated no difference in the number of correct recognitions over trials, $F(2, 22) = 2.81$, $MSE = 0.555$, $p > .05$.

SUMMARY

- In a one-factor within-subjects design a single group of participants is given each level of the independent variable.
- The one-factor within-subjects analysis of variance is used to analyze scores from a one-factor multilevel within-subjects design.
- Three mean squares are generated in a one-factor within-subjects analysis of variance: MS_A, which varies with the effect of the independent variable and treatments by subjects interaction, MS_S, which varies with differences among subjects, and $MS_{A \times S}$, which varies with the interaction of treatments with subjects and provides a measure of the error variation in the experiment.
- The F statistic used in the one-factor within-subjects analysis of variance is $F = MS_A / MS_{A \times S}$.
- Using the F statistic follows the usual steps of formulating statistical hypotheses, setting a significance level, locating a rejection region, calculating F_{obs}, and making decisions concerning the statistical hypotheses.
- A statistically significant F when three or more levels of an independent variable are manipulated requires a multiple comparison test to find the statistically significant pairwise differences.
- The Tukey test is used for all possible pairwise post hoc comparisons.

- η^2 may be used as a measure of the strength of a treatment effect.
- Choosing between a between-subjects or a within-subjects design requires considering the number of subjects needed, the anticipated effectiveness of the independent variable, and the possibility of occurrence of multiple treatment effects.

KEY TERMS AND SYMBOLS

critical difference (CD) (346)
df_A (350)
df_S (350)
$df_{A \times S}$ (350)
df_{Total} (350)
eta squared (η^2) (347)
factor A (337)
factor S (337)
MS_A (337)

MS_S (337)
$MS_{A \times S}$ (337)
multiple treatment effects (356)
n_A (334)
practice effect (356)
repeated measures design (334)
SS_A (338)
SS_S (338)
$SS_{A \times S}$ (338)

SS_{Total} (338)
treatment carry-over effect (356)
treatments-by-subjects design (334)
treatments-by-subjects interaction ($A \times S$) (339)
within-subjects design (334)

CHAPTER SUPPLEMENT: CALCULATING A ONE-FACTOR WITHIN-SUBJECTS ANALYSIS OF VARIANCE WITH COMPUTATIONAL FORMULAS

This supplement provides the computational format for a one-factor within-subjects analysis of variance. An experiment with four levels of an independent variable A and five participants in each level is represented as follows:

	Factor A				
Subject	A_1	A_2	A_3	A_4	
S_1	X_{11}	X_{12}	X_{13}	X_{14}	T_{S1}
S_2	X_{21}	X_{22}	X_{23}	X_{24}	T_{S2}
S_3	X_{31}	X_{32}	X_{33}	X_{34}	T_{S3}
S_4	X_{41}	X_{42}	X_{43}	X_{44}	T_{S4}
S_5	X_{51}	X_{52}	X_{53}	X_{54}	T_{S5}
	T_{A1}	T_{A2}	T_{A3}	T_{A4}	G

where X_{ij} = score of a subject.
 T_A = total of scores for a level of the independent variable.
 T_S = total of scores for a subject.
 G = grand total of the scores.
 n_A = number of scores in a level of the independent variable.
 a = number of levels of the independent variable.
 N = total number of scores.

Four numerical values are found using these terms:

$$[1] = \sum \sum X_{ij}^2 \qquad \text{the sum of all the scores squared,}$$

$$[2] = \frac{\sum T_A^2}{n_A} \qquad \text{the sum of each level of the independent variable total squared, divided by the number of subjects,}$$

$$[3] = \frac{\sum T_S^2}{a} \qquad \text{the sum of each subject's scores squared, divided by the number of levels of factor } A,$$

$$[4] = \frac{G^2}{N} \qquad \text{the grand total squared, divided by the total number of scores.}$$

Using these numerical values, an analysis of variance is obtained as follows:

Source of Variance	SS	df	MS	F
Factor A	$[2] - [4]$	$a - 1$	$\dfrac{SS_A}{df_A}$	$\dfrac{MS_A}{MS_{A \times S}}$
Subjects (S)	$[3] - [4]$	$n_A - 1$	$\dfrac{SS_S}{df_S}$	
$A \times S$	$[1] - [2] - [3] + [4]$	$(a - 1)(n_A - 1)$	$\dfrac{SS_{A \times S}}{df_{A \times S}}$	
Total	$[1] - [4]$	$N - 1$	Not calculated	

To illustrate the computations, I use the example scores given in Table 12.2 for which an analysis of variance is summarized in Table 12.3.

	Illusion Condition (A)				
Subject	**Standard** A_1	**Subjective Contours** A_2	**Solid Dots** A_3	**Control** A_4	**Subject Totals**
1	16.6	15.8	14.7	14.4	$T_{S1} = 61.50$
2	16.9	15.6	15.1	13.8	$T_{S2} = 61.40$
3	17.1	16.1	14.8	13.9	$T_{S3} = 61.90$
4	17.2	16.3	15.2	14.1	$T_{S4} = 62.80$
5	16.8	15.7	15.3	14.3	$T_{S5} = 62.10$
	$T_A = 84.60$	79.50	75.10	70.50	$G = 309.70$

$n_A = 5$, $a = 4$, and $N = 20$.

The values of the numerical computational terms are:

$$[1] = [(16.6)^2 + \cdots + (16.8)^2 + (15.8)^2 + \cdots + (15.7)^2 + (14.7)^2 + \cdots$$
$$+ (15.3)^2 + (14.4)^2 + \cdots + (14.3)^2] = 4818.630$$

$$[2] = \frac{(84.60)^2 + (79.50)^2 + (75.10)^2 + (70.50)^2}{5} = 4817.534$$

$$[3] = \frac{(61.50)^2 + (61.40)^2 + (61.90)^2 + (62.80)^2 + (62.10)^2}{4} = 4796.018$$

$$[4] = \frac{(309.70)^2}{20} = 4795.704$$

Then

$$SS_A = [2] - [4] = 4817.534 - 4795.704 = 21.830,$$
$$df_A = a - 1 = 4 - 1 = 3,$$
$$MS_A = \frac{21.830}{3} = 7.277.$$

$$SS_S = [3] - [4] = 4796.018 - 4795.704 = 0.314,$$
$$df_S = n_A - 1 = 5 - 1 = 4,$$
$$MS_S = \frac{0.314}{4} = 0.078.$$

$$SS_{A \times S} = [1] - [2] - [3] + [4]$$
$$= 4818.630 - 4817.534 - 4796.018 + 4795.704 = 0.782,$$
$$df_{A \times S} = (a - 1)(n_A - 1) = (4 - 1)(5 - 1) = 12,$$
$$MS_{A \times S} = \frac{0.782}{12} = 0.065.$$

$$SS_{Total} = [1] - [4] = 4818.630 - 4795.704 = 22.926,$$
$$df_{Total} = N - 1 = 20 - 1 = 19,$$
$$F_{obs} = \frac{MS_A}{MS_{A \times S}} = \frac{7.277}{0.065} = 111.95.$$

The summary of the analysis of variance is

Source	SS	df	MS	F
Factor A	21.830	3	7.277	111.95*
Subjects	0.314	4	0.078	
$A \times S$	0.782	12	0.065	
Total	22.926	19		

*$p < .01$.

The values obtained by this computational approach are identical to those presented in Table 12.3 from the definitional formulas of an analysis of variance.

REVIEW QUESTIONS

1. Suppose that you are interested in whether the type of mood reflected by a word (happy, neutral, or sad) affects how well the word is remembered from a list. You construct a list composed of six happy words (e.g., joyful, bright), six neutral words (e.g., derive, convey) and six sad words (e.g., gloomy, lonely). Each of eight participants then learns the list to a criterion of two complete correct recitations. One week later each person attempts to recall the list. The number of items correctly recalled as a function of the type of word was as follows:

	Type of Word		
Participant	Happy	Neutral	Sad
1	5	4	3
2	6	3	4
3	4	5	2
4	5	3	1
5	3	1	2
6	6	3	4
7	2	2	3
8	5	3	1

   a. Find the mean and standard deviation for each type of word condition. Then analyze the scores with a one-factor within-subjects analysis to answer the following question: Does the type of word affect recall? Use a .05 significance level. If needed, use the Tukey HSD test for multiple comparisons.
   b. What is the strength of effect of the independent variable of type of word?
   c. Describe the results following the style illustrated in the Reporting the Results of the Analysis of Variance section of this chapter.

2. Example Problem 10.3 introduced a within-subjects design study on the Morinaga misalignment illusion [see Figure 10.3, panel (a), page 258]. Suppose an experimenter wants to know if instructing subjects about the illusion changes their perception of it. The experimenter first had 12 subjects align the points of the angles and measured the amount of error in adjustment for each person. After subjects aligned the points, they were then told about the illusion and asked to align the points again. The two error measurements (in millimeters) for each subject were as follows.

	Instructional Condition (A)	
Subject	Before Instructions (A_1)	After Instructions (A_2)
1	1.3	1.4
2	2.1	2.0
3	2.5	2.7
4	1.9	2.0
5	3.0	3.4
6	2.5	2.8
7	1.8	1.6
8	2.4	2.5
9	3.1	3.3
10	3.4	3.4
11	2.5	2.3
12	2.9	2.8

a. Find the mean and standard deviation for each instructional condition. Then analyze the scores with a one-factor within-subjects analysis to answer the question: Did the instructions affect the amount of the illusions perceived? Use a .05 significance level.

b. Compare F_{obs} to t_{obs} for Chapter 9 Review Question 4. Does $\sqrt{F_{obs}} = t_{obs}$?

c. Do you reach the same or different conclusions about the effect of the independent variable from the analysis of variance and the t_{rel} test?

d. Describe the results of this experiment following the style illustrated in the Reporting the Results of the Analysis of Variance section of this chapter.

3. Assume that you plan to conduct a one-factor within-subjects experiment with five levels of the independent variable and 12 participants.

a. Write the statistical hypothesis tested by the analysis of variance on the scores that you would obtain.

b. Find the *df* for the analysis of variance of this design.

c. What is the value of F_{crit} at the .05 significance level for the analysis of variance of this design?

d. Suppose that the value of F_{obs} was larger than F_{crit}. What decision would you make about H_0 and H_1?

e. Suppose that you reject H_0 and accept H_1 for this experiment. What inference would you make about the treatment means from these decisions?

4. The following tables are incomplete summary tables for an analysis of variance. By using the relationships among SS, *df*, and MS, provide the missing values in each table. Then answer the following questions for each table.

a. How many levels of the independent variable were manipulated?

b. How many scores were obtained in each level of the independent variable?

c. How many subjects participated in the study?

d. Is the value of F_{obs} statistically significant at the .05 level?

e. What decision do you make for H_0 and H_1 for each analysis?

TABLE 1

Source	SS	df	MS	F
Factor A	—	—	11.00	—
Factor S	138.00	23	6.00	
A × S	253.00	46	—	
Total	—	71		

TABLE 2

Source	SS	df	MS	F
Factor A	60.00	—	—	—
Factor S	133.00	19	7.00	
A × S	—	95	—	
Total	573.00	—		

5. Several experimenters recently investigated an infant's interest in unfamiliar faces in comparison to familiar faces. Each of 14 infants viewed photographs of familiar faces (e.g., photographs of the mother and father), unfamiliar faces (e.g., photographs of males and females unknown to the infant), and a blank oval the same size as a face. The experimenters recorded the amount of time each infant fixated on the face. The stimulus conditions and the mean duration of time fixated on the stimulus for each condition are presented in Table 1. An analysis of variance on these data is presented in Table 2.

TABLE 1
Mean fixation time (in seconds) as a function of stimulus condition.

Stimulus Condition		
Familiar Face (A_1)	Unfamiliar Face (A_2)	Blank Oval (A_3)
34.2	26.8	18.5

TABLE 2
Analysis of variance summary for mean fixation times presented in Table 1.

Source	SS	df	MS	F
Stimulus condition (A)	1727.32	2	863.66	15.99*
Subjects (S)	2047.37	13	157.49	
A × S	1404.52	26	54.02	
Total	5179.21	41		

*$p < .01$.

A Tukey HSD gave a $CD = 6.9$ seconds at the .05 significance level.
a. What is the effect of the stimulus conditions on fixation time?
b. Describe the results of this experiment following the style illustrated in the Reporting the Results of the Analysis of Variance section of this chapter.

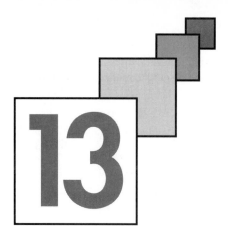

Correlation

Chapters 9 through 12 dealt with the use of statistics in experiments in which an independent variable is manipulated and a dependent variable measured. In many studies, however, a researcher is interested only in finding whether two variables are related. **Correlational studies** involve research in which two or more variables are measured to find the direction and degree to which they are related. Neither variable is manipulated; thus, there is no independent or dependent variable in these studies. In this chapter I introduce concepts of correlation needed to understand such research and a statistic called the correlation coefficient. Using correlated scores to predict one score from another is introduced in Chapter 14. The simplest instance of a correlational study involves obtaining measures on two different variables from each of a number of participants. The paired measures then are statistically analyzed to determine if any relationship exists between them. Consider the following example.

Correlational studies: Studies in which two or more variables are measured to find the direction and degree to which they covary.

Loneliness is a psychological state that all of us experience at one time or another. For many, loneliness appears to be a long-lasting state and may be related to mental health problems (Roberts, Lewinsohn, & Seeley, 1993). Suppose that we are interested in exploring the relationship between loneliness and psychological depression. I obtain a sample of 10 people and measure both their loneliness and depression levels. Loneliness is measured by asking the person to respond to 10 statements similar to

"I feel left out of activities with others"

with Never (0), Rarely (1), Sometimes (2), or Often (3). The numbers in parentheses indicate the numerical weight assigned to the response. A person who answers with "never" to all 10 statements will receive a zero for loneliness, whereas someone who responds with "often" for all 10 statements will receive a 30 for loneliness. Depression is measured similarly with 10 statements, such as "I feel sad." Again the participant responds with Never (1), Rarely (2), Sometimes (3), or Often (4). Notice, however, in this scale that the numerical values assigned to the responses differ from those assigned for the loneliness scale. The lowest score is 10, obtained by someone who answers "never" to all 10 statements and the highest is 40, obtained by a person who answers "often" to all 10 statements. Thus, for each participant two scores were obtained, one a score on loneliness and the other a score on depression.

Suppose that the loneliness scores (designated variable X) and the depression scores (designated variable Y) obtained are those presented in Table 13.1. The designation of a variable as either X or Y is arbitrary. In general, however, a researcher asks the question, What is the level of Y as a function of X?

This statement indicates the researcher is interested in predicting the value of one variable (Y) from the value of the other variable (X). The variable we wish to use as the predictor is usually designated the X variable and the predicted variable as Y. Thus, if a researcher asks the question, "What is the depression score for a certain loneliness score?" he or she is attempting to predict the level of depression (Y) from the level of loneliness (X). The details of using one score to predict another are presented in Chapter 14.

Bivariate distribution: A distribution in which two scores are obtained from each subject.

The paired scores in Table 13.1 represent a **bivariate distribution** of scores. The prefix *bi* means "two"; thus, these scores are bivariate in that two scores are obtained from each participant. Are these scores related? Are higher loneliness scores associated with higher

TABLE 13.1
Hypothetical scores for 10 subjects on loneliness and depression.

Subject	Loneliness Score: X	Depression Score: Y
1	4	16
2	27	37
3	18	33
4	7	23
5	30	34
6	12	32
7	18	24
8	23	29
9	19	26
10	12	26

depression scores and lower loneliness scores related to lower scores on depression? Or perhaps the relationship is the inverse; that is, higher loneliness scores are associated with lower depression scores, and lower scores on loneliness are related to higher scores on depression. It also is possible that the scores do not covary, that loneliness and depression scores are independent of each other. To find if the scores are related I first construct a graph of the scores, called a *scatterplot;* then I calculate a statistic called a *Pearson correlation coefficient* on the scores.

SCATTERPLOTS

Scatterplot: A graph of a bivariate distribution in which the X variable is plotted on the horizontal axis and the Y variable is plotted on the vertical axis.

A scatterplot of the scores of Table 13.1 is presented in Figure 13.1. In a **scatterplot** (sometimes called a *scattergram* or a *scatter diagram*), the variable labeled X (in the example, the loneliness score) is plotted on the horizontal axis (the abscissa), and the Y variable (in the example, the depression score) is plotted on the vertical axis (the ordinate). The score of a person on each of the two measures is indicated by one point on the scatterplot. For example, in Figure 13.1 the scores for subject 1 are plotted at the point that intersects a value of 4 on the loneliness score and 16 on the depression scale. To illustrate how the scatterplot was constructed, I have identified each person by placing the number of the subject from Table 13.1 next to the point that represents his or her scores on the scatterplot. Typically, however, subjects are not identified by name or number on a scatterplot.

Positive Relationships

The scatterplot indicates that the example scores tend to covary: Higher depression scores tend to be related to higher loneliness scores, and lower depression scores tend to be related

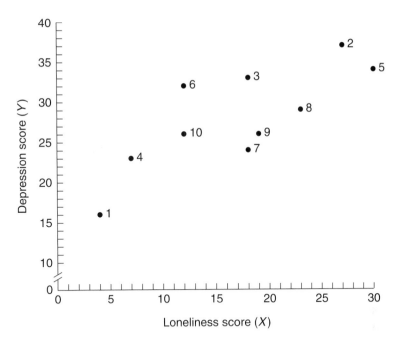

FIGURE 13.1
Scatterplot of loneliness and depression scores for 10 participants. The numbers next to the plotted scores identify the participants. The scores are from Table 13.1.

Covary: Two variables covary when a change in one variable is related to a consistent change in the other variable.

Positive relationship: A relationship between two variables in which, as the value of one variable increases, the value of the other variable tends to increase also.

Linear relationship: A relationship between two variables that can be described by a straight line.

to lower loneliness scores. Scores **covary** when a change in one score is accompanied by a consistent change in the other score. The relationship among the scores in Figure 13.1 is also positive. In a **positive relationship** (also called a *direct relationship*), as the value of variable X increases, the value of variable Y tends to increase also. Thus, in Figure 13.1, as the loneliness scores increase, the depression scores also tend to increase. Because both variables are measured and not manipulated, it is equally appropriate to state that as the depression scores increase the loneliness scores tend to increase also. But in Figure 13.1 the positive relationship is not perfect. Participant 9, for example, has a higher loneliness score than person 10, but both have a depression score of 26. Similarly, participants 6 and 10 both have loneliness scores of 12, but depression scores of 32 and 26, respectively.

A perfect positive relationship between depression and loneliness scores is illustrated in Figure 13.2. In this instance the scatterplot results in a straight line. Relationships between two variables that can be described by a straight line are called **linear relationships**. In a perfect positive relationship, such as that illustrated in Figure 13.2, for every value of X, there is only one corresponding value of Y. Thus, knowing the value of one score permits us to know or predict perfectly the score on the second variable. For example, a person who obtained a loneliness score of 8 scored 18 on the depression measurement. Or a

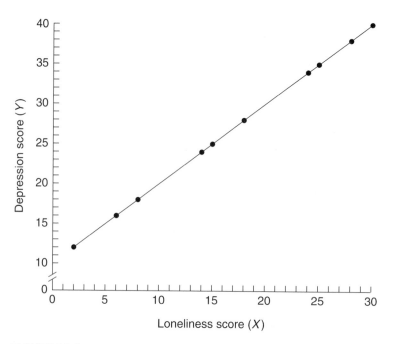

FIGURE 13.2
A perfect positive relationship between loneliness scores and depression scores for 10 participants.

person who scored 24 on depression obtained a 14 on loneliness. There is no error in predicting one score from the other in a perfect relationship. Perfect positive relationships seldom, if ever, occur between scores obtained in actual research, however.

Negative Relationships

Negative relationship: A relationship between two variables in which, as the value of one variable increases, the value of the other variable tends to decrease.

Suppose that the relationship obtained between the loneliness and depression scores was that shown in Figure 13.3. This figure illustrates a **negative relationship** between the two variables: As the value of variable X increases, the value of variable Y tends to decrease. In Figure 13.3 you can see that low scores on loneliness tend to be associated with high depression scores, and high loneliness scores are associated with low depression scores. Negative relationships sometimes are identified as *inverse relationships*, for the variables are oppositely related: low values on X are related to high values on Y, and high values on X are related to low values on Y.

The negative relationship illustrated in Figure 13.3 is not a perfect relationship between loneliness and depression scores. For example, two people have loneliness scores of 20, but depression scores of 17 and 24, respectively. Similarly, two participants have depression scores of 32, but one has a loneliness score of 5 and the other a loneliness score of 12.

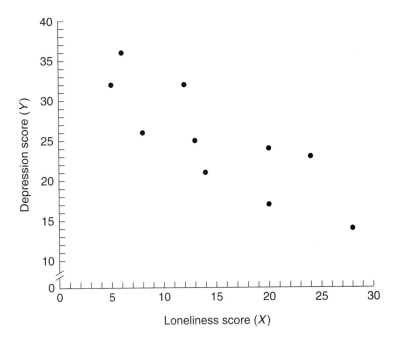

FIGURE 13.3
A negative relationship between loneliness scores and depression scores
for 10 participants.

A perfect negative relationship between depression and loneliness scores is illustrated in Figure 13.4. In this instance the scatterplot again creates a straight line, and knowing one score allows a perfect prediction of the other score. For example, if I know that a person obtained 8 on loneliness, I know also that his or her depression score was 32. Similarly, if I know someone obtained a depression score of 22, then his or her loneliness score was 18. As with perfect positive relationships, perfect negative relationships rarely occur with actual scores. Notice that *positive* or *negative* applied to a scatterplot indicates only the direction, not the strength, of a relationship. For predicting one score from another, positive and negative relationships are equally useful.

TESTING YOUR KNOWLEDGE 13.1

1. Define: bivariate distribution of scores, correlational study, covary, direct relationship, inverse relationship, linear relationship, negative relationship, positive relationship, scatterplot.
2. Reverse the designation of the X and Y variables for Table 13.1 (i.e., call the depression score X and the loneliness score Y) and then construct a scatterplot of the scores similar to Figure 13.1. Does the designation of a variable as X or Y change the relationship between the scores?

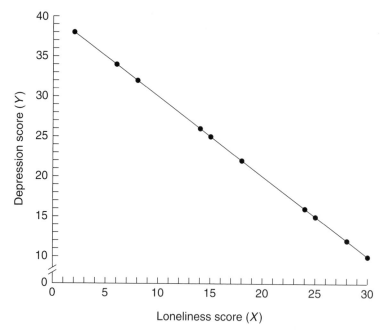

FIGURE 13.4
A perfect negative relationship between loneliness scores and depression scores for 10 participants.

3. For Tables 1 and 2, construct a scatterplot of the scores on a sheet of graph paper; then answer the following questions for each table.
    a. Does the relationship between the scores appear to be positive or negative, or is there no relationship between the scores?
    b. Is the relationship between the scores perfect or less than perfect?
    c. Would knowing the loneliness score of a subject increase the accuracy of predicting the depression score for that subject?

TABLE 1

Subject	Loneliness	Depression
1	4	19
2	12	20
3	28	33
4	18	32
5	14	26
6	6	19
7	22	28
8	23	36
9	15	30
10	18	27

TABLE 2

Subject	Loneliness	Depression
1	5	29
2	11	31
3	23	23
4	17	17
5	28	16
6	13	21
7	12	26
8	4	28
9	21	14
10	16	25

4. The following scores represent the body weight in pounds and self-esteem scores from a sample of 10 people.

Person	Body Weight	Self-Esteem
1	100	39
2	111	47
3	117	54
4	124	23
5	136	35
6	139	30
7	143	48
8	151	20
9	155	28
10	164	46

a. Plot a scatterplot of the scores on a sheet of graph paper. Does the relationship between the scores appear to be positive or negative, or is there no relationship between the scores?

b. Is the relationship between the scores perfect or less than perfect?

c. Would knowing the body weight of a person increase the accuracy of predicting the self-esteem score for that person?

THE PEARSON CORRELATION COEFFICIENT

An inspection of a scatterplot gives an impression of whether two variables are related and the direction of their relationship. But it alone is not sufficient to determine whether there is an association between two variables. The relationship depicted in the scatterplot needs to be described quantitatively. Descriptive statistics that express the degree of relation between two variables are called **correlation coefficients**. A commonly used correlation

Pearson correlation coefficient: A statistic, symbolized by r, that indicates the degree of linear relationship between two variables measured at the interval or ratio level.

coefficient for scores at the interval or ratio level of measurement is the **Pearson correlation coefficient**, symbolized as r. This statistic is named after Karl Pearson (1857–1936), a British statistician who devised the formula for its computation. The **Pearson correlation coefficient** is defined as

$$\text{Pearson correlation coefficient} = r = \frac{\sum (X - \overline{X})(Y - \overline{Y})}{\sqrt{[\sum (X - \overline{X})^2][\sum (Y - \overline{Y})^2]}}$$

where

X = score of a participant on the X variable.
$\overline{X}$ = mean of all scores on the X variable.
Y = score of a participant on the Y variable.
$\overline{Y}$ = mean of all scores on the Y variable.

This formula may be written using simpler notation as

$$r = \frac{CP_{XY}}{\sqrt{(SS_X)(SS_Y)}},$$

where

$CP_{XY} = \sum (X - \overline{X})(Y - \overline{Y})$, the cross products of X and Y (the subscripts X and Y indicate that the cross products are calculated on variables identified as X and Y).
SS_X = sum of squares for the X scores [i.e., $\sum (X - \overline{X})^2$].
SS_Y = sum of squares for the Y scores [i.e., $\sum (Y - \overline{Y})^2$].

The definitional formula is not usually used to actually calculate r. Instead either a standard score formula or a computational formula given later in this chapter is used. But the definitional formula illustrates what the correlation coefficient is measuring. I will work through the derivation of this formula and then present the standard score and computational formulas.

Obtaining a Measure of Covariation: Cross Products

To see how r provides a measure of how much two variables covary, return to the scores of Table 13.1. The scatterplot of these scores (see Figure 13.1) indicated that the scores tend to be positively related: Low scores on loneliness are related to low depression scores, and higher scores on loneliness are related to higher depression scores. I develop a statistic that indicates how much the two variables covary by using a difference score: how much a score differs from the mean of the scores, either $X - \overline{X}$ or $Y - \overline{Y}$. For example, the mean of the loneliness scores in Table 13.1 is 17. Person 2 obtained a loneliness score of 27. If I find $X_2 - \overline{X}$, or $27 - 17 = +10$, we see that person 2 obtained a loneliness score 10 points above the mean of the loneliness scores. Similarly, person 4 obtained a loneliness score of 7. This person's loneliness score could also be expressed as $X_4 - \overline{X}$; in this case, $7 - 17 = -10$, or 10 points below the mean loneliness score. Converting a score into a difference from the mean of the scores indicates both whether the score is above or below the mean and how far below or above it is.

The Y scores could be indexed similarly with respect to their mean, $\overline{Y}$. For example, the mean of the depression scores is 28. Person 2 obtained a depression score of 37. Converting this score to a difference from the mean, I obtain $Y_2 - \overline{Y} = 37 - 28 = +9$. On the other hand, person 4 obtained a depression score of 23. Expressed as a difference from the mean, this score is $Y_4 - \overline{Y} = 23 - 28 = -5$, or 5 points below the mean depression score.

From these difference scores we see that person 2 was above the mean on both loneliness and depression, whereas person 4 was below the mean on both scores. Suppose that I obtain difference scores for both loneliness and depression for all the participants as shown in columns b and d, respectively, of Table 13.2. Notice that four of the six people who are above the mean on loneliness (column b, participants 2, 3, 5, and 8) are also above the mean on depression (column d). Likewise, three of the four participants below the mean on loneliness (column b, subjects 1, 4, and 10) are also below the mean on depression (column d).

A measure of how much the scores covary can be obtained by multiplying each person's difference from the mean on the X variable by his or her difference from the mean on the Y variable and then summing the product of each multiplication over all the subjects. This process is illustrated in column e of Table 13.2. For example, for person 4, $(X - \overline{X})(Y - \overline{Y}) = (-10)(-5) = +50$. The sum of the products in this column is $+367$.

The $\sum (X - \overline{X})(Y - \overline{Y})$ is called the **cross products of X and Y**, symbolized as CP_{XY}, and it forms the numerator of the formula for r. The CP_{XY} reflect the amount and direction of a relationship between two sets of scores. If the scores are positively related as in Table 13.2, the cross products take on a positive value; the more strongly the X and Y

Cross products of X and Y: The value of $\sum (X-\overline{X})(Y-\overline{Y})$ for variables X and Y.

TABLE 13.2
Calculation of the cross products of X and Y. Scores in columns a and c are the loneliness scores and depression scores of Table 13.1, respectively.

	(a) Loneliness	(b) Loneliness	(c) Depression	(d) Depression	(e)
Subject	X	$X - \overline{X}$	Y	$Y - \overline{Y}$	$(X - \overline{X})(Y - \overline{Y})$
1	4	-13	16	-12	$+156$
2	27	$+10$	37	$+9$	$+90$
3	18	$+1$	33	$+5$	$+5$
4	7	-10	23	-5	$+50$
5	30	$+13$	34	$+6$	$+78$
6	12	-5	32	$+4$	-20
7	18	$+1$	24	-4	-4
8	23	$+6$	29	$+1$	$+6$
9	19	$+2$	26	-2	-4
10	12	-5	26	-2	$+10$
$\overline{X}$	17		$\overline{Y}$ 28	Sum	$+367$

scores covary, the larger the CP_{XY} becomes. For negatively related scores, the CP_{XY} is negative and becomes larger as the negative relationship becomes stronger. The value of the CP_{XY} for a negative relationship of X and Y is illustrated in Table 13.3a with the scores of the negative relationship in Figure 13.3. The CP_{XY} is -399 for these scores.

TABLE 13.3

(a) Cross products of X and Y for a negative relationship between loneliness and depression scores.

Subject	Loneliness		Depression		
	X	$X - \overline{X}$	Y	$Y - \overline{Y}$	$(X - \overline{X})(Y - \overline{Y})$
1	5	-10	32	$+7$	-70
2	24	$+9$	23	-2	-18
3	20	$+5$	17	-8	-40
4	12	-3	32	$+7$	-21
5	14	-1	21	-4	$+4$
6	20	$+5$	24	-1	-5
7	28	$+13$	14	-11	-143
8	13	-2	25	0	0
9	6	-9	36	$+11$	-99
10	8	-7	26	$+1$	-7
$\overline{X}$	15		$\overline{Y}$ 25	Sum	-399

(b) Cross products of X and Y for no relationship between loneliness and depression scores.

Subject	Loneliness		Depression		
	X	$X - \overline{X}$	Y	$Y - \overline{Y}$	$(X - \overline{X})(Y - \overline{Y})$
1	24	$+7$	14	-12	-84
2	16	-1	36	$+10$	-10
3	4	-13	24	-2	$+26$
4	12	-5	16	-10	$+50$
5	22	$+5$	28	$+2$	$+10$
6	30	$+13$	26	0	0
7	10	-7	34	$+8$	-56
8	28	$+11$	30	$+4$	$+44$
9	14	-3	28	$+2$	-6
10	10	-7	24	-2	$+14$
$\overline{X}$	17		$\overline{Y}$ 26	Sum	-12

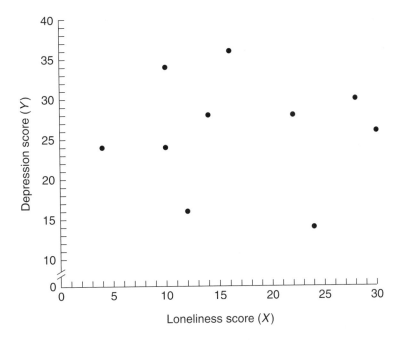

FIGURE 13.5
No relationship between loneliness scores and depression scores for 10 participants. The scores are from Table 13.3b.

When the X and Y scores are not related, the CP_{XY} will be closer to zero. The CP_{XY} for an instance when X and Y are not related is presented in Table 13.3b. Figure 13.5 is a scatterplot of these scores. Notice that the X and Y scores do not covary: High scores on X are not related consistently to either high or low scores on Y. Similarly, low scores on X are not related consistently to either high or low scores on Y. The $CP_{XY} = -12$ calculated in Table 13.3b corresponds to this lack of relationship.

r: Comparing the CP_{XY} with a Measure of the Total Variation in Scores

The CP_{XY} indicates the direction of a relationship between two variables, but the numerical value of the CP_{XY} depends on the units of measurement of X and Y and the number of scores obtained. Two different sets of scores may have the same degree of relationship, but different values of CP_{XY}, because the scores measure different units or because one set of scores involves a larger sample than the other. To be useful as a measure of the covariation of X and Y, CP_{XY} must be put into a form that will take on a common range of values regardless of the unit of measurement used or the number of scores obtained.

The cross products take on a common range of values when they are compared to a measure of the total variation in each set of scores. One measure of variation we have consistently used is the sum of squares (SS). For scores identified as the X variable, $SS_X = \sum (X - \overline{X})^2$, and for the scores identified as the Y variable, $SS_Y = \sum (Y - \overline{Y})^2$. To put the SS into the same units as the cross products, I take the square root of each SS. Then, by multiplying the square root of SS_X by the square root of SS_Y, I obtain a measure of the total variation in the two sets of scores, $\sqrt{(SS_X)(SS_Y)}$. The Pearson correlation coefficient, r, is a ratio of the CP_{XY} to this measure of the total variation. Accordingly, we see that the two definitional formulas for r,

$$r = \frac{\sum (X - \overline{X})(Y - \overline{Y})}{\sqrt{[\sum (X - \overline{X})^2][\sum (Y - \overline{Y})^2]}}$$

and

$$r = \frac{CP_{XY}}{\sqrt{(SS_X)(SS_Y)}},$$

use identical numerical values to obtain r.

Notice that because the denominator of the formula for r involves squared differences it always takes on positive values. Hence, the sign of the correlation coefficient, either positive ($+$) or negative ($-$), is determined by the sign of the numerator. The computation of r on the 10 scores of Table 13.1 using the definitional formula is illustrated in Table 13.4. For each subject,

- Column a is the loneliness score.
- Column b is the difference between the subject's loneliness score and the mean of the loneliness scores (i.e., $X - \overline{X}$).
- Column c is the squared value of column b.
- Column d is the depression score, Y.
- Column e is the difference between the depression score and the mean of the depression scores (i.e., $Y - \overline{Y}$).
- Column f is the squared value of column e.
- Column g presents column b multiplied by column e [i.e., $(X - \overline{X})(Y - \overline{Y})$], or the CP_{XY}.

The SS_X is obtained by summing the values of column c, the SS_Y by summing the values of column f, and the CP_{XY} by summing the values of column g. These sums are then substituted into the formula to obtain a numerical value of r, identified as r_{obs} (see step 2 of Table 13.4). For the scores of Table 13.1, $r_{obs} = +.78$. Before I discuss the interpretation of r_{obs}, however, I present two alternative formulas frequently used to calculate the correlation coefficient.

TABLE 13.4
Calculating r on the loneliness and depression scores of Table 13.1 using the definitional formula.

Step 1. Finding $SS_X = \Sigma (X - \overline{X})^2$, $SS_Y = \Sigma (Y - \overline{Y})^2$, $CP_{XY} = \Sigma (X - \overline{X})(Y - \overline{Y})$

	(a)	(b)	(c)	(d)	(e)	(f)	(g)
	Loneliness			**Depression**			
Subject	X	$X - \overline{X}$	$(X - \overline{X})^2$	Y	$Y - \overline{Y}$	$(Y - \overline{Y})^2$	$(X - \overline{X})(Y - \overline{Y})$
1	4	-13	169	16	-12	144	$+156$
2	27	$+10$	100	37	$+9$	81	$+ 90$
3	18	$+1$	1	33	$+5$	25	$+ 5$
4	7	-10	100	23	-5	25	$+ 50$
5	30	$+13$	169	34	$+6$	36	$+ 78$
6	12	-5	25	32	$+4$	16	$- 20$
7	18	$+1$	1	24	-4	16	$- 4$
8	23	$+6$	36	29	$+1$	1	$+ 6$
9	19	$+2$	4	26	-2	4	$- 4$
10	12	-5	25	26	-2	4	$+ 10$
$\overline{X}$ 17			SS_X 630	$\overline{Y}$ 28		SS_Y 352	CP_{XY} $+367$

Step 2. Calculating r:

$$\Sigma (X - \overline{X})^2 = SS_X = 630,$$

$$\Sigma (Y - \overline{Y})^2 = SS_Y = 352,$$

$$\Sigma (X - \overline{X})(Y - \overline{Y}) = CP_{XY} = +367,$$

and

$$r = \frac{\Sigma (X - \overline{X})(Y - \overline{Y})}{\sqrt{[\Sigma (X - \overline{X})^2][\Sigma (Y - \overline{Y})^2]}}$$

or

$$r = \frac{CP_{XY}}{\sqrt{(SS_X)(SS_Y)}}.$$

Substituting numerical values,

$$r_{obs} = \frac{+367}{\sqrt{(630)(352)}} = +.779 = +.78.$$

ALTERNATIVE FORMULAS FOR THE PEARSON CORRELATION

Standard Scores Formula for r

The definitional formula for r may be rewritten separating the denominator into its two separate sums of squares as follows:

$$r = \frac{\sum (X - \overline{X})(Y - \overline{Y})}{\sqrt{[\sum (X - \overline{X})^2]}\sqrt{[\sum (Y - \overline{Y})^2]}}$$

or

$$r = \frac{\sum (X - \overline{X})(Y - \overline{Y})}{(\sqrt{SS_X})(\sqrt{SS_Y})}.$$

Notice that $(X - \overline{X})/\sqrt{SS_X}$ appears very similar to a standard score, $z = (X - \overline{X})/S$, introduced in Chapter 6. All that is needed to make this expression a standard score is to divide the SS_X by N, the number of scores entering into SS_X, to obtain S_X, the sample standard deviation of the X scores. A similar argument follows for $(Y - \overline{Y})/\sqrt{SS_Y}$. Accordingly, the **standard score formula** for r is

$$r = \frac{\sum (z_X z_Y)}{N_{\text{pairs}}},$$

where
$$z_X = (X - \overline{X})/S_X.$$
$$z_Y = (Y - \overline{Y})/S_Y.$$
$$N_{\text{pairs}} = \text{number of pairs of scores.}$$

The sample standard deviation for the X scores, S_X, is found by

$$S_X = \sqrt{\frac{\sum (X - \overline{X})^2}{N}}$$

and S_Y, the sample standard deviation for the Y scores, by

$$S_Y = \sqrt{\frac{\sum (Y - \overline{Y})^2}{N}}.$$

Table 13.5 illustrates the use of this formula for finding r_{obs} on the scores of Table 13.1. The first step is to obtain S_X and S_Y needed to find the z scores. The values of $\sum (X - \overline{X})^2 = 630$ and $\sum (Y - \overline{Y})^2 = 352$ in this step were obtained from Table 13.4. From these calculations we find that to convert X scores into standard scores $z_X = (X - 17)/7.937$. Similarly, for the Y scores $z_Y = (Y - 28)/5.933$ (see step 2 of the table).

The third step is to convert each raw score into a standard score using the z formulas. Column a of step 3 in Table 13.5 presents the X score for each subject. Column b presents the $X - \overline{X}$ differences for each subject and column c the z score for each X. Similarly,

TABLE 13.5
Calculating r on the loneliness and depression scores of Table 13.1 using the standard score formula.

Step 1: Obtaining S_X and S_Y

$$S_X = \sqrt{\frac{\sum (X - \overline{X})^2}{N_{pairs}}}, \qquad S_Y = \sqrt{\frac{\sum (Y - \overline{Y})^2}{N_{pairs}}}.$$

From Column c of Table 13.4	From Column f of Table 13.4
$\sum (X - \overline{X})^2 = 630$	$\sum (Y - \overline{Y})^2 = 352$
$N_{pairs} = 10$	$N_{pairs} = 10$
$S_X = \sqrt{\dfrac{630}{10}} = 7.937$	$S_Y = \sqrt{\dfrac{352}{10}} = 5.933$

Step 2: Finding z_X, z_Y, and $\sum z_X z_Y$:

To convert X scores to standard scores

$$\overline{X} = 17, \qquad S_X = 7.937.$$

Thus,

$$z_X = \frac{X - 17}{7.937}.$$

To convert Y scores to standard scores:

$$\overline{Y} = 28, \qquad S_Y = 5.933.$$

Thus,

$$z_Y = \frac{Y - 28}{5.933}.$$

Step 3: Converting raw scores to z scores:

	(a)	(b)	(c)	(d)	(e)	(f)	(g)
		Loneliness			Depression		
Subject	X	$X - \overline{X}$	z_X	Y	$Y - \overline{Y}$	z_Y	$z_X z_Y$
1	4	−13	−1.638	16	−12	−2.023	+3.314
2	27	+10	+1.260	37	+9	+1.517	+1.911
3	18	+1	+0.126	33	+5	+0.843	+0.106
4	7	−10	−1.260	23	−5	−0.843	+1.062
5	30	+13	+1.638	34	+6	+1.011	+1.656
6	12	−5	−0.630	32	+4	+0.674	−0.425
7	18	+1	+0.126	24	−4	−0.674	−0.085
8	23	+6	+0.756	29	+1	+0.169	+0.128
9	19	+2	+0.252	26	−2	−0.337	−0.085
10	12	−5	−0.630	26	−2	−0.337	+0.212
$\overline{X}$	17			$\overline{Y}$	28	Sum	+7.794

Step 4: Calculating r:

$\sum (z_X z_Y) = +7.794$ (see column g),

$N_{pairs} = 10$,

$r = \dfrac{\sum (z_X z_Y)}{N_{pairs}}.$

Substituting numerical values,

$$r_{obs} = \frac{+7.794}{10}$$
$$= +.779$$
$$= +.78.$$

column d presents the Y score for each subject. Column e presents the $Y - \overline{Y}$ differences for each subject, and column f the z score for each Y. The z_X and z_Y scores of each subject are multiplied in column g, and the sum of this column, $+7.794$, provides the value of $\sum (z_X z_Y)$ needed for the numerator of the formula for r.

Step 4 of the table illustrates substituting $\sum (z_X z_Y)$ and N_{pairs} into the formula. The $r_{obs} = +.78$, the same value obtained using the definitional formula in Table 13.4. I recommend the standard score method when you have data expressed as standard scores. If scores are not standard scores, then I recommend you use the computational formula that follows.

Computational Formula for r

The value of r using a **computational formula** is given by

$$r = \frac{(N_{pairs})(\sum XY) - (\sum X)(\sum Y)}{\sqrt{[(N_{pairs})(\sum X^2) - (\sum X)^2][(N_{pairs})(\sum Y^2) - (\sum Y)^2]}}.$$

This formula works directly with the raw scores and does not require finding the difference between a score and the mean of the scores. Table 13.6 illustrates using this formula on the scores of Table 13.1. Columns a and b of Table 13.6 present the loneliness (X) and depression (Y) scores, respectively. The sums of these columns, $\sum X = 170$ and $\sum Y = 280$, provide the $\sum X$ and $\sum Y$ needed in the formula. Column c shows each X^2, and the sum of this column, 3520, provides the value of $\sum X^2$. Column d obtains each Y^2, and the sum of this column, 8192, is the value of $\sum Y^2$. Column e obtains the value of XY for each subject, and the sum of this column, 5127, provides the value of $\sum XY$.

Step 2 of Table 13.6 illustrates substituting numerical values into the formula for r. The $r_{obs} = +.78$. Notice that, regardless of the formula used (definitional, z score, or computational), $r_{obs} = +.78$ for the scores of Table 13.1.

There is an additional important point to notice here also. Earlier I indicated that the designation of a variable as X or Y is entirely arbitrary. For the example the loneliness score was designated as X and the depression score as Y. If, however, I had reversed the designation and identified the depression score as X and the loneliness score as Y, the results of the computations for each formula would be identical to those found in Tables 13.4, 13.5, and 13.6. The correlation between the loneliness and depression scores of Table 13.1 is $+.78$ regardless of which variable is designated as X or Y for the computations.

SUMMARY OF FORMULAS FOR r

The four different formulas for r are summarized in Table 13.7. All the formulas produce the same value of r_{obs} when applied to a set of scores.

TABLE 13.6
Calculating r on the loneliness and depression scores of Table 13.1 using the computational formula.

Step 1: Finding $\sum X, \sum Y, \sum X^2, \sum Y^2, \sum XY$:

Subject	(a) X	(b) Y	(c) X^2	(d) Y^2	(e) XY
1	4	16	16	256	64
2	27	37	729	1369	999
3	18	33	324	1089	594
4	7	23	49	529	161
5	30	34	900	1156	1020
6	12	32	144	1024	384
7	18	24	324	576	432
8	23	29	529	841	667
9	19	26	361	676	494
10	12	26	144	676	312
Sums	170	280	3520	8192	5127

Step 2: Calculating r:

$$\sum X = 170 \qquad\qquad \sum Y = 280$$

$$(\sum X)^2 = (170)^2 = 28{,}900 \qquad (\sum Y)^2 = (280)^2 = 78{,}400$$

$$\sum X^2 = 3520 \qquad\qquad \sum Y^2 = 8192$$

$$\sum XY = 5127$$

$$N_{pairs} = 10$$

$$r = \frac{(N_{pairs})(\sum XY) - (\sum X)(\sum Y)}{\sqrt{[(N_{pairs})(\sum X^2) - (\sum X)^2][(N_{pairs})(\sum Y^2) - (\sum Y)^2]}}$$

Substituting numerical values, we obtain

$$r_{obs} = \frac{(10)(5127) - (170)(280)}{\sqrt{[(10)(3520) - 28{,}900][(10)(8192) - 78{,}400]}}$$

$$= \frac{51{,}270 - 47{,}600}{\sqrt{(35{,}200 - 28{,}900)(81{,}920 - 78{,}400)}} = \frac{+3670}{4709.14} = +.779 = +.78$$

TABLE 13.7
Summary of formulas for r.

Definitional formula

$$r = \frac{\sum (X - \bar{X})(Y - \bar{Y})}{\sqrt{[\sum (X - \bar{X})^2][\sum (Y - \bar{Y})^2]}}$$

Definitional formula expressed as CP_{XY} and SS_X, SS_Y

$$r = \frac{CP_{XY}}{\sqrt{(SS_X)(SS_Y)}}$$

Standard scores formula

$$r = \frac{\sum (z_X z_Y)}{N_{\text{pairs}}}$$

Computational formula

$$r = \frac{(N_{\text{pairs}})(\sum XY) - (\sum X)(\sum Y)}{\sqrt{[(N_{\text{pairs}})(\sum X^2) - (\sum X)^2][(N_{\text{pairs}})(\sum Y^2) - (\sum Y)^2]}}$$

TESTING YOUR KNOWLEDGE 13.2

1. Define: cross product, CP_{XY}, r, SS_X, SS_Y.
2. Explain why the cross products provide a measure of the covariation of two sets of scores.
3. Given the following scores:

Subject	Loneliness	Depression
1	4	19
2	12	20
3	28	33
4	18	32
5	14	26
6	6	19
7	22	28
8	23	36
9	15	30
10	18	27

    a. Use the definitional formula to find r_{obs} for these scores.
    b. The scores for this question were drawn from Testing Your Knowledge 13.1, question 3, Table 1. Compare r_{obs} to the scatterplot of the scores constructed for that question. Use this comparison to visualize the relationship a value of r_{obs} describes.
4. Given the following scores:

Subject	Loneliness	Depression
1	5	29
2	11	31
3	23	23
4	17	17
5	28	16
6	13	21
7	12	26
8	4	28
9	21	14
10	16	25

   a.   Use the standard score formula to find r_{obs} for these scores.
   b.   The scores for this question were drawn from Testing Your Knowledge 13.1, question 3, Table 2. Compare r_{obs} to the scatterplot of the scores constructed for that question. Use this comparison to visualize the relationship a value of r_{obs} describes.
5. Given the following scores:

Person	Body Weight	Self-Esteem
1	100	39
2	111	47
3	117	54
4	124	23
5	136	35
6	139	30
7	143	48
8	151	20
9	155	28
10	164	46

   a.   Use the computational formula to find r_{obs} for these scores.
   b.   The scores for this question were drawn from Testing Your Knowledge 13.1, question 4. Compare r_{obs} to the scatterplot of the scores constructed for that question. Use this comparison to visualize the relationship a value of r_{obs} describes.

CHARACTERISTICS OF r

The correlation coefficient reveals both the direction and the degree of linear relationship between two variables. The direction of the relationship is indicated by the positive or negative sign of the correlation coefficient. The degree to which the points on the scatterplot lie on a straight line is given by the absolute value of r, a value that may vary from .00 to 1.00. Combining the sign (+ or −) with the numerical values of r allows r to vary from −1.00 through .00 to +1.00.

Direction of Relationship

Earlier I discussed positive and negative relationships among the scores in a scatterplot. The correlation coefficient indicates the direction of the relationship by the plus or minus sign of the coefficient. A positive r (e.g., $r_{obs} = +.86$) indicates that there is a positive relationship between variables X and Y; as the scores on variable X increase, the scores on variable Y tend to increase also. The scores in Figures 13.1 and 13.2 illustrate positive relationships; $r_{obs} = +.78$ for Figure 13.1 and $r_{obs} = +1.00$ for Figure 13.2.

A negative r (e.g., $r_{obs} = -.86$) indicates an inverse relationship between the variables; as scores increase on variable X, they tend to decrease on variable Y. A negative relation is illustrated in Figures 13.3 and 13.4. Here $r_{obs} = -.83$ for Figure 13.3 and -1.00 for Figure 13.4.

Degree of Relationship

The numerical value of r indicates how well the relationship between variables X and Y is described by a straight line. An r of 1.00 means that the relationship is perfectly linear; all points in the scatterplot lie in a straight line. Figure 13.2 portrays a scatterplot showing a perfect positive correlation, $r_{obs} = +1.00$, for loneliness and depression scores. A perfect negative correlation, $r_{obs} = -1.00$, is illustrated in Figure 13.4. When r equals either plus or minus 1.00, for every value of X there is only one corresponding value of Y. You can see this relationship in either Figure 13.2 or 13.4. For every loneliness score there is only one depression score. This relation allows us to predict perfectly the Y from the X scores. In either Figure 13.2 or 13.4, if you are given a loneliness score, then you can predict perfectly the depression score associated with that loneliness score.

At the other extreme, if the variables are unrelated, then the value of the correlation coefficient approaches zero. When r is about zero, a value of one score is not systematically associated with a value of the other score. Such an instance is shown in Figure 13.5, where $r_{obs} = -.02$.

Values of the correlation coefficient between .00 and 1.00 indicate that there is some, but not a perfect, relationship between X and Y. To illustrate, we notice in Figure 13.1, for which $r = +.78$, that the X and Y variables are not perfectly related. As the loneliness scores increase, the depression scores tend to increase, but knowing a loneliness score does not allow perfect prediction of the depression score. For example, two people obtained a loneliness score of 12, but one subject had a depression score of 32 and the other a depression score of 26.

An analogous negative correlation is demonstrated in Figure 13.3, for which $r_{obs} = -.83$. Here, as loneliness scores increase, depression tends to decrease. But again the relationship is not perfect; knowing the loneliness score does not allow us to perfectly predict the associated depression score. As an example, notice that two people obtained a score of 20 on loneliness, but one subject had a 17 on depression, the other a 24.

It is often difficult to visualize what a value of r might look like if the scores were placed on a scatterplot. This ability is gained only by comparing values of r to a scatterplot of the scores that produced the correlation. Figure 13.6 presents several scatterplots exhibiting different values of r. Panels (a) to (e) of this figure illustrate correlations decreasing from 1.00 to .00. Notice that as r decreases the linear relationship between X and Y becomes less strong, until $r_{obs} = .00$ and there is no relationship remaining.

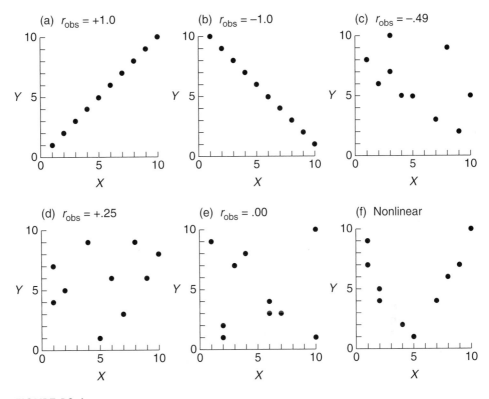

FIGURE 13.6
Scatterplots illustrating various correlations between scores on variable *X* and variable *Y* for 10 scores. The value of the Pearson correlation coefficient between the sets of scores is given by r_{obs}.

The Pearson *r* is a measure of the linear or straight-line relationship between variables *X* and *Y*. Figure 13.6f presents a nonlinear, U-shaped relationship between the *X* and *Y* variables. In this relation, low values of *X* are associated with high values of *Y*. As *X* increases, *Y* decreases to a point; then further increases in *X* are associated with increases in *Y*. This relationship between *X* and *Y* cannot be represented by a straight line, and *r* cannot be used to describe such a relationship.

Restriction of Range and the Value of *r*

The value of *r* is sensitive to the range of values that either the *X* or *Y* variable may take on. As the range of values for one or both of the variables becomes smaller or restricted, the value of *r* also becomes smaller. To illustrate this relationship, consider the scores in Figure 13.1 with $r_{obs} = +.78$. Suppose that I want to examine the relationship of loneliness and depression on only the six participants highest on loneliness. These are loneliness scores that range from 18 to 30 (i.e., loneliness scores from subjects 2, 3, 5, 7, 8, and 9). The range of depression scores for these six people is from 24 to 37. In comparison to the range of loneliness and depression scores for the full 10 participants, the range of both the loneliness and depression scores for the top 6 people has become restricted or truncated (i.e., shortened). The r_{obs} of these six scores is $+.69$, less than the r_{obs} of $+.78$ on the full set of scores.

The implication of this illustration is clear. Correlation coefficients calculated on scores that have a restricted range may lead us to believe that there is no relationship between two variables, when, had a larger range of scores been employed, a relationship would have been found. Accordingly, before calculating a correlation coefficient, carefully examine the scores obtained to determine if they represent a limited range of values.

Coefficient of Determination

Coefficient of determination: The value of r^2 indicating the common variance of variables X and Y.

In Chapter 9, I introduced eta squared as a measure of the strength of the effect of an independent variable on a dependent variable in an experiment. In correlational studies, the **coefficient of determination, r^2** (the squared value of r), provides an analogous measure of the strength of association between X and Y.

The interpretation of r^2 is similar to that of η^2. That is, r^2 indicates the proportion of variance in one set of scores that is related to the variance in the other set of scores. To illustrate, for the scores of Table 13.1 $r_{obs} = +.78$; thus, r_{obs}^2 is equal to $(+.78)^2$, or .61. This value means that these pairs of scores have 61 percent of their variance in common. In other words, 61 percent of the variance in scores for loneliness is associated with the variance in depression scores.

Correlation and Causality

Many variables are highly correlated, but the existence of a correlation between variables X and Y does not imply that one causes the other. If variables X and Y are correlated, then at least three possibilities exist with respect to a causal relation between the variables:

- X causes Y.
- Y causes X.
- Neither X nor Y causally affect each other, but both are caused by a third variable, Z.

Consider the example problem of the correlation between loneliness (variable X) and depression (variable Y). The example resulted in a correlation of $+.78$, indicating that people who are more lonely tend also to be more depressed. Which variable, if either, causally affects the other? Does being lonely cause depression? Or does being depressed cause loneliness? Or does neither of these relationships apply, and a third variable, Z, such as lack of social skills appropriate for forming friendships, cause a person to be both lonely and depressed? These three possible causal relationships are illustrated in Table 13.8. A correlation between two variables indicates only that they are linearly related; it does not provide any information about what causes them to be related.

As another example, smoking (variable X) and stress levels (variable Y) are positively correlated; cigarette smokers typically report higher stress levels than do nonsmokers (Parrott, 1999). This relationship is correlational, found simply by questioning individuals on both their smoking habits and stress levels. The relationship itself is not in question, but the cause of the relationship is (Kassel, 2000). One explanation proposed for this relationship is that smokers have higher stress levels for multiple reasons (variable Z), such as higher job or family stresses than nonsmokers, and smoking is a method used to reduce this stress. A

TABLE 13.8
Possible causal relationships from an observed correlation of
two variables, loneliness (X) and depression (Y).

A. *The observed correlation:*

Positive correlation obtained
between variables X and Y

Individuals high in
loneliness (X) are high
in depression (Y)

Individuals low in
loneliness (X) are low
in depression (Y)

B. *Possible causal relationships that may explain the
observed relationship:*

Possibility 1

variable X causes   variable Y

Loneliness (X) causes a person to be depressed (Y).

Possibility 2

variable Y causes   variable X

Being depressed (Y) causes a person to be lonely
(X).

Possibility 3

variable Z causes   both variables X and Y

The lack of appropriate social skills (variable Z)
causes a person to be both lonely (X) and
depressed (Y).

second explanation that has been offered is that the higher stress level is actually caused by the smoking itself, a product of nicotine dependency. A simple correlational finding, however, cannot answer the question of which, if either, explanation is correct.

Other research studies have indicated a negative correlation between the reported amount of sleep per night (variable X) and energy levels during the day (variable Y); people who sleep less also report higher daytime energy levels. Should you conclude from this relationship that if you lack energy during the day then you should sleep less during the night? The answer is no, for a correlational relationship does not allow such a causal conclusion. Probably a third variable, such as a physiological condition (variable Z) that affects both daytime energy level and the amount of sleep needed, accounts for the observed relationship. These examples illustrate that we must always be aware that a correlational relationship only indicates that two variables are related but tells us nothing about the cause of the relationship.

TESTING YOUR KNOWLEDGE 13.3

1. What does the plus or minus sign of r tell you about the relationship of variables X and Y?
2. What does the numerical value of r tell you about the relationship of variables X and Y?
3. What effect may restricting the range of scores on either the X or Y variable have on the value of r?
4. Calculate the coefficient of determination for the following values of r_{obs}:
   a. $+.12$ **b.** $-.74$ **c.** $-.59$
   d. $-.36$ **e.** $+.23$ **f.** $+.19$
5. You observe a correlation between variables X and Y. Identify the three possible causal relationships that may explain the correlation.
6. Various researchers have reported the following correlations. Identify a third variable that may be responsible for the observed correlation.
   a. A negative correlation between income and blood pressure.
   b. A positive correlation between coffee drinking and cigarette smoking.
   c. A positive correlation between exposure to violence on television and aggressive behavior in children.

TESTING THE STATISTICAL SIGNIFICANCE OF THE PEARSON r

The Population Correlation, ρ

ρ: Rho, the symbol for the population correlation coefficient.

The Pearson r describes the linear relationship between the X and Y scores of a sample. As with any set of scores, the sample is drawn from a larger population of scores, and I may wish to test if a correlation exists among the X and Y scores in the population. In a population, a linear correlation between X and Y scores is represented by the parameter ρ (the seventeenth letter of the Greek alphabet, *rho*, pronounced "row"). In the example problem of the correlation between loneliness and depression, $r_{obs} = +.78$ provides an estimate of ρ. As with any statistic, r_{obs}, because it is obtained from a sample, will vary from sample to sample, even though the samples are from the same population and, thus, it is unlikely that r_{obs} will be equal to ρ. Accordingly, I may test a statistical hypothesis that r_{obs} represents a sample from a population with a specific ρ. Although it is possible to test hypotheses concerning any value of ρ, the most commonly tested hypothesis is that ρ equals zero in the population sampled.

Testing for a Nonzero Correlation in the Population

The statistical test to determine if r is a chance difference from a zero correlation in the population is straightforward. The familiar steps of statistical hypothesis testing are followed:

- A null hypothesis, H_0, and an alternative hypothesis, H_1, are formulated.
- The sampling distribution of r, assuming that H_0 is true, is obtained. This distribution is given in Table A.5.
- A significance level is selected.
- A critical value of r, identified as r_{crit}, is found from the sampling distribution of r given in Table A.5.

- A rejection region is located in the sampling distribution of r.
- The correlation coefficient, identified as r_{obs}, is calculated from the sample data.
- A decision to reject or not reject H_0 is made on the basis of whether or not r_{obs} falls into the rejection region.

Statistical Hypotheses

Null Hypothesis.   The null hypothesis is

$$H_0: \rho = 0.$$

This hypothesis states that the correlation between the X and Y variables is zero in the population.

Alternative Hypothesis.   The alternative hypothesis is

$$H_1: \rho \neq 0.$$

This hypothesis states that the correlation between the X and Y variables is not zero in the population.

Sampling Distribution of r and Critical Values

Because r may take on values only between .00 to 1.00, its sampling distribution under H_0: $\rho = 0$ may be determined readily. As is the case with most other statistical tests, however, the sampling distribution of r depends on its degrees of freedom. The **df for r are equal to $N_{pairs} - 2$**, where N_{pairs} is the number of pairs of scores from which r is calculated. Critical values of r, identified as r_{crit}, from sampling distributions of r with df ranging from 1 to 100 are presented in Table A.5 for $\alpha = .05$ and .01.

Locating a Rejection Region

If H_1 is true, I expect to obtain values of r greater than zero. Accordingly, the rejection region for r_{obs} is a value of r equal to or greater than r_{crit}. An r_{obs} equal to or larger in absolute value (that is, ignoring the $+$ or $-$ sign of r_{obs}) than r_{crit} falls into the rejection region. The probability of such an r_{obs} is equal to or less than the value of alpha if H_0 is true.

Decision Rules

The decision rules for the statistical hypotheses follow the common pattern:

- If r_{obs} falls into the rejection region, then:
    Reject $H_0 : \rho = 0$.
    Accept $H_1 : \rho \neq 0$.
- If r_{obs} does not fall into the rejection region, then:
    Do not reject H_0.
    Do not accept H_1.

I illustrate this process in the example problems that follow. Table 13.9 summarizes the decisions and conclusions reached from a statistical test on r.

TABLE 13.9
Summary of decisions and conclusions in statistical hypothesis testing with r. A .05 significance level is illustrated.

If r_{obs} falls into the rejection region for $\alpha = .05$, then:	If r_{obs} does not fall into the rejection region for $\alpha = .05$, then:
Probability of r_{obs} is less than or equal to .05, or $p \leq .05$.	Probability of r_{obs} is greater than .05, or $p > .05$.
$H_0 : \rho = 0$ is rejected.	H_0 is not rejected.
$H_1: \rho \neq 0$ is accepted. The r_{obs} is treated as estimating a population ρ different from zero.	H_1 is not accepted.
r_{obs} is statistically significant at the .05 level.	r_{obs} is not statistically significant at the .05 level.
It is decided that the X and Y variables are correlated in the population from which the sample was selected.	It is decided that the X and Y variables are not correlated in the population from which the sample was selected.

Assumptions of the Test for Statistical Significance of r

The test for statistical significance of r assumes that X and Y form a bivariate normal distribution in the population. A **bivariate normal distribution** possesses the following characteristics:

Bivariate normal distribution: A distribution of X and Y variables in which (1) the X scores are normally distributed in the population sampled, (2) the Y scores are normally distributed in the population sampled, (3) for each X score the distribution of Y scores in the population is normal, and (4) for each Y score the distribution of X scores in the population is normal.

- The X scores, loneliness scores in the example, are normally distributed in the population sampled.
- The Y scores, depression scores in the example, are normally distributed in the population sampled.
- For each X score, the distribution of Y scores in the population is normal. Using the example, this assumption means that for each loneliness score in the population there is a normal distribution of depression scores.
- For each Y score, the distribution of X scores in the population is normal. This assumption is similar to the previous assumption, except now for each depression score in the population there is a normal distribution of loneliness scores.

For many paired measures of behavior, we may assume that they form a bivariate normal distribution in the population and thus test for a nonzero correlation of the scores in the population.

Example Problem 13.1

Testing the Statistical Significance of r_{obs} between Loneliness and Depression

Problem: The Pearson correlation for the loneliness and depression scores of Table 13.1 was found to be $r_{obs} = +.78$. Does this sample value indicate the presence of a nonzero correlation between loneliness and depression scores in the population from which the participants were sampled? Use a .05 significance level.

Solution: The problem requires that I test the statistical hypothesis that the population correlation, ρ, for loneliness and depression scores is zero.

Statistic to Be Used: $r_{obs} = +.78$.

Assumptions for Use: Loneliness and depression scores possess a bivariate normal distribution in the population from which the scores were sampled.

Statistical Hypotheses:

$$H_0: \rho = 0$$
$$H_1: \rho \neq 0$$

Significance Level: $\alpha = .05$.

df: $df = N_{pairs} - 2 = 10 - 2 = 8$.

Critical Value of r: $r_{crit}(8) = .632$ from Table A.5.

Rejection Regions: Values of r_{obs} equal to or greater in absolute value than .632.

Decision: The $r_{obs} = +.78$ is greater in absolute value than $r_{crit} = .632$. Accordingly, it falls into the rejection region. Therefore, we

$$\text{Reject } H_0 : \rho = 0,$$
$$\text{Accept } H_1 : \rho \neq 0.$$

Conclusion: Loneliness and depression scores are significantly correlated in the population; the $r_{obs} = +.78$ is not simply a chance difference from a true population correlation of zero. The best estimate I have of the population correlation is provided by $r_{obs} = +.78$. Lonely people tend to be depressed. The coefficient of determination $r_{obs}^2 = (+.78)^2 = .61$, indicating that loneliness and depression have 61 percent of their variance in common.

Example Problem 13.2

Is a Sense of Humor Related to Physical Health?

Problem: One characteristic often noted about others is their sense of humor. Carroll and Shmidt (1992) hypothesized that having a good sense of humor may be related to good physical health, for those who can deal with anxiety-evoking situations with humor may be able to control the stresses of life more easily. Suppose that you test this hypothesis by measuring 16 people on their sense of humor and their physical health. Sense of humor is measured using the Situation Humor Response Questionnaire (Martin & Lefcourt, 1984). This questionnaire presents descriptions of 18 situations and asks a person to rate each situation on a scale from 1 to 5 on how amusing they would find the situation. Accordingly, scores on this questionnaire may range from 18 to 90, with higher scores indicating more use of humor in dealing with situations. Physical health is measured by having participants complete a 20-item self-report inventory on health problems. Scores on this inventory may range from zero (no reported health problems) to 20 (20 reported health problems). You obtain the following scores on these two measures.

Participant	Humor Questionnaire: X	Physical Health: Y
1	36	9
2	68	3
3	61	12
4	47	12
5	35	15
6	48	17
7	42	10
8	30	17
9	56	11
10	39	17
11	51	14
12	54	8
13	60	3
14	29	13
15	65	7
16	47	8

Is the humor questionnaire score related to the number of reported health problems? Use a .05 significance level.

Solution: The problem requires testing a statistical hypothesis that the population correlation, ρ, for humor questionnaire and health problems scores is zero.

Statistic to Be Used: r.

Assumption for Use: The humor questionnaire and health problems scores possess bivariate normal distributions in the populations from which the scores were sampled.

Statistical Hypotheses: $H_0: \rho = 0$

$H_1: \rho \neq 0$

Significance Level: $\alpha = .05$.

df: $df = N_{pairs} - 2 = 16 - 2 = 14$.

Critical Value of r: $r_{crit}(14) = .497$ from Table A.5.

Rejection Regions: Values of r_{obs} equal to or greater in absolute value than .497.

Calculation: The computational formula

$$r = \frac{(N_{pairs})(\sum XY) - (\sum X)(\sum Y)}{\sqrt{[(N_{pairs})(\sum X^2) - (\sum X)^2][(N_{pairs})(\sum Y^2) - (\sum Y)^2]}}$$

will be used to obtain r_{obs}. The numerical values needed for this formula are

$$N_{pairs} = 16$$

$$\sum XY = 7908$$

$$\sum X = 768$$

$$\sum Y = 176$$

$$\sum X^2 = 39,092$$

$$\sum Y^2 = 2242$$

$$(\sum X)^2 = 589,824$$

$$(\sum Y)^2 = 30,976.$$

Substituting values into the formula,

$$r_{obs} = \frac{16(7908) - (768)(176)}{\sqrt{[16(39,092) - 589,824][16(2242) - 30,976]}} = \frac{-8640}{13,211.079} = -.65$$

$$r_{obs}^2 = (-.65)^2 = .42.$$

Decision: The value of $r_{obs} = -.65$ is greater in absolute value than $r_{crit} = .497$ and, thus, falls into the rejection region. The decisions with respect to H_0 and H_1 are

$$\text{Reject } H_0: \rho = 0,$$
$$\text{Accept } H_1: \rho \neq 0.$$

Conclusion: There is a significant negative correlation between humor questionnaire scores and self-reported health problems in the population sampled. People who scored higher on the humor questionnaire reported fewer physical health problems than did those who obtained lower humor questionnaire scores. The coefficient of determination indicates that the humor questionnaire and health scores have 42 percent of their variance in common.

REPORTING THE RESULTS OF A CORRELATIONAL STUDY

The report of a correlational study should include the value of r_{obs}, the *df* for r_{obs}, the significance level used, and whether or not r_{obs} was statistically significant. Often, the mean and standard deviation for each set of scores are included in the report. To illustrate, I use the example of the correlation between loneliness and depression.

> With an alpha level of .05, there was a significant correlation between the loneliness $(M = 17.0, SD = 8.4)$ and depression scores $(M = 28.0, SD = 6.3)$, $r(8) = +.78$, $p < .01$. The loneliness and depression scores were significantly positively related.

THE SPEARMAN RANK-ORDER CORRELATION COEFFICIENT

Spearman rank-order correlation coefficient (r_s):
A correlation coefficient used with ordinal measurements.

The Pearson r is appropriate when scores on the variables to be correlated are interval or ratio measures. Sometimes, however, measures represent rank ordering on both the X and Y variables. When ranked scores are obtained, the **Spearman rank-order correlation coefficient**, symbolized by r_s, is commonly used to quantify the relationship between the two sets of scores. The Spearman rank-order correlation coefficient is found from the formula

$$r_s = 1 - \left[\frac{6 \sum D^2}{(N_{pairs})(N^2_{pairs} - 1)} \right],$$

where D = difference in a pair of ranked scores for a subject.

N_{pairs} = number of pairs of ranks in the study.

As with the Pearson r, values of r_s may be positive or negative and range from -1.00 through .00 to $+1.00$.

An Example of the Use of r_s

We have all observed that animals within a species behave differently from each other. To study differences in animal behaviors, Feaver, Mendl, and Bateson (1986) developed a method of measuring behaviors such as playing, chasing, fleeing, crouching, and so forth. Suppose that an investigator using this technique hypothesizes that playing (X) and chasing (Y) behaviors are related in cats. Ten cats are observed for a period of time in the same environment and ranked separately on playing and chasing behaviors. The most playful cat receives a rank of 1 and the least playful a rank of 10. Similarly, the cat that chases most is ranked 1 and the cat that chases least is ranked 10.

Ranks of the 10 cats on playing and chasing behaviors are presented in columns a and b of Table 13.10. Cats 1 and 10 were judged to be equal in chasing behavior. Therefore, both cats were assigned the same rank, 6.5, which is the average of the two ranks, 6 and 7, that would be assigned to them if they were not tied.

The procedures involved in calculating r_s are illustrated in the remainder of Table 13.10. The first step is to find the difference, D, in each pair of ranks by subtracting one rank from the other. This step is shown in column c, where the chasing rank (Y) is subtracted from the playing rank (X) for each cat. Then each D is squared, as shown in column d. The sum of this column, 80.50, provides the value of $\sum D^2$. The $\sum D^2$ and N_{pairs} are substituted into the formula, and r_s is calculated; $r_{s\,obs} = +.51$.

TABLE 13.10
Calculating the Spearman rank-order correlation coefficient (r_s) on playing and chasing behavior of 10 cats. Columns a and b present ranks of each cat on chasing and playing behavior, respectively.

Cat	(a) Playing: X	(b) Chasing: Y	(c) $D = (X - Y)$	(d) $D^2 = (X - Y)^2$
1	2	6.5	−4.5	20.25
2	6	8	−2	4.00
3	8	4	4	16.00
4	4	1	3	9.00
5	7	5	2	4.00
6	5	9	−4	16.00
7	10	10	0	0.00
8	3	2	1	1.00
9	1	3	−2	4.00
10	9	6.5	2.5	6.25
			Sum	80.50

The formula for r_s is

$$r_{s\,obs} = 1 - \left[\frac{6 \sum D^2}{(N_{pairs})(N_{pairs}^2 - 1)} \right]$$

Substituting the values of $\sum D^2 = 80.50$ and $N_{pairs} = 10$,

$$r_{s\,obs} = 1 - \left[\frac{(6)(80.50)}{(10)(10^2 - 1)} \right] = 1 - 0.488$$

$$= +.512 = +.51, \text{ rounded to two decimal places.}$$

Statistical Significance of the Spearman Rank-Order Correlation

The test for the statistical significance of r_s is similar to that for the Pearson r. The null hypothesis is that the rank-order correlation in the population, symbolized by ρ_s, is zero, or $H_0 : \rho_s = 0$. The alternative hypothesis is that the population correlation is not zero, or $H_1 : \rho_s \neq 0$. Critical values of r_s for the .05 and .01 levels are presented in Table A.6. The critical values are based on N_{pairs} rather than degrees of freedom. If $r_{s\,obs}$ is equal to or larger in absolute value than the critical value, then the decision is to reject H_0 and accept H_1.

For the example, the critical value of r_s for $N_{pairs} = 10$ and $\alpha = .05$ is .648. Because $r_{s\,obs} = +.51$ is smaller than the critical value, the null hypothesis is not rejected at the .05 level. The relationship between the ranks on playing and chasing is not statistically significant; playing and chasing behaviors were not related in the sample observed.

Characteristics of r_s

The Spearman correlation coefficient shows the agreement of the ranks of two variables. If variables X and Y are ranked identically, then r_s will be $+1.00$. If the variables are ranked oppositely, so that a rank of 1 on variable X corresponds to the lowest rank on variable Y, and the lowest rank on variable X corresponds to a rank of 1 on variable Y, then r_s will be -1.00. If there is no agreement on the rankings, then r_s will be about zero. When there is some, but not perfect, agreement on the ranks, then r_s will take on a value between $.00$ and 1.00. The direction of the relationship is indicated by the plus or minus sign of the correlation.

TESTING YOUR KNOWLEDGE 13.4

1. Define: bivariate normal distribution, ρ.
2. Identify the statistical hypotheses needed to test if r_{obs} differs significantly from zero.
3. For each of the following values of N_{pairs}, determine the df and then find the r_{crit} for $\alpha = .05$ and $\alpha = .01$ from Table A.5. $N_{pairs} =$

    a. 8   b. 15   c. 20
    d. 32   e. 43   f. 75

4. For each of the following r_{obs} and N_{pairs}, identify the statistical null and alternative hypotheses; then find r_{crit} at the .05 significance level. Indicate whether the r_{obs} falls into a rejection region and then indicate your decisions with respect to the statistical hypotheses.

	r_{obs}	N_{pairs}
a.	+.580	12
b.	−.346	12
c.	−.682	20
d.	+.204	24
e.	+.249	80
f.	−.731	9

5. College professors often believe that class attendance and course grades are correlated. Suppose that a professor maintained attendance records and found the following number of absences from class and examination averages for 12 students:

Student	Absences	Exam Average
1	22	72
2	6	88
3	1	99
4	8	78
5	6	66
6	11	77
7	10	52
8	6	78
9	10	76
10	0	96
11	5	91
12	10	86

a. Find the value of r_{obs} for these scores using the computational formula.
b. Test to determine if r_{obs} differs significantly from a population correlation of zero.
c. What do you conclude about the relationship of absences and exam averages?

6. For each of the following observed values of r_s and N_{pairs}, identify the statistical null hypotheses; then find r_{crit} at the .05 significance level. Indicate whether the observed r_s falls into a rejection region and then indicate your decisions with respect to the statistical hypotheses.

	r_s	N_{pairs}
a.	+.401	17
b.	−.620	12
c.	+.541	24
d.	−.366	10
e.	+.544	21
f.	−.377	30

SUMMARY

- Correlational studies attempt to find the extent to which two or more variables are related.
- In a scatterplot, one of the two scores (variable X) is represented on the horizontal axis (the abscissa) and the other measure (variable Y) is plotted on the vertical axis (the ordinate). The score of a subject on each of the two variables is represented by one point on the scatterplot.
- In a positive or direct relationship, as the value of variable X increases, the value of variable Y also increases.
- In a negative or inverse relationship, as the value of variable X increases, the value of variable Y decreases.
- The Pearson correlation coefficient is defined as

$$r = \frac{\sum (X - \overline{X})(Y - \overline{Y})}{\sqrt{[\sum (X - \overline{X})^2][\sum (Y - \overline{Y})^2]}}.$$

- The $\sum (X - \overline{X})(Y - \overline{Y})$ is the cross product of X and Y and is symbolized as CP_{XY}. Thus, the correlation coefficient also may be expressed as

$$r = \frac{CP_{XY}}{\sqrt{(SS_X)(SS_Y)}}.$$

- The value of r using standard scores is given by

$$r = \frac{\sum (z_X z_Y)}{N_{pairs}}.$$

- The value of r using a computational formula is given by

$$r = \frac{(N_{pairs})(\sum XY) - (\sum X)(\sum Y)}{\sqrt{[(N_{pairs})(\sum X^2) - (\sum X)^2][(N_{pairs})(\sum Y^2) - (\sum Y)^2]}}.$$

- The direction of a relationship is indicated by the positive or negative sign of r.
- The degree to which the points on the scatterplot lie on a straight line is given by the absolute value of r, a value that may vary from .00 to 1.00.
- A linear correlation between variables X and Y is represented in a population by ρ.
- The statistical significance of r is tested using Table A.5.
- The coefficient of determination, r^2, indicates the proportion of variance in the X variable that is related to the variance in the Y variable.
- If variables X and Y are correlated, then at least three possibilities exist with respect to the causal relations among the variables:
    - X causally affects Y.
    - Y causally affects X.
    - Neither X nor Y causally affect each other, but both are causally affected by a third variable, Z.
- The Spearman rank-order correlation coefficient is found by

$$r_s = 1 - \left[\frac{6 \sum D^2}{(N_{pairs})(N_{pairs}^2 - 1)} \right].$$

- The statistical significance of r_s is tested using Table A.6.

KEY TERMS AND SYMBOLS

bivariate distribution (367)
bivariate normal distribution (392)
coefficient of determination (r^2) (388)
correlation coefficient (373)
correlational study (367)
covary (369)

cross products of X and Y (CP_{XY}) (375)
linear relationship (369)
negative relationship (370)
Pearson correlation coefficient (r) (374)
positive relationship (369)
ρ (390)

ρ_s (397)
scatterplot (368)
Spearman rank-order correlation coefficient (r_s) (396)
SS_X (378)
SS_Y (378)

REVIEW QUESTIONS

1. Review Question 3 of Chapter 1 indicated that a recent study reported a relationship between anger levels and blood pressure for males. Suppose an experimenter

interested in this topic obtains anger level scores and systolic blood pressure in millimeters of mercury from 16 male participants. Anger level scores were obtained using a rating scale in which scores could range from 10 to 100 with higher scores indicating higher levels of anger. The following scores were obtained.

Participant	Anger Level	Blood Pressure
1	64	170
2	30	132
3	37	129
4	39	144
5	17	145
6	29	122
7	36	124
8	34	145
9	44	137
10	32	115
11	37	127
12	47	148
13	50	148
14	41	144
15	46	133
16	61	158

   a. Construct a scatterplot of the anger score (on the abscissa) and blood pressure (on the ordinate).

   b. Does the relationship between the scores on the scatterplot appear to be positive or negative, or is there no relationship apparent?

   c. Calculate r_{obs} using the computational formula and test to find if it differs significantly from a correlation of zero in the population at the .05 significance level.

   d. What conclusion do you reach about the relationship of anger level and systolic blood pressure scores in the sample?

   e. Calculate r^2. What proportion of the variation in anger level and systolic blood pressure is common to the two measures?

   f. Report the results of your study following the example in the Reporting the Results of a Correlational Study section of this chapter.

2. Our reaction to others is often based on their physical appearance. For males, at least, tallness frequently seems to evoke positive reactions from others. As the old adage says, "tall, dark, and handsome." Following this line of thinking, Villimez, Eisenberg, and Carroll (1986) were interested in finding if any relationships exist between physical size and academic performance for primary school children. They obtained a number of measures of childrens' size and related them to test scores and report card grades. Holding age constant to control for height differences related to age, they found an r_{obs} of $-.12$ between height and report card grades for 53 third-grade girls and an r_{obs} of $+.32$ for 42 third-grade boys.

a. Test each correlation coefficient to find if it differs significantly at the .05 level from a correlation of zero in the population sampled.

b. Calculate the coefficient of determination for each value of r_{obs}.

c. What conclusion do you reach concerning the relationship between height and report card grades in primary school children?

3. Students are often interested in predicting their final examination grade from the grade received on a midterm examination. To make such predictions, grades on the midterm and final exam must be correlated. Suppose that for an elementary statistics class the following grades were obtained for 10 students on a midterm and final examination.

	Examination	
Student	**Midterm: X**	**Final: Y**
1	87	84
2	89	91
3	97	96
4	80	87
5	73	66
6	85	90
7	81	79
8	74	80
9	80	89
10	89	86

a. Plot a scatterplot of the midterm exam (on the abscissa) and final exam (on the ordinate).

b. Does the relationship between the scores on the scatterplot appear to be positive or negative, or is no relationship apparent?

c. Calculate r_{obs} using the computational formula and test to find if it differs significantly from a correlation of zero in the population at the .05 significance level.

d. What conclusion do you reach about the relationship of midterm exam grades and final exam grades in the sample?

4. Krantz (1987) found that physical attractiveness and popularity are positively correlated for kindergarten girls, but not for kindergarten boys. Suppose that you conducted a similar study and had an observer rank kindergarten children on physical attractiveness and popularity. Twelve girls and 14 boys were ranked, and you found the following rankings.

Girls

Child	Physical Attractiveness: X	Popularity: Y
1	3	1
2	6	7
3	2	3
4	9	10
5	12	11
6	1	3
7	7	8
8	8	7
9	4	5
10	10	9
11	5	6
12	11	12

Boys

Child	Physical Attractiveness: X	Popularity: Y
1	5	9
2	11	1
3	3	10
4	9	4
5	4	6
6	8	12
7	12	5
8	1	13
9	14	8
10	10	14
11	6	2
12	13	11
13	2	7
14	7	3

a. Calculate $r_{s\,obs}$ on the scores of the girls and test to find if it differs significantly from a correlation of zero in the population at the .05 significance level.

b. What conclusion do you reach about the relationship of physical attractiveness and popularity rankings for the girls?

c. Calculate $r_{s\,obs}$ on the scores of the boys and test to find if it differs significantly from a correlation of zero in the population at the .05 significance level.

d. What conclusion do you reach about the relationship of physical attractiveness and popularity rankings for the boys?

5. A study by Wong (1993) measured 76 college students with the Wechsler Adult Intelligence Scale—Revised and correlated the resulting IQ scores with the students' grade-point averages. The range of IQ scores was from 83 to 133. The r_{obs} between IQ score and grade-point average was +.18, which is nonsignificant at the .05 level. Identify one reason why there may be no correlation between the two variables in this study.

6. As computers become more common in the workplace and home, there is increasing interest in the possible effects of prolonged viewing of a computer screen on perceptual abilities. A study by Weiss, Kimmel, and Stein (1993) correlated a measure of depth perception to the number of hours a person had spent working on a computer immediately prior to the test of depth perception. They measured the number of hours a participant had been working on a computer and the amount of error (in centimeters) in aligning two vertical rods in a depth-perception test. If the participant had perfect depth perception, the error score would be zero centimeters. If a participant was unable to align the two rods perfectly, there would be an error; the larger the error, the poorer the depth perception. Suppose that you measured 13 people on the number of hours they had worked on a computer and on a test of depth perception immediately after they had finished on the computer and obtained the following scores.

Participant	Hours of Computer Use: X	Depth-Perception Error (cm): Y
1	0.5	4.3
2	1.7	3.1
3	4.2	2.1
4	6.0	0.4
5	2.8	6.3
6	5.3	3.7
7	0.9	1.6
8	3.4	1.2
9	1.4	2.4
10	5.1	5.2
11	1.9	0.6
12	4.8	4.1
13	2.6	5.4

a. Construct a scatterplot of the hours of computer use (on the abscissa) and depth-perception error (on the ordinate).

b. Does the relationship between the scores on the scatterplot appear to be positive or negative, or is no relationship apparent?

c. Calculate r_{obs} using the computational formula and test to find if it differs significantly from a correlation of zero in the population at the .05 significance level.

d. What conclusion do you reach about the relationship of the hours of computer use and depth-perception error in the sample?

7. Huebner and McCullough (2000) investigated factors affecting adolescents' satisfaction with school. One of the variables studied was the number of negative daily events associated with school. Negative daily events include such aspects as worrying about performance in a class, having a bad teacher, or interacting with disliked people. Suppose an investigator interested in this problem asks 15 adolescents to keep a record of the negative daily events associated with school and to evaluate their school satisfaction on a summated rating scale in which scores may range from 6 (very low satisfaction) to 48 (very high satisfaction) and obtained the following scores:

Student	Negative Events	School Satisfaction
1	7	34
2	14	14
3	8	24
4	19	15
5	6	29
6	10	27
7	17	14
8	7	38
9	12	19
10	17	21
11	6	29
12	9	27
13	13	18
14	22	18
15	5	30

a. Construct a scatterplot of the number of negative events (on the abscissa) and school satisfaction (on the ordinate).

b. Does the relationship between the scores on the scatterplot appear to be positive or negative, or is there no relationship apparent?

c. Calculate r_{obs} using the computational formula and test to find if it differs significantly from a correlation of zero in the population at the .05 significance level.

d. What conclusion do you reach about the relationship between the number of negative events and school satisfaction in the sample?

8. Chapter 1 introduced the work of Woehr and Cavell (1993) and Cavell and Woehr (1994) on the correlates of performance on the first exam in an introductory psychology course. One variable measured was the number of hours of TV a student reported watching per week. Suppose you asked 17 of your friends to record the number of hours of TV they watched per week so you could correlate it against their first exam grade in a course. From the scores, you obtained the following values: For TV watching, $SS_X = 652$; for first exam grade, $SS_Y = 2094$; and $CP_{XY} = -859$.

a. Use these values to find r_{obs} between TV watching and exam grade.

b. Is the value of r_{obs} statistically significant at the .05 level?

c. Suppose one friend reported watching TV 4 hours per week whereas another friend reported watching TV 15 hours per week. What would the correlation you found lead you to predict about their first exam score?

9. A teacher interested in finding if a relationship exists between how well children are liked by others in their class and a child's participation in class activities ranked fifth grade students on the two dimensions. Suppose the following ranks were obtained for 16 children:

Child	Liking Rank	Participation Rank
1	6	8
2	9	12
3	1	2
4	2	4
5	16	14
6	3	1
7	8	11
8	4	3
9	10	5
10	5	6
11	15	13
12	12	9
13	7	7
14	13	10
15	14	16
16	11	15

a. Find the value of r_s for these scores.

b. Test to determine if the observed r_s differs significantly from a population correlation of zero.

c. What do you conclude about the relationship of liking and class participation?

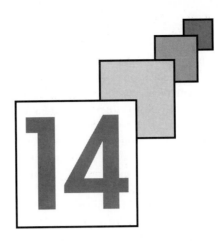

Regression and Prediction

The discussion of correlation in Chapter 13 indicated that if two variables were correlated perfectly, such as the scores in Figures 13.2 and 13.4, then knowing the value of one variable permits a perfect prediction of the value of the other variable. But even if variables X and Y are not correlated perfectly, I still may use the score on one variable to predict the score on the second when a statistically significant correlation exists between the two variables. There are many reasons why we want to predict one variable from another. Suppose, for example, that you want to know what your first examination score in a course might indicate about your final grade. Here you want to predict your final course grade from the first examination grade. College admission officers want to predict grade-point averages from standardized achievement tests. Personnel managers may predict employee performance from employment test scores. And your doctor may predict your risk of developing a certain disease from the results of a medical test. Other examples are given later in the chapter.

This chapter deals with predicting one variable from another when the two variables are related linearly. The approach I take is to fit a straight line, called a *linear regression line*, to a scatterplot of the two variables and use this regression line to predict one score from the other. Two variables may be related in a nonlinear way also, but the following discussion is limited only to straight-line relationships. I begin with several simple examples of linear relationships; then I introduce an example of predicting depression scores from responses to a questionnaire on loneliness.

LINEAR RELATIONS

Definition of a Linear Relation

Linear relation: A relation between two variables such that each time that variable X changes by 1 unit, variable Y changes by a constant amount.

A linear relationship between two variables is a straight-line relationship between the variables. Figure 14.1 illustrates two variables, X and Y, that are perfectly positively linearly related. This figure permits us to more completely define a linear relation. In a **linear relation**, each time one variable changes by one unit there is a constant change in the second variable. In Figure 14.1, for each 1-unit increase in X, Y increases by 0.5 unit. For example, as X increases from 2 to 3 (1 unit on the X measurement), Y increases from 1.0 to 1.5 (0.5 unit on the Y measurement). Similarly, as X increases from 4 to 5 (1 unit on the X measurement), Y increases from 2.0 to 2.5 (0.5 unit on the Y measurement). In this illustration, then, a change in X of 1 unit of its measurement results in a constant change of 0.5 unit on the Y measure.

The requirement of a linear relationship that a change of 1 unit in the X variable be accompanied by a constant amount of change in the Y variable applies whether the relationship is positive or negative. Figure 14.2 illustrates a perfect negative linear relationship between X and Y. Each time X changes by 1 unit, Y also changes by a constant amount. For example, as X changes 1 unit from 2 to 3, Y changes from 9.4 to 8.6, a change of -0.8 on the Y measurement. Similarly, a change of X from 8 to 9 results in a change of Y from 4.6 to 3.8, again a change of -0.8 on the Y measurement. For the linear relationship in Figure 14.2, every change in X of 1 unit is accompanied by a corresponding and constant change of Y of -0.8 unit.

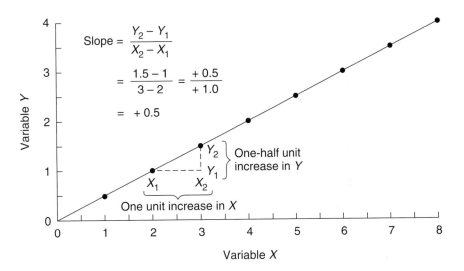

FIGURE 14.1
A perfect positive linear relationship between variable X and variable Y with a slope of +0.5.

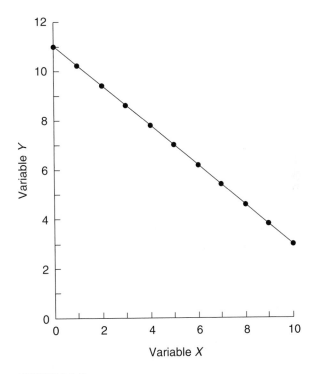

FIGURE 14.2
A perfect negative linear relationship between variable X and variable Y with a slope of −0.8 and a Y-intercept of +11.

The **general equation of a straight line** is given by

$$Y = bX + a,$$

where $Y =$ score on the Y variable.

$X =$ score on the X variable.

$b =$ slope of the line.

$a =$ constant called the Y-intercept.

This equation is used to predict the value of variable Y from the value of variable X.

Slope of a Line

In Figures 14.1 and 14.2, every change in X by 1 unit of its measure is accompanied by a corresponding and constant change in the Y variable. The relationship of the change in the Y variable corresponding to a change in the X variable is the **slope of the straight line** relating the two variables. Specifically, the slope of a line relating variables X and Y is symbolized by b and defined as

$$\textbf{Slope} = \boldsymbol{b} = \frac{\textbf{Change in value of } Y}{\textbf{Change in value of } X}$$

This relationship is expressed as

$$b = \frac{Y_2 - Y_1}{X_2 - X_1},$$

where X_1 and $X_2 =$ two values of X.

Y_1 and $Y_2 =$ values of Y corresponding to X_1 and X_2, respectively.

The numerical values presented in Figure 14.1 allow us to find the slope of the line relating X and Y using the values of $X_1 = 2$ and $X_2 = 3$. The values of Y corresponding to these X values are $Y_1 = 1$ and $Y_2 = 1.5$, respectively. Thus,

$$b = \frac{Y_2 - Y_1}{X_2 - X_1} = \frac{1.5 - 1}{3 - 2} = \frac{+0.5}{+1} = +0.5.$$

The slope of this straight line is $+0.5$; for every increase of 1 unit in X, Y increases by 0.5 unit. The slope of a straight line is constant over its length. Thus, regardless of the values of X used, b will be $+0.5$ for this example. For instance, suppose I use $X_1 = 3$ and $X_2 = 5$. For these values of X, the corresponding Y values are $Y_1 = 1.5$ and $Y_2 = 2.5$. Hence,

$$b = \frac{2.5 - 1.5}{5 - 3} = \frac{+1}{+2} = +0.5.$$

Knowing the slope of the line in Figure 14.1, I can write an equation relating the value of Y to X for this line. This equation is

$$Y = +0.5X.$$

For each value of X, this equation provides the corresponding value of Y, and I can solve $Y = +0.5X$ for different values of X as follows:

If $X = $ _____,	Then $Y = $ _____
0	0
1	0.5
2	1.0
3	1.5
4	2.0
5	2.5
6	3.0
7	3.5
8	4.0

Compare these values of Y with the values of Y plotted in Figure 14.1 for each X value. Notice that $Y = +0.5X$ provides the equation describing the linear relationship plotted in Figure 14.1. Thus, if I knew only this equation and the X score, I could predict the Y score perfectly.

The equation $Y = bX$ provides part of the general equation for a straight line and describes any linear relationship between X and Y provided that $Y = 0$ when $X = 0$. But what if Y does not equal zero when $X = 0$? I turn to this problem next.

The Y-Intercept of a Line

Look at the relationship between variables X and Y presented in Figure 14.3. The slope of this line is also $+0.5$, for every change of 1 unit in X, Y changes by $+0.5$ unit. But this line cannot be described by the equation $Y = +0.5X$, for this equation indicates that Y should equal zero when $X = 0$. But, looking at Figure 14.3, we see that $Y = 3$ when $X = 0$. Let us substitute another value for X, say $X = 10$, into the equation $Y = +0.5X$. Doing so, I find that Y should be 5 when $X = 10$. From Figure 14.3, however, we see that $Y = 8$ when $X = 10$. By comparing Y found from the equation $Y = +0.5X$ with the values of Y plotted in Figure 14.3, we find that the equation $Y = +0.5X$ gives a value of Y that is 3 units less than the Y plotted on the figure. Suppose, then, that I use the equation $Y = +0.5X$ and add 3 to each value of Y obtained from it. Then the equation is

$$Y = +0.5X + 3.$$

This equation now describes the relationship between X and Y in Figure 14.3. To demonstrate, solving $Y = +0.5X + 3$ for different values of X, I obtain the following:

If $X =$ _____ ,	Then $Y =$ _____
0	3.0
2	4.0
4	5.0
10	8.0
13	9.5
19	12.5
24	15.0
26	16.0
30	18.0

These values of Y for each value of X correspond perfectly with the values of Y plotted on Figure 14.3. Thus, $Y = 0.5X + 3$ is the equation describing the line shown in Figure 14.3.

This example provides a specific instance of the equation for a linear relationship between X and Y. To express the general equation for a straight line, I substitute the letter b for the slope of $+0.5$ and the letter a for the constant of 3 in the equation $Y = +0.5X + 3$. Doing so, I obtain $Y = bX + a$, the general equation of a straight line with slope b, and Y-intercept, a. The **Y-intercept** is the value of Y when $X = 0$. When $X = 0$, the line intercepts, or intersects, the Y axis, and the value of Y at this point is the Y-intercept. In Figure 14.3 the Y-intercept is $+3$, whereas in Figure 14.1 the Y-intercept is 0.

Y-intercept: The value of Y when $X = 0$ in the equation $Y = bX + a$.

Example Linear Relations and Their Equations

To gain familiarity with linear relationships and the equations describing them, Figure 14.4 provides examples of both positive and negative linear relationships between X and Y. The

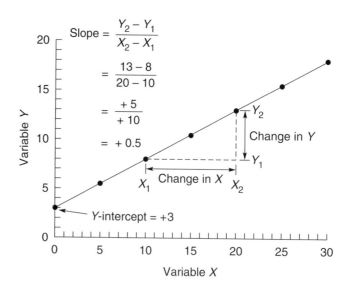

FIGURE 14.3
A linear relationship between X and Y with a slope of $+0.5$ and a Y-intercept of $+3$.

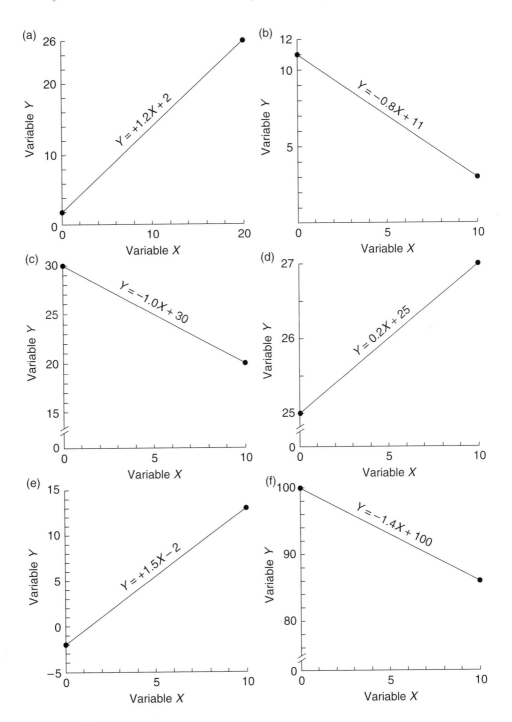

FIGURE 14.4
Various linear relationships between variables X and Y: (a) $Y = +1.2X + 2$; (b) $Y = -0.8X + 11$; (c) $Y = -1.0X + 30$; (d) $Y = +0.2X + 25$; (e) $Y = +1.5X - 2$; (f) $Y = -1.4X + 100$.

equation of the straight line with the slope and Y-intercept is given for each relationship illustrated. For example, panel (b) presents the linear relationship used in Figure 14.2 to illustrate a negative relationship between X and Y. The equation for this relationship is $Y = -0.8X + 11$. Here we see that the slope is –0.8; the minus sign indicates the relationship is negative. For every increase of 1 unit in X, Y decreases by 0.8 unit. When X is zero, the line intercepts the Y axis at a value of +11; thus, the Y-intercept for this equation is +11. Study each example and ensure that you can obtain the value of b and a for each relationship presented.

TESTING YOUR KNOWLEDGE 14.1

1. Define: a, b, linear relation, slope of a straight line, Y-intercept.
2. Write the general equation for a straight line.
3. Write the equation for the slope of a straight line.
4. For each of the following graphs, find the slope and Y-intercept. Then write the equation for each line.

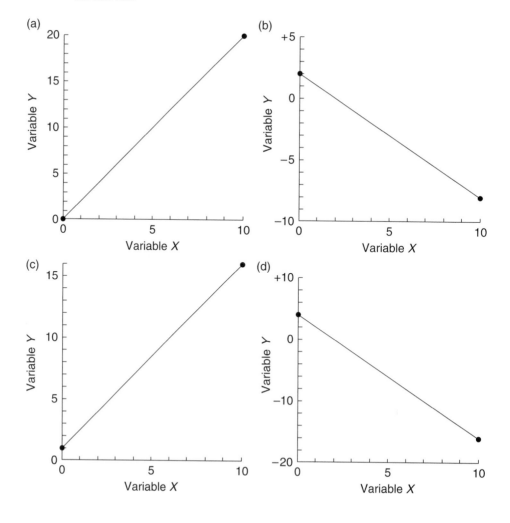

FINDING A LINEAR REGRESSION LINE

An Example Problem

The previous examples involved variables identified simply as X and Y and the equation $Y = bX + a$ was used to predict Y from X. To introduce how we find the equation that describes the linear relationship of two sets of scores, I return to the problem introduced in Chapter 13, the relationship between loneliness and depression scores. Our goal is to develop an equation allowing us to predict depression scores from loneliness scores.

Suppose, for a moment, that the scores in Table 14.1 were obtained from 10 people. These scores are perfectly positively related, $r_{obs} = +1.00$. Consequently, I expect a scatterplot to reveal that the scores fall on a straight line, as Figure 14.5 illustrates. I obtain the equation for the linear relationship between loneliness and depression scores by finding the slope and Y-intercept of the line. Both values were found on the figure: $b = +1$ and $a = +10$. Thus, the equation relating the depression scores (Y) to the loneliness scores (X) for Table 14.1 is

$$Y = 1X + 10$$

or

$$\text{Depression score} = (+1)(\text{loneliness score}) + 10.$$

Because the correlation of the scores is $+1.00$, I can use this equation to predict perfectly each person's depression score knowing only his or her loneliness score. The predicted

TABLE 14.1
Hypothetical scores for 10 participants on loneliness and depression.

Participant	Loneliness Score: X	Depression Score: Y
1	6	16
2	15	25
3	28	38
4	2	12
5	24	34
6	8	18
7	25	35
8	30	40
9	14	24
10	18	28

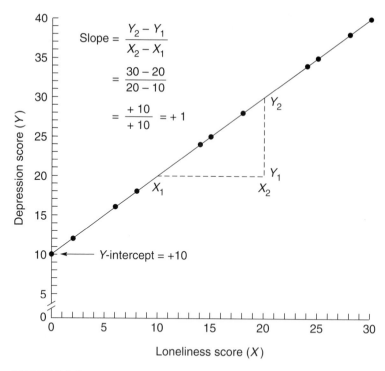

FIGURE 14.5
Scatterplot of the loneliness and depression scores given in Table 14.1.

depression scores are given in column b of Table 14.2. For example, person 1 has a loneliness score of 6. Applying the equation,

$$\text{Predicted depression score} = (+1)(\text{loneliness score}) + 10,$$

we find

$$\text{Predicted depression score} = (+1)(6) + 10$$
$$= 6 + 10 = 16.$$

The depression score predicted from the loneliness score of 6 is 16. The depression scores predicted from the other loneliness scores are presented in column b of Table 14.2. These predicted scores are identified with the letter Y' (read as "Y prime" or "Y predicted") to indicate that they have been predicted from the X score of loneliness using the equation

Y': The value of Y predicted from X using a linear regression equation.

$$Y' = 1X + 10.$$

The actual depression score obtained by each person (symbolized by Y) is presented in column c. Notice that the predicted and actual depression scores are identical. Because

TABLE 14.2

Depression scores predicted from loneliness scores using the equation

Depression score = (+1)(loneliness score) + 10.

Column a identifies the obtained loneliness score, column b the depression score predicted from the equation, and column c the actual depression score from Table 14.1.

Participant	(a) Loneliness Score: X	(b) Predicted Depression: Y'	(c) Actual Depression: Y
1	6	16	16
2	15	25	25
3	28	38	38
4	2	12	12
5	24	34	34
6	8	18	18
7	25	35	35
8	30	40	40
9	14	24	24
10	18	28	28

$r_{obs} = +1.00$, Y' and Y are the same and there is no error in predicting depression scores from loneliness scores.

A More Realistic Example Problem

From an applied perspective, the scores in Table 14.1 are unusual. Rarely, if ever, are two variables perfectly correlated as they are in Table 14.1. More realistically, scores on two variables will exhibit a less than perfect correlation, such as the scores presented in Table 14.3. These scores were used in Chapter 13 to present the Pearson correlation coefficient (see Table 13.1). The r_{obs} for these scores is +.78, which is statistically significant at the .05 level.

The scores of Table 14.3 are presented in a scatterplot in Figure 14.6. As $r_{obs} = +.78$ indicates, these scores are positively related; higher depression scores are associated with higher scores on loneliness, and lower depression scores are related to lower loneliness scores. Although the relationship between the loneliness and depression scores in Figure 14.6 is not perfect, it does appear to be linear. But what would be the best straight line to describe these scores? Obviously, a number of straight lines could be drawn on the scatterplot. For example, I have drawn two different straight lines labeled A and B on the figure. The lines were drawn arbitrarily, except that each line passes through $\overline{X} = 17$ and $\overline{Y} = 28$. Does line A appear to "fit" or describe the scores better or worse than line B? To answer this question, I need a criterion to decide how well a particular straight line fits a set of correlated scores.

TABLE 14.3
Hypothetical scores for 10 subjects on loneliness and depression. The mean and estimated population standard deviation are given for each set of scores.

Subject	Loneliness Score: X	Depression Score: Y
1	4	16
2	27	37
3	18	33
4	7	23
5	30	34
6	12	32
7	18	24
8	23	29
9	19	26
10	12	26
	$\overline{X}$ 17	$\overline{Y}$ 28
	s_X 8.37	s_Y 6.25

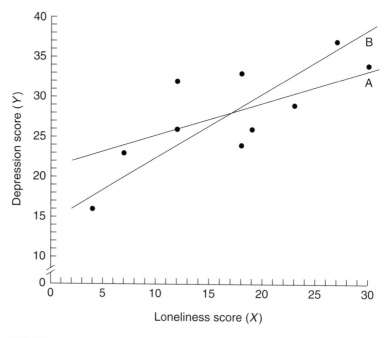

FIGURE 14.6
Scatterplot of the loneliness and depression scores given in Table 14.3. Lines A and B were drawn arbitrarily on the scatterplot.

The Least-Squares Criterion

Each line, A and B, in Figure 14.6 allows predicting a value of Y (that is, a Y') for each value of X. For example, for a loneliness score of 7, line A predicts a Y' of 24.0, and for a loneliness score of 27, a Y' equal to 32.0. On the other hand, line B predicts Y' equal to 20.0 for an X of 7 and Y' equal to 36.0 for a loneliness score of 27. These predicted Y scores are presented in column c of Table 14.4 for line A and in column f for line B. Each Y' score is in error in comparison with the Y score actually obtained, and the difference $Y - Y'$ is a measure of the error in prediction of the Y score from the X score. Table 14.4 illustrates the errors in prediction of each Y score from the X scores using either line A (see column d) or line B (see column g) of Figure 14.6.

Each line leads to errors in prediction. But does one line lead to smaller errors in prediction than the other? I might try to answer this question by adding up the errors in columns d and g, respectively, of Table 14.4. But if I sum the columns, as I have done in Table 14.4, I find that the sum of the errors, $\sum (Y - Y')$, is zero for each line. Thus, the sum of the errors cannot be used as a criterion to determine the fit of a straight line to the points in a scatterplot; it will always be equal to zero. A similar problem occurred in Chapter 5 when attempting to find a measure of the variation of scores about the mean of a distribution. In that

TABLE 14.4

Error of prediction of Y scores from the X scores of Figure 14.6 using either line A or line B. The error is given by the difference between the obtained Y score and the Y score predicted from X, or $Y - Y'$. Columns a and b identify the obtained X and Y scores, respectively, column c the Y predicted from line A, columns d and e the error and squared error of the predicted score from line A, respectively, column f the Y predicted from line B, and columns g and h the error and squared error of the predicted score from line B, respectively.

	(a)	(b)	(c)	(d)	(e)	(f)	(g)	(h)
			Predicted from Line A			Predicted from Line B		
	Obtained Scores		Scores	Error		Scores	Error	
Subject	X	Y	Y'	$Y - Y'$	$(Y - Y')^2$	Y'	$Y - Y'$	$(Y - Y')^2$
1	4	16	22.8	−6.8	46.24	17.6	−1.6	2.56
2	27	37	32.0	+5.0	25.00	36.0	+1.0	1.00
3	18	33	28.4	+4.6	21.16	28.8	+4.2	17.64
4	7	23	24.0	−1.0	1.00	20.0	+3.0	9.00
5	30	34	33.2	+0.8	0.64	38.4	−4.4	19.36
6	12	32	26.0	+6.0	36.00	24.0	+8.0	64.00
7	18	24	28.4	−4.4	19.36	28.8	−4.8	23.04
8	23	29	30.4	−1.4	1.96	32.8	−3.8	14.44
9	19	26	28.8	−2.8	7.84	29.6	−3.6	12.96
10	12	26	26.0	0.0	0.00	24.0	+2.0	4.00
			Sum	0.0	159.20		0.0	168.00

instance we found that $\sum (X - \overline{X})$ was always equal to zero. The problem was resolved by squaring each $X - \overline{X}$ before the differences were summed. Then I used $\sum (X - \overline{X})^2$ to develop a measure of error variation in the scores.

The current problem may be resolved similarly by squaring each $Y - Y'$ difference and summing the squared $Y - Y'$ differences. Then I will use $\sum (Y - Y')^2$ to determine which line best fits the scatterplot. Table 14.4 illustrates obtaining $\sum (Y - Y')^2$ for each line, A and B in columns e and h, respectively. The $\sum (Y - Y')^2$ for line A is 159.20 (see column e), whereas for line B it is 168.00 (see column h). Based on $\sum (Y - Y')^2$ as a measure of error in prediction, line A produces less error than line B. However, although line A produces less error than line B, we cannot be sure it is the line that produces the least error. Our task, then, is to find the straight line relating the X and Y scores that produces the smallest value of $\sum (Y - Y')^2$.

Least-squares regression line: A straight line that minimizes the value of $\sum (Y - Y')^2$.

A straight line that minimizes the value of $\sum (Y - Y')^2$ is called a **least-squares regression line**, for it minimizes the value of the sum of the squared differences of every predicted Y' score from the obtained Y score. The word *regression* is used in statistics to refer to the relationship between correlated variables. Figure 14.7 illustrates a least-squares regression line fitted to the scatterplot of the scores in Table 14.3. The equation for this line is $Y' = +0.583X + 18.1$. This line possesses the characteristic that $\sum (Y - Y')^2$ is a minimum; no other straight line fitted to the scores of Table 14.3 will produce a smaller value of $\sum (Y - Y')^2$. I now explain how to find the slope and Y-intercept for a least-squares regression line.

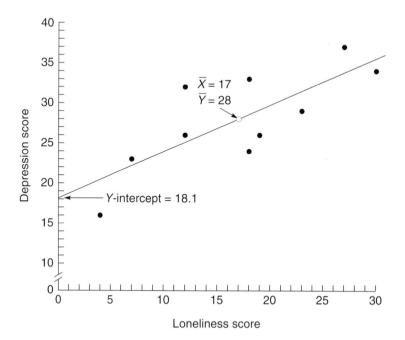

FIGURE 14.7
The least-squares regression line for the loneliness and depression scores of Table 14.3.

The Slope and Y-Intercept of a Least-Squares Regression Line for Predicting Y from X

To find a least-squares regression line to predict variable Y from variable X, I must determine the slope (b) and Y-intercept (a) of a straight line that minimizes the value of $\sum (Y - Y')^2$.

Slope of a Least-Squares Regression Line

There are several alternative formulas for finding the slope of a least-squares regression line; each formula produces the same value for b for a set of scores.

Deviational and Cross-Products Formula.   The slope of the least-squares regression line for two variables using deviations of scores from their mean is given by

$$\text{Slope} = b = \frac{\sum (X - \overline{X})(Y - \overline{Y})}{\sum (X - \overline{X})^2}.$$

Recall that the numerator of this formula, $\sum (X - \overline{X})(Y - \overline{Y})$, is the cross product of X and Y and is symbolized as CP_{XY}. The denominator of the formula,

$$\sum (X - \overline{X})^2,$$

is the sum of squares for X, or SS_X. Thus, I may also write an equation for b in cross-products and sum-of-squares form as

$$\text{Slope} = b = \frac{CP_{XY}}{SS_X}.$$

Computational Formula.   A formula that provides easier computations is

$$\text{Slope} = b = \frac{(N_{\text{pairs}})(\sum XY) - (\sum X)(\sum Y)}{(N_{\text{pairs}})(\sum X^2) - (\sum X)^2},$$

where N_{pairs} is the number of pairs of scores.

Correlation Formula.   The value of b may also be obtained from r by using the equation

$$\text{Slope} = b = r \left(\frac{s_Y}{s_X} \right),$$

where $r = r_{\text{obs}}$ between two sets of scores.
s_Y = estimated population standard deviation for the Y scores.
s_X = estimated population standard deviation for the X scores.

I illustrate the use of this equation in Example Problem 14.1.

Which Formula Should You Use to Find b?   Table 14.5 presents each of the preceding formulas for the slope. Each formula provides the same value of b when applied to a set of scores. Which formula should you choose to calculate b from a set of scores? In general, the computations needed for the computational formula are easier to perform and less likely to lead to an error than those needed for the deviational or cross-products formulas. Consequently, the computational formula is the approach you would most likely use to obtain b from a set of scores, and I illustrate its use next. If, however, you have already found the value of r_{obs} on the scores, then the correlation formula would be easiest, for it requires only that you find s_X and s_Y in addition to the value of r_{obs}.

Finding b Using the Computational Formula

Table 14.6 illustrates using the computational formula to find the slope of the least-squares regression line shown in Figure 14.7 fitted to the loneliness and depression scores of Table 14.3. Columns a and b of Table 14.7 present the X and Y scores, respectively. The sums of these columns provide the $\sum X$ and $\sum Y$ needed: $\sum X = 170$ and $\sum Y = 280$. Column c obtains each X^2, and the sum of this column, 3520, provides $\sum X^2$. Column d gives the value of each XY (i.e., each X score multiplied by its corresponding Y score), and the sum of this column, 5127, provides the $\sum XY$.

Step 2 of Table 14.6 illustrates substituting values of $\sum X, \sum Y, \sum XY$, and $\sum X^2$ into the equation. The value of b obtained for the scores of Table 14.3 is $+0.583$. The plus sign indicates that the slope is positive.

TABLE 14.5
Formulas for the slope of a least-squares regression line.

Deviational formula

$$b = \frac{\sum (X - \overline{X})(Y - \overline{Y})}{\sum (X - \overline{X})^2}$$

Cross-products and sum-of-squares formula

$$b = \frac{CP_{XY}}{SS_X}$$

Computational formula

$$b = \frac{(N_{pairs})(\sum XY) - (\sum X)(\sum Y)}{(N_{pairs})(\sum X^2) - (\sum X)^2}$$

N_{pairs} is the number of pairs of scores

Correlation formula

$$b = r\left(\frac{s_Y}{s_X}\right)$$

TABLE 14.6
Calculating b using the computational formula. The loneliness scores (X) in column a and depression scores (Y) in column b are from Table 14.3.

Step 1. Finding $\sum X, \sum Y, \sum X^2, \sum XY$:

Subject	(a) X	(b) Y	(c) X^2	(d) XY
1	4	16	16	64
2	27	37	729	999
3	18	33	324	594
4	7	23	49	161
5	30	34	900	1020
6	12	32	144	384
7	18	24	324	432
8	23	29	529	667
9	19	26	361	494
10	12	26	144	312
Sums	170	280	3520	5127

Step 2. Calculating b:

$$\sum X = 170,$$
$$(\sum X)^2 = 170^2 = 28{,}900,$$
$$\sum Y = 280,$$
$$\sum X^2 = 3520,$$
$$\sum XY = 5127,$$
$$N_{pairs} = 10,$$

and

$$b = \frac{(N_{pairs})(\sum XY) - (\sum X)(\sum Y)}{(N_{pairs})(\sum X^2) - (\sum X)^2}.$$

Substituting numerical values,

$$b = \frac{(10)(5127) - (170)(280)}{(10)(3520) - 28{,}900}$$
$$= \frac{+3670}{6300} = +0.583.$$

Y-Intercept of a Least-Squares Regression Line

The Y-intercept of a least-squares regression line is calculated from the value of b by the formula

$$a = \overline{Y} - b\overline{X},$$

where $\overline{Y}$ = mean of the Y scores.

$\overline{X}$ = mean of the X scores.

b = slope of the least-squares regression line obtained by using one of the formulas given in the previous section.

To illustrate the use of this formula for the scores of Table 14.3, $\overline{Y} = 28$, $\overline{X} = 17$, and $b = +0.583$. Thus,

$$a = 28 - (+0.583)(17) = 28 - 9.911 = 18.089 = 18.1$$

rounded to one decimal place. The least-squares regression line for these scores intersects the Y axis at a value of $Y = 18.1$.

Equation for the Least-Squares Regression Line

When the values of b and a are substituted into the equation for a straight line,

$$Y' = bX + a,$$

we find

$$Y' = +0.583X + 18.1.$$

Hence, the least-squares regression line for the scores of Table 14.3 is described by the equation $Y' = +0.583X + 18.1$. To obtain predicted values of Y, a value of X is entered into the equation and the equation solved for Y'. Predicted values of Y for the scores of Table 14.3 are as follows:

Subject	If X = _____,	Then Y' = _____
1	4	20.4
2	27	33.8
3	18	28.6
4	7	22.2
5	30	35.6
6	12	25.1
7	18	28.6
8	23	31.5
9	19	29.2
10	12	25.1

The Y' values lie on the regression line illustrated in Figure 14.7.

Fitting a Least-Squares Regression Line to Scores

I now illustrate how the least-squares regression line given by $Y' = +0.583X + 18.1$ is fitted to the scores plotted in Figure 14.7. If any two points on a straight line are known, then we have sufficient information to plot the line on a figure. For the regression line, one point on the line is the Y-intercept, the value of Y' when $X = 0$. For the example, the Y-intercept is 18.1. Thus, one point on the line has the coordinates $X = 0$, $Y = 18.1$.

A second point may be obtained by substituting a different value of X and solving for Y'. Although I may substitute any value for X, I use the value of $\overline{X}$, where $\overline{X} = 17$ for the example. Substituting $\overline{X} = 17$ into the equation, I obtain

$$Y' = +0.583(17) + 18.1 = 28.0 \quad \text{rounded to one decimal place}$$

Consequently, when $\overline{X} = 17$, $Y' = 28.0$. Notice this predicted value of $Y' = 28.0$ is also the value of $\overline{Y}$. For any least-squares regression line, when the value of X is the mean of the X scores, Y' will be equal to the mean of the obtained Y scores. Therefore, a second point on the regression line will always be a point with coordinates of $\overline{X}$, $\overline{Y}$. For the scores in Figure 14.7, $\overline{X} = 17$, $\overline{Y} = 28$, and the regression line on Figure 14.7 passes through these coordinates.

TESTING YOUR KNOWLEDGE 14.2

1. Define: least-squares regression line, Y'.
2. Write the general equation for predicting a value of Y from X with a straight line.
3. The slope and Y-intercept for the regression of Test 2 (Y) on Test 1 (X) grades are $b = +0.8$ and $a = 9$.
   a. Write the equation for the regression line of Test 2 on Test 1 grades.
   b. Find values of predicted Test 2 grades (i.e., Y') for the following Test 1 scores (i.e., X): 60, 65, 80, 85, 90.
   c. Plot the regression line on a sheet of graph paper. The value of $\overline{X} = 76$.
4. The slope and Y-intercept for the regression of Task 2 (Y) on Task 1 (X) scores are $b = -1.4$ and $a = 23$.
   a. Write the equation for the regression line of Task 2 on Task 1 scores.
   b. Find values of predicted Task 2 scores (i.e., Y') for the following Task 1 scores (i.e., X): 5, 8, 11, 14, 17.
   c. Plot the regression line on a sheet of graph paper. The value of $\overline{X} = 11$.

ERROR IN PREDICTION

Residuals: A Measure of the Error in Prediction

As we saw from Figure 14.7, using variable X to predict variable Y leads to some error in prediction, unless, of course, X and Y are perfectly correlated. The difference between a score and its predicted value, $Y - Y'$, is a measure of this error and is called the **residual**. The residual is used as the basis for a measure of the accuracy of prediction called the *standard error of estimate*. To develop the standard error of estimate, I turn to Table 14.7.

Table 14.7 presents the loneliness and depression scores of Table 14.3 in columns a and b, respectively. Predicted depression scores (i.e., Y') obtained from the regression

Residual: The value of $Y - Y'$.

TABLE 14.7

Calculating the residual for the predicted depression scores (Y', column c) from the loneliness scores (X, column a) of Table 14.3 using the regression equation Y' = +0.583X + 18.1. The residual, or error in prediction, is presented in column d, and the squared value of the residual is presented in column e.

Subject	(a) X	(b) Y	(c) Y'	(d) Y − Y'	(e) (Y − Y')²
1	4	16	20.43	−4.43	19.6249
2	27	37	33.84	+3.16	9.9856
3	18	33	28.59	+4.41	19.4481
4	7	23	22.18	+0.82	0.6724
5	30	34	35.59	−1.59	2.5281
6	12	32	25.10	+6.90	47.6100
7	18	24	28.59	−4.59	21.0681
8	23	29	31.51	−2.51	6.3001
9	19	26	29.18	−3.18	10.1124
10	12	26	25.10	+0.90	0.8100
					138.1597 Sum

equation $Y' = +0.583X + 18.1$ are shown in column c. For example, Y' for person 6 with a loneliness score of 12 is

$$Y'_6 = (+0.583)(12) + 18.1 = 25.10.$$

To minimize rounding error in later calculations the predicted values in column c were carried to two decimal places. You should calculate the remaining Y' values in column c to ensure that you are able to work with the regression equation for these scores.

The residual, $Y - Y'$, is shown in column d for each person. The sum of these residuals is equal to zero (within the limits of rounding error), so I cannot use this sum as a measure of error in prediction. Therefore, to develop a measure of error in prediction, I square the residuals as shown in column e. Summing the squared values of $Y - Y'$ in column e results in a sum of squares called the SS_{Residual}, the sum of squared residuals. The SS_{Residual} is equal to $\sum (Y - Y')^2$, or 138.1597 for the example.

SS_{Residual}: The value of $\sum (Y - Y')^2$.

The Standard Error of Estimate

In Chapter 5 I developed a measure of error variation for a set of scores, the standard deviation, s, by dividing the SS for a set of scores by its degrees of freedom and then taking the square root of the obtained value. I obtain a similar measure of error variation in the prediction of Y from X, the *standard error of estimate*, by finding the square root of the quotient of the SS_{Residual} divided by its degrees of freedom. The df for SS_{Residual} are $N_{\text{pairs}} - 2$, where N_{pairs} is the number of pairs of scores. Accordingly, the **standard error of estimate**, symbolized as $s_{Y \cdot X}$ to indicate that Y is predicted from X, is defined as

Standard error of estimate ($s_{Y \cdot X}$): The value of $\sqrt{\dfrac{\sum (Y - Y')^2}{N_{\text{pairs}} - 2}}$.

$$\text{Standard error of estimate} = s_{Y \cdot X} = \sqrt{\frac{SS_{\text{Residual}}}{N_{\text{pairs}} - 2}},$$

or, equivalently,

$$\text{Standard error of estimate} = s_{Y \cdot X} = \sqrt{\frac{\sum (Y - \overline{Y}')^2}{N_{\text{pairs}} - 2}}.$$

In the example, $SS_{\text{Residual}} = 138.1597$, and $N_{\text{pairs}} = 10$; thus, the standard error of estimate of predicting depression scores from loneliness scores is

$$s_{Y \cdot X} = \sqrt{\frac{138.1597}{10 - 2}} = 4.16 \quad \text{rounded to two decimal places.}$$

The definition of $s_{Y \cdot X}$ as

$$s_{Y \cdot X} = \sqrt{\frac{\sum (Y - Y')^2}{N_{\text{pairs}} - 2}}$$

illustrates that it is a measure of error variation of the predicted scores compared with the actual scores. Because this formula requires finding $Y - Y'$ differences, however, it is both time consuming and open to computational error. Thus, two alternative formulas have been developed, one a computational formula that can be applied to scores without obtaining $Y - Y'$ differences and the other a formula using r.

Computational Formula for Calculating $s_{Y \cdot X}$

A computational formula for calculating $s_{Y \cdot X}$ directly from the scores without finding residuals is

$$s_{Y \cdot X} = \sqrt{\left[\frac{1}{N_{\text{pairs}}(N_{\text{pairs}} - 2)}\right]\left[N_{\text{pairs}} \sum Y^2 - (\sum Y)^2 - \frac{[N_{\text{pairs}}(\sum XY) - (\sum X)(\sum Y)]^2}{N_{\text{pairs}} \sum X^2 - (\sum X)^2}\right]},$$

where N_{pairs} is the number of pairs of scores.

This equation is not as difficult to use as it may first appear. The computations using this equation to find $s_{Y \cdot X}$ for the example loneliness and depression scores are illustrated in Table 14.8. Step 1 of the table obtains the numerical values needed to solve the formula. For each subject:

- Column a presents the loneliness score, X.
- Column b is the depression score, Y.
- Column c is the loneliness score squared (X^2).
- Column d is the depression score squared (Y^2).
- Column e is the loneliness score multiplied by the depression score (XY).

The $\sum X$ is the sum of column a, $\sum Y$ is the sum of column b, $\sum X^2$ is the sum of column c, $\sum Y^2$ is the sum of column d, and $\sum XY$ is the sum of column e. Step 2 illustrates substituting these values into the formula. The obtained value of $s_{Y \cdot X}$ is 4.16, the same as found using the definitional formula.

TABLE 14.8

Calculating $s_{Y \cdot X}$ using the computational formula. The loneliness scores (X, column a) and depression scores (Y, column b) are from Table 14.3.

Step 1. Finding $\sum X, \sum Y, \sum X^2, \sum Y^2$, and $\sum XY$:

Subject	(a) X	(b) Y	(c) X^2	(d) Y^2	(e) XY
1	4	16	16	256	64
2	27	37	729	1369	999
3	18	33	324	1089	594
4	7	23	49	529	161
5	30	34	900	1156	1020
6	12	32	144	1024	384
7	18	24	324	576	432
8	23	29	529	841	667
9	19	26	361	676	494
10	12	26	144	676	312
Sums	170	280	3520	8192	5127

Step 2. Calculating $s_{Y \cdot X}$:

$$\sum X = 170 \qquad\qquad \sum Y = 280$$

$$(\sum X)^2 = 170^2 = 28{,}900 \qquad\qquad (\sum Y)^2 = 280^2 = 78{,}400$$

$$\sum X^2 = 3520 \qquad\qquad \sum Y^2 = 8192$$

$$\sum XY = 5127$$

$$N_{\text{pairs}} = 10$$

and

$$s_{Y \cdot X} = \sqrt{ \left[\frac{1}{N_{\text{pairs}}(N_{\text{pairs}} - 2)} \right] \left[N_{\text{pairs}} \sum Y^2 - (\sum Y)^2 - \frac{[N_{\text{pairs}}(\sum XY) - (\sum X)(\sum Y)]^2}{N_{\text{pairs}} \sum X^2 - (\sum X)^2} \right] }$$

$$= \sqrt{ \left[\frac{1}{10(8)} \right] \left[10(8192) - 78{,}400 - \frac{[10(5127) - (170)(280)]^2}{10(3520) - 28{,}900} \right] }$$

$$= \sqrt{ \left[\frac{1}{80} \right] \left[3520 - \frac{(3670)^2}{6300} \right] } = \sqrt{ \left(\frac{1}{80} \right) 1382.079 }$$

$$= 4.16 \quad \text{rounded to two decimal places.}$$

Calculating $s_{Y\cdot X}$ from r

The standard error of estimate also may be calculated from the value of r_{obs} between X and Y and the standard deviation of the Y variable with the formula

$$s_{Y\cdot X} = s_Y \sqrt{\left[\frac{N_{pairs} - 1}{N_{pairs} - 2}\right](1 - r_{obs}^2)}.$$

For the scores of Table 14.3,

$$s_Y = 6.25,$$
$$r_{obs} = +.78,$$
$$N_{pairs} = 10.$$

Thus,

$$s_{Y\cdot X} = (6.25)\sqrt{\left[\frac{10 - 1}{10 - 2}\right][1 - (+.78)^2]} = (6.25)(0.6638) = 4.15,$$

which, within the limits of rounding error, is the same as the value found by either the definitional or computational formulas.

When N_{pairs} is large, the ratio of $N_{pairs} - 1$ to $N_{pairs} - 2$ approaches 1.0 and the formula is often written as

$$s_{Y\cdot X} = s_Y \sqrt{1 - r_{obs}^2}.$$

Table 14.9 summarizes the various formulas for calculating $s_{Y\cdot X}$.

Information Provided by the Standard Error of Estimate

To understand what information the standard error of estimate provides, I return briefly to a consideration of the standard deviation, s. The standard deviation for a set of scores provides a measure of error variation for those scores. If I know nothing about the scores other than the mean, then the best prediction I can make for any score is the mean. Of course, this prediction will likely be in error; and, on the average, the error will be the value of the standard deviation. For example, suppose that you are told that the mean depression score for Table 14.3 is 28. If you are asked to predict an individual score knowing nothing other than $\overline{Y} = 28$, your best prediction is 28. But for any score in Table 14.3 this prediction is in error; no subject obtained a depression score of 28. The average error in this prediction is the value of the standard deviation, $s_Y = 6.25$, for this set of scores.

Suppose now you are told that there is a linear relation between the loneliness and depression scores given by

$$Y' = +0.583X + 18.1.$$

TABLE 14.9
Formulas for the standard error of estimate, $s_{Y \cdot X}$.

Residuals formula

$$s_{Y \cdot X} = \sqrt{\frac{SS_{\text{Residual}}}{N_{\text{pairs}} - 2}}$$

or

$$s_{Y \cdot X} = \sqrt{\frac{\sum (Y - Y')^2}{N_{\text{pairs}} - 2}}.$$

Computational formula

$$s_{Y \cdot X} = \sqrt{\left[\frac{1}{N_{\text{pairs}}(N_{\text{pairs}} - 2)} \right] \left[N_{\text{pairs}} \sum Y^2 - \left(\sum Y \right)^2 - \frac{[N_{\text{pairs}}(\sum XY) - (\sum X)(\sum Y)]^2}{N_{\text{pairs}} \sum X^2 - (\sum X)^2} \right]}$$

Formula using r_{obs}

$$s_{Y \cdot X} = s_Y \sqrt{\left[\frac{N_{\text{pairs}} - 1}{N_{\text{pairs}} - 2} \right] (1 - r_{\text{obs}}^2)}$$

Further suppose that you are told that person 1 has a loneliness score of 4. Using this score and applying the regression equation, you predict this person's Y score to be 20.43. Although this prediction, too, is in error (the person's actual score was 16), the prediction of 20.43 is closer to the actual score than is the prediction of 28.0 made from $\overline{Y}$. The standard error of estimate is the standard deviation of the error in the predicted scores. Thus, $s_{Y \cdot X}$ indicates the average error in predictions from the linear regression line. Notice in the example that $s_{Y \cdot X} = 4.16$ is smaller than $s_Y = 6.25$. Accordingly, if I predict Y from X, the error in prediction typically will be less than if I simply used $\overline{Y}$ as a predictor for all the Y values. Table 14.10 presents the relationship between s_Y and $s_{Y \cdot X}$ as a function of the correlation between variables X and Y. The table was constructed by substituting values of r_{obs} into the formula

$$s_{Y \cdot X} = s_Y \sqrt{1 - r_{XY \text{ obs}}^2}.$$

The first column of this table presents values of r_{obs} ranging from 0 to 1.0. The second column shows the proportion of s_Y that $s_{Y \cdot X}$ will be for the value of r_{obs}. Notice that when r_{obs} is zero, $s_{Y \cdot X} = s_Y$, and knowing the loneliness score for a person does not improve the accuracy of prediction of the person's depression score. For small values of r (e.g., $r = .1, .2,$ or $.3$), knowing the X variable score does little to improve the accuracy of prediction of the Y variable score. On the other hand, large values of r (e.g., $r = .7, .8,$ or $.9$) improve the accuracy considerably. For example, if the correlation between X and Y is .8, then $s_{Y \cdot X}$ is only .6

TABLE 14.10
Relationship between $s_{Y \cdot X}$ and s_Y as a function of r.

If r_{obs} = _____ ,	Then $s_{Y \cdot X}$ = _____ s_Y.
0	1.000
.1	.995
.2	.980
.3	.954
.4	.917
.5	.866
.6	.800
.7	.714
.8	.600
.9	.436
1.0	.000

of s_Y. When r is 1.00, then $s_{Y \cdot X} = 0$; prediction of the Y score from the X score is perfect and there is no error of prediction.

PREDICTING X FROM Y

The examples to this point have used the loneliness scores (X) to predict depression scores (Y). But we could reverse the process and use the depression scores to predict loneliness. This would result in a different regression equation from the one predicting depression from loneliness. Table 14.11 presents the loneliness and depression scores with the X and Y designation reversed from Table 14.3; depression scores are now designated X (column a) and loneliness scores Y (column b). Columns c and d present the values of $\sum X^2$ and $\sum XY$ needed to obtain the slope using the computational formula as illustrated in Step 2 of the table. Step 3 obtains the value of the Y-intercept, a. The regression line for predicting loneliness from depression is presented in Step 4. This regression line was used to calculate the Y' values shown in column e of the table. Residuals are presented in column f and the squared value of the residuals in column g. Step 5 illustrates calculating $s_{Y \cdot X}$ from the residuals.

Notice that the slope and Y-intercept of the regression line depend on which variable is designated as X and which as Y. If loneliness is designated as the X variable, then the regression line is $Y' = +0.583X + 18.1$. If, however, depression is designated as the X variable, then the regression line is $Y' = +1.043X - 12.2$. Each line allows prediction of the variable designated Y with equal accuracy, however. This characteristic can be seen by comparing $s_{Y \cdot X}$ to s_Y for each line. If loneliness is the X variable, then $s_{Y \cdot X}$ is 4.16 and s_Y is 6.25. Here $s_{Y \cdot X} / s_Y$ equals 4.16/6.25, which equals .67. On the other hand, if depression is the X variable, then $s_{Y \cdot X}$ is 5.56 and s_Y is 8.37. Here $s_{Y \cdot X} / s_Y$ equals 5.56/8.37, which equals .66. Within the limits of rounding error, each regression line allows a similar reduction in error in predicting scores. In most instances, a researcher will have a particular reason to designate a variable as X to be used to predict Y. Thus, for most data sets only one regression line will be found.

TABLE 14.11

Calculating the least-squares regression line, predicted scores, and residuals for loneliness scores from depression scores.

Step 1. Finding $\sum X, \sum Y, \sum X^2$, and $\sum XY$:

	(a) Depression	(b) Loneliness	(c)	(d)	(e)	(f)	(g)
Participant	(X)	(Y)	X^2	XY	Y'	Y − Y'	$(Y - Y')^2$
1	16	4	256	64	4.488	−0.488	0.238
2	37	27	1369	999	26.391	0.609	0.371
3	33	18	1089	594	22.219	−4.219	17.800
4	23	7	529	161	11.789	−4.789	22.935
5	34	30	1156	1020	23.262	6.738	45.401
6	32	12	1024	384	21.176	−9.176	84.199
7	24	18	576	432	12.832	5.168	26.708
8	29	23	841	667	18.047	4.953	24.532
9	26	19	676	494	14.918	4.082	16.663
10	26	12	676	312	14.918	−2.918	8.515
Sums	280	170	8192	5127			247.362

Step 2. Calculating b using the computational formula:

$\sum X = 280$

$(\sum X)^2 = 280^2 = 78{,}400$

$\sum Y = 170$

$\sum X^2 = 8192$

$\sum XY = 5127$

$N_{\text{pairs}} = 10.$

$$b = \frac{(N_{\text{pairs}})(\sum XY) - (\sum X)(\sum Y)}{(N_{\text{pairs}})(\sum X^2) - (\sum X)^2}$$

Substituting numerical values,

$$b = \frac{(10)(5127) - (280)(170)}{(10)(8192) - 78400}$$

$$= +\frac{3670}{3520}$$

$$= +1.043$$

Step 3. Calculating a:

$\overline{X} = 28, \overline{Y} = 17$

$a = \overline{Y} - b\overline{X}$

$= 17 - 1.043(28) = -12.2.$

Step 4. Regression Line:

$Y' = +1.043X - 12.2.$

Step 5. Calculating $s_{Y \cdot X}$ from the residuals:

$\sum (Y - Y')^2 = 247.362$

$N_{\text{pairs}} - 2 = 8$

$$s_{Y \cdot X} = \sqrt{\sum (Y - Y')^2 \div (N_{\text{pairs}} - 2)}$$

$$= \sqrt{247.362 \div 8} = 5.56$$

USING A LINEAR REGRESSION LINE

Two conditions are required for appropriate use of linear regression. First, r_{obx} for the scores must be statistically significant. If the scores are not correlated, then the best prediction for a Y score is to use the mean of the Y scores. If the X and Y scores are not correlated, then if you are given an X score and asked to predict a Y score, the best prediction of Y is simply $\overline{Y}$. The knowledge of X does not give you any information about the value of Y.

A second requirement is that the relationship between the X and Y scores must be linear. The least-squares regression line is a straight line. If the X and Y scores are not linearly related, then it is inappropriate to fit a least-squares regression line to them. For example, if X and Y are related in a U-shaped or an inverted U-shaped (i.e., ∩) fashion, then constructing a least-squares regression line for the scores will not lead to accurate predictions, for the scores are not linearly related.

We must be cautious also not to predict beyond the range of scores encompassed in the sample from which the prediction equation was developed. The relationship may be nonlinear for values outside the range in the sample.

TESTING YOUR KNOWLEDGE 14.3

1. Define: least-squares regression line, residual, SS_{Residual}, standard error of estimate, $s_{Y \cdot X}$, $Y - Y'$.
2. Why is $\sum (Y - Y')$ not used as a measure of error for predicting Y from X?
3. Why may $\sum (Y - Y')^2$ be used as a measure of error for predicting Y from X?
4. Give the definitional formula for the standard error of estimate.
5. In a study attempting to predict examination grades from the number of hours devoted to studying for the examination, the following values were found for 16 pairs of scores: $\sum X = 72$, $\sum X^2 = 408$, $(\sum X)^2 = 5184$, $\sum Y = 1264$, $\sum Y^2 = 102{,}636$, $(\sum Y)^2 = 1{,}597{,}696$, and $\sum XY = 6140$. What is the value of $s_{Y \cdot X}$ for this study?
6. An exercise physiologist found a correlation of $r_{\text{obs}} = +.41$ between the amount of exercise and weight loss in a sample of 45 people over a three-month period. The value of s_Y was 5.2 pounds. What is the value of $s_{Y \cdot X}$ for this study?
7. An instructor attempting to predict final exam grades from midsemester exam grades for a class of 27 students found that $SS_{\text{Residual}} = 462.25$. What is the value of $s_{Y \cdot X}$ for this study?

Example Problem 14.1

Finding a Regression Line from the Correlation Coefficient

Problem: One avenue of research into the problem of eating disorders, such as anorexia and bulimia, has been to investigate the relationship of a person's body image to other attributes of the individual, such as sex role, perceived attractiveness, or self-esteem. Mintz and Betz (1986), for example, measured body satisfaction and depression proneness in college students using self-report rating scales. Body satisfaction scores could range from 1 (indicating strong positive feelings toward one's body) to 7 (indicating strong negative feelings toward one's body). Depression proneness scores also ranged from 1 (indicating strong resistance to depression) to 7 (indicating proneness to depression). For a group of 23 slightly underweight females, Mintz and Betz found a statistically significant correlation of body satisfaction ratings (variable X) with depression proneness ratings (variable Y) of $r_{\text{obs}} = +.44$. Suppose that I replicated this study for a group of 15 slightly underweight females and found r_{obs} between body satisfaction and depression proneness of +.58. For 13 df, $r_{\text{crit}} = .514$; thus, r_{obs} is statistically significant. The mean of the body satisfaction scores was $\overline{X} = 3.7$ with a standard deviation of 1.8. For depression proneness, $\overline{Y} = 3.8$ and $s_Y = 1.9$. Find (a) the least-squares regression line of depression proneness on body satisfaction, (b) predicted depression proneness scores as a function of body satisfaction scores, and (c) the standard error of estimate.

Solution: The problem requires finding values for the slope and Y-intercept of the regression line. Because r_{obs} is given, I find the slope using the correlational formula shown in Table 14.5.

Finding the Slope: The slope, b, of the regression line is found from r by

$$b = r\left(\frac{s_Y}{s_X}\right).$$

Substituting values of r_{obs}, s_X, and s_Y, I obtain

$$b = +.58\left(\frac{1.9}{1.8}\right) = +0.61.$$

Finding the Y-Intercept: The Y-intercept is found from

$$a = \overline{Y} - b\overline{X} = 3.8 - (+0.61)(3.7) = 1.54.$$

Obtaining the Regression Equation: The regression equation of depression proneness (Y) on body satisfaction (X) is given by

$$Y' = +0.61X + 1.54.$$

Obtaining Predicted Depression Proneness Scores (Y'): Depression proneness scores (Y') predicted from body satisfaction scores (X) are obtained by solving the regression equation for a value of X. For example, for a body satisfaction rating score of 1, the regression equation becomes

$$Y' = +0.61(1) + 1.54 = 2.15.$$

The depression proneness rating predicted from a body satisfaction rating of 1 is 2.15 or, rounding to one decimal place, 2.2.

Plotting the Regression Line: The regression line given by

$$Y' = +0.61X + 1.54$$

is plotted in Figure 14.8. Values of the predictor variable, body satisfaction (X), are placed on the abscissa, and values of the predicted variable, depression proneness score (Y'), are placed on the ordinate. The regression line is located on the graph by identifying the Y-intercept (1.54) and the coordinates of $\overline{X}$, $\overline{Y}$ (3.7 and 3.8, respectively) and drawing a straight line connecting these two points. The predicted depression proneness scores for each value of X are identified by the dots on the line.

Finding the Standard Error of Estimate: The $s_{Y \cdot X}$ is found by

$$s_{Y \cdot X} = s_Y \sqrt{\left[\frac{N_{pairs} - 1}{N_{pairs} - 2}\right](1 - r_{obs}^2)}.$$

FIGURE 14.8
The least-squares regression line for body image and
depression proneness ratings. Predicted values of depression
proneness for each body image rating are indicated by the
dots on the regression line.

Substituting $s_Y = 1.9$, $N_{\text{pairs}} = 15$, and $r_{\text{obs}} = +.58$, I obtain

$$s_{Y \cdot X} = (1.9)\sqrt{\left[\frac{15 - 1}{15 - 2}\right][1 - (+.58)^2]} = 1.6 \quad \text{rounded to one decimal place.}$$

This $s_{Y \cdot X}$ is less than $s_Y = 1.9$. Knowing a person's body satisfaction score increases the
accuracy of predicting depression proneness in comparison to using $\overline{Y} = 3.8$ as a predicted
value for all scores.

Example Problem 14.2

Finding a Regression Line and the Standard Error of Estimate with the Computational Formula

Problem: Example Problem 14.1 introduced the research of Mintz and Betz (1986) on the
relationship of body satisfaction and depression proneness scores. They also obtained self-rat-
ings of social self-esteem from their participants. The self-esteem rating scales gave scores
ranging from 20 (indicating low self-esteem) to 100 (indicating high self-esteem). Body satisfaction scores could range from 1 (indicating strong positive feelings toward one's body) to

7 (indicating strong negative feelings toward one's body). For slightly underweight females, Mintz and Betz obtained a statistically significant correlation between body satisfaction (X) scores and social self-esteem (Y) scores of $r_{obs} = -.60$. Suppose in a replication of this study with 15 students that I obtained the following body satisfaction and social self-esteem scores:

Student	Body Satisfaction: X	Self-Esteem: Y
1	2	76
2	4	48
3	6	27
4	1	70
5	3	41
6	5	38
7	6	37
8	3	61
9	7	33
10	1	91
11	4	36
12	2	55
13	3	49
14	5	51
15	4	52

We want to find: (a) the least-squares regression line of social self-esteem scores on body satisfaction scores, (b) predicted self-esteem scores as a function of body satisfaction, (c) the value of $s_{Y \cdot X}$ from the residuals $Y - Y'$, and (d) the value of $s_{Y \cdot X}$ using the computational formula.

Solution: Table 14.12 provides the values necessary to find the information requested. In this table, the following values are given:

Column

a	Body satisfaction scores (X) and the $\sum X$
b	Self-esteem scores (Y) and the $\sum Y$
c	Body satisfaction scores squared (X^2) and the $\sum X^2$
d	Self-esteem scores squared (Y^2) and the $\sum Y^2$
e	Cross products of the body satisfaction and self-esteem scores and the $\sum XY$
f	Values of Y' predicted from the regression line found
g	Residual for each self-esteem score

Finding the Regression Line
Calculating b using the computational formula:

TABLE 14.12
Calculating the least-squares regression line, predicted scores, and residuals for self-esteem scores from body image scores.

Student	(a) X	(b) Y	(c) X^2	(d) Y^2	(e) XY	(f) Y'	(g) $Y - Y'$
1	2	76	4	5776	152	64.859	+11.141
2	4	48	16	2304	192	48.837	−0.837
3	6	27	36	729	162	32.815	−5.815
4	1	70	1	4900	70	72.870	−2.870
5	3	41	9	1681	123	56.848	−15.848
6	5	38	25	1444	190	40.826	−2.826
7	6	37	36	1369	222	32.815	+4.185
8	3	61	9	3721	183	56.848	+4.152
9	7	33	49	1089	231	24.804	+8.196
10	1	91	1	8281	91	72.870	+18.130
11	4	36	16	1296	144	48.837	−12.837
12	2	55	4	3025	110	64.859	−9.859
13	3	49	9	2401	147	56.848	−7.848
14	5	51	25	2601	255	40.826	+10.174
15	4	52	16	2704	208	48.837	+3.163
Sums	56	765	256	43,321	2480		
Mean	3.73	51.00					
s	1.83	17.54					

$$\sum X = 56,$$
$$(\sum X)^2 = 56^2 = 3136,$$
$$\sum X^2 = 256,$$
$$\sum Y = 765,$$
$$\sum XY = 2480,$$
$$N_{pairs} = 15,$$

and

$$b = \frac{(N_{pairs})(\sum XY) - (\sum X)(\sum Y)}{(N_{pairs})(\sum X^2) - (\sum X)^2}.$$

Substituting numerical values,

$$b = \frac{(15)(2480) - (56)(765)}{(15)(256) - 3136} = \frac{-5640}{704} = -8.011.$$

Calculating a: $\overline{X} = 3.73$ and $\overline{Y} = 51.00$. Substituting these values into $a = \overline{Y} - b\overline{X}$, I obtain

$$a = 51.00 - (-8.011)(3.73) = 80.881.$$

Regression line: The regression line is given by

$$Y' = -8.011X + 80.881.$$

Predicted Self-Esteem Scores: Predicted self-esteem scores from the regression equation are given in column f of the table. To minimize rounding error in finding $s_{Y \cdot X}$ from the residuals, the Y' values were carried to three decimal places.

$s_{Y \cdot X}$ **from the Residuals:** The residual values are presented in column g of the table. The value of $s_{Y \cdot X}$ is obtained from these residuals by

$$s_{Y \cdot X} = \sqrt{\frac{\sum (Y - Y')^2}{N_{pairs} - 2}}.$$

To obtain $\sum (Y - Y')^2$, each residual in column g is squared and the 15 squared values are summed. The $\sum (Y - Y')^2 = 1293.7380$. $N_{pairs} - 2 = 15 - 2 = 13$. Substituting numerical values,

$$s_{Y \cdot X} = \sqrt{\frac{1293.7380}{13}} = 9.98.$$

$s_{Y \cdot X}$ **from the Computational Formula:** The computational formula is

$$s_{Y \cdot X} = \sqrt{\left[\frac{1}{N_{pairs}(N_{pairs} - 2)}\right]\left[N_{pairs}\sum Y^2 - (\sum Y)^2 - \frac{[N_{pairs}(\sum XY) - (\sum X)(\sum Y)]^2}{N_{pairs}\sum X^2 - (\sum X)^2}\right]}.$$

Substituting numerical values

$$s_{Y \cdot X} = \sqrt{\left[\frac{1}{(15)(13)}\right]\left[15(43,321) - (765)^2 - \frac{[(15)(2480) - (56)(765)]^2}{(15)(256) - (56)^2}\right]}$$

$$= \sqrt{\left[\frac{1}{195}\right]\left[64,590 - \frac{(-5640)^2}{704}\right]}$$

$$= \sqrt{\left(\frac{1}{195}\right)19,405.909} = 9.98.$$

The value of $s_{Y \cdot X}$ from this formula is the same as the value obtained using the definitional formula and residuals.

Conclusion: The regression equation

$$Y' = -8.011X + 80.881$$

allows prediction of self-esteem scores from body satisfaction scores with considerable reduction in the error of prediction. The value of $s_{Y \cdot X} = 9.98$, the average error associated with a predicted self-esteem score from the regression equation, is smaller than $s_Y = 17.54$, the average amount of error that is associated with using $\overline{Y}$ (i.e., 51.0) as the predicted value of self-esteem for all individuals.

Example Problem 14.3

Predicting Job Performance with a Regression Equation

Problem: A major aspect of industrial psychology is predicting the work success of applicants to business and governmental organizations. Regression analysis is often used to make these predictions. Applicants may take a work-related test, and scores from the test are used to predict potential success on the job. Consider a simple example. Suppose that a business gives job applicants a work-sample test. A work-sample test is a miniature version of the job. Performance on the work-sample test (variable X) is used to predict actual job proficiency (Y') with the regression equation

$$Y' = +0.76X + 55.$$

Suppose 12 applicants are given the work-sample test and the following scores were obtained.

Applicant	Work-Sample Test Score: X
1	12
2	37
3	27
4	34
5	17
6	39
7	24
8	40
9	47
10	15
11	31
12	21

The company will not hire anyone whose predicted job proficiency is less than 75. Which applicants are eligible for hiring based on their work-sample test scores?

Solution: The solution requires applying the regression equation to each applicant's work-sample test score to obtain a predicted job-proficiency score. The predicted job-proficiency score for each applicant is shown next.

Applicant	Predicted Job-Proficiency Score: Y'
1	64.1
2	83.1
3	75.5
4	80.8
5	67.9
6	84.6
7	73.2
8	85.4
9	90.7
10	66.4
11	78.6
12	71.0

The predicted scores of applicants 1, 5, 7, 10, and 12 are below the required predicted score of 75; hence, these applicants would not be eligible for hiring. The scores of all other applicants are 75 or above; thus, these applicants are eligible for hiring. The regression line for $Y' = +0.76X + 55$ is illustrated in Figure 14.9. Notice that a predicted job-proficiency score of 75 corresponds to a work-sample score of 26.3. Any work-sample test score below 26.3 leads to a predicted job-proficiency score of less than 75. Accordingly, applicants with work-sample test scores less than 26.3 would not be hired.

MULTIPLE REGRESSION

Regression analysis is widely used in the behavioral sciences and in an array of practical settings. While the example problems have presented both X and Y variables, in practice, only the X variable and a regression equation for predicting Y from this X may be known, the regression equation having been developed from previous instances where both X and Y were known. For example, a heating fuel dealer may predict how much fuel oil she needs to order for a subsequent week (variable Y) based on the mean daily temperature of the previous week (variable X). Or a retailer may attempt to predict sales volume (variable Y) from the amount of money spent on advertising (variable X). Each of our examples used only one X variable to predict the Y variable. In practice, however, regression equations typically are more complex than those that I introduced and use several X variables to predict Y. This approach is called **multiple regression** because multiple predictors are used. For example, an employer may want to predict potential employee performance as a function of an aptitude test score, a score on a standardized interview, and a score on a work-sample test. The general regression equation for representing this approach is

Multiple regression:
Predicting the value of Y scores using several X variables.

$$Y' = b_1 X_1 + b_2 X_2 + b_3 X_3 + a,$$

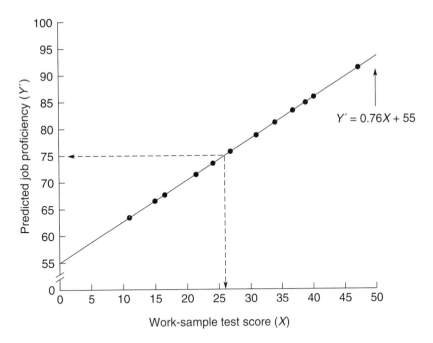

FIGURE 14.9
The regression line $Y' = +0.76X + 55$ used to predict job proficiency (Y') from a work-sample test (X). Predicted values of job proficiency for work-sample scores are indicated by dots on the regression line.

where Y' is the predicted job performance; X_1, X_2, and X_3 are predictor variables (in this example, X_1 is the score on the aptitude test, X_2 is the score on the standardized interview, and X_3 is the score on the work-sample test); b_1, b_2, and b_3 are regression coefficients for X_1, X_2, and X_3, respectively; and a is the Y-intercept.

The regression coefficients weight each X variable in the prediction of Y. For example, if $b_1 = +0.18$, $b_2 = +0.10$, $b_3 = +0.34$, and $a = 30.3$, then the equation becomes

$$Y' = +0.18X_1 + 0.10X_2 + 0.34X_3 + 30.3.$$

If an applicant obtains an aptitude test score of 75, an interview score of 20, and a work-sample test score of 90, then

$$Y' = (0.18)(75) + (0.10)(20) + (0.34)(90) + 30.3$$
$$= 13.5 + 2.0 + 30.6 + 30.3 = 76.4.$$

Multiple regression equations are widely used for prediction in the behavioral sciences. Friedman et al. (1993), for example, used seven dimensions of childhood personality—sociability, physical energy, cheerfulness, conscientiousness, motivation, permanency of mood, and intelligence—to predict longevity. As another example, in an attempt to predict cigarette smoking among adolescents, Williams and Covington (1997) used the variables of race, age, peer involvement, family closeness, number of friends smoking, number of family members smoking, and an adolescent's perception of the health risks of smoking to develop a multiple regression equation. Obtaining the regression coefficients for these complex equations, however, requires knowledge beyond the scope of this introductory chapter.

TESTING YOUR KNOWLEDGE 14.4

1. Personality attributes and performance of specific tasks are often related. For example, Gormly and Gormly (1986) correlated ratings of social introversion to performance on a block design test measuring spatial abilities. They found a statistically significant positive correlation: More socially introverted individuals created the required block designs more quickly. Suppose that you replicated this study rating subjects on a 9-point social introversion scale, where 1 indicates highly socially introverted and 9 indicates not at all socially introverted. The amount of time in seconds each subject took to create a particular design with nine colored blocks was recorded. The scores obtained for 12 subjects were as follows:

Subject	Introversion: (X)	Block Design Times: (Y)
1	6	217
2	3	230
3	9	315
4	1	224
5	4	271
6	2	198
7	3	256
8	5	263
9	8	321
10	7	289
11	8	265
12	6	291

The mean block design time was 261.67 seconds, with $s_Y = 38.82$ seconds. The r_{obs} for these scores is statistically significant at the .05 level. Using the computational formula for b, construct the regression line of block design on introversion scores.

a. What is the slope of the regression line?
b. What is the Y-intercept of the regression line?
c. Write the equation for the regression line.
d. Plot a scatterplot of the introversion and block design scores. Place the regression line on this plot.
e. What is the predicted block design score (Y') for each introversion score?
f. Use the Y' given to find the residual for each subject.
g. Find the $SS_{Residual}$.
h. Find $s_{Y \cdot X}$ using the $SS_{Residual}$.
i. Compare $s_{Y \cdot X}$ to the s_Y, 38.82, for these scores. Does the use of the regression equation to predict block design scores from introversion scores reduce the error of prediction in comparison to using the mean block design score (i.e., 261.7 seconds) as the predicted value for all block design scores?

2. Bird watchers notice that many species spend a great deal of time scanning the environment. Elgar, McKay, and Woon (1986) observed house sparrows to find the relationship between amount of scanning and feeding rate. They found a statistically significant negative correlation between the two variables. Suppose that you replicated this study observing 15 house sparrows. You recorded the number of scans of the environment each bird made per minute (variable X) and the number of pecks at food each bird made per minute (variable Y) and found the mean scan rate ($\overline{X}$) was 26.2 scans per minute with $s_X = 8.7$. The mean pecks per minute ($\overline{Y}$) was 13.3 with $s_Y = 4.5$. The r_{obs} between the two variables was −.84. Using the correlational formula to find b, construct the regression line of pecking rate (Y) on scans per minute (X).

   a. What is the slope of the regression line?
   b. What is the Y-intercept of the regression line?
   c. Write the equation for the regression line.
   d. What is the predicted pecking rate for a scan rate of 41 scans per minute? For 18 scans per minute?

SUMMARY

- In a linear relation, each time that variable X changes by 1 unit there is a constant change in variable Y.
- The general equation of a straight line is given by $Y = bX + a$.
- The slope, b, is defined as

$$b = \frac{\text{change in value of } Y}{\text{change in value of } X}.$$

- The Y-intercept, a, is the value of Y when $X = 0$.
- The general equation of a straight line may be used to predict Y scores from known X scores: $Y' = bX + a$. Y' represents the predicted value of Y.
- The residual, $Y - Y'$, is the difference between an obtained Y score and Y' predicted from X.
- A least-squares regression line minimizes the value of the sum of the squared residuals.
- The standard error of estimate is found by

$$s_{Y \cdot X} = \sqrt{\frac{SS_{\text{Residual}}}{N_{\text{pairs}} - 2}}$$

or

$$s_{Y \cdot X} = \sqrt{\frac{\sum (Y - Y')^2}{N_{\text{pairs}} - 2}}.$$

- The standard error of estimate indicates the average amount of error when predicting Y scores from X.
- Multiple regression involves using several X variables to predict variable Y.

KEY TERMS AND SYMBOLS

general equation of a straight
  line (410)
least-squares regression line (420)
linear relation (408)

multiple regression (440)
residual $(Y - Y')$ (425)
slope of a straight line (b) (410)
SS_{Residual} (426)

standard error of estimate $(s_{Y \cdot X})$
  (426)
Y-intercept (a) (411)
Y' (416)

REVIEW QUESTIONS

1. Jamie received her midterm grade in her statistics class. Her instructor said that
   for a previous semester the following midterm and final examination grades were
   obtained by 10 students in the class.

| | Examination | |
Student	Midterm: X	Final: Y
1	87	84
2	89	91
3	97	96
4	80	87
5	73	66
6	85	90
7	81	79
8	74	80
9	80	89
10	89	86

   a. Find the slope of the least-squares regression line for predicting final exam
      grades from midterm grades using the computational formula.
   b. The r_{obs} for these scores is $+.781$, $s_X = 7.37$, and $s_Y = 8.34$. Find b using
      the correlational formula.
   c. Find the equation of the least-squares regression line for predicting Y from X
      for these scores.
   d. Jamie received a 77 on her midterm examination. Based on the regression
      line found in part c, what is her predicted final examination score?
   e. What is the value of $s_{Y \cdot X}$ for this regression line?

2. An investigator observed 12 students on the amount of time playing video games
   per week (variable X) and correlated this time with their semester grade-point
   averages (variable Y). For a range of 0 to 15 hours per week of video-game playing, r_{obs} was $-.632$ ($p < .05$). The $s_X = 4.10$ hours and $s_Y = 0.75$. The Y-inter-
   cept of the regression line was 3.23.

a. Find the least-squares regression line for predicting grade-point average from video-game playing time.

b. Brian plays video games about 3 hours per week. What is his predicted grade-point average?

c. The mean video-game playing time in the sample observed was 5.1 hours per week. What is the mean grade-point average for the sample?

3. One study found a linear relationship between amount of smoking by a pregnant woman and the amount of weight loss of the neonate ("Birth Weight," 1986). For each cigarette smoked per day during pregnancy by the mother the baby's birth weight is reduced by 4.3 ounces. Thus, if a mother smoked an average of two cigarettes per day during pregnancy, the baby's birth weight would be reduced by 8.6 ounces. Assume that if the pregnant mother does not smoke the average weight of the neonate is 128 ounces.

a. Write the equation for the linear relationship for these data. (*Hint:* Both the slope and the Y-intercept are given.)

b. Plot the linear regression line on a sheet of graph paper. Place the number of cigarettes smoked (X) on the abscissa.

c. What is the predicted birth weight of a baby whose mother smoked the following number of cigarettes per day during pregnancy?

$$0 \quad 1 \quad 5 \quad 8 \quad 10 \quad 13 \quad 20$$

4. In Chapter 13, Review Question 1, I gave the following values of anger level scores and systolic blood pressure for 16 males.

Participant	Anger Level	Blood Pressure
1	64	170
2	30	132
3	37	129
4	39	144
5	17	145
6	29	122
7	36	124
8	34	145
9	44	137
10	32	115
11	37	127
12	47	148
13	50	148
14	41	144
15	46	133
16	61	158

    a. Find the equation for the regression of blood pressure (Y) on anger level (X) for these scores. Use the computational formula for the slope.

    b. What is the predicted blood pressure for each person as a function of anger level?

    c. Plot a scatterplot of anger level (on the abscissa) and blood pressure (on the ordinate). Place the regression line on this plot also.

    d. What proportion of s_Y is $s_{Y \cdot X}$ for these scores?

5. Exercise 2 of Testing Your Knowledge 14.4 presented a study on the relationship of the number of scans per minute (X) and number of pecks per minute (Y) for 15 house sparrows. Suppose you made similar observations with 13 wrens and obtained the following scores.

Bird	Scans: X	Pecks: Y
1	29	12
2	34	8
3	24	14
4	14	20
5	37	11
6	22	13
7	11	23
8	33	9
9	24	11
10	30	14
11	36	9
12	20	23
13	32	7

    a. What is the slope of the regression line?

    b. What is the Y-intercept of the regression line?

    c. Write the equation for the regression line.

    d. Plot a scatterplot of the scans and pecks scores. Place the regression line on this plot.

    e. Use the computational formula to find $s_{Y \cdot X}$ for this set of scores.

    f. Compare $s_{Y \cdot X}$ to $s_Y = 5.41$ for these scores. Does use of the regression equation to predict pecks from scans reduce the error of prediction in comparison to using the mean number of scans (i.e., 13.4) as the predicted value for all scan scores?

6. A company uses a score on a standardized interview to predict work performance of job applicants. The regression equation used is $Y' = +1.2X + 18$, where Y' is the predicted job performance and X is the job applicant's score on the standardized interview. The company will hire only applicants whose predicted job performance is 60 or better. The standardized interview scores of eight applicants are as follows. Which of the applicants will the company hire?

Applicant	Standardized Interview Score: X
Dianne	31
Rodrigo	36
Colin	30
Maria	41
Ruben	39
Luke	29
Holly	27
Blythe	44

7. Review Question 8 of Chapter 13 presented a study on the correlation of the number of hours of TV watched per week and the first exam grade in a course for 17 students. The value of r_{obs} for the scores was $-.735$, the mean number of hours of TV watched ($\overline{X}$) was 10.0 with s_X equal to 6.38, and the mean exam grade ($\overline{Y}$) was 76.0 with s_Y equal to 11.44. The SS_X was 652.0 and CP_{XY} was -859.0.

   a. Find the equation for the regression line for predicting exam grades from the number of hours of TV watched for these scores.

   b. Find the predicted exam scores for students who watch 4 and 15 hours of TV per week, respectively.

   c. What is the value of $s_{Y \cdot X}$ for these scores? What proportion of s_Y is $s_{Y \cdot X}$ for these scores?

Nonparametric Statistical Tests

Chapter 8 to 12 developed statistical hypothesis testing emphasizing the *t* test and the analysis of variance. Both tests are **parametric tests**, for they use sample statistics (e.g., $\overline{X}$) to make inferences about population parameters (μ). **Nonparametric statistical tests** involve hypotheses that do not state relationships about population parameters. They also make fewer assumptions about the shapes of populations than do parametric tests. For this reason, nonparametric tests are sometimes called **distribution-free tests**.

Nonparametric statistical test: A statistical test involving hypotheses that do not state a relationship about a population parameter.

Recall that parametric tests assume the following:

- The scores in the populations sampled are normally distributed.
- The variances of scores in the populations are equal.

In practice the data collected may not meet these assumptions. Yet, because parametric tests are thought to be robust, researchers may use the *t* test or analysis of variance on the data even if the assumptions are not fully met.

In some instances, however, these assumptions are not met sufficiently to allow using a parametric test. For example, in measuring the reaction time of an individual, most reaction times are likely to be short (e.g., perhaps about 500 milliseconds or less). No reaction time can be less than 0 seconds; but there is no upper limit on the maximum time that may be measured. A few individuals may have very long reaction times compared to other people. Thus, a frequency distribution of reaction-time measures is likely to be positively skewed; most reaction times are very short, and a few may be much longer. Such a distribution clearly is not an approximately normal distribution.

Parametric tests also assume that it is appropriate to compute a mean (i.e., $\overline{X}$) on the scores obtained. This requirement implies that the scores should achieve either an interval or ratio scale of measurement. But often behaviors cannot be measured at these levels. An experimenter simply may count the number of people displaying a certain behavior, thus obtaining frequencies of occurrence of the behavior, a nominal measurement. Or the scores obtained may represent an ordinal scale, such as rank ordering individuals on a certain personality trait. Because parametric tests require $\overline{X}$ to be calculated, they are not appropriate for use if the scores represent nominal or ordinal measurements. Thus, nonparametric tests are used when:

- The assumptions of parametric tests are not met, or
- Scores are at either the nominal or ordinal level of measurement.

Table 15.1 presents parametric tests and corresponding nonparametric tests for one-factor designs. I discuss the chi-square, Mann–Whitney *U*, and the Wilcoxon signed-ranks tests in this chapter. A nonparametric test of correlation, the Spearman rank-order correlation coefficient, was presented in Chapter 13.

ANALYSIS OF FREQUENCY DATA: THE CHI-SQUARE TEST

Many studies lead to scores that indicate only whether a behavior occurred or not. For example, when observing animals in the wild, a scientist may record only whether an

TABLE 15.1
Parametric and nonparametric tests for one-factor designs as a function of type of design and scale of measurement.

| | | Type of Design | | | |
| | | Between Subjects | | Within Subjects | |
Scale of Measure of Data		Two Levels	Three or More Levels	Two Levels	Three or More Levels
Parametric tests	**Ratio or interval**	t_{ind} or between-subjects ANOVA	Between-subjects ANOVA	t_{rel} or within-subjects ANOVA	Within-subjects ANOVA
Nonparametric tests	**Ordinal**	Mann–Whitney U	Kruskal–Wallis ANOVA by ranks	Wilcoxon signed ranks	Friedman ANOVA by ranks
	Nominal	Chi square	Chi square		

animal does or does not behave in a certain way. These scores achieve nominal measurement; they simply represent the occurrence of mutually exclusive categories of behavior. The frequency of occurrence of responses in the various categories may be obtained, but an individual score indicates only whether a behavior occurred or not; it conveys no numerical information about the response. A nonparametric test, the **chi-square test** (pronounced "ky square") provides an appropriate test for these scores when a between-subjects design is used and the scores are nominal measures representing only the frequency of occurrence of a response. I discuss two forms of the chi-square test, the chi-square test of independence and the chi-square test for goodness of fit.

Chi-square test: A statistical test used to analyze nominal level of measurement scores where frequencies of occurrence of the various categories are obtained.

The Chi-Square Test of Independence

Chi-square test of independence: The chi square used when a score is categorized on two independent dimensions.

The **chi-square test of independence** (also called a *two-way chi square*) is used when a score is categorized on two independent dimensions. The following example illustrates its use. Much of what we know and believe about the world arises from what we see on television. Because of its informational capabilities, behavioral scientists are concerned that television may often present an inaccurate portrait of society. Consider something as simple as the hair color of a TV character. In the general population the proportion of men and women with specific hair colors is about equal (e.g., the proportion of men and women having grey hair is about equal). Yet for TV characters, Davis (1990) found that female characters were about five times more likely to have blonde hair than were male characters, but males were six times more likely to be grey haired than were female characters. Similarly, Elasmar, Hasegawa, and Brain (1999) found that a significantly larger proportion of blonde-haired female characters were successful at achieving their goals identified in the plot than were dark-haired females. Suppose, then, a researcher is interested in finding if there is a relationship between hair color and career status for female characters on TV shows. She hypothesized that female TV characters with blonde hair would more frequently have professional-level jobs than characters with dark hair. To test this hypothesis, she randomly sampled a number of TV shows featuring adult female characters and then categorized these characters by hair color, either blonde or dark haired, and career level, either professional or nonprofessional. Each character was counted only once in the sample.

Hypothetical results for this study are shown in Table 15.2. A TV character is categorized on two dimensions in this table: (1) hair color, blonde or dark, and (2) job level, professional or nonprofessional. The values in this table designated by O (for *observed frequency*) represent the frequency of observations in each category. There was a total of 180 female characters observed in the study and each character contributed only one response to the table, the character was either blonde or dark haired, and her job was either professional or nonprofessional.

Contingency Tables

Rows-by-columns contingency table: A rows-by-columns table presenting the frequency of each category formed by the intersection of the row and column variables in the table.

Marginal frequencies: The row totals and the column totals of the observed frequencies in a contingency table.

Table 15.2 is called a **rows-by-columns contingency table** or a *two-way frequency table.* The rows of the table (symbolized by r) represent one category into which TV characters may be placed. The columns (symbolized by c) provide a second category for the character. Table 15.2 is, thus, a 2 rows ($r =$ two categories of job level, professional or nonprofessional) by 2 columns ($c =$ two categories of the hair color of the character, blonde or dark). It is called a contingency table because we are trying to find if the character's job level, professional or nonprofessional, is related to the character's hair color. The **marginal frequencies** shown in the table are the row totals (i.e., the *row marginals*) and the column totals (i.e., the *column marginals*) of the obtained frequencies.

TABLE 15.2

Hypothetical data for categorization of adult female TV characters by hair color and career level. The values given for O are the observed frequencies and the values given for E are the expected frequencies obtained from the marginal frequencies.

	Hair Color		
	Blonde	**Dark**	**(Marginal)**
Professional	$O = 36$	$O = 48$	84
Career Level	$E = 28$	$E = 56$	
Nonprofessional	$O = 24$	$O = 72$	96
	$E = 32$	$E = 64$	
(Marginal)	60	120	(Total) 180

Expected Frequencies

There are 60 blonde-haired characters and 120 dark-haired characters represented in Table 15.2. Of the total of 180 characters categorized, 84, or 46.7 percent, had a professional-level job and 96, or 53.3 percent, had nonprofessional jobs. If hair color is not related to the job level, then I expect that about 46.7 percent (i.e., 84/180) of the 60 blonde-haired characters, or 28 characters, should have professional-level jobs. Similarly, about 53.3 percent (i.e., 96/180) of the 60 blonde-haired characters, or 32 characters, should have nonprofessional-level jobs. A similar expectation holds for dark-haired characters if there is no relation between hair color and job level. In this instance I expect about 46.7 percent of the 120 dark-haired characters, or 56 females, to have nonprofessional-level jobs and about 53.3 percent of the 120 dark-haired characters, or 64 females, to have nonprofessional-level jobs. These values are called **expected frequencies**, the frequencies of response expected if hair color is not related to job level. Expected frequencies are indicated by the value of **E** (for *expected frequency*) in each cell of the table. Expected frequencies are obtained assuming there is no relationship between the two dimensions on which the participant is categorized. In this example, the expected frequencies assume that hair color and job level are independent of each other.

Expected frequencies: The frequencies in a contingency table obtained assuming that the two dimensions of the table are independent.

The chi-square test uses expected and observed frequencies to develop a test statistic. If there is no relation between the two dimensions in the population sampled, then the observed frequencies should be about the same as the expected frequencies. Large differences of the observed from the expected frequencies should occur only rarely by chance if the column and row variables are not associated. But if the column and row variables are related in the population sampled, then the observed frequencies should differ from the expected frequencies by larger amounts. For example, if the frequency of hair color is related to career level as hypothesized, then it is likely that the blonde-haired characters will have more professional-level jobs than the 28 expected by chance and fewer nonprofessional jobs than the 32 expected by chance. Similarly, if the hypothesized relationship between hair color and job level exists, then it is also likely that the dark-haired characters will have fewer than the 56 professional-level jobs and more than the 64 nonprofessional jobs that are expected by chance.

The χ^2 Statistic

The chi-square (symbolized as χ^2) test measures the difference of the obtained frequencies from the expected frequencies with the test statistic:

$$\chi^2 = \sum_{r=1}^{r} \sum_{c=1}^{c} \frac{(O_{rc} - E_{rc})^2}{E_{rc}},$$

where χ = *chi*, the twenty-second letter of the Greek alphabet (pronounced "ky").

O_{rc} = observed frequency in the *rc* cell, where *r* represents the row number and *c* the column number.

E_{rc} = expected frequency of the *rc* cell.

r = number of categories of the row variable ($r = 2$, job level in this example).

c = number of levels of the columns variable ($c = 2$, hair color in this example).

The double summation signs and limits (i.e., $\sum_{r=1}^{r} \sum_{c=1}^{c}$) indicate that the $(O_{rc} - E_{rc})^2/E_{rc}$ values are summed over all rows and columns of the contingency table.

Statistical Hypothesis Testing with χ^2

Using χ^2 to determine whether hair color is related to job level in the example requires statistical hypothesis testing following the familiar steps:

- A null hypothesis, H_0, and an alternative hypothesis, H_1, are formulated. The null hypothesis provides the sampling distribution of the χ^2 statistic.
- A significance level is selected.
- A critical value of χ^2, identified as χ^2_{crit}, is found from the sampling distribution of χ^2 in Table A.7.
- Using the value of χ^2_{crit}, a rejection region is located in the sampling distribution of χ^2.
- χ^2_{obs} is calculated from the frequencies in the contingency table.
- A decision to reject or not reject H_0 is made on the basis of whether χ^2_{obs} falls into the rejection region.

Statistical Hypotheses

Null Hypothesis.   The null hypothesis under which the sampling distribution of χ^2 is developed and under which expected frequencies for each cell are found is

H_0:   The row variable and the column variable are independent in the population.

For the example study, H_0 may be stated specifically as

H_0:   The job level of the character is independent of hair color of the character.

Alternative Hypothesis.   The alternative hypothesis is

H_1:   The row and column variables are related in the population.

For the example study, H_1 may be stated specifically as

H_1:   The job level of the character is related to the hair color of the character.

Selecting a Significance Level

The process of selecting a significance level is identical to that discussed in earlier chapters. In line with common practice, I choose $\alpha = .05$.

Finding χ^2_{crit} and Locating a Rejection Region

Degrees of Freedom of χ^2.   The specific sampling distribution of χ^2 and, thus, the value of χ^2_{crit} depends on the degrees of freedom of the statistic. The *df* for χ^2 are given by

$$\text{Degrees of freedom} = (r - 1)(c - 1)$$

where r represents the number of rows and c represents the number of columns in the contingency table. For the example, $r = 2$ and $c = 2$; thus, $df = (2 - 1)(2 - 1)$, which equals 1. Values of χ^2_{crit} for $\alpha = .05$ and $.01$ from the sampling distribution of χ^2 at various df are given in Table A.7. The critical value of χ^2 for 1 df and $\alpha = .05$ from Table A.7 is 3.84146 or 3.84 rounded to two decimal places.

Locating a Rejection Region.   If the null hypothesis is true and job level is independent of hair color, then χ^2_{obs} should be relatively small; the expected and observed frequencies for each cell of the contingency table should be much alike. On the other hand, if H_1 is true and the row variable is related to the column variable, then χ^2_{obs} should become larger because the expected and observed frequencies will differ from each other. Consequently, relatively large values of χ^2_{obs} should be rare if the null hypothesis is true but common if the alternative hypothesis is true. Thus, a value of χ^2_{obs} equal to or greater than χ^2_{crit} is statistically significant at the value of α selected. Accordingly, for the example, if χ^2_{obs} is equal to or greater than 3.84, it falls into the rejection region and will lead to rejection of H_0 and acceptance of H_1.

Calculating χ^2_{obs}

Calculating χ^2_{obs} requires knowing both the observed and expected frequencies of responses. The expected frequencies for each cell of a contingency table are obtained from the marginal frequencies by

$$\textbf{Expected frequency of a cell} = \frac{\textbf{(Row marginal for cell)(Column marginal for cell)}}{\textbf{Total number of responses}}.$$

For example, the expected frequency for the blonde hair/professional-level job cell (row 1, column 1) is found by:

$$E_{11} = \frac{(\text{row 1 marginal})(\text{column 1 marginal})}{\text{total}} \quad \text{or}$$

$$E_{11} = \frac{(84)(60)}{180} = \frac{5040}{180} = 28.$$

This expected frequency is the E in the blonde hair/professional-level job cell of Table 15.2. After expected frequencies for each cell are obtained, χ^2_{obs} is found using the statistic

$$\chi^2_{obs} = \sum_{r=1}^{r} \sum_{c=1}^{c} \frac{(O_{rc} - E_{rc})^2}{E_{rc}}.$$

To calculate χ^2_{obs}:

- Subtract the expected frequency (E) from the observed frequency (O) for each cell.
- Square each $O - E$ difference.
- Divide each squared $O - E$ difference by the expected frequency of the cell.
- Sum the resulting $(O - E)^2/E$ values over all cells in the contingency table to obtain χ^2_{obs}.

The numerical value of χ^2_{obs} for the frequencies shown in Table 15.2 is calculated as follows:

$$\chi^2_{obs} = \left[\frac{(36-28)^2}{28}\right] + \left[\frac{(24-32)^2}{32}\right] + \left[\frac{(48-56)^2}{56}\right] + \left[\frac{(72-64)^2}{64}\right],$$

$$= \frac{8^2}{28} + \frac{(-8^2)}{32} + \frac{(-8^2)}{56} + \frac{8^2}{64},$$

$$= 2.286 + 2.000 + 1.143 + 1.000,$$

$$= 6.43 \text{ rounded to two decimal places.}$$

Decisions About the Statistical Hypotheses

The χ^2_{obs} of 6.43 is larger than χ^2_{crit} of 3.84 and, thus, falls into the rejection region. Accordingly, H_0 is rejected and H_1 is accepted. There is a statistically significant relationship between the row and column variables.

Conclusion from the Test

The rejection of H_0 indicates that hair color and job level are related. The nature of the relationship is seen by examining Table 15.2: A greater than chance frequency of a professional-level job is associated with blonde hair and a greater than chance frequency of a nonprofessional job is associated with dark hair.

Assumptions for the Use of the Chi-Square Test

A chi-square test of independence may be used on a contingency table of any size (e.g., 2×3, 3×4, or 4×4). Several assumptions apply to its use, however.

- Each participant may contribute only one response to the contingency table.
- The number of responses obtained should be large enough so that no expected frequency is less than 10 in a 2×2 contingency table or less than 5 in a contingency table larger than 2×2. If this condition is not met, then either more responses should be collected or an alternative test, such as the Fisher exact test, should be used.

Further details of the use of chi-square and alternative tests for frequency data may be found in most advanced statistics texts.

Example Problem 15.1

Using the Chi-Square Test with a 3 × 2 Contingency Table

Problem: Being a firstborn often appears to confer certain advantages to a child. Several studies have indicated that firstborn children typically perform better on academic-type measures than do later-born children, and Eisenman (1987) found a relationship between birth order and creativity among college males. Firstborn males' scores were more frequently above the median on creativity, and later-born males' creativity scores were more frequently below the median in his sample. Suppose that you extend this research by testing 100 firstborn and 100 later-born adult males by asking them for creative uses of common objects. You categorize their responses as being either in the top, middle, or bottom one-third of the scores for creativity. The categorization by birth order and creativity test score resulted in the following observed frequencies.

		Birth Order	
		Firstborn	Later Born
Creativity test score	Top one-third	47	29
	Middle one-third	29	35
	Bottom one-third	24	36

Is there a relationship between birth order and creativity in males? Use a .05 significance level.

Solution: One categorization of a subject in this study is birth order with two levels, first-born and later born. The second categorization was based on the creativity test score being in the top, middle, or bottom one-third of scores for a college population. Each subject contributes only one score or count to the frequency; hence, the chi-square test is an appropriate statistical test for these data.

Statistic to Be Used: χ^2.

Assumptions for Use
1. Each person contributes only one response to the contingency table.
2. No expected frequency will be less than 5. This minimum expected frequency applies because the contingency table, a 3×2, is greater than a 2×2.

Statistical Hypotheses
H_0:   Birth order and creativity are independent in the male population sampled.
H_1:   Birth order and creativity are related in the male population sampled.

Significance Level: $\alpha = .05$.

df: $df = (r - 1)(c - 1) = (3 - 1)(2 - 1) = 2$.

Critical Value: $\chi^2_{\text{crit}}(2) = 5.99146$ from Table A.7 or 5.99 rounded to two decimal places.

Rejection Region: Values of χ^2_{obs} equal to or greater than 5.99.

Calculation: The formula for χ^2_{obs} requires finding expected frequencies; to do so I must find the marginal frequencies. The observed frequencies (indicated by O), the expected frequencies (indicated by E), and the marginal frequencies are provided in the following contingency table:

| | | Birth Order | | |
		Firstborn	Later Born	(Row Marginals)
Creativity test score	**Top one-third**	$O = 47$ $E = 38$	$O = 29$ $E = 38$	76
	Middle one-third	$O = 29$ $E = 32$	$O = 35$ $E = 32$	64
	Bottom one-third	$O = 24$ $E = 30$	$O = 36$ $E = 30$	60
	(Column marginals)	100	100	(Total) 200

Column marginals are obtained by summing the observed frequencies in each column. Row marginals are obtained analogously by summing the observed frequencies in each row. Given the marginal frequencies, expected frequencies are found using

$$\text{Expected frequency of a cell} = \frac{\text{(Row marginal for cell)(Column marginal for cell)}}{\text{Total number of responses}}.$$

Expected frequencies for each cell of the table are then as follows:

Firstborn—top $\frac{1}{3}$ cell: $E_{11} = \dfrac{(76)(100)}{200} = \dfrac{7600}{200} = 38,$

Later born—top $\frac{1}{3}$ cell: $E_{12} = \dfrac{(76)(100)}{200} = \dfrac{7600}{200} = 38,$

Firstborn—middle $\frac{1}{3}$ cell: $E_{21} = \dfrac{(64)(100)}{200} = \dfrac{6400}{200} = 32,$

Later born—middle $\frac{1}{3}$ cell: $E_{22} = \dfrac{(64)(100)}{200} = \dfrac{6400}{200} = 32,$

Firstborn—bottom $\frac{1}{3}$ cell: $E_{31} = \dfrac{(60)(100)}{200} = \dfrac{6000}{200} = 30,$

Later born—bottom $\frac{1}{3}$ cell: $E_{32} = \dfrac{(60)(100)}{200} = \dfrac{6000}{200} = 30.$

The value of χ^2_{obs} is found by

$$\chi^2_{obs} = \sum_{r=1}^{3} \sum_{c=1}^{2} \frac{(O_{rc} - E_{rc})^2}{E_{rc}}.$$

Substituting numerical values,

$$\chi^2_{obs} = \frac{(47 - 38)^2}{38} + \frac{(29 - 38)^2}{38} + \frac{(29 - 32)^2}{32} + \frac{(35 - 32)^2}{32} + \frac{(24 - 30)^2}{30} + \frac{(36 - 30)^2}{30},$$

$$= 2.13 + 2.13 + 0.28 + 0.28 + 1.20 + 1.20,$$

$$= 7.22.$$

Decision: The $\chi^2_{obs} = 7.22$ is greater than $\chi^2_{crit} = 5.99$; thus, it falls into the rejection region. I reject H_0 and accept H_1.

Conclusion: Birth order and creativity are related in the male population sampled. By examining the table of observed and expected frequencies, we see that firstborn males' scores occur more frequently and later-born males' scores occur less frequently in the top one-third of the scores than expected by chance. We notice also that firstborn males' scores occur less frequently and later-born males' more frequently in the bottom one-third of scores than a chance hypothesis predicts.

THE χ^2 TEST FOR GOODNESS OF FIT

Chi-square test for goodness of fit: The chi square used when a score is categorized on only one dimension.

In the chi-square test of independence, participants were categorized on two different dimensions, for example whether a TV character was blonde or dark haired, and whether the character's career was professional or nonprofessional. With the **chi-square test for goodness of fit**, scores are categorized on only one dimension or variable. Consider an example.

Many people believe that abnormal behavior is more likely to occur during a full moon. As a test for empirical evidence to support this belief, suppose that you categorized the admission of new clients into a mental health unit over a one-year period by lunar phases and found the following distribution of admissions.

Lunar Phase

Full Moon	New Moon	First Quarter	Third Quarter
62	50	60	56

Do admissions vary with the phase of the moon? The chi-square goodness of fit test may be used to answer this question.

The observed frequencies categorize behavior only by lunar phase. To use a chi-square test, I need to find expected frequencies of admissions for each lunar phase. Because I do not have row and column marginals to obtain expected frequencies, I must have some other basis for predicting expected frequencies. For this example, I use the following reasoning to obtain the expected frequencies. If admission into the mental health unit is unrelated to phase of the moon, then the frequency of new admissions should be equal in each phase, with any observed differences reflecting only sampling error. This reasoning may be expressed in the null hypothesis:

H_0:   New admissions to the mental health unit and phase of the moon are independent in the population sampled.

The alternative hypothesis, then, is

H_1: New admissions to the mental health unit and phase of the moon are related in the population sampled.

If this alternative hypothesis is true, then new admissions should not be equal among the lunar phases. But if H_0 is true, then one-fourth of the new admissions should occur in each lunar phase. Hence, expected frequencies of admissions incidents may be obtained by dividing the total frequency of admissions by 4, the number of lunar phases. Applying this reasoning to our example, there are 228 total new admissions, so the expected frequency for each phase is $\frac{228}{4}$ or 57. The observed and expected frequencies for each lunar phase are then as follows:

Lunar Phase

Full Moon	New Moon	First Quarter	Third Quarter
$O = 62$	$O = 50$	$O = 60$	$O = 56$
$E = 57$	$E = 57$	$E = 57$	$E = 57$

Chi square may be obtained from these data by

$$\chi^2 = \sum_{c=1}^{c} \frac{(O_c - E_c)^2}{E_c} \quad \text{with } c - 1 \text{ df.}$$

Accordingly,

$$\chi^2_{\text{obs}} = \frac{(62 - 57)^2}{57} + \frac{(50 - 57)^2}{57} + \frac{(60 - 57)^2}{57} + \frac{(56 - 57)^2}{57},$$

$$= \frac{(5)^2}{57} + \frac{(-7)^2}{57} + \frac{(3)^2}{57} + \frac{(-1)^2}{57},$$

$$= \frac{25}{57} + \frac{49}{57} + \frac{9}{57} + \frac{1}{57},$$

$$= \frac{84}{57} = 1.47.$$

The degrees of freedom for this χ^2_{obs} are $c - 1$, where c represents the number of categories used. For the example, $c = 4$; thus, $df = 4 - 1 = 3$. The critical value of χ^2 for 3 df and $\alpha = .05$ is given in Table A.7; $\chi^2_{\text{crit}}(3) = 7.81$ rounded to two decimal places. $\chi^2_{\text{obs}} = 1.47$ is less than χ^2_{crit} and does not fall into the rejection region. I fail to reject the null hypothesis. There is no evidence that the frequency of new admissions to the mental health unit is related to phases of the moon in the population sampled.

The assumptions for the chi-square goodness of fit test are similar to those for the chi-square test of independence; each participant must contribute only one observation to the data, and the expected frequencies should not be less than 10 if there are only two categories or not less than 5 if there are three or more categories.

REPORTING THE RESULTS OF THE CHI-SQUARE TEST

The *Publication Manual of the American Psychological Association* (1994) requires that a report of the chi-square test include the *df* and the sample size on which χ^2_{obs} is based. To illustrate, I use the example of the chi-square test for independence on the TV characters problem.

Table 1 presents the observed frequencies for hair color and career level. With alpha equal to .05, a chi-square test on these frequencies was statistically significant, $\chi^2(1, N = 180) = 6.43$, $p < .05$. Blonde-haired female TV characters were more likely to have professional-level careers than were dark-haired characters.

TABLE 1
Hypothetical data for categorization of adult female TV characters by hair color and career level.

Career Level	Hair Color	
	Blonde	Dark
Professional	36	48
Nonprofessional	24	72

In this report:

Table 1	Provides the observed frequencies of the responses.
$\alpha = .05$	Indicates the significance level selected for the test.
$\chi^2(1, N = 180)$	Identifies the test statistic as the chi square. The 1 in parentheses indicates the test was based on 1 *df* and the $N = 180$ gives the total sample size.
$= 6.43$	Gives the value of χ^2_{obs} (not the χ^2_{crit} value of Table A.7).
$p < .05$	Indicates that

    a.   the probability of χ^2_{obs} if H_0 is true is less than or equal to .05. This value is the probability of χ^2_{obs} or an even more extreme value of χ^2_{obs} if H_0 is true; it may not be the same as the value of α selected.

    b.   "H_0: The job level of the character is independent of hair color of the character" was rejected.

         "H_1: The job level of the character is related to the hair color of the character" was accepted.

TESTING YOUR KNOWLEDGE 15.1

1. Define: c, chi-square test, expected frequencies, marginal frequencies, nonparametric test, observed frequencies, parametric test, r, rows-by-columns contingency table, two-way frequency table.
2. Under what circumstances is a nonparametric test used to analyze data from an experiment?

3. Identify the appropriate statistical test for each of the following one-factor designs with two levels of the independent variable and the level of measurement of the scores indicated.
    a. Within-subjects, ratio measurement.
    b. Between-subjects, nominal measurement.
    c. Between-subjects, ratio measurement.
    d. Between-subjects, ordinal measurement.
    e. Within-subjects, ordinal measurement.
4. What form of data is suitable for analysis by the chi-square test?
5. What is represented by the columns of a rows-by-columns contingency table?
6. What is represented by the rows of a rows-by-columns contingency table?
7. The following are values of χ^2_{obs} for various degrees of freedom (given in parentheses).

$$\chi^2_{obs}(2) = 7.26 \qquad \chi^2_{obs}(4) = 8.33$$
$$\chi^2_{obs}(7) = 14.19 \qquad \chi^2_{obs}(20) = 26.94$$

For each value of χ^2_{obs} and df, find the value of χ^2_{crit} at the .05 level. Then indicate whether χ^2_{obs} falls into the rejection region and the decisions you make concerning H_0 and H_1.
8. For each of the following contingency tables, calculate expected frequencies; then find χ^2_{obs} and indicate whether it is statistically significant at the .05 level. The values in each cell represent observed frequencies.

a.

		Column	
		1	2
Row	1	12	32
	2	16	38

b.

		Column	
		1	2
Row	1	27	22
	2	17	46

c.

		Column	
		1	2
Row	1	33	66
	2	27	14

9. Complete the following problem using the chi-square test following the format illustrated in the example problem. Use a .05 significance level. Have you ever run a traffic stop sign while driving? Perhaps not, but no doubt you have seen others do so. How frequently do drivers fail to stop for stop signs, and does the frequency of occurrence of such behaviors depend on the time of day or day of the week? Suppose that a researcher investigated this problem by observing the number of vehicles not stopping for a stop sign at

an intersection. He observed traffic from 10:00 A.M. to 11:00 A.M. and from 2:00 P.M. to 3:00 P.M. on Tuesday, Wednesday, and Thursday of one week. Car licenses were noted and each car was counted only on its first trip through the intersection for the week. Suppose that the investigator reported the following frequency of vehicles ignoring the stop sign during the two times on each of the days of the week observed.

| | | Day of Week | | |
		Tuesday	Wednesday	Thursday
Time	10:00 to 11:00 A.M.	38	46	58
	2:00 to 3:00 P.M.	46	54	63

Is there a relationship between day of the week and time of day with respect to drivers ignoring stop signs?

10. Complete the following problem using the chi-square test following the format illustrated in the example problem. Use a .05 significance level. Psychologists have hypothesized that one cause for eating disorders among females is the many cues that stress thinness as desirable for females. Smith, Waldorf, and Trembath (1990) investigated one form of cue, the personal ad, to see if these ads indicated weight as an important characteristic of a desired partner. They hypothesized that ads placed by males seeking females would more likely indicate a weight requirement than would an ad placed by a female seeking a male. To test this hypothesis, they examined a set of personal ads and categorized them by gender of the person placing the ad and whether or not the ad expressed a weight preference. The following hypothetical frequencies typify the outcome of their study. Does the hypothesized relationship exist in these scores?

| | Preference for Weight Indicated | |
	Yes	No
Ad placed by male	89	186
Ad placed by female	6	219

MANN–WHITNEY *U* TEST

Mann–Whitney *U* test: A nonparametric test for a between-subjects design using two levels of an independent variable with scores representing at least ordinal measurement.

The **Mann–Whitney *U* test** is a nonparametric test for a between-subjects design using two levels of an independent variable with scores representing at least ordinal measurement. I develop the Mann–Whitney *U* test using an example of research on perceiving reversible figures (Reisberg, 1983; Strueber and Stadler, 1999).

Reversible figures are stimuli that offer two or more possible perceptual organizations. For example, Figure 15.1 illustrates the Schroeder staircase. This figure has two possible perceptual organizations: In one, a set of stairs appears normal; in the other, the stairs seem upside down. The stairs will reverse perceptually if you view them for a while. If

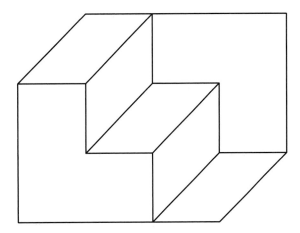

FIGURE 15.1
The Schroeder staircase, an ambiguous figure.

attention and memory are required to reverse the perception from one organization to the other, then an additional task that occupies attention and memory should lengthen the time needed to reverse the perception. To test this hypothesis, suppose I created two equivalent groups of participants were created. Both groups viewed the Schroeder staircase and reported when they had seen both organizations of the stimulus. The independent variable was the type of interfering task. Participants in the control group (A_1) simply viewed the figure and reported the reversal. Participants in the experimental group (A_2) counted backward by threes from a three-digit number, a task requiring both attention and memory, while they viewed the stimulus. If perceiving reversal of the figure also requires attention and memory, then counting backward should interfere with perception of the figure and delay the reports of a reversal. The amount of time it took each person to report a reversal was recorded. This time is called the *latency* of a response. If a participant did not report a reversal at the end of 2 minutes, the test was stopped and the person assigned an "infinite" (∞) latency.

Table 15.3 presents hypothetical data for this experiment, with nine people in each of the two groups. The scores are shown in order of increasing latency in each group, although they would not occur in this order as they actually were recorded from participants. Notice that for the experimental group one person did not report a reversal within 2 minutes. This person was assigned an infinite latency without a numerical value. Because both the *t* test and the analysis of variance require numerical values from each participant, they cannot be used to analyze these data if this participant's score is included. The Mann–Whitney *U* test, however, only requires that scores be ranked, and an infinite latency can be ranked. Thus, the scores are analyzed with the Mann–Whitney *U* test.

Statistical Hypothesis Testing with the Mann–Whitney *U*

I first present a conceptual overview of the *U* test and then a computational format. Both approaches require ranking scores to develop a test statistic and a sampling distribution of

TABLE 15.3

Hypothetical perceptual reversal latencies (in seconds) of the Schroeder staircase figure. Participants in the control group simply viewed the figure. Participants in the experimental group counted backward by threes while viewing the figure.

Group	
Control (A_1)	Experimental (A_2)
2	4
5	10
6	11
8	12
9	14
13	17
15	85
21	98
42	∞[a]

For ease of discussion, the scores are presented in order of increasing latency in each treatment group.

[a]This score represents an "infinite" reversal latency; this person did not see the reversal within the 2-minute time limit.

that statistic. This ranking is done even if the scores represent an interval or ratio measurement; the scores are converted to ordinal measurement by ranking them.

Ranking Scores

The first step in ranking the scores is to combine the scores of both groups (for a total of N scores) and then place the scores in order of increasing magnitude from smallest to largest. This procedure is shown in row 1 of Table 15.4 for the data of Table 15.3. In performing the ranking, the group identity of the scores is maintained (see row 2 of Table 15.4). Then the ranks from 1 to N are assigned to the scores, giving the smallest score the rank of 1 and the largest score the rank of N. This ranking is shown in row 3 of Table 15.4. Often there may be tied scores, such as two people obtaining a latency of 12 seconds. Table 15.5 describes the procedure for dealing with such ties and Example Problem 15.2 illustrates this procedure.

The *U* Statistic

The U statistic is the number of times that the rank of a score in one group precedes the rank of a score in the other group. This calculation is illustrated in rows 4 and 5 of Table 15.4. For example, the score of 2 (shown in row 1) from the A_1 group (identified in row 2) precedes all the A_2 scores in rank (given in row 3). Thus, this score precedes nine of the A_2 scores in rank. Scores of 5, 6, 8, and 9 from the A_1 group each precede eight of the scores in

TABLE 15.4
Rank ordering scores of Table 15.3.

1. Latency scores ordered from smallest to largest	2	4	5	6	8	9	10	11	12	13	14	15	17	21	42	85	98	∞
2. Group identity[a]	1	2	1	1	1	1	2	2	2	1	2	1	2	1	1	2	2	2
3. Rank	1	2	3	4	5	6	7	8	9	10	11	12	13	14	15	16	17	18
4. Number of times an A_1 score precedes A_2 scores	9		8	8	8	8				5		4		3	3			
5. Number of times an A_2 score precedes A_1 scores		8					4	4	4		3		2					

[a]A 1 indicates the score is from group A_1, control; 2 indicates the score is from group A_2, experimental.

the A_2 group in rank. Row 4 of Table 15.4 presents the number of times that an A_1 score precedes an A_2 score in rank. Examine the numerical values in this row to be sure to understand how they were obtained. The total number of times that an A_1 score precedes an A_2 score in rank is 56, the total of the values in row 4 (i.e., $9 + 8 + 8 + 8 + 8 + 5 + 4 + 3 + 3 = 56$). Thus, the value of $U_{A1\,obs}$ (for the U observed on group A_1) is 56.

There is also a value of U for the A_2 group. This value represents the number of times that the rank of an A_2 score precedes the rank of an A_1 score. Row 5 of Table 15.4 indicates the number of times that an A_2 score precedes an A_1 score in rank. The sum of the values in this row (i.e., $8 + 4 + 4 + 4 + 3 + 2 = 25$) provides $U_{A2\,obs} = 25$.

Characteristics of the U Statistic

If a treatment has no effect, then it is expected that, when the scores are combined and ordered as they are in Table 15.4, scores from each group will be approximately equally distributed over the rankings. I do not expect the scores from one group to be represented exclusively among the lower ranks and the scores of the other condition to be exclusively among the higher ranks. Consequently, the value of $U_{A1\,obs}$ should be about equal to $U_{A2\,obs}$. For example, if the treatment had no effect in the example, then $U_{A1\,obs}$ and $U_{A2\,obs}$ would each equal about 40. If the treatment had an exceptionally strong effect, however, and all the A_1 scores had lower ranks than the A_2 scores, then $U_{A1\,obs}$ would be 81 and $U_{A2\,obs}$ would be equal to 0. The values of $U_{A1\,obs}$ and $U_{A2\,obs}$ are perfectly inversely related. As $U_{A1\,obs}$ increases, $U_{A2\,obs}$ decreases by an equal amount. Hence, only one value of U, the smaller value, is used in a statistical test. I can easily determine if the smaller value has been calculated by using the relation

$$U_{A2\,obs} = n_{A1}n_{A2} - U_{A1\,obs},$$

where n_{A1} is the number of scores in group A_1 and n_{A2} is the number of scores in group A_2. In the example, $U_{A2\,obs}$ is found from $U_{A1\,obs}$ by

$$U_{A2\,obs} = (9)(9) - 56 = 81 - 56 = 25,$$

and 25 is the smaller of the two values of U for the data of Table 15.3. Thus, $U_{obs} = 25$.

This U statistic is used in a statistical hypothesis test by following the steps of statistical hypothesis testing.

Statistical Hypotheses

Null Hypothesis.   The null hypothesis under which the sampling distribution of U is developed is

> H_0:   The population distribution of A_1 scores is identical to the population distribution of A_2 scores.

If H_0 is true, then the value of $U_{A1\,obs}$ should be about the same as $U_{A2\,obs}$.

Alternative Hypothesis.   The alternative hypothesis for the U test is

> H_1:   The population distribution of A_1 scores is not identical to the population distribution of A_2 scores.

If H_1 is true, then $U_{A1\,obs}$ and $U_{A2\,obs}$ should differ from each other.

Sampling Distributions and Critical Values of U

The sampling distribution of U varies with n_{A1} and n_{A2}. To simplify the use of the U statistic, tables of its sampling distribution and critical values of U at the .01 and .05 levels have been developed for various sizes of n_{A1} and n_{A2}. Because the maximum value of U is determined by n_{A1} and n_{A2}, tables of the sampling distribution of U present only the smaller of the two values of U that may be obtained from a study. The sampling distribution for the smaller value of U for groups ranging in size from 1 to 20 for $\alpha = .01$ and $\alpha = .05$ is presented in Table A.8. The values in this table present the critical value of U, identified as U_{crit}, for the smaller U_{obs}. Values of the smaller U_{obs} **less than or equal to U_{crit}** are statistically significant for the value of α selected. Notice, in contrast to the t, F, and χ^2 statistics, that the rejection region for U_{obs} consists of values of the smaller U_{obs} that are *less than or equal to U_{crit}*. For the example data, $n_{A1} = 9$ and $n_{A2} = 9$; thus, $U_{crit} = 17$ at the .05 significance level.

Decisions about the Statistical Hypotheses

Decisions about the statistical hypotheses are made using the smaller of the two values of U_{obs}, as follows:

Value of Smaller U_{obs}	Statistical Decision
Less than or equal to U_{crit}	Reject H_0 Accept H_1
Greater than U_{crit}	Do not reject H_0 Do not accept H_1

For our example of the reversal latency scores of Table 15.3, $U_{A1\,obs} = 56$ and $U_{A2\,obs} = 25$. $U_{A2\,obs}$ is the smaller of the two values, and this value is used as U_{obs} for the statistical hypothesis test. $U_{obs} = 25$ is larger than $U_{crit} = 17$. Accordingly, the value of U_{obs} does not fall into the rejection region; I fail to reject H_0 and I do not accept H_1.

Conclusion from the Test

Failing to reject H_0 leads to the conclusion that there is no evidence to indicate that the population distribution of the control group scores differs from the population distribution of experimental group scores in the example. Counting backward did not change the latency of a reversal in comparison to the control condition.

Assumptions of the Mann–Whitney U Test

The assumptions applying to the U test are the following:

- Each participant contributes only one score to the data.
- Scores are at least ordinal measurement and represent a continuous variable. In many instances, as in the example problem, scores will be either interval or ratio measurements, and these measures will be converted to ranks for application of the U test.

Computational Formulas for U

The approach taken in Table 15.4 to obtain U_{A1} and U_{A2} is cumbersome, but it illustrates what U_{A1} and U_{A2} represent. For computational purposes, however, simplified formulas have been developed.

$U_{A1\,obs}$

The value of $U_{A1\,obs}$ is found from the formula

$$U_{A1\,obs} = n_{A1}n_{A2} + \frac{n_{A1}(n_{A1} + 1)}{2} - \sum R_{A1},$$

where n_{A1} = number of scores in group A_1

n_{A2} = number of scores in the A_2 group

$\sum R_{A1}$ = sum of the ranks assigned to scores in group A_1

The $\sum R_{A1}$ is obtained by adding the ranks assigned to the A_1 scores in row 3 of Table 15.4. For the example, the ranks of the scores in the A_1 group are 1, 3, 4, 5, 6, 10, 12, 14, and 15. The sum of these ranks is 70; thus, $\sum R_{A1} = 70$. Substituting values into the equation for U_{A1} provides

$$U_{A1\,obs} = (9)(9) + \frac{9(9 + 1)}{2} - 70 = 56.$$

$U_{A2\,obs}$

The value of $U_{A2\,obs}$ is obtained from the formula

$$U_{A2\,obs} = n_{A1}n_{A2} + \frac{n_{A2}(n_{A2} + 1)}{2} - \sum R_{A2},$$

where $\sum R_{A2}$ is the sum of the ranks assigned to scores in A_2. For the example, the ranks of the scores in the A_2 group are 2, 7, 8, 9, 11, 13, 16, 17, and 18 (see row 3 in Table 15.4). The sum of these ranks is 101; thus, $\sum R_{A2} = 101$. Substituting into the formula,

$$U_{A2\,obs} = (9)(9) + \frac{9(9 + 1)}{2} - 101 = 25.$$

Alternatively, if $U_{A1\,obs}$ is known, $U_{A2\,obs}$ may be obtained from the formula given earlier:

$$U_{A2\,obs} = n_{A1}n_{A2} - U_{A1\,obs}.$$

Each formula provides the same value of $U_{A2\,obs}$.

Table 15.5 summarizes the U test using these computational formulas. This table also includes the procedure to be followed if ranks are tied. Example Problem 15.2 illustrates the steps in this table.

TABLE 15.5
Using the Mann–Whitney U test with computational formulas.

Step 1: Rank order the combined scores of both groups from the smallest score (rank = 1) to the largest score (rank = N). Maintain the group designation (A_1 or A_2) of each score. Assign tied scores the mean of the ranks they would have been assigned if they were not tied.

Step 2: Find $\sum R_{A1}$ and $\sum R_{A2}$.

Step 3: Compute $U_{A1\,obs}$.

$$U_{A1\,obs} = n_{A1}n_{A2} + \frac{n_{A1}(n_{A1} + 1)}{2} - \sum R_{A1}.$$

Step 4: Compute $U_{A2\,obs}$.

$$U_{A2\,obs} = n_{A1}n_{A2} + \frac{n_{A2}(n_{A2} + 1)}{2} - \sum R_{A2}$$

or

$$U_{A2\,obs} = n_{A1}n_{A2} - U_{A1}.$$

Step 5: Choose the smaller of the two values of U_{obs}. This U_{obs} is compared with the U_{crit}.

Example Problem 15.2

Using the Mann–Whitney *U* Test

Problem: At many colleges and universities the major drug-use problem of students is alcohol abuse. Suppose that a counselor developed an alcohol education program for students. At the beginning of an academic year the counselor randomly selected 8 first-year males and presented the educational program to them. Six weeks after presenting the program, she gave the students a questionnaire on their alcohol consumption. At the same time she randomly chose 10 other first-year males who had not been given the alcohol education program and also gave them the questionnaire. The estimated daily alcohol consumption of the two groups in ounces of pure alcohol was as follows:

Educational Program Condition

Program Given (A_1)	No Program Given (A_2)
0.31	0.41
0.53	0.63
0.58	1.14
0.14	0.21
0.16	0.89
0.52	0.55
0.53	0.89
0.02	0.91
	0.08
	0.59

Because these scores are estimates of a behavior, the counselor believed that they do not meet the requirements of interval measurement. Consequently, she treated them as presenting ordered information only. Did the educational program condition affect the estimated alcohol consumption of those students exposed to it? Use a .05 significance level.

Solution: The research design is a between-subjects design with two levels of the independent variable, educational program condition. The dependent variable, estimated alcohol consumption, is considered an ordinal measure. Accordingly, the Mann–Whitney *U* test is an appropriate statistical test for these data.

Statistic to Be Used: Smaller U_{obs}.

Assumptions for Use
1. Each subject is measured in only one treatment condition.
2. The dependent variable is at least ordinal measurement and represents a continuous variable.

Statistical Hypotheses

H_0:   The population distribution of the educational-program-given (A_1) scores is identical to the population distribution of the no-educational-program-given (A_2) scores.

H_1:   The population distribution of the educational-program-given (A_1) scores is not identical to the population distribution of the no-educational-program-given (A_2) scores.

Significance Level: $\alpha = .05$.

Critical Value of U: For $n_{A1} = 8$, $n_{A2} = 10$, and $\alpha = .05$, $U_{crit} = 17$ from Table A.8.

Rejection Region: Values of the smaller U_{obs} equal to or less than 17.

Calculation: The steps of Table 15.5 are followed to calculate U_{obs}.

Step 1:   Rank order the combined scores of both groups from smallest to largest.

Ordered scores:	0.02	0.08	0.14	0.16	0.21	0.31	0.41	0.52	0.53	0.53	0.55	0.58	0.59	0.63	0.89	0.89	0.91	1.14
Group identity:	1	2	1	1	2	1	2	1	1	1	2	1	2	2	2	2	2	2
Rank:	1	2	3	4	5	6	7	8	9.5	9.5	11	12	13	14	15.5	15.5	17	18

Two sets of scores are tied, 0.53 and 0.89. For 0.53, the scores occupy the ranks of 9 and 10; hence, each score was assigned the mean (i.e., 9.5) of the two ranks. Similarly, the two scores of 0.89 occupy the ranks of 15 and 16; thus, each score was assigned the mean (i.e., 15.5) of the two ranks.

Step 2:   Obtain the sum of the ranks for each group.

$$\Sigma R_{A1} = 1 + 3 + 4 + 6 + 8 + 9.5 + 9.5 + 12 = 53.$$

$$\Sigma R_{A2} = 2 + 5 + 7 + 11 + 13 + 14 + 15.5 + 15.5 + 17 + 18 = 118.$$

Step 3:   Compute $U_{A1\,obs}$.

$$U_{A1\,obs} = (8)(10) + \frac{8(8+1)}{2} - 53$$

$$= 80 + (72/2) - 53$$

$$= 80 + 36 - 53 = 63.$$

Step 4:   Compute $U_{A2\,obs}$.

$$U_{A2\,obs} = (8)(10) + \frac{10(10+1)}{2} - 118$$

$$= 80 + (110/2) - 118$$

$$= 80 + 55 - 118 = 17.$$

Step 5:   Choose the smaller U_{obs}.

$$U_{A2\,obs} = 17 \text{ is the smaller } U_{obs}.$$

Decision: $U_{obs} = 17$ is equal to $U_{crit} = 17$. Thus, it falls into the rejection region; H_0 is rejected and H_1 is accepted.

Conclusion: Rejection of H_0 indicates that the distribution of estimates from the educational program group is different from the distribution of estimates of the no educational program group. The alcohol education program reduced the amount of alcohol consumed as measured by students' estimates of daily alcohol consumption.

REPORTING THE RESULTS OF THE MANN–WHITNEY U TEST

The journal presentation of the U test follows the general guidelines for statistical presentations. I illustrate using the example problem on the effect of counting backward on the perception of reversals in the Schroeder staircase figure.

A Mann–Whitney U test was used to compare the distributions of the reversal latencies of the control ($n = 9$) and experimental groups ($n = 9$). With an alpha level of .05, the distributions did not differ significantly, $U = 25, p > .05$.

This presentation provides the typical information about the test used. The value of $U = 25$ is the smaller U_{obs}, and the $p > .05$ indicates that this U is nonsignificant at the .05 level. The group size information ($n_{A1} = n_{A2} = 9$) provides the information needed to look up U_{crit} in Table A.8.

TESTING YOUR KNOWLEDGE 15.2

1.   Combine the following scores of groups A_1 and A_2 and rank order from 1 to N. Maintain the group identity of each score. Then find $U_{A1\,obs}$, the number of times an A_1 score precedes an A_2 score, and $U_{A2\,obs}$, the number of times an A_2 score precedes an A_1 score.

Group	
A_1	A_2
15	7
23	26
10	14
19	16

a.   Which value of U_{obs} is the smaller value?

b.   Is the smaller U_{obs} statistically significant at the .05 level?

2. Find $U_{A1\,obs}$ and $U_{A2\,obs}$ for the scores of question 1 using the computational formulas for U.
   a. Do the values of $U_{A1\,obs}$ and $U_{A2\,obs}$ obtained with the computational formulas agree with those obtained in question 1?
3. Write the statistical hypotheses for the Mann–Whitney U test.
4. If H_0 is true, then what should be the relation of $U_{A1\,obs}$ to $U_{A2\,obs}$?
5. If H_1 is true, then what should be the relation of $U_{A1\,obs}$ to $U_{A2\,obs}$?
6. Given in the following table are the smaller values of U_{obs} for various group sizes. For each set of U_{obs} and group sizes, find the value of U_{crit} at the .01 level. Then indicate whether U_{obs} falls into the rejection region and the decisions you make concerning H_0 and H_1.

	U_{obs}	n_{A1}	n_{A2}
a.	3	6	4
b.	12	10	10
c.	28	16	9
d.	21	7	19
e.	4	13	19
f.	126	18	19

7. Complete the following problem using the Mann–Whitney U test following the format illustrated in the example problem. Use a .05 significance level. The use of music to induce relaxation in dental patients is becoming more widespread. Suppose that a dentist tested the effectiveness of music in relaxing patients by randomly assigning patients to one of two groups. Thirteen patients in a music condition listened to music while dental proce-dures were performed; 12 patients in a no music condition did not listen to music while similar dental procedures were performed. Midway through the appointment, each patient was asked to estimate his or her anxiety on a scale of 1 (not at all anxious) to 100 (extremely anxious). The anxiety estimates obtained were as follows:

Music Condition

No Music	Music
52	44
75	21
66	66
33	54
17	37
78	84
94	30
89	29
27	54
49	49
53	33
78	10
	78

Do the groups differ in their distributions of anxiety estimates?

THE WILCOXON SIGNED-RANKS TEST

Wilcoxon signed-ranks test: A nonparametric test for within-subjects designs with two levels of an independent variable.

The **Wilcoxon signed-ranks test** is a nonparametric test for within-subjects designs with two levels of an independent variable. Thus, it is a nonparametric analog of the t_{rel}. The Wilcoxon test assumes only that the underlying dimension of behavior measured is continuous and that scores may be placed in rank order.

To illustrate the Wilcoxon signed-ranks test, I introduce an experiment on the expression of emotion in voice patterns (Cosmides, 1983). Suppose a psychologist hypothesized that vocal frequencies will change with different emotional states. To test this hypothesis, she uses a one-factor within-subjects design with two levels of an independent variable, the type of script a person is to read, either a script reflecting a happy scene (A_1) or a script reflecting a sad scene (A_2). The purpose of the script is to induce either a happy or sad emotion in the subject. In each condition the person's task is to read the script silently and, on a signal from the experimenter, say aloud the words "I'm still reading." The frequency span of the vocal expression of "I'm still reading" is the dependent variable for each subject and is measured in cycles per second (cps, or hertz). Thus, a score is the range of the highest vocal frequency minus the lowest vocal frequency in a subject's expression of the three words.

Suppose that the frequency spans for 10 people tested under both script conditions are those presented in Table 15.6. The means, standard deviations, and variances for these scores are also shown here. Notice that not only do the mean frequency ranges appear to differ, but there is a large difference in the variability of the two conditions. Recall that t_{rel}

TABLE 15.6
Hypothetical scores for vocal-frequency span (in hertz) as a function of type of script read.

Person	Happy (A_1)	Sad (A_2)
1	305	214
2	275	385
3	360	519
4	299	307
5	317	483
6	326	454
7	284	501
8	347	463
9	331	382
10	314	297
$\overline{X}_A$	315.80	400.50
s_A	26.54	101.40
s^2	704.37	10,281.96

The column header above the two data columns reads **Type of Script**.

requires the variances of the two populations to be equal. In this example, however, the two variances differ considerably (704.37 and 10,281.96 for the happy and sad scripts, respectively). Thus, one of the assumptions of t_{rel} is violated by these data. The Wilcoxon signed-ranks test does not make assumptions about the variances; accordingly, it is an appropriate test for these scores.

Statistical Hypothesis Testing with the Wilcoxon Signed-Ranks Test

The T Statistic
The Wilcoxon test uses ranked scores to obtain a test statistic called the T, which is the smaller sum of the ranks from the two treatment conditions.

Statistical Hypotheses

Null Hypothesis.   The null hypothesis tested with the T is

H_0:   The population distributions of the related A_1 and A_2 scores are identical.

Alternative Hypothesis.   The alternative hypothesis is

H_1:   The population distributions of the related A_1 and A_2 scores are not identical.

Sampling Distribution and Critical Values of T
Values of T_{crit} for $\alpha = .05$ and $\alpha = .01$ are presented in Table A.9 for samples from 6 to 50. This table is entered with the value of N_{pairs}, the number of pairs of scores or, equivalently, the number of participants. Values of T_{obs} **less than or equal to** T_{crit} fall into the rejection region and are statistically significant for the value of α selected. In the example with $N_{pairs} = 10$ and $\alpha = .05$, $T_{crit} = 8$. The rejection region is, thus, defined by values of T_{obs} less than or equal to 8.

Calculating T
The computations for obtaining T_{obs} involve the following steps. The result of each step is shown in Table 15.7 using the example vocal-frequency-span scores.

Step 1:   Find $d = X_{A1} - X_{A2}$, the difference between the A_1 and A_2 scores for each subject as shown in column a of Table 15.7. Maintain the + or − sign of the difference.

Step 2:   Find the absolute value of each difference ($|d|$, the value without regard to sign) as shown in column b.

Step 3:   Rank the absolute differences from smallest (rank = 1) to largest (rank = N) as shown in column c. Differences of zero are not ranked, and the value of N used to find T_{crit} is reduced by the number of zero differences occurring. Tied values of d are assigned the mean of the ranks that would have been assigned had no tie occurred.

Step 4:   Give each rank in column c the sign of the difference in column a. The signed ranks are shown in column d.

TABLE 15.7
Computation of the Wilcoxon *T* on the scores of Table 15.6.

Person	Type of Script Happy (A_1)	Type of Script Sad (A_2)	(a) d	(b) |d|	(c) Ranked |d|	(d) Signed Rank
1	305	214	+91	91	4	+4
2	275	385	−110	110	5	−5
3	360	519	−159	159	8	−8
4	299	307	−8	8	1	−1
5	317	483	−166	166	9	−9
6	326	454	−128	128	7	−7
7	284	501	−217	217	10	−10
8	347	463	−116	116	6	−6
9	331	382	−51	51	3	−3
10	314	297	+17	17	2	+2

Step 5:   Sum the ranks of like sign (i.e., the sum of the positive-signed ranks and the sum of the negative-signed ranks) in column d. For example, the sum of the positive-signed ranks in column d equals 6 [i.e., $(+4) + (+2)$] and the sum of the negative-signed ranks equals -49 [i.e., $(-5) + (-8) + (-1) + (-9) + (-7) + (-10) + (-6) + (-3)$].

Step 6:   Find the absolute value of each sum of the ranks. Then choose the smaller of the two sums of the ranks. In this case it is 6, the sum of the positive ranks. This sum is T_{obs}; thus, $T_{obs} = 6$.

Decisions about the Statistical Hypotheses

The $T_{obs} = 6$ is less than $T_{crit} = 8$; accordingly, T_{obs} falls into the rejection region. I reject H_0 and accept H_1.

Conclusion from the Test

Rejection of H_0 and acceptance of H_1 lead to the conclusion that the two distributions of scores differ; the type of script produced differences in the vocal-frequency span. The vocal-frequency span for a sad script is larger than for a happy script.

Example Problem 15.3

Using the Wilcoxon Signed-Ranks Test

Problem: It has been hypothesized that music tempo affects the speed of behaviors, with fast-tempo music increasing the speed with which a behavior may occur (McElrea & Standing, 1992; Roballey et al., 1985). To investigate this hypothesis, suppose a researcher conducted the following study. Eleven cafeteria patrons were observed eating on two different days with two different background music conditions, slow music on day 1 (A_1) and fast music on day 2 (A_2). The same people were observed unobtrusively on both days. The number of bites per minute taken by each person under each music condition was recorded. Suppose that the following median bites per minute were observed for each person under the two music tempo conditions.

	Music Tempo	
Person	**Slow** (A_1)	**Fast** (A_2)
1	3	4
2	4	6
3	2	3
4	3	3
5	3	8
6	4	2
7	1	4
8	5	4
9	3	6
10	5	9
11	2	8

The experimenter considered the scores to achieve ordinal measurement. Does music tempo affect biting rate? Use a .05 significance level.

Solution: The research design is a one-factor within-subjects design with two levels of the independent variable, music tempo. The dependent variable is measured at least at the ordinal level; thus, the Wilcoxon signed-ranks test is an appropriate statistical test for these data.

Statistic to Be Used: T, the smaller sum of the ranks.

Assumptions for Use
  1. Each subject is measured on both levels of the independent variable.
  2. The dependent variable is measured at least at the ordinal level.

Statistical Hypotheses
  H_0: The population distributions of the related A_1 and A_2 scores are identical.
  H_1: The population distributions of the related A_1 and A_2 scores are not identical.

Significance Level: $\alpha = .05$.

Critical Value of T: For $N_{pairs} = 11$ and $\alpha = .05$, $T_{crit} = 10$. In the calculation of T, however, person 4 shows a zero change between the music conditions. This participant is dropped from the analysis. Accordingly, N_{pairs} becomes 10 and T_{crit} for $N = 10$ is 8 from Table A.9.

Rejection Region: Values of T_{obs} less than or equal to 8.

Calculation

Step 1: The value of $d = X_{A1} - X_{A2}$ is found for each person (column a of Table 15.8).

Step 2: Absolute values of d are obtained (column b of Table 15.8).

Step 3: The absolute values of d are ranked from 1 to 10; $d = 0$ is not included in the ranking (column c). Notice the ranking of the several sets of tied d values. Tied scores are given the mean of the ranks that they occupy. For example, there are three differences of $|d| = 1$ in column b. These values occupy the ranks 1, 2, and 3. The mean of these ranks is 2; thus, each value of $|d| = 1$ is assigned a rank of 2.

Step 4: The sign of each d (from column a) is attached to the rank of d (column d).

Step 5: Like-signed ranks are summed. The absolute value of the sum of the positive-signed ranks $= 6.5$ [i.e., $(+4.5) + (+2) = 6.5$]. The absolute value of the sum of the negative-signed ranks $= 48.5$ [i.e., $(-2) + (-4.5) + (-2) + (-9) + (-6.5) + (-6.5) + (-8) + (-10) = 48.5$].

Step 6: The absolute value of the sum of the positive-signed ranks is the smaller sum of the ranks; hence, $T_{obs} = 6.5$.

Decision: $T_{obs} = 6.5$ is less than $T_{crit} = 8$ and falls into the rejection region; H_0 is rejected and H_1 accepted.

Conclusion: The distributions of the number of bites taken per minute differ significantly under the two music tempos; more bites are taken per minute under a fast tempo than under a slow tempo.

TABLE 15.8
Computation of the Wilcoxon T on the number of bites taken as a function of music tempo.

Person	Music Tempo Slow (A_1)	Fast (A_2)	(a) d	(b) $\lvert d \rvert$	(c) Ranked $\lvert d \rvert$	(d) Signed Rank
1	3	4	−1	1	2	−2
2	4	6	−2	2	4.5	−4.5
3	2	3	−1	1	2	−2
4	3	3	0	0	—	—
5	3	8	−5	5	9	−9
6	4	2	+2	2	4.5	+4.5
7	1	4	−3	3	6.5	−6.5
8	5	4	+1	1	2	+2
9	3	6	−3	3	6.5	−6.5
10	5	9	−4	4	8	−8
11	2	8	−6	6	10	−10

REPORTING THE RESULTS OF THE WILCOXON SIGNED-RANKS TEST

I illustrate the reporting of the Wilcoxon signed-ranks test using the example manipulating the type of script and measuring the vocal-frequency span of subjects.

> A Wilcoxon signed-ranks test was used to compare the vocal-frequency spans of the happy and sad script conditions. With an alpha level of .05, the script conditions differed significantly, $T = 6$ ($N = 10$), $p < .05$. There was a significantly greater range of frequencies in the sad-script condition compared to the happy-script condition.

Again, this presentation provides the information needed to interpret the value of T_{obs}. Knowing the value of N_{pairs}, I can look up the value of T_{crit} if necessary.

USING NONPARAMETRIC TESTS

As we have seen, nonparametric tests do not make assumptions about the population distribution of scores for a sample. Furthermore, they usually require only that we be able to rank order the scores obtained. Parametric tests, such as the t or analysis of variance, require stronger assumptions about the nature of scores in an experiment, assumptions that sometimes may be questionable for the scores collected in a study. Nevertheless, nonparametric statistical tests are less widely used in behavioral science research than are parametric statistical tests. Why?

There are several answers to this question. In general, if the assumptions for a parametric test are met by the scores being analyzed, then a nonparametric test is less likely to detect an effect of the independent variable than its corresponding parametric test. That is, nonparametric tests typically are less powerful and, thus, more likely to lead to Type II errors than parametric tests when the assumptions for parametric tests are met by the data. Because most parametric tests are considered robust with respect to violation of assumptions, many researchers routinely analyze their data with parametric tests.

Nonparametric tests also provide different information than do parametric tests. For example, the t_{ind} leads to conclusions about the equality or inequality of the population means, but conclusions with the U test concern the equality or inequality of the population distributions. In addition, for more complex designs, such as the factorial designs discussed in Chapter 11, there are no nonparametric tests that provide as much information as the parametric factorial analysis of variance.

As I have suggested, there are no hard and fast rules about when a nonparametric test should be used. The perception of reversals in the Schroeder staircase example presented to introduce the U test in this chapter provides an unusually clear-cut instance when a nonparametric statistical test is necessary. One of the scores in this experiment was an infinite value. With such a value, a mean or standard deviation of scores cannot be computed. Obviously, then, a parametric test cannot be used on these data.

Other instances are often not so straightforward. For example, how much must the underlying distribution of a population of scores differ from a normal distribution before the use of a parametric test is inappropriate? When are the variances of two or more populations considered to be unequal? Behavioral scientists are not in agreement on the answers to these questions; consequently, they may not agree on whether a parametric or nonparametric test should be used to analyze a set of scores.

TESTING YOUR KNOWLEDGE 15.3

1. For what type of research design is the Wilcoxon test appropriate?
2. What is the test statistic used by the Wilcoxon signed-ranks test?
3. Write the statistical hypotheses for the Wilcoxon signed-ranks test.
4. Given next are the smaller absolute values of the sum of the signed ranks for experiments of different group sizes. For each smaller rank and value of N_{pairs}, identify the value of T_{obs}. Then find T_{crit} for the .05 significance level and indicate whether T_{obs} falls into the rejection region. Finally, identify the decisions you make concerning H_0 and H_1.

	Smaller Rank	N_{pairs}
a.	2	8
b.	9	10
c.	17	13
d.	40	19
e.	98	25

5. Complete the following problem using the Wilcoxon signed-ranks test following the format illustrated in the example problem. Use a .05 significance level.

Sport psychologists are interested in the relationship of anxiety to performance in sports competition. For example, Maynard and Howe (1987) measured anxiety of rugby players before games 1 and 2 of a playoff series. Suppose that you attempted a similar study and found the following anxiety scores. The range of possible scores is from 12 (very low reported anxiety) to 84 (very high reported anxiety).

Player	Game 1	Game 2
1	68	72
2	56	65
3	78	77
4	49	54
5	66	64
6	43	53
7	77	70
8	68	78
9	28	29
10	69	75
11	75	78
12	80	72
13	75	75
14	65	76
15	71	70

It is likely that the population distribution of anxiety of scores is negatively skewed (most players reporting very high anxiety, a few reporting very low anxiety levels); thus, you plan to use a nonparametric statistical analysis for these scores. Do the distributions of anxiety scores differ from game 1 to game 2?

SUMMARY

- The chi-square test is used for scores that represent the frequency of occurrence of a response.
- The chi-square test of independence is used to test for a relationship between categories on two independent dimensions.
- The chi-square test of independence is obtained by

$$\chi^2_{obs} = \sum_{r=1}^{r} \sum_{c=1}^{c} \frac{(O_{rc} - E_{rc})^2}{E_{rc}}.$$

- The chi-square goodness of fit test is used to determine how well scores categorized on one dimension agree with theoretically derived expected frequencies for those categories.
- The chi-square test for goodness of fit is obtained by

$$\chi^2_{obs} = \sum_{c=1}^{c} \frac{(O_c - E_c)^2}{E_c}.$$

- The Mann–Whitney U test is a nonparametric test for a between-subjects design using two levels of an independent variable and scores at least at an ordinal level.
- The U statistic is the number of times that the rank of a score in one group precedes the rank of a score in the other group.
- The value of $U_{A1\,obs}$ is found from

$$U_{A1\,obs} = n_{A1}n_{A2} + \frac{n_{A1}(n_{A1} + 1)}{2} - \sum R_{A1}$$

and the value of $U_{A2\,obs}$ from

$$U_{A2\,obs} = n_{A1}n_{A2} + \frac{n_{A2}(n_{A2} + 1)}{2} - \sum R_{A2}.$$

The smaller U_{obs} is used as the test statistic.

- The Wilcoxon signed-ranks test is a parametric test for within-subjects designs with two levels of an independent variable.

- The test statistic used in the Wilcoxon signed-ranks test is the T, the smaller sum of the ranks from the two treatment conditions.
- When the assumptions for a parametric test are met by the data being analyzed, a parametric test is more powerful than its corresponding nonparametric test.

KEY TERMS AND SYMBOLS

chi-square test (450)
chi-square test for goodness of
  fit (458)
chi-square test of independence
  (450)
χ^2 (452)
χ^2_{crit} (453)
χ^2_{obs} (453)
distribution-free tests (449)

expected frequencies (E) (452)
Mann–Whitney U test (462)
marginal frequencies (451)
nonparametric statistical test
  (449)
parametric test (449)
rows-by-columns contingency
  table (451)
T (474)

T_{crit} (474)
T_{obs} (474)
U (464)
U_{crit} (466)
$U_{A1\,obs}$ (465)
$U_{A2\,obs}$ (465)
Wilcoxon signed-ranks test
  (473)

REVIEW QUESTIONS

1. Many individuals in psychotherapy terminate the therapy before its scheduled completion. These people (known as psychotherapy dropouts) appear to comprise a substantial minority of those in psychotherapy (Stahler & Eisenman, 1987). Suppose that to gain more knowledge of this problem you obtain the records of several community mental health centers and categorize dropouts and nondropouts by gender and severity of the problem that they exhibit.

   a. You obtained the following frequencies of dropouts and nondropouts for males and females.

	Gender	
	Male	**Female**
Nondropout	99	130
Dropout	75	78

   Is the dropout frequency related to gender at the .05 significance level? If so, what is the relationship?

   b. The subjects were then categorized by the severity of their psychological problem: mild, moderate, and severe. The following frequencies were obtained:

Severity of Psychological Problem

	Mild	Moderate	Severe
Nondropout	51	66	112
Dropout	64	54	35

Is the dropout rate related to severity of the psychological problem at the .05 significance level? If so, what is the relationship?

2. Example Problem 12.2 introduced a study testing whether yawning is a sign of boredom. Using a one-factor within-subjects design, participants saw a 30-minute rock music video (A_1, the interesting stimulus) and 30 minutes of a color-bar test pattern without sound (A_2, the uninteresting stimulus). The number of times a person yawned during the two sessions was observed and recorded. Suppose that we replicated this experiment using 11 subjects and observed the following number of yawns for each session:

Type of Video (A)

Person	Interesting	Uninteresting
1	5	7
2	2	1
3	4	7
4	3	8
5	0	2
6	4	5
7	7	6
8	6	23
9	3	3
10	1	4
11	8	9

a. Use the Wilcoxon signed-ranks test and a .05 significance level to find if the type of task affects the amount of yawning that occurs.

b. Why might the Wilcoxon signed-ranks test be more appropriate for these data than t_{rel}? (*Hint:* Examine the distribution of the scores.)

c. What conclusions do you reach from the Wilcoxon test?

3. Chapter 9, Review Question 1, presented a study to determine the effect of noise on blood pressure. Two groups of subjects were formed. Participants in the quiet group relaxed in a comfortable chair for 30 minutes, and at the end of the 30 minutes their systolic blood pressure was measured. Participants in the noise group also sat in the same chair for 30 minutes. During the 30-minute wait, however, they listened to a recording of traffic noise from a large city during rush hour. After listening to the noise for 30 minutes, the systolic blood pressure of these

individuals was also recorded. Suppose that the following blood pressure measures (in millimeters of mercury) were obtained:

Group

Quiet	Noise
106	141
117	136
124	124
129	139
115	121
147	119
121	147
115	128
128	115
136	134
127	140

Use the U test and a .05 significance level to find if the distributions differ. Describe your conclusions.

4. To find if sex differences exist in trait anxiety, a researcher gave an anxiety inventory to 9 females and 13 males. The scores on the inventory may range from 20 (low anxiety) to 80 (high anxiety). Suppose that the following scores were obtained.

Gender

Female	Male
36	54
25	70
47	34
39	53
55	41
41	56
29	32
59	44
38	40
	61
	50
	30
	37

Use the Mann–Whitney U test and a .05 significance level to find if the distribution of female anxiety scores differs from that of the males. Describe your conclusions.

5. In Chapter 9, I presented a problem dealing with weight gain after the cessation of smoking. In that study, the weights of eight people were measured at the time they entered a smoking cessation program and one year later. The following weights were obtained.

Time of Weight Measurement

Person	Entering Program	One Year after Stopping
1	122.4	127.9
2	117.1	119.4
3	127.8	127.1
4	123.2	126.5
5	112.5	114.6
6	118.7	125.3
7	121.4	119.8
8	131.7	134.2

Analyze the scores with the Wilcoxon signed-ranks test to see if the distributions differ at the .05 level. Describe your conclusions.

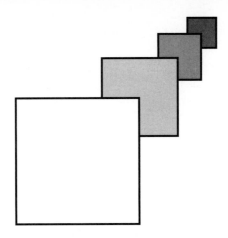

Appendixes

Appendix A
Statistical Tables

TABLE A.1
Proportions of area under the standard normal distribution.

(a) Value of +z	(b)	(c)	(a) Value of +z	(b)	(c)	(a) Value of +z	(b)	(c)
.00	.0000	.5000	.28	.1103	.3897	.56	.2123	.2877
.01	.0040	.4960	.29	.1141	.3859	.57	.2157	.2843
.02	.0080	.4920	.30	.1179	.3821	.58	.2190	.2810
.03	.0120	.4880	.31	.1217	.3783	.59	.2224	.2776
.04	.0160	.4840	.32	.1255	.3745	.60	.2257	.2743
.05	.0199	.4801	.33	.1293	.3707	.61	.2291	.2709
.06	.0239	.4761	.34	.1331	.3669	.62	.2324	.2676
.07	.0279	.4721	.35	.1368	.3632	.63	.2357	.2643
.08	.0319	.4681	.36	.1406	.3594	.64	.2389	.2611
.09	.0359	.4641	.37	.1443	.3557	.65	.2422	.2578
.10	.0398	.4602	.38	.1480	.3520	.66	.2454	.2546
.11	.0438	.4562	.39	.1517	.3483	.67	.2486	.2514
.12	.0478	.4522	.40	.1554	.3446	.68	.2517	.2483
.13	.0517	.4483	.41	.1591	.3409	.69	.2549	.2451
.14	.0557	.4443	.42	.1628	.3372	.70	.2580	.2420
.15	.0596	.4404	.43	.1664	.3336	.71	.2611	.2389
.16	.0636	.4364	.44	.1700	.3300	.72	.2642	.2358
.17	.0675	.4325	.45	.1736	.3264	.73	.2673	.2327
.18	.0714	.4286	.46	.1772	.3228	.74	.2704	.2296
.19	.0753	.4247	.47	.1808	.3192	.75	.2734	.2266
.20	.0793	.4207	.48	.1844	.3156	.76	.2764	.2236
.21	.0832	.4168	.49	.1879	.3121	.77	.2794	.2206
.22	.0871	.4129	.50	.1915	.3085	.78	.2823	.2177
.23	.0910	.4090	.51	.1950	.3050	.79	.2852	.2148
.24	.0948	.4052	.52	.1985	.3015	.80	.2881	.2119
.25	.0987	.4013	.53	.2019	.2981	.81	.2910	.2090
.26	.1026	.3974	.54	.2054	.2946	.82	.2939	.2061
.27	.1064	.3936	.55	.2088	.2912	.83	.2967	.2033

(continued)

TABLE A.1 Continued

(a) Value of +z / −z	(b)	(c)	(a) Value of +z / −z	(b)	(c)	(a) Value of +z / −z	(b)	(c)
.84	.2995	.2005	1.53	.4370	.0630	2.22	.4868	.0132
.85	.3023	.1977	1.54	.4382	.0618	2.23	.4871	.0129
.86	.3051	.1949	1.55	.4394	.0606	2.24	.4875	.0125
.87	.3078	.1922	1.56	.4406	.0594	2.25	.4878	.0122
.88	.3106	.1894	1.57	.4418	.0582	2.26	.4881	.0119
.89	.3133	.1867	1.58	.4429	.0571	2.27	.4884	.0116
.90	.3159	.1841	1.59	.4441	.0559	2.28	.4887	.0113
.91	.3186	.1814	1.60	.4452	.0548	2.29	.4890	.0110
.92	.3212	.1788	1.61	.4463	.0537	2.30	.4893	.0107
.93	.3238	.1762	1.62	.4474	.0526	2.31	.4896	.0104
.94	.3264	.1736	1.63	.4484	.0516	2.32	.4898	.0102
.95	.3289	.1711	1.64	.4495	.0505	2.33	.4901	.0099
.96	.3315	.1685	1.65	.4505	.0495	2.34	.4904	.0096
.97	.3340	.1660	1.66	.4515	.0485	2.35	.4906	.0094
.98	.3365	.1635	1.67	.4525	.0475	2.36	.4909	.0091
.99	.3389	.1611	1.68	.4535	.0465	2.37	.4911	.0089
1.00	.3413	.1587	1.69	.4545	.0455	2.38	.4913	.0087
1.01	.3438	.1562	1.70	.4554	.0446	2.39	.4916	.0084
1.02	.3461	.1539	1.71	.4564	.0436	2.40	.4918	.0082
1.03	.3485	.1515	1.72	.4573	.0427	2.41	.4920	.0080
1.04	.3508	.1492	1.73	.4582	.0418	2.42	.4922	.0078
1.05	.3531	.1469	1.74	.4591	.0409	2.43	.4925	.0075
1.06	.3554	.1446	1.75	.4599	.0401	2.44	.4927	.0073
1.07	.3577	.1423	1.76	.4608	.0392	2.45	.4929	.0071
1.08	.3599	.1401	1.77	.4616	.0384	2.46	.4931	.0069
1.09	.3621	.1379	1.78	.4625	.0375	2.47	.4932	.0068
1.10	.3643	.1357	1.79	.4633	.0367	2.48	.4934	.0066
1.11	.3665	.1335	1.80	.4641	.0359	2.49	.4936	.0064
1.12	.3686	.1314	1.81	.4649	.0351	2.50	.4938	.0062

z			z			z		
1.13	.3708	.1292	1.82	.4656	.0344	2.51	.4940	.0060
1.14	.3729	.1271	1.83	.4664	.0336	2.52	.4941	.0059
1.15	.3749	.1251	1.84	.4671	.0329	2.53	.4943	.0057
1.16	.3770	.1230	1.85	.4678	.0322	2.54	.4945	.0055
1.17	.3790	.1210	1.86	.4686	.0314	2.55	.4946	.0054
1.18	.3810	.1190	1.87	.4693	.0307	2.56	.4948	.0052
1.19	.3830	.1170	1.88	.4699	.0301	2.57	.4949	.0051
1.20	.3849	.1151	1.89	.4706	.0294	2.58	.4951	.0049
1.21	.3869	.1131	1.90	.4713	.0287	2.59	.4952	.0048
1.22	.3888	.1112	1.91	.4719	.0281	2.60	.4953	.0047
1.23	.3907	.1093	1.92	.4726	.0274	2.61	.4955	.0045
1.24	.3925	.1075	1.93	.4732	.0268	2.62	.4956	.0044
1.25	.3944	.1056	1.94	.4738	.0262	2.63	.4957	.0043
1.26	.3962	.1038	1.95	.4744	.0256	2.64	.4959	.0041
1.27	.3980	.1020	1.96	.4750	.0250	2.65	.4960	.0040
1.28	.3997	.1003	1.97	.4756	.0244	2.66	.4961	.0039
1.29	.4015	.0985	1.98	.4761	.0239	2.67	.4962	.0038
1.30	.4032	.0968	1.99	.4767	.0233	2.68	.4963	.0037
1.31	.4049	.0951	2.00	.4772	.0228	2.69	.4964	.0036
1.32	.4066	.0934	2.01	.4778	.0222	2.70	.4965	.0035
1.33	.4082	.0918	2.02	.4783	.0217	2.71	.4966	.0034
1.34	.4099	.0901	2.03	.4788	.0212	2.72	.4967	.0033
1.35	.4115	.0885	2.04	.4793	.0207	2.73	.4968	.0032
1.36	.4131	.0869	2.05	.4798	.0202	2.74	.4969	.0031
1.37	.4147	.0853	2.06	.4803	.0197	2.75	.4970	.0030
1.38	.4162	.0838	2.07	.4808	.0192	2.76	.4971	.0029
1.39	.4177	.0823	2.08	.4812	.0188	2.77	.4972	.0028
1.40	.4192	.0808	2.09	.4817	.0183	2.78	.4973	.0027
1.41	.4207	.0793	2.10	.4821	.0179	2.79	.4974	.0026
1.42	.4222	.0778	2.11	.4826	.0174	2.80	.4974	.0026
1.43	.4236	.0764	2.12	.4830	.0170	2.81	.4975	.0025
1.44	.4251	.0749	2.13	.4834	.0166	2.82	.4976	.0024
1.45	.4265	.0735	2.14	.4838	.0162	2.83	.4977	.0023
1.46	.4279	.0721	2.15	.4842	.0158	2.84	.4977	.0023
1.47	.4292	.0708	2.16	.4846	.0154	2.85	.4978	.0022
1.48	.4306	.0694	2.17	.4850	.0150	2.86	.4978	.0021
1.49	.4319	.0681	2.18	.4854	.0146	2.87	.4979	.0021
1.50	.4332	.0668	2.19	.4857	.0143	2.88	.4979	.0020
1.51	.4345	.0655	2.20	.4861	.0139	2.89	.4980	.0019
1.52	.4357	.0643	2.21	.4864	.0136	2.90	.4981	.0019

(continued)

TABLE A.1 Continued

(a) Value of +z / −z	(b)	(c)	(a) Value of +z / −z	(b)	(c)	(a) Value of +z / −z	(b)	(c)
2.91	.4982	.0018	3.18	.4993	.0007	3.45	.4997	.0003
2.92	.4982	.0018	3.19	.4993	.0007	3.46	.4997	.0003
2.93	.4983	.0017	3.20	.4993	.0007	3.47	.4997	.0003
2.94	.4984	.0016	3.21	.4993	.0007	3.48	.4997	.0003
2.95	.4984	.0016	3.22	.4994	.0006	3.49	.4998	.0002
2.96	.4985	.0015	3.23	.4994	.0006	3.50	.4998	.0002
2.97	.4985	.0015	3.24	.4994	.0006	3.51	.4998	.0002
2.98	.4986	.0014	3.25	.4994	.0006	3.52	.4998	.0002
2.99	.4986	.0014	3.26	.4994	.0006	3.53	.4998	.0002
3.00	.4987	.0013	3.27	.4995	.0005	3.54	.4998	.0002
3.01	.4987	.0013	3.28	.4995	.0005	3.55	.4998	.0002
3.02	.4987	.0013	3.29	.4995	.0005	3.56	.4998	.0002
3.03	.4988	.0012	3.30	.4995	.0005	3.57	.4998	.0002
3.04	.4988	.0012	3.31	.4995	.0005	3.58	.4998	.0002
3.05	.4989	.0011	3.32	.4995	.0005	3.59	.4998	.0002
3.06	.4989	.0011	3.33	.4996	.0004	3.60	.4998	.0002
3.07	.4989	.0011	3.34	.4996	.0004	3.61	.4998	.0002
3.08	.4990	.0010	3.35	.4996	.0004	3.62	.4999	.0001
3.09	.4990	.0010	3.36	.4996	.0004	3.63	.4999	.0001
3.10	.4990	.0010	3.37	.4996	.0004	3.64	.4999	.0001
3.11	.4991	.0009	3.38	.4996	.0004	3.65	.4999	.0001
3.12	.4991	.0009	3.39	.4997	.0003	3.66	.4999	.0001
3.13	.4991	.0009	3.40	.4997	.0003	3.67	.4999	.0001
3.14	.4992	.0008	3.41	.4997	.0003	3.68	.4999	.0001
3.15	.4992	.0008	3.42	.4997	.0003	3.69	.4999	.0001
3.16	.4992	.0008	3.43	.4997	.0003	3.70	.4999	.0001
3.17	.4992	.0008	3.44	.4997	.0003			

Source: Reprinted with permission from Table II.1, The normal probability function and related functions. *CRC Handbook of Tables for Probability and Statistics* (2nd ed., 1968). Copyright CRC Press, Boca Raton, Florida.

TABLE A.2

Critical values of the t distribution for $\alpha = .05$ and $\alpha = .01$. A value of $t_{obs}(df)$ equal to or greater than the tabled value is statistically significant at the α level selected.

	Two-Tailed Test			One-Tailed Test	
df	$\alpha = .05$	$\alpha = .01$	df	$\alpha = .05$	$\alpha = .01$
1	12.706	63.657	1	6.314	31.821
2	4.303	9.925	2	2.920	6.965
3	3.182	5.841	3	2.353	4.541
4	2.776	4.604	4	2.132	3.747
5	2.571	4.032	5	2.015	3.365
6	2.447	3.707	6	1.943	3.143
7	2.365	3.499	7	1.895	2.998
8	2.306	3.355	8	1.860	2.896
9	2.262	3.250	9	1.833	2.821
10	2.228	3.169	10	1.812	2.764
11	2.201	3.106	11	1.796	2.718
12	2.179	3.055	12	1.782	2.681
13	2.160	3.012	13	1.771	2.650
14	2.145	2.977	14	1.761	2.624
15	2.131	2.947	15	1.753	2.602
16	2.120	2.921	16	1.746	2.583
17	2.110	2.898	17	1.740	2.567
18	2.101	2.878	18	1.734	2.552
19	2.093	2.861	19	1.729	2.539
20	2.086	2.845	20	1.725	2.528
21	2.080	2.831	21	1.721	2.518
22	2.074	2.819	22	1.717	2.508
23	2.069	2.807	23	1.714	2.500
24	2.064	2.797	24	1.711	2.492
25	2.060	2.787	25	1.708	2.485
26	2.056	2.779	26	1.706	2.479
27	2.052	2.771	27	1.703	2.473
28	2.048	2.763	28	1.701	2.467
29	2.045	2.756	29	1.699	2.462
30	2.042	2.750	30	1.697	2.457
40	2.021	2.704	40	1.684	2.423
60	2.000	2.660	60	1.671	2.390
120	1.980	2.617	120	1.658	2.358
∞	1.960	2.576	∞	1.645	2.326

TABLE A.3a

Critical values of the F distribution for $\alpha = .05$. A value of F_{obs} ($df_{numerator}$, $df_{denominator}$) equal to or greater than the tabled value is statistically significant at the .05 significance level.

								Degrees of Freedom for the Numerator											
	1	2	3	4	5	6	7	8	9	10	12	15	20	24	30	40	60	120	∞
1	161.4	199.5	215.7	224.6	230.2	234.0	236.8	238.9	240.5	241.9	243.9	245.9	248.0	249.1	250.1	251.1	252.2	253.3	254.3
2	18.51	19.00	19.16	19.25	19.30	19.33	19.35	19.37	19.38	19.40	19.41	19.43	19.45	19.45	19.46	19.47	19.48	19.49	19.50
3	10.13	9.55	9.28	9.12	9.01	8.94	8.89	8.85	8.81	8.79	8.74	8.70	8.66	8.64	8.62	8.59	8.57	8.55	8.53
4	7.71	6.94	6.59	6.39	6.26	6.16	6.09	6.04	6.00	5.96	5.91	5.86	5.80	5.77	5.75	5.72	5.69	5.66	5.63
5	6.61	5.79	5.41	5.19	5.05	4.95	4.88	4.82	4.77	4.74	4.68	4.62	4.56	4.53	4.50	4.46	4.43	4.40	4.36
6	5.99	5.14	4.76	4.53	4.39	4.28	4.21	4.15	4.10	4.06	4.00	3.94	3.87	3.84	3.81	3.77	3.74	3.70	3.67
7	5.59	4.74	4.35	4.12	3.97	3.87	3.79	3.73	3.68	3.64	3.57	3.51	3.44	3.41	3.38	3.34	3.30	3.27	3.23
8	5.32	4.46	4.07	3.84	3.69	3.58	3.50	3.44	3.39	3.35	3.28	3.22	3.15	3.12	3.08	3.04	3.01	2.97	2.93
9	5.12	4.26	3.86	3.63	3.48	3.37	3.29	3.23	3.18	3.14	3.07	3.01	2.94	2.90	2.86	2.83	2.79	2.75	2.71
10	4.96	4.10	3.71	3.48	3.33	3.22	3.14	3.07	3.02	2.98	2.91	2.85	2.77	2.74	2.70	2.66	2.62	2.58	2.54
11	4.84	3.98	3.59	3.36	3.20	3.09	3.01	2.95	2.90	2.85	2.79	2.72	2.65	2.61	2.57	2.53	2.49	2.45	2.40
12	4.75	3.89	3.49	3.26	3.11	3.00	2.91	2.85	2.80	2.75	2.69	2.62	2.54	2.51	2.47	2.43	2.38	2.34	2.30
13	4.67	3.81	3.41	3.18	3.03	2.92	2.83	2.77	2.71	2.67	2.60	2.53	2.46	2.42	2.38	2.34	2.30	2.25	2.21
14	4.60	3.74	3.34	3.11	2.96	2.85	2.76	2.70	2.65	2.60	2.53	2.46	2.39	2.35	2.31	2.27	2.22	2.18	2.13
15	4.54	3.68	3.29	3.06	2.90	2.79	2.71	2.64	2.59	2.54	2.48	2.40	2.33	2.29	2.25	2.20	2.16	2.11	2.07
16	4.49	3.63	3.24	3.01	2.85	2.74	2.66	2.59	2.54	2.49	2.42	2.35	2.28	2.24	2.19	2.15	2.11	2.06	2.01
17	4.45	3.59	3.20	2.96	2.81	2.70	2.61	2.55	2.49	2.45	2.38	2.31	2.23	2.19	2.15	2.10	2.06	2.01	1.96
18	4.41	3.55	3.16	2.93	2.77	2.66	2.58	2.51	2.46	2.41	2.34	2.27	2.19	2.15	2.11	2.06	2.02	1.97	1.92
19	4.38	3.52	3.13	2.90	2.74	2.63	2.54	2.48	2.42	2.38	2.31	2.23	2.16	2.11	2.07	2.03	1.98	1.93	1.88
20	4.35	3.49	3.10	2.87	2.71	2.60	2.51	2.45	2.39	2.35	2.28	2.20	2.12	2.08	2.04	1.99	1.95	1.90	1.84
21	4.32	3.47	3.07	2.84	2.68	2.57	2.49	2.42	2.37	2.32	2.25	2.18	2.10	2.05	2.01	1.96	1.92	1.87	1.81
22	4.30	3.44	3.05	2.82	2.66	2.55	2.46	2.40	2.34	2.30	2.23	2.15	2.07	2.03	1.98	1.94	1.89	1.84	1.78
23	4.28	3.42	3.03	2.80	2.64	2.53	2.44	2.37	2.32	2.27	2.20	2.13	2.05	2.01	1.96	1.91	1.86	1.81	1.76
24	4.26	3.40	3.01	2.78	2.62	2.51	2.42	2.36	2.30	2.25	2.18	2.11	2.03	1.98	1.94	1.89	1.84	1.79	1.73
25	4.24	3.39	2.99	2.76	2.60	2.49	2.40	2.34	2.28	2.24	2.16	2.09	2.01	1.96	1.92	1.87	1.82	1.77	1.71
26	4.23	3.37	2.98	2.74	2.59	2.47	2.39	2.32	2.27	2.22	2.15	2.07	1.99	1.95	1.90	1.85	1.80	1.75	1.69
27	4.21	3.35	2.96	2.73	2.57	2.46	2.37	2.31	2.25	2.20	2.13	2.06	1.97	1.93	1.88	1.84	1.79	1.73	1.67
28	4.20	3.34	2.95	2.71	2.56	2.45	2.36	2.29	2.24	2.19	2.12	2.04	1.96	1.91	1.87	1.82	1.77	1.71	1.65
29	4.18	3.33	2.93	2.70	2.55	2.43	2.35	2.28	2.22	2.18	2.10	2.03	1.94	1.90	1.85	1.81	1.75	1.70	1.64
30	4.17	3.32	2.92	2.69	2.53	2.42	2.33	2.27	2.21	2.16	2.09	2.01	1.93	1.89	1.84	1.79	1.74	1.68	1.62
40	4.08	3.23	2.84	2.61	2.45	2.34	2.25	2.18	2.12	2.08	2.00	1.92	1.84	1.79	1.74	1.69	1.64	1.58	1.51
60	4.00	3.15	2.76	2.53	2.37	2.25	2.17	2.10	2.04	1.99	1.92	1.84	1.75	1.70	1.65	1.59	1.53	1.47	1.39
120	3.92	3.07	2.68	2.45	2.29	2.17	2.09	2.02	1.96	1.91	1.83	1.75	1.66	1.61	1.55	1.50	1.43	1.35	1.25
∞	3.84	3.00	2.60	2.37	2.21	2.10	2.01	1.94	1.88	1.83	1.75	1.67	1.57	1.52	1.46	1.39	1.32	1.22	1.00

Degrees of Freedom for the Denominator

Source: Reprinted from Table 18. Percentage points of the *F*-distribution (variance ratio). Upper 5% points. *Biometrika Tables for Statisticians,* Volume 1, Copyright 1976, Cambridge University Press. Reprinted by permission of the Biometrika Trustees.

TABLE A.3b

Critical values of the F distribution for $\alpha = .01$. A value of F_{obs} ($df_{numerator}$, $df_{denominator}$) equal to or greater than the tabled value is statistically significant at the .01 significance level.

Degrees of Freedom for the Numerator

	1	2	3	4	5	6	7	8	9	10	12	15	20	24	30	40	60	120	∞
1	4052	4999.5	5403	5625	5764	5859	5928	5981	6022	6056	6106	6157	6209	6235	6261	6287	6313	6339	6366
2	98.50	99.00	99.17	99.25	99.30	99.33	99.36	99.37	99.39	99.40	99.42	99.43	99.45	99.46	99.47	99.47	99.48	99.49	99.50
3	34.12	30.82	29.46	28.71	28.24	27.91	27.67	27.49	27.35	27.23	27.05	26.87	26.69	26.60	26.50	26.41	26.32	26.22	26.13
4	21.20	18.00	16.69	15.98	15.52	15.21	14.98	14.80	14.66	14.55	14.37	14.20	14.02	13.93	13.84	13.75	13.65	13.56	13.46
5	16.26	13.27	12.06	11.39	10.97	10.67	10.46	10.29	10.16	10.05	9.89	9.72	9.55	9.47	9.38	9.29	9.20	9.11	9.02
6	13.75	10.92	9.78	9.15	8.75	8.47	8.26	8.10	7.98	7.87	7.72	7.56	7.40	7.31	7.23	7.14	7.06	6.97	6.88
7	12.25	9.55	8.45	7.85	7.46	7.19	6.99	6.84	6.72	6.62	6.47	6.31	6.16	6.07	5.99	5.91	5.82	5.74	5.65
8	11.26	8.65	7.59	7.01	6.63	6.37	6.18	6.03	5.91	5.81	5.67	5.52	5.36	5.28	5.20	5.12	5.03	4.95	4.86
9	10.56	8.02	6.99	6.42	6.06	5.80	5.61	5.47	5.35	5.26	5.11	4.96	4.81	4.73	4.65	4.57	4.48	4.40	4.31
10	10.04	7.56	6.55	5.99	5.64	5.39	5.20	5.06	4.94	4.85	4.71	4.56	4.41	4.33	4.25	4.17	4.08	4.00	3.91
11	9.65	7.21	6.22	5.67	5.32	5.07	4.89	4.74	4.63	4.54	4.40	4.25	4.10	4.02	3.94	3.86	3.78	3.69	3.60
12	9.33	6.93	5.95	5.41	5.06	4.82	4.64	4.50	4.39	4.30	4.16	4.01	3.86	3.78	3.70	3.62	3.54	3.45	3.36
13	9.07	6.70	5.74	5.21	4.86	4.62	4.44	4.30	4.19	4.10	3.96	3.82	3.66	3.59	3.51	3.43	3.34	3.25	3.17
14	8.86	6.51	5.56	5.04	4.69	4.46	4.28	4.14	4.03	3.94	3.80	3.66	3.51	3.43	3.35	3.27	3.18	3.09	3.00
15	8.68	6.36	5.42	4.89	4.56	4.32	4.14	4.00	3.89	3.80	3.67	3.52	3.37	3.29	3.21	3.13	3.05	2.96	2.87
16	8.53	6.23	5.29	4.77	4.44	4.20	4.03	3.89	3.78	3.69	3.55	3.41	3.26	3.18	3.10	3.02	2.93	2.84	2.75
17	8.40	6.11	5.18	4.67	4.34	4.10	3.93	3.79	3.68	3.59	3.46	3.31	3.16	3.08	3.00	2.92	2.83	2.75	2.65
18	8.29	6.01	5.09	4.58	4.25	4.01	3.84	3.71	3.60	3.51	3.37	3.23	3.08	3.00	2.92	2.84	2.75	2.66	2.57
19	8.18	5.93	5.01	4.50	4.17	3.94	3.77	3.63	3.52	3.43	3.30	3.15	3.00	2.92	2.84	2.76	2.67	2.58	2.49
20	8.10	5.85	4.94	4.43	4.10	3.87	3.70	3.56	3.46	3.37	3.23	3.09	2.94	2.86	2.78	2.69	2.61	2.52	2.42
21	8.02	5.78	4.87	4.37	4.04	3.81	3.64	3.51	3.40	3.31	3.17	3.03	2.88	2.80	2.72	2.64	2.55	2.46	2.36
22	7.95	5.72	4.82	4.31	3.99	3.76	3.59	3.45	3.35	3.26	3.12	2.98	2.83	2.75	2.67	2.58	2.50	2.40	2.31
23	7.88	5.66	4.76	4.26	3.94	3.71	3.54	3.41	3.30	3.21	3.07	2.93	2.78	2.70	2.62	2.54	2.45	2.35	2.26
24	7.82	5.61	4.72	4.22	3.90	3.67	3.50	3.36	3.26	3.17	3.03	2.89	2.74	2.66	2.58	2.49	2.40	2.31	2.21
25	7.77	5.57	4.68	4.18	3.85	3.63	3.46	3.32	3.22	3.13	2.99	2.85	2.70	2.62	2.54	2.45	2.36	2.27	2.17
26	7.72	5.53	4.64	4.14	3.82	3.59	3.42	3.29	3.18	3.09	2.96	2.81	2.66	2.58	2.50	2.42	2.33	2.23	2.13
27	7.68	5.49	4.60	4.11	3.78	3.56	3.39	3.26	3.15	3.06	2.93	2.78	2.63	2.55	2.47	2.38	2.29	2.20	2.10
28	7.64	5.45	4.57	4.07	3.75	3.53	3.36	3.23	3.12	3.03	2.90	2.75	2.60	2.52	2.44	2.35	2.26	2.17	2.06
29	7.60	5.42	4.54	4.04	3.73	3.50	3.33	3.20	3.09	3.00	2.87	2.73	2.57	2.49	2.41	2.33	2.23	2.14	2.03
30	7.56	5.39	4.51	4.02	3.70	3.47	3.30	3.17	3.07	2.98	2.84	2.70	2.55	2.47	2.39	2.30	2.21	2.11	2.01
40	7.31	5.18	4.31	3.83	3.51	3.29	3.12	2.99	2.89	2.80	2.66	2.52	2.37	2.29	2.20	2.11	2.02	1.92	1.80
60	7.08	4.98	4.13	3.65	3.34	3.12	2.95	2.82	2.72	2.63	2.50	2.35	2.20	2.12	2.03	1.94	1.84	1.73	1.60
120	6.85	4.79	3.95	3.48	3.17	2.96	2.79	2.66	2.56	2.47	2.34	2.19	2.03	1.95	1.86	1.76	1.66	1.53	1.38
∞	6.63	4.61	3.78	3.32	3.02	2.80	2.64	2.51	2.41	2.32	2.18	2.04	1.88	1.79	1.70	1.59	1.47	1.32	1.00

Degrees of Freedom for the Denominator

Source: Reprinted from Table 18, Percentage points of the *F*-distribution (variance ratio). Upper 1% points. *Biometrika Tables for Statisticians*, Volume 1, Copyright 1976, Cambridge University Press. Reprinted by permission of the Biometrika Trustees.

TABLE A.4a

Values of the studentized range statistic, q, for $\alpha = .05$.

| | | \multicolumn{9}{c}{**Number of Means Being Compared**} | | | | | | | | |
		2	3	4	5	6	7	8	9	10
	1	17.97	26.98	32.82	37.08	40.41	43.12	45.40	47.36	49.07
	2	6.08	8.33	9.80	10.88	11.74	12.44	13.03	13.54	13.99
	3	4.50	5.91	6.82	7.50	8.04	8.48	8.85	9.18	9.46
	4	3.93	5.04	5.76	6.29	6.71	7.05	7.35	7.60	7.83
	5	3.64	4.60	5.22	5.67	6.03	6.33	6.58	6.80	6.99
	6	3.46	4.34	4.90	5.30	5.63	5.90	6.12	6.32	6.49
	7	3.34	4.16	4.68	5.06	5.36	5.61	5.82	6.00	6.16
Degrees	8	3.26	4.04	4.53	4.89	5.17	5.40	5.60	5.77	5.92
of	9	3.20	3.95	4.41	4.76	5.02	5.24	5.43	5.59	5.74
Freedom	10	3.15	3.88	4.33	4.65	4.91	5.12	5.30	5.46	5.60
for	11	3.11	3.82	4.26	4.57	4.82	5.03	5.20	5.35	5.49
MS_{Error}	12	3.08	3.77	4.20	4.51	4.75	4.95	5.12	5.27	5.39
	13	3.06	3.73	4.15	4.45	4.69	4.88	5.05	5.19	5.32
	14	3.03	3.70	4.11	4.41	4.64	4.83	4.99	5.13	5.25
	15	3.01	3.67	4.08	4.37	4.59	4.78	4.94	5.08	5.20
	16	3.00	3.65	4.05	4.33	4.56	4.74	4.90	5.03	5.15
	17	2.98	3.63	4.02	4.30	4.52	4.70	4.86	4.99	5.11
	18	2.97	3.61	4.00	4.28	4.49	4.67	4.82	4.96	5.07
	19	2.96	3.59	3.98	4.25	4.47	4.65	4.79	4.92	5.04
	20	2.95	3.58	3.96	4.23	4.45	4.62	4.77	4.90	5.01
	24	2.92	3.53	3.90	4.17	4.37	4.54	4.68	4.81	4.92
	30	2.89	3.49	3.85	4.10	4.30	4.46	4.60	4.72	4.82
	40	2.86	3.44	3.79	4.04	4.23	4.39	4.52	4.63	4.73
	60	2.83	3.40	3.74	3.98	4.16	4.31	4.44	4.55	4.65
	120	2.80	3.36	3.68	3.92	4.10	4.24	4.36	4.47	4.56
	∞	2.77	3.31	3.63	3.86	4.03	4.17	4.29	4.39	4.47

If Appendix A.4 is used to find q for the CD of a test of simple effects in a factorial design, use the following conversion to find the column to be used.

Type of Design	Use q from Table A.4 Found in the Column for ___ Levels of the Independent Variable
2×2	3
2×3	5
3×2	5
3×3	7
3×4	8
4×3	8
4×4	10

TABLE A.4b
Values of the studentized range statistic, q, for $\alpha = .01$.

		Number of Means Being Compared								
		2	3	4	5	6	7	8	9	10
	1	90.03	135.0	164.3	185.6	202.2	215.8	227.2	237.0	245.6
	2	14.04	19.02	22.29	24.72	26.63	28.20	29.53	30.68	31.69
	3	8.26	10.62	12.17	13.33	14.24	15.00	15.64	16.20	16.69
	4	6.51	8.12	9.17	9.96	10.58	11.10	11.55	11.93	12.27
	5	5.70	6.98	7.80	8.42	8.91	9.32	9.67	9.97	10.24
	6	5.24	6.33	7.03	7.56	7.97	8.32	8.61	8.87	9.10
	7	4.95	5.92	6.54	7.01	7.37	7.68	7.94	8.17	8.37
Degrees	8	4.75	5.64	6.20	6.62	6.96	7.24	7.47	7.68	7.86
of	9	4.60	5.43	5.96	6.35	6.66	6.91	7.13	7.33	7.49
Freedom	10	4.48	5.27	5.77	6.14	6.43	6.67	6.87	7.05	7.21
for	11	4.39	5.15	5.62	5.97	6.25	6.48	6.67	6.84	6.99
MS_{Error}	12	4.32	5.05	5.50	5.84	6.10	6.32	6.51	6.67	6.81
	13	4.26	4.96	5.40	5.73	5.98	6.19	6.37	6.53	6.67
	14	4.21	4.89	5.32	5.63	5.88	6.08	6.26	6.41	6.54
	15	4.17	4.84	5.25	5.56	5.80	5.99	6.16	6.31	6.44
	16	4.13	4.79	5.19	5.49	5.72	5.92	6.08	6.22	6.35
	17	4.10	4.74	5.14	5.43	5.66	5.85	6.01	6.15	6.27
	18	4.07	4.70	5.09	5.38	5.60	5.79	5.94	6.08	6.20
	19	4.05	4.67	5.05	5.33	5.55	5.73	5.89	6.02	6.14
	20	4.02	4.64	5.02	5.29	5.51	5.69	5.84	5.97	6.09
	24	3.96	4.55	4.91	5.17	5.37	5.54	5.69	5.81	5.92
	30	3.89	4.45	4.80	5.05	5.24	5.40	5.54	5.65	5.76
	40	3.82	4.37	4.70	4.93	5.11	5.26	5.39	5.50	5.60
	60	3.76	4.28	4.59	4.82	4.99	5.13	5.25	5.36	5.45
	120	3.70	4.20	4.50	4.71	4.87	5.01	5.12	5.21	5.30
	∞	3.64	4.12	4.40	4.60	4.76	4.88	4.99	5.08	5.16

Source: Reprinted from Table 29, Percentage points of the studentized range, $q = (x_n - x_1)/s_y$. Upper 1% points. *Biometrika Tables for Statisticians*, Volume 1, Copyright 1976, Cambridge University Press. Reprinted by permission of the Biometrika Trustees.

If Appendix A.4 is used to find q for the *CD* of a test of simple effects in a factorial design, use the following conversion to find the column to be used.

Type of Design	Use q from Table A.4 Found in the Column for ___ Levels of the Independent Variable
2×2	3
2×3	5
3×2	5
3×3	7
3×4	8
4×3	8
4×4	10

TABLE A.5

Critical values of r for $\alpha = .05$ and $\alpha = .01$ (two-tailed test). A value of r_{obs} equal to or greater than the tabled value is statistically significant at the α level selected.

df^a	$\alpha = .05$	$\alpha = .01$
1	.99692	.999877
2	.9500	.99000
3	.878	.9587
4	.811	.9172
5	.754	.875
6	.707	.834
7	.666	.798
8	.632	.765
9	.602	.735
10	.576	.708
11	.553	.684
12	.532	.661
13	.514	.641
14	.497	.623
15	.482	.606
16	.468	.590
17	.456	.575
18	.444	.561
19	.433	.549
20	.423	.537
25	.381	.487
30	.349	.449
35	.325	.418
40	.304	.393
45	.288	.372
50	.273	.354
60	.250	.325
70	.232	.302
80	.217	.283
90	.205	.267
100	.195	.254

[a]df are equal to $N_{pairs} - 2$ where N_{pairs} is the number of paired observations.

Source: Reprinted from Table 13, Percentage points for the distribution of the correlation coefficient, r, when $\rho = 0$. *Biometrika Tables for Statisticians,* Volume 1, Copyright 1976, Cambridge University Press. Reprinted by permission of the Biometrika Trustees.

TABLE A.6
Critical values of r_s for $\alpha = .05$ and $\alpha = .01$ (two-tailed test). A value of $r_{s\,obs}$ equal to or greater than the tabled value is statistically significant at the α level selected.

N_{pairs}	$\alpha = .05$	$\alpha = .01$
5	—	—
6	.886	—
7	.786	.929
8	.738	.881
9	.700	.833
10	.648	.794
11	.618	.818
12	.591	.780
13	.566	.745
14	.545	.716
15	.525	.689
16	.507	.666
17	.490	.645
18	.476	.625
19	.462	.608
20	.450	.591
21	.438	.576
22	.428	.562
23	.418	.549
24	.409	.537
25	.400	.526
26	.392	.515
27	.385	.505
28	.377	.496
29	.370	.487
30	.364	.478

Source: E. G. Olds, Distribution of sums of squares of rank differences for small numbers of individuals. *Annals of Mathematical Statistics,* Volume 9, 1938, 133–148, and E. G. Olds. The 5% significance levels for sums of squares of rank differences and a correction. *Annals of Mathematical Statistics,* Volume 20, 1949, 117–118 as reprinted with permission from Table X.12, Critical values of Spearman's rank correlation coefficient. *CRC Handbook of Tables for Probability and Statistics* (2nd ed. 1968). Copyright CRC Press, Boca Raton, Florida.

TABLE A.7

Critical values of the chi-square distribution for $\alpha = .05$ and $\alpha = .01$. A value of $\chi^2_{obs}(df)$ equal to or greater than the tabled value is statistically significant at the α level selected.

df	$\alpha = .05$	$\alpha = .01$
1	3.84146	6.63490
2	5.99146	9.21034
3	7.81473	11.3449
4	9.48773	13.2767
5	11.0705	15.0863
6	12.5916	16.8119
7	14.0671	18.4753
8	15.5073	20.0902
9	16.9190	21.6660
10	18.3070	23.2093
11	19.6751	24.7250
12	21.0261	26.2170
13	22.3620	27.6882
14	23.6848	29.1412
15	24.9958	30.5779
16	26.2962	31.9999
17	27.5871	33.4087
18	28.8693	34.8053
19	30.1435	36.1909
20	31.4104	37.5662
21	32.6706	38.9322
22	33.9244	40.2894
23	35.1725	41.6384
24	36.4150	42.9798
25	37.6525	44.3141
26	38.8851	45.6417
27	40.1133	46.9629
28	41.3371	48.2782
29	42.5570	49.5879
30	43.7730	50.8922
40	55.7585	63.6907
50	67.5048	76.1539
60	79.0819	88.3794
70	90.5312	100.425
80	101.879	112.329
90	113.145	124.116
100	124.342	135.807

Source: Reprinted from Table 8, Percentage points of the χ^2-distribution. *Biometrika Tables for Statisticians*, Volume 1, Copyright 1976, Cambridge University Press. Reprinted by permission of the Biometrika Trustees.

TABLE A.8a

Critical values of U in the Mann–Whitney U test for $\alpha = .05$ (two-tailed test). If the group sizes are unequal, n_1 is the smaller group. A value of U_{obs} equal to or less than the tabled value is statistically significant at the .05 significance level.

												n_2								
	1	2	3	4	5	6	7	8	9	10	11	12	13	14	15	16	17	18	19	20
1																				
2								0	0	0	0	1	1	1	1	1	2	2	2	2
3					0	1	1	2	2	3	3	4	4	5	5	6	6	7	7	8
4				0	1	2	3	4	4	5	6	7	8	9	10	11	11	12	13	13
5			0	1	2	3	5	6	7	8	9	11	12	13	14	15	17	18	19	20
6			1	2	3	5	6	8	10	11	13	14	16	17	19	21	22	24	25	27
7			1	3	5	6	8	10	12	14	16	18	20	22	24	26	28	30	32	34
8		0	2	4	6	8	10	13	15	17	19	22	24	26	29	31	34	36	38	41
9		0	2	4	7	10	12	15	17	20	23	26	28	31	34	37	39	42	45	48
10		0	3	5	8	11	14	17	20	23	26	29	33	36	39	42	45	48	52	55
11		0	3	6	9	13	16	19	23	26	30	33	37	40	44	47	51	55	58	62
12		1	4	7	11	14	18	22	26	29	33	37	41	45	49	53	57	61	65	69
13		1	4	8	12	16	20	24	28	33	37	41	45	50	54	59	63	67	72	76
14		1	5	9	13	17	22	26	31	36	40	45	50	55	59	64	67	74	78	83
15		1	5	10	14	19	24	29	34	39	44	49	54	59	64	70	75	80	85	90
16		1	6	11	15	21	26	31	37	42	47	53	59	64	70	75	81	86	92	98
17		2	6	11	17	22	28	34	39	45	51	57	63	67	75	81	87	93	99	105
18		2	7	12	18	24	30	36	42	48	55	61	67	74	80	86	93	99	106	112
19		2	7	13	19	25	32	38	45	52	58	65	72	78	85	92	99	106	113	119
20		2	8	13	20	27	34	41	48	55	62	69	76	83	90	98	105	112	119	127

(n_1 labels the rows.)

Source: D. Auble, Critical values of U in the Wilcoxon (Mann–Whitney) two-sample statistic, Institute of Educational Research, Indiana University, Bloomington, Indiana, Volume 1, Number 2, 1953 as reprinted with permission from Table X.4, Critical values of U in the Wilcoxon (Mann–Whitney) two-sample statistic. *CRC Handbook of Tables for Probability and Statistics* (2nd ed., 1968). Copyright CRC Press, Boca Raton, Florida.

TABLE A.8b

Critical values of U in the Mann–Whitney U test for $\alpha = .01$ (two-tailed test). If the group sizes are unequal, n_1 is the smaller group. A value of U_{obs} equal to or less than the tabled value is statistically significant at the .01 significance level.

n_1																n_2				
	1	2	3	4	5	6	7	8	9	10	11	12	13	14	15	16	17	18	19	20
1																				
2																			0	0
3									0	0	0	1	1	1	2	2	2	2	3	3
4						0	0	1	1	2	2	3	3	4	5	5	6	6	7	8
5					0	1	1	2	3	4	5	6	7	7	8	9	10	11	12	13
6				0	1	2	3	4	5	6	7	9	10	11	12	13	15	16	17	18
7				0	1	3	4	6	7	9	10	12	13	15	16	18	19	21	22	24
8				1	2	4	6	7	9	11	13	15	17	18	20	22	24	26	28	30
9			0	1	3	5	7	9	11	13	16	18	20	22	24	27	29	31	33	36
10			0	2	4	6	9	11	13	16	18	21	24	26	29	31	34	37	39	42
11			0	2	5	7	10	13	16	18	21	24	27	30	33	36	39	42	45	48
12			1	3	6	9	12	15	18	21	24	27	31	34	37	41	44	47	51	54
13			1	3	7	10	13	17	20	24	27	31	34	38	42	45	49	53	56	60
14			1	4	7	11	15	18	22	26	30	34	38	42	46	50	54	58	63	67
15			2	5	8	12	16	20	24	29	33	37	42	46	51	55	60	64	69	73
16			2	5	9	13	18	22	27	31	36	41	45	50	55	60	65	70	74	79
17			2	6	10	15	19	24	29	34	39	44	49	54	60	65	70	75	81	86
18			2	6	11	16	21	26	31	37	42	47	53	58	64	70	75	81	87	92
19		0	3	7	12	17	22	28	33	39	45	51	56	63	69	74	81	87	93	99
20		0	3	8	13	18	24	30	36	42	48	54	60	67	73	79	86	92	99	105

Source: D. Auble, Critical values of *U* in the Wilcoxon (Mann–Whitney) two-sample statistic, Institute of Educational Research, Indiana University, Bloomington, Indiana, Volume 1, Number 2, 1953 as reprinted with permission from Table X.4, Critical values of *U* in the Wilcoxon (Mann–Whitney) two-sample statistic. *CRC Handbook of Tables for Probability and Statistics* (2nd ed., 1968). Copyright CRC Press, Boca Raton, Florida.

TABLE A.9

Critical values of T in the Wilcoxon test for $\alpha = .05$ and $\alpha = .01$ (two-tailed test). A value of T_{obs} equal to or less than the tabled value is statistically significant at the α level selected. Dashes indicate that statistical significance cannot be attained at this level for this group size.

N_{pairs}	$\alpha = .05$	$\alpha = .01$	N_{pairs}	$\alpha = .05$	$\alpha = .01$
6	0	—	29	126	100
7	2	—	30	137	109
8	3	0	31	147	118
9	5	1	32	159	128
10	8	3	33	170	138
11	10	5	34	182	148
12	13	7	35	195	159
13	17	9	36	208	171
14	21	12	37	221	182
15	25	15	38	235	194
16	29	19	39	249	207
17	34	23	40	264	220
18	40	27	41	279	233
19	46	32	42	294	247
20	52	37	43	310	261
21	58	42	44	327	276
22	65	48	45	343	291
23	73	54	46	361	307
24	81	61	47	378	322
25	89	68	48	396	339
26	98	75	49	415	355
27	107	83	50	434	373
28	116	91			

Source: Robert L. McCornack, Extended Tables of the Wilcoxon Matched Pair Signed Rank Statistic. *Journal of the American Statistical Association*, 1965, *60*, 864–871. Reprinted with permission from *The Journal of the American Statistical Association*. Copyright 1965 by the American Statistical Association. All rights reserved.

Appendix B
Mathematics Review

This review briefly covers the mathematics needed to understand the statistics presented in this text.

STATISTICAL SYMBOLS

A **symbol**, sometimes called a **sign**, is a letter or character used to represent something. The following table presents the common symbols used in statistics.

Symbol and Example	Description
X or X_i	X is used to represent a score or a measurement obtained from a participant. The subscript i, when used, indicates the score of a particular participant. For example, X_1 represents the score of participant number 1.
$=$	Equals sign.
$X_1 = 3$	The score of subject 1 equals 3.
$X_5 = 27$	The score of subject 5 equals 27.
$a = 2$	The value of a equals 2.
$\neq$	Does not equal sign.
$6 \neq 3$	6 is not equal to 3.
$+$	Plus sign. This sign indicates that the numbers joined by the $+$ should be added. The result of addition is called the *sum*. A statement such as "The sum of 5 and 1" indicates that the numbers are to be added together.
$5 + 1 = 6$	The sum of 5 plus 1 equals 6.
$5 + 1 + 6 = 12$	The sum of 5 plus 1 plus 6 equals 12.
$a + b$	a plus b: The value of b is to be added to the value of a.
$-$	Minus sign. This sign indicates that the number that follows the $-$ should be subtracted from the number preceding the $-$ sign. The result of subtraction is called the *difference*. A statement such as

"The difference of 5 and 1" indicates that one number is to be subtracted from the other.

$5 - 1 = 4$ The difference of 5 minus 1 is 4.

$a - b$ a minus b: The value of b is to be subtracted from the value of a.

$(\ )(\ )$ or $\times$ Multiplication or times sign. The values in parentheses or separated by the $\times$ are multiplied. The result of multiplication is called a *product*.

$(2)(3) = 6$ The product of 2 multiplied by 3 is 6.

$2 \times 3 = 6$ The product of 2 multiplied by 3 is 6.

$(a)(b)$ or $a \times b$ a times b: The value of a is to be multiplied by the value of b.

Exception to the rule: In a factorial design the interaction of factors A and B is indicated by $A \times B$. In this instance, the term should be read as "the A by B interaction." It does not mean that A is multiplied by B.

$\div$ or $/$ or —   Division sign. The number preceding the $\div$ or the $/$ or the number above the — (the *numerator*) is divided by the number following the $\div$ or the $/$ or the number below the — (the *denominator*), respectively. The result of division is called the *quotient*.

$6 \div 2 = 3$ The quotient of 6 divided by 2 is 3.

$6/2 = 3$ The quotient of 6 divided by 2 is 3.

$\frac{6}{2} = 3$ The quotient of 6 divided by 2 is 3.

$a \div b$, or a/b, or $\frac{a}{b}$ The quotient of a divided by b.

$<$ Less than symbol. The number preceding the $<$ is less than the number following the $<$.

$2 < 3$ 2 is less than 3.

$a < b$ The value of a is less than the value of b.

$X_3 < 10$ The score of subject 3 is less than 10.

$>$ Greater than symbol. The number preceding the $>$ is greater than the number following the $>$.

$3 > 2$ 3 is greater than 2.

$a > b$ The value of a is greater than the value of b.

$X_3 > 10$ The score of subject 3 is greater than 10.

$\leq$ Less than or equal to symbol. The number preceding the $\leq$ is less than or equal to the number following the $\leq$.

$2 \leq 3$ 2 is less than or equal to 3.

$4 \leq 4$ 4 is less than or equal to 4.

$a \leq b$ The value of a is less than or equal to the value of b.

$X_3 \leq 10$ The score of subject 3 is less than or equal to 10.

$\geq$	Equal to or greater than symbol. The number preceding the $\geq$ is equal to or greater than the number following the $\geq$.
$3 \geq 2$	3 is equal to or greater than 2.
$4 \geq 4$	4 is equal to or greater than 4.
$a \geq b$	The value of a is equal to or greater than the value of b.
$X_3 \geq 10$	The score of subject 3 is equal to or greater than 10.
$5 < X_1 < 10$	The greater than and less than symbols may be placed in one term as illustrated. This term is read as "The score of subject 1 is greater than 5 and less than 10."
$5 \leq X_1 \leq 10$	The equal to or greater than and less than or equal to symbols may also be placed in one term as illustrated. This term is read as "The score of subject 1 is equal to or greater than 5 and equal to or less than 10."
$\mid\ \ \mid$	Absolute value symbol. This symbol indicates that we ignore the $+$ or $-$ sign attached to a number.
$\mid -6 \mid = 6$	The absolute value of minus 6 is 6.
$\mid +6 \mid = 6$	The absolute value of plus 6 is 6.
$(\ \ )^2$	The number enclosed in parentheses is squared, or multiplied by itself. Sometimes the parentheses are not used, and the square indicator, ^{2}, simply follows the number to be squared.
$(5)^2 = 25$	5 squared, which is 5×5, equals 25.
$5^2 = 25$	5 squared equals 25.
$\sqrt{\ \ }$	Square root symbol. The $\sqrt{\ \ }$ indicates finding the number that, when multiplied by itself (i.e., when squared), equals the number under the $\sqrt{\ \ }$ symbol.
$\sqrt{25} = 5$	The square root of 25 equals 5, for 5 multiplied by itself (i.e., 5×5) equals 25.
$\sqrt{36} = 6$	The square root of 36 equals 6, for 6 multiplied by itself (i.e., 6×6) equals 36.
Σ	Summation symbol. The numbers following the Σ should be added together.
$\Sigma (3 + 2) = 5$	The sum of 3 plus 2 is 5.
$\Sigma (3 + 2 + 4) = 9$	The sum of 3 plus 2 plus 4 is 9.
ΣX or ΣX_i	The sum of X. Add all the scores that are represented by X. For example, if the scores of three subjects are $X_1 = 3$, $X_2 = 6$, and $X_3 = 4$, then $\Sigma X = 3 + 6 + 4 = 13$. Sometimes limits are placed on the summation sign, such as $\sum_{i=1}^{3} X_i$. These limits indicate to add the scores of subjects 1 to 3. If limits are not used, then ΣX means to add all the scores designated by X.

MATHEMATICAL OPERATIONS

Negative Numbers

A negative number may occur as a result of subtraction, such as $6 - 8 = -2$. The 8, which is larger than the 6 by 2, results in a difference of -2 when it is subtracted from the 6. Negative numbers occur often in statistics and then are used in basic mathematical operations. If a number is not preceded by a minus sign, it is assumed to be positive.

Adding Negative Numbers

$6 + (-4) = 2$ Adding a negative number to a positive number is equivalent to subtracting the negative number from the positive number. Thus, $6 + (-4) = 6 - 4 = 2$.

$(-6) + (-4) = -10$ In this instance, the -4 is subtracted from the -6, or $(-6) + (-4) = -6 - 4 = -10$.

Subtracting Negative Numbers

$6 - (-4) = 10$ Subtracting a negative number is equivalent to adding the absolute value of the negative number. Thus, $6 - (-4) = 6 + |-4| = 6 + 4 = 10$.

Multiplying Negative Numbers

$(-6)(-4) = 24$ If both numbers to be multiplied are negative, then the product is positive.

$(6)(-4) = -24$ If only one of the two numbers is negative, then the product is negative.
$(-6)(4) = -24$

Dividing Negative Numbers

$-10 \div 5 = -2$ If either the numerator or the denominator is negative, then the quotient is negative.
$10 \div -5 = -2$

$-10 \div -5 = 2$ If both the numerator and the denominator are negative, then the quotient is positive.

Fractions

The easiest approach to working with fractions is to convert the fraction to a decimal by dividing the numerator by the denominator, for example, $\frac{1}{4} = 0.25$, $\frac{2}{4} = 0.50$, and $\frac{3}{4} = 0.75$. If the decimal is to be involved in further calculations, then it should be carried to at least four decimal places (e.g., $\frac{4}{11} = 0.3636$). Thus, $\frac{2}{5} + \frac{1}{8} + \frac{1}{3}$ equals $0.4000 + 0.1250 + 0.3333 = 0.8583$.

Proportions and Percents

Proportion

A proportion is a part of a whole. As an example, if 100 people answer a questionnaire and 45 of them are males, then the proportion of male respondents is $\frac{45}{100}$ or .45. The proportion of female respondents is $\frac{55}{100}$ or .55.

Percent

A percent is formed when a proportion is multiplied by 100. Thus, a proportion of .45 male respondents equals $.45 \times 100$ or 45 percent male respondents. The percentage of female respondents is $.55 \times 100 = 55$ percent.

Order of Mathematical Operations

The following examples illustrate the order in which mathematical operations are performed with common statistical terms.

Term	Order of Mathematical Operations
$\sum (X - \overline{X})$	1. The mean is subtracted from each score in a set of scores. 2. The differences are summed.
$\sum (X - \overline{X})^2$	1. The mean is subtracted from each score in a set of scores. 2. Each difference is squared. 3. The squared differences are summed.
$\sum X^2$	1. Each X value is squared. 2. The squared X values are summed.
$(\sum X)^2$	1. The X values are summed. 2. The sum of the X values (i.e., $\sum X$) is squared.
$\sum XY$	1. The corresponding X and Y values are multiplied for the set of scores. 2. The multiplied XY values are summed for the set of scores.
$(\sum X)(\sum Y)$	1. The X values are summed to obtain $\sum X$. 2. The Y values are summed to obtain $\sum Y$. 3. The sum of the X values (i.e., $\sum X$) is multiplied by the sum of the Y variables (i.e., $\sum Y$).

Appendix C
Glossary

Alpha or α: The value of the significance level stated as a probability.

Alternative hypothesis: A statement of what must be true if the null hypothesis for a statistical test is false.

Analysis of variance (ANOVA): A statistical test used to analyze multilevel designs.

Archival records: Research using existing records.

Artifactual main effect: A main effect that does not give meaningful information about the effect of an independent variable in a factorial design.

Asymptotic distribution: A distribution for which the tails of the distribution never touch the X axis.

Bar graph: A graph used to present a frequency distribution when the variable measured is qualitative in nature. The frequency of occurrence of scores in a category is given by the height of the bar.

Beta (β): The probability of a Type II error.

Between-groups variance: The variance calculated using the variation of the group means about the grand mean.

Between-subjects design: An experiment in which two or more groups are created.

Bimodal distribution: A distribution with two modes.

Bivariate distribution: A distribution in which two scores are obtained from each subject.

Bivariate normal distribution: A distribution of X and Y variables in which (1) the X scores are normally distributed in the population sampled, (2) the Y scores are normally distributed in the population sampled, (3) for each X score the distribution of Y scores in the population is normal, and (4) for each Y score the distribution of X scores in the population is normal.

Cell mean: The mean of the n_{AB} scores for a treatment combination in a factorial design.

Cell or treatment condition: A combination formed from one level of each independent variable in a factorial design.

Central limit theorem: A mathematical theorem stating that, as sample size increases, the sampling distribution of the mean approaches a normal distribution.

Chance difference: A difference between equivalent groups due to random variation.

Chi-square test: A statistical test used to analyze nominal level of measurement scores where frequencies of occurrence of the various categories are obtained.

Chi-square test of goodness of fit: The chi square used when a score is categorized on only one dimension.

Chi-square test of independence: The chi square used when a score may be categorized on two independent dimensions.

Class interval: The width of the interval used in a grouped frequency distribution.

Coefficient of determination: The value of r^2 indicating the common variance of variables X and Y.

Confidence interval: A range of score values expected to contain the value of mu with a certain level of confidence.

Confidence limits: The lower and upper scores defining the confidence interval.

Confounded experiment: An experiment in which an extraneous variable is allowed to vary consistently with the independent variable.

Consistent estimator: A statistic for which the probability that the statistic has a value closer to the parameter increases as the sample size increases.

Continuous distribution: A distribution for which, if any two scores in the distribution are chosen, another score that lies between them can always be found.

Continuous variable: A variable that can take on an infinite set of values between any two levels of the variable.

Convenience sampling: Obtaining subjects from among people who are accessible or convenient to the researcher.

Correlation coefficient: A statistic that provides a numerical description of the extent of the relatedness of two sets of scores and the direction of the relationship.

Correlational studies: Studies in which two or more variables are measured to find the direction and degree to which they covary.

Covary: Two variables covary when a change in one variable is related to a consistent change in the other variable.

Critical difference: The minimum numerical difference between two treatment means that is statistically significant.

Critical value: The specific numerical values that define the boundaries of the rejection region.

Cross products of X and Y: The value of $\sum (X - \overline{X})(Y - \overline{Y})$ for variables X and Y.

Cumulative frequency of a class interval: The frequency of occurrence of scores in that interval plus the sum of the frequencies of scores of lower class intervals.

Cumulative frequency of a score: The frequency of occurrence of that score plus the sum of the frequencies of all the scores of lower value.

Cumulative grouped percentage frequency of a class interval: The percentage frequency of the scores in that interval plus the sum of the percentage frequencies of all the class intervals of lower value.

Cumulative grouped relative frequency of a class interval: The relative frequency of the scores in that interval plus the sum of the relative frequencies of class intervals of lower value.

Data: The scores or numerical measurements of behavior or characteristics obtained from observations of a sample of people or animals.

Degrees of freedom: The number of scores free to vary when calculating a statistic.

Dependent variable: The variable in an experiment that depends on the independent variable.

In most instances the dependent variable is some measure of a behavior.

Descriptive statistics: Statistical procedures used to summarize and describe the data from a sample.

Discrete outcomes: Outcomes in a distribution that have a countable set of values.

Discrete variable: A variable that can take on only a finite or potentially countable set of values.

Empirical data: Scores or measurements based on observation and sensory experience.

Empirical probability distribution: A probability distribution found by counting actual occurrences of an event.

Equivalent groups: Groups of subjects that are not expected to differ in any consistent or systematic way prior to receiving the independent variable of the experiment.

Error rate in an experiment: The probability of making at least one Type I error in the statistical comparisons conducted in an experiment.

Estimated population standard deviation (s): The square root of the estimated population variance.

Estimated population variance (s^2): A measure of variability obtained by subtracting the mean of a distribution from each score in the distribution, squaring each difference, summing the differences, and then dividing the sum by the number of scores minus 1.

Estimated standard error of the difference between means: The standard error of the difference between means obtained by using s^2 to estimate σ^2.

Estimated standard error of the mean: The standard error of the mean obtained by using s to estimate σ.

Event: The occurrence of a specified set of outcomes in a probability distribution.

Expected frequencies: The frequencies in a contingency table obtained assuming that the two dimensions of the table are independent.

Experiment: A controlled situation in which one or more independent variables are manipulated to observe the effect on the dependent variable.

Extraneous variables: Any variables, other than the independent variable, that can affect the dependent variable in an experiment.

Factor: An alternative name for an independent variable.

Factorial design: A research design in which two or more independent variables are varied simultaneously.

Frequency distribution: A table showing each score in a set of scores and how frequently each score occurred.

Frequency polygon: A graph constructed by placing the midpoints of each class interval of a frequency distribution on the abscissa and indicating the frequency of a class interval by placing a dot at the appropriate frequency above the midpoint. The dots are connected with straight lines.

General equation of a straight line: $Y = bX + a$.

Grand mean: The mean of all scores in an experiment.

Grouped frequency distribution: A frequency distribution in which scores are grouped together in class intervals and the frequency of scores occurring within each class is tabulated.

Grouped percentage frequency distribution: A grouped frequency distribution obtained by multiplying the relative frequency values by 100 to obtain percentages.

Grouped relative frequency distribution: A grouped frequency distribution obtained by dividing the frequency of scores in an interval by the total number of scores in the distribution.

Histogram: A form of bar graph in which the frequency of occurrence of scores in a class interval is given by the height of the bar and the size of each class interval is represented by the width of the bar on the abscissa.

Independent variable: A variable manipulated in an experiment to determine its effect on the dependent variable.

Interaction: A situation in a factorial design when the effect of one independent variable depends on the level of the other independent variable with which it is combined.

Interquartile range: The range of values for the middle 50 percent of the scores in a distribution.

Interval measurement: The amount of a variable is ordered along a dimension and the differences between the assigned numbers represent equal amounts in the magnitude of the variable measured. The zero point of an interval scale is an arbitrary starting point.

Least-squares regression line: A straight line that minimizes the value of $\sum (Y - Y')^2$.

Level of an independent variable: One value of the independent variable. To be a variable, an independent variable must take on at least two different levels.

Linear relation: A relation between two variables such that each time variable X changes by 1 unit variable Y changes by a constant amount.

Linear relationship: A relationship between two variables that can be described by a straight line.

Lower real limit of a number: The point midway between a number and the next lower number.

Main effect of factor A: The difference between $\overline{X}_{A1}$ and $\overline{X}_{A2}$ in a factorial design, symbolized by $\overline{X}_{A1} - \overline{X}_{A2}$.

Main effect of factor B: The difference between $\overline{X}_{B1}$ and $\overline{X}_{B2}$ in a factorial design, symbolized by $\overline{X}_{B1} - \overline{X}_{B2}$.

Main effect mean: The mean of all subjects given one level of an independent variable, ignoring the classification by the other independent variable in a factorial design.

Mann–Whitney U test: A nonparametric test for a between-subjects design using two levels of an independent variable with the scores representing at least ordinal measurement.

Marginal frequencies: The row totals and the column totals of the observed frequencies in a contingency table.

Mean square: The name used for a variance in the analysis of variance.

Measurement: Assigning numbers to variables following a set of rules.

Measures of central tendency: Numbers that represent the average or typical score obtained from measurements of a sample.

Measures of variability: Numbers that indicate how much scores differ from each other and the measure of central tendency in a set of scores.

Median: A score value in the distribution with an equal number of scores above and below it. The median is the 50th percentile in a distribution.

Midpoint of a class interval: The point midway between the real limits of the class interval.

Mode: The most frequently occurring score in a distribution of scores.

Multimodal distribution: A distribution with more than two modes.

Multiple comparison tests: Statistical tests used to make pairwise comparisons to find which means differ significantly from one another in a one-factor multilevel design.

Multiple regression: Predicting the value of Y scores using several X variables.

Multiple treatment effects: Changes in subjects' performance in a within-subjects design that are due to being tested in each level of the independent variable.

Mutually exclusive outcomes: Outcomes that cannot occur at the same time.

Naturalistic observation: Research involving the observation of behaviors occurring in natural settings.

Negative relationship: A relationship between two variables in which as the value of one variable increases the value of the other variable tends to decrease.

Nominal measurement: A classification of the measured variable into different categories.

Nonparametric test: A statistical test involving hypotheses that do not state a relationship about a population parameter.

Nonsignificant difference: The observed value of the test statistic does not fall into a rejection region and the null hypothesis is not rejected.

Normal distribution: A theoretical mathematical distribution that specifies the relative frequency of a set of scores in a population.

Null hypothesis: A statement of a condition that a scientist tentatively holds to be true about a population. The null hypothesis is the hypothesis tested by a statistical test.

One-factor between-subjects design: A research design in which one independent variable is manipulated and two or more groups are created.

One-factor multilevel design: An experiment with one independent variable and three or more levels of that independent variable.

One-sample t test: A t test used to test the difference between a sample mean and an hypothesized population mean for statistical significance when $\sigma_{\overline{X}}$ is estimated by $s_{\overline{X}}$.

One-tailed test: A statistical test employing a rejection region in only one tail of the sampling distribution of the test statistic.

Operational definition: A specification of the operations used to make observations, to manipulate an independent variable, or to measure the dependent variable.

Ordinal measurement: The amount of a variable is placed in order of magnitude along a dimension.

Outcome: Each possible occurrence in a probability distribution.

Pairwise comparisons: Statistical comparisons involving two means.

Parameter: A number that describes a characteristic of a population.

Parametric test: A statistical test involving hypotheses that state a relationship about a population parameter.

Participant or subject: The person who participates in an experiment.

Pearson correlation coefficient: A statistic, symbolized by r, that indicates the degree of linear relationship between two variables measured at the interval or ratio level.

Percentage frequency distribution: The frequency of occurrence of a score expressed as a percentage of the total number of scores obtained.

Percentile: The score at or below which a specified percentage of scores in a distribution fall.

Percentile rank of a score: The percentage of scores in the distribution that are equal to or less than that score.

Placebo control: A simulated treatment condition.

Point estimation: Estimating the value of a parameter as a single point from the value of a statistic.

Population: A complete set of people, animals, objects, or events that share a common characteristic.

Population mean (μ):   The sum of all the scores in a population divided by the number of scores summed.

Population standard deviation (σ):   The square root of the population variance.

Population variance (σ²):   The variance obtained by measuring all scores in a population.

Positive relationship: A relationship between two variables in which as the value of one variable increases the value of the other variable tends to increase also.

Post hoc comparisons: Statistical tests that make all possible pairwise comparisons after a statistically significant F_{obs} has occurred for the overall analysis of variance.

Power: The probability of rejecting H_0 when H_0 is false and H_1 is true. The power of a statistical test is given by $1 - \beta$.

Practice effect: A multiple treatment effect that occurs because subjects may become more practiced or fatigued on the experimental task.

Probability of an event:

$$p(\text{event}) = \frac{\text{Number of outcomes comprising the event}}{\text{Total number of possible outcomes}}.$$

Qualitative data: Data obtained from nominal measurement indicating that variables differ in quality.

Quantitative data: Data obtained from ordinal, interval, or ratio measurements indicating how much of a variable exists.

Random assignment: A method of assigning subjects to treatment groups so that any individual selected for the experiment has an equal probability of assignment to any of the groups and the assignment of one subject to a group does not affect the assignment of any other individual to that same group.

Random sample: A sample in which individuals are selected so that each member of the population has an equal chance of being selected for the sample, and the selection of one member is independent of the selection of any other member of the population.

Random sampling: A sampling method in which individuals are selected so that each member of the population has an equal chance of being selected for the sample, and the selection of one member is independent of any other member of the population.

Range: The numerical difference between the lowest and highest score in a distribution.

Ratio measurement: The amount of a variable is ordered along a dimension, the differences between the assigned numbers represent equal amounts in the magnitude of the variable measured, and a true zero point exists, which represents the absence of the characteristic measured.

Raw data or raw scores: The scores obtained from all the subjects before the scores have been analyzed statistically.

Real limit of a class interval: The point midway between the stated limit of a class interval and the stated limit of the next lower or upper class interval.

Real limits of a number: The points midway between the number and the next lower and the next higher numbers on the scale used to make the measurements.

Regression analysis: The use of statistical methods to predict one set of scores from a second set of scores.

Rejection region: Values on the sampling distribution of the test statistic that have a probability equal to or less than α if H_0 is true. If the test statistic falls into the rejection region, H_0 is rejected.

Relative frequency: The frequency of a score divided by the total number of scores obtained.

Research hypothesis: A statement of an expected, or predicted, relationship between two or more variables. In an experiment, a research hypothesis is a predicted relationship between an independent variable and a dependent variable.

Research method: An approach used to collect data.

Residual: The value of $Y - Y'$.

Robustness: A term used to indicate that violating the assumptions of a statistical test has little effect on the probability of a Type I error.

Rows-by-columns contingency table: A rows-by-columns table presenting the frequency of each category formed by the intersection of the row and column variables in the table.

Sample: A subset, or subgroup, selected from a population.

Sample mean ($\overline{X}$):   The sum of a set of scores divided by the number of scores summed.

Sample standard deviation (S):   The square root of the sample variance.

Sample variance (S^2):   A measure of variability obtained by subtracting the mean of a distribution from each score in the distribution, squaring each difference, summing the differences, and then dividing the sum by the number of scores in the distribution.

Sampling distribution: A theoretical probability distribution of values of a statistic resulting from selecting all possible samples of size n from a population.

Sampling distribution of the difference between means: The distribution of $\overline{X}_{A1} - \overline{X}_{A2}$ differences when all possible pairs of samples of size n are selected from a population and $\overline{X}_{A1} - \overline{X}_{A2}$ found for each pair of samples.

Sampling distribution of the mean: The distribution of $\overline{X}$ values when all possible samples of size n are selected from a population.

Sampling error: The amount by which a sample mean differs from the population mean.

Scatterplot: A plot of a bivariate distribution in which the X variable is plotted on the horizontal axis and the Y variable is plotted on the vertical axis.

Score: The measurement obtained on the subject's performance of a task.

Semi-interquartile range: One-half of the interquartile range.

Significance level: A probability value that provides the criterion for rejecting a null hypothesis in a statistical test.

Simple effect of an independent variable: The effect of one independent variable at only one level of the other independent variable in a factorial design.

Simple random sampling: Selecting members from a population such that each member of the population has an equal chance of being selected for the sample, and the selection of one member is independent of the selection of any other member of the population.

Skewed distribution: A frequency distribution in which scores are clustered at one end of the distribution with scores occurring infrequently at the other end of the distribution.

Slope of a straight line: The slope of a straight line is given by

$$b = \frac{\text{Change in value of } Y}{\text{Change in value of } X}.$$

Spearman rank-order correlation coefficient: A correlation coefficient used with ordinal measures.

Standard error of estimate: The value of

$$\sqrt{\frac{\sum (Y - Y')^2}{N_{\text{pairs}} - 2}}.$$

Standard error of the difference between means, or the standard error of the difference: The standard deviation of a theoretical sampling distribution of $\overline{X}_{A1} - \overline{X}_{A2}$ values.

Standard error of the mean: The standard deviation of the sampling distribution of the mean found by dividing σ by the square root of the size of the sample.

Standard normal deviate: The value of z_{obs} when a score is transformed into a score on the standard normal distribution.

Standard normal distribution: A normal distribution with $\mu = 0$ and $\sigma = 1$.

Standard score: A score obtained by using the transformation $z = (X - \overline{X})/S$.

Stated limits of a class interval: The highest and lowest scores that could fall into that class interval.

Statistic: A single number used to describe a set of data from a sample or to analyze those data more fully.

Statistical hypothesis: A statement about a population parameter (for a parametric test).

Statistical hypothesis testing: Procedures used to determine the anticipated size of chance differences between groups.

Statistical inference: Estimating population values from statistics obtained from a sample.

Statistically significant difference: The observed value of the test statistic falls into a rejection region and H_0 is rejected.

Statistics: The methods or procedures used to summarize, analyze, and draw inferences from data.

Stem-and-leaf display: A display of data in which the first (or second) digit of a score is the stem and the second (or last) digit is the leaf.

Stratified random sampling: A sampling method in which members of a population are categorized into homogeneous subgroupings called strata. Members of the population are randomly sampled from the strata in the proportion to which the strata occur in the population.

Strength of effect: The strength of an independent variable as measured by one of the strength of effect statistics.

Sum of squares: A numerical value obtained by subtracting the mean of a distribution from each score in the distribution, squaring each difference, and then summing the differences.

Sum of squares residual: The value of $\sum (Y - Y')^2$.

Survey research: Research involving obtaining data from either oral or written interviews with people.

Symmetrical frequency distribution: A frequency distribution that when folded in half about a midpoint produces two halves identical in shape.

Test statistic: A number calculated from the scores of the sample that allows testing a statistical null hypothesis.

Theoretical probability distribution: A probability distribution found from the use of a theoretical probability model.

Treatment carry-over effect: A multiple treatment effect that occurs when the effect of one level of the independent variable carries over to affect performance in the next level of the independent variable.

Treatments-by-subject interaction: A situation in a one-factor within-subjects design where the effect of the independent variable depends on the subject.

Tukey HSD test: A statistical test used for post hoc comparisons between treatment means in a one-factor multilevel design or to test for differences between cell means in a factorial design.

Two-tailed test: A statistical test using rejection regions in both tails of the sampling distribution of the test statistic.

Type I error: The error in statistical decision making that occurs if the null hypothesis is rejected when actually it is true of the population.

Type II error: The error in statistical decision making that occurs if H_0 is not rejected when it is false and the alternative hypothesis (H_1) is true.

Unbiased estimator: A statistic with a mean value over an infinite number of random samples equal to the parameter it estimates.

Unimodal distribution: A distribution with one mode.

Upper real limit of a number: The point midway between a number and the next larger number.

Variable: Any environmental condition or event, stimulus, personal characteristic or attribute, or behavior that can take on different values at different times or with different people.

Variability: How much scores differ from each other and the measure of central tendency in a distribution.

Wilcoxon signed-ranks test: A nonparametric test for within-subjects designs with two levels of an independent variable.

Within-groups error variance: The variance of the scores in a group calculated about the group mean.

Within-subjects design: A research design in which one group of subjects is exposed to and measured under each level of an independent variable. In a within-subjects design, each subject receives each treatment condition.

Y-intercept: The value of Y when $X = 0$ in the equation $Y = bX + a$.

Appendix D
Statistical Symbols

A	Factor A, the independent variable in an experiment.
A_1, A_2, A_3	Levels of factor A in either a one-factor or a factorial design.
α	Alpha, the probability of a Type I error.
$A \times B$	The representation of the interaction of factors A and B in a factorial design.
a	(1) Number of levels of factor A or (2) Y-intercept of an equation for a straight line in a regression analysis.
B	Factor B, the second independent variable in a factorial design.
B_1, B_2, B_3	Levels of factor B in a factorial design.
b	(1) Number of levels of factor B or (2) Slope of a straight line in a regression analysis.
β	Beta, the probability of a Type II error.
χ^2	Chi-squared statistic.
χ^2_{crit}	Critical value of χ^2.
χ^2_{obs}	Value of χ^2 statistic obtained from data.
CD	Critical difference in a multiple comparison test.
CP_{XY}	Cross products of X and Y in a correlational study.
$cum\ f$ or cf	Cumulative frequency of a score.
cf_L	Cumulative frequency of scores up to the lower real limit of an interval in a grouped frequency distribution.
$cum\ rf$ or crf	Cumulative relative frequency of a score.
$cum\ \%f$ or $c\%f$	Cumulative percentage frequency of a score.
D	(1) Difference in a pair of ranked scores for an individual; used in Spearman rank-order correlation coefficient or (2) Difference between two scores

	obtained from a subject in a within-subjects design.
df	Degrees of freedom. In an analysis of variance, the df are usually subscripted, such as df_A, df_B, $df_{A \times B}$, df_{Error}, or df_{Total}, to indicate which source of variance they correspond to.
η^2	Eta squared.
E_{rc}	Expected frequency of a score in row r, column c of a chi-square test contingency table.
f	Frequency of a score.
f_i	Frequency of scores in an interval of a grouped frequency distribution.
F	The F statistic in the analysis of variance.
F_{crit}	Critical value of F.
F_{obs}	Value of F obtained from data.
H_0	Statistical null hypothesis.
H_1	Statistical alternative hypothesis.
IQR	Interquartile range.
i	Size or width of the class interval in a grouped frequency distribution.
M	Sample mean. The symbol used in publications following the editorial style of the *Publication Manual of the American Psychological Association* (1994).
Mdn	Median.
MS	Mean square, a variance estimate in the analysis of variance. Mean squares typically are subscripted, such as MS_A, MS_B, $MS_{A \times B}$, or MS_{Error}, to indicate which source of variance they represent.
MSE	Mean square error. The symbol used to identify the MS_{Error} for an analysis of variance in publications following the

	editorial style of the *Publication Manual of the American Psychological Association* (1994).
μ	Mu, the population mean.
$\mu_{\overline{X}}$	Mean of the theoretical sampling distribution of the mean.
N	Total number of scores in a sample or the total number of scores in an experiment.
N_{pairs}	Number of pairs of scores.
n	Number of scores in a subgroup of a larger sample.
n_A	Number of scores in a level of a one-factor design.
n_{AB}	Number of scores in a cell of a two-factor design.
O_{rc}	Observed frequency of a score in row r, column c of a chi-square test contingency table.
$\%f$	Percentage frequency of a score.
P	A percentile point expressed as a proportion. Used to obtain the score at a specified percentile point.
P_X	Percentile rank of score of X.
p	Probability.
q	Studentized range statistic used in the Tukey HSD test.
r	Pearson correlation coefficient for a sample.
r_{crit}	Critical value of Pearson correlation coefficient.
r_{obs}	Observed value of a Pearson correlation between variables X and Y.
rf	Relative frequency of a score.
ρ	Rho, the population correlation coefficient.
ρ_S	Population Spearman rank-order correlation coefficient.
r_S	Spearman rank-order correlation coefficient.
r^2	Coefficient of determination.
σ	Sigma, the population standard deviation.
σ^2	Population variance.

$\sigma_{\overline{X}}$	Standard error of the mean.
$\sigma_{\overline{X}A1-\overline{X}A2}$	Standard error of the difference between means.
$\displaystyle\sum_{i=1}^{N}$	Summation notation from $i = 1$ to N.
S	Sample standard deviation.
s	Estimated population standard deviation.
SD	Standard deviation. The symbol used in publications following the editorial style of the *Publication Manual of the American Psychological Association* (1994).
S^2	Sample variance.
s^2	Estimated population variance.
s^2_{pooled}	Pooled variance estimate for the difference between two population means.
$s_{\overline{X}}$	Estimated standard error of the mean.
SE	Standard error of the mean. The symbol used in publications following the editorial style of the *Publication Manual of the American Psychological Association* (1994).
$s_{\overline{X}A1-\overline{X}A2}$	Estimated standard error of the difference between means.
$s_{Y \cdot X}$	Standard error of estimate when predicting Y from X.
$SIQR$	Semi-interquartile range.
$\sum R$	Sum of ranks.
SS	Sum of squares. In an analysis of variance a SS is usually subscripted such as SS_A, SS_B, $SS_{A \times B}$, SS_{Error}, or SS_{Total} to indicate which source of variation it represents.
SS_{Residual}	The value of $\sum (Y - Y')^2$.
SS_X	Sum of squares of the X variable in a correlation.
SS_Y	Sum of squares of the Y variable in a correlation.
t	t statistic in the t test.
t_{crit}	Critical value of t.
t_{ind}	t statistic obtained in the t test for independent groups.
t_{obs}	Value of t obtained from data.

t_{rel} — t statistic obtained in the t test for related measures.

T — Wilcoxon T statistic.

T_{crit} — Critical value of T.

T_{obs} — Value of T obtained from data.

U — Mann–Whitney U statistic.

U_{crit} — Critical value of U.

U_{obs} — The smaller value of U obtained from data.

X — A subject's score on the variable identified as the X variable. Depending on the design used, a score may be represented by X_i, X_{ij}, or X_{ijk}.

$X_{Highest}$ — The highest score in a distribution of scores.

X_{Lowest} — The lowest score in a distribution of scores.

X_L — Lower real limit of an interval containing the score X in a frequency distribution.

X_P — Score at the P percentile point in a distribution.

X_{25} — Score corresponding to the 25th percentile of a distribution.

X_{50} — Score corresponding to the median of a distribution.

X_{75} — Score corresponding to the 75th percentile of a distribution.

$\overline{X}$ — X bar, the sample mean.

$\overline{X}_{A1}, \overline{X}_{A2}, \overline{X}_{A3}$ — Main effect means for levels of factor A.

$\overline{X}_{B1}, \overline{X}_{B2}, \overline{X}_{B3}$ — Main effect means for levels of factor B.

$\overline{X}_{AB}$ — Cell mean in a two-factor design.

$\overline{X}_G$ — Grand mean.

$\overline{X}_S$ — Subject mean in a within-subjects design.

$\overline{X}_{\overline{X}}$ — Mean of the empirical sampling distribution of the mean.

$\overline{X}_{\overline{X}A1 - \overline{X}A2}$ — Mean of an empirical sampling distribution of the difference between means.

Y — A subject's score on the variable identified as the Y variable.

$\overline{Y}$ — Y bar. The sample mean for scores identified as the Y variable.

Y' — Predicted value of Y from a linear regression line.

z — Value of a score obtained from using the z transformation.

Appendix E
Answers for Computational Problems

Solutions are given for most of the numerical problems in the Testing Your Knowledge and Chapter Review Questions sections. For formulas and explanations, see the relevant sections of the text.

CHAPTER 1
Testing Your Knowledge 1.1

2. **b.** From a sample statistic of 52 percent to a population parameter of 52 percent.

Testing Your Knowledge 1.2

2. **a.** Type of feedback given.
   b. Duration of foot pronation.
   c. The study involved the creation of two equivalent groups in a between-subjects design and the manipulation of an independent variable.
   d. To determine if the pronation durations differed more than expected by chance.

Testing Your Knowledge 1.3

2. **a.** To find if belief in paranormal phenomena and number of science courses taken are related.
   b. Belief in paranormal phenomena; number of science courses taken.

Review Questions

3. **a.** Correlation and regression.
   c. Anger level; blood pressure.
4. **a.** Description and statistical hypothesis testing.
   b. Type of treatment given a child.
   c. Child's body temperature.
5. **a.** Description.   **c.** Percentage.
6. **a.** Raw data.   **b.** Inference.
   c. Statistic.   **d.** Raw data.
   e. Inference.   **f.** Statistic.

CHAPTER 2
Testing Your Knowledge 2.1

2. **a.** Survey research.   **b.** Experiment.
   c. Archival records.
   d. Naturalistic observation.

Testing Your Knowledge 2.2

3. People are assigned to the same category although they do not possess the same amount of the variable being measured.
5. **b.** No.

Testing Your Knowledge 2.3

2. **a.** Yes, the scale is interval.
   b. No.   **c.** No.
3. **a.** Yes, the scale is ratio.
   b. Yes.   **c.** Yes.

Testing Your Knowledge 2.4

2. **a.** Continuous.   **b.** Continuous.
   c. Discrete.   **d.** Continuous.
   e. Continuous.   **f.** Discrete.
   g. Discrete.   **h.** Discrete.
3. **a.** 152.35 to 152.45 cm.
   b. 17.25 to 17.35 sec.
   c. 3.5 to 4.5.   **d.** 0.4365 to 0.4375 sec.
   e. 6.85 to 6.95 mm. **f.** 67.805 to 67.815 lb.
4. **a.** 27.44.   **b.** 119.028.
   c. 1.44.   **d.** 1263.7592.
   e. 0.35.   **f.** 13.27.

Review Questions

1. **a.** Survey research.   **b.** Archival records.
   c. Experiment.
   d. Naturalistic observation.

3. **a.** Career orientation.
   b. Ordinal.
4. **a.** Body weight.
   b. Ratio.
   c. 134.55 to 134.65 lb.
   d. 127.6 or 127.65 lb. depending on the convention followed.
5. **a.** Emotional stability.
   b. Rating scale: gray area between ordinal and interval scale.
   c. 7.5 to 8.5.
   d. No, it should be rounded to 5.8 or 5.83 depending on the convention followed.
6. **a.** Ratio.
   b. 96.5 to 97.5 minutes.
   c. 82.7 or 82.67 minutes depending on the convention followed.
7. Ordinal.
8. Nominal.
9. **a.** Discrete.   **b.** Continuous.
   c. Discrete.   **d.** Continuous.
10. **a.** 141.25 to 141.35 lb.
    b. 33.5 to 34.5 minutes.
    c. 175.55 to 175.65 yards.
    d. 98.15 to 98.25°F.
    e. 108.5 to 109.5 mm of mercury.
11. **a.** 42.26.   **b.** 1.16.
    c. 163.65.   **d.** 27.43.
    e. 13.90.   **f.** 24.62.
    g. 19.28.
13. **a.** Ordinal.   **b.** Ratio.

CHAPTER 3

Testing Your Knowledge 3.1

2. **a.**

Score	Tally	f	rf	$\%f$
19	/	1	.05	5
18		0	.00	0
17		0	.00	0
16		0	.00	0
15	/	1	.05	5
14	/	1	.05	5
13	/	1	.05	5
12	/	1	.05	5
11	/	1	.05	5
10	/	1	.05	5
9	//	2	.10	10
8	////	4	.20	20
7		0	.00	0
6	//	2	.10	10
5	//	2	.10	10
4	//	2	.10	10
3	/	1	.05	5
2		0	.00	0

   b. Lowest = 3; highest = 19.
   c. 8.

Testing Your Knowledge 3.2

2. 10 to 20.   3. 5.   4. 11.
6. **a.** 123, 125.   **b.** 129, 131.
   c. 122.5, 125.5.   **d.** 128.5 to 131.5.
   e. 121.   **f.** 3.
7. **a.** $i = 10$.

Class Interval	Real Limits Lower	Real Limits Upper	Midpoint of Class	Tally	f	rf	$\%f$	cf	crf	$c\%f$
200–209	199.5	209.5	204.5	/	1	.02	2	50	1.00	100
190–199	189.5	199.5	194.5	/	1	.02	2	49	.98	98
180–189	179.5	189.5	184.5		0	.00	0	48	.96	96
170–179	169.5	179.5	174.5		0	.00	0	48	.96	96
160–169	159.5	169.5	164.5		0	.00	0	48	.96	96
150–159	149.5	159.5	154.5	/	1	.02	2	48	.96	96
140–149	139.5	149.5	144.5	/	1	.02	2	47	.94	94
130–139	129.5	139.5	134.5		0	.00	0	46	.92	92
120–129	119.5	129.5	124.5		0	.00	0	46	.92	92

(answer continues)

Class Interval	Real Limits		Midpoint of Class	Tally	f	rf	$\%f$	cf	crf	$c\%f$
	Lower	Upper								
110–119	109.5	119.5	114.5		0	.00	0	46	.92	92
100–109	99.5	109.5	104.5		0	.00	0	46	.92	92
90–99	89.5	99.5	94.5	//	2	.04	4	46	.92	92
80–89	79.5	89.5	84.5	///	3	.06	6	44	.88	88
70–79	69.5	79.5	74.5	//////	6	.12	12	41	.82	82
60–69	59.5	69.5	64.5	///////////	11	.22	22	35	.70	70
50–59	49.5	59.5	54.5	////////	8	.16	16	24	.48	48
40–49	39.5	49.5	44.5	//////	6	.12	12	16	.32	32
30–39	29.5	39.5	34.5	///////	7	.14	14	10	.20	20
20–29	19.5	29.5	24.5	//	2	.04	4	3	.06	6
10–19	9.5	19.5	14.5	/	1	.02	2	1	.02	2

b. The large majority of stotting distances were 99 meters or less. Distances in the interval of 60 to 69 meters occurred most frequently. No distance was less than 10 meters or greater than 209 meters.

c. $P_{68} = 67$.   **d.** $X_{50} = 60.4$ meters.

Testing Your Knowledge 3.3

2. a.

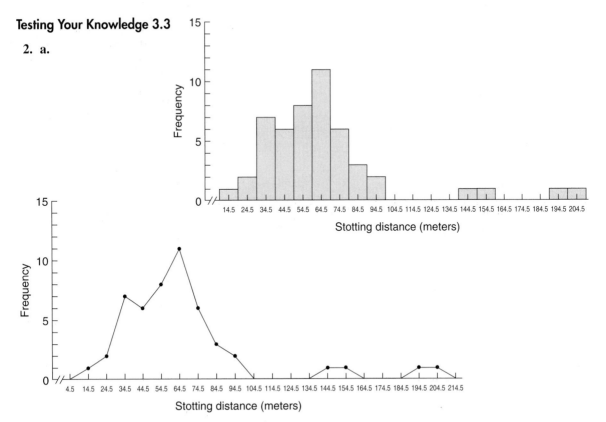

b. The distributions are similar to those in 2a except that relative frequencies are portrayed on the ordinate.

c. The majority of stotting distances were less than 104.5 meters. The most frequently occurring distances were in the interval with a midpoint of 64.5 meters. No distance was less than 9.5 meters or greater than 209.5 meters.

3.

Stem	Leaf
20	5
19	0
18	
17	
16	
15	4
14	0
13	
12	
11	
10	
9	11
8	133
7	022256
6	11234666778
5	04456789
4	237899
3	1377889
2	59
1	8

a. 18 meters.   **b.** 205 meters.
c. 66 and 72 meters.

Testing Your Knowledge 3.4

2. a. Symmetrical, unimodal.
 b. Asymmetrical, positively skewed, unimodal.
 c. Asymmetrical, positively skewed, bimodal.
 d. Asymmetrical, negatively skewed, unimodal.

Review Questions

1. a. Size of class interval = 20; class intervals start at stated limit of 220; first midpoint at 229.5; upper stated limit of last class interval = 499.
 b. 400 to 419; midpoint = 409.5; yes.

c. Value will be in interval 340 to 359.
d. $X_{50} = 356.2$.   **e.** $P_{431} = 89$.
2. a. Size of class interval = 5; class intervals start at stated limit of 0; first midpoint at 2.0; upper stated limit of last class interval = 64.
 b. 0 to 4.   **c.** $X_{50} = 6.2$.
 d. $P_{24} = 86$.
 e.

Stem		Leaf
6	*	
	•	3
5	*	8
	•	1
4	*	67
	•	
3	*	7
	•	
2	*	66
	•	114
1	*	5778
	•	0124
0	*	5555566666678899
	•	00000000111122333344444

Lowest score = 0; highest score = 63.
Most frequently occurring score = 0.

4. a.

Number of Days Absent	Reward-policy School	No-reward-policy School
More than 25	.02	.03
24–25	.00	.03
22–23	.02	.005
20–21	.00	.04
18–19	.01	.00
16–17	.00	.02
14–15	.02	.11
12–13	.00	.05
10–11	.03	.09
8–9	.08	.10
6–7	.04	.015
4–5	.13	.07
2–3	.23	.17
0–1	.42	.27

b. $X_{50} =$ 2.2   5.2
c. $P_4 =$ 68   46

d. For the reward-policy school, 78% of the students are absent 5 days or less with a median absence of 2.2 days. For the no-reward-policy school, only 51% of the students are absent 5 days or less, and the median number of absences is 5.2 days.

5. b. Lowest score = 5; highest score = 29.
   c. 20.

6. a. $i = 30$.   **b.** 209.5; 239.5.
   c. 224.5.   **e.** 340 minutes.
   f. $P_{264} = 53$.

7. a. 40.   **c.** $P_{78} = 69$.
   d. 79.3 minutes.

CHAPTER 4

Testing Your Knowledge 4.1

3. a. 49.   **b.** Unimodal.
4. a. 27.   **b.** Unimodal.
5. a. 24, 27, 49.   **b.** Multimodal.
7. 46.   **8.** 42.   **9.** 46.

Testing Your Knowledge 4.2

2. a. $\overline{X} = 88.0$.   **c.** 262.
3. a. 41.7.   **b.** 39.5.
   c. 37.7.

Testing Your Knowledge 4.3

1. a. Median.   **b.** Mean.
   c. Mode.   **d.** Mean.
2. Smaller than median.
3. Positively skewed.

Review Questions

1. Possibly negatively skewed because the mean is less than the median.
2. Positively skewed because the mean is considerably larger than the median.
3. Positively skewed because the mean is considerably larger than the median.
4. *Set 1*
   b. Mode = 38, Mdn = 38, $\overline{X}$ = 38.6.
   c. Approximately symmetrical; all measures of central tendency are about the same.

Set 2
   b. Mode = 28, Mdn = 29, $\overline{X}$ = 33.5.
   c. Positively skewed; mean is larger than the median.

Set 3
   b. Mode = 52, Mdn = 50, $\overline{X}$ = 46.7.
   c. Negatively skewed; mean is less than the median.

Set 4
   b. Mode = bimodal, 26, 52; Mdn = 40; $\overline{X}$ = 38.6.
   c. Approximately symmetrical, bimodal.
   d. Because the distribution is bimodal, neither the Mdn nor the $\overline{X}$ represents the typical score of a subject very well.

5.

	$\overline{X}$	Mdn	Mode	
Roberto	64	65	90	Mode
Dimitrios	58	65	None	Median
Karen	71	67	56	Mean

6. a. It is likely that some subjects estimated very high numbers of drinks consumed each week, thus positively skewing the distribution.
   b. Median number of drinks per week.
7. a. Mode or median.
   b. Mode = 793, Mdn = 832.

CHAPTER 5

Testing Your Knowledge 5.1

2. Range = 44, IQR = 18, $SIQR$ = 9.
3. a. Range = 287 ms, IQR = 85 ms, $SIQR$ = 42.5 ms.

Testing Your Knowledge 5.2

2. a and b.

	Read by Themselves	Read by Teacher
$\overline{X}$	59.00	57.00
s	5.54	10.23
s^2	30.69	104.65

c. Read by teacher group.
d. 10.23.

3. a.

	Male	Female
$\overline{X}$	15.55	7.05
s	7.41	2.59
s^2	54.91	6.71

b. Males.

c. 7.41 minutes.

d. Females; the s is smaller for females than for males.

Testing Your Knowledge 5.3

1. a. *Mdn, SIQR.*   **b.** *Mdn, SIQR.*
c. $\overline{X}, s.$ **d.** *Mdn, SIQR.*
e. $\overline{X}, s.$ **f.** *Mdn, SIQR.*
g. *Mdn, SIQR.*

Review Questions

1. a. $Mdn = 50, \overline{X} = 49.60, IQR = 10, s = 7.26.$
b. Both are equally good.
2. a. $Mdn = 50, \overline{X} = 49.45, IQR = 10, s = 11.56.$
b. Both are equally good.
c. The *IQR* is not affected by scores in the tails of the distribution.
3. a. Range.   **b.** *IQR.*
c. *SIQR.*   **d.** $s^2.$
e. $s.$ **f.** *IQR.*
g. Range.   **h.** $S^2.$
i. $s^2.$ **j.** $S.$
k. $s.$ **l.** *SIQR.*
m. $\sigma.$ **n.** $\sigma^2.$
4. a. 15.4 drinks per week.
b. Large.
c. The large standard deviations indicate that the distributions were positively skewed. Some subjects estimated a very large number of drinks per week and inflated the value of s. This result indicates that the median would be a better measure of central tendency for the scores.
5. The *IQR* or *SIQR* because they do not require knowing the numerical value of the score assigned to the ninth patient.

CHAPTER 6

Testing Your Knowledge 6.1

4. a. .3413.   **b.** .4772.
c. .4987.   **d.** .3413.
e. .4772.   **f.** .4987.
g. .8400.   **h.** .9544.
i. .9974.   **j.** .1359.
k. .1574.   **l.** .0215.

Testing Your Knowledge 6.2

2.

	z	Area 0 to z	Area beyond z
a.	$+1.90$	.4713	.0287
b.	-0.52	.1985	.3015
c.	$+0.77$	.2794	.2206
d.	-1.83	.4664	.0336
e.	$+1.75$	.4599	.0401
f.	-1.26	.3962	.1038

3. a. .0401.
b. .1465.
c. .3345.
d. Approximately 58.8 to 85.2 using $z = +$ or $-1.65.$

Testing Your Knowledge 6.3

3. .0014.

4.

	z	p
a.	$+1.90$	.0287
b.	-0.52	.3015
c.	$+0.77$	.2206
d.	-1.83	.0336
e.	$+1.75$	.0401
f.	-1.26	.1038

5. a. .0668.
b. .1865.
c. .2426.

Review Questions

3. a. .1587.   **b.** .0228.
   c. .0038.   **d.** .4082.
   e. .4525.
   f. Approximately 80.8 to 119.2 using $z = +$ or -1.28.
   g. .6568.   **h.** .0918.
   i. .0475.   **j.** .0038.
4. a. .016.   **b.** .018.
5. a. $p = .06$.   **b.** $p = .08$.
   c. $p = .54$.
6. a. .0968.   **b.** .0968.
   c. .8064.
7. a. .0668.   **b.** .0401.
   c. .9544.   **d.** .8664.
   e. .2266.   **f.** .3085.

8. a.

	Video Games	GPA
$\overline{X}$	8.0	2.7
S	5.86	0.87
Alex	-0.34	-0.23
Lauren	0.00	-0.80
Yvonne	-1.37	$+1.38$
Laval	$+1.19$	$+0.80$
Bonnie	-0.85	$+0.46$
Jason	$+1.37$	-1.61

   b. That she is at the mean of the group for video-game playing.
   c. That she is 1.38 standard deviations above the mean GPA of the group.
   d. That the person's GPA is below the mean of the group.
   e. That the person's video-game playing time is above the mean of the group.

9.

English Literature	World History
$z = +0.83$	$z = +1.00$

World history, where your score is one standard deviation above the class mean.

10. a. $p = .206$.   **b.** $p = .045$.
11. a. $p = .458$.   **b.** $p = .267$.

CHAPTER 7

Testing Your Knowledge 7.1

2.

	(a) Proportion	(b) Number
Generalized anxiety disorder	.27	27
Agoraphobia	.23	23
Simple phobia	.19	19
Panic disorder	.22	22
Obsessive-compulsive	.09	9

Testing Your Knowledge 7.2

2. Biased; underestimates.
3. Unbiased.
4. Biased; slightly underestimates.
7. a. .6826.   **b.** .1587.
   c. .0228.   **d.** .0475.
   e. .4525.
8. a. 9, 6, 3 seconds, respectively.
   b. As N increases, $s_{\overline{X}}$ decreases.
9. a. $s = 10$, $s_{\overline{X}} = 2$.
        $s = 15$, $s_{\overline{X}} = 3$.
        $s = 20$, $s_{\overline{X}} = 4$.
   b. As s increases, $s_{\overline{X}}$ also increases.
10. Population A_2 because it has a larger value of σ.

Testing Your Knowledge 7.3

2. a. 73.0.
   b. 69.1 to 76.9.
   c. 67.8 to 78.2.
   d. 73.0.
   e. 71.0 to 75.0.
   f. 70.4 to 75.6.
   g. The value of $\sigma_{\overline{X}}$ becomes smaller as N increases.

Review Questions

1. a. σ.   **b.** μ.
c. σ^2.   **d.** $\sigma_{\overline{X}}$.
2. $N = 24$, because $\overline{X}$ is a consistent estimator.
3. Stratified; see text for explanation.
5. a. 9.0 cigarettes per day.
  b. 7.5 to 10.5 cigarettes per day.
6. a. 0.3.   **b.** .0013.
  c. .1587.   **d.** .9544.

8. Sample

Sample	a.	b.	d.
A	2.00	.1587	.3413
B	1.33	.0668	.4332
C	1.00	.0228	.4772
D	0.80	.0062	.4938
E	0.40	< .0001	> .4999

CHAPTER 8

Testing Your Knowledge 8.1

3. a. H_0: $\mu = 100$.
    H_1: $\mu \neq 100$.
  b. H_0: $\mu = 4.4$ hours
    H_1: $\mu \neq 4.4$ hours
  c. H_0: $\mu = 423.0$ milliseconds.
    H_1: $\mu \neq 423.0$ milliseconds.

4. z_{obs}
  a. -2.13 Falls into rejection region; reject H_0, accept H_1.
  b. -1.20 Does not fall into rejection region; do not reject H_0, do not accept H_1.
  c. $+2.25$ Falls into rejection region; reject H_0, accept H_1.
  d. $+1.72$ Does not fall into rejection region; do not reject H_0, do not accept H_1.

5. a. $z = (\overline{X} - \mu)/\sigma_{\overline{X}}$.
  b. H_0: $\mu = 100$; H_1: $\mu \neq 100$.
  c. $\alpha = .05$.
  d. $z_{crit} = 1.96$.
  e. Values of z_{obs} more extreme than $z = -1.96$ or $+1.96$.
  f. $z_{obs} = +2.50$.
  g. Reject H_0; accept H_1.

h. The sample mean differs significantly from the population mean.

Testing Your Knowledge 8.2

3. a. 7.   **b.** 6.
  c. 6.
4. a. 9.   **b.** 15.
  c. 6.   **d.** 53.
  e. 119.   **f.** 29.
5. The distribution with 13 df.
6. When the $df = \infty$.

Testing Your Knowledge 8.3

1. a. H_0: $\mu = 493$; H_1: $\mu \neq 493$.
  b. H_0: $\mu = 36.1$; H_1: $\mu \neq 36.1$.
  c. H_0: $\mu = 100$; H_1: $\mu \neq 100$.
2. a. 2.447.   **b.** 2.898.
  c. 2.069.   **d.** 2.042.
  e. 2.042.   **f.** 2.660.
  g. 2.000.   **h.** 1.980.

3.

	Falls into Rejection Region	Decision
a.	Yes	Reject H_0 Accept H_1
b.	No	Fail to reject H_0 Do not accept H_1
c.	Yes	Reject H_0 Accept H_1
d.	No	Fail to reject H_0 Do not accept H_1
e.	Yes	Reject H_0 Accept H_1
f.	Yes	Reject H_0 Accept H_1
g.	No	Fail to reject H_0 Do not accept H_1
h.	Yes	Reject H_0 Accept H_1
i.	Yes	Reject H_0 Accept H_1
j.	Yes	Reject H_0 Accept H_1
k.	Yes	Reject H_0 Accept H_1

5. **a.** $t = (\bar{X} - \mu)/s_{\bar{X}}$.   **b.** See text.
   c. $H_0: \mu = 7.0$; $H_1: \mu \neq 7.0$.
   d. $\alpha = .05$.   **e.** $t_{crit}(10) = 2.228$.
   f. Values of t_{obs} more extreme than -2.228 or $+2.228$.
   g. $t_{obs} = -4.979$.   **h.** Reject H_0; accept H_1.
   i. The sample mean of 5.8 minutes differs significantly from the population mean of 7.0 minutes.

6. *Report 1*
   a. 70.4 kg.   **b.** 7.6 kg.
   c. One-sample t.
   d. $H_0: \mu = 75$ kg; $H_1: \mu \neq 75$ kg.
   e. 6.   **f.** -1.48.
   g. 5.   **h.** 2.571.
   i. Fail to reject H_0.
   j. Do not accept H_1.
   k. The sample mean does not differ significantly from the population mean.

Report 2
   a. 10.4 days.   **b.** 2.3 days.
   c. One-sample t.
   d. $H_0: \mu = 8.7$ days; $H_1: \mu \neq 8.7$ days.
   e. 25.   **f.** $+3.70$.
   g. 24.   **h.** 2.064.
   i. Reject H_0.   **j.** Accept H_1.
   k. The sample mean differs significantly from the population mean; 10.4 days is significantly longer than the hypothesized mean of 8.7 days.

Testing Your Knowledge 8.4

2. **b.** $p = \alpha$.
   c. A Type I error cannot occur if H_0 is false.
   e. No.
4. 80.1 to 113.9 minutes.

Chapter Review

5. **a.** Reject H_0; accept H_1.
   b. Fail to reject H_0; do not accept H_1.
7. **a.** The sample mean differs significantly from the hypothesized population mean.
   b. The sample mean does not differ significantly from the hypothesized population mean.
8. Rejection region consists of values of z_{obs} more extreme than $z = -2.58$ or $+2.58$.

z_{obs}	Falls into Rejection Region	Decision
$+3.71$	Yes	Reject H_0 Accept H_1
-2.60	Yes	Reject H_0 Accept H_1
$+1.74$	No	Fail to reject H_0 Do not accept H_1
-3.05	Yes	Reject H_0 Accept H_1
-1.96	No	Fail to reject H_0 Do not accept H_1
$+2.58$	Yes	Reject H_0 Accept H_1

9. $z_{obs} = -1.52$; nonsignificant; fail to reject H_0.
11. **a.** The sample mean differs significantly from the hypothesized population mean.
   b. The sample mean does not differ significantly from the hypothesized population mean.

12.

	Falls into Rejection Region	Decision
a.	Yes	Reject H_0 Accept H_1
b.	No	Fail to reject H_0 Do not accept H_1
c.	Yes	Reject H_0 Accept H_1
d.	Yes	Reject H_0 Accept H_1
e.	No	Fail to reject H_0 Do not accept H_1
f.	No	Fail to reject H_0 Do not accept H_1

13. **a.** $t_{obs}(8) = -2.924$; significant at the .05 level; reject H_0, accept H_1.
   c. Yes.   **d.** No.
   e. 6.81 to 7.59 hours; $\mu = 7.7$ is not included in this interval.
14. **a.** $t_{obs}(11) = +3.139$; significant at the .05 level; reject H_0, accept H_1.
   b. No.
15. **a.** Type I error.   **b.** Type II error.
   c. Correct decision.   **d.** Correct decision.

CHAPTER 9

Testing Your Knowledge 9.1

6. a. Extraneous variable = age; groups differ systematically in average age as well as noise condition.

b. Extraneous variable = experimenter's encouragement; groups differ systematically in encouragement as well as noise condition.

c. Extraneous variable = gender; groups differ systematically in gender as well as noise condition.

d. Extraneous variable = college major; groups differ systematically in college major as well as noise condition.

e. Extraneous variable = time of day when the experiment was conducted; groups differ systematically in time of day as well as noise condition.

Testing Your Knowledge 9.2

3. a. 3.77.

b. 3.56.

c. 3.81.

d. 2.25.

Testing Your Knowledge 9.3

6.

Sample Set	df	t_{crit}	Falls into Rejection Region	Decision
1.	18	2.101	Yes	Reject H_0 Accept H_1
2.	18	2.101	No	Fail to reject H_0 Do not accept H_1
3.	28	2.048	Yes	Reject H_0 Accept H_1
4.	28	2.048	Yes	Reject H_0 Accept H_1
5.	68	2.000	Yes	Reject H_0 Accept H_1
6.	33	2.042	No	Fail to reject H_0 Do not accept H_1
7.	127	1.980	Yes	Reject H_0 Accept H_1
8.	148	1.980	Yes	Reject H_0 Accept H_1

9. *Problem 1*

a. $H_0: \mu_{A1} = \mu_{A2}$; $H_1: \mu_{A1} \neq \mu_{A2}$.

b. $t_{obs}(34) = -3.656$.

c. 34.

d. 2.042.

e. Values of t_{obs} more extreme than -2.042 or $+2.042$.

f. Yes.

g. Reject H_0; accept H_1.

h. Different populations.

i. Yes.

j. Yes; the control group estimated a statistically significant shorter time interval than the experimental group.

Problem 2

a. $H_0: \mu_{A1} = \mu_{A2}$; $H_1: \mu_{A1} \neq \mu_{A2}$.

b. $t_{obs}(28) = -1.742$.

c. 28.

d. 2.048.

e. Values of t_{obs} more extreme than -2.048 or $+2.048$.

f. No.

g. Fail to reject H_0; do not accept H_1.

h. There is no evidence that they are not from the same population.

i. No; it is nonsignificant.

j. No; the difference between the group means is treated as a chance difference.

Testing Your Knowledge 9.4

2. a. Set 2.

b. Set 2.

c. Set 1.

3. $n_{A1} = n_{A2} = 20$ expected to have a smaller $s_{\bar{X}A1 - \bar{X}A2}$ and lead to a more powerful statistical test.

4. a. .42.

b. .27.

c. .19.

d. .23.

e. .08.

7. *Report 1*

a. 2.

b. 62.

c. 79.7; 73.0.

d. 8.57; 5.85.

e. 3.60.

f. 2.000.

g. Reject H_0.

h. Accept H_1.

i. Statistically significant.

j. The effect of the treatment.

Report 2

a. 2.

b. 30.

c. 22.78; 24.33.

d. 5.23; 5.14.

e. -0.82.

f. 2.048.

g. Fail to reject H_0.   **h.** Do not accept H_1.
i. Nonsignificant.   **j.** Sampling error.

Testing Your Knowledge 9.5

2. a. H_0: $\mu_{A1} = \mu_{A2}$; H_1: $\mu_{A1} \neq \mu_{A2}$.
  b. $t_{obs}(10) = -3.148$.
  c. 10.   **d.** 2.228.
  e. Values of t_{obs} more extreme than -2.228 or $+2.228$.
  f. Yes.   **g.** Reject H_0; accept H_1.
  h. Different populations.
  i. Yes.
  j. Yes; the control group responded with statistically significant shorter reaction times than the experimental group.
  k. .50.   **l.** -41.8 to -7.2 ms.

Review Questions

1.

	Group	
	Quiet	**Noise**
$\overline{X}$	122.64	131.27
s	8.76	10.45

  a. $t_{obs}(20) = -2.099, p < .05$. The mean blood pressure of the quiet group is significantly lower than that of the noise group.
  b. $\eta^2 = .18$; 18% of the variance in the dependent variable.
  c. 0.05 to 17.21.

2.

	Group	
	Quiet	**Noise**
$\overline{X}$	113.09	115.27
s	4.55	6.48

$t_{obs}(20) = -0.913$, $p > .05$. The mean blood pressures of the two groups do not differ significantly.

3.

	Gender	
	Male	**Female**
$\overline{X}$	17.77	18.59
s	4.99	5.32

$t_{obs}(28) = -0.429, p > .05$. Males and females do not differ significantly on the rated need for solitude.

4. a.

	Instructional Condition	
	Before	**After**
$\overline{X}$	2.45	2.52
s	.604	.677

  b. With an alpha level of .05 and a two-tailed test, the mean error for judgments made before instructions ($M = 2.45$ mm, $SD = .604$ mm) did not differ significantly from the mean error for judgments made after instructions were given ($M = 2.52$ mm, $SD = .677$ mm), $t(11) = -1.261, p > .05$.

5. a. $t_{obs}(88) = +3.170, p < .01$. The mean locus of control score for the foster parents group was significantly higher than the mean locus of control score for the biological parents group.
  b. $\eta^2 = .10$.   **c.** 1.29 to 5.69.

6. a. $t_{obs}(5398) = -25.003, p < .001$; the GPAs of the two groups differ significantly. The GPA of students involved in residence hall disruptions is significantly lower than the GPA of students not involved in disruptions.
  b. $\eta^2 = .10$.   **c.** 0.47 to 0.55.

7. $t_{obs}(32) = -0.818, p > .05$. The nonsignificant t indicates that the group means do not differ significantly at the .05 level.

8. a. $t_{obs}(24) = -3.744, p < .05$. The mean trustworthiness rating of the speaker demonstrating immediacy behaviors is significantly higher than the rating of the speaker in the no immediacy behavior conditions.
  b. $\eta^2 = .37$.   **c.** -3.223 to -0.931.
  d. With an alpha level of .05 and a two-tailed test, the mean trustworthiness rating of the speaker demonstrating immediacy behaviors ($M = 6.9, SD = 1.41$) was significantly higher than the rating of the speaker in the no immediacy behavior condition ($M = 4.8, SD = 1.42$), $t(24) = -3.744, p < .01, \eta^2 = .37$.

CHAPTER 10

Testing Your Knowledge 10.1

6. $a = 4$, $n_A = 11$, $N = 44$.

11. 150.00.

12. 25.00.

13. 79.

14. 25.00.

15. 10.00.

16. $df_A = 3$, $df_{Error} = 40$, $df_{Total} = 43$.

17.

Source	SS	df	MS	F
Factor A	24.00	1	24.00	6.00
Error	16.00	4	4.00	
Total	40.00	5		

18.

Source	SS	df	MS	F
Factor A	42.00	2	21.00	5.25
Error	24.00	6	4.00	
Total	66.00	8		

19. *Table 1*

Source	SS	df	MS	F
Factor A	50.00	1	50.00	5.00
Error	260.00	26	10.00	
Total	310.00	27		

a. 2.   **b.** 14.

c. 28.

Table 2

Source	SS	df	MS	F
Factor A	18.00	3	6.00	3.00
Error	152.00	76	2.00	
Total	170.00	79		

a. 4.   **b.** 20.   **c.** 80.

Testing Your Knowledge 10.2

6. Approximately 1.00.

7. It becomes greater than 1.00.

8. a. H_0: $\mu_{A1} = \mu_{A2}$;
     H_1: The μ_A's are not equal.

b. H_0: $\mu_{A1} = \mu_{A2} = \mu_{A3} = \mu_{A4}$;
     H_1: The μ_A's are not all equal.

c. H_0: $\mu_{A1} = \mu_{A2} = \mu_{A3} = \mu_{A4} = \mu_{A5} = \mu_{A6}$;
     H_1: The μ_A's are not all equal.

9. The independent variable has no effect.

10. The independent variable has an effect.

11. Zero.

12. No upper limit.

13.

Experiment	F_{crit}	Falls into Rejection Region	Decision
1.	4.96	Yes	Reject H_0 Accept H_1
2.	3.40	No	Fail to reject H_0 Do not accept H_1
3.	4.26	Yes	Reject H_0 Accept H_1
4.	3.15	Yes	Reject H_0 Accept H_1
5.	3.89	Yes	Reject H_0 Accept H_1
6.	3.68	No	Fail to reject H_0 Do not accept H_1
7.	2.61	No	Fail to reject H_0 Do not accept H_1
8.	3.10	No	Fail to reject H_0 Do not accept H_1
9.	2.25	Yes	Reject H_0 Accept H_1
10.	2.53	No	Fail to reject H_0 Do not accept H_1

Testing Your Knowledge 10.3

1.

	Group	
	Control	Experimental
$\overline{X}$	7.09	8.82
s	1.30	1.47

a. H_0: $\mu_{A1} = \mu_{A2}$;
     H_1: The μ_A's are not equal.

b. $F_{obs}(1, 20) = 8.51$.

c. $df_A = 1$, $df_{Error} = 20$.

d. $F_{crit}(1, 20) = 4.35$.

e. Values of $F_{obs} \geq 4.35$.

f. Yes.   **g.** Reject H_0; accept H_1.

h. Different populations.

i. Yes.

j. They differ; the control group estimated a shorter time interval.

k. No, because only two levels of the independent variable were manipulated.

l. $\eta^2 = .30$.   **m.** 30 percent.

2.

	Grade		
	2nd	**4th**	**6th**
$\overline{X}$	565.80	530.60	501.00
s	32.410	28.99	24.42

a. H_0: $\mu_{A1} = \mu_{A2} = \mu_{A3}$.
H_1: The μ_A's are not all equal.

b. $F_{obs}(2, 39) = 17.76$.

c. $df_A = 2$, $df_{Error} = 39$.

d. $F_{crit}(2, 39) = 3.32$ (critical value for 2, 30 df).

e. Values of F_{obs} equal to or greater than 3.32.

f. Yes.   **g.** Reject H_0; accept H_1.

h. There is at least one significant difference among the means.

i. Yes; because F_{obs} is statistically significant and there are three means being compared in the experiment.

j. $CD = 26.86$.

k. Each group differs significantly from each other group.

l. The sleep periods from longest to shortest are 2nd graders, 4th graders, 6th graders.

m. $\eta^2 = .48$.   **n.** 48 percent.

3.1. a. 2.   **b.** 62.

c. 14.15.   **d.** 4.00.

e. Reject H_0.   **f.** Accept H_1.

g. Yes.

h. The familiar and unfamiliar poetry passage group means.

3.2. a. 4.   **b.** 40.

c. 1.13.   **d.** 2.92.

e. Fail to reject H_0.   **f.** Do not accept H_1.

g. No.

h. There are no significant differences among the means.

3.3. a. 3.   **b.** 39.

c. 33.94.   **d.** 3.32.

e. Reject H_0.   **f.** Accept H_1.

g. Yes.

h. The Tukey CD indicates that the mean for the hard rock music (29.9) was significantly higher than the mean for either classical music (18.5) or the mean for the no-music control group (17.5). The classical and no-music control group means did not differ significantly.

Review Questions

1. a.

	Treatment Group		
	No Music	**Oldies**	**Hard Rock**
$\overline{X}$	36.0	35.6	22.9
s	3.70	3.50	3.60

$F_{obs}(2, 21) = 34.39, p < .01$. Tukey $CD = 4.6$. The hard rock music group detected significantly fewer errors than did either the no music or the oldies music groups. The no music and oldies music groups means do not differ significantly.

b. $\eta^2 = .77$.

2. a.

	Instructional Condition		
	No Videotape	**Soccer Videotape**	**Throwing, Catching Videotape**
$\overline{X}$	45.22	44.33	57.11
s	5.63	5.74	6.68

$F_{obs}(2, 24) = 12.57, p < .01$. Tukey $CD = 7.1$. The throwing, catching videotape mean differs significantly from both the no videotape and the soccer videotape means. The no videotape and soccer videotape means do not differ significantly.

b. $\eta^2 = .51$.

3. a.

	Group	
	Quiet	**Noise**
$\overline{X}$	122.64	131.27
s	8.76	10.45

$F_{obs}(1, 20) = 4.41, p < .05$. The mean for the quiet group is significantly lower than the mean for the noise group.

b. Yes, $t = \sqrt{F} = \sqrt{4.41} = 2.10$.

4. a. $a = 6, n_A = 7, N = 42$.

b. $df_A = 5, df_{Error} = 36, df_{Total} = 41$.

5. *Table 1*

Source	SS	df	MS	F
Factor A	50.00	2	25.00	2.50
Error	270.00	27	10.00	
Total	320.00	29		

a. 3. **b.** 10.

c. 30.

d. $F_{crit}(2, 27) = 3.35$; F_{obs} is nonsignificant.

e. Fail to reject H_0; do not accept H_1.

Table 2

Source	SS	df	MS	F
Factor A	60.00	5	12.00	4.00
Error	216.00	72	3.00	
Total	276.00	77		

a. 6. **b.** 13.

c. 78.

d. $F_{crit}(5, 72) = 2.37$; F_{obs} is statistically significant.

e. Reject H_0; accept H_1.

Table 3

Source	SS	df	MS	F
Factor A	45.00	3	15.00	3.00
Error	320.00	64	5.00	
Total	365.00	67		

a. 4. **b.** 17.

c. 68.

d. $F_{crit}(3, 64) = 2.76$; F_{obs} is statistically significant.

e. Reject H_0; accept H_1.

7. $F_{obs}(1, 18) = 4.00$.

8. $t_{obs}(22) = 3.00$.

10. The statistically significant $F_{obs}(3, 64) = 21.64$ indicates that there is at least one significant difference between the groups. Applying the $CD = 5.0$ minutes to the pairwise comparisons reveals that the Behavior Modification and Cigarettes Anonymous Club have significantly longer mean times between smoking cigarettes than either the Control group or the Smoke-Stop Gum group. The Behavior Modification and Cigarettes Anonymous means do not differ significantly from each other, and the Control group and Smoke-Stop Gum group means also do not differ significantly from each other.

CHAPTER 11

Testing Your Knowledge 11.1

2.

	Number of Independent Variables	Levels	Number of Subjects Needed
a.	2	$A = 3$; $B = 3$	90
b.	2	$A = 3$; $B = 2$	60
c.	2	$A = 2$; $B = 3$	60
d.	2	$A = 6$; $B = 2$	120
e.	2	$A = 4$; $B = 4$	160
f.	3	$A = 2$; $B = 2$ $C = 2$	80
g.	3	$A = 2$; $B = 4$ $C = 3$	240
h.	3	$A = 3$; $B = 3$ $C = 2$	180

3. *Table 1*

	Factor A A_1	Factor A A_2	Main Effect Means for Factor B
Factor B B_1	13.3	20.2	16.8
Factor B B_2	16.8	22.8	19.8
Main Effect Means for Factor A	15.1	21.5	$\overline{X}_G = 18.3$

Table 2

	Factor A		Main Effect Means for Factor B
	A_1	A_2	
Factor B B_1	18.9	30.1	24.5
B_2	31.3	33.9	32.6
Main Effect Means for Factor A	25.1	32.0	$\overline{X}_G = 28.6$

Testing Your Knowledge 11.2

8. 240.00.

9. 45.00.

10. 55.00.

11. 60.00.

12. $df_A = 1$, $df_B = 2$, $df_{A \times B} = 2$, $df_{Error} = 30$, $df_{Total} = 35$.

13. $df_A = 2$, $df_B = 1$, $df_{A \times B} = 2$, $df_{Error} = 72$, $df_{Total} = 77$.

14. 79.

15. $MS_A = 14.00/1 = 14.00$;
$MS_B = 26.00/2 = 13.00$;
$MS_{A \times B} = 44.00/2 = 22.00$;
$MS_{Error} = 480.00/60 = 8.00$.

16. a.

Source	SS	df	MS	F
Factor A	108.00	1	108.00	27.00
Factor B	0.00	1	0.00	0.00
$A \times B$	12.00	1	12.00	3.00
Error	32.00	8	4.00	
Total	152.00	11		

b. Both main effect means for factor B are equal to 32.0.

17. *Table 1*

Source	SS	df	MS	F
Factor A	32.00	2	16.00	2.00
Factor B	24.00	1	24.00	3.00
$A \times B$	24.00	2	12.00	1.50
Error	480.00	60	8.00	
Total	560.00	65		

a. 3.

c. 11.

b. 2.

d. 66.

Table 2

Source	SS	df	MS	F
Factor A	36.00	2	18.00	4.50
Factor B	24.00	4	6.00	1.50
$A \times B$	160.00	8	20.00	5.00
Error	840.00	210	4.00	
Total	1060.00	224		

a. 3.

c. 15.

b. 5.

d. 225.

Testing Your Knowledge 11.3

10. *Table 1*

Source	df	F_{obs}	F_{crit}	F_{obs} Falls into Rejection Region	Decision
Factor A	1	4.63	4.08	Yes	Reject H_0 Accept H_1
Factor B	3	2.11	2.84	No	Fail to reject H_0 Do not accept H_1
$A \times B$	3	3.97	2.84	Yes	Reject H_0 Accept H_1

Table 2

Source	df	F_{obs}	F_{crit}	F_{obs} Falls into Rejection Region	Decision
Factor A	3	1.42	2.68	No	Fail to reject H_0 Do not accept H_1
Factor B	2	3.51	3.07	Yes	Reject H_0 Accept H_1
$A \times B$	6	2.37	2.17	Yes	Reject H_0 Accept H_1

Table 3

Source	df	F_{obs}	F_{crit}	F_{obs} Falls into Rejection Region	Decision
Factor A	2	4.12	3.07	Yes	Reject H_0 Accept H_1
Factor B	4	2.83	2.45	Yes	Reject H_0 Accept H_1
$A \times B$	8	1.87	2.02	No	Fail to reject H_0 Do not accept H_1

Testing Your Knowledge 11.4

Figure 11.2

a. Yes.   **b.** No.

c. Yes.

d. Because of the statistically significant interaction, the effect of the type of teaching method depends on the type of material, factor B. For mathematical material (B_1), computer-assisted teaching (A_1) leads to significantly higher test scores than does noncomputer-assisted teaching (A_2). For social studies material (B_2), however, the teaching methods do not differ from each other.

e. The statistically significant interaction indicates that the effect of type of material depends on the type of teaching, factor A. For computer-assisted teaching (A_1), mathematical material (B_1) leads to significantly higher test scores compared to social studies material (B_2). For noncomputer-assisted teaching (A_2), there is no difference between the types of materials.

f. No; the main effect for factor A indicates an overall superiority for computer-assisted teaching, but computer-assisted teaching leads to significantly higher test scores only with mathematical material. Thus the main effect for factor A is an artifact of the interaction; it conveys no meaningful information about the effect of factor A on test scores.

Figure 11.3

a. No.   **b.** Yes.

c. Yes.

d. The statistically significant interaction indicates that the effect of type of teaching depends on the type of material, factor B. For mathematical material (B_1), the teaching methods do not differ significantly. For social studies material (B_2), noncomputer-assisted teaching (A_2) leads to significantly higher test scores than does computer-assisted teaching (A_1).

e. The statistically significant interaction indicates that the effect of type of material depends on the type of teaching, factor A. Both types of teaching lead to higher test scores for mathematical material, but the difference between mathematical and social studies material is larger for computer-assisted teaching than it is for noncomputer-assisted teaching.

f. Yes; the main effect for factor B indicates an overall superiority for mathematical material, and mathematical material leads to significantly higher test scores for both types of teaching. The interaction, however, indicates that the difference between mathematical and social studies material depends on the type of teaching method.

2. *Table 1*

a. Yes.   **b.** No.

c. No.

d. Computer-assisted teaching (A_1) leads to significantly higher test scores than does noncomputer-assisted teaching (A_2).

e. No effect.

f. Yes; there is no interaction of A and B.

Table 2

a. No.   **b.** Yes.

c. No.   **d.** No effect.

e. Mathematical material (B_1) leads to significantly higher test scores than does social studies material (B_2).

f. Yes; there is no interaction of A and B.

Table 3

a. Yes.   **b.** Yes.

c. No.

d. Noncomputer-assisted teaching (A_2) leads to significantly higher test scores than does computer-assisted teaching (A_1).

e. Mathematical material (B_1) leads to significantly higher test scores than does social studies material (B_2).

f. Yes; there is no interaction of A and B.

Table 4

a. No.   **b.** No.

c. Yes.

d. Because of the statistically significant interaction, the effect of teaching method depends on the type of material, factor B. For mathematical material (B_1), computer-assisted teaching (A_1) leads to significantly higher test scores than does noncomputer-assisted teaching (A_2). For social studies material (B_2), however, noncomputer-assisted teaching (A_2) leads to significantly higher test scores than does computer-assisted teaching (A_1).

e. Because of the statistically significant interaction, the effect of the type of material depends on the type of teaching, factor A. For computer-assisted teaching (A_1), mathematical material (B_1) leads to significantly higher test scores than social studies material. For noncomputer-assisted teaching (A_2), social studies material (B_2) leads to significantly higher test scores than mathematical material.

f. No; the main effect for each independent variable indicates no overall effect of the independent variable. However, each independent variable does have an effect, but the effect of each independent variable depends on the level of the other independent variable.

Table 5

a. Yes.   **b.** Yes.

c. Yes.

d. Because of the statistically significant interaction, the effect of the type of teaching method depends on the type of material. For mathematical material (B_1), the difference between computer-assisted (A_1) and noncomputer-

assisted (A_2) teaching is nonsignificant. For social studies material, however, noncomputer-assisted teaching (A_2) leads to significantly higher test scores compared to computer-assisted teaching (A_1).

e. Because of the statistically significant interaction, the effect of the type of material depends on the type of teaching. For both computer-assisted (A_1) and noncomputer-assisted (A_2) teaching, mathematical material (B_1) leads to significantly higher test scores than does social studies material (B_2). However, the difference between mathematical and social studies scores is greater for computer-assisted teaching (A_1) than it is for noncomputer-assisted teaching (A_2).

f. The main effect of factor A, teaching method, is artifactual because it indicates an overall superiority for noncomputer-assisted teaching. But noncomputer-assisted teaching leads to significantly higher performance only with social studies material. The main effect of factor B, type of material, is meaningful; mathematical material leads to significantly higher performance for both computer-assisted and noncomputer-assisted teaching.

Table 6

a. Yes.   **b.** Yes.

c. Yes.

d. Because of the statistically significant interaction, the effect of the type of teaching method depends on the type of material. For mathematical material (B_1), computer-assisted teaching (A_1) leads to significantly higher test scores compared to noncomputer-assisted teaching (A_2). For social studies material, however, there is no effect of teaching method.

e. The effect of type of material depends on the type of teaching. For computer-assisted teaching (A_1), mathematical material (B_1) leads to significantly higher test scores than does social studies material (B_2). For noncomputer-assisted teaching (A_2), the difference between mathematical material (B_1) and social studies material (B_2) scores is nonsignificant.

f. The main effects for both factor A, teaching method, and factor B, type of material, are artifactual.

Testing Your Knowledge 11.5

1. Analysis of variance summary.

Source	SS	df	MS	F
Locus of control (A)	704.167	1	704.167	1.15
Instructions (B)	1,472.667	1	1,472.667	2.41
$A \times B$	46,112.666	1	46,112.666	75.39*
Error	12,233.000	20	611.650	
Total	60,522.500	23		

*$p < .01$.

a. (1) No significant main effect for either independent variable.
   (2) Significant interaction.
b. ($CD = 36.15$). The statistically significant interaction indicates that the effect of instructions depends on the locus of control. For internal locus of control subjects, skill instructions led to significantly more time spent on the task than did chance instructions. For external locus of control subjects, however, chance instructions led to significantly more time spent on the task than did skill instructions.
c. Because of the interaction, the nonsignificant main effects do not provide useful information for interpreting the outcome.
d. $\eta^2 = .76$ for the interaction of factors A and B.

2. Analysis of variance summary.

Source	SS	df	MS	F
Instruction (A)	191.361	1	191.361	23.61*
Crime (B)	1667.361	1	1667.361	205.75*
$A \times B$	210.250	1	210.250	25.94*
Error	259.333	32	8.104	
Total	2328.305	35		

*$p < .01$.

a. (1) Significant main effects for both factors A and B.
   (2) Significant interaction.

b. ($CD = 3.31$). The statistically significant interaction indicates that the effect of type of instructions depends on the type of crime; the difference between the filmed and normal instructions for auto theft is nonsignificant, but a significantly longer term is assigned with filmed instruction compared to normal instructions for aggravated assault.
c. The statistically significant interaction indicates that the effect of type of crime depends on the type of instructions. For both types of instructions, aggravated assault leads to significantly longer prison terms than does auto theft. However, the difference between the prison terms for auto theft and aggravated assault is larger for filmed instructions than it is for normal instructions.
d. The statistically significant main effect for type of crime is meaningful; significantly longer terms are assigned for aggravated assault under both normal and filmed instructions. The main effect for type of instruction is artifactual; there is no difference between the filmed and normal instructions for auto theft, but a significantly longer term is assigned with filmed instruction for aggravated assault.
e. $\eta^2 = .72$ for type of crime. $\eta^2 = .09$ for the interaction of factors A and B.

3.1. a. 3.   b. 2.
   c. 42.

d.

	F_{crit}
A	3.32
B	4.17
$A \times B$	3.32

e. Yes.   f. Yes.
g. No.

3.2. a. 2.   b. 4.
   c. 96.

d.

	F_{crit}
A	4.00
B	2.76
$A \times B$	2.76

e. Yes.   **f.** No.
g. Yes.
3.3. a. 2.   **b.** 2.
c. 60.

d.

	F_{crit}
A	4.08
B	4.08
$A \times B$	4.08

e. No.   **f.** No.
g. Yes.

Review Questions

1. Analysis of variance summary.

Source	SS	df	MS	F
Eye contact (A)	24.500	1	24.500	0.76
Affect (B)	780.125	1	780.125	24.17*
$A \times B$	325.125	1	325.125	10.07*
Error	903.750	28	32.277	
Total	2033.500	31		

*$p < .01$.

a. Yes; there is a significant interaction of factors A and B (Tukey $CD = 7.1$). For positive affect conditions, the no-eye-contact mean is significantly higher than the eye-contact mean. For negative affect conditions, the eye-contact condition means do not differ significantly.

b. For the no-eye-contact condition, there is no significant difference between positive and negative affect conditions. For the eye-contact condition, however, negative affect leads to a significantly higher heart rate than does positive affect.

c. The statistically significant main effect for affect condition is artifactual; there is no significant difference between the affect conditions in the no-eye-contact condition, but in the eye-contact condition, the negative affect cell mean is significantly higher than the positive affect cell mean.

d. $\eta^2 = .16$ for the interaction of factors A and B.

2. Analysis of variance summary.

Source	SS	df	MS	F
Personality type (A)	36.750	1	36.750	6.58*
Background noise (B)	30.083	1	30.083	5.38*
$A \times B$	27.000	1	27.000	4.83*
Error	245.833	44	5.587	
Total	339.666	47		

*$p < .05$.

a. The analysis of variance reveals a statistically significant interaction; thus, a Tukey CD for simple effects is necessary. This CD for 3, 44 df equals 2.35. The analysis of the simple effects indicates that the mean for the introverts in the noisy background condition ($M = 8.2$ items correct) is significantly lower than the mean for the introverts in the quiet condition ($M = 11.3$ items correct) and also significantly lower than the mean for the extroverts in the noisy condition ($M = 11.4$ items correct). The mean for the introverts in the quiet background condition did not differ significantly from the mean of the extroverts in the quiet condition ($M = 11.5$ items correct) and the mean of the extroverts in the quiet background did not differ significantly from the mean of the extroverts in the noisy background condition.

b. $\eta^2 = .08$.

c. Both main effects are statistically significant but are artifactual and cannot be meaningfully interpreted.

3. Analysis of variance summary.

Source	SS	df	MS	F
Instructional method (A)	436.594	2	218.297	47.78*
Practice (B)	60.168	1	60.168	13.17*
$A \times B$	69.777	2	34.888	7.64*
Error	219.332	48	4.569	
Total	785.871	53		

*$p < .01$.

a. There is a statistically significant interaction; thus, the effect of instructional method depends on the level of practice. For the traditional method the one-week practice mean ($M = 13.1$ words correct) was significantly less than the six-week practice mean ($M = 17.9$ words correct; $CD = 2.9$). However, there was no significant difference between the one- and six-week practice conditions for either the word box ($M = 18.7$ words correct; $M = 21.0$ words correct; respectively) or word sort ($M = 22.8$ words correct; $M = 22.0$ words correct; respectively) methods. In addition, the differences between instructional methods depend on the amount of practice. For the one-week practice condition, each instructional method group differed significantly from the others; the word sort subjects obtained the highest score, the word box method the next highest score, and the traditional method the lowest score. For the six-week practice condition, the traditional method mean was significantly less than either the word box or word sort mean. The word box and word sort means did not differ significantly, however.

b. $\eta^2 = .09$.

c. Both main effects are artifactual.

4. $a = 2$, $b = 3$, $n_{AB} = 8$, $N = 48$, $df_A = 1$, $df_B = 2$, $df_{A \times B} = 2$, $df_{Error} = 42$, $df_{Total} = 47$.

5. *Table 1*

Source	SS	df	MS	F
Type of task (A)	15.00	3	5.00	2.50
Noise level (B)	16.00	2	8.00	4.00*
A × B	36.00	6	6.00	3.00*
Error	120.00	60	2.00	
Total	187.00	71		

*$p < .05$.

a. 4.	**b.** 3.
c. 6.	**d.** 72.

e. F_{obs} for factor B and the $A \times B$ interaction are statistically significant.

f. Factor A: Fail to reject H_0
                    Do not accept H_1
  Factor B: Reject H_0
                    Accept H_1
  $A \times B$:   Reject H_0
                    Accept H_1

Table 2

Source	SS	df	MS	F
Training length (A)	40.00	4	10.00	0.50
Skill level (B)	120.00	3	40.00	2.00
A × B	960.00	12	80.00	4.00*
Error	3200.00	160	20.00	
Total	4320.00	179		

*$p < .01$.

a. 5.	**b.** 4.
c. 9.	**d.** 180.

e. F_{obs} for the $A \times B$ interaction is statistically significant.

f. Factor A: Fail to reject H_0
                    Do not accept H_1
  Factor B: Fail to reject H_0
                    Do not accept H_1
  $A \times B$:   Reject H_0
                    Accept H_1

Table 3

Source	SS	df	MS	F
Type of feedback (A)	200.00	4	50.00	2.50*
Task difficulty (B)	160.00	2	80.00	4.00*
A × B	240.00	8	30.00	1.50
Error	2700.00	135	20.00	
Total	3300.00	149		

*$p < .05$.

a. 5.	**b.** 3.
c. 10.	**d.** 150.

e. F_{obs} for factor A and factor B are statistically significant.

f. Factor A: Reject H_0
                       Accept H_1
    Factor B: Reject H_0
                       Accept H_1
    $A \times B$:   Fail to reject H_0
                       Do not accept H_1

6. a. Because of the statistically significant interaction, the effect of type of imagery depends on the amount of elaboration. For low elaboration, ordinary imagery leads to significantly greater recall than does bizarre imagery. For high elaboration, however, ordinary imagery leads to significantly less recall than does bizarre imagery. The main effect of type of imagery is artifactual.

  b. Again, because of the statistically significant interaction, the effect of amount of elaboration depends on the type of imagery. For ordinary imagery, low elaboration leads to significantly higher recall than does high elaboration. For bizarre imagery, an opposite relation holds; low elaboration leads to significantly lower recall than does high elaboration.

7. a. The statistically significant interaction indicates that the effect of type of gauge depends on the amount of sleep deprivation. For no sleep deprivation, the difference between the number of correct readings for analog and digital gauges is nonsignificant. For 24 hours of sleep deprivation, digital gauges result in significantly more correct readings than do analog gauges. The main effect of type of gauge is artifactual.

  b. Again, the statistically significant interaction indicates that the effect of amount of sleep deprivation depends on the type of gauge. For both analog and digital gauges, 24 hours of sleep deprivation results in significantly fewer correct readings than does no sleep deprivation. However, the difference between the number of correct readings for no and 24 hours of sleep deprivation is greater for analog gauges than it is for digital gauges. Because 24 hours of sleep deprivation results in fewer correct readings for both analog and digital gauges, the main effect of amount of sleep deprivation is meaningful.

CHAPTER 12

Testing Your Knowledge 12.1

4. 199.00.
5. 33.00.
6. 25.00.
7. 96.00.
8. $df_A = 4$, $df_S = 12$, $df_{A \times S} = 48$, $df_{Total} = 64$.
9. 59.
10. $MS_A = 11.00$, $MS_S = 2.00$, $MS_{A \times S} = 2.00$.
11. *Table 1*

Source	SS	df	MS	F
Factor A	48.00	4	12.00	6.00
Factor S	27.00	9	3.00	
$A \times S$	72.00	36	2.00	
Total	147.00	49		

  a. 5.   **b.** 10.
  c. 10.

Table 2

Source	SS	df	MS	F
Factor A	6.00	2	3.00	2.00
Factor S	36.00	12	3.00	
$A \times S$	36.00	24	1.50	
Total	78.00	38		

  a. 3.   **b.** 13.
  c. 13.

Testing Your Knowledge 12.2

3. H_0: $\mu_{A1} = \mu_{A2} = \mu_{A3} = \mu_{A4} = \mu_{A5}$; H_1: The μ_A's are not all equal.

Testing Your Knowledge 12.3

2.

	City (A)		
	Dallas	**Tijuana**	**Tripoli**
$\overline{X}$	30.8	21.6	22.6
s	4.14	3.15	3.55

a. H_0: $\mu_{A1} = \mu_{A2} = \mu_{A3}$
H_1: The μ_A's are not all equal.

b.

Source	SS	df	MS	F
City (A)	709.000	2	354.500	37.52*
Subjects (S)	269.333	13	20.718	
A × S	245.667	26	9.449	
Total	1224.000	41		

*$p < .01$.

c. 2, 26.
d. $F_{crit}(2, 26) = 3.37$.
e. Values of F_{obs} equal to or greater than 3.37.
f. Yes.
g. Reject H_0; accept H_1.
h. Different populations.
i. Yes.
j. Yes, because the F_{obs} is statistically significant and three levels of the independent variable are varied.
k. Tukey $CD = 2.90$.
l. The mean estimated latitude for Dallas is significantly higher than the means for either Tijuana or Tripoli. The means for Tijuana and Tripoli do not differ significantly.
m. $\eta^2 = .74$.

3. a. 2.　　　　　　**b.** 19.
　c. 4.76.　　　　　**d.** 4.41.
　e. Reject H_0.　　**f.** Accept H_1.
　g. Yes.
　h. The simple and complex stimulus conditions.

4. a. 3.　　　　　　**b.** 12.
　c. 2.81.　　　　　**d.** 3.44.
　e. Fail to reject H_0.　**f.** Do not accept H_1.
　g. No.
　h. No treatment conditions differ significantly.

Review Questions

1. a.

	Type of Word		
	Happy	**Neutral**	**Sad**
$\overline{X}$	4.5	3.0	2.5
s	1.41	1.20	1.20

Source	SS	df	MS	F
Type word (A)	17.333	2	8.666	7.00*
Subjects (S)	16.667	7	2.381	
A × S	17.333	14	1.238	
Total	51.333	23		

*$p < .05$.

Tukey $CD = 1.5$. The mean for happy words is significantly greater than the mean for either neutral or sad words. The neutral and sad words means do not differ significantly.

b. $\eta^2 = .50$.

2.

	Instructional Condition	
	Before Instructions	**After Instructions**
$\overline{X}$	2.45	2.52
s	0.60	0.68

a.

Source	SS	df	MS	F
Instructions (A)	0.027	1	0.027	1.50
Subjects (S)	8.843	11	0.804	
A × S	0.203	11	0.018	
Total	9.073	23		

F_{obs} is nonsignificant at the .05 level. There is no evidence that instructions affected the magnitude of the perceived illusion.

b. $t_{obs}(11) = 1.261$. $\sqrt{F} = \sqrt{1.50} = 1.225$. (The slight difference in values between t and F is due to rounding errors in computations.)

b. Same conclusions.

3. a. H_0: $\mu_{A1} = \mu_{A2} = \mu_{A3} = \mu_{A4} = \mu_{A5}$. H_1: The μ_A's are not all equal.

b. $df_A = 4$, $df_S = 11$, $df_{A \times S} = 44$, $df_{Total} = 59$.

c. $F_{crit}(4, 44) = 2.61$.

d. Reject H_0; accept H_1.

e. There is at least one significant difference among the means. A Tukey HSD test is necessary to locate the specific significant differences.

4. *Table 1*

Source	SS	df	MS	F
Factor A	22.00	2	11.00	2.00
Factor S	138.00	23	6.00	
A × S	253.00	46	5.50	
Total	413.00	71		

a. 3.   b. 24.

c. 24.   d. No.

e. Fail to reject H_0; do not accept H_1.

Table 2

Source	SS	df	MS	F
Factor A	60.00	5	12.0	3.00
Factor S	133.00	19	7.0	
A × S	380.00	95	4.0	
Total	573.00	119		

a. 6.   c. 20.

b. 20.   d. Yes.

e. Reject H_0; accept H_1.

5. The statistically significant $F_{obs}(2, 26) = 15.99$ indicates that there is at least one significant difference among the means. Pairwise comparisons with the Tukey CD indicate that each mean differs significantly from each other mean. Consequently, infants fixated on the familiar face for the longest duration. The duration of fixation on the unfamiliar face was significantly less than the fixation on the familiar face, and the duration of fixation on the blank oval was significantly less than the fixation on either the familiar or unfamiliar face.

CHAPTER 13

Testing Your Knowledge 13.1

2. No, the relationship between the two scores does not change.

3. *Table 1*

   a. Positive relationship.

   b. Less than perfect.

   c. Yes. Knowing the loneliness score allows better prediction of depression than can be achieved without knowing it.

Table 2

   a. Negative relationship.

   b. Less than perfect.   c. Yes.

4. a. Weak negative relationship.

   b. Less than perfect.

   c. No, it would do little to increase the accuracy of the prediction.

Testing Your Knowledge 13.2

3. a. $r_{obs} = +.870$.

4. a. $r_{obs} = -.764$.

5. a. $r_{obs} = -.277$.

Testing Your Knowledge 13.3

4. r^2

   a. .0144

   b. .5476

   c. .3481

   d. .1296

   e. .0529

   f. .0361

Testing Your Knowledge 13.4

2. $H_0: \rho = 0; H_1: \rho \neq 0$.

3.

df	Critical Value .05	.01
a. 6	.707	.834
b. 13	.514	.641
c. 18	.444	.561
d. 30	.349	.449
e. 41	.304	.393
f. 73	.232	.302

4.

Statistical Hypotheses	Critical Value	Falls into Rejection Region	Decision
a. $H_0: \rho = 0$	.576	Yes	H_0: Reject
$H_1: \rho \neq 0$			H_1: Accept
b. $H_0: \rho = 0$	.576	No	H_0: Fail to reject
$H_1: \rho \neq 0$			H_1: Do not accept
c. $H_0: \rho = 0$	.444	Yes	H_0: Reject
$H_1: \rho \neq 0$			H_1: Accept
d. $H_0: \rho = 0$	.423	No	H_0: Fail to reject
$H_1: \rho \neq 0$			H_1: Do not accept
e. $H_0: \rho = 0$	.232	Yes	H_0: Reject
$H_1: \rho \neq 0$			H_1: Accept
f. $H_0: \rho = 0$	.666	Yes	H_0: Reject
$H_1: \rho \neq 0$			H_1: Accept

5. a. $r_{obs} = -.550$.
b. $r_{crit}(10) = .576$; r_{obs} is nonsignificant.
c. There is no evidence for a relationship between absences and test scores for the population from which these scores were sampled.

6.

Statistical Hypotheses	Critical Value	Falls into Rejection Region	Decision
a. $H_0: \rho_s = 0$	.490	No	H_0: Fail to reject
$H_1: \rho_s \neq 0$			H_1: Do not accept
b. $H_0: \rho_s = 0$	.591	Yes	H_0: Reject
$H_1: \rho_s \neq 0$			H_1: Accept
c. $H_0: \rho_s = 0$	.409	Yes	H_0: Reject
$H_1: \rho_s \neq 0$			H_1: Accept
d. $H_0: \rho_s = 0$	.648	No	H_0: Fail to reject
$H_1: \rho_s \neq 0$			H_1: Do not accept
e. $H_0: \rho_s = 0$	.438	Yes	H_0: Reject
$H_1: \rho_s \neq 0$			H_1: Accept
f. $H_0: \rho_s = 0$	.364	Yes	H_0: Reject
$H_1: \rho_s \neq 0$			H_1: Accept

Review Questions

1. b. Positive.
  c. $r_{obs} = +.655$; $r_{crit}(14) = .497$; r_{obs} is statistically significant.
  d. There is a positive relationship between anger level and systolic blood pressure. Higher anger levels are associated with higher systolic blood pressure.
  e. $r^2 = .43$.

2. a. $r_{obs} = -.12$ for girls; $r_{crit}(51) = .273$; r_{obs} is nonsignificant. $r_{obs} = +.32$ for boys; $r_{crit}(40) = .304$; r_{obs} is statistically significant.
  b. $r^2 = .01$ for girls. $r^2 = .10$ for boys.
  c. There is no relationship for girls. For boys, the relationship is positive; taller boys tend to obtain higher report card grades.

3. b. Positive.
  c. $r_{obs} = +.781$; $r_{crit}(8) = .632$; r_{obs} is statistically significant.
  d. They are positively related; the higher the midterm grade, the higher the final exam grade tends to be.

4. a. $r_{s\,obs} = +.937$; $r_{crit}(12) = .591$; $r_{s\,obs}$ is statistically significant.
  b. Popularity and physical attractiveness are positively related in the population of girls from which the sample was drawn.
  c. $r_{s\,obs} = -.134$; $r_{crit}(14) = .545$; $r_{s\,obs}$ is nonsignificant.
  d. There is no relationship between popularity and physical attractiveness of boys in the population from which the sample was drawn.

5. The IQ of college students involves a restricted range of that variable. Very low and very high IQ scores were not included in the sample. It is also possible that the grade-point averages are similarly restricted in range.

6. b. No relationship.
  c. $r_{obs} = -.001$; $r_{crit}(11) = .553$; r_{obs} is nonsignificant.
  d. The number of hours of computer use and depth perception error are not related in the sample measured.

7. b. The relationship appears to be negative.

c. $r_{obs} = -.807$. $r_{crit}(13) = .514$. r_{obs} is statistically significant.

d. The number of negative daily events and school satisfaction are negatively related. More negative daily events are associated with lower school satisfaction.

8. a. $r_{obs} = -.735$.

b. $r_{crit}(15) = .482$. r_{obs} is statistically significant.

c. A negative correlation indicates that higher scores on variable X are associated with lower scores on variable Y. Thus, you expect a lower grade for the friend who watches 15 hours of TV per week than you do for the friend who watches 4 hours per week.

9. a. $r_{s\,obs} = +.847$.

b. $r_{s\,crit}(16) = .507$. $r_{s\,obs}$ is statistically significant.

c. There is a positive correlation between liking rank and participation rank. Higher liking ranks are associated with higher participation ranks.

CHAPTER 14

Testing Your Knowledge 14.1

4. a. $b = +2$; $a = 0$; $Y = +2X$.

b. $b = -1$; $a = +2$; $Y = -1X + 2$.

c. $b = +1.5$; $a = +1$; $Y = +1.5X + 1$.

d. $b = -2$; $a = +4$; $Y = -2X + 4$.

Testing Your Knowledge 14.2

3. a. $Y' = +0.8X + 9$.

b.

X	Y'
60	57
65	61
80	73
85	77
90	81

c. $\overline{Y} = 69.8$. The regression line passes through the points $X = 0, Y = 9$; $\overline{X} = 76, \overline{Y} = 69.8$.

4. a. $Y' = -1.4X + 23$.

b.

X	Y'
5	16.0
8	11.8
11	7.6
14	3.4
17	-0.8

c. $\overline{Y} = 7.6$. The regression line passes through the points $X = 0, Y = 23$; $\overline{X} = 11, \overline{Y} = 7.6$.

Testing Your Knowledge 14.3

5. 4.98.

6. 4.80.

7. 4.30.

Testing Your Knowledge 14.4

1. a. $+11.507$.

b. 202.215.

c. $Y' = +11.507X + 202.215$.

d. The regression line passes through the points $X = 0, Y = 202.215$; $\overline{X} = 5.17, \overline{Y} = 261.7$.

e.

X	Y'
6	271.3
3	236.7
9	305.8
1	213.7
4	248.2
2	225.2
3	236.7
5	259.8
8	294.3
7	282.8
8	294.3
6	271.3

f.

Subject	Residual $(Y - Y')$
1	-54.3
2	-6.7
3	+9.2
4	+10.3
5	+22.8
6	-27.2
7	+19.3
8	+3.2
9	+26.7
10	+6.2
11	-29.3
12	+19.7

g. 6824.43.

h. 26.12.

i. Yes; $s_{Y \cdot X}$ is smaller than s_Y.

2. a. $b = -0.43$.

b. $a = 24.6$.

c. $Y' = -0.43X + 24.6$.

d. 41 scans, $Y' = 7.0$.
18 scans, $Y' = 16.9$.

Review Questions

1. a. $+0.884$.   **b.** $+0.884$.
c. $Y' = +0.884X + 10.96$.
d. 79.0.   **e.** 5.52.
2. a. $Y' = -0.116X + 3.23$.
b. 2.88.   **c.** 2.64.
3. a. $Y' = -4.3X + 128$, where $X =$ number of cigarettes smoked per day.

c.

Cigarettes per Day	Predicted Birth Weight (oz)
0	128.0
1	123.7
5	106.5
8	93.6
10	85.0
13	72.1
20	42.0

4. a. $Y' = +0.786X + 107.16$.

b.

Participant	Predicted Blood Pressure
1	157.5
2	130.7
3	136.2
4	137.8
5	120.5
6	130.0
7	135.5
8	133.9
9	141.7
10	132.3
11	136.2
12	144.1
13	146.5
14	139.4
15	143.3
16	155.1

d. $s_{Y \cdot X}$ is .78 of s_Y.

5. a. -0.562.
b. 28.33.
c. $Y' = -0.562X + 28.33$.
e. 2.90.

6.

Applicant	Predicted Job Performance: Y'
Dianne	55.2
Rodrigo	61.2
Colin	54.0
Maria	67.2
Ruben	64.8
Luke	52.8
Holly	50.4
Blythe	70.8

The predicted job performance scores of Rodrigo, Maria, Ruben, and Blythe are greater than 60. Thus, these applicants will be hired.

7. a. $Y' = -1.317X + 89.17$.
b. Y' for 4 hours $= 83.9$; Y' for 15 hours $= 69.4$.
c. $s_{Y \cdot X} = 8.01$; $s_{Y \cdot X}$ is .70 of s_Y.

CHAPTER 15

Testing Your Knowledge 15.1

7.

χ^2_{obs}	df	χ^2_{crit}	Falls into Rejection Region	Decisions
7.26	2	5.99	Yes	H_0: Reject H_1: Accept
8.33	4	9.49	No	H_0: Fail to reject H_1: Do not accept
14.19	7	14.1	Yes	H_0: Reject H_1: Accept
26.94	20	31.4	No	H_0: Fail to reject H_1: Do not accept

8. The values in each cell are expected frequencies.

a.

	Column	
	1	**2**
Row 1	12.6	31.4
Row 2	15.4	38.6

$\chi^2_{obs}(1) = 0.073$, $p > .05$; nonsignificant.

b.

	Column	
	1	**2**
Row 1	19.2	29.8
Row 2	24.8	38.2

$\chi^2_{obs}(1) = 9.256$, $p < .01$; statistically significant.

c.

	Column	
	1	**2**
Row 1	42.4	56.6
Row 2	17.6	23.4

$\chi^2_{obs}(1) = 12.442$, $p < .01$; statistically significant.

9. $\chi^2_{obs}(2) = 0.168$. This χ^2_{obs} is nonsignificant; there is no relationship between day of the week and time of day for cars passing stop signs in this example.

10. $\chi^2_{obs}(1) = 70.914$, $p < .01$; the hypothesized relationship exists.

Testing Your Knowledge 15.2

1. Scores ordered from smallest

to largest	7	10	14	15	16	19	23	26
Group identity	2	1	2	1	2	1	1	2
Rank	1	2	3	4	5	6	7	8

Number of times an A_1 score precedes

A_2 scores	3		2		1	1

Number of times an A_2 score precedes

A_1 scores	4		3		2

$U_{A1} = 7$; $U_{A2} = 9$.

   a. U_{A1}.   **b.** No.

2. $U_{A1} = 7$; $U_{A2} = 9$.

   a. Yes.

4. U_{A1} should be about equal to U_{A2}.

5. They should differ considerably.

6.

	U_{crit}	Falls into Rejection Region	Decision
a.	0	No	H_0: Fail to reject H_1: Do not accept
b.	16	Yes	H_0: Reject H_1: Accept
c.	27	No	H_0: Fail to reject H_1: Do not accept
d.	22	Yes	H_0: Reject H_1: Accept
e.	56	Yes	H_0: Reject H_1: Accept
f.	87	No	H_0: Fail to reject H_1: Do not accept

7. Smaller $U = U_{A1} = 54.5$; $U_{crit} = 41$; U_{A1} does not fall into the rejection region. There is no evidence that the groups differ in their anxiety estimates.

Testing Your Knowledge 15.3

4.

	T_{crit}	Falls into Rejection Region	Decision
a.	3	Yes	H_0: Reject H_1: Accept
b.	8	No	H_0: Fail to reject H_1: Do not accept
c.	17	Yes	H_0: Reject H_1: Accept
d.	46	Yes	H_0: Reject H_1: Accept
e.	89	No	H_0: Fail to reject H_1: Do not accept

5. $T_{obs}(14) = 27$; $T_{crit}(14) = 21$; T_{obs} is not statistically significant. The anxiety level did not change from game 1 to game 2 in this sample.

Review Questions

1. a. $\chi^2_{obs}(1) = 1.235$, $p > .05$. The frequency of dropout is not related to gender.

  b. $\chi^2_{obs}(2) = 28.990$, $p < .01$. The frequency of dropout is related to the severity of the problem. A larger than expected number of individuals with mild problems drop out; fewer than expected individuals with severe problems drop out.

2. $\sum(-R) = 50$, $\sum(+R) = 5$; therefore, $T_{obs}(11) = 5$, $p < .01$. Reject H_0; the type of task affects yawning.

  a. The uninteresting video condition scores are positively skewed.

  b. The distributions of the number of yawns differ. More yawns occur with an uninteresting stimulus than with an interesting stimulus.

3. $U_{A2} = 38.5$, $p > .05$. The distributions do not differ significantly.

4. $U_{A2} = 44.5$, $p > .05$. The distributions do not differ significantly.

5. $T_{obs} = 3$; $T_{crit}(8) = 3$. T_{obs} falls into the rejection region; thus, H_0: The population distributions of the related A_1 and A_2 scores are identical is rejected.

Appendix F
Commonly Used Formulas

FREQUENCY DISTRIBUTIONS

Ungrouped Frequency Distributions

rf of a score $= f$ of a score$/N$

$\%f$ of a score $= (rf$ of a score$) \times 100$

Grouped Frequency Distributions

$$\text{size of class interval} = i = \frac{X_{\text{highest}} - X_{\text{lowest}}}{\text{number of intervals}}$$

$$rf \text{ of scores in an interval} = \frac{f \text{ of scores in interval}}{N}$$

$\%f$ of scores in an interval $= (rf$ of scores in interval$) \times 100$

Percentile Rank

$$P_X = \frac{cf_L + [(X - X_L)/i]f_i}{N} \times 100$$

Percentile Point

$$X_P = X_L + \left(\frac{P(N) - cf_L}{f_i}\right)i$$

MEASURES OF CENTRAL TENDENCY

Median

$$Mdn = X_{.50} = X_L + \left(\frac{.50(N) - cf_L}{f_i}\right)i$$

Mean

$$\overline{X} = \frac{\sum X}{N}$$

MEASURES OF VARIABILITY

Range

$$\text{range} = X_{\text{highest}} - X_{\text{lowest}}$$

Interquartile Range

$$IQR = X_{75} - X_{25}$$

Semi-Interquartile Range

$$SIQR = \frac{IQR}{2} = \frac{X_{75} - X_{25}}{2}$$

Variance

Population Variance

$$\sigma^2 = \frac{\sum (X - \mu)^2}{N_{\text{population}}}$$

Sample Variance

$$S^2 = \frac{\sum (X - \overline{X})^2}{N}$$

Estimated Population Variance

Definitional formula: $s^2 = \sum (X - \overline{X})^2 / (N - 1)$

Sum of squares formula: $s^2 = SS / (N - 1)$

Computational formula: $s^2 = \dfrac{\sum X^2 - [(\sum X)^2 / N]}{N - 1}$

Standard Deviation

Population Standard Deviation

$$\sigma = \sqrt{\sigma^2}$$

Sample Standard Deviation

$$S = \sqrt{S^2} = \sqrt{\frac{\sum (X - \overline{X})^2}{N}}$$

Estimated Population Standard Deviation

Definitional formula: $s = \sqrt{\sum (X - \bar{X})^2 / (N - 1)}$

Sum of squares formula: $s = \sqrt{SS/(N - 1)}$

Computational formula: $s = \sqrt{\dfrac{\sum X^2 - [(\sum X)^2/N]}{N - 1}}$.

Standard Error of the Mean

σ Known

$\sigma_{\bar{X}} = \sigma/\sqrt{N}$

σ Unknown

$s_{\bar{X}} = s/\sqrt{N}$

Standard Error of the Difference between Means

σ Known

$\sigma_{\bar{X}A1 - \bar{X}A2} = \sqrt{\dfrac{\sigma_{A1}^2}{n_{A1}} + \dfrac{\sigma_{A2}^2}{n_{A2}}}$

σ Unknown

$s_{\bar{X}A1 - \bar{X}A2} = \sqrt{\left[\dfrac{(n_{A1} - 1)s_{A1}^2 + (n_{A2} - 1)s_{A2}^2}{n_{A1} + n_{A2} - 2}\right]\left[\dfrac{1}{n_{A1}} + \dfrac{1}{n_{A2}}\right]}$

PROBABILITY

Probability (p) of Occurrence of an Event

$p(\text{event}) = \dfrac{\text{number of outcomes comprising the event}}{\text{total number of possible outcomes}}$

z SCORES AND STANDARD SCORES

Single Score

$z = \dfrac{X - \mu}{\sigma}$

Standard Score

$$z = \frac{X - \overline{X}}{S} \text{ or } z = \frac{X - \overline{X}}{\sqrt{\sum (X - \overline{X})^2/N}}$$

Sample Mean

$$z = (\overline{X} - \mu)/\sigma_{\overline{X}}$$

t TESTS

One-Sample *t* Test

$$t = \frac{\overline{X} - \mu}{s_{\overline{X}}} \text{ or } t = \frac{\overline{X} - \mu}{s/\sqrt{N}}, \quad df = N - 1$$

t Test for Independent Groups

Definitional formula: $t_{\text{ind}} = \dfrac{\overline{X}_{A1} - \overline{X}_{A2}}{s_{\overline{X}A1 - \overline{X}A2}}$

Computational formula:
$$t_{\text{ind}} = \frac{\overline{X}_{A1} - \overline{X}_{A2}}{\sqrt{\left[\dfrac{(n_{A1} - 1)s_{A1}^2 + (n_{A2} - 1)s_{A2}^2}{n_{A1} + n_{A2} - 2}\right]\left[\dfrac{1}{n_{A1}} + \dfrac{1}{n_{A2}}\right]}}, \quad df = N - 2$$

t Test for Related Groups

$$t_{\text{rel}} = \frac{\overline{X}_{A1} - \overline{X}_{A2}}{\sqrt{\dfrac{\sum D^2 - (\sum D)^2/N_{\text{pairs}}}{N_{\text{pairs}}(N_{\text{pairs}} - 1)}}}, \quad df = N_{\text{pairs}} - 1$$

ANALYSIS OF VARIANCE

One-Factor Between-Subjects Design

Source	SS	df[a]	MS	F
Factor *A*	$\sum\sum (\overline{X}_A - \overline{X}_G)^2$	$a - 1$	SS_A/df_A	MS_A/MS_{Error}
Error	$\sum\sum (X - \overline{X}_A)^2$	$N - a$	$SS_{\text{Error}}/df_{\text{Error}}$	
Total	$\sum\sum (X - \overline{X}_G)^2$	$N - 1$	Not calculated	

[a]a = number of levels of factor *A*, *N* = total number of scores.

Two-Factor Between-Subjects Design

Source	SS	df[a]	MS	F
Factor A	SS_A	$a - 1$	$\dfrac{SS_A}{df_A}$	$\dfrac{MS_A}{MS_{Error}}$
Factor B	SS_B	$b - 1$	$\dfrac{SS_B}{df_B}$	$\dfrac{MS_B}{MS_{Error}}$
Interaction of A and B	$SS_{A \times B}$	$(a - 1)(b - 1)$	$\dfrac{SS_{A \times B}}{df_{A \times B}}$	$\dfrac{MS_{A \times B}}{MS_{Error}}$
Error	SS_{Error}	$ab(n_{AB} - 1)$	$\dfrac{SS_{Error}}{df_{Error}}$	
Total	SS_{Total}	$N - 1$	Not calculated	

[a] a = number of levels of factor a; b = number of levels of factor B; n_{AB} = number of scores in each cell; N = total number of scores.

One-Factor Within-Subjects Design

Source	SS	df[a]	MS	F
Factor A	SS_A	$a - 1$	$\dfrac{SS_A}{df_A}$	$\dfrac{MS_A}{MS_{A \times S}}$
Factor S	SS_S	$n_A - 1$	$\dfrac{SS_S}{df_S}$	
$A \times S$	$SS_{A \times S}$	$(a - 1)(n_A - 1)$	$\dfrac{SS_{A \times S}}{df_{A \times S}}$	
Total	SS_{Total}	$N - 1$	Not calculated	

[a] a = number of levels of factor A; n_A = number of scores in a treatment condition or, equivalently, the number of subjects; N = total number of scores.

TUKEY HSD MULTIPLE COMPARISON TESTS

For One-Factor Between-Subjects Designs

$$CD = q\sqrt{\frac{MS_{Error}}{n_A}}$$

For One-Factor Within-Subjects Designs

$$CD = q \sqrt{\frac{MS_{A \times S}}{n_A}}$$

For Simple Effects in a Factorial Between-Subjects Design

$$CD = q \sqrt{\frac{MS_{\text{Error}}}{n_{AB}}}$$

STRENGTH OF EFFECT MEASURES

Eta Squared for *t* Test

$$\eta^2 = \frac{t^2_{\text{obs}}}{t^2_{\text{obs}} + df}$$

Eta Squared for One-Factor Between-Subjects Analysis of Variance

$$\eta^2 = \frac{SS_A}{SS_{\text{Total}}}$$

or

$$\eta^2 = \frac{(df_A)(F_{\text{obs}})}{(df_A)(F_{\text{obs}}) + df_{\text{Error}}}$$

Eta Squared for One-Factor Within-Subjects Analysis of Variance

$$\eta^2 = \frac{SS_A}{SS_A + SS_{A \times S}}$$

Eta Squared for Two-Factor Between-Subjects Analysis of Variance

$$\eta^2 = \frac{SS_A}{SS_{\text{Total}}} \quad \text{For factor } A$$

$$\eta^2 = \frac{SS_B}{SS_{\text{Total}}} \quad \text{For factor } B$$

$$\eta^2 = \frac{SS_{A \times B}}{SS_{\text{Total}}} \quad \text{For the interaction of factors } A \text{ and } B$$

CORRELATION

Pearson Correlation Coefficient

Definitional formula: $r = \dfrac{\sum (X - \overline{X})(Y - \overline{Y})}{\sqrt{[\sum (X - \overline{X})^2][\sum (Y - \overline{Y})^2]}}$

Cross-products formula: $r = \dfrac{CP_{XY}}{\sqrt{(SS_X)(SS_Y)}}$

Computational formula: $r = \dfrac{(N_{\text{pairs}})(\sum XY) - (\sum X)(\sum Y)}{\sqrt{[(N_{\text{pairs}})(\sum X^2) - (\sum X)^2][(N_{\text{pairs}})(\sum Y^2) - (\sum Y)^2]}}$

Standard score formula: $r = \dfrac{\sum (z_X z_Y)}{N_{\text{pairs}}}$,

$df = N_{\text{pairs}} - 2$ for all formulas

Coefficient of Determination

r^2

Spearman Rank-Order Correlation Coefficient

$r_s = 1 - \left[\dfrac{6 \sum D^2}{(N_{\text{pairs}})(N_{\text{pairs}}^2 - 1)} \right]$

REGRESSION

Equation of a Straight Line

$Y = bX + a$

Slope of a Straight Line

$b = \dfrac{\text{change in value of } Y}{\text{change in value of } X} = \dfrac{Y_2 - Y_1}{X_2 - X_1}$

Equation of Least-Squares Linear Regression Line

$Y' = bX + a$

Slope of Least-Squares Linear Regression Line

Deviational formula: $b = \dfrac{\sum (X - \bar{X})(Y - \bar{Y})}{\sum (X - \bar{X})^2}$

Cross-products formula: $b = \dfrac{CP_{XY}}{SS_X}$

Computational formula: $b = \dfrac{(N_{pairs})(\sum XY) - (\sum X)(\sum Y)}{(N_{pairs})(\sum X^2) - (\sum X)^2}$

Correlation formula: $b = r \left(\dfrac{s_Y}{s_X} \right)$

Y-Intercept of Least-Squares Linear Regression Line

$a = \bar{Y} - b\bar{X}$

Standard Error of Estimate

Definitional formula: $s_{Y \cdot X} = \sqrt{\dfrac{SS_{Residual}}{N_{pairs} - 2}}$ or $s_{Y \cdot X} = \sqrt{\dfrac{\sum (Y - Y')^2}{N_{pairs} - 2}}$

Computational formula:

$$s_{Y \cdot X} = \sqrt{\left[\dfrac{1}{N_{pairs}(N_{pairs} - 2)} \right] \left[N_{pairs} \sum Y^2 - (\sum Y)^2 - \dfrac{[N_{pairs}(\sum XY) - (\sum X)(\sum Y)]^2}{N_{pairs} \sum X^2 - (\sum X)^2} \right]}$$

Correlation formula: $s_{Y \cdot X} = s_Y \sqrt{\left[\dfrac{N_{pairs} - 1}{N_{pairs} - 2} \right](1 - r_{obs}^2)}$

NONPARAMETRIC TESTS

Chi-Square Test for Independence

$\chi^2 = \sum \sum \dfrac{(O_{rc} - E_{rc})^2}{E_{rc}}, \quad df = (r - 1)(c - 1)$

$\begin{array}{l} \text{Expected} \\ \text{frequency} \\ \text{of a cell} \end{array} = \dfrac{\text{(Row marginal for cell)(Column marginal for cell)}}{\text{Total number of responses}}$

Chi-Square Test for Goodness of Fit

$\chi^2 = \sum \dfrac{(O_c - E_c)^2}{E_c}, \quad df = c - 1$

Mann–Whitney *U* Test

$$U_{A1} = n_{A1}n_{A2} + \frac{n_{A1}(n_{A1} + 1)}{2} - \sum R_{A1}$$

$$U_{A2} = n_{A1}n_{A2} + \frac{n_{A2}(n_{A2} + 1)}{2} - \sum R_{A2}$$

or

$$U_{A2} = n_{A1}n_{A2} - U_{A1}$$

Wilcoxon Signed-Ranks Test

$$T = \text{smaller of } \sum (-R) \text{ or } \sum (+R)$$

References

Abelson, R. P. (1997). On the surprising longevity of flogged horses: Why there is a case for the significance test. *Psychological Science, 8,* 12–15.

American Psychological Association. (1994). *Publication Manual of the American Psychological Association* (4th ed.). Washington, DC: Author.

Artis, J. B. (1993, January 28). A fat promise in the dark days of January. *Boston Globe,* p. 45.

Becoña, E., & Vázquez, F. L. (1998). Smoking cessation and weight gain in smokers participating in a behavioral treatment at 3-year follow-up. *Psychological Reports, 82,* 999–1005.

Birth weight, secondary smoke linked. (1986, August 22). *Boston Globe,* p. 83.

Bond, C. F., Jr., & Anderson, E. L. (1987). The reluctance to transmit bad news: Private discomfort or public display? *Journal of Experimental Social Psychology, 23,* 176–187.

Borgia, G., & Gore, M. A. (1986). Feather stealing in the satin bowerbird (Ptilonorhynchus violaceus): Male competition and the quality of display. *Animal Behaviour, 34,* 727–738.

Bower, G. H. (1981). Mood and memory. *American Psychologist, 36,* 129–148.

Bradley, J. V. (1980). Nonrobustness in classical tests on means and variances: A large-scale sampling study. *Bulletin of the Psychonomic Society, 15,* 275–278.

Bradley, J. V. (1984). The complexity of nonrobustness effects. *Bulletin of the Psychonomic Society, 22,* 250–253.

Brunner, B. (Ed.). (1999). *Time Almanac 2000.* Boston, MA: Information Please.

Cafardo, N. (1994, August 12). What they're forfeiting. *Boston Globe,* p. 41.

Caro, T. M. (1986). The functions of stotting in Thompson's gazelles: Some tests of the predictions. *Animal Behaviour, 34,* 663–684.

Carroll, J. L., & Shmidt, J. L., Jr. (1992). Correlation between humorous coping style and health. *Psychological Reports, 70,* 402.

Cavell, T. A., & Woehr, D. J. (1994). Predicting introductory psychology test scores: An engaging and useful topic. *Teaching of Psychology, 21,* 108–110.

Clarkson, P. M., James, R., Watkins, A., & Foley, P. (1986). The effect of augmented feedback on foot pronation during barre exercise in dance. *Research Quarterly for Exercise and Sport, 57,* 33–40.

Cohen, J. (1994). The Earth is round ($p < .05$). *American Psychologist, 49,* 997–1003.

Cortina, J. M., & Dunlap, W. P. (1997). On the logic and purpose of significance testing. *Psychological Methods, 2,* 161–172.

Cosmides, L. (1983). Invariance in the acoustic expression of emotion during speech. *Journal of Experimental Psychology: Human Performance and Perception, 9,* 864–881.

Coulter, R. G., Coulter, M. L., & Glover, J. A. (1984). Details and picture recall. *Bulletin of the Psychonomic Society, 22,* 327–329.

Craik, F. I. M., & Tulving, E. (1975). Depth of processing and the retention of words in episodic memory. *Journal of Experimental Psychology: General, 104,* 268–294.

Davis, D. M. (1990). Portrayals of women in prime-time network television: Some demographic characteristics. *Sex Roles, 23,* 325–331.

Day, R. H., & Kasperczyk, R. T. (1984). The Morinaga misalignment effect with circular stimulus elements. *Bulletin of the Psychonomic Society, 22,* 193–196.

Dihoff, R. E., Hetznecker, W., Brosvic, G. M., Carpenter, L. N., & Hoffman, L. S. (1993). Ordinal measurement of autistic behavior: A preliminary report. *Bulletin of the Psychonomic Society, 31,* 287–290.

Dudycha, A. L., & Dudycha, L. W. (1972). Behavioral statistics. In R. E. Kirk (ed.) *Statistical issues: A reader for the behavioral sciences* (pp. 2–25). Monterey, CA: Brooks/Cole.

Egli, E. A., & Meyers, L. S. (1984). The role of video game playing in adolescent life: Is there reason to be concerned? *Bulletin of the Psychonomic Society, 22,* 309–312.

Eisenman, R. (1987). Creativity, birth order, and risk taking. *Bulletin of the Psychonomic Society, 25,* 87–88.

Elasmar, M., Hasegawa, K., & Brain, M. (1999). The portrayal of women in U.S. prime time television. *Journal of Broadcasting & Electronic Media, 44*(1), 20–34.

Elgar, M. A., McKay, H., & Woon, P. (1986). Scanning, pecking, and alarm flights in house sparrows. *Animal Behaviour, 34,* 1892–1894.

Feaver, J., Mendl, M., & Bateson, P. (1986). A method for rating the individual distinctiveness of domestic cats. *Animal Behaviour, 34,* 1016–1025.

Frick, R. W. (1996). The appropriate use of null hypothesis testing. *Psychological Methods, 1,* 379–390.

Friedman, A., & Brown, N. R. (2000). Reasoning about geography. *Journal of Experimental Psychology: General, 129,* 193–219.

Friedman, H. S., Tucker, J. S., Tomlinson-Keasey, C., Schwartz, J. E., Wingard, D. L., & Criqui, M. H. (1993). Does childhood personality predict longevity? *Journal of Personality and Social Psychology, 65,* 176–185.

Fudin, R., & Levinson, H. (1994). Note on 1993 salaries of major league baseball players. *Perceptual and Motor Skills, 78,* 1085–1086.

Gaito, J. (1977). Directional and nondirectional alternative hypotheses. *Bulletin of the Psychonomic Society, 9,* 371–372.

Gardner, P. L. (1975). Scales and statistics. *Review of Educational Research, 45,* 43–57.

Geban, O., Askar, P., & Özkan, I. (1992). Effects of computer simulations and problem-solving approaches on high school students. *Journal of Educational Research, 86*(1), 5–10.

Good, L. R., & Good, K. C. (1973). An objective measure of the motive to avoid success. *Psychological Reports, 33,* 1009–1010.

Gormly, J., & Gormly, A. (1986). Social introversion and spatial abilities. *Bulletin of the Psychonomic Society, 24,* 273–274.

Gross, W. C. (1993). Gender and age differences in college students' alcohol consumption. *Psychological Reports, 72,* 211–216.

Gustafson, R. (1987a). Alcohol and aggression: A test of an indirect measure of aggression. *Psychological Reports, 60,* 1241–1242.

Gustafson, R. (1987b). Alcohol and the acceptance of social influence: A preliminary study. *Psychological Reports, 60,* 488–490.

Gwartney-Gibbs, P. A. (1986). The institutionalization of premarital cohabitation: Estimates from marriage license applications, 1970 and 1980. *Journal of Marriage and the Family, 48,* 423–434.

Haase, R. F., Waechter, D. M., & Solomon, G. S. (1982). How significant is a significant difference? Average effect size of research in counseling psychology. *Journal of Counseling Psychology, 29,* 58–65.

Hagen, R. L. (1997). In praise of the null hypothesis statistical test. *American Psychologist, 52,* 15–24.

Harris, L. J., & Blaiser, M. J. (1997). Effects of a mnemonic peg system on the recall of daily tasks. *Perceptual and Motor Skills, 84,* 721–722.

Harris, R. J. (1997). Significance tests have their place. *Psychological Science, 8,* 8–11.

Hicks, R. A., Mistry, R., Lucero, K., Marical, C., & Pellegrini, R. J. (1990). Self-reported sleep durations of college students: Normative data for 1978–79 and 1988–89. *Perceptual and Motor Skills, 70,* 370.

Homan, S. P., Topping, M., & Hall, B. W. (1986). Does teacher oral reading of test items affect the performance of students of varying reading ability? *Journal of Educational Research, 79,* 363–365.

Huebner, E. S., & McCullough, G. (2000). Correlates of school satisfaction among adolescents. *Journal of Educational Research, 93,* 331–335.

Hughey, A. W. (1985). Further inquiry into the relationship between GPA and undesirable behavior in residence halls. *Psychological Reports, 56,* 510.

Hunter, J. E. (1997). Needed: A ban on the significance test. *Psychological Science, 8,* 3–7.

Infoplease.com. (2000). Weekly TV viewing by age. Retrieved May 16, 2000 from the World Wide Web: www.infoplease.com/ipea/A0772264.html.

Jacoby, S. (2000, July–August). The allure of money. *Modern Maturity. 43R*(4). 34–41.

Jenkins, C. D., Zyzanski, S. J., & Rosenman, R. H. (1979). *Jenkins activity survey.* New York: Psychological Corporation.

Joseph, L. M. (2000). Developing first graders phonemic awareness, word identification and spelling: A comparison of two contemporary phonic instructional approaches. *Reading Research and Instruction, 39*(2), 160–169.

Kassel, J. D. (2000). Smoking and stress: Correlation, causation, and context. *American Psychologist, 55,* 1155–1156.

Keppel, G. (1991). *Design and analysis: A researcher's handbook* (3rd ed.). Englewood Cliffs, NJ: Prentice Hall.

Kleinkrecht, R. A., & Donaldson, D. A. (1975). A review of the effects of diazepam on cognitive and psychomotor performance. *Journal of Nervous and Mental Diseases, 161,* 399–411.

Krantz, M. (1987). Physical attractiveness and popularity: A predictive study. *Psychological Reports, 60,* 723–726.

Lindner, D., & Hynan, M. T. (1987). Perceived structure of abstract paintings as a function of structure of music listened to on initial viewing. *Bulletin of the Psychonomic Society, 25,* 44–46.

Martin, R. A., & Lefcourt, H. M. (1984). Situational humor response questionnaire: Quantitative measure of sense of humor. *Journal of Personality and Social Psychology, 47,* 145–155.

Maynard, I. W., & Howe, B. L. (1987). Interrelations of trait and state anxiety with game performance of rugby players. *Perceptual and Motor Skills, 64,* 599–602.

McCarthy, P. R., & Schmeck, R. R. (1982). Effects of teacher self-disclosure on student learning and perceptions of teacher. *College Student Journal, 16,* 45–49.

McElrea, H., & Standing, L. (1992). Fast music causes fast drinking. *Perceptual and Motor Skills, 75,* 362.

McKelvey, M. W., & McKenry, P. C. (2000). The psychosocial well-being of Black and White mothers following marital dissolution, *Psychology of Women Quarterly, 24,* 4–14.

Meyer, G. E. (1986). Interactions of subjective contours with the Ponzo, Müller–Lyer, and vertical–horizontal illusions. *Bulletin of the Psychonomic Society, 24,* 39–40.

Mintz, L. B., & Betz, N. E. (1986). Sex differences in the nature, realism, and correlates of body image. *Sex Roles, 15,* 185–195.

Mishra, R. (2000, June 21). U.S. health care system ranked 37th. *The Boston Globe,* p. A2.

Morrison, C., & Reeve, J. (1986). Effect of instructional units on the analysis of related and unrelated skills. *Perceptual and Motor Skills, 62,* 563–566.

Newburger, J. W., Takahashi, M., Burns, J. C., Beiser, A. S., Chung, K. J., Duffy, C. E., Glode, M. P., Mason, W. H., Reddy, V., Sanders, S. P., Shulman, S. T., Wiggins, J. W., Hicks, R. V., Fulton, D. R., Lewis, A. B., Leung, D. Y. M., Colton, T., Rosen, F. S., & Melish, M. E. (1986). The treatment of Kawasaki syndrome with intravenous gamma globulin. *New England Journal of Medicine, 315,* 341–347.

O'Brien, E. J., & Wolford, C. R. (1982). Effect of delay in testing on retention of plausible versus bizarre mental images. *Journal of Experimental Psychology: Learning, Memory, and Cognition, 8,* 148–152.

Parrott, A. C. (1999). Does cigarette smoking *cause* stress? *American Psychologist, 54,* 817–820.

Pedersen, D. M. (1979). Dimensions of privacy. *Perceptual and Motor Skills, 48,* 1291–1297.

Pedersen, D. M. (1987). Sex differences in privacy preferences. *Perceptual and Motor Skills, 64,* 1239–1242.

Pfendler, C., & Widdel, H. (1986). Vigilance performance when using colour on electronic displays. *Perceptual and Motor Skills, 63,* 939–944.

Provine, R. R., & Hamernik, H. B. (1986). Yawning: Effects of stimulus interest. *Bulletin of the Psychonomic Society, 24,* 437–438.

Reisberg, D. (1983). General mental resources and perceptual judgments. *Journal of Experimental Psychology: Human Performance and Perception, 9,* 966–979.

Roballey, T. C., McGreevy, C., Rongo, R. R., Schwantes, M. L., Steger, P. J., Wininger, M. A., & Gardner, E. B. (1985). The effect of music on eating behavior. *Bulletin of the Psychonomic Society, 23,* 221–222.

Roberts, R. E., Lewinsohn, P. M., & Seeley, J. R. (1993). A brief measure of loneliness suitable for use with adolescents. *Psychological Reports, 72,* 1379–1391.

Rotton, J., & Kelly, I. W. (1985). A scale for assessing belief in lunar effects: Reliability and concurrent validity. *Psychological Reports, 57,* 239–245.

Sadeh, A., Raviv, A., & Gruber, R. (2000). Sleep patterns and sleep disruptions in school-age children. *Developmental Psychology, 36,* 291–301.

Senders, V. L. (1958). *Measurement and statistics.* New York: Oxford University Press.

Smith, J. E., Waldorf, V. A., & Trembath, D. L. (1990). "Single white male looking for thin, very attractive. . . ." *Sex Roles, 23,* 675–683.

Spielberger, C. D. (1980). *Test anxiety inventory.* Palo Alto, CA: Consulting Psychologists Press.

Stahler, G. J., & Eisenman, R. (1987). Psychotherapy dropouts: Do they have poor psychological adjustment? *Bulletin of the Psychonomic Society, 25,* 198–200.

Standing, L., Lynn, D., & Moxness, K. (1990). Effects of noise upon introverts and extroverts. *Bulletin of the Psychonomic Society, 28,* 138–140.

Stigler, S. M. (1986). *The history of statistics: The measurement of uncertainty before 1900.* Cambridge, MA: Harvard University Press.

Streiner, D. L. (1996). Maintaining standards: Differences between the standard deviation and standard error, and when to use each. *Canadian Journal of Psychiatry, 41,* 498–502.

Strueber, D., & Stadler, M. (1999). Differences in top-down influences on the reversal rate of different categories of reversible figures. *Perception, 28,* 1185–1196.

Sturgeon, R., & Beer, J. (1990). Attendance reward and absenteeism in high school. *Psychological Reports, 66,* 759–762.

The wizards of odds. (1989, June). *Aide Magazine,* pp. 9–13.

Thorson, J. A. (1993). To die with your boots on: Relative lethality of the states. *Psychological Reports, 72,* 843–854.

Tobacyk, J., Miller, M. J., & Jones, G. (1984). Paranormal beliefs of high school students. *Psychological Reports, 55,* 255–261.

Trinkhaus, J. (1982). Stop sign compliance: An informal look. *Psychological Reports, 50,* 288.

Trinkhaus, J. (1983). Stop sign compliance: Another look. *Psychological Reports, 57,* 922.

Trinkhaus, J. (1988). Stop sign compliance: A further look. *Perceptual and Motor Skills, 67,* 670.

Trinkhaus, J. (1993). Stop sign compliance: A follow-up look. *Perceptual and Motor Skills, 76,* 1218.

Trinkaus, J. (1997). Stop sign compliance: A final look. *Perceptual and Motor Skills, 85,* 217–218.

Tukey, J. W. (1977). *Exploratory data analysis.* Reading, MA: Addison-Wesley.

Unrug-Neervoort, A., Kaiser, J., & Coenen, A. (1992). Influence of diazepam on prospective time estimation. *Perceptual and Motor Skills, 75,* 993–994.

U.S. Bureau of Labor Statistics. (2000, April 19). Usual weekly earning summary. Retrieved May 16, 2000 from the World Wide Web: stats.bls.gov/newsrels.htm.

U.S. Bureau of Labor Statistics. (2000). Labor force statistics from the current population survey. Table 4. Quartiles and selected deciles of usual weekly earnings of full-time and salary workers by selected characteristics, first quarter 2000 averages, not seasonally adjusted. Retrieved May 17, 2000 from the World Wide Web: stats.bls.gov/news.release/wkyeng.t04.htm.

U.S. Census Bureau. (1998, March). Household and family characteristics: March 1998 update. Retrieved August 18, 2000 from the World Wide Web: www.census.gov/prod/3/98pubs/p20-515u.pdf.

U.S. Census Bureau. (1999). *Statistical abstract of the United States: 1999.* Author, pp. 868–889.

Villimez, C., Eisenberg, N., & Carroll, J. L. (1986). Sex differences in the relation of children's height and weight to academic performance and others' attributions of competence. *Sex Roles, 15,* 667–681.

Wainer, H. (1999). One cheer for null hypothesis significance testing. *Psychological Methods, 4,* 212–213.

Wang, A. Y., Thomas, M. H., & Ouellette, J. A. (1992). Keyword mnemonic and retention of second language vocabulary words. *Journal of Educational Psychology, 84,* 520–528.

Weiss, B. A., Kimmel, D., & Stein, J. (1993). Psychology of computer use: XXVII: Effect of computer use on depth perception. *Perceptual and Motor Skills, 77,* 175–178.

Wellens, A. R. (1987). Heart-rate changes in response to shifts in interpersonal gaze from liked and disliked others. *Perceptual and Motor Skills, 64,* 595–598.

Wiehe, V. R. (1986). *Loco Parentis* and locus of control. *Psychological Reports, 59,* 169–170.

Wilkinson, L., & The Task Force on Statistical Inference. (1999). Statistical methods in psychology journals: Guidelines and explanations. *American Psychologist, 54,* 594–604.

Williams, J. G., & Covington, C. J. (1997). Predictors of cigarette smoking among adolescents. *Psychological Reports, 80,* 481–482.

Woehr, D. J., & Cavell, T. A. (1993). Self-report measures of ability, effort, and nonacademic activity as predictors of introductory psychology test scores. *Teaching of Psychology, 20,* 156–160.

Wong, J. L. (1993). Comparison of the Shipley versus WAIS—R subtests and summary scores in predicting college grade point average. *Perceptual and Motor Skills, 76,* 1075–1078.

Yarnold, P. R., Grimm, L. G., & Mueser, K. T. (1986). Social conformity and the Type A behavior pattern. *Perceptual and Motor Skills, 62,* 99–104.

Zuckerman, M. (1979). *Sensation seeking: Beyond the optimal level of arousal.* Hillsdale, NJ: Erlbaum.

Zusne, L. (1986–87). Some factors affecting the birthday–deathday phenomenon. *Omega, 17,* 9–26.

Name Index

Subject Index